Dedicated to

Sri Raja Rajeshwari, Mata Sharda Devi and Sri Sai Baba

Whose blessings will overcome all the hurdles in life

PREFACE

This book is an up-to-date edition based on NIELIT '*O*' *Level* Module-3 (M3–R5) syllabus for **Programming and Problem Solving through 'Python' Language**. This is a text book that explains this highly technical subject in very simple language. The complicated concepts for solving problems using the 'Python' language are brought out in an easy-to-understand manner through various examples and diagrams. It is felt that most of the books available in the market do not cover the entire syllabus of the course.

The 'O' Level Module-3 (M3–R5) course revised by NIELIT is very comprehensive and needs very thorough study of the applied knowledge of both the Programming techniques and 'Python' language. We have made great efforts to cover the entire syllabus so that students would get hands on experience in the Python programming.

There are rapid changes in the field of programming and many new concepts are introduced from time to time. Accordingly, there is a major change in the syllabus for 'O' Level Module-3 (M3–R5). Hence, the scope for the questions set in the examination will cover many more new terms. This has prompted us to bring out this book by inserting prescribed topics and latest concepts. It focuses on teaching the Python language and help students learn programming concepts and develop problem solving skills. Algorithms and flowcharts are very important to understand the logic of the programming. Therefore, a separate chapter is included on this important topic. In addition, the book contains ample concise and practical example programs. Also many solved and unsolved examples are provided at the end of each chapter. An effort is made to explain all topics in layman's language with a large number of illustrations and examples.

A special feature throughout this book is that the salient and crucial information has been encapsulated within parallel and horizontal lines with a (☞) mark to draw the attention of the reader .

We shall feel obliged if you could send us your critical opinion regarding the presentation, readability and coverage in this book and request you to mail your suggestions, if any, to improve the same.

16th January, 2020 Authors

Based on

NIELIT 'O' Level Revised Syllabus of year 2020 for M3–R5

'O' LEVEL *made simple* MODULE - 3

PROGRAMMING AND PROBLEM SOLVING THROUGH 'PYTHON' LANGUAGE

by

Satish Jain

B.Sc., B.E.(IISc), M.E.(IISc), M.Tech.(IIT Kanpur),
Ex-Professor of Information Technology,
Institute of Information Technology & Management
GGS Indraprastha University, Delhi.

Shashi Singh

MCA, M.Phil

bpb

Reprinted 2026

First Edition 2020

Second Revised & Updated Edition 2022

Third Revised & Updated Edition 2023

ISBN: 978-93-89845-10-5

Distributors:

BPB PUBLICATIONS
20, Ansari Road, Darya Ganj
New Delhi-110002
Ph: 23254990/23254991

DECCAN AGENCIES
4-3-329, Bank Street,
Hyderabad-500195
Ph: 24756967/24756400

MICRO MEDIA
Shop No. 5, Mahendra Chambers,
150 DN Rd. Next to Capital Cinema,
V.T. (C.S.T.) Station, MUMBAI-400 001
Ph: 22078296/22078297

NIELIT is in no way connected with this book. This book is written solely for the benefit and guidance of students appearing of NIELIT Examination

Published by Manish Jain for BPB Publications, 20 Ansari Road, Darya Ganj, New Delhi-110002 and Printed at Akash Press, Delhi

www.bpbonline.com

M3-R5 : Programming and Problem Solving through 'Python' Language

Outline of Course

S.No.	TOPIC	Written Marks (Max.)
1.	Introduction to Programming, Algorithm and Flowcharts to solve problems	20
2.	Introduction to Python, Operators, Expressions and Python Statements, Sequence data types	30
3.	Functions, File Processing, Modules	40
4.	NumPy Basics	10
	Total Marks	**100**

Detailed Syllabus

1. Introduction to Programming

Introduction to Programming The basic Model of computation, algorithms, flowcharts, Programming Languages, compilation, testing &debugging and documentation.

2. Algorithms and Flowcharts to Solve Problems

Flow Chart Symbols, Basic algorithms/flowcharts for sequential processing, decision-based processing and iterative processing. Some examples like:
Exchanging values of two variables, summation of a set of numbers, Decimal Base to Binary Base conversion, Reversing digits of an integer, GCD (Greatest Common Division) of two numbers, Test whether a number is prime, factorial computation, Fibonacci sequence, Evaluate 'sin x' as sum of a series, Reverse order of elements of an array, Find largest number in an array, Print elements of upper triangular matrix, etc.

3. Introduction to Python

Python Introduction, Technical Strength of Python, Introduction to Python Interpreter and program execution, Using Comments, Literals, Constants, Python's Built-in Data types, Numbers (Integers, Floats, Complex Numbers, Real, Sets), Strings (Slicing, Indexing, Concatenation, other operations on Strings), Accepting input from Console, printing statements, Simple 'Python' programs.

4. Operators, Expressions and Python Statements

Assignment statement, expressions, Arithmetic, Relational, Logical, Bitwise operators and their precedence, Conditional statements: if, if-else, if-elif-else; simple programs, Notion of iterative computation and control flow -range function, While Statement, For loop, break statement, Continue Statement, Pass statement, else, assert.

5. Sequence Data Types

Lists, tuples and dictionary, (Slicing, Indexing, Concatenation, other operations on Sequence data type), concept of mutability, Examples to include finding the maximum, minimum, mean; linear search on list/tuple of numbers, and counting the frequency of elements in a list using a dictionary.

6. Functions

Top-down approach of problem solving, Modular programming and functions, Function parameters, Local variables, the Return statement, DocStrings, global statement, Default argument values, keyword arguments, VarArgs parameters.
Library function-input(), eval(),print(), String Functions: count(), find(), rfind(), capitalize(), title(), lower(), upper(), swapcase(), islower(), isupper(), istitle(), replace(), strip(), lstrip(), rstrip(), aplit(), partition(), join(), isspace(), isalpha(), isdigit(), isalnum(), startswith(), endswith(), encode(), decode(), String: Slicing, Membership, Pattern Matching, Numeric Functions: eval(), max(), min(), pow(), round(), int(), random(), ceil(), floor(), sqrt(), Date & Time Functions, Recursion.

7. File Processing

Concept of Files, File opening in various modes and closing of a file, Reading from a file, Writing onto a file, File functions-open(), close(), read(), readline(), readlines(),write(), writelines(), tell(),seek(), Command Line arguments.

8. Scope and Modules

Scope of objects and Names, LEGB Rule Module Basics, Module Files as Namespaces, Import Model, Reloading Modules.

9. NumPy Basics

Introduction to NumPy, ndarray, datatypes, array attributes, array creation routines, Array From Existing Data, Array From Numerical Ranges, Indexing & Slicing.

USEFUL TIPS FOR THE EXAMINEE

Dear Reader,

Every examination has its peculiarity and the best results are often obtained by identifying that particular feature and working with the help of right strategies, which in turn can be adopted by correctly analyzing the question paper.

The 'O' Level Examination being no exception to this rule, the authors present an effective aid to guide you to analyze the question paper and thus help to chalk out your own effective plan of action.

The instructions given on the first page of the question paper should always be read *very* carefully. As the answer sheets of Part ONE will be evaluated with the help of a computer, you have to be extra cautious.

The answer sheet contains separate boxes for writing answers to each question in this part. You should read the following paragraphs to avoid mistakes and clear the first part without any difficulty.

How to avoid mistakes?

If you are not sure about a particular answer - *do not fill* the box in the first try itself, but make an attempt later. After having given an initial reading to all the questions, first attempt only those questions about which you are very ***sure*** regarding the correct answer. It is while taking a second go at the questions, that you answer the remaining ones, always making sure that you spend only a *limited* amount of time on each one of them. Finally, go through all the answers once decided and fill the boxes with black ink as per the instructions given in the question paper.

How to answer the questions of Part TWO?

Once you have done well in Part ONE, rest assured, passing Part TWO will not pose much of a problem, if you have effectively followed the instructions given below. While answering Part TWO, the time limit should be strictly kept in mind and every effort must be made to complete all the questions, by keeping the answers brief and to the point. Remember you can also resort to making a sketch/diagram in your answer wherever possible, instead of describing it in words, because "a thousand words of description can be effectively expressed by a small diagram." As the number of questions are normally more for an average student, this precious time saved, enables you to have a wider coverage of the paper.

While attempting the descriptive type of questions, keep a check on the length of your answers and keep in mind the time frame available for answering the remaining questions.

The last stage, being the revision stage, you should save at least 5 to 10 minutes to revise all your answers. Try to find the gross errors, like units of measurement, or wrong question number you might have put for a specific answer, etc. This does happen because of the inherent tension of the examination.

This book has covered the complete syllabus in an easy to understand manner. It is advised, however, that in addition to this book, you should also refer to a few books on 'Python' Language. This will enable you to broaden the horizon of your knowledge.

Make your own notes, by reading each topic from this book and other standard books. Once you are quite sure about the comprehension of the topic, try to answer the Exercises given at the end of each chapter of this book.

In the second reading, go through the sample papers given at the end of the book. Solve these papers without consulting any book. After you have answered them, compare your response with the relevant matter available in the text of this book. Where you find your answers differ, re-study that part again.

WISH YOU A GRAND SUCCESS in the 'O' Level Examination, and a very bright future in the field of computer science.

Authors

Contents

Programming and Problem Solving through 'Python' Language

Module 3: M3–R5

Chapter 7. List Manipulation 199

Chapter 8. Tuples 238

Chapter 9. Dictionaries 255

Chapter 10. Functions 274

CHAPTER 1

Introduction to Programming

1.1 THE BASIC MODEL OF COMPUTATION

A program is a set of instructions, written in a computer language, to perform a specific task. In an attempt to solve problems on a computer, one has to write a step-by-step solution using simple instructions for operations and thus, obtain the results. There would be a number of methods to solve a given problem, and therefore, solutions may differ from person-to-person. However, in all cases, the basic steps remain the same. These basic steps are as follows:

a. Formulating the problem and deciding the data types to be inputted.
b. Identifying the steps of computation that are necessary for getting the solution.
c. Identifying decision points, i.e., under what circumstances a particular operation is to be performed and when not to be performed.
d. Knowing the expected results and verifying with the actual values.

1.1.1 Procedure for Problem Solving

Problem-solving is the process involving basic sequential steps necessary to arrive at the solution of the given problem.

It is a logical process of breaking down the problem into small parts which can be solved step-by-step to obtain the result. This does not involve the computer.

Though every problem is unique in itself, a few basic steps for solving the problem are common. These steps should be understood thoroughly and practiced effectively. Using these steps, your problem solving capability will improve with time.

The six basic steps in solving a problem are as follows:

a. Spend sometime in understanding the problem thoroughly. In this step, you are not required to use the computer. Instead, you should try to answer what is expected and how to obtain it. This means, try to solve the problem manually.
b. Construct a list of variables that are needed to get the solution of the problem.
c. Decide the layout for the output presentation.
d. Select the programming technique which is best suited to solve the problem and, then only carry out the coding, using a suitable programming language.
e. Test the program. Select test data so that each part of the program can be checked for correctness.
f. Finally, use data validation steps to prevent processing of wrongly entered data.

The above mentioned six steps are further elaborated in the following sections:

Step 1. Understanding the Problem

Read each *statement* given in the problem carefully so that you can answer the first question "What is expected by solving the problem?" Do not start drawing a flowchart or a decision table straight away. Instead, read each statement of the problem slowly and carefully by understanding the *keywords*. Use paper and pencil to solve the problem manually for some test data. Let us understand this point by solving the problem given in Example 1.

Example 1

Accept a value M and find out the sum of the first M even integers.

Solution

The solution of this problem requires you to draw a flowchart so that if you input 6 as the value of M (See Figure 1.1), the flowchart should give you the sum of the first 6 even integers. In the first step, you should be able to answer the following two questions:

"What are the first 6 even integers?"
These are 2, 4, 6, 8, 10, and 12.
"What is their sum?"

Their sum is 42. Hence, the flowchart is to be framed in such a way that the sum of the first 6 even integers comes out to be 42.

Step 2. Construction of the List of Variables

In this step, you should think in advance the number of variables required and the name of the variables before drawing the flowchart. The names chosen for variables should be an aid to memory. For example, in the case of the problem stated in Step 1 given above, the variables may be I, SUM, and COUNT as given below.

1. To generate even integers 2, 4, 6,...(I)
2. To obtain the sum of even integers 2 + 4 + 6 + ... (SUM)
3. To count the number of even integers, i.e., count 1, 2, 3,... (COUNT)

Thus, it is clear that you need to use the above-mentioned three variables and one more variable "M" whose value will be input by the user of the program from the keyboard. Finally, the four variables are:

M	To be inputted from the keyboard
I	To generate even integers
COUNT	A counter to keep a track of the number of even integers that have been summed up
SUM	An accumulator that contains the current total of even integers

☞ *A problem solver has to decide the various kinds of variables that take different values for finding the solution.*

Step 3. Output Design

Often, the 'output' format is specified in the problem itself, but sometimes, it may not be so. If the output format is not specified, you must keep in mind that the output report should easily be understandable to a reader. The headings should not cause any doubt or confusion in the mind of the reader.

In the problem given in step 1 the output format could be as follows:

No. of Integers-6 Total Value-42

You should keep one point in mind. The programs and problem solutions are for other people (teachers, supervisors, contractors, etc.). They will appreciate you only if they can understand the results and analyze them. Hence, the output format should have the following characteristics:

a. Attractive
b. Easy-to-read
c. Self-explanatory

Step 4. Program Development

You should now draw a flowchart for the procedure that you have just made in Steps 1, 2 and 3. Standard symbols should be used for drawing the flowchart. If the problem is complex, you should divide it into several simpler parts. Then, draw a flowchart for each part separately and join them together using connectors.

The flowchart for the problem given in Example 1 is shown in Figure 1.1. Now, write the code in the prescribed high level language to translate the flowchart into the program.

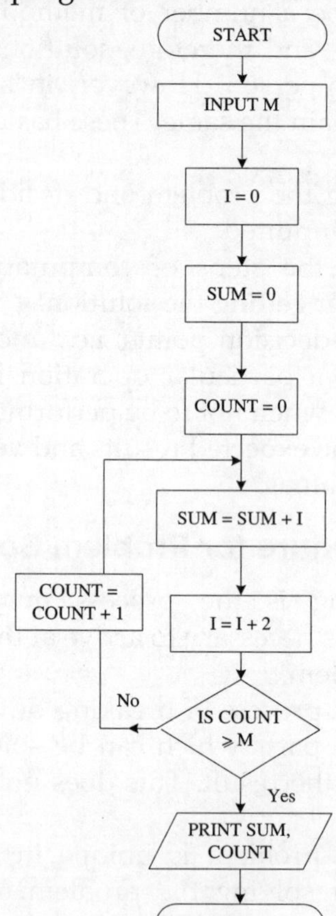

Figure 1.1 Flowchart to Find the sum of M Even Integers

Step 5. Testing the Program

You should give a *dry* run to the program developed in Step 4. This means giving some known values to the variables and checking the result by comparing with manually calculated values. Test values are selected such that each part of the flowchart is tested, and consequently, the program is confirmed to be free from any logical errors.

Step 6. Validating the Data

It is quite likely that the user of your program may enter values that are not expected by the program. Such values should be rejected by the procedure created by you. This is known as validation of data. For example, in the problem stated in Step 1 given above, you may give the limit to the value of "M" and "M" should be an integer value. Such types of validation checks can be included in our program.

1.1.2 Problem Definition and use of Examples for Problem-Solving

Let us take an example of a problem faced in day-to-day life. Suppose, you want to reach your computer laboratory by 8 AM. You would lay out a plan to get ready by 7 AM; then take a bus/rikshaw to reach at the gate of your college. Then, climb up the stairs to arrive at the laboratory. You will note the time taken for each part. If due to some reason, you are unable to get ready by 7 AM, and you already know that it takes one hour to reach college laboratory by bus/rikshaw, then you will take a faster means of transportation. You may take an auto-rikshaw or a taxi. Thus, a very simple problem of reaching the computer laboratory by 8 AM will need several steps to reach a solution. Each step is to be accurately defined/marked so that no guess work is required. You can thus represent the solution of this problem in three steps as shown in Figure 1.2.

In Figure 1.2, Steps 1, 2 and 3 appear to be very simple. In actual practice, when you have to give instructions to a student who is going for the first time, it may not be so easy. For example, you have to define the word "READY" precisely so that he knows exactly what he has to do by 7 AM to get READY. Similarly, in Step 2, you may have to clearly specify the bus route number, the bus stop to board the bus, the place to get down from the bus, etc. You would also like to tell that the bus is not to be boarded, if it is overcrowded. The word "overcrowded" needs to be exactly defined. Finally, Step 3 needs further elaboration about the floor and room number where the computer laboratory is located and how to reach there.

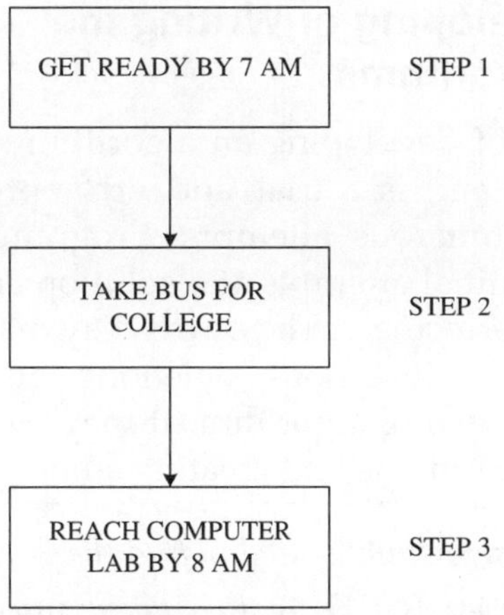

Figure 1.2 Step-by-Step Solution to Reach computer Laboratory (LAB)

You can explain all this to a person who does not know anything about the computer laboratory, provided you know it correctly. In the same way, you can solve the problem on the computer, if you know exactly what it is and how to solve it manually. Let us solve a few problems using these methods.

1.2 ALGORITHMS

A set of instructions which describes the steps to be followed to carry out an activity is called an *algorithm* or *procedure* for solving a problem. If the algorithm is written in the computer programming language, then such a set of instructions is called a *program*. The task of writing the computer program involves going through several stages. So, programming requires more than just writing programs. That means it requires writing algorithms, as well as testing the program for all types of errors.

☞ *Algorithm is a stepwise presentation of program in simple English.*

1.2.1 Characteristics of Algorithm

(a) Language independent.
(b) Simple, complete, unambiguous, step-by-step program flow.
(c) No standard format or syntax required.
(d) Helpful to understand problems and plan out solution.

1.2.2 Developing or Writing the Algorithms

The process of developing an algorithm (to solve a specific problem) is a trial–and–error process that may need numerous attempts. Programmers will make some initial attempts at a solution and review it to test its correctness. The errors they discover will usually lead to insertions, deletions, or modifications in the existing algorithm. It may even lead to scrapping the old one and creating a new.

☞ *Euclid's algorithm is used to find the Greatest Common Divisor (GCD) of two given integer values. GCD is also known as the Greatest Common Factor (GCF) or Highest Common Factor (HCF).*

1.3 FLOWCHARTS

A flowchart is a graphical or symbolic representation of a process. Each step in the process is represented by a different symbol and contains a short description of the process step. The flowchart symbols are linked together with arrows showing the flow of the process.

☞ *Flowchart is basically a plan to be followed when the program is being written. It acts like a road map for a programmer and guides him on how to go about it from the starting point to the final point while writing the computer program.*

For a beginner, it is strongly recommended that the flowchart must be drawn first before writing the program to reduce errors and omissions. Moreover, the flowchart is helpful in testing and modifying the program.

1.3.1 Guidelines for Drawing a Flowchart

(a) There should be only one entry/starting point and one exit point of the flowchart.
(b) Use the correct symbol at each stage in the flowchart.
(c) The logical flow should clearly be shown using arrows.
(d) Use connectors to reduce the number of flowlines.
(e) Lines should ideally be vertical or horizontal.

☞ *A cross-functional flowchart, also known as deployment flowchart, is a business process mapping tool.*

1.3.2 Flowcharting Rules

a. First think of the main line of logic, and then incorporate details.
b. Do not give every detail on the flowchart. A reader who is interested in greater details can refer to the program itself.
c. Statements in the flowchart symbols should be precise and easy-to-understand.
d. Be consistent in using names and variables in the flowchart. Use descriptive variable names.
e. Go from left-to-right and top-to-bottom while constructing flowcharts.
f. Keep the flowchart simple. The crossing of flow lines should be avoided.
g. If a new flowcharting page is needed, it is recommended that the flowchart be broken at an input or output point. Moreover, properly labeled connectors should be used to link the portions of the flowchart on different pages.

1.3.3 Advantages of using Flowcharts

Convey Better Meaning

Since a flowchart is a pictorial representation of the solution of a problem, it is easier for a programmer to understand the logic of the program.

Effective Joining of Parts of a System

A number of programmers are normally associated with the design of a software package. Each programmer is responsible for designing only a part of the entire system. So initially, if each programmer draws a flowchart for his part of design, the flowcharts of all the programmers can be placed together to visualize the overall system design. Any problem in linking the various parts of the system can easily be detected at this stage, and the design can be modified accordingly.

☞ *Flowcharts can thus be used as working models in the design of new programs and software systems.*

Efficient Coding

Once a flowchart is correctly drawn, programmers find it very easy to write the concerned program because the flowchart acts as a roadmap for them. It guides them how to go ahead from the starting point of the program to the final point ensuring that no steps are omitted. The ultimate result is an error free program developed at a faster rate.

Systematic Debugging

Even after taking full care in a program design, some errors may remain in the program because the designer might never have thought about a particular case. These errors are detected only when you start executing the program on a computer. Such types of program errors are called *bugs*, and the process of removing these errors is known as *debugging*. A flowchart is very helpful in detecting, locating, and removing mistakes (bugs) in a program in a systematic manner.

Systematic Testing

Testing is the process of confirming if a program will successfully do all the jobs for which it has been designed under the specified constraints. For testing a program, different varieties of data are fed as input to that program to test all the paths in the program logic.

1.3.4 Limitations of Flowcharts

Takes More Time to Draw

Flowcharts are very time-consuming and laborious to draw with proper symbols and spacing, especially for large and complex systems.

Difficult to Make Changes

Any changes or modifications in the program logic will usually require a completely new flowchart. Redrawing a flowchart is a tedious job, and many companies either do not change it or produce the flowchart by using a computer program to draw it.

Non-standardization

There are no standards determining the amount of details that should be included in a flowchart.

1.4 PSEUDOCODE

A pseudocode is a set of statements written in a human readable language, expressing the processing logic of a program.

General rules used for writing pseudocodes are as follows:

(a) **Imperative Sentence**: The imperative sentences are used to show actions. For example: Add x to sum, Display result, Sort list, Calculate, etc.

(b) **Operators**: Mostly arithmetic operators (+, -, *, / etc.) and relational operators (=, =>, =>, <, > etc.) are used.

(c) **Decision**: IF, THEN, ELSE, CASE, ENDCASE are used for decision-making.

(d) **Looping**: The looping or repetition of statements is shown by FOR, WHILE, etc.

Example 2

Display "Selected for National scholarship Examination"

Solution

Display "Selected for National Scholarship Examination"
FOR roll1 to roll10 DO
Display Roll, Name, Address
ENDFOR.

Example 3

Print if candidate can vote or not.

Solution

IF age >=18
THEN Display "Can Vote"
ELSE
Display " Cannot Vote"

1.5 PROGRAMMING LANGUAGES

A computer can only do what a program can make it do. To perform a particular task, the programmer writes a sequence of instructions called *program*.

☞ *An instruction is a command given to the computer to perform a certain specified operation on given data. A set of programs written to perform a specific task in a computer is called software.*

A computer contains a Central Processing Unit (CPU) which interprets each instruction in a program serially, sets up an internal route for flow of data, manipulates data and stores it in the main memory. Thereafter, it fetches the next instruction. This process continues till the last instruction has been executed.

Basically, a processor is designed to understand a specified set of instruction codes, and each of these instructions are stored in the main memory in the form of binary numbers. Microprocessors have input/output instructions to manipulate characters. Usually, the number and type of instructions for different types of microprocessors are not the same.

Each natural language has a systematic method of using the symbols of that language. In English, the method is given by the rules of grammar. These rules tell us which word to use when and how to use it. Similarly, the symbols of a particular computer language must also be used as per the set of rules which are known as the "syntax rules" of the language. In case of a natural language, people can use poor or incorrect vocabulary and grammar, and still make themselves understood. However, computers, being machines, can accept only exact vocabulary governed by strict syntax rules of the language being used. Thus, in case of a computer language, you must adhere to the syntax of the language, if you want it to be understood by the computer.

Computer languages can be classified into three broad categories:

a. Machine language
b. Assembly language
c. High-level language

1.5.1 Machine or Low-Level Language

The set of instruction codes, whether in binary or in decimal notation, which can be directly understood by the computer without the help of a translator is called a *machine code* or *machine/Low-Level language program.*

The computer understands information composed of only zeros and ones, and hence it uses binary digits for its operation. The computer instructions are therefore coded and stored in the memory in the form of 0's and 1's. A program written in the form of 0's and 1's is called a *machine language program.* There is a specific binary code for each instruction. For example, to add the contents of register A and register B, the binary code is 10000000 for Intel 8085. The binary code (machine code or object code) for a certain operation differs from computer to computer. Each microprocessor has its own instruction set and corresponding machine codes.

Machine code is the fundamental language of a computer and is normally written as strings of 1's and 0's. However, a machine language program need not necessarily be coded as strings of binary digits (1's and 0's). It can also be written using decimal digits if the circuitry of the computer being used permits this.

The circuitry of the computer is wired in such a way that it immediately recognizes the machine language and converts it into the electrical signals needed to run the computer. An instruction prepared in any machine language has a two-part format, as shown in Figure 1.3. The first part is the command or operation, and it tells the computer what function to perform. Every computer has an operation code or opcode for each of its functions. The second part of the instruction is the operand, and it tells the computer where to find or store the data or other instructions that are to be manipulated. Thus, each instruction tells the control unit of the CPU what to do, and the length and location of the data fields that are involved in the operation. Typical operations involve reading, adding, subtracting, writing, and so on.

OPCODE	OPERAND
(Operation code)	(Address/Location)

Figure 1.3 Instruction format

☞ *All computers use binary digits (0's and 1's) for performing internal operations.*

Hence, most computers machine languages consist of strings of binary numbers. This is the only language which the CPU directly understands. When stored inside the computer, the symbols which make up the machine language program are made up of 1's and 0's. For example, a typical program instruction to print out a number on the printer might be:

1011001111110100111101100

The program to add two numbers in memory and print the result might look like the following:

0010000000000011001110010011000000000100001000001
0110000000000011100101110101000111111011100101110
0000000000000000000000000

☞ *Machine language is not a very easy language to learn because it is difficult to read and understand, and it is written in a number system with which you are not familiar with.*

Since programmers are more familiar with the decimal number system and English language, most of them prefer to write the computer instructions in high-level language using decimal numbers.

Advantages and Disadvantages of using Machine Language

Programs written in machine language are executed very fast by the computer. This is mainly because machine instructions are directly understood by the CPU, and no translation of the program is required. However, writing a program in machine language has several disadvantages which are discussed below.

Machine Dependent: Since the internal design of every type of processor is different from that of every other type of processor, each type needs different electrical signals to operate. The machine language is also different from one type of computer to another. It is determined by the actual design or construction of the Arithmetic Logic Unit (ALU), the Control Unit, and the size as well as the word length of the Memory Unit. Hence, it is important to note that after becoming proficient in the machine code of a particular computer, the programmer will be required to learn a new machine code and would have to write all the existing programs again, in case the computer system is changed.

Difficult to Program: Although machine language is easily understood by the computer, it is very difficult for a human programmer to write a program in this language. It is necessary for the programmer either to memorize many dozens of code numbers for the commands in the machine instruction set or to constantly refer to a reference card. A programmer is also forced to keep track of the storage locations of data and instructions. The machine language programmer must also be an expert who knows about the hardware structure of the computer.

Errorprone: Since the machine language programmer has to remember opcodes and storage locations of data and instructions, it therefore becomes very difficult for him to concentrate fully on the logic of the problem. This frequently causes errors in programming.

Difficult to Modify: It is very difficult to debug or modify machine language programs. Checking machine instructions to locate errors is also as tedious as writing them initially. Similarly, modifying a machine language program at a later date is so difficult that many programmers would prefer coding the logic afresh instead of incorporating the necessary modifications in the old program.

In short, writing a program in machine language is so difficult and time-consuming that it is rarely used today.

1.5.2 Assembly Language

Programs can easily be written in alphanumeric symbols instead of 0's and 1's. Meaningful and easily rememberable symbols are selected for this purpose. For example, ADD for addition, SUB for subtraction, CMP for comparison, etc. Such symbols are known as *mnemonics*. A program written in mnemonics is called *assembly language program*. The writing of programs in assembly language is easier and faster as compared to the writing of programs in machine language.

Advantages of Assembly Language

The advantage of assembly language over machine language is that the computation time of an assembly language program is less. The assembly language program runs faster to produce the desired result.

Disadvantages of Assembly Language

a. Programming is difficult and time-consuming.
b. Assembly language is machine-dependent. The programmer must have detailed knowledge of the structure of the computer he is using. He must have the knowledge of registers and instruction sets of the computer, connections of ports to the peripherals, etc.
c. The program written in assembly language for one computer cannot be used in any other computer, i.e., the assembly language program is not portable. Each processor has its own instruction sets and hence, its own assembly language.
d. An assembly language program contains more instructions as compared to a high-level language program. Each statement of a program in the high-level language corresponds to many instructions in assembly language program.
e. In case of an assembly language, instructions are still written at the machine code level. This means that one assembly language instruction is substituted for one machine code instruction.

1.5.3 High-Level Languages

A language in which each statement is directly translated into a *single* machine code is known as *low-level language*. Examples of low-level languages are the assembly languages of various processors. The basic problem of an assembly language is that it is more closely related to the structure of a computer than to the performance of the task which is to be performed. The programmer spends more time in manipulating registers and considering instruction sequences than solving the actual problem.

To overcome the difficulties associated with *assembly languages, high-level* or *procedure-oriented* languages were developed. High-level languages permit programmers to describe tasks in a form which is problem-oriented rather than computer-oriented. A programmer can formulate problems more efficiently in a high-level language.

The instructions written in a high-level language are called *statements*. The statements more closely resemble English and mathematics as compared to mnemonics in assembly languages. Examples of latest high-level languages are Java, C, C++, C#, Python, Visual Basic, Delphi, Perl, Ruby, PHP, etc.

High-level languages are independent of computer architecture. The same program will run on any other computer which has a compiler for that language. The compiler is machine-dependent but not the language.

Advantages of High-Level Languages

High level languages have the following advantages over assembly and machine languages:

Machine Independent: High-level languages are machine independent. It means that a company changing computers – even to the one from a different manufacturer – will not be required to rewrite all the programs that it is currently using. In other words, a program written in a high-level language can be run on many different types of computers with very little or practically no modification.

Easy to Learn and Use: These languages are very similar to English language used by us. Hence, they are easy to learn and use. The programmer need not worry about how to store the numbers in the computer, where to store them, what to do with them, etc.

Few Errors: The programs written in high-level languages are much less prone to errors, since the programmer need not write all the small steps carried out by the computer. Therefore, he is much less likely to make an error. The computer takes care of all the little details and will not introduce any error of its own unless something breaks down. Furthermore, compilers are so designed that they automatically catch and point out the errors made by the programmer. Hence, diagnostic errors, if any, can be easily located and corrected by the programmer.

Lower Program Preparation Cost: Writing programs in high-level languages requires less time and effort, which ultimately leads to lower program preparation cost. Generally, the cost of all phases of program preparation (coding, debugging, testing, etc.) is lower with a high-level language than with an assembly language or a machine language.

Better Documentation: A high-level language is designed in such a way that its instructions may be written similar to the language of the problem. Thus, the statements of a program written in a high-level language can easily be understood by a person familiar with the problem. For the documentation of such programs, very few or practically no separate comment statements are required.

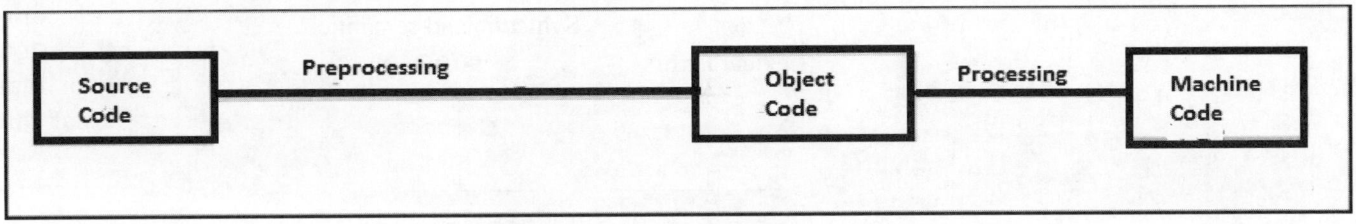

Figure 1.4 Compilation Process

Easier to Maintain: Programs written in high-level languages are easier to maintain than assembly language or machine language programs. This is mainly because they are easier to understand, and hence it is easier to locate, correct, or modify instructions as and when desired. Insertion or removal of certain instructions from a program is also possible without any complication. Thus, major changes can be incorporated with very little effort.

Disadvantages of High-Level Languages

Lower Efficiency: The programs written in high-level languages take more time to execute and require more computer main memory.

Lack of Flexibility: Since the automatic features of high-level languages are always not under the control of the programmer, the programs written in these languages are less flexible as compared to those written in assembly languages. An assembly language provides programmers access to all the special features of the machine they are using. Certain types of operations, which are easily programmed using the assembly language, are impractical to attempt using a high-level language. This lack of flexibility means that some tasks cannot be done in a high-level language, or can be done only with great difficulty.

Source and Object Language

The language in which a programmer writes programs is called *source language*. It may be a high-level language or an assembly language. The language in which the computer works is called *object language* or machine language. Machine codes are also known as *object codes*. A program written in a source language is called a *source program*. When a source program is converted into machine code by an assembler or compiler, it is known as an *object program*. In other words, a machine language program ready for execution is called an object program.

1.6 COMPILER

A program which translates a high-level language program into a machine language program is called a *compiler*. It checks all kinds of limits, ranges, errors, etc. But its program execution time is more and occupies a larger part of the memory. It has slow speed and low efficiency in memory utilization. If a compiler runs on a computer for which it produces the object code, then it is known as a *self* or *resident compiler*. If a compiler runs on a computer other than that for which it produces object code, then it is called a *cross-compiler*. The process of producing an object program using compiler is called compilation. After compilation, you get a file known as object file which is in machine language. There are two steps in executing a program, compilation phase and then execution phase. Compilation is required to detect syntax and semantic errors in a program. The compiler converts the program into machine language so that it can execute the program on machine. (See Figure 1.4).

☞ *A compiler is nearly 5 to 25 times faster than an interpreter. An interpreter is a small program as compared to the compiler.*

The tasks performed by a compiler are shown in Figure 1.5. These may be divided into two main categories.

The compilation process consists of two steps:

(a) The Analysis Phase

(b) The Synthesis Phase

Analysis Phase

The Analysis phase consists of the following tasks:

(a) Lexical Analysis

(b) Syntax Analysis

(c) Semantic Analysis

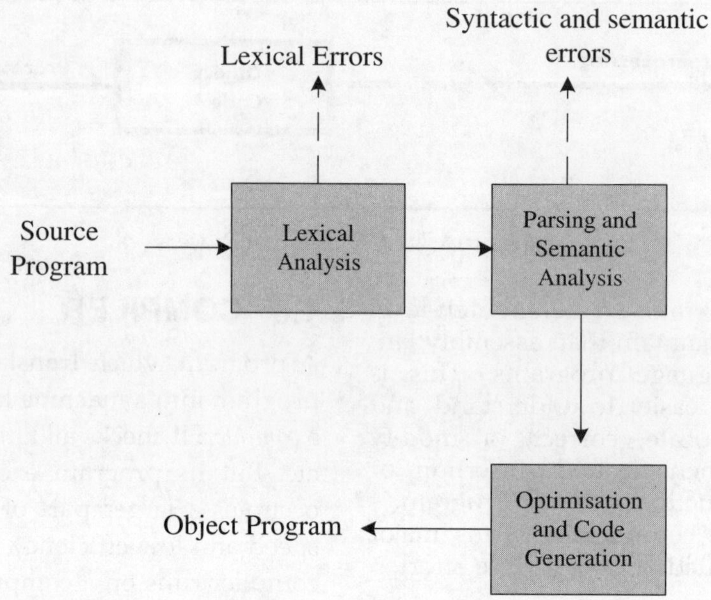

Figure 1.5 Block Diagram of tasks done by a Compiler

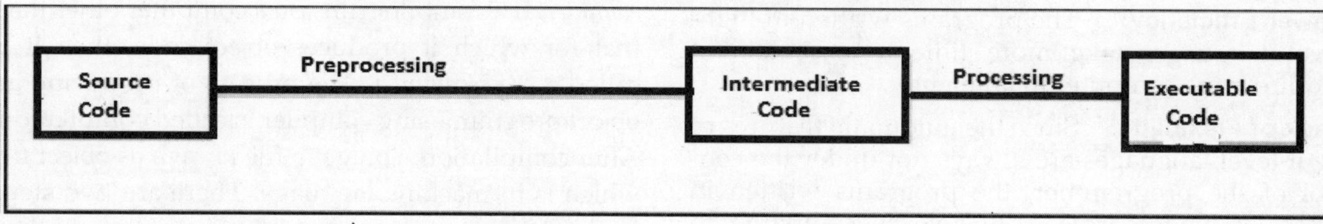

Figure 1.6 Interpretation process

Synthesis Phase

The Synthesis Phase refers to the synthesis of the object program. It generates code and does optimization. This phase takes the parse tree and data type information as input and generates the object code as output. The object code can either be in machine language or in assembly language. The compiler writes machine or symbolic instructions for each HLL statement.

This phase is also concerned with code optimization for generation of faster and more compact code. Unlike assembler, compilers need multiple passes to translate the program. It needs to scan the program many times to generate an efficient code, in terms of both execution time and memory requirements.

1.6.1 Basic Flow of Compilation

The basic flow of program execution is as follows:

Program (Source code) → Binary → Execution

So, Source code is converted into binary form using some special software known as translator, and computer executes the code.

1.7 INTERPRETER

An *interpreter* is a program which translates statements of a high-level language program into machine code. It translates one statement of the program at a time. It reads one statement of a high-level language program, translates it into machine code, and executes it. Then, it reads the next statement of the program, again translates and executes it. In this way, it proceeds further till all the statements of the program are translated and executed. On the other hand, the compiler goes through the entire high-level language program once or twice and then translates the entire program into machine codes. A compiler is 5 to 25 times faster than an interpreter.

The object program produced by the compiler is permanently saved for future reference. On the other hand, the object code of the statement produced by the interpreter is not saved. If an instruction is used the next time, it must be interpreted once again and translated into machine code. For example, during the repetitive processing of the steps in a loop, each instruction in the loop must be re-interpreted as the loop is executed.

Interpreter, unlike compiler, does not generate any intermediate code; it directly executes program statements line-by-line. Note that Python supports interpreter, so programs are executed directly. (See Figure 1.6).

☞ *An interpreter is a small program as compared to compiler. It occupies less memory space, so it can be used in a smaller system which has limited memory space.*

Python is an interpreter language. It means it executes the code line by line. Python provides a Python Shell (also known as Python Interactive Shell) which is used to execute a single Python command and get the result.

1.8 LINKER

Usually a longer program is divided into a number of smaller sub-programs called *modules*. It is easier to develop, test and debug smaller programs. A *linker* is a program that links (combines) smaller programs to form a single program. While developing a program, subroutines are frequently used. The subroutines are stored in a library file. The linker also links subroutines with the main program. It links machine codes of the programs. Therefore, it accepts user's programs after editor has edited the program and compiler has produced machine codes of the program. The process is called linking.

1.9 LOADER

The *loader* is a program that loads machine codes of a program into the system memory. It accepts programs either in absolute or relocatable format. If a program is in absolute format (i.e., the actual addresses of the instructions and data are supplied by the programmer), the loader simply loads the program into the system memory. If a program is in relocatable format, the locater assigns specific addresses to each instruction and data before the loader loads the program into memory. The process performed by the loader is known as loading.

☞ *A locater is a program that assigns specific memory address to each machine code of a program which is to be loaded into system memory.*

Difference between Compiler and Interpreter

1. A program which translates high level language program into machine language program is called a *compiler*. The compiler goes through the entire program and then translates the entire program into machine codes. It generates intermediate object code for the whole program.
   An *interpreter* is a program which translates one statement of a high level language program into machine code and executes it at a time. It does not generate any intermediate object code.
2. Compiler shows list of errors along with line numbers at the end of program execution where-as interpreter shows errors line-by-line.
3. The interpreter is a small program as compared to the compiler.
4. The compiler is faster than the interpreter.
5. Compiler needs more memory during compilation whereas interpreter requires less memory during interpretation as it interprets single unit of code at a time.
6. The object code program produced by the compiler is permanently saved for future reference, whereas the object code of the statement produced by the interpreter is not saved. Thus, the presence of source program is always required for the interpreter. If the instruction is used next time, it must be interpreted once again and then translated into machine code.

1.10 TESTING AND DEBUGGING

Even after taking full care in program design, some errors may remain in the program as the program designer might never have thought about a particular case. These errors are detected only when you start executing the program on a computer. Such types of program errors are called *bugs*, and the process of removing these errors is known as *debugging*. A flowchart is very helpful in detecting, locating, and removing mistakes (bugs) in a program in a systematic manner.

☞ *Program debugging is the process of finding and correcting errors ("bugs") in a computer program.*

Every program, written in any language, after locating errors, if any and removing them, must be executed to see the output.

Testing and debugging are vital steps in developing computer programs. They are also time-consuming steps. In fact, the time spent in testing and debugging often equals or exceeds the time spent in program writing.
There are three types of errors that occur in a computer program. These are:

a. Syntax Errors
b. Run-time Errors
c. Logical Errors

1.10.1 Syntax Errors

Syntax errors occur in the programs when the rules or syntax of the programming language is not followed. Such programming errors typically involve incorrect punctuation, incorrect word sequence, undefined terms, or misuse of terms. The Python interpreter immediately reports it, usually along with the reason. For example, you get this error message when you try to use an equals sign (=) to do an arithmetic calculation:

```
>>> 5 - 6 =
SyntaxError: invalid syntax
```

or

```
>>> print "hello"
SyntaxError: Missing parentheses in call
to 'print'. Did you mean print("hello")?
```

In Python 3.x, print is a built-in function and requires parentheses. The statement above violates this usage and hence syntax error is displayed.
All *syntax errors* must be found and corrected before a program is made to run. Almost all language processors are designed to detect syntax errors. The error messages are useful as they help the programmers rectify all syntax errors in their programs. Thus, it is a relatively easy task to detect and correct syntax errors.

☞ *A syntax error can also occur in a calculator when an invalid equation is entered into it. This can be caused either by opening brackets without closing them or by entering several decimal points in one number.*

1.10.2 Runtime Errors

Runtime errors occur when a program is executed on the computer, but the desired results are not achieved due to some misinterpretation of a particular instruction. This could be something like dividing a number by zero which results in a very large value of quotient. It may also be any other instruction which the computer is not able to understand. For example, during run time if you try to open a file that does not exist in the hard disk, then it will create runtime error. To overcome this problem, there is a built-in error detector in the language interpreter or compiler which will give the message that reflects the reason for the runtime error. Most runtime errors are easy to identify because program halts when it encounters them. For example, an infinite loop or wrong input value say, dividing a number by 0 will produce runtime error.

```
>>> a = 1
>>> b = 0
>>> print(a/b)
Trackback (most recent call last):
   File "<pyshell#1>", line 1,in <module>
      print(a/b>
ZeroDivisionError: division by zero
```

☞ *ZeroDivisionError is thrown when the second operator in the division is zero.*

Runtime error, is also called an exception. A number of built-in exceptions are defined in the Python library. For example TypeError is thrown when an operation or function is applied to an object of an inappropriate type.

```
>>> '2'+2
Traceback (most recent call last):
File "<pyshell#5>", line 1, in <module>
'2'+2
TypeError: unsupported operand type(s)
for +: 'int' and 'str'
```

☞ *A runtime error is an error that causes abnormal termination of program during execution of a code.*

1.10.3 Logical Errors

Logical errors are the errors that occur in planning the program logic. In this case, the language processor successfully translates the source code into machine code. The computer actually does not know that an error has been made. It follows the program instructions and outputs the results, but the result of the output may not be correct.
The problem is that the logic being followed in the

solution of the problem does not produce the desired results. When the logical error occurs, the computer does not print the correct output. The computer does not tell you what is wrong. For example, if instruction should be:

```
a = b * c
```

but has been written as:

```
a = b + c
```

This error will not be detected by the language processor since no language rules have been broken. However, the output will produce the wrong result. Thus, it is an example of the logical error. Logical error in program source code results in incorrect or unexpected result. It is a type of runtime error that may simply produce the wrong output or may cause a program to crash while running.

In the following program, the *while* loop will not execute even a single time since the initial value of i is 100.

```
i = 100
while i<10:
      i= i+2
      print(i)
```

☞ *A logical error is a mistake in a program source code that results in incorrect or unexpected behavior.*

Semantic error is the error that occurs when a particular statement is unable to provide a meaning. For example, the following statement is semantically incorrect since an expression cannot come on the left side of assignment statement.

```
a + b = c
```

This can be written as follows:

```
c = a + b
```

Now, this is both semantically and syntactically correct.

☞ *Semantic error is an error in a program that makes it do something other than what the programmer intended. Syntax errors are caused by invalid syntax. Semantic (logical) errors are caused by errors in program logic.*

How to locate Logical Errors?

In order to determine whether or not the logical error exists, the program must be tested. The purpose of testing is to determine whether the results are correct or not. The testing procedure involves running the program to process input test data that will produce known results. By running the program and comparing the results, the accuracy of the program logic can be determined.

Logical errors occur typically due to either incorrect logic or missing logic. If the logic is wrong, the answers generated from the test data will be wrong. Errors caused by missing logic result from logical situations that the program was not designed to handle.

As an example, suppose that a numeric field (like a number 1234) is to be used in an arithmetic process, and the data entry operator enters a value that is not numeric for the field (such as 1-2-3-4). The program logic should determine that the data is not numeric prior to attempting the arithmetic process. If that logic is missing and non-numeric data is used in the arithmetic operation, the program will fail. This error occurred only because the non-numeric data was entered into a numeric field.

1.11 TESTING A PROGRAM

In order to completely test a program logic, the test data must test each logical path of the program. Hence, the selection of proper test data is very important in program testing. In general, the test data selected for testing a program should include:

a. Normal data, which will test the generally used program paths.

b. Unusual but valid data, which will test the program paths used to handle exceptions. Such data might be encountered occasionally while running the program.

c. Incorrect, incomplete, or inappropriate data, which will test the error-handling capabilities of the program. This is done in order to see how the program reacts in abnormal and unusual circumstances.

If a program runs successfully with the test data and produces correct results, it is normally released for use. However, even at this stage, errors may remain in the program. In the case of complex systems, there may be thousands of different possible paths through which the program is to be tested, and it may not be practical to trace through all these paths during testing.

1.11.1 Methods of Correcting Logical Errors

Some ways to locate and correct logical errors are briefly described below:

a. One approach is to study the source code producing the incorrect results and try to determine the cause of the problem.
b. Put several print or write statements in the program that indicate the values of intermediate computations. Once the errors have been found and corrected, such print or write statements are removed from the program.
c. Use of tracing routines which are software tools provided to the programmer to help in debugging the program logic. Tracing routines or debug packages assist the programmer in following the logic by printing out intermediate calculated results and field values that are used in making logical decisions in the program. Using these techniques, the programmer can follow the program execution step-by-step in order to determine where the logic has an error.
d. Look at a printout of the contents of memory. This printout is called a storage dump or memory dump. The memory dump lists the instructions and data held in the computer memory in their raw form, that is, their binary or equivalent hexadecimal or octal form. The programmer can then study this listing for possible clues to the cause of the programming error(s). Most programmers of high-level languages resort to the use of memory dumps only when all other methods of detecting the logical error fail.

1.11.2 Differences between Testing and Debugging

Testing and debugging are two separate tasks. The differences between these two processes are outlined in Table 1.1.

Table 1.1 Differences between Testing and Debugging

	Testing	Debugging
1.	Testing is the process in which a program is validated.	Debugging is the process in which program errors are removed.
2.	Testing is complete when all desired verifications in terms of the specifications have been performed.	Debugging is a process that ends only temporarily, as subsequent execution of a program may uncover other errors, thereby restarting the debugging process.
3.	Testing can and should be planned. It is a definable task in which how and what to test can be specified. It can be scheduled to take place at a specific time in the development cycle.	Debugging is a reactive procedure which stems from testing. It cannot be planned ahead of time. The best that can be done is to establish guidelines of how to debug and develop a list of "what to look for."'
4.	Testing can begin in the early stages of the development effort. Of course, the tests themselves must be run near the end of the project, but the decisions of what to test, how to test, with what kind of data it is to be tested and should be completed before the coding is started.	Debugging, on the other hand, cannot begin until the end of the development cycle because it requires an executable program.

1.12 DOCUMENTATION

Documentation of a software system involves collecting, organizing, storing, and maintaining a complete historical record of programs and other documents used or prepared during different phases of the system development.

The documentation of a program is a continuous process. The program specifications, the algorithmic representation, and the program itself can all be considered part of the documentation of a program. However, after successfully completing the program, you must ensure that our documentation is compete and in a finished, usable form. This, includes both technical documentation for the programmers who may be working with and modifying the completed program and user-level documentation for the users of the programme.

Documentation starts when you first begin to formulate a problem statement and continues as you devise a solution, express the solution algorithmically, and code the algorithm as a computer program. In other words, documentation is an inherent part of a program.

Most programs that are written by professional programmers are used in a production environment. This means that once a program is deemed operational it is used on a regular basis, usually by people other than the author(s). For example, programs to process payrolls, maintain inventories, or handle hotel or airline reservations are invariably used by people who did not write them.

Moreover, these people are usually not even programmers. In this sort of environment you can see the need for the following two different kinds of documentation.

- User documentation
- Technical documentation

1.12.1 User Documentation

It provides the information that one needs in order to use a program. This information includes a number of different items. These items are as follows:

a. A description of the application area of the program or what this program will do.
b. A description of the input data that the program requires.
c. A description of the output produced by the program.
d. A description of the commands needed to start the program.
e. A description of the kinds of interactions that are possible with the program.
f. An explanation of all the messages that the program can produce.
g. An account (in non-technical terms) of the performance capabilities and limitations of the program.

1.12.2 Technical Documentation

This kind of documentation is addressed to programmers who might get the task of modifying the program at some time. Perhaps, a mistake will become apparent after the program has been placed into use, or a decision may be made to enhance the program by adding a new feature. In either case, good technical documentation is a necessity.

1.12.3 Aims of Documentation

The aims of documentation are as follows:

a. To make available a clear description of the work done so far and help in the design of the system by working to a set of standards. The documentation needs to be kept up-to-date throughout the project.
b. Good documentation ensures that everyone involved in the system (system designers, programmers, and users) fully understands how their aspect of the system will work. For example, what type of data will be inputted and how, and what information will be available from the system. This brings any misunderstandings or disagreements to surface before they become deeply entrenched in the system.
c. To ensure that the system can be maintained after completion, even though the programmers involved in the original design or programming of the system may not be available. It is essential that proper documentation is kept to enable a newcomer to make necessary corrections, alterations, or enhancements.

Program Maintenance

Program maintenance covers a wide range of activities, including correcting coding and design errors, updating documentation and test data, and upgrading user's support. In other words, maintenance may be viewed as enhancements i.e. adding, modifying or developing the code to support changes in the specifications.

REVIEW QUESTIONS WITH ANSWERS

1. Multiple Choice Questions

1. A program which translates a high-level language program into a machine language program is called

   a. Compiler b. Interpreters
   c. Both a and b d. None of the above

2. A sequence of instructions, in a computer language, to get the desired result is known as:

a. An algorithm b. A decision table
c. A program d. None of the above

3. Which type of errors are flagged by compilers?
a. Logical errors b. Syntax errors
c. Both a and b d. None of these

4. An algorithm is best described as
a. A computer language
b. A step by step procedure for solving a problem
c. A branch of mathematics
d. None of the above

5. Bug means:
a. A logical error in a program.
b. A difficult syntax error in a program.
c. Both a and b
d. None of the above

6. The part of a machine level instruction, which tells the central processor what has to be done, is:
a. An operation code b. An address
c. An operand d. None of the above

7. Which of the following is not true about an interpreter?
a. Interpreter generates an object program from the source program
b. Interpreter is a kind of translator
c. Interpreter analyzes each source statement every time it is to be executed
d. None of the above

8. The errors that can be pointed out by the compiler are:
a. Syntax errors b. Semantic errors
c. Logical errors d. None of the above

9. Which is not true about a compiler?
a. It converts one statement of a program into machine language.
b. An object code produced by a compiler is permanently saved for future.
c. It reports all errors in a program with line numbers.
d. It produces faster object code than an interpreter.

10. Which of the following is a language processor?
a. Assembler b. Interpreter
c. Compiler d. All of these

11. A program that converts a high-level language program to a set of instructions that can run on a computer is called a:
a. Compiler b. Debugger
c. Editor d. None of the above

12. The name given to a sequence of instructions in a computer language to get the desired result is
a. A program b. An algorithm
c. A pseudocode d. A decision table

13. The language understood by a computer without translation is called:
a. Command language
b. High-level language
c. Assembly language
d. Machine language

14. The mapping from assembly language instructions into machine language instructions is
a. Many-one b. One-many
c. One-one d. Many-many

15. A compiler is:
a. Machine-independent and OS-independent
b. Machine-dependent and OS-dependent
c. Machine-dependent and OS-independent
d. Machine-independent and OS-dependent

16. Which one of the following statements is incorrect?
a. A compiler compiles the source program.
b. An assembler takes an assembly program as input.
c. A compiler does the same type of function as interpreter.
d. None of these

17. Which one is not a high level programming language?
a. Perl b. Python
c. Ruby d. Diamond

18. A translator which reads an entire program written in high-level and converts it into machine language code is:
a. Assembler b. Translator
c. Compiler d. System software

19. Which of the following is not one of the processes that a high-level language program must go through before it is ready to be executed?
a. Translation b. Controlling
c. Loading d. Linking

20. Which of the following is related to machine language?
    a. Difficult to learn
    b. First generation language
    c. Machine dependent
    d. All of the above

2. State True or False for the following:

1. An assembly language program runs faster than high-level language programs.
2. It is easy to correct or modify machine language programs.
3. An assembly language program contains more instructions as compared to a high level language program.
4. Set of instructions given to a computer is known as program.
5. The instructions written in high-level language are called statements.
6. High-level language is machine-independent.
7. The language in which a programmer writes program is called object program.
8. Python is a machine level language.
9. An interpreter converts one instruction at a time.
10. A compiler is more intelligent than an assembler.

3. Match the following:

1.	Machine language	a.	A sequence of instructions which when followed properly, solves a problem.
2.	Algorithm	b.	A translator which translates a high-level language into a particular computer's machine language.
3.	Bug	c.	One of the latest high level languages
4.	Compiler	d.	The language which communicates with the computer, using only the binary digits 1 and 0.
5.	Assembly language	e.	The graphical representation of a program.
6.	Delphi	f.	Error in a computer program.
7.	Object code	g.	Executes instructions line-by-line.
8.	It is written using letter code	h.	Machine language program
9.	Interpreter	i.	Low level language.
10.	Translators	j.	Language for real time and system programming.
11.	Flowchart	k.	Compilers, interpreters, assemblers.
12.	High Level Language	l.	Assembly language

4. Fill in the blanks:

1. A set of instructions which describes the steps to be followed to carry out an activity is called ________.
2. Algorithm if written in computers language, then such set of instructions is called a ________.
3. In ________ language, each instruction is written in the form of a string of 0's and 1's.
4. A ________ language is machine-dependent.
5. ________ languages are similar to the English language.
6. Program errors are called ________.
7. The process of removing bugs is known as ________.
8. A ________ program runs faster than an interpreted program.
9. Binary number uses only ________ digits .
10. A program written in mnemonics is called ________ program.

Answers

1. 1. c 2. c 3. b 4. b 5. c 6. a 7. a 8. a 9. a 10. d 11. a 12. a 13. d 14. c 15. b 16. c 17. d 18. c 19. b 20. d

2. 1. T 2. F 3. T 4. T 5. T 6. T 7. F 8. F 9. T 10. T

3. 1. d 2. a 3. f 4. b 5. i 6. c 7. h 8. l 9. g 10. k 11. e 12. j

4. 1. Algorithm 2. Program 3. Machine 4. Low-level 5. High-level 6. Bugs

7. Debugging 8. Compiled 9. Two
10. Assembly language

Short Answer Questions

1. Discuss the advantages of assembly language over machine language.

Ans Advantages of assembly language over machine language are as follows:

a. Programs can easily be written in alphanumeric symbols instead of 0's and 1's. Meaningful and easily rememberable symbols are selected for this purpose. For example, ADD for addition, SUB for subtraction, CMP for comparison, etc. Such symbols are known as mnemonics.
b. Writing programs in assembly language saves programmer's time. Fewer errors are made, and those that are made are easier to locate. Thus, writing of programs in assembly language is easier and faster as compared to writing programs in a machine language.
c. Modification of assembly language programs is easier than machine language programs.

2. Differentiate between syntax errors and runtime error.

Ans (a) Syntax error messages

Syntax or compilation errors, are detected and displayed by the compiler as it attempts to translate our program. If a statement has a syntax error, it cannot be translated and our program will not be executed.

(b) Runtime error messages

Runtime errors are detected by the computer and are displayed during execution of the program. The runtime error occurs when the program directs the computer to perform an illegal operation, such as dividing a number by zero. When runtime error occurs, the computer will stop executing our program and will print a diagnostic message that indicates the line where the error was detected.

3. Write the names of few high-level programming languages.

Ans Examples of latest high-level languages are Java, C, C++, C#, Python, Visual Basic, Delphi, Perl, Ruby, PHP, etc.

4. What do you understand by compilation and execution of a program?

Ans To translate the source code of a program written in a high-level language into object code prior to execution of the program is known as *compilation*. The program that performs this task is known as compiler. Now, the object code made after compilation, is linked with other library codes which are needed for execution of the program. The resulting code is known as *executable code*. After successful compilation, we get file with `.obj` extension and after linking, a file with `.exe` is created. After executing the `.exe` file, the result is obtained.

5. What do you mean by documentation of a program? What is the importance of documentation?

Ans Documentation of a program involves collecting, organizing, storing and maintaining a complete historical record of programs and other documents used or prepared during different phases of the system development. The main aims of documentation are as follows:

(a) To make available a clear description of the work done so far and help in the design of the system by working to a set of standards. The documentation needs to be kept up-to-date throughout the project.
(b) Good documentation ensures that everyone involved in the system design (namely system designers, programmers and users) fully understands how their part of the system will work. For example, what data will be inputted and how, and what information will be available from the system.

6. How do syntax errors occur? Explain with an example.

Ans Syntax errors are caused by invalid syntax, for example, entering *prnt* instead of *print* in Python. Since a translator cannot understand instructions containing syntax errors, it terminates when it encounters such errors, indicating the place where in the program the problem has occurred.

7. Differentiate between Interpreter and Compiler.

Ans Differences between Interpreter and compiler are as follows:

(a)	Translates program one statement at a time.	Scans the entire program and translates it as a whole into machine code.
(b)	It takes less amount of time to analyze the source code, but the overall execution time is slower.	It takes large amount of time to analyze the source code, but the overall execution time is comparatively faster.
(c)	No intermediate object code is generated; hence, it is memory efficient.	Generates intermediate object code which further requires linking; hence, it requires more memory.
(d)	Continues translating the program until the first error is found, in which case it stops. Hence, debugging is easier.	It generates the error message only after scanning the whole program. Hence, debugging is comparatively harder.
(e)	Programming languages like Python and Ruby use interpreters.	Programming languages like C and C++ use compilers.

8. What do you mean by semantic errors (logical errors)? Explain with example.

Ans Semantic errors (logical errors) are the errors in program logic. Such errors cannot automatically be detected, since translators do not understand the intent of the given computation. For example, if a program computed the average of three numbers as:

(num1 + num2 + num3) / 2.0

the translator would have no means of determining that the divisor should be 3, not 2. Computers do not understand what a program is meant to do; they only follow the instructions given. It is up to the programmer to detect such errors.

9. What is program maintenance?

Ans *Program maintenance* covers a wide range of activities, including correcting coding and design errors, updating documentation and test data, and upgrading user's support. In other words, maintenance may be viewed as enhancements i.e. adding, modifying or developing the code to support changes in the specifications.

EXERCISE

A. Fill in the blanks

a. In ________ language, programming address is symbolic not absolute.
b. The object program is executed at ________.
c. With an ________ the source program needs to be interpreted every time it is to be run.
d. ________ produces faster object program.
e. An assembler translates ________ language programs into machine language.
f. Assembly language instructions use ________ addresses.
g. The ________ analysis phase of the compilation process groups the characters of the source code into tokens.
h. The language that the computer understands, without requiring any translation, is called ________.
i. The term used to denote an error in a computer program is ________.
j. A source program contains instructions written in a ________ language like BASIC or COBOL.
k. Machine language codes are ________ dependent.
l. ________ is the output of a compiler.
m. There exists a ________ correspondence between high-level language statements and machine language statements.

B. State True or False for the following:

a. Programming languages like Python and Ruby use interpreters.
b. An algorithm is nothing but a sequence of instructions telling the computer what to do and how to do.
c. Assembly language instructions are written in binary digits.
d. An algorithm should terminate after a finite number of steps.
e. A computer is intelligent enough to understand an ambiguity in an algorithm.
f. A program written in a machine language of a particular computer can be executed on a different computer.
g. The use of machine language requires some knowledge of different registers in the CPU.
h. Assembly language allows us to use symbolic names for operands.
i. A system software package that converts a high-level language program into machine language program is called an assembler.
j. A software used to convert source program instructions into machine language instructions is called a language processor.
k. An object program is created by a compiler from a source program at runtime.
l. An interpreter creates an object program from a source program.
m. Compiler translates pseudocode into machine language.
n. Interpreter produces object program slowly.
o. A program written in a high-level language is called source code.
p. Machine language is a machine-dependent language, while assembly language is machine-independent language.
q. The mnemonic code does not vary from computer-to-computer.
r. Logical errors in a program can be identified by the compiler.
s. Assembly language is called low-level language because the CPU directly understands it.
t. Translations through an interpreter are faster than a compiler.

C. Answer the following questions

1. What do you understand by the term problem definition? Explain it with an example.
2. What is an algorithm? Why is it necessary to write an algorithm before program coding?
3. What are the major differences between compilation and interpretation? Which process takes more time by repeated processing and why?
4. Differentiate between high-level and low-level languages. Which is more user-friendly?
5. Differentiate between source code and object code.
6. Give a brief description of any two high-level languages.
7. Write any two points about machine language.
8. Give three factors that make high level language more advantageous than machine level language.
9. Differentiate between testing and debugging a program. Can the logical errors be located at the testing stage?
10. What is an execution error? Differentiate it from syntactic error. Give examples.
11. Distinguish between compiler-time error and run-time error with the help of an example.
12. How are Compilation, Linking and Loading related? Also, explain the basic task of a Compiler, Linker and Loader.
13. Write any five flowcharting rules.
14. Write the basic steps in solving a problem.
15. Write the purpose of testing.
16. What is meant by dry run?
17. What are bugs?
18. What is debugging?
19. Name the three types of errors that occur in a computer program.
20. Write any three advantages of flowchart.
21. What is semantic error?
22. How do you locate logical errors?

CHAPTER 2

Flowcharts and Algorithms to Solve Problems

2.1 INTRODUCTION

A flowchart is a graphical representation of an algorithm. It shows different subtasks with different symbols. A few symbols are needed to indicate the necessary operations in the flowchart. These symbols have been standardized by the American National Standards Institute (ANSI). These symbols are shown in Figure 2.1, and their functions are discussed below.

Terminal

Terminal symbol is used to indicate the starting (BEGIN) and stopping (END) in the logic flow of a program. It is the first and also the last symbol in the program logic.

Input/Output

Input/output symbol is used to indicate an input/output operations in the program. If there is a program instruction to input data from any type of input device, then that step will be indicated in the flowchart with the input/output symbol. Similarly, all output instructions are indicated in the flowchart with the input/output symbol.

Processing

Processing symbol is used to represent arithmetic and data movement instructions in a flowchart. Thus, all arithmetic processes such as addition, subtraction, multiplication and division are shown by the processing symbols. The logical process of moving data from one location of the main memory to another is also denoted by this symbol.

☞ *In the flowchart, the trapezoid symbol represents a manual operation.*

Flow lines

Flow lines with arrowheads indicate the exact sequence in which the instructions are to be executed. This indication is also called flow of instructions. Normally, the flow of instructions in a flowchart is from top-to-bottom and left-to-right. Arrowheads are generally required when the normal top-to-bottom flow is not to be followed. However, as a good practice and in order to avoid any confusion, flow lines are drawn with an arrowhead at the point of entry to a symbol.

☞ *Note that in flowchart, the flow lines should not cross each other, and that such intersections should be avoided whenever possible.*

Decision

In a flowchart decision symbol is used to indicate a point at which a decision has to be made and to jump to one of the alternatives. Figure 2.2 shows three different ways in which the decision symbol can be used. It may be noted that the criterion for making the decision should clearly be indicated within the decision box. Moreover, the condition upon which each of the possible *exit paths* will be followed, should also be identified. During execution, the correct path is followed based on the decision.

Connector

If the flowchart becomes too long or the flow lines start *criss-crossing* at many places, then it causes confusion and reduces understandability of the flowchart. Moreover, there may be instances when the flowchart becomes too long to fit in a single page. Whenever the flowchart becomes complex enough, and the number and direction of flow lines are confusing or spread over more than one page, it is recommended to utilize the connector symbol as a

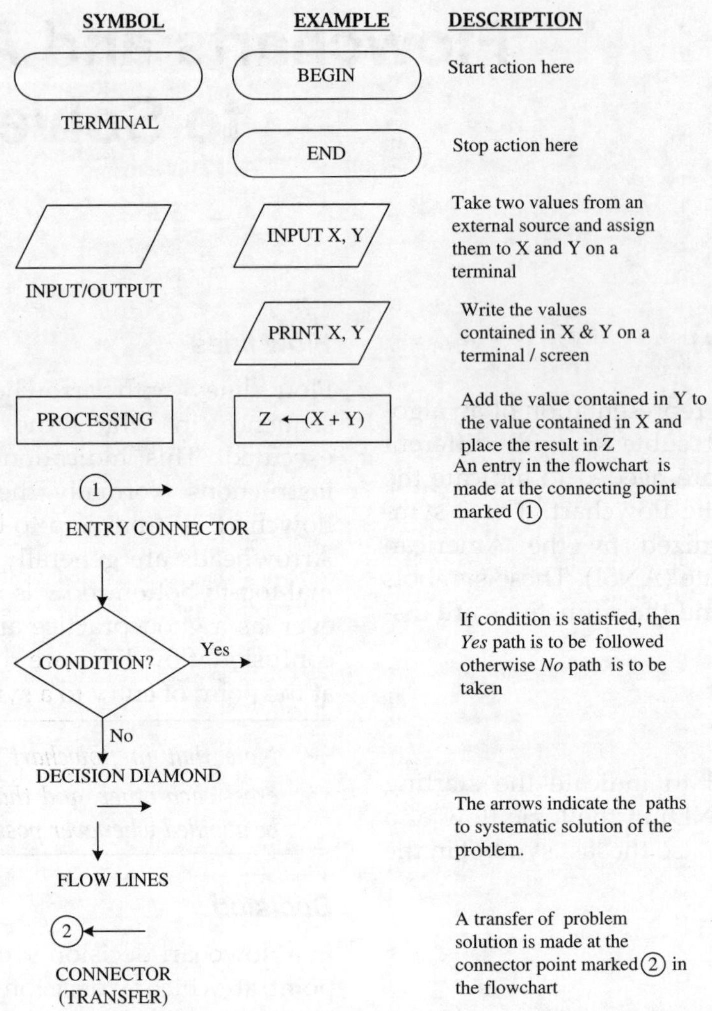

Figure 2.1 Flowchart Symbols and their Functions

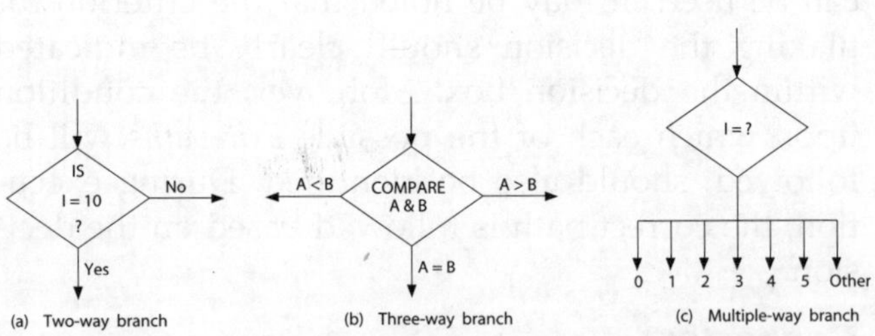

Figure 2.2 Decision Symbols used with Different Ways of Branching

substitute for flow lines. This symbol represents an entry from, or an exit to, another part of the flowchart.

> ☞ *A connector symbol is represented by a circle, and a letter or digit is placed within the circle to indicate the link. (See Figure 2.1)*

A pair of identically labeled connector symbols is commonly used to indicate a continued flow when the use of a line is confusing. So, two connectors with identical labels serve the same function as a long flow line. It may be noted that connectors do not represent any operation, and their use in a flowchart is only for the sake of convenience and clarity.

> ☞ *A letter or digit placed within the circle is used to indicate the link in the flowchart.*

2.2 FLOWCHARTS FOR SEQUENTIAL, DECISION-BASED and ITERATIVE PROCESSING

2.2.1 Sequential Processing

The Sequential (Sequence) construct means the statements are being executed sequentially. This is the default flow of statements.

Control structures allow you to change the sequence of instructions for execution. They also implement decisions and repetitions in programs.

Decision-based (Conditional/Selection) Controls allow the computer to decide as to which statement is to be executed next depending upon a condition-test.

Iterative construct (Looping) allows the computer to execute a group of statements repeatedly till the condition is true. However, power of programming languages lies in their ability to instruct a computer to perform the same basic operation again and again till the specific condition is satisfied.

In real-life applications, sometimes, you will need to change the sequence of execution according to conditions. For example,

"If you pass in the examination, then you will get a mobile".

In this statement, the resultant action is taken if the condition is evaluated to *true*.

2.2.2 Decision-based Processing

Conditional/Selection logic, also known as decision logic, is used for making decisions. It is used for selecting the appropriate path out of the two or more alternative paths in the program logic. It is depicted as either an IF...THEN...ELSE or IF.....THEN structure. The flowcharts shown in Figures 2.3 and 2.4 illustrate the logic of these structures. Their corresponding pseudocode, i.e., statement in English language is also given in these figures.

FLOWCHART

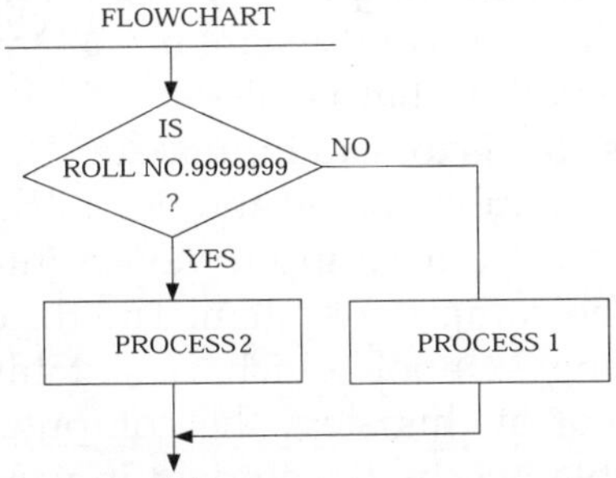

PSEUDOCODE

```
•
•
•
If Condition
THEN
    process1
ELSE
    process2
END IF
•
•
•
```

Figure 2.3 Flowchart for Decision-based Logic with Pseudocode

The IF...THEN structure says that if the condition is true, then perform process 1; and if it is not true, then skip over process 1.

FLOWCHART

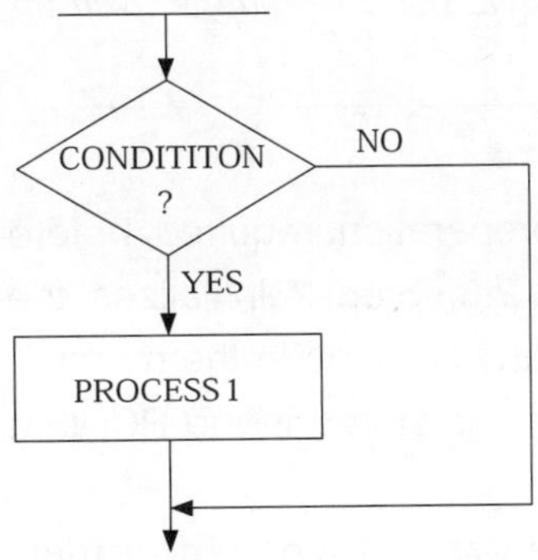

PSEUDOCODE

```
•
•
•
IF CONDITION
    THEN PROCESS 1
END IF
•
•
•
```

Figure 2.4 Decision Logic Flowchart with Pseudocode (If-Then Selection Structure)

The IF...THEN...ELSE construct says that if the condition is true, then perform process 1, else (if the condition is not true) perform process 2. Thus, in this case either process 1 or process 2 will be executed depending on whether the specified condition is true or false. However, if you do not want to choose between the two processes, and you simply want to decide if a process is to be performed or not, then use IF...THEN structure only.

In both the structures, process 1 and process 2 can actually be one or more processes. They are not limited to a single process. END IF is used to indicate the end of the decision structures.

2.2.3 Iterative (Looping) Processing

Many jobs that are required to be done with the help of a computer are *repetitive* in nature. For example, calculation of salary of different workers in a factory is done by the (No. of hours worked) × (wage rate). This calculation will be performed by an accountant for each worker every month. Such types of repetitive calculations can easily be done using a program that has a loop built into the solution of the problem. The loop is defined as a block of processing steps repeated a certain number of times. An *endless* loop repeats infinitely and is always the result of an error. Figure 2.5 illustrates a flowchart depicting the concept of looping. It shows the flowchart for printing values 1, 2, 3..., 20.

In Step 5 of Figure 2.5, the current value of A is compared with 21. If the current value of A is less than 21, steps 3 and 4 are repeated. As soon as the current value of A becomes more than 21, the path corresponding to "NO" is followed, and the repetition process stops.

☞ *In programming language, the 'for' loop is used for an iteration technique.*

Terms Used in Looping

Initialization : It is the preparation required before entering a loop. In Figure 2.5, Step 2 initializes the value of A as 1. If there is any garbage in the memory location where the value of A is stored in the PC, that will be changed as 1.

Incrementation : It is the process wherein numerical value is added to the variable each time one goes round the loop. Step 4 in Figure 2.5 shows the increment of A by 1.

The Loop Variable : It is an active variable in the loop. In Figure 2.5, A is the active variable.

Loop Exit Test : There must be some method of leaving the loop after it has revolved the requisite number of times. In Figure 2.5, Step 5 is the decision diamond, where the value of A is compared with 21. As soon as the condition becomes false, control comes out of the loop, and the process stops.

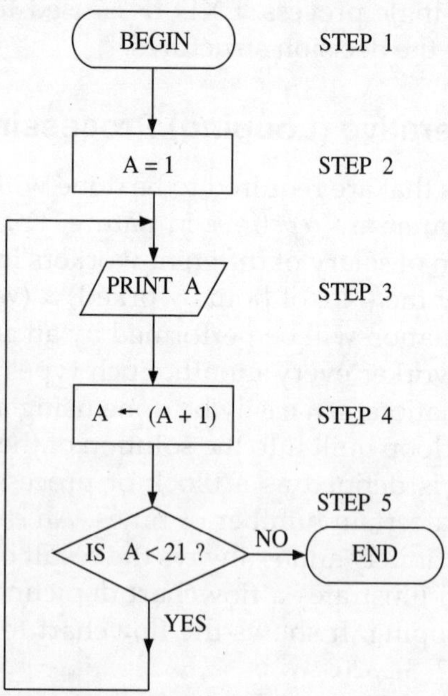

Figure 2.5 Concept of Looping

Example 1

Draw a flowchart for adding marks in ten subjects obtained by a student in an examination. The output should print the percentage of marks of the student in the examination. The flowchart for this problem is shown in Figure 2.6.

Solution

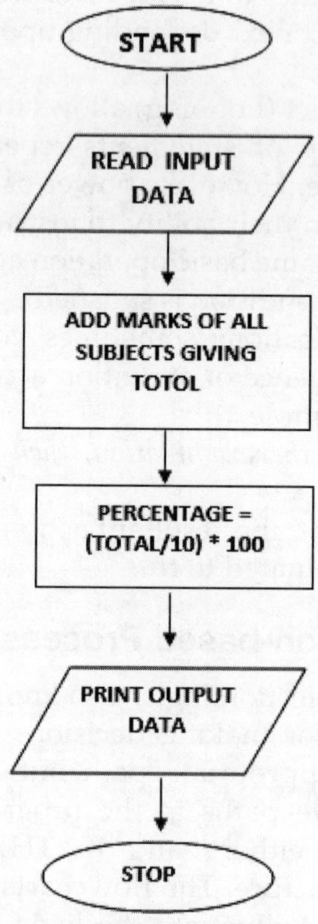

Figure 2.6 Flowchart for Calculating Percentage of Marks

In Figure 2.6, the first symbol is a terminal symbol. It shows that this is the starting point or beginning of the flowchart. The second symbol is an Input/Output (I/O) symbol that is labeled specifically to show that this step is to read input data. This step will input the roll number, name and the marks obtained by the student from an input device into the main storage of the computer system. The third symbol is a processing symbol which is suitably labeled to indicate that at this step, the computer will add the marks obtained by the student in various subjects and then store the sum in a memory location which has been given the name TOTAL. The fourth symbol is again a processing symbol. The label inside it clearly indicates that the percentage of marks obtained by a student is calculated at this stage by dividing TOTAL by 10 and multiplying the result by 100. The result is stored in a memory location which has been given the name PERCENTAGE. The fifth symbol is an input/output symbol and is labeled as PRINT OUTPUT.

Example 2

Draw a flowchart for calculating the average and the percentage marks of 50 students. Each student appeared in ten subjects. The flowchart should show the counting of the number of students who appeared in the examination, and the calculation should stop when the number of students reaches 50. (See Figure 2.7).

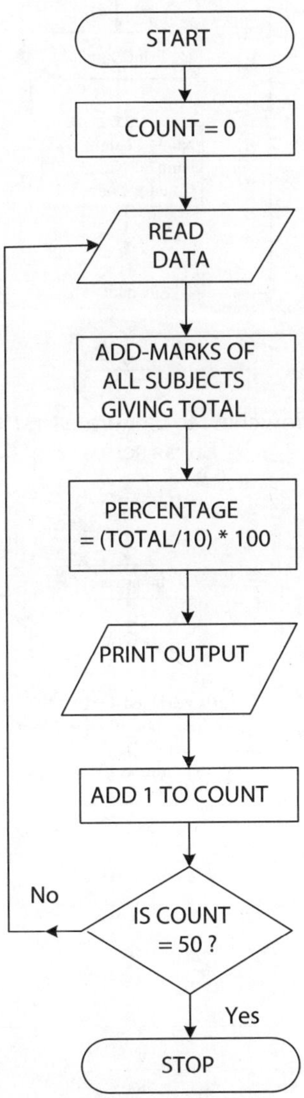

Figure 2.7 Flowchart for Calculating Percentage for 50 Students

In Figure 2.7, since all the students have appeared in the same examination, the process of calculation and printing the percentage of marks obtained by each student will basically remain the same. (The process of reading the input data; adding the marks of all subjects; calculating the percentage and then writing the output data). This is to be repeated for all the 50 students. In this situation where the same logical steps can be repeated, the flow line symbols are used in a flowchart to indicate the repetitive nature of the logic in the form of a loop.

Figure 2.7 shows a flowchart which uses a decision step to terminate the algorithm. In this flowchart, another variable COUNT has been introduced which is initialized to zero outside the loop process and is incremented by 1 after processing the data for each student. Thus, the value of COUNT will always be equal to the number of students whose data has already been processed. At the decision step, the value of COUNT is compared with 50 which is the total number of students who have appeared for the examination. The steps within the loop process are repeated until the value of COUNT becomes equal to 50. As soon as the value of COUNT becomes equal to 50, the instruction at the decision step causes the control to come out of the loop and the processing stops because a terminal symbol labeled STOP is encountered.

2.2.4 How to Write a General Flowchart?

The flowchart shown in Figure 2.8 is a general flowchart for calculating the percentage of marks of any number of students appearing in the examination. A good program should be general in nature. For example, in this case you should write a program that need not be modified every time the total number of students appearing in an examination changes.

To overcome these drawbacks, another method can be adopted to control the loop. In this method, the end of input data is marked by a trailer record, that is, the last data record in the input is followed by a record whose main purpose is to indicate that the end of the input data has been reached. Suppose the first 7 characters of the input record of a student represent his roll number (ROLL NO). Since 0000000 is never used as a roll number, a value of 0000000 as the first 7 characters can be used to represent the *trailer* record. As each input record is processed, the ROLL NO can be compared with 0000000 to determine if processing is complete. The logic of this process is shown in flowchart of Figure 2.8.

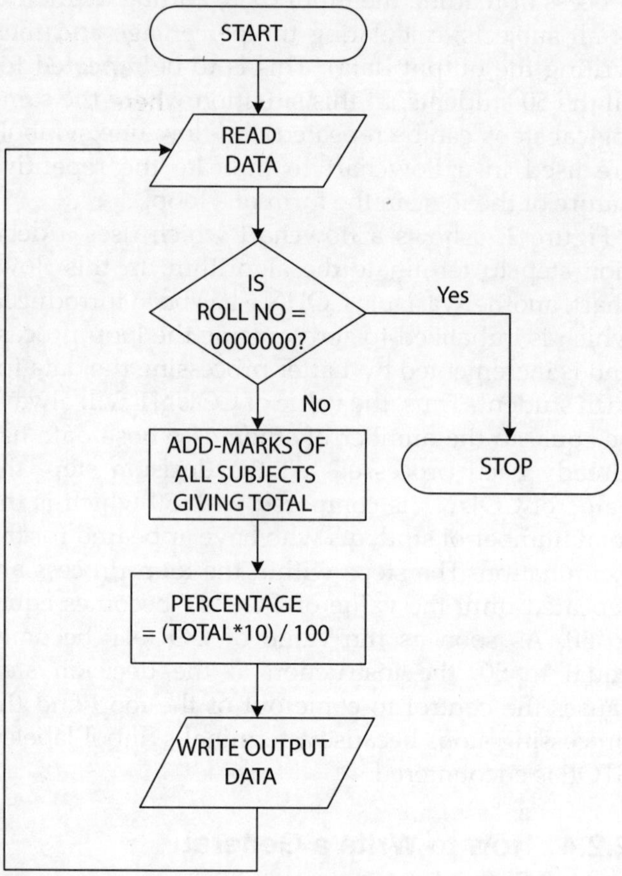

Figure 2.8 General Flowchart for Calculating Percentage

What is a Trailer Record?

The concept of a trailer record centers around the notion of selecting a field (a particular item of data) in the input record which will be used to indicate the end of data and then selecting a trailer value, also known as *sentinel* value, which will never occur as normal data value for that field. The roll number 0000000 is a trailer record in Figure 2.8.

Example 3

Draw a flowchart to generate first 13 members of Lucas series:

1, 3, 4, 7, 11, 18, 29, ... (See Figure 2.9).

Example 4

Draw a flowchart that reads a year and determines whether it is a leap year or not (See Figure 2.10).

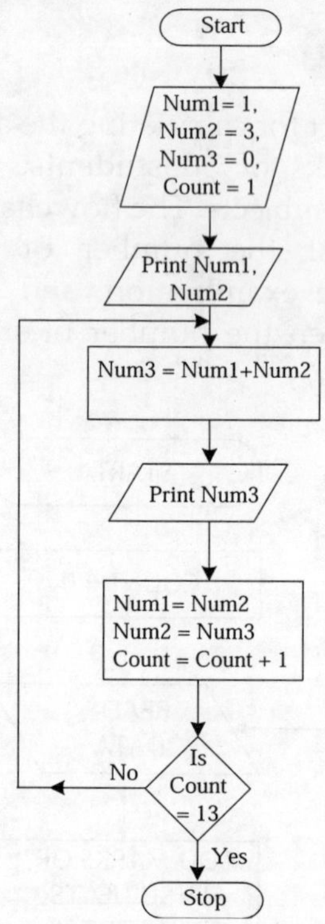

Figure 2.9 Flowchart to Generate first 13 members of Lucas series

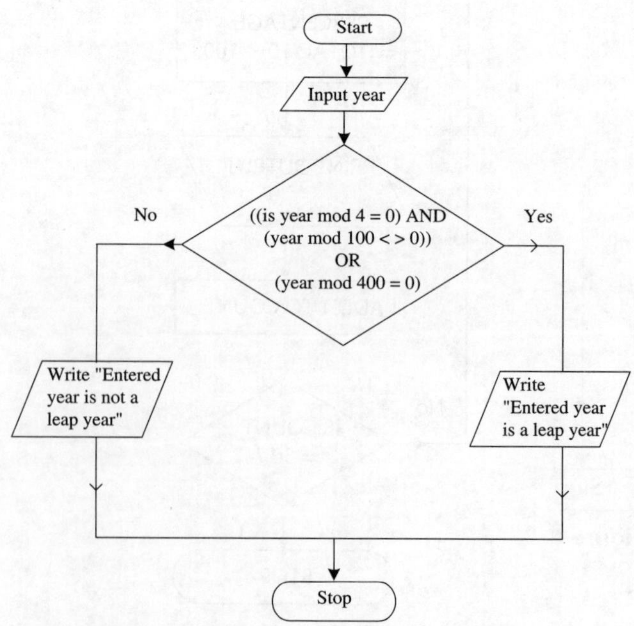

Figure 2.10 Flowchart to Find whether the given year is a leap year or not

Example 5

Draw a flowchart that swaps two numbers without using a temporary variable (See Figure 2.11).

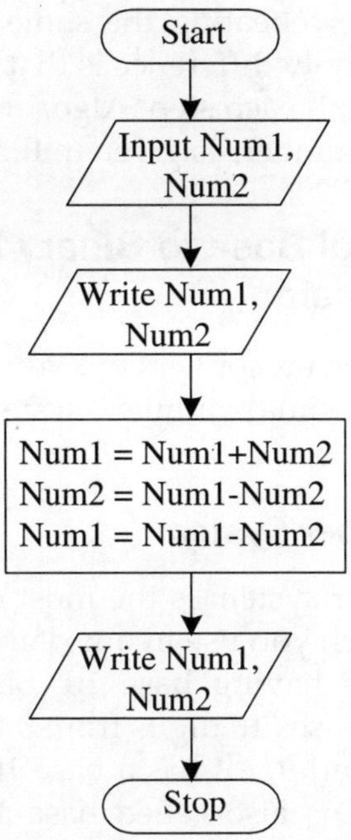

Figure 2.11 Flowchart for Swapping two numbers without using Temporary Variable

Example 6

Draw a flowchart to read any number. If the number is greater than 10, it displays its square and cube (See Figure 2.12).

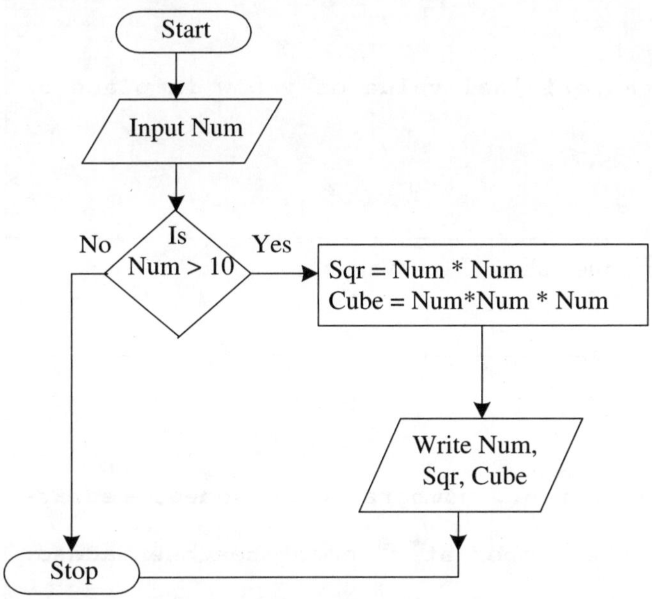

Figure 2.12 Flowchart for Displaying Square and Cube of a Number Greater than 10

2.3 SAMPLE ALGORITHMS

A set of instructions which describes the steps to be followed to carry out an activity is called an *algorithm* or *procedure* for solving a problem. Some examples of algorithms are given in the following sub-sections:

2.3.1 Exchanging the Values of Two Variables

Exchanging the values of two variables means interchanging their values. You can clearly understand this by an example.

Suppose you have two variables *x* and *y*. Our aim is to swap or interchange the values of *x* and *y*.

The original values of *x* and *y* are:

11	58
x	y

After swapping, the result should be:

58	11
x	y

To do so, you need one temporary variable, i.e., *t*. First, copy the value of *x* into *t*, i.e.,

11 →	11
x	t

Then copy the value of *y* into *x*, i.e.,

58 →	58
y	x

Now copy the value of *t* into *y* i.e.,

11 →	11
t	y

At last, you shall get the new values in *x* and *y* as shown below:

58	11
x	y

You find that the values of *x* and *y* have now been interchanged or swapped as desired. Algorithm for exchanging the values of two variables is given in Figure 2.13.

2.3.2 Summation of a Set of Numbers

Summation of a set of numbers is like adding numbers given in a series. To add a set of numbers manually, you start adding the digits in the right most column. For example:

```
 782
 222
 565
-----
 ...9
-----
```

When using computer, you must design an algorithm to perform this task with a different approach. Computer can add two numbers at a time and return the sum of two numbers.

So to add n numbers, you initialize the variable location S, where you are going to store the sum, by the assignment $S = 0$. Now, you first do the following:

$$S = S + a_1 \text{ where } a_1 \text{ is the first number}$$

then we do $S = S + a_2$ (The new value of S contains $a_1 + a_2$)

then $S = S + a_3$ (The new value of S contains $a_1 + a_2 + a_3$)

and so on till $S = S + a_n$

Here, you are repeating the same process again and again. The only difference is that the values of a and S change with each step. Algorithm for summation of a set of numbers is given in Figure 2.14.

2.3.3 Decimal Base to Binary Base Conversion

Before doing such a conversion, you need to know definition of decimal number system and binary number system.

Decimal Number System

Decimal number system is the most common number system which you use in our daily lives. It is the set of numbers having base 10. Since a decimal number system uses 10 digits from 0 to 9, i.e., 0, 1, 2, 3, 4, 5, 6, 7, 8, and 9, it has a base 10. The decimal number system is also called base 10 system. For example, 6598, 75, 100567, etc., are examples of decimal numbers.

☞ *The base or radix of decimal number system is 10.*

Algorithm

```
1.   Begin.
2.   Get the values of variables x and y.
3.   Assign the value of x to t.
4.   Assign the value of y to x. So x has the original value of y now in place of
     the original value of x.
5.   Assign the value of t to y.
6.   Show the values of x and y.
7.   Stop.
```

Figure 2.13 Algorithm for Exchanging the Values of Two Variables

Algorithm

```
1.   Begin.
2.   Read n numbers to be summed.
3.   Initialize sum as 0.
4.   Initialize 'count' as 1.
5.   While 'count' is less than or equal to n, i.e., numbers to be added, repeat-
     edly do:
6.   Calculate the sum of n numbers. (After the number at nth count has been added,
     the control will shift to Step 7.)
     a. Read the number at position 'count', i.e., when count is 1 read first
     number, when count is 2, read second number and so on.
     b. Update the current sum by adding to it the read number.
     c. Add 1 to 'count'.
7.   Stop.
```

Figure 2.14 Algorithm for Summation of a Set of Numbers

Algorithm

```
1.    Begin.
2.    Get the decimal number whose binary equivalent you want.
3.    Divide the decimal number by 2.
4.    Write the remainder.
5.    Quotient of previous stage becomes the dividend and again divide it by 2 at
      next stage.
6.    Write the remainder to right hand side of previous remainder.
7.    Repeat the process successively till quotient is zero.
8.    The set of digits formed by the remainders at different stages, when placed
      in the reverse order, will form the binary equivalent of the decimal number.
9.    Stop.
```

Figure 2.15 Algorithm for Conversion of Decimal Number to Binary Number

Binary Number System

Binary means 2. The set of numbers having base 2 is called binary number system.

Binary numbers consist of only two digits, i.e., 0 and 1. Each one of these is also called bit, a short form of **bi**nary digi**t**.

☞ *For storing the binary number, the electronic elements of a computer need to have only two stable states. The output of such electronic circuits at any time is either high or low. These states represent 1 and 0 respectively. High is represented by 1 and low is represented by 0.*

The computer understands only binary number system. But you use data in the form of decimal digits. All such numbers are converted to binary codes within the computer because computers can operate using binary numbers only.

Conversion of Decimal Number to Binary Number

To convert a decimal number to a binary number, the decimal number is divided by 2 successively. The quotient and remainders are noted down at each stage. The quotient of the preceding stage is divided by 2 at the next stage. The process is repeated until the quotient becomes zero. Now, to make binary equivalent, put the remainders in reverse order. For example, the binary representation of the decimal number 13 is shown here.

	Quotient	Remainder	
$13 \div 2 =$	6	1	↑ LSB
$6 \div 2 =$	3	0	
$3 \div 2 =$	1	1	
$1 \div 2 =$	0	1	MSB

MSB = Most Significant Bit
LSB = Least Significant Bit

So binary representation of $(13)_{10}$ will be $(1101)_2$. Algorithm for conversion of decimal number to binary number is given in Figure 2.15.

2.3.4 Reversing Digits of an Integer Number

Reversing digits basically means changing the digits order backward. For example:

Input 3 5 6 8
Result 8 6 5 3 (Each digit placed in the reverse)

To do so, you divide the number by 10 and get the remainder.

```
                      Dividend
                     /
Divisor ——→10 | 3568 | 356 ←—— Quotient
                30
                ——
                 56
                 50
                 ——
                  68
                  60
                  ——
                   8 ←—— Remainder
```

You can get the remainder by mod() function:

$r = 3568 \bmod (10)$
$= 8$

Now remove 8 from the original integer. So you next get 356 (number to be reversed).

again
$r = 356 \bmod (10)$
$= 6$

Successively, you find out the remainders until the dividend is less than 10. Now place the digits of the remainders in the reverse order.

Number to be Changed	Reversed-digits Number
3568	8
356	86
35	865
3 (i.e., less than 10)	8653

Algorithm for reversing digits of an integer number is given in Figure 2.16.

Algorithm

```
1.    Begin.
2.    Get positive integer number to be reversed.
3.    While the integer number being reversed is greater than 10 repeatedly do:
      a. Extract the right most digit of the number to be reversed by remainder
      function, i.e., mod() function.
      b. Construct the reversed integer by writing the extracted digit to right
      hand side of the current reversed number.
4.    Write the integer (dividend which is less than 10) to the RHS of the reversed
      number.
5.    Stop.
```

Figure 2.16 Algorithm for Reversing Digits of an Integer Number

2.3.5 GCD (Greatest Common Divisor) of Two Numbers

The greatest number which is a common factor of two or more given numbers is called GCD (Greatest Common Divisor).

How to find GCD?

Suppose two numbers are given. Now, divide the greater number by the smaller one. Next, divide the divisor by the remainder. Continue on repeating the process of dividing the preceding divisor by the remainder last obtained, till the remainder zero is obtained. Then, the last divisor is the required GCD of the given numbers. Suppose, you want to find GCD of 136 and 170, then

Say, $a = 136$
$b = 170$

Greater number is b, i.e., 170; so b will be dividend. Smaller number is a, i.e., 136; so a will be divisor.

Dividend
Divisor → 136 | 170 | 1
136
34 ← Remainder

Remainder, i.e., 34 is now divisor.

Dividend
Divisor → 34 | 136 | 4
136
0 ← Remainder

Therefore, the greatest common divisor (GCD) is 34.

Algorithm

```
1.   Begin.
2.   Get 1st and 2nd (non-zero) integers, i.e., a and b.
3.   Check which integer is larger.
4.   Get the remainder by dividing the greater integer by the smaller integer.
5.   Now make smaller integer dividend and divide the dividend by the divisor get
     the remainder. Let remainder be the divisor.
6.   Repeat Steps 4, 5, and 6 until a 'zero' remainder is obtained. Now, the last
     divisor is the GCD.
8.   Stop.
```

Figure 2.17 Algorithm for finding GCD (Greatest Common Divisor) of Two Numbers

2.3.6 Test whether the Given Number is a Prime Number

The natural number 1 has only one factor. Except 1, every decimal number has two or more factors. For example, 2 has two factors 1 and 2; the number 3 has the factors 1 and 3. The number 4 has three factors 1, 2 and 4; the number 5 has two factors 1 and 5. The positive numbers which have only two factors, i.e., 1 and that number itself are called prime numbers. The example of prime numbers are 2, 3, 5, 7, 11, 13, 17, etc.

☞ ***Prime numbers** are any of the positive integer numbers greater than 1, each divisible only by itself and by 1. Thus, 2, 3, 5 ,7,....... etc., are prime numbers.*

The aim here is to find the prime numbers. A Greek mathematician Eratosthenes who lived in the 3rd century BC (Before Christ) gave a very simple method for finding a prime number. The method is known as "*Sieve method*". Suppose you have to find all the prime numbers in the range of 1 to 20. To find the prime number, follow the steps:

1. Strike out 1 because it is not a prime number.
2. Encircle 2 and strike out all the multiples of 2, i.e., 4, 6, 8, 10, 12, ... 20.

   ~~1~~ ② 3 4 5 ~~6~~ 7 ~~8~~ 9 ~~10~~
   11 ~~12~~ 13 ~~14~~ 15 ~~16~~ 17 ~~18~~ 19 ~~20~~
3. Encircle 3 and strike out all the multiples of 3.

   ② ③ 5 7 ~~9~~ 11 13 ~~15~~ 17 19

You continue the process of encircling and striking till every number in list is either encircled or struck out.

(2) (3) (5) (7) (11) (13) (17) (19)

All the circled number are thus prime numbers and the numbers that are struck out except 1 are composite numbers. This method is given as an algorithm below.

Algorithm

```
1.   Begin.
2.   Get the number which you want to check whether it is prime or not.
3.   Set the value of divisor to 2.
4.   Divide the number by divisor (i.e., 2 first)
     If remainder is zero, then the given number is not prime; else the process is
     to be continued.
5.   Increment divisor by 1; divide the number by the incremented divisor; and
     check if remainder is zero. Keep repeating the process till either the
     remainder becomes zero or until divisor is equal to the number itself. If
     remainder becomes zero at any stage, the number is not prime; else it is prime
     if carried to the last stage, till incremented divisor is the number itself.
6.   Stop.
```

Figure 2.18 Algorithm to Test whether the Given Number is a Prime Number or not

2.3.7 Organize Numbers in Order (Sorting)

Sorting of numbers means to arrange a given set of numbers either in ascending or in descending order. To sort the data, selection-sort method is popularly used. On the computer systems, selection sort is implemented in the form of exchange selection sort that requires a single array to work with. In this technique, computer keeps on finding the next smallest element and brings it at its appropriate position. To sort data in ascending order, you do the following:

1. Place the values in the form of one dimensional array as shown in Figure 2.19(a).

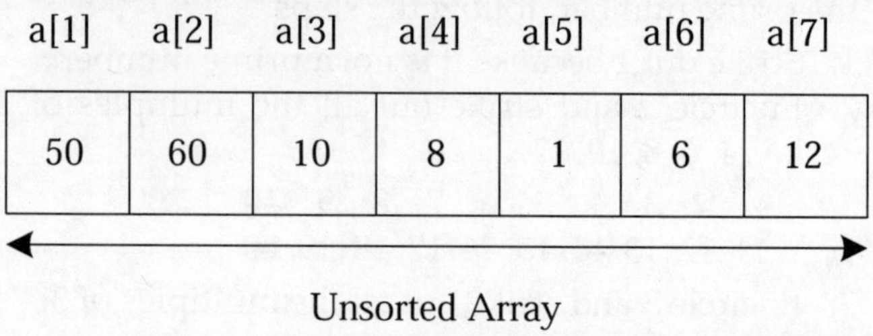

Figure 2.19(a)

2. Find the smallest value and place it as first item in the array. At the same time, move the value of the first location of the array to the location where smallest value was stored. It means interchange the value of *a*[5] with *a*[1] as shown in Figure 2.19(b).

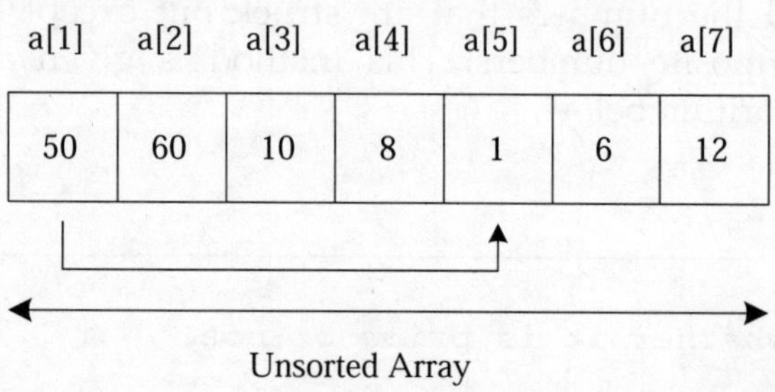

Figure 2.19(b)

3. Now *a*[1] element has the smallest value. See Figure 2.19(c).

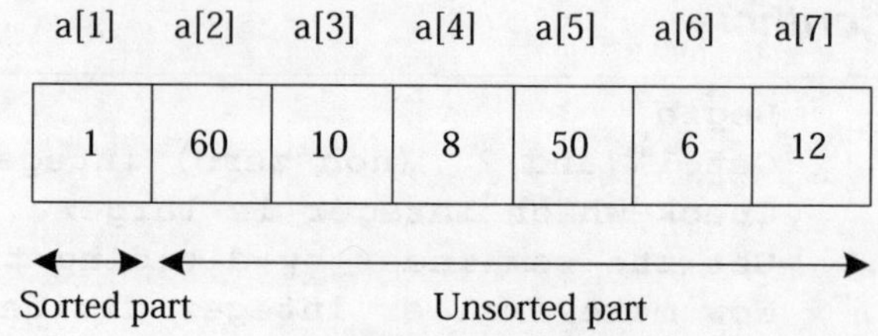

Figure 2.19(c)

Next, compare element of *a*[2] with other elements in the unsorted array. You get the array as shown in Figure 2.19(d).

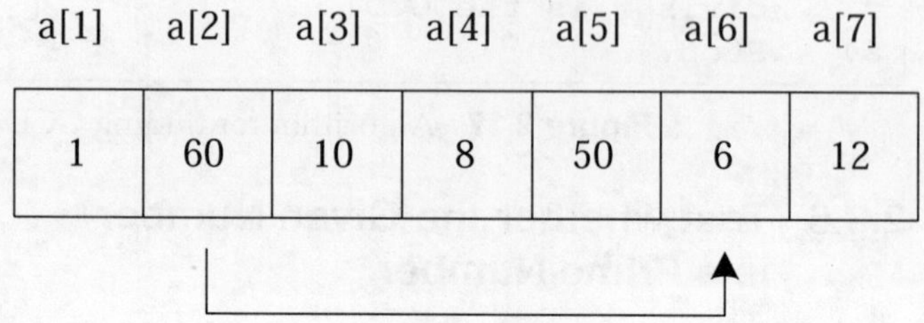

Figure 2.19(d)

Swap the value of *a*[2] and *a*[6] with the help of temporary variable, *temp*. See Figure 2.19(e).

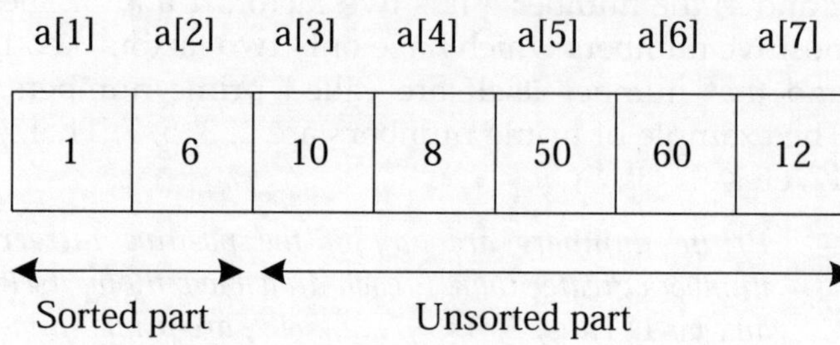

Figure 2.19(e)

Repeat the above steps to get the 3rd element, then 4th, and so on. See Figure 2.19(f).

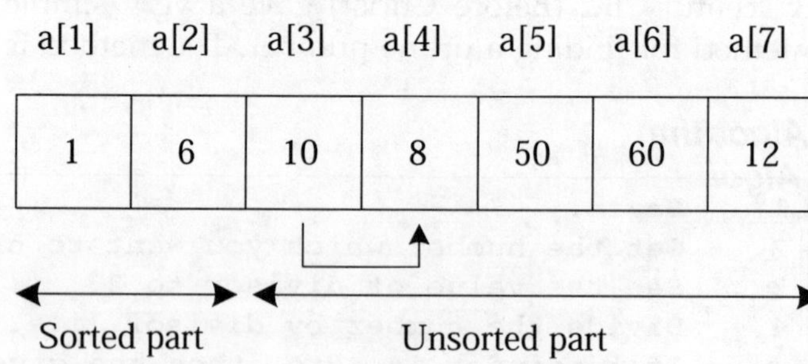

Figure 2.19(f)

Note that you need to process the unsorted array only (n–1) times. All the elements of the array would now be in the ascending order. See Figure 2.19(g).

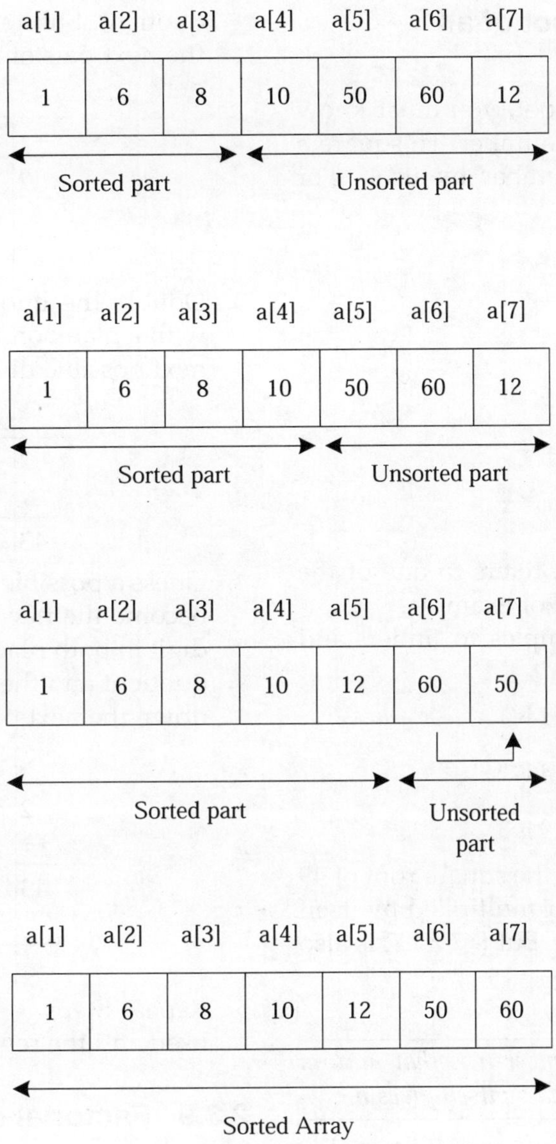

Figure 2.19(g)

Algorithm

```
1.   Begin.
2.   Read numbers and store them in an array of n elements, i.e., size of array a
     is n with elements as a[1], a[2], a[3], ....., a[n].
3.   Find the smallest element within unsorted array.
4.   Exchange, i.e., swap smallest value of the array element with that of the 1st
     element i.e., store it in 1st element of the unsorted part of array.
5.   Repeat Steps 3 and 4 until all the elements in the array are arranged in the
     ascending order.
6.   Stop.
```

Figure 2.20 Algorithm for Sorting

2.3.8 Find the Square Root of an Integer Number

Before understanding square root, you must know what you mean by squaring a number. To square a number is to multiply the number by itself. For example:

$1^2 = 1 \times 1$

$= 1$

$2^2 = 2 \times 2$

$= 4$

$3^2 = 3 \times 3$

$= 9$

Square root, on the contrary, refers to one of the two equal factors of a number. For example,

Let us read some more examples to understand square root.

$1^2 = 1 \times 1 = 1$ The square root of 1 is 1.

$2^2 = 2 \times 2 = 4$ The square root of 4 is 2.

$3^2 = 3 \times 3 = 9$ The square root of 9 is 3.

Therefore, if you have to find the square root of 49 then you will see "what number multiplied by itself will give 49". Certainly $7 \times 7 = 49$. But (-7×-7) is also 49.

So, ± 7 is the square root of 49.

☞ *A square root of a given number **n** is that natural number which when multiplied by itself gives **n**.*

You can say that if *a* is the square root of *b* then *b* is the square of *a*. For example,

$\sqrt{49} = \pm 7$ (±7 is square root of 49; 49 is square of +- 7)

$\sqrt{64} = 8$ (±8 is square root of 64; 64 is square of +- 8)

Algorithm

1. Place bar over every pair of digits starting with the right hand side. The number of bars indicates the number of digits in the square root.

   $\overline{5}\;\overline{29}$

2. Find the largest square root for the first pair that is less than or equal to the first pair. Take the square root of this number as divisor and get quotient. Subtract the product and bring down the next pair of digits to the right of the remainder.

$$\begin{array}{r|l} & 2 \\ \hline 2 & \overline{5}\;\overline{29} \\ & 4 \\ \hline & 129 \end{array}$$

3. Double the quotient as it appears and enter it with a blank on the right for the next digit, as the next possible divisor.

$$\begin{array}{r|l} & 23 \\ \hline 2 & \overline{5}\;\overline{29} \\ & 4 \\ \hline 43 & 129 \end{array}$$

4. Guess a possible digit to fill the blank and also to become the new digit in the quotient. Enter this digit in both places. Multiply the new digit in the quotient and the new divisor. Subtract and bring down the next period.

$$\begin{array}{r|l} & 23 \\ \hline 2 & \overline{5}\;\overline{29} \\ & 4 \\ \hline 43 & 129 \\ & 129 \\ \hline & 0 \end{array}$$

5. Repeat Steps 3 and 4 till the last pair has been used and the remainder comes to zero.

2.3.9 Factorial of a Given Number

The product of all positive integers from 1 to *n* is called the 'factorial *n*' or '*n* factorial'. It is denoted by *n*!. For example,

$5! = 1 \times 2 \times 3 \times 4 \times 5$

$= 120$

$n! = 1 \times 2 \times 3.....(n-2) \times (n-1) \times n$

Here, *n* is a positive integer.

☞ *It may be noted that 0! = 1, which means factorial zero is equal to 1.*

Let us take an example. Suppose you want to find out the value of factorial 5.

Initially assign the value of $i = 1$ and *factorial* = 1. So method will be to successively go on increasing the value of i by 1 and keep updating the value of *factorial* by multiplying the current value of i by the value of factorial till the incremented value of i equals to the number desired for finding the factorial.

Thus,factorial = previous value of factorial $\times i$, i.e., start with $i = 1$, giving factorial $1 = 1 \times 1$.

Now increment the value of i by 1, giving updated

$$\text{factorial } 2 = 1 \times 2 = 2$$

Again increase the value of i by 1, giving

$$\text{factorial } 3 = 2 \times 3 = 6$$

Increment the value of i until the value of i becomes 5 and corresponding value of factorial is obtained.

To summarize, the factorial will be calculated in the following way:

factorial $1 = 1 \times 1 = 1$
factorial $2 = 1 \times 2 = 2$
factorial $3 = 2 \times 3 = 6$
factorial $4 = 6 \times 4 = 24$
factorial $5 = 24 \times 5 = 120$

Hence, 5! = 120

Algorithm

```
1.  Begin.
2.  Get the number of which the factorial is to be calculated, i.e., n.
3.  Assign the value as i = 1 and factorial = 1.
4.  Calculate factorial n = factorial (n-1) × i
5.  Increment the value of i by 1, i.e., i = i + 1.
6.  Repeat Steps 4 and 5 till Step 4 has been executed with the value of i = n.
7.  Write the value of factorial.
8.  Stop.
```

Figure 2.21 Algorithm to find Factorial of a Given Number

2.3.10 Fibonacci Sequence

In a Fibonacci sequence, the previous two numbers are added to generate the next Fibonacci number.

$f_1 = 1$ (1st number in the Fibonacci series)

$f_2 = 2$ (2nd in the Fibonacci series)

$f_3 = f_2 + f_1 = 2 + 1 = 3$

$f_4 = f_3 + f_2 = 3 + 2 = 5$

$f_5 = f_4 + f_3 = 5 + 3 = 8$, and so on.

f_1	f_2	f_3	f_4	f_5	f_6	f_7 ....
1	2	3	5	8	13	21 ....

In other words, to get next fibonacci number, you have to do sum of previous two numbers in the series.

☞ *The Fibonacci sequence is named after Fibonacci.*

Algorithm

```
1.  Assign sum = 0, A = 0, B = 1, i = 1
2.  Get the number up to which you want to generate the Fibonacci series, i.e., n.
3.  Add A and B to get next Fibonacci number in sum.

4.  Assign the value of B to A, i.e, A = B.
5.  Assign the value of sum to B, i.e., B = sum.
```

(Conti..)

```
6.   Write the value of sum to get next Fibonacci number in the series.
7.   Increment i with 1 i.e. i = i + 1 and repeat Steps 3, 4, 5, 6 till the last
     value of i = n.
8.   Stop.
```

Figure 2.22 Algorithm to generate the Fibonacci number series

2.3.11 Evaluate 'sin (*x*)' as Sum of a Series

You know that

$$\sin x = \frac{x}{1!} - \frac{x^3}{3!} + \frac{x^5}{5!} - \frac{x^7}{7!} + \frac{x^9}{9!}$$

Here, *x* is in radians.

Understanding the problem

1. Read X.
2. Keep accumulating a product of integers (PRODUCT) in such a way that PRODUCT is initially 1, then $1 \times 2 \times 3$, then $1 \times 2 \times 3 \times 4 \times 5$, and so on.
   PRODUCT serves as the denominator in terms of the formula.
3. Accumulate the terms:
   $$\frac{X}{PRODUCT}, \frac{X^3}{PRODUCT}, \frac{X^5}{PRODUCT}, \ldots$$
4. Compute $X^1, X^3, X^5 \ldots$ through the use of X^i where i is initially set to 1 and incremented by 2's to obtain X and odd power of X.
5. Generate the oscillating sequence of terms
   $X,\ -X^3,\ +X^5,\ -X^7,\ + \ldots$
   To do that, you note that $(X)^1, (-X)^3, (X)^5, (-X)^7$ gives rise to $X, -X^3, X^5, -X^7$.

Hence, you use –1 as successive multiplier to generate successive terms of the sequence from their magnitude.

The algorithm is given below.

Algorithm

```
1.   Read x in radians.
2.   Read n where 'n' is the number of terms of series which you may like to add-up
     to get desired precision of sum.
3.   For 1st term,
          sum = x
          product = 1  (variable 'product' used for
                                denominator)
          num = x (variable 'num' used for numerator)
          power = 1
4.   For next term,
          num = num × (-x³)
          power = power + 2
          product = product × (power - 1) × power
          next_term = num/product
5.   Then,
          sum = sum + next_term
6.   Repeat Steps 4 and 5, looping 'n - 1' times to get the sum of first 'n' terms
     of the series.
7.   Print sum.
8.   Stop.
```

Figure 2.23 Algorithm to Evaluate 'sin (*x*)' as Sum of a Series

2.3.12 Reverse the Order of Elements of an Array

Reverse order of elements means value of 1st position of the array is exchanged with last element of the array, 2nd element of array is exchanged with '2nd last' and so on.
For example, see Figure 2.24(a).

a[1]	a[2]	a[3]	a[4]	a[5]
1	3	4	8	9

Before Reverse

Figure 2.24(a)

a[1]	a[2]	a[3]	a[4]	a[5]
9	8	4	3	1

After Reverse

Figure 2.24(b)

Here,

$a[1] \Leftrightarrow a[5]$ (Swap element 5 value with element 1 value)
$a[2] \Leftrightarrow a[4]$
$a[3] \Leftrightarrow a[3]$

Here, you can see the suffixes/subscripts on left hand side are in increasing order and the suffixes/subscripts on right hand side are in decreasing order. (See Figure 2.24(b)).

For determining the reverse-array subscript values, you can use the formula $[n - i + 1]$ where 'n' is total number of elements an 'i' is the subscript of the element of original array.

$n - i + 1$
$5 - 1 + 1 = 5$
$5 - 2 + 1 = 4$
$5 - 3 + 1 = 3$

Swapping the values of that elements in the array would thus be reversed.

To exchange the values of the elements of the array, you need one temporary variable. Then you do the swapping as given below.

$\therefore$ $\text{temp} = a[i]$

$a[i] = a[n - i + 1]$

$a[n - i + 1] = \text{temp}$

Algorithm

1. **Begin.**
2. **Get the values and store them in an array with elements a[1], a[2], a[3], a[4], ..., a[*n*]**
   where *n* is the number of elements.
3. **Compute *r*, the number of exchange needed to reverse the array *r* = integer value of n/2.**
4. **Exchange the ith element with [*n* - *i* + 1] using**
   $\text{temp} = a[i]$
   $a[i] = a[n - i + 1]$
   $a[n - i + 1] = \text{temp}$
5. **Carry out Step 4 *r* times, increasing *i* by 1.**
6. **Print the reversed array elements a[1], a[2], a[3], a[4], ..., a[*n*].**
7. **Stop.**

Figure 2.25 Algorithm to Reverse the Order of Elements

2.3.13 Find Largest Number in an Array

Largest number means the number which is greater than all other numbers in the array elements. Another number(s) in the set may be equal to this number but cannot be greater than this number. For example, in the following array:

Array	10	11	15	19	2
	a[1]	**a[2]**	**a[3]**	**a[4]**	**a[5]**

you find that the number 19 is the largest number.

From small set of numbers stored in the array, it is easy to find largest number, but finding the largest value from thousands of numbers stored in the array may take long time. But using following logic, you can get the answer in a short time.

Logic

Assign the value of the first element of the array to variable *temp;* then compare the value of *temp* to those of other elements in the array in order, one-by-one. If any element value is greater than *temp* then put that value in *temp* and continue comparison.

For the array shown above value of *temp* = 10 taken from first element of the array.

Compare value in *temp* to 2nd element value of the array. Here, 11 is greater than 10, so delete the original value of *temp* and write down the 2nd element, i.e., 11 in *temp.* Then compare the 3rd element value with the new *temp* value. The procedure will be continued till all the elements in the array have been examined. In the end, you will get the largest value in the *temp* variable.

Algorithm

```
1.   Begin.
2.   Get the value of element in an array and store them in the array elements
     a[1], a[2]..... a[n]   where n is the number of elements.
3.   Set temporary variable and assign the value of 1st array element a[1] to temp.
4.   Compare temp with the next element a[2] of the array.
5.   If the element is having greater value than temp, assign that value to temp.
6.   Repeat Steps 4 and 5 till last element a[n] of the array is encountered.
7.   Final value of temp is the largest value stored in the array.
8.   Stop
```

Figure 2.26 Algorithm to Find Largest Number in an Array

2.3.14 Multiplication of Two Matrices

Arthur Kelley was the first person to introduce the concept of matrix. Later on, the study of matrix was utilized to solve different types of linear equation problems.

How to form a Matrix?

$$\left.\begin{aligned} 8x + 5y &= 2 \\ 6x + y &= 3 \end{aligned}\right\}$$

is a system of two linear equations. Arrange the coefficient of x and y in the following way:

$$\begin{bmatrix} 8 & 5 \\ 6 & 1 \end{bmatrix}$$

[8 5] in the top horizontal line is called 1st row.
[6 1] in the second horizontal line is called 2nd row.

$\begin{bmatrix} 8 \\ 6 \end{bmatrix}$ is called 1st column.

$\begin{bmatrix} 5 \\ 1 \end{bmatrix}$ is called 2nd column.

A matrix is a two-dimensional array having m rows and n columns. So, you have $m \times n$ positions. Each row consists of m elements, and each column consists of n elements.

Matrix Multiplication

Figure 2.27 shows the elements of a 3×3 matrix.

Let $A = A_{ij}, i = 1, 2, \ldots, m;$

$j = 1, 2, \ldots, n$

Let $B = B_{jk}, j = 1, 2, \ldots, n;$

$k = 1, 2, \ldots, p$

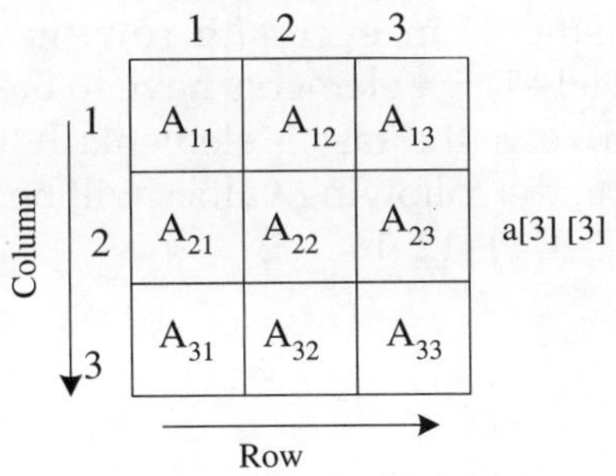

A(i, j) where i = 1, 2, 3 and j = 1, 2, 3

Figure 2.27

The product AB of matrices A and B will have *i* rows and *k* columns.

The two matrices A $(m \times n)$ and B $(n \times p)$ are such that the number of rows of B is same as the number of columns of A. Then the product of these two matrices can be carried out and it is defined as:

$C = AB = C_{ik}$, where i changes from $1, \ldots m$ and

$k = 1, \ldots p$

Thus, $C_{ik} = a_{i1}b_{1k} + a_{i2}b_{2k} + \ldots + a_{in}b_{nk}$

C_{ik} is obtained by multiplying the values/elements in the ith row of A with the corresponding values/elements in the kth column of B and then adding them.

☞ *The matrix **A** is said to be compatible for multiplication with the matrix **B** if the number of columns of **A** is equal to the number of rows of **B**.*

It should be noted that there can be matrices which are not compatible for multiplication, and in that case you can say that the multiplication, of matrices is not defined.

For example, if

$$A = \begin{bmatrix} 5 & 8 & 9 \\ 6 & 9 & 5 \end{bmatrix} \quad B = \begin{bmatrix} 5 & 5 \\ 4 & 8 \\ 7 & 9 \\ 6 & 8 \end{bmatrix}$$

Here, A is a matrix of size 2 × 3, i.e., 2 rows and 3 columns.

B is a matrix of size 4 × 2, i.e., 4 rows and 2 columns.

You know that for obtaining the product of two matrices, the number of columns of the matrix A must be equal to the number of rows of matrix B.

But, A has 3 columns and B has 4 rows, so A and B are not compatible for multiplication.

Let us take an example where the multiplication of matrices is defined.

$$A = \begin{bmatrix} 0 & 2 & 3 \\ 1 & 3 & 1 \\ 2 & 5 & 2 \end{bmatrix} \quad B = \begin{bmatrix} 1 & 0 \\ 0 & 2 \\ 2 & 2 \end{bmatrix}, \text{ then}$$

Here, A and B are compatible. The product is as follows:

$$A \times B = \begin{bmatrix} 0\times1+2\times0+3\times2 & 0\times0+2\times2+3\times2 \\ 1\times1+3\times0+1\times2 & 1\times0+3\times2+1\times2 \\ 2\times1+5\times0+2\times2 & 2\times0+5\times2+2\times2 \end{bmatrix}$$

$$= \begin{bmatrix} 6 & 10 \\ 3 & 8 \\ 6 & 14 \end{bmatrix}$$

Here 6 is the value of the element lying in the 1st row and 1st column of the *product matrix* $(A \times B)$. This is the sum of the products of the corresponding elements of 1st row of A with 1st column of B.

Algorithm

```
1.  Get 1st and 2nd matrices.
2.  Check if the number of columns of 1st matrix is equal to the number of rows in
    2nd matrix. Then matrices are compatible for multiplication. Otherwise, prod-
    uct is not possible.
3.  If matrices are compatible then find the sum of the product of corresponding
    element of each row of A with the corresponding element of each column of B.
```

Figure 2.28 Algorithm for Matrix Multiplication

2.3.15 Print Elements of Upper Triangle Matrix

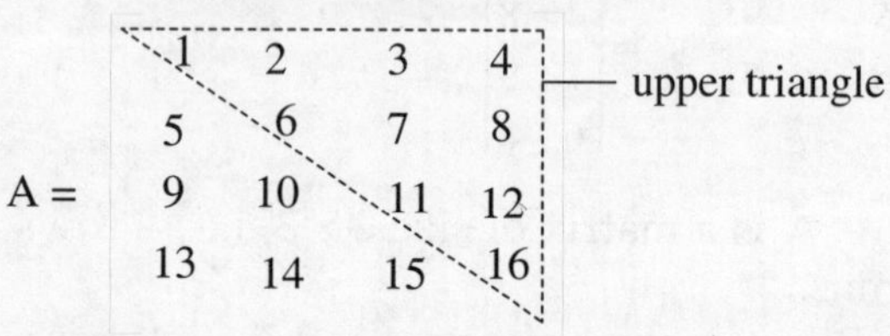

Let us consider 4 × 4 square matrix. Now, to print last (4-*i*+1) elements in every *i*th row, in the first row, the last (4-1+1) = 4 elements have to be printed. In the second row, the last 3 elements have to be printed. Hence, the following values will be printed.

1 2 3 4 6 7 8 11 12 16

Algorithm

```
1.    Begin.
2.    Read the order of square matrix, n.
3.    Read the contents of the matrix in
           A[i] [j] form
4.    Initialize i to 0 and j to 1.
5.    Repeat Steps 6, and 7, until i is less than or equal to n.
6.    Repeat the following steps until j is less than or equal to n.
      (i)  print a[i][j]
      (ii) Increment j by 1
7.    Stop.
```

Figure 2.29 Algorithm to Print Elements of Upper Triangle Matrix

2.3.16 Evaluate the Salesman's Wage

Suppose a salesman earns a basic wage of Rs. 1000 in a week. He also earns a commission of 25% of the value of all the goods he sells. If he sells more than Rs. 1000 of goods in any week, he receives a bonus of Rs. 50. Write the algorithm.

Algorithm

```
1.    Input Salesman's name and the value of the goods sold.
2.    Calculate the total wage. If the value of goods sold is less than or equal to
      Rs. 1000, then
          wage = 1000 + 25% of value
3.    If value of goods sold is greater than Rs. 1000, then
          wage = 1000 + 25% of value + 50
4.    Print the total wage.
```

Figure 2.30 Algorithm to Evaluate the Salesman's Wage

2.3.17 Finding Maximum Among Three Numbers

To determine maximum out of three numbers, you have to assume three numbers, such as a, b and c and follow the algorithm given below.

Algorithm

```
1.    Begin
2.    Read the three numbers, i.e., a, b and c.
```

(Conti..)

```
3.     If a>b
       i.     If a > c, then a is the greatest number.
       ii.    else, c is the greatest number.
4.     else
       i.     If b > c, then b is the greatest number.
       ii.    else, c is the greatest number.
5.     Stop.
```

Figure 2.31 Algorithm to Determine Maximum out of Three Numbers

2.3.18 Finding the Sum of First n Even Numbers

To get the sum of first n even numbers, you assume an array A of n elements and follow the algorithm given below:

Algorithm

```
1.     Begin.
2.     Initialize evensum as 0 and Read N.
3.     Repeat for I = 1,2,...,N
       i.     If (A[I] % 2 == 0  then
       ii.    evensum = evensum + A[I]
       iii.   I=I + 1
4.     Display evensum
5.     Stop.
```

Figure 2.32 Algorithm to find Sum of Even Numbers

2.3.19 Conversion of Temperature

Let us assume *temp* to be temperature given in Celsius To convert it into Fahrenheit follow the algorithm given below:

Algorithm

```
1.     Begin.
2.     Read the value of Celsius temperature (temp).
3.     Fahren = 1.8 * temp + 32
4.     Print 'Converted Temperature is ', Fahren
5.     Stop.
```

Figure 2.33 Algorithm for Conversion of Temperature

2.3.20 Finding the Average Height of Boys and Girls in a Class

To find the average height of boys and girls in a class, follow the algorithm given below:

Algorithm

```
1.     Begin.
2.     Initialize the counters to accumulate total number of girls and boys in the
       class and also their respective heights, i.e., sum_boys_height,
       sum_girls_height, heightb, heightg.
```

(Conti..)

```
3.    While inputting data is left repeat steps 4 and 5.
4.    Read rno, sex_code, heightb, heightg.
5.    if sex_code = 1 then
                sum_boys_height = sum_boys_height + heightb
                ++total_boys
      else
                sum_girls_height = sum_girls_height + heightg
                ++total_girls
6.    Avg_boys_height = sum_boys_height / total_boys
7.    Avg_girls_height = sum_girls_height / total_girls
8.    Print total_boys, Avg_boys_height, total_girls, Avg_girls_height
9.    Stop.
```

Figure 2.34 Algorithm for Finding the Average Height of Boys and Girls in a Class

2.3.21 Finding Average of Random *N* Numbers

To calculate average of random *n* numbers, follow the algorithm given below:

Algorithm

```
1.    Begin.
2.    Read random n integers.
3.    Calculate sum of these n integers.
4.    Divide the sum by n.
5.    Print the final value as average.
6.    Stop.
```

Figure 2.35 Algorithm for Finding Average of Random *n* Numbers

2.3.22 Checking Given Number is Palindrome or Not

A palindrome is a number which appears same when it is read from left to right or from right to left.

For example, 1234321 is a palindrome number. To check whether the given number is palindrome or not, follow the algorithm given below:

Algorithm

```
1.    Begin.
2.    Read the value of number, say num.
3.    Store the value of num in n, and initialize rev to 0.
               digit = num % 10
               rev = rev * 10 + digit
               num = num / 10
4.    if (n == rev)
               Print "the number is a palindrome"
5.    else
               Print "the number is not a palindrome"
6.    Stop.
```

Figure 2.36 Algorithm for Checking whether Given Number is Palindrome or Not

2.3.23 Checking the Given Number is Odd or Even

To check whether the given number is odd or even, follow the algorithm given below:

Algorithm

```
1.    Begin.
2.    Read the value of number, say num.
3.    Divide the number by 2.
4.    if the remainder is 1 then
            Print "the number is odd"
5.    else
            Print "the number is even"
6.    Stop.
```

Figure 2.37 Algorithm for Checking whether Given Number is Odd or Even

2.3.24 Checking the Given Number is Positive, Negative or Zero

To check whether the given number is positive, negative or zero, follow the algorithm given below:

Algorithm

```
1.    Begin.
2.    Read the value of number, say num.
3.    if num > 0 , print "the value of num is positive"
4.    else
3.    If num < 0 , print "the value of num is negative"
5.    else, print "the value of num is zero".
6.    Stop.
```

Figure 2.38 Algorithm for Checking whether Given Number is Positive, Negative or Zero

2.3.25 Finding the Maximum and Minimum Number

To find maximum and minimum number, follow the algorithm given below:

Algorithm

```
1.    Begin.
2.    Read the value of first number, say num.
3.    Store the value of num in Max and Min.
4.    for (count = 1; count < 100; count = count + 1)
            Read the next number, num.
            if max < num
                      max = num
            else if min > num
                      min = num
5.    Print 'the value of largest number', max
6.    Print 'the value of smallest number', min
7.    Stop
```

Figure 2.39 Algorithm for Finding the Maximum and Minimum Number

2.3.26 Finding Grade for Given Total Marks

To find grade for given total marks, follow the algorithm given below:

Algorithm

```
1.    Begin.
2.    Read the value of total marks, say total.
3.    if (total > 100) print "Error: total is out of range"
      else if (total >= 90) print "Grade A"
      else if (total >= 80) print "Grade B"
      else if (total >= 70) print "Grade C"
      else if (total >= 60) print "Grade D"
      else if (total >= 50) print "Grade E"
      else if (total >= 0) print "Grade F"
      else print "Error: total is out of range"
4.    Stop.
```

Figure 2.40 Algorithm for Finding Grade for Given Total Marks

REVIEW QUESTIONS WITH ANSWERS

1. Multiple Choice Questions

1. A natural number 1 is also a/an:
   a. Prime number
   b. Real number
   c. Integer number
   d. None of the above
2. Prime number is a number:
   a. Divisible by 1
   b. Divisible by 1 and by itself
   c. Divisible by 1 and by itself except the number 1
   d. None of the above
3. Swapping of two numbers is done by:
   a. Directly interchanging their values with each other
   b. Storing the value of one in a temporary variable and shifting the value of the other into the first and then copying the value of temporary to the other
   c. Transferring one number to other number without storing any number in the temp variable
   d. None of the above
4. Sorting an array in the ascending order of numbers is the process of:
   a. Putting the largest number first and smallest in the last
   b. Putting the smallest number first and the largest number in the last
   c. Putting the numbers in any way you desire
   d. None of the above
5. GCD of two numbers is:
   a. The smallest number which is a common factor of the given numbers
   b. The largest number which is a common factor of the given numbers
   c. 1 for all numbers
   d. None of the above
6. Product of matrices A (m × n) and B (n × p) will be matrix C with row and columns as:
   a. m and p   b. n and p
   c. p and n   d. none of the above
7. The product of all natural numbers from 1 to n is called:
   a. n!
   b. n × n
   c. n^n
   d. none of the above

2. State True or False for the following:

1. The elements of an array A of dimension N are represented as A[1], A[2], ... A[N].
2. The product of two matrices A[ij] and B[jk] is a matrix C[ik].
3. The series 1, 2, 3, 4, 8, 13 is a Fibonacci series.

4. In an array of ascending order of numbers, the largest number is the last element of the array and smallest number is the first element of the array.
5. Multiplication of two matrices is possible only when they are compatible.
6. Algorithm is the graphical representation of logic.
7. Algorithm is helpful to understand problems and plan out solution.

3. Match the following:

1. 5!	a. 1
2. 1, 1, 2, 3, 5, 8	b. Fibonacci series
3. $\sin\left(\frac{\pi}{2}\right)$	c. 120
4. $\begin{bmatrix}1 & 2\\3 & 4\end{bmatrix} \times \begin{bmatrix}2 & 1\\3 & 4\end{bmatrix}$	d. Sorted array
5. | 1 | 5 | 9 | 11 | 15 |	e. Square matrix $\begin{bmatrix}8 & 9\\18 & 19\end{bmatrix}$
6. Pictorial representation of program	f. Algorithm
7. Language independent	g. Flowchart

4. Fill in the blanks:

1. The GCD of the numbers 120 and 64 is ________.
2. The number 31 is a ________ because it is divisible by 1 or by itself only.
3. In Fibonacci series, the ________ two numbers are added to generate the Fibonacci number.
4. Square root of a number is that number which multiplied by ________ gives the original number.
5. Sin (x) is defined as $x - \frac{x^3}{3!} + \frac{x^5}{5!} - \frac{x^7}{7!}$ where x is expressed in ________.
6. The ________ symbol is used to indicate the beginning and end of the flowchart.
7. A ________ symbol is represented by a circle and a letter or digit placed within the circle.
8. ________ is a program analysis tool that is used for planning program logic.
9. Pictorial representation of an algorithm is ________.
10. Diamond shape is used to show ________ in a flowchart.
11. Flowchart tool is used for ________ designing.

Answers

1. 1. c 2. b 3. b 4. b 5. b 6. a 7. a

2. 1. T 2. T 3. F 4. T 5. T 6. F 7. T

3. 1. c 2. b 3. a 4. e 5. d 6. g 7. f

4. 1. 8 2. Prime number 3. Previous 4. Itself 5. Radians 6. Terminal 7. Connector 8. Pseudocode 9. Flowchart 10. Condition 11. Program

Short Answer Questions

1. Write an algorithm to sort an array in the descending order.

Ans Algorithm to sort an array in descending order.

1. Begin.
2. Read numbers and store them in an array of n elements, i.e., size of array a is n with elements as a[1], a[2], a[3], ... , a[n].
3. Find the largest element within unsorted array.
4. Exchange i.e., swap largest value of the array element with that of the 1st element, i.e., store it in the 1st element of the unsorted part of array.
5. Repeat Steps 3 and 4 until all the elements in the array are arranged in the descending order.
6. Stop.

2. Write an algorithm that reads a year and determines whether it is a leap year or not.

Ans Algorithm to determine whether the year is a leap year or not.

1. Begin.
2. Prompt the user to enter four digit year.
3. Read the year.
4. if (year %100 = = 0 ‖ year % 400 = = 0 ‖ year %4 = = 0)

return true ('The year is a leap year')
else
return false ('The year is not a leap year')
5. Stop.

3. Write an algorithm to calculate the volume and surface area of sphere, assuming PI = 3.14.

Ans

1. Begin.
2. Read the value of radius (r) of the sphere.
3. volume = (4 * PI * r * r * r) / 3
4. area = 4 * PI * r * r
5. Print 'volume of sphere', volume
6. Print 'area of sphere', area
7. Stop.

4. Write an algorithm to calculate area of rectangle(area). Read the value of length(l) and breadth(b).

Ans

1. Begin.
2. Read the value of length(l) and breadth(b) of a rectangle.
3. area = l * b
4. Print 'area of rectangle', area
5. Stop.

5. Write an algorithm to calculate simple interest. Read the values of principal amount(p), number of years(n) and rate of interest(r).

Ans

1. Begin.
2. Read the value of principal amount(p), number of years(n) and rate of interest(r).
3. si = (p * n * r) / 100
4. Print 'Simple Interest is ', si
5. Stop.

6. What is flowchart? Explain its different symbols.

Ans A flowchart is a graphical or symbolic representation of a process. Each step in the process is represented by a different symbol and contains a short description of the process step. The flowchart symbols are linked together with arrows showing the flow of the process. The most common flowchart symbols are as follows:

(a) **Terminator**: An oval-shaped symbol indicates the start or end of the process.

(b) **Process**: A rectangular-shaped symbol indicates all kinds of arithmetic and logical processes.

(c) **Decision**: A diamond-shaped symbol indicates a decision to be made.

(d) **Connector**: A small, labeled, circular symbol is used to indicate a jump in the flowchart.

(e) **Input/Output**: A parallelogram indicates data input or output (I/O) for a process.

7. What is an algorithm?

Ans A set of instructions which describes the steps to be followed to carry out an activity is called an *algorithm* or *procedure* for solving a problem.

8. Name the symbol used in the flowchart to represent arithmetic and data movement instructions.

Ans Processing symbol

9. Draw a flowchart to print sum of numbers between 1 and the entered number. For example, if you enter 5, then it will find the sum of 1, 2, 3, 4 and 5, i.e., 1 + 2 + 3 + 4 + 5 = 15

Ans Flowchart is given in Figure 1.

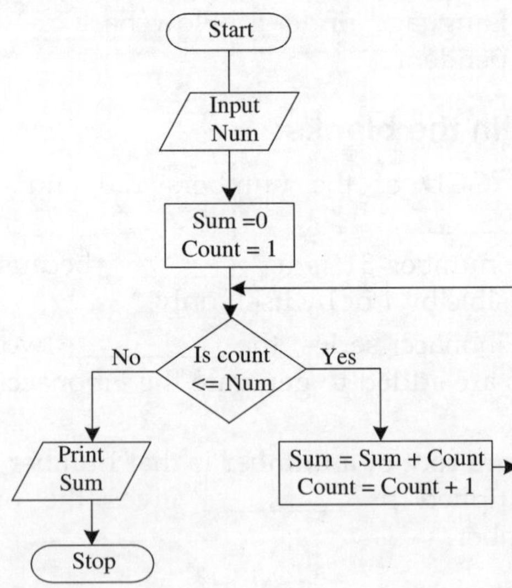

Figure 1 Flowchart to Print Sum of numbers between 1 and the Entered Number

10. Make the flowchart to solve the following cosine series.
$S = 1 - x^2/2! + x^4/4! - x^6/6! + \ldots$ 100 terms

Ans Flowchart is given in Figure 2.

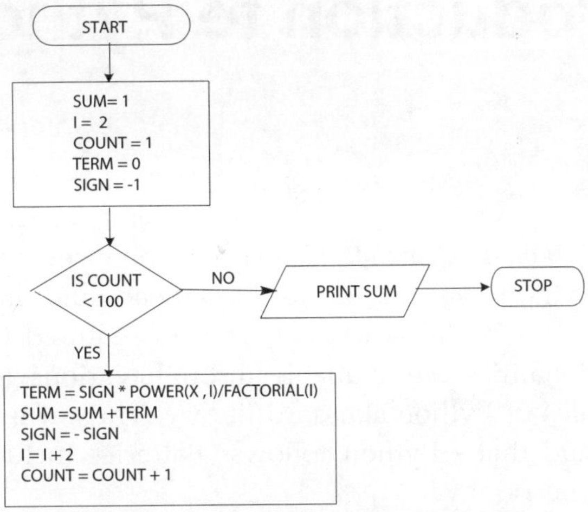

Figure 2 Flowchart for Cosine Series

EXERCISE

1. What is an algorithm? Write an algorithm to find out the value of cos(x) with the help of the following series.

$$\cos(x) = x - \frac{x^3}{3!} + \frac{x^5}{5!} - \frac{x^7}{7!} \cdots\cdots\cdots$$

2. Write an algorithm which computes the roots of a quadratic equation.

$$ax^2 + bx + c = 0$$

Hint: The roots of the quadratic equation can be computed by the following formulas:

$$x_1 = -b + \sqrt{\frac{b^2 - 4ac}{2a}}$$

$$x_2 = -b - \sqrt{\frac{b^2 - 4ac}{2a}}$$

The roots x_1 and x_2 are:

a. Real and equal for $b^2 - 4ac = 0$

b. Real and unequal for $b^2 - 4ac > 0$

c. Imaginary $b^2 - 4ac < 0$

3. Write an algorithm to find area of triangle.
4. Develop an algorithm to test whether a given number is a prime number or not.
5. What is a flowchart? Explain any four symbols used in flowchart.
6. What do you mean by looping control in a program? Explain the different terms which are used in looping.
7. Draw a flowchart to generate first 10 members of Lucas series.
8. Explain looping with the help of an example.
9. What are advantages and limitations of flow-chart?
10. Draw a flowchart to find the fibonacci series till term <=10000.

CHAPTER 3

Introduction to Python

3.1 PYTHON INTRODUCTION

Python is a powerful high-level, interpreted, interactive and object-oriented-scripting language. It was designed to be easily readable; it uses English keywords frequently whereas other languages use punctuation. It has fewer syntactical constructions than other languages. It has simple easy-to-use syntax to learn computer programming.

3.1.1 Features of Python Language

(a) *Python is Interpreted:* This means that it is processed at runtime by the interpreter, and you do not need to compile your program before executing it. Interpreted languages run directly from source code that humans generate whereas programs written in compiled languages, like C++, must be translated into machine code before they can be executed. Python is considered an interpreted language because Python programs are executed by an interpreter.

(b) *Python is Interactive:* This means that you can actually work at a Python prompt and interact with the interpreter directly to execute your programs and get the output.

(c) *Python is Object-oriented:* Python supports procedure-oriented programming as well as object-oriented programming. In procedure-oriented languages, the program is built around procedures or functions, which are reusable codes of programs. In object-oriented languages, the program is built around objects which combine data and functionality.

(d) *Python is Beginner's Language:* Python is a great language for beginner programmers as the language is interpreted, hence gives immediate results. It also supports the development of a wide range of applications, from simple text processing to WWW (World Wide Web) browsers to games.

(e) *Python is Complete Language:* When you install Python, you need not download and install additional libraries. All types of required functionalities are available through various modules of Python standard library. Thus, it is also said that - Python follows "Batteries Included" Philosophy.

3.1.2 History of Python

Python was developed by Guido van Rossum in the late eighties and early nineties at the National Research Institute for Mathematics and Computer Science in the Netherlands. Python 1.0 was released in November 1994. In 2000, Python 2.0 was released. Later on, Python 3.0 was released in 2008. The most recent major version of Python is Python 3. Python 3 is not backward compatible with Python 2. It is available for Windows, Mac OS and most of the versions of Linux operating system. It is well supported and freely available at www.python.org.

Python is derived from many other languages, including ABC, Modula-3, C, C++, Algol-68, SmallTalk, and UNIX shell and other scripting languages. It is copyrighted. Similar to Perl, Python source code is now available under the GNU General Public License (GPL).

☞ *Python 3.0 has new major features, including a full garbage collector and support for Unicode.*

Who uses Python?

Python provides powerful programming features, and is widely used. Companies and Organizations that use Python include YouTube, Google, Yahoo, and NASA. Python is used for web development (server-side), software development, mathematics, and system scripting. The popular YouTube video sharing service is largely written in Python. Google makes extensive use of Python in its web search systems. Dropbox storage service codes both its server and desktop client software, primarily, in Python. The NSA uses Python for cryptography and intelligence analysis. Today Python has become the language of choice for data scientists. Python libraries like NumPy, Pandas and Matplotlib are extensively used in the process of data analysis. Machine Learning is another key application area of Python. Some of the real-world applications of machine learning include medical diagnosis, sales prediction etc. Python can also be used to develop Android apps.

3.2 TECHNICAL STRENGTH OF PYTHON

Python has following technical features:

(a) *Easy-to-learn, Use and Read:* Python has relatively few keywords, simple structure, and a clearly defined syntax. So, it is easy to learn and use. To run a Python program, you simply type it and execute it. There are no intermediate compile and link steps as there are for languages such as C or C++. Python executes programs immediately. Python code is much more clearly defined and visible to the eyes. So, programs written in Python are easily readable and understandable.

(b) *Easy-to-maintain:* Python is successful as its source code is fairly easy-to-maintain. It can be used as a scripting language or can be compiled to byte-code for building large applications.

(c) *A Wide Standard Library:* One of Python's greatest strengths is the availability of bulk of the library with add-on modules present. It is very portable and cross-platform i.e., compatible with UNIX, Windows, and Macintosh.

(d) *Interactive Mode:* It supports an interactive mode in which you can enter results from a terminal right to the program, allowing interactive testing and debugging of code.

(e) *Portable:* Python can run on a wide variety of hardware platforms and has the same interface on all platforms. So, it is called platform independent programming language. It runs on Windows, Linux/Unix, Mac OS X, and has been ported to the Java and .NET virtual machines also. Since Python can run equally well on a variety of platforms such as Windows, Linux/UNIX, Macintosh, Supercomputer, and smart phones, it is also called a true cross-platform language.

(f) *Extendable:* Additional functionality (other than what is provided in the core language) can be made available through modules and packages written in other languages (C, C++, Java etc). You can add low-level modules to the Python interpreter. These modules enable programmers to add to or customize their tools to be more efficient.

(g) *Databases:* Python provides interfaces to all major commercial databases available today.

(h) *GUI Programming:* Python supports Graphical User Interface or GUI applications that can be created and ported to many system calls, libraries, and windows systems, such as Windows MFC (Microsoft Foundation Class(es)), Macintosh, and the X Window system of UNIX.

(i) *Free and Open Source*: Python is an example of a FLOSS (Free/Libre and Open Source Software). In simple terms, you can freely distribute copies of this software, read its source code, make changes to it, and use pieces of it in new free programs. A large programming community is actively involved in the development and support of Python libraries for various applications such as web frameworks, mathematical computing and data science.

(j) *Variety of Usage and Applications*: Python is general purpose programming language which can be used for both scientific and non-scientific programming. This language is used by companies in real revenue generating products, such as operation of Google search engine and YouTube. Intel, Cisco, HP (Hewlett-Packard), and IBM (International Business Machines) use Python for hardware testing. NASA (National Aeronautics and Space Administration) and others use Python for their scientific programming task. It is also used in Rapid Prototyping, Database applications, Game development, Web applications, System Administrations, etc.

(k) *Scalable:* Python provides a better structure and support for large programs than shell scripting.

(l) *Dynamic typing:* One of the important features of Python is that it is a dynamically-typed language. Programming languages such as C, C++, Java, and C# are statically-typed languages. A variable in these languages is a user-friendly name given to a memory location and is intended to store the value of a particular data type. A variable in Python is not bound permanently to a specific data type. Python keeps track of the kinds of objects your program uses when it executes; it does not require complicated type and size declarations in your code.

(m) *Automatic memory management:* Python automatically allocates and reclaims (" garbage collector") objects when no longer used, and most grow and shrink on demand.

(n) *Supports multiple programming paradigms* : Python supports multiple programming paradigms including imperative, procedural, object-oriented and functional programming styles.

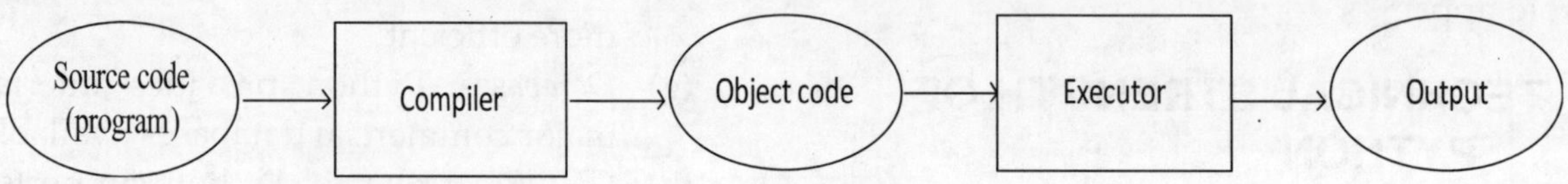

Figure 3.1 A Compiler Translates Source Code into Object Code

☞ *Python provides options, such as Tkinter (Python interface for Tk GUI toolkit), wxPython (Python interface for wxWindows), and JPython (a Python port for Java) to develop Graphical User Interfaces (GUIs).*

3.3 INTRODUCTION TO PYTHON INTERPRETER AND PROGRAM EXECUTION

A *program* is a sequence of instructions given to the computer to perform a specific task. A programming language consists of a set of codes for writing down the instructions that the computer will follow. Programmers also refer to their programs as computer code, and the process of writing an algorithm in a programming language is called coding.

Python is a powerful high-level, object-oriented programming language. It has simple easy-to-use syntax to learn computer programming. For example, the addition of two numbers can be expressed more logically and is easier to understand. You know that computer understands only the machine language (also known as low level language). So, you need to translate the high-level language into the machine language that the computer can execute. The high-level program is called *source code*, and the resulting machine code (object code) is a program that the computer can directly execute.

There are two ways to do this: a high-level language can either be compiled or interpreted. In compilation, source code is first converted to object code (See Figure 3.1). Then the object code is executed to get the output. An interpreted language is a language that is read in its raw form and executes statement at a time without being first compiled. An interpreter is a program that translates one statement of a high-level language program into machine code and executes it, and then translates and executes the next statement of the program and so on and so forth.

In this way, it proceeds further till all the statements of the program are translated and executed one after the other. Figure 3.2 shows the structure of interpreter.

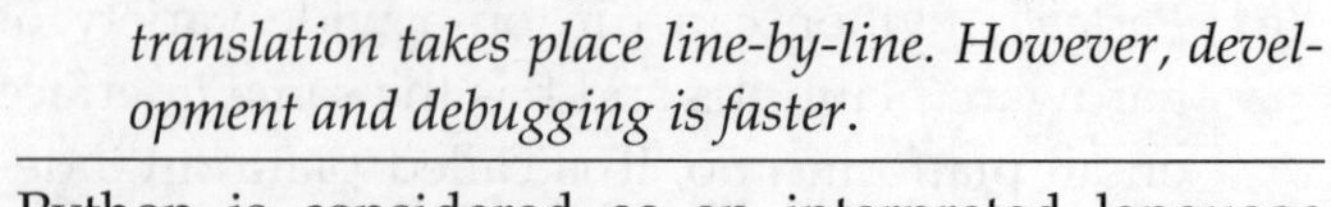

Figure 3.2 An Interpreter Translates one Statement at a time, alternately Reading lines and Performing computation

☞ *Interpreted languages run more slowly because the translation takes place line-by-line. However, development and debugging is faster.*

Python is considered as an interpreted language because:

(a) Python programs are executed by interpreter, not by compiler.

(b) A program written in a compiled language, such as C or C++ is converted from the source language, i.e., C or C++ into a binary code, i.e., 0s and 1s) using a compiler. When you run the program, the linker/loader software copies the program from hard disk to memory and starts running it.
Python, on the other hand, does not need to be converted into binary. You just run the program directly from the source code.

Python is an interpreted, object oriented, and high-level programming language with dynamics semantics.

3.4 HOW TO DOWNLOAD AND INSTALL PYTHON?

To use Python, you need to install Python on your computer. There are multiple Python distributions available today.

Anaconda is one of several Python distributions. It is a new distribution of the Python and R programming languages for data science package machine and learning related applications.

The free version of Anaconda distribution community edition can be downloaded directly from Anaconda website. For the enterprise edition, one needs professional support from Anaconda sales team. (See Figure 3.3).

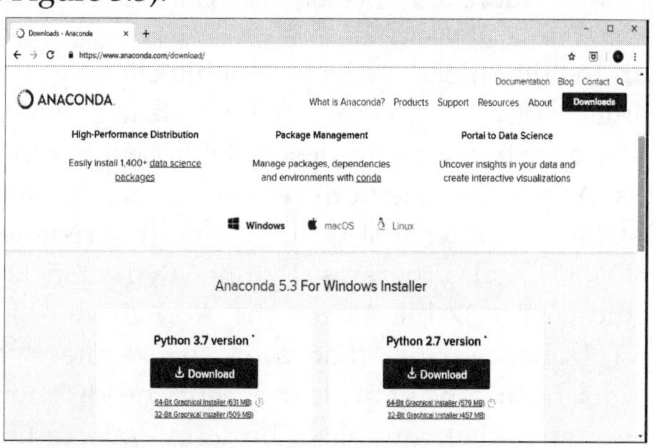

Figure 3.3 Anaconda Installation Screen

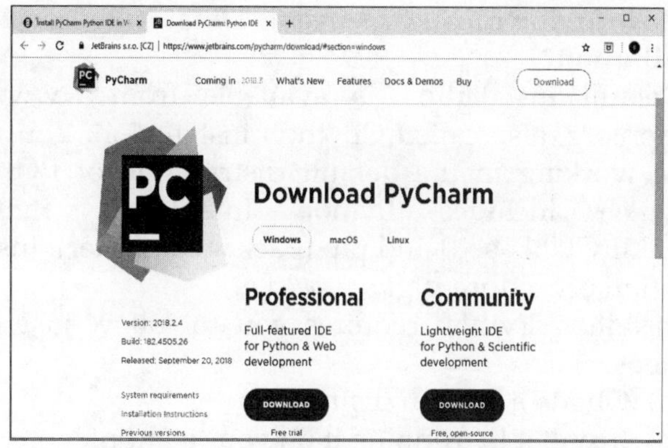

Figure 3.4 PyCharm Installation Screen

How to download and Install Anaconda?

Download the .exe files, of Anaconda, run through the installer and accept the terms, and finish installation. To check, close the browser and pull up the terminal. Once the installation is complete, it should have automatically added that to the path. To test this, go ahead and type 'python'. The version of Python i.e., 3 will be shown and also the Anaconda distribution will be seen. If you install the 4 versions of Anaconda, then all the packages, which are there, can also be imported easily.

Many popular IDEs are also available such as PyCharm (See Figure 3.4). PyCharm is an integrated development environment (IDE) used in computer programming, specifically for the Python language. The web developers can use the live editing preview option provided by the IDE to view a single web page simultaneously in the editor and browser. At the same time, the live edit feature provided by the IDE enables programmers to see the changes made to the code instantaneously on the web browser.

How to download and install PyCharm?

To download PyCharm, visit the website https://www.jetbrains.com/pycharm/download/ and click the "DOWNLOAD" link under the Community Section. Once the download is complete, run the exe to install PyCharm. It will display setup wizard; follow the instruction and click on Next. Wait for the installation to finish. Once the installation is finished, you should receive a message on screen that PyCharm is installed.

How to download and install Default Python Distribution?

Default installation is available from www.python.org, also called CPython installation. You will be working in the default distribution of Python, which includes Python Interpreter, Python IDLE(GUI Based) and pip (package installer). Installation procedure is given below:

Installing Python requires you to follow just two steps:

(a) Obtain a Python distribution.

(b) Install it by running it on your computer.

Python distribution is available for a wide variety of platforms. Python runs on Windows, Linux/UNIX, MAC OS X, and has been ported to the Java and .NET virtual machines also, with no special hardware requirement. The most up-to-date and current source code, binaries, documentation, news, etc., can be downloaded from the official Website of Python:

http://www.python.org/

To install Python on Windows machine, open a Web browser and go to following website:

http://www.python.org/download/

Now, download the installer based on your local machines hardware architecture.

Figure 3.5 Python Installation Screen 1

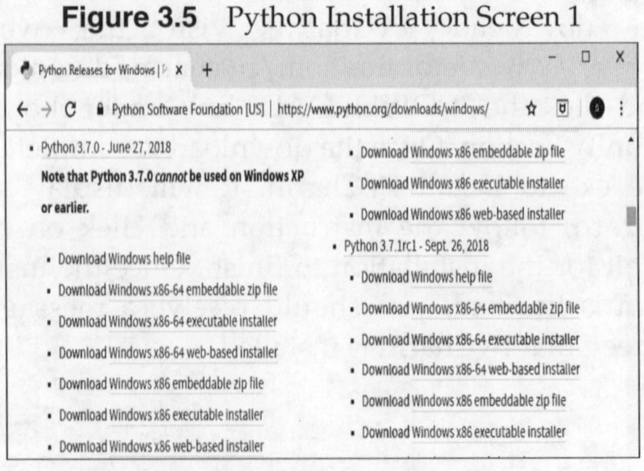

Figure 3.6 Python Installation Screen 2

After downloading the desired Python version for specific platform, you can install it by running the downloaded installer files by following the instructions. You will install Python 3.7.0. for Windows which was released on June 27, 2018.

☞ *In order to install Python 3.5.1 and above, minimum OS requirement is Windows 7 with SP2. For versions 3.0 to 3.4.x, Windows XP is acceptable.*

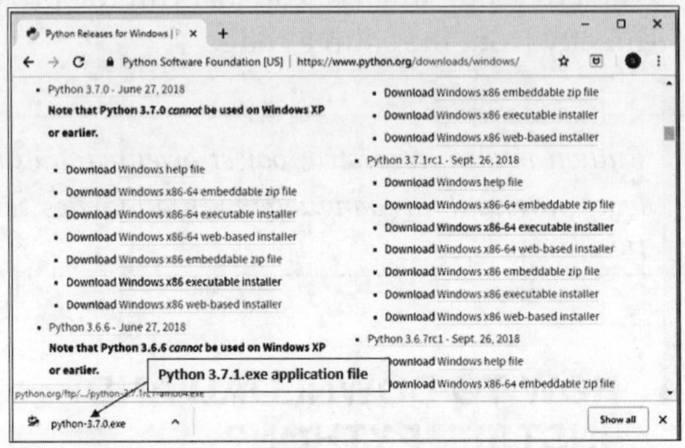

Figure 3.7 Python Installation Screen 3

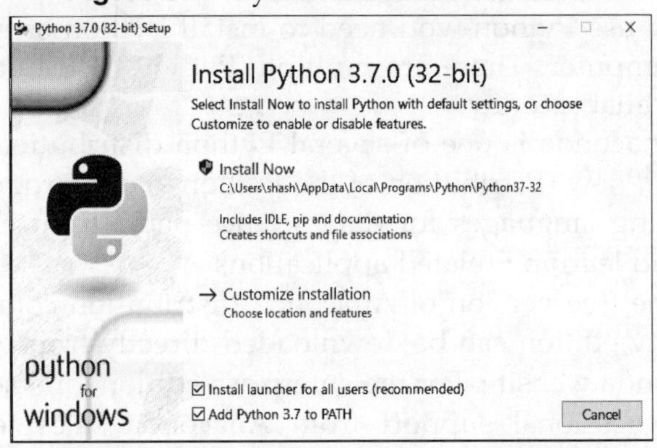

Figure 3.8 Python Installation Screen 4

Run the downloaded file by double-clicking it. This brings forth the Python install wizard, which is really easy to use as it is a simple wizard-based process. As you can see in the above figure, the default installation folder will be C:\Users\{UserName}\AppData\Local\Programs\Python\Python37-32 for Python 3.7.0 32 bit. Check the Add Python 3.7 to PATH checkbox, so that you can execute Python scripts from any path. Just accept the default settings, and click on Next button. Wait until the installation is finished. Figures from Figure 3.5 to Figure 3.10 show you Python 3.7.0 installation process. After successful installation, you can start working with Python on your local machine.

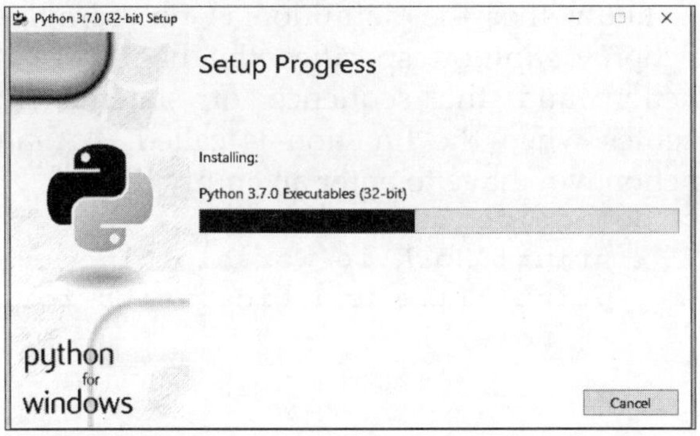

Figure 3.9 Python Installation Screen 5

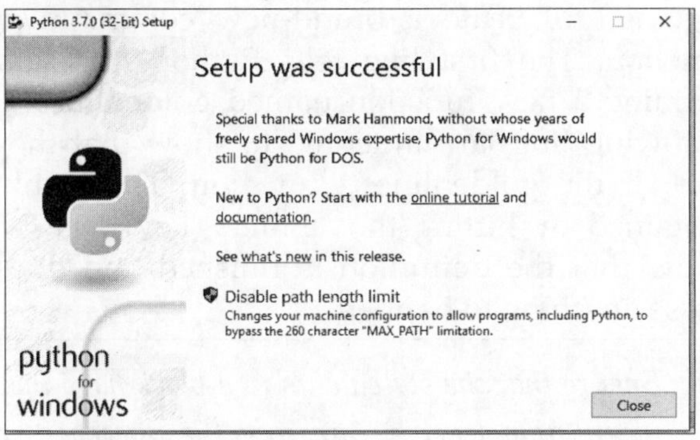

Figure 3.10 Python Installation Screen 6

3.5 HOW TO START PYTHON?

After installation is successfully completed, you can start Python in the following ways (see Figure 3.11). These are:

(a) Python Shell - Interactive mode (Command-line)

(b) Python Editor - Script mode (Integrated Development Environment - IDLE)

Python Shell is used to execute a single Python command and get the result in the same window. It waits for the input command from the user. As soon as the user enters the command, it executes it and displays the result.

IDLE is a simple Integrated Development Learning Environment that comes with Python. The important feature of IDLE is that it is a program that allows the user to edit, run, browse and debug a Python program from a single interface.

3.5 1 Interactive Mode (Command-line)

Interactive mode of working means you type the command one at a time, and the Python executes the given command and gives you output. Interactive interpreter of Python is also called Python Shell.

Follow these steps to work in interactive mode while using Python:

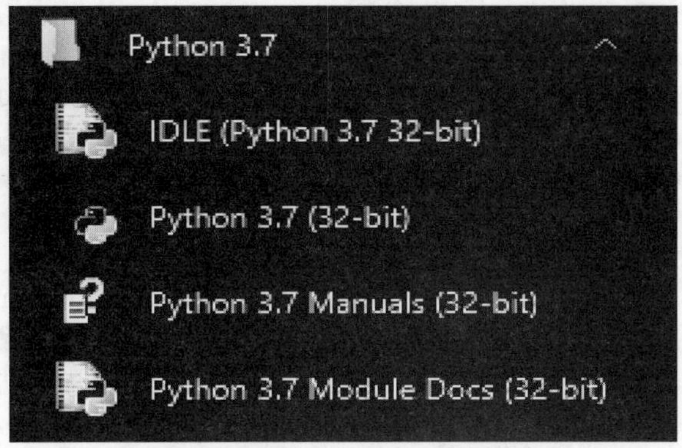

Figure 3.11 Starting Python

Figure 3.12 Python Interactive Mode

(a) Click on **Start** Button → **All Programs** → **Python 3.7(32 bit)**. It will give you the screen similar to the one shown in Figure 3.12.

Python shell is an interactive window where you can type Python code and see the output in the same window by pressing Enter key. When Python interactive mode starts up, it tells you which version is running, the date on which it was released, and a few hints about what to do next. Then, it displays the Python prompt: >>> also known as primary prompt indicating that Python is ready to take commands from the user. When you use interactive mode, Python processes each line of code you type as soon as you press Enter key.

You can enter Python and start coding right away from the command line in the interactive interpreter. In Interactive mode, when you type Python command in front of Python command prompt >>>, the Python executes the given command there, and then gives the output. For example, if you type 2+3 in front of Python prompt, it will display result 5.

```
>>> 2+3
5
```

The Python interpreter can be used like a calculator. If you just want to do simple calculations, you can type numbers and operators and press Enter key to see the result, as shown in Figure 3.13. The >>>, is the prompt the interpreter uses to indicate that it is ready. If you type 2 + 2, the interpreter displays result 4. (See Figure 3.13).

In Programming languages, a complete command is called a *statement*. In Python, you can also print statements. Type the following text to the right of Python prompt and press Enter Key.

```
>>> print("Hello World")
```

☞ *The quotation marks in the program indicate the beginning and end of the text to be displayed. They do not appear in the result.*

It will display the result as shown in Figure 3.14.

Figure 3.13 Python Interpreter used like a Calculator

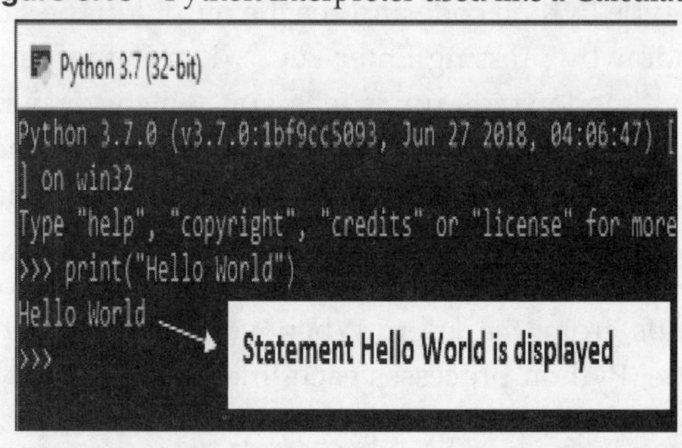

Figure 3.14 Python Interpreter used to Print Statement

How to write multi-line code in Interactive mode?

You can write multi-line code in interactive mode. However, note that interactive mode does not let you save your work. When you write multi-line statements, the ... (continuation prompt) will be displayed. This ... (continuation prompt) is also called secondary prompt indicating that interpreter is waiting for additional input to execute the current statement. If you type a function definition in interactive mode, the interpreter prints ellipses (...) to let you know that the definition is not complete. A function definition specifies the name of a new function and the sequence of statements that executes when the function is called. To end the function, you have to enter an empty line.

```
>>> def goldenlines():
...     print("Work is worship.")
...     print("Time and tide waits for
          none.")
...
>>>
```

Python allows us to put a sequence of statements together to create a brand-new command called function. The first line tells Python that you are defining a new function named goldenlines(). The following lines are indented to show that they are part of the goldenlines() function. The blank line (obtained by hitting the <Enter> key) lets Python know that the definition is finished and does not cause anything to happen.

☞ *Ensure that the statements in a block have the same indentation level by pressing the Spacebar or Tab key. The Python interpreter will throw an error if the indentation level in the block is not same.*

The function is invoked by typing its name.

```
>>> goldenlines()
Work is worship.
Time and tide waits for none.
>>>
```

>>> is the default Python prompt of the interactive shell. It is often seen for code examples which can be executed interactively in the interpreter.

... is the default Python prompt of the interactive shell while entering code for an indented code block or within a pair of matching left and right delimiters (i.e., parentheses, square brackets or curly braces).

Working in interactive mode is convenient for beginners and for testing small piece of code, as you can test them immediately. But for writing more than few lines, you should always use script mode. In script mode, you type Python program in a file and save our code so that you can modify and reuse the code later and then execute the content from the file.

Quitting Interactive Mode

To exit Python interactive mode, press Ctrl-Z or type quit(), as shown below:

```
>>> quit()
```

3.5 2 Script Mode (Integrated Development Learning Environment-IDLE)

IDLE (Integrated Development and Learning Environment) is an integrated development environment (IDE) for Python. The Python installer for Windows contains the IDLE module by default.

Interactive mode does not save commands entered by the user. But if you want to save all the commands in the form of program file and see all output lines together then script mode of Python is used. A program stored in a file (usually one that will be interpreted) is called *script*. Python script mode is basically used for writing programs, i.e., a set of instructions that can be saved for further use. This file is saved on a disk so that it can be used over and over again. Since Python interactive mode does not save any of your work when you quit, you may want to store your important work in text files. Text files that contain Python code are called scripts (if they are whole programs) or modules (if they contain chunks of code meant to be imported into other programs). Both scripts and modules end with the suffix .py.

☞ *A user can switch to script mode by creating a file from File -> New option.*

To run Python from a Graphical User Interface (GUI) environment, you need a GUI application on your system that supports Python. A special type of program known as a Programming environment is specifically designed to help programmers to write programs and include features, such as automatic indenting, color highlighting, and interactive development. To create and run a Python script, you will use IDLE.

When you write multi-line statements, IDLE does not display the ... continuation prompt. IDLE automatically indents lines for you.

IDLE uses colored syntax to highlight your code. By default, built-in functions are *purple*; strings are *green*; and language keywords (such as like print, if and else) are *orange*. Any results produced are in *blue*. The code you type is colorized to make it easier to distinguish one part of a statement from another.

☞ *The IDLE development environment includes Python interactive mode and more tools for writing and running programs and for keeping track of names.*

☞ *The Python code contained in script is executed by including a file system path (absolute or relative) referring to either a Python file, a directory containing a __main__.py file, or a zipfile containing a __main__.py file.*

3.6 CREATING A SIMPLE "Hello World" PROGRAM

IDLE has two window types, the Shell window and the Editor window. Python shell window is an interactive interpreter. IDLE includes a text/editor window for opening, editing, and creating modules and scripts. Let us create and save program in text editor. To do so, follow the instructions given below:

(a) Click on **Start** button → **All Programs** → **IDLE(Python 3.7 32-bit**. It will display IDLE as shown in Figure 3.15.

When you open IDLE, you will see a window called Python Shell, as shown in Figure 3.15. The Python Shell window runs in interactive mode; it displays the Python prompt, >>>. Typing statements and programs in the Python Shell Interactive mode in IDLE works much the same as interactive mode in command line window.

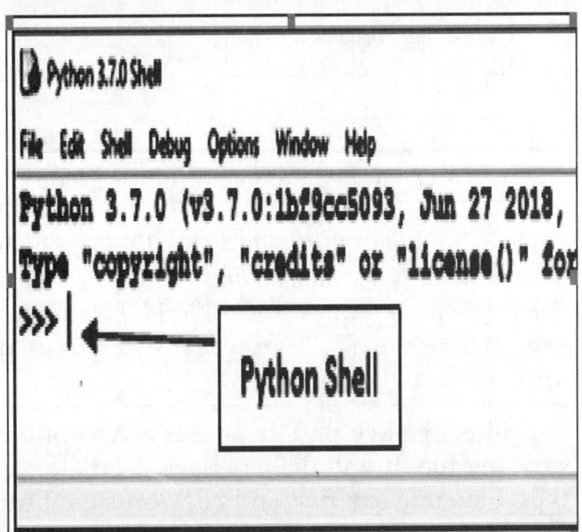

Figure 3.15 Python's IDLE

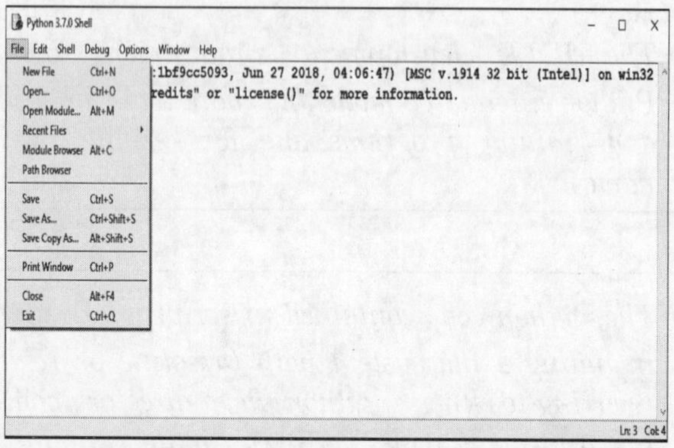

Figure 3.16 Python's New Text Editor

3.6.1 Process of Writing a Program

(b) To open a new text editing window, choose **File** → **New File** as shown in Figure 3.16.

In Python, # symbol is used to add comment. Everything from the # to the end of the line is ignored. A comment is the text that you insert into the program for documentation purpose. In this new window, type the following statements:

```
# My First Program
print ("Hello World")
```

After typing two lines of code, your screen appears as shown in Figure 3.17.

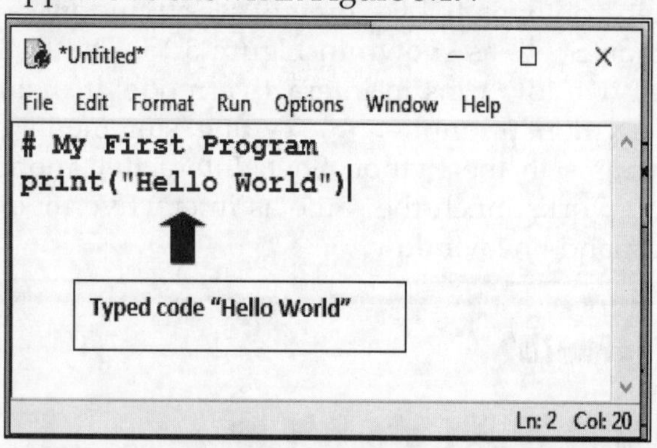

Figure 3.17 Typed Program in Script Mode

☞ *Note : In Python, print and Print are two different things. print is a command and Print is just a word. So, if you write Print ("Hello World"), - it will display* `NameError : name 'Print' is not defined`.

(c) Use **File** → **Save** or **File** → **Save As** option to save the file. It will display Save As dialog box; type filename say *first* and click on **save** button (See Figure 3.18). Note that all Python programs are saved with .py extension.

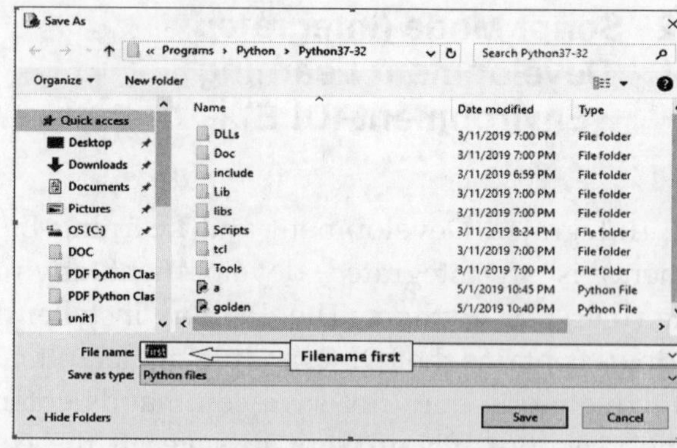

Figure 3.18 Save As Dialog Box

3.6.2 Running a Program

(a) To run a program, module or script, make sure it is opened in the text editor, and choose **Run** → **Run Module** or Press F5 key. See Figure 3.19.

☞ *Note : The =RESTART= line means that Python is clearing all the work you have previously done before it starts running your program.*

If file is not opened then Click on **File** → **Open** option to open the saved program, module or script. The Python Shell restarts (clearing any names that it was storing from the previous session), and Python executes the code as shown in Figure 3.20.

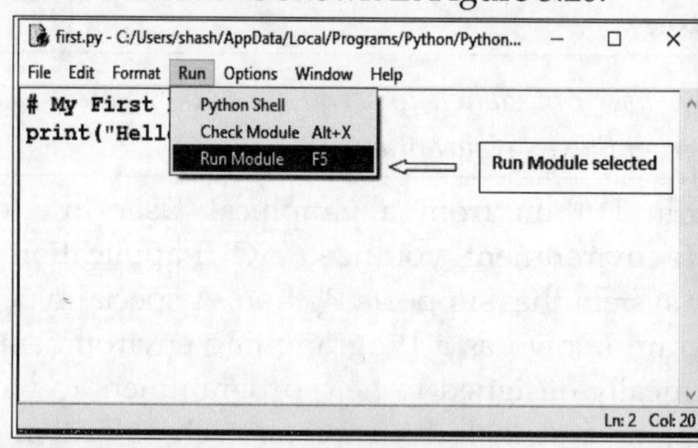

Figure 3.19 Running Program, Module or Script

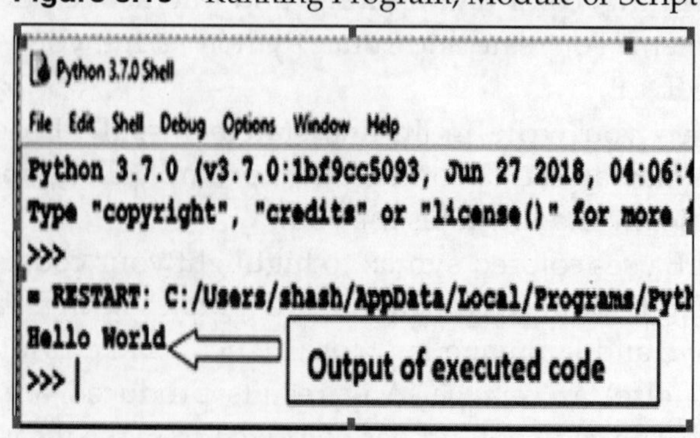

Figure 3.20 Output Shown in Python Shell Window

3.7 WORK EFFECTIVELY WITH IDLE

IDLE has lots of features, but you need to know about only a few of them.

3.7.1 TAB Completion

Start typing in some code, and then press the TAB key. IDLE will offer suggestions to help you complete your statement.

Type `pr` and then TAB at the >>> prompt to see IDLE list of command completion suggestions.

3.7.2 Recall Code Statements

Press Alt-P to recall the previous code statement entered into IDLE, or press Alt-N to move to the next code statement (assuming there is one). Both key combinations can be used to cycle rapidly through all of the code you have entered into IDLE, re-executing any code statements as needed.

3.7.3 Edit Recalled Code

Once you recall your code statement, you can edit it and move around the statement using the arrow keys. It's possible to edit any statement that you have previously entered, even code statements that span multiple lines.

3.8 IDLE MENUS

IDLE has two window types, the Shell window and the Editor window. It is possible to have multiple editor windows simultaneously. IDLE's menus dynamically change based on the window that is currently selected. Each menu documented below indicates which window type it is associated with.

The *File* menu provides the ability to open, save, print, close files, etc.

The *Edit* menu provides options for the usual editing commands such as Undo, Redo, Copy, Cut, Paste, Find, and Replace.

The *Format* menu provides options for indenting, commenting, uncommenting a section of code, etc.

The *Run* menu provides the Run Module, which executes the Python code currently in the Editor window. The F5 shortcut key is a convenient way to execute a program. If the module has not been saved, IDLE will prompt the user to save the code.

The *Options* menu provides the option Configure IDLE for configuring various aspects of IDLE, including the fonts used, the color of keywords, the color of comment lines, etc., and the number of spaces used for each tab character (for indentation of program lines) etc.

The *Windows* menu provides options for controlling the height of the window. It also provides a list of all currently opened Python windows (by file name), including the Python Shell. This provides an easy way to switch from one window to another.

Finally, the *Help* menu includes About IDLE, which consists of the version number of installed IDLE; and IDLE Help, which gives a brief summary of the commands of the menu bar.

3.9 PYTHON STYLE RULES AND CONVENTIONS

Table 3.1 summarizes the list of some of the Python style rules and conventions.

Table 3.1 List of Python Style Rules and Conventions

Elements	Description
Semicolons	The Python statement written in the form of sentence must not be terminated with semicolons. Semicolons should not be used as separator to put two commands on the same line.
Line length	The line length should be of maximum 79 characters, if you use Python.
Indentation	In Python, indentation is used to form suites, i.e., block of statements, and it is treated as a unit. The code blocks are indented with spaces.
Blank Lines	The two blank lines should be between top level definitions, and one blank line should be between method definitions.
Whitespace	Standard typographic rules are used for spaces around punctuation.

Comments	The right style for module, function, method and in-line comments should always be used.
Statements	Generally only one statement per line should be written.
Case Sensitive	Python is case sensitive, i.e., it treats upper and lower case characters differently. Therefore, case of statement is very important. Always be careful while declaring code and identifier names.

3.10 USING COMMENTS

Comments are the entries in a computer program for the purpose of documentation or explanation. They should be written in such a way that even a beginner can understand the logic of the program easily. Any text contained within comments is ignored by the Python interpreter. Every programming language has different ways to give the comment in programs. Comments should be used intelligently to improve the quality and understandability of the program.

In Python, the line after # (hash) is called a comment. Use # to comment-out a line of code or to add a short, one-line comment to your program. For example,

```
# Compute the average of the values
avg = sum / number
```

The above line here is a comment that explains what the statement that follows is supposed to do. The comment begins with the # symbol and continues until the end of that line. The interpreter will ignore the # symbol and the contents of the rest of the line.

You may also append a short comment to the end of the statement:

```
x=5 # assign 5 to x
avg = sum / number # Compute the average
per= (total*100)/500 # Compute percentage
```

Here, an executable statement and the comment appear on the same line. The interpreter will read the assignment statement, but it will ignore the comment.

In Python, use a triple quote for multi-line comments. For example,

```
'''
This is
an example of
multi-line comment
'''
print ("Hello World")
```

☞ *Good programmers clarify their code by inserting remarks that explain the purpose of a section of code.*

3.11 PYTHON CHARACTER SET

Character set is a set of valid characters that a language can recognize. Python uses the character set to declare identifier. There are two types of character sets in Python language. These are:

(a) Source characters
(b) Execution characters/Escape sequences

3.11.1 Source Characters

Using source characters, source text is created. Following is the list of source characters:

Alphabets : A to Z, a to z and _ (underscore)
Numbers : 0 to 9
Special characters : + - * / ^ ~ % = ! & | ( ) { } [ ] ? ' ', ; : \ # blank "

3.11.2 Execution Characters / Escape Sequences

These characters are interpreted at the time of execution. The values of execution characters are implementation-defined.

The characters on the keyboard can be printed or displayed by pressing the key. But some characters, such as line feed, form feed, and tab, cannot be printed or displayed directly. Python provides the mechanism to get such characters that are invisible or difficult to represent directly through execution characters. In Python \n, \r, \t, \f and \v are considered as whitespace characters. Execution characters and escape sequences are used inter-changeably.

Table 3.2 Escape Sequence Characters

Execution Character	Meaning	Result at Execution Time
\n	End of a line	Moves the active position to the initial position of the next line. (See Figure 3.21).
\r	Carriage return	Moves the active position to the initial position of the next paragraph.
\f	Form feed	Moves the active position to the initial position of the next logical page.
\v	Vertical tab	Moves the active position to the next vertical tabulation position.
\t	Horizontal tab	Moves the active position to the next horizontal tabulation position. (See Figure 3.21).
\b	Backspace	Moves the active position to the previous position on the current line.
\a	Alert	Produces an audible alert.

Example 1 –**Demo of backslash (\).**

```
# Demo of backslash (\)
print('A\nB\nC')
print('a\tb\tc')

RUN
>>>
A
B
C
a	b	c
>>>
```

Figure 3.21 Program Demonstrating Working of Backslash

Escape codes are embedded inside string literals and start with a backslash character (\). They are used to embed characters that are either unprintable or have a special syntactic meaning to Python that you want to suppress. Each of the escape sequences shall produce a unique implementation-defined value which can be stored in a single character. These escape sequences are represented by a backslash (\) followed by a character. Though there are two or more characters in an escape sequence, they are considered as a single character. Some of them are shown in Table 3.2.

Many other characters, after backslash (\), in output statements will result in display of the character itself. For example, the execution of \k will result in displaying of k.

3.12 TOKEN

The smallest individual unit or element in a program is known as a *token* a lexical unit. Each token should be separated from the other by a space, tab or carriage return, which are collectively termed as white space. Python has the following tokens which are discussed below: keywords, identifiers, literals (constants), punctuators and operators.

Keywords: At the time of designing a language, some words are reserved to do specific tasks. Such words are called as *keywords* or *reserved* words. Keywords are the reserved words in Python. They are used to define the syntax and structure of the Python language.

Identifiers: Identifier is user-defined name given to different parts of program, namely variable, class, object, and function.

Literals: Literals can be defined as a data that is given in a variable or constant.

Punctuators: Punctuators are symbols that are used in programming languages to organize sentence structure, and indicate the rhythm and emphasis of expression, statements and program structure. For example '(Single Quote), " (Double Quote), # (Hash), \ (forward slash), () (parenthesis), [] (Square bracket), {} (Curly bracket), (comma), : (colon), = (Assignment) etc.

Operators: Operators are special symbols in Python that carry out arithmetic or logical computation.

3.13 IDENTIFIERS

An identifier is a unique name that enables you to identify something. Identifiers are used to label variables, functions, classes, objects, and modules. They begin with either a letter or an underscore, and they can contain letters, underscores, or digits. This implies that a single identifier cannot contain any space. They cannot contain punctuation marks. Python is a case-sensitive programming language. Thus AGE, Age and age are three different identifiers in Python. Some legal identifiers are x, age, marks2, and Total_Marks.

☞ *Variables are examples of identifiers. Identifiers are names given to identify something.*

3.13.1 Points to be Remembered While using Identifiers

The following points should be kept in mind while using identifiers:

(a) Allowable characters in identifiers are the letters from A to Z, a to z, and the digits from 0 to 9. Identifiers must begin with a letter or underscore (_) but not with a digit in Python.
(b) The identifier must not be a keyword of Python.
(c) Python is case sensitive language. Therefore, you have to be very careful while using names for identifiers. Identifiers, such as name, Name and NAME are three different variable names.
(d) Special characters, such as @, ? and (), are not allowed as variable names.
(e) A variable name cannot contain spaces.

Let's Try

Determine whether the following are Valid or Invalid Identifiers.

myName	_CHK
marks_1	variable1
else	9file
First.rec	Data-file
print_my_name	1variable
True	false

Let's Try

Which of the following can be used as valid variable identifier(s) in Python?

4thSum	_Cost
Total	Price*Qty
Number#	float
_Data	Address One
for	Number12
true	None

Table 3.3 List of Python Keyword/Reserved Words

False	None	True	and	as
assert	async	await	break	class
continue	def	del	elif	else
except	finally	for	from	global
if	import	in	is	lambda
nonlocal	not	or	pass	raise
return	try	while	with	yield

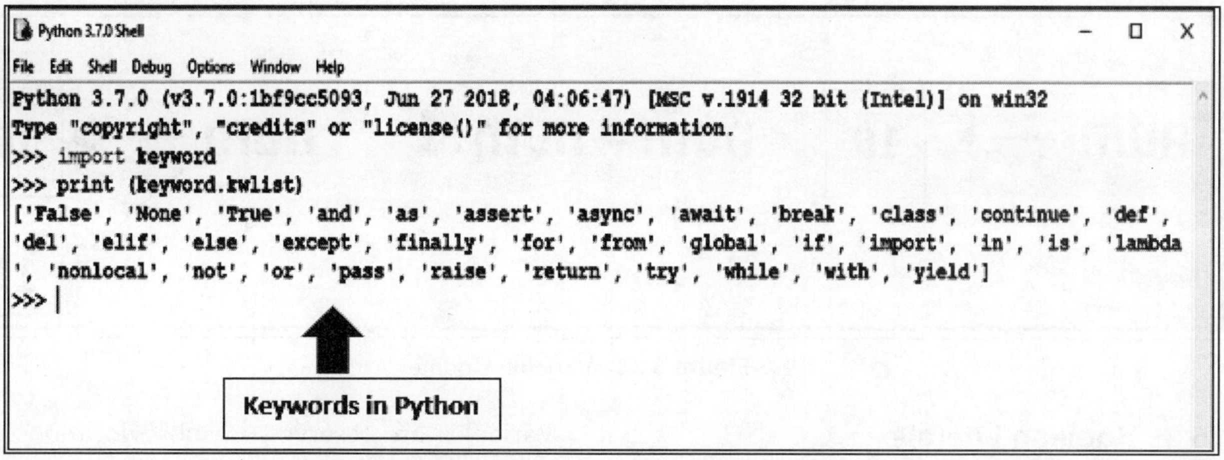

Figure 3.22 List of Keywords Available in Python

3.14 KEYWORDS/RESERVED WORDS

At the time of designing a language, some words are reserved to do specific tasks. Such words are called as *keywords* or *reserved* words. Keywords cannot be used as variable name. In Python, they are case sensitive. Table 3.3 shows a list of Python language keywords. Note that all keywords are in small case except *False*, *None* and *True*. To display list of keywords in Python write the following commands:

```
>>> import keyword
>>> print (keyword.kwlist)
```

List of Python keywords will appear as shown in Figure 3.22

Difference between Keywords and Identifiers

Keywords are the words used by Python interpreter to recognize the structure of program. As these words have specific meaning for interpreter, they cannot be used for any other purpose. So, keywords are reserved. The are in-built.

An identifier is a unique name that enables you to identify something. Identifiers are used to label variables, functions, classes, objects, and modules. They begin with either a letter or an underscore. They can contain letters, underscores, or digits but they cannot contain punctuation marks. They are user-defined.

☞ *Identifier is a user-defined name given to part of program namely variable, object, function etc.*

3.15 LITERALS

Literals can be defined as a data which is given in a variable or constant. For example 7, -2.9, "xyz", 'Hello' are literals. Literals are fixed numeric or non-numeric value. Python supports the following literals:

3.15.1 String Literals

Strings are the only literal sequence type that contains, a sequence of characters. However, characters are not a type. So strings are the lowest-level primitive for character storage and manipulation. String literals are formed by enclosing text in the single or double or both a single and double quote. For example, "Abhishek", '3784', 'Some "quoted" \'extra\' text.'.

A string literal can also span multiple lines. It can also be enclosed in matching groups of three single or double quotes (generally referred to as triple-quoted string). For example,

```
"""This string
spans several lines
because it is a little long.
"""
```

3.15.2 Numeric Literals

Python supports three types of numeric literals integer, float and complex. For example,

```
a = 7  #Integer literal
b = 25.7 #Float Literal
x = 3.14j #Complex Literal
```

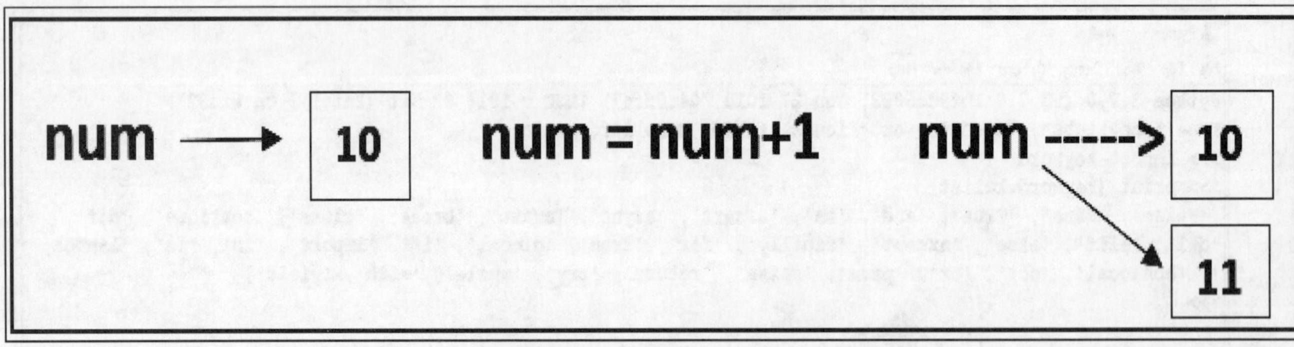

Figure 3.23 Variable Update

3.15.3 Boolean Literals

Boolean literals are used to denote boolean values. They contain either *True* or *False*.

```
isboolean = True   # Boolean literal
```

3.16 VARIABLE

A variable is basically a name that represents (or refers to) some value. For example, you might want the name x to represent 5. To do so, simply execute the following:

```
>>> x = 5
```

This is called an assignment. You assign the value 5 to the variable x. In other words, you bind the variable x to the value (or object) 5. After you have assigned the value to the variable, you can use the variable in expressions:

```
>>> x * 2
10
```

A value is one of the basic things a program works with, like letter or a number. These values belong to different types, such as 7 is an integer, 3.5 is float (number with decimal point), and 'Hello, Python' is a string, as it contains string of letters. Variable is a name that refers to a value.

3.16.1 Notion of a Variable

In Python, a name refers to an object. The name is actually a label for a memory location in the computer that stores something. A value is a chunk of code or any sort of thing that Python understands. For example, when you enter a statement such as x = 5 in Python, you are binding a name (x) to an object (5).

☞ *In Python, object is simply a collection of data (variables) and methods (functions) that act on those data. Hence, a variable is also an object in Python.*

Variables are reserved memory locations to store values. This means that when you create a variable, you reserve some space in memory. Based on the data type of the variable, the interpreter allocates memory and decides what can be stored in the reserved memory. Therefore, by declaring variable with different data types, you can store integers, decimals, or characters in these variables.

However, Python variables do not have to be explicitly declared to reserve memory space. The declaration happens automatically when you assign a value to a variable. The equal sign (=) is used to assign values to variables. The operand to the left of the = operator is the name of the variable, and the operand to the right of the = operator is the value stored in the variable.

For example:

```
counter = 100 # An integer assignment
miles = 1000.0 # A floating point
                 assignment
name = "Abhishek" # A string assignment
```

Here 100, 1000.0 and "Abhishek" are the values assigned to counter, miles and name variables, respectively.

☞ *Initialization is the process that sets the initial value of a variable. It is done only once for each variable, when that variable is created.*

Identity of variable refers to the variable address in the memory which does not change once it has been created. To check address of variable id() method is used. For example to check the addresses of above declared variables use id() method as follows:

```
>>> id(counter)
1481522992
>>> id(miles)
57358912
>>> id(name)
23268752
```

3.16.2 Methods to Manipulate Variable

You can think variable as named storage location in computer memory. Notice that in Figure 3.23 an arrow is used to show which value a variable refers to and old value does not get replaced by new one. It simply switches to refer to the new value. When a value is no longer referred to by any variable, Python automatically clears these values out of memory so that space is used for new values.

☞ *The equal to sign (=) is used to assign values to variables.*

Assigning same value to multiple variables:
Python allows you to assign a single value to several variables simultaneously. For example:

```
a = b = c = 1
```

Here, an integer object is created with the value 1, and all three variables are assigned to the same memory location.

Let's Try

Assigning the same text to multiple variables:

```
a = b = c = "same"
print (a)
print (b)
print (c)
```

Assigning multiple values to multiple variables:
You can also assign multiple objects to multiple variables. For example:

```
a, b, c = 1, 2, "Abhishek"
```

Here, two integer objects with values 1 and 2 are assigned to variables a and b, and one string object with the value "Abhishek" is assigned to the variable c.

Let's Try

Assigning multiple values to multiple variables:

```
x, y, z = 2, 4.7, "Welcome"
print (x)
print (y)
print (z)
```

Assigning None to variable:
In Python, *None* is a special data type with a single value. For example,

```
begin = None
```

The line assigns a special value called *None* to variable begin. None is Python's way of representing nothing. It makes a good placeholder for a value. It also evaluates to false when treated as a condition.

Remember the following points while creating variable name:

(a) They begin with either an alphabet letter (lower or upper case) or an underscore (_), but they cannot start with a digit. Generally, they are written in lower case letters.
(b) The variable name can consist of alphabet letter(s), number(s) and underscore(s) only. For example, myVar, MyVar, _myVar, MyVar123, name_23, and _my_name are valid variable names. But m*var, my-var, 1myVar are invalid variable names.
(c) They cannot contain punctuation marks.
(d) Variable name should be meaningful and short, and it cannot contain spaces.
(e) Identifiers in Python are case sensitive. So, NAME, name, nAME, and nAmE are treated as different variable names.
(f) A Python keyword cannot be used as a variable name.

☞ *Starting the name with a single or double underscore has a special meaning in Python.*

3.16.3 L-value and R-value

Every assignment statement has two parts: a left-hand side and a right-hand side. Any kind of code that could go on the right hand side of an assignment operator is called an R-value. Similarly, anything that could appear on its left is called an L-value.

Rvalues are the literals and expressions that are assigned to lvalues. They can come only on RHS of an assignment statement.

Lvalues are the objects to which you can assign a value or expression. They can come on LHS or RHS of an assignment statement.

Example:

```
a=2 # valid assignment
b=7 # valid assignment
2=a # invalid and produces an error
7=b # invalid and produces an error
```

Note in an assignment statement, the variable that is receiving the value must appear on the left side of the = operator, otherwise it will generate error as shown in above examples.

☞ *Note : L-value is an expression that refers to storage area, and R-value is an expression that denotes value.*

3.16.4 Mutable and Immutable Variables

A *mutable variable* is one whose value may change in place whereas in an *immutable variable* change of value will not happen in place. Modifying an immutable variable will rebuild the same variable. For example,

```
>>> x=5 # will create a value 5 refer-
enced by x
>>> y=x # will make y refer to 5 of x
>>> x= x+y # in this statement LHS(x),
will rebuild to 10
>>> print(x)
10
>>> print(y)
5
```

so,

x → 10
y → 5

Immutable is an object with a fixed value. Immutable objects include numbers, strings and tuples. Such an object cannot be altered. A new object has to be created if a different value has to be stored.

☞ *In Python language, variables do not need declaration to reserve memory space. The "variable declaration" or "variable initialization" happens automatically when you assign a value to a variable.*

3.16.5 Variable Assignment and Accepting input

An assignment statement creates a variable and sets its value, or changes the value of an existing variable. The value that is assigned to a given variable does not have to be specified in the program, as demonstrated in previous examples. The value can come from the user by using input function.

```
print("Enter your name:")
x = input()
print("Hello, " + x)
Hello, Shashi
```

Let's Try

Assigning string by accepting it from the user through the input function.

```
print("Enter your first name:")
a = input()
print("Hello, " + a)
```

Let's Try

Assigning values by accepting them from the user through the input function.

```
x = int(input("Input first number: "))
y = int(input("Input second number: "))
z = int(input("Input third number: "))
print("Numbers are: ", x, y, z)
```

3.16.6 Working with Dynamic Typing

There are two approaches to data typing in programming languages. You know that a variable is defined by assigning it some value. In *static typing*, a variable is declared as a certain type before it is used and can be assigned values of that type. However, Python uses dynamic typing. In *dynamic typing*, the data type of a variable depends only on the type of value that the variable is currently holding. Thus, the same variable may be assigned values of different type during the execution of a program. Once a value has been assigned to a variable, the interpreter will then decide what sort of value it is (i.e., number, string, etc.).

Dynamic typing makes it easier to handle different types of unpredictable user input. The interpreter can accept user input in many different forms, to which it assigns a type dynamically, i.e., words, numbers, or any other data type. This need not be decided by the programmer in the beginning of program in order to assign it to a variable.

For example, in the following Python statements, an integer value is assigned to a variable 'x'. Now, the Python interpreter won't object if the same variable is used to store a reference to a string.

```
x=20
print (x)
x = "Seven"
print (x)
```

The above mentioned code will display:

```
20
Seven
```

This means variable x is earlier pointing to an integer value 20 and then to a string value "Seven". That is why Python is called a dynamically-typed language.

3.17 CONSTANTS

Constants are the items which represent values directly and whose values cannot be changed during the execution of the program. Fixed values such as numbers, letters, and strings are called *constants* because their value does not change. String constants use single-quotes (') or double-quotes ("). For example:

```
>>> print(123)
123
>>> print(98.6)
98.6
>>> print('Hello world')
Hello world
>>> VOWELS = "aeiou"
```

Variable name in all caps is called constant and refers to the value that is not meant to change (i.e., their value is constant).

Let's Try

What will be the output of the following print statements?

```
>>> print(63)
>>> print(75.5)
>>> print('Hello! How are you?')
>>> name = "Shiva"
>>> print(name)
```

Constants are valuable to programmers in two ways:

(a) They make program clearer. Here, variable name VOWELS can be used anywhere you need the sequence of vowels instead of string "aeiou"

(b) They save retyping. They are especially useful if you have a long value such as like very long number or string.

☞ *Note : Use a constant in programs where you have the same, unchanging value used in multiple places. Note that when you create constants use all caps variable name.*

3.17.1 Literal Constants

An example of a literal constant is a number, such as 5, 1.23, or a string such as 'This is a string', or "It's a string!". It is called a literal because it will use its value literally. The number 2 always represents itself and nothing else; it is a constant because its value cannot be changed. Hence, all these are referred to as literal constants.

String Literals & String value

A string literal is a sequence of characters surrounded by quotes. You can use single, double or triple quotes for a string. And, a character literal is a single character surrounded by single or double quotes.

You get a string value when you call the print() function and run the program.

```
>>> print("Hello, World!")
Hello, World!
```

Here, the string literal is "Hello, World!", while the string value is Hello, World! without the quotation marks.

Generally, the string value which you get as the output in the terminal window when you run a Python program does not include quotation marks. But some string values may need to include quotation marks, like when you are quoting a source. Since string literals and string values are not equivalent, it is often necessary to add additional formatting to string literals to ensure that string values are displayed the way in which you intend to.

Quotes and Apostrophes

Since you can use single quotes or double quotes, in Python, it is simple to embed quotes in a string by using double quotes within a string enclosed by single quotes:

'Vivek says, "Hello!"'

Or, you can use an apostrophe in a string enclosed by double quotes:

"Vivek's shirt is blue."

In the way you combine single and double quotes, you can control the display of quotation marks and apostrophes within your strings.

With multiple lines, strings can be grouped into clean and orderly text, formatted as a letter, or used to maintain the line breaks of a poem or song lyrics. Strings on multiple lines can make text more readable to humans. To create strings that span multiple lines, triple single quotes ''' or triple double quotes """ are used to enclose the string.

☞ *Note : With triple quotes, you can print strings on multiple lines to make text, especially lengthy text, easier to read.*

Using Escape characters is another way to format strings. All Escape characters start with the backslash (\) combined with another character within a string to format the given string a certain way.

By using the escape character \" you are able to use double quotes to enclose a string that includes in the text quoted between double quotes. Similarly, you can use the escape character \' to add an apostrophe in a string that is enclosed in single quotes.

```
>>> print("Vivek says, \"Hello!\"")
Vivek says, "Hello!"
>>> print('Vivek\'s shirt is blue.')
Vivek's shirt is blue.
```

A raw string tells Python to ignore all formatting within a string, including escape characters. You create a raw string by putting an *r* in front of the string, just before the beginning quotation mark:

```
>>> print(r"Vivek says,\"The shirt\'s colour is blue.\"")
Vivek says,\"The shirt\'s colour is blue.\"
```

By constructing a raw string by using *r* in front of the given string, you can retain backslashes and other characters that are used as escape characters.

3.18 KNOWLEDGE OF DATA TYPES

The kind of data that a variable holds in a programming language is called the *data type*. Data types are the classification or categorization of data items. Every value in Python has a data type. The ability to divide data into different types in Python enables you to work with complex objects.

3.19 STANDARD DATA TYPES

The data stored in memory can be of many types. For example, a person's age is stored as a numeric value, and his or her address is stored as alphanumeric characters. Python is known as a dynamically typed language, which means that you do not have to explicitly identify the data type when you initialize a variable. Python knows, based on the value it has been given, that it should allocate memory for a string, integer or float. It has various standard types that are used to define the operations possible on them and the storage method for each of them. It has different data types such as Number, String, List, Tuple and Dictionary.

☞ *Note that everything is an object in Python programming; data types are actually classes and variables are instances (objects) of these classes like most other languages.*

3.19.1 Number

Number data types store numeric values. They are immutable (value of its object cannot be changed) data types, which means that changing the value of a number data type results in a newly allocated object. Number objects are created when you assign a value to them. For example,

num1 = 5
num2 = 7

Python automatically converts different types of numbers so that you (usually) do not need to think about the compatibility of different number types. For example, if you do a mathematical operation with both integers and floats, Python converts the integers into floats and gives the result as a float. There are three numeric types in Python: int, float and complex. Variables of numeric types are created when you assign a value to them. To verify the type of any object in Python, use the type() function:

x = 1 # int
y = 2.8 # float
z = 1j # complex

The three numerical types of Python are discussed below:

int (integer)

Positive or negative whole numbers (without a fractional part) are called integer. Integers are of two types Integers-(signed) and Booleans. *int* is the basic integer data type. It is a whole number, positive or negative, without decimals, of unlimited length. It cannot hold fractional values. Examples of integer are 5, 34, 92, -43, -3255522, etc. Do not use commas to separate digits and also integers should not have leading zeroes.

Boolean type can take only one of two values, True and False. These correspond to 1 and 0. This is the most appropriate return type for a function that uses its return value to express whether some condition holds true or not.

The following integer literals are recognized by Python:

a. **Decimal Integer literals (base 10)**: An integer literals consists of a sequence of digits. For example, 245, -96, 53, etc.
b. **Octal Integer literals (base 8)** : An octal value can contain digits 0 to 7. 8 and 9 are invalid digits in octal integer. To indicate an octal number,

you will use the prefix 0o or 0O (zero followed by either a lowercase or uppercase letter 'o'). For example, 0O4, 0o14, etc.

c. **Hexadecimal Integer literals (base 16)**: To indicate hexadecimal literals, you will use the prefix '0X' or '0x' (zero and uppercase or lowercase letter 'x').

float (floating point real values)

Numbers with fractions or decimal point are called floating point number. For example, 0.34, .07, -12.9, 34.2963, etc. Float numbers can be positive or negative. They can also be used to represent a number in scientific or exponent notation. For example, -3.0 X 10^5 is represented as -3.0e5.

complex (complex numbers)

Complex number is an extension of the familiar real number system in which all numbers are expressed as a sum of a real part and an imaginary part. A complex number consists of an ordered pair of real floating point numbers denoted by a + bj, where *a* is the real part and *b* is the imaginary part of the complex number. The imaginary part is written with a j suffix, e.g., 3+1j. Python has built-in support for complex numbers.

For example,

```
>>> x=3+1j
>>> print(x.real,x.imag)
3.0 1.0
```

There may be times when you want to specify a type for a variable. This can be done with casting. Python is an object-orientated language, and it uses classes to define data types, including its primitive types. It provides a special function called *type* that tells us the data type of any value.

```
>>> type(72)
<class 'int'>
>>>
>>> type("string")
<class 'str'>
>>>
>>> type(98.7)
<class 'float'>
>>>
```

<class 'int'> indicates that the type of 72 is int. Similarly, <class 'str'> and <class 'float'> indicate that "string" and 98.7 are of type str and float, respectively.

☞ *In Python, the floating point numbers have precision of 15 digits, i.e., double precision.*

Integers and floats are data types that deal with numbers. Sometimes you need to convert an integer to a float or vice-versa. To convert integer to float, use the float() function; and to convert a float to an integer, use the int() function. You can also convert numbers to strings by using the str() method.

Let's Try

Write datatype for the following:

```
>>> type(4)
>>> type(3.14)
>>> type (2.0)
>>> a= -53
>>> type(a)
```

What is typecasting?

Typecasting is a process of explicitly specifying types of variables in a programming language.

Example 2 –**Program demonstrating working of typecasting.**

```
# Program demonstrating working of typecasting
x=10
y="2"
z=int(y) # convert string to integer using int()
sum=x+z
print(sum)

RUN
>>>
12
>>>
```

Figure 3.24 Program Demonstrating Working of Typecasting

Sometimes you need to convert data type. For example, if you want to add two numbers in which one value of a variable is an integer, and the second is a string. Then you need to use typecasting to convert string data type into integer before you perform addition (See Figure 3.24). Casting in Python is done using constructor functions as given below:

int() - It constructs an integer number from an integer literal, a float literal (by rounding down to the previous whole number) or a string literal (provided that the string represents a whole number). For example,

```
x = int(1)   # x will be 1
y = int(2.8) # y will be 2
z = int("3") # z will be 3
```

float() - It constructs a float number from an integer literal, a float literal or a string literal (provided that the string represents a float or an integer). For example,

```
x = float(1)      # x will be 1.0
y = float(2.8)    # y will be 2.8
z = float("3")    # z will be 3.0
w = float("4.2") # w will be 4.2
```

str() - It constructs a string from a wide variety of data types, including strings, integer literals and float literals. For example,

```
x = str("s1") # x will be 's1'
y = str(2)    # y will be '2'
z = str(3.0)  # z will be '3.0'
```

☞ *Converting one data type to another data type is called typecasting.*

Let's Try

What will be the output of the following *float* casting operations?

```
# float casting operations
x=float(5)
y=float(20.0)
z=float("80")
print(x)
print(y)
print(z)
```

Let's Try

What will be the output of the following *int* casting operations?

```
# int casting operations
x=int(5)
y=int(20.0)
z=int("80")
print(x)
print(y)
print(z)
```

Let's Try

What will be the output of the following *string* casting operations?

```
# string casting operations
x=str(5)
y=str(20.0)
z=str("80")
print(x)
print(y)
print(z)
```

The range of Python numbers

The range of numbers supported by Python numeric data types is discussed below:

a. *Integer* numbers can be of any length, only limited by available memory.
b. *Booleans* can have only two permissible values True(1) or False(0).
c. *Float* numbers can be of unlimited range, depending on machine architecture.
d. *Complex numbers* range is same as floating point numbers because the real part and imaginary part both are represented internally as float values.

Real

Real numbers, or floating point numbers, are represented in Python according to the IEEE 754 double-precision binary floating-point format, which is stored in 64 bits of information divided into three sections: sign, exponent, and mantissa.

Sets

Python has a data type called a set. Sets work like mathematical sets. They are a lot like lists with no repeats. Sets are denoted by curly braces.

3.19.2 String

Strings in Python are identified as a contiguous set of characters in between quotation marks. Python allows for either pairs of single or double quotes.

Example 3 – Program demonstrating working with string.

```
# Program demonstrating working with string
str = 'Hello Python'
print(str) # Prints complete string
print(str[0]) # Prints first character of the string
print(str[2:5])# Prints characters starting from 3rd to 5th
print(str[2:]) # Prints string starting from 3rd character
print(str * 2) # Prints string two times
print(str + "PROGRAMMING") # Prints concatenated string

RUN
>>>
Hello Python
H
llo
llo Python
Hello PythonHello Python
Hello PythonPROGRAMMING
>>>
```

Figure 3.25 Program Demonstrating Working with String

So 'hello' is same as "hello". A string can have any number of characters in it, including 0. The empty string is '' (two quote characters with nothing between them). The string with length 1 represents a character in Python. The plus (+) sign is the string concatenation operator, and the asterisk (*) is the repetition operator. Strings are defined using quotes (", ', or """).

```
>>> st = "Hello World"
>>> st = 'Hello World'
>>> st = """This is a multi-line
string that uses triple quotes."""
```

Strings can be displayed on screen using the print function. For example:

```
print("hello") # It will print hello
```

☞ *In Python, # symbol is used to add comment. Every thing from the # to the end of the line is ignored.*

Like many other popular programming languages, strings in Python are arrays of bytes representing Unicode characters. However, Python does not have a character data type; a single character is simply a string with a length of one. For example 'a', 'b', 'c' are strings of length one. Square brackets can be used to access elements of the string.

☞ *In Python, there are no limits to the number of characters you can put in a string. A string, having 0 characters, is known as an empty string.*

```
a = "hello"
print(a[1]) # it will print e
```

Slicing is a mechanism used to select a range of items from sequence type like list, tuple, and string. It is beneficial and easy to get elements from a range by using slice way. It requires a : (colon) which separates the start and end index of the field in square brackets.

3.19.3 List

Python has a basic notation of a kind of data structure called a container, which is basically any object that can contain other objects. The two main kinds of containers are sequences (such as, lists and tuples) and mappings (such as, dictionaries).

Lists are the most versatile form of Python compound data types. A list contains items separated by commas and enclosed within square brackets ([]). For example,

```
>>> li = ["abc", 34, 4.34, 23]
```

To some extent, lists are similar to arrays in C. Difference between them is that all the items belonging to a list can be of different data type (heterogeneous). The values stored in a list can be accessed using the slice operator ([ ] and [:]) with indexes starting at 0 in the beginning of the list and working their way to end-1. The plus (+) sign is the list concatenation operator, and the asterisk (*) is the repetition operator.

You can access individual members of a list in the following way:

```
>>> li = ["abc", 34, 4.34, 23]
>>> li[1] # Second item in the list.
34
```

Unlike strings which are immutable, it is possible to change individual elements and size of the list.

3.19.4 Tuples

A tuple is like a list whose values cannot be modified once they have been created (enclosed in regular brackets). In other words, the tuple is immutable. Another way to think about tuples is to consider them to be a constant list. Tuples have elements which are indexed starting at 0. Items in a tuple are accessed using a numeric index.

```
>>> x = ('Vivek', 'Abhishek', 'Arti')
>>> print(x[2])
Arti
>>> y = (1, 9, 2 )
>>> print(y)
(1, 9, 2)
>>> print(max(y))
9
```

3.19.5 Dictionary

Dictionaries are Python's most powerful data collection. Dictionaries store a mapping between a set of keys and a set of values. They allow us to do fast database-like operations in Python. They literals use curly braces and have a list of key : value pairs. You can make an empty dictionary also. Dictionaries are written like this:

```
>>> pword = { 'Amit' : 'chuck' , 'Beena'
: 'permit', 'Deepak': 'grant'}
>>> print(pword)
{ 'Amit' : 'chuck' , 'Beena' : 'permit',
'Deepak': 'grant'}
>>> ooo = { }
>>> print(ooo)
{}
```

Dictionaries consist of pairs (called items) of keys and their corresponding values. In this example, the names are the keys and the passwords are the values. Each key is separated from its value by a colon (:); the items are separated by commas and the whole thing is enclosed in curly braces. An empty dictionary (without any items) is written with just two curly braces, like this: {}.

3.19.6 Sets

Python also includes a data type for sets. A set is an unordered collection with no duplicate elements. Basic uses include membership testing and eliminating duplicate entries. Set objects also support mathematical operations like union, intersection, difference, and symmetric difference.

Curly braces or the set() function can be used to create sets. To create an empty set, you have to use set(), not {}; the latter creates an empty dictionary, a data structure that you discussed earlier.

```
fruits = {"apple", "banana", "cherry"}
print(fruits)
{'cherry','banana','apple'}
```

The set list is unordered, so the items will appear in a random order. The items in the set are not displayed in the order that they were defined. Sets, like dictionaries, do not maintain a logical ordering. The order in which items are stored is determined by Python, and not by the order in which they were provided. Therefore, it is invalid and makes no sense to access an element of the set by index value.

☞ *A set is a collection which is unordered and unindexed. In Python, sets are written with curly brackets.*

3.20 print STATEMENT

print is a function which prints something on the screen. To print any message as it is on screen, just type *print* and that message or argument in (' ') or (" ").

```
print ("Hello World")
```

For example, in the above-mentioned program, "Hello World" is a string and *print* is a Python command to write a string in quotes on the console or terminal window.

☞ *print() statement without any argument will simply jump to the next line.*

Now, let us consider some more examples of how to use print command. Type the following print statements and run the program to see the output:

Example 4 –**Program to display string using print command.**

```
print ("Hello, How are you?")
print ("I am learning Python language.")

RUN
>>>
Hello, How are you?
I am learning Python language.
>>>
```

Figure 3.26 Program Demonstrating print command

Let's do something more advanced:

Example 5 –**Program to display sum of two numbers using print command.**

```
x = 2
y = 3
print ("Sum of",x,"and",y,"is",x+y)
RUN
>>>
Sum of 2 and 3 is 5
>>>
```

Figure 3.27 Program to Print Sum of Two Numbers

Note that whatever you write in (" ") or (' ') will be printed as it is and is not evaluated. So, 'Sum of' gets printed as it is without quotes and then the value of 'x' gets printed (i.e., 2); then 'and' is printed as it is. Then value of y is printed (i.e., 3) and at the end x+y is calculated and printed (i.e., 5).

Multiple values can be displayed by the single print() function separated by comma. Python will automatically insert spaces between them. The following example displays values of name and age variables using the single print() function.

```
>>> name="Aman"
>>> age=19
>>> print("Name:", name, "Age:",age)
Name: Aman Age: 19
```

By default, a single space (' ') acts as a separator between values. However, any other character can be used by providing a sep, short for separator, parameter to change that space to something else. For example, using sep=':' would separate the arguments by a colon and sep='##' would separate the arguments by two hash signs. In the following example "," is used as a separator character.

```
>>> name="Aman"
>>> age=19
>>> print(name,age)
Aman 19
>>> print(name,age,sep=",")
Aman,19
```

The output of the print() function always ends by a newline character. The print() function has another optional parameter end, whose default value is "\n". This value can be substituted by any other character such as a single space (' ') to display the output of the subsequent print() statement in the same line.

Let's Try

Write the following print statements and check the output:

(a)

```
print ("You are Welcome!")
print ("I am enjoying learning Python language.")
```

(b)

```
num1 = 10
num2 = 7
print ("Sum of",num1,"and",num2,"is",num1+num2)
```

(c)

```
n1 = 5
n2 = 3
print ("Product of",n1,"and",n2,"is",n1*n2)
```

As print() is used to print output on screen, to input data into a program, i.e., to get data from the user you use input(). This function reads a single line of text as a string. If the input function is called, the program flow will be stopped until the user has given an input and pressed Enter key. The text of the optional parameter, i.e., the prompt, will be printed on the screen.

Let's Try

Write the following print statements and check the output:

(a)

```
person = input('Enter your name:')
print('Hello', person, '!')
```

```
person = input('Enter your name:')
print('Hello', person, '!', sep='')
```

3.21 ACCEPTING INPUT FROM THE CONSOLE

In Python, input is used to request and get information from the user, and print is used to display information on the screen.

3.21.1 input()

In Python, input is accomplished by using an assignment statement combined with a special function called input(). Syntax of input() is as follows:

```
variable = input(<prompt>)
```

Here, prompt is an expression that serves to ask the user for input; this is almost always a string literal (i.e., some text inside quotation marks). When Python encounters an input expression, it evaluates the prompt and displays the result of the prompt on the screen. It then pauses and waits for the user to type an expression and press the Enter key. The expression typed by the user is then evaluated to produce the result. As the input provided is evaluated, Python expects valid expression. If the input provided is not correct then either syntax error or exception is raised by Python.

```
>>> name = input('Enter your name: ')
Enter your name: Vivek
>>> print('Hello', name)
Hello Vivek
```

Note that a comma is used to separate the individual items being printed, causing a space to appear between each when displayed. Thus, the output of the print function in this case is Hello Vivek, and not HelloVivek. Let us take some more examples:

```
>>> x=input("something:")
something:10
>>> x
'10'
>>> x=input("something:")
something:'10' # entered data is treated as string with or without ''
>>> x
"'10'"
>>> x = input("x: ")
x: 34
type(x)
<class 'str'> # input() function always returns a value of string type
>>> y = input("y: ")
y: 42
type(y)
<class 'str'>
>>> print(x + y)
3442
```

Here, the values entered (34 and 42) would be supplied by the user. Your program would then print out the value 3442, which is the concatenation, i.e., joining of two strings. In order to add them, you need to turn them into numbers. That can be done using int() or float().

```
>>> x = int(input("x: "))
x: 34
type(x)
<class 'int'>
>>> y = int(input("y: "))
y: 42
type(y)
<class 'int'>
>>> print(x + y)
76
```

Now, type the following:

```
>>> price=float(input('Enter price: '))
Enter price: 12.50
>>> qty=int(input('Enter quantity: '))
Enter quantity: 3
>>> print(price * qty)
37.5
```

Let's Try

Type the following code and write the output.

```
print('Enter an integer value:')
x = input()
print('Enter another integer value:')
y = input()
num1 = int(x)
num2 = int(y)
print(num1, '+', num2, '=', num1 + num2)
```

Example 6 –Program to demonstrate how to enter data using input command.

```
print('What is your name?')
name = input()
print('Hello!' + name + 'Nice to meet you!')

RUN
>>>
What is your name?
Priya
Hello! Priya Nice to meet you!
>>>
```

Figure 3.28 Program to Enter Data using input command

In the above program 'What is your name?' is printed as it is without quotes. input() reads a single line and stores it in the variable "name". Then 'Hello!' is printed as it is, value of name is printed (i.e. Priya) and 'Nice to meet you!' is printed as it is.

Example 7 –Program to demonstrate input command with message.

```
name = input("Enter Your Name : ")
print("You are Welcome", name)

RUN
>>>
Enter Your Name : Puja
You are Welcome Puja
>>>
```

Figure 3.29 Program to Demonstrate input command with Message

Example 8 –**Program to accept student's detail using the input function and display it.**

```
name    = input("Enter Student Name : ")
marks   = input("Enter Total Marks: ")
address = input ("Enter Address: ")
print("Printing Student's Details")
print ("Name",   "Marks", "Address")
print (name, marks, address)
RUN
>>>
Enter Student Name : Dev
Enter Total Marks: 467
Enter Address: C2, Janak Puri
Printing Student's Details
Name Marks Address
Dev 467 C2, Janak Puri
>>>
```

Figure 3.30 Program to Accept and Print Student's Details

The input() function reads a line from input and converts it into a string and returns it. Then, you can use this input string in your Python program.

Let's Try

Write the following code and check the output:

(a)
```
age = input("Your age? ")
print("You are " + age + " years old.")
```

(b)
```
emp_name = input("Enter Employee Name: ")
salary  = input("Enter salary :")
print ("Employee Name", "Salary")
print (emp_name, salary)
```

Whatever you enter as input, input function converts it into a string. Even if you enter an integer value, still input() function will convert it into the string. You need to explicitly convert it into the integer in your code. Let's understand this with an example.

Example 9 –**Program to check input type in Python.**

```
# Program to check input type in Python
number = input ("Enter a number :")
name   = input("Enter name :")
print("Printing type of input value")
print ("Type of number", type(number))
print ("Type of name", type(name))
RUN
>>>
Enter a number :25
Enter name : Ansh
Printing type of input value
Type of number <class 'str'>
Type of name <class 'str'>
>>>
```

Figure 3.31 Program to Check Input Type in Python

Note that in the above-mentioned program, both number and name variable types are *str*, i.e., string. You know that whatever you enter either any number (integer or float) or string as input, input() function always converts it into a string. So, let's understand how to accept integer value from a user in Python.

```
>>> num = input('Enter a number: ')
Enter a number: 10
>>> num
'10'
```

Here, you can see that the entered value 10 is a string, not a number. To convert this into a number, you can use int() or float() functions.

```
>>> int('10')
10
>>> float('10')
10.0
```

This same operation can be performed using the eval() function.

Example 10 **–Program to add two inputted numbers by converting both the numbers into an int type using int().**

```
# Program to add two inputted numbers
first_num = int ( input ("Enter first number : ") )
second_num = int ( input ("Enter second number : ") )
sum = first_num + second_num
print("Addition of two number is: ", sum)

RUN
>>>
Enter first number : 12
Enter second number : 10
Addition of two number is:  22
>>>
```

Figure 3.32 Program to Add Two Inputted Numbers

Note that in Figure 3.32 you have explicitly added a cast of an integer type to an input function, i.e., you converted input value to the integer type using int(). Now if you print the type of first_num, you will get type as "int".

```
>>> type(first_num)
<class 'int'>
```

You can also accept float value from a user in Python and convert user input into float number using float() function.

Let's Try

Write the following code in Python and check the output:

```
# Program to accept float value from the user
float_num = float (input("Enter any float number :") )
print ("Input float number is: ", float_num )
print ("Type is:", type(float_num) )
```

Write the following codes in Python and run the program assuming a=2 and b=4. Also, write the reason behind the first program producing incorrect output.

a = input() b = input() s = a + b print(s)	a = int(input()) b = int(input()) s = a + b print(s)

3.21.2 eval()

eval() function is used to evaluate the value of a string. It takes a string as an argument, evaluates this string as number, and returns the numeric result. It can evaluate even expressions, provided the input is a string:

```
>>> eval('27')
27
>>> eval('27.67')
27.67
>>> eval('5+2')
7
>>> eval("7*4+2")
30
```

Example 11 –**Program to convert given temperature in Celsius into Fahrenheit. Use eval() for input.**

```
# Program to convert temperature in Celsius into Fahrenheit
temp = eval(input('Enter a temperature in Celsius: '))
print('In Fahrenheit, that is', 9/5*temp+32)

RUN
>>>
Enter a temperature in Celsius: 0
In Fahrenheit, that is 32.0
>>>
```

Figure 3.33 Program to Convert Temperature given in Celsius into Fahrenheit

Example 12 –**Program to calculate average of two inputted numbers. Use eval() to input numbers.**

```
# Program to calculate average of two inputted numbers
num1 = eval(input('Enter the first number: '))
num2 = eval(input('Enter the second number: '))
print('The average of the numbers you entered is', (num1+num2)/2)

RUN
>>>
Enter the first number: 65
Enter the second number: 72
The average of the numbers you entered is 68.5
>>>
```

Figure 3.34 Program to Calculate Average of Two Inputted Numbers

3.22 SIMPLE PYTHON PROGRAMS

Example 13 –**Program to add two numbers given by user.**

```
# Program to add two numbers given by user
print('Please enter an integer value:')
x = input()
print('Please enter another integer value:')
y = input()
num1 = int(x)
num2 = int(y)
print(num1, '+', num2, '=', num1 + num2)
```

(Conti...)

```
RUN
>>>
Please enter an integer value:
56
Please enter another integer value:
32
56 + 32 = 88
>>>
```

Figure 3.35 Program to Add Two Numbers Given by User

Example 14 –**Program to display months and days for entered no. of days.**

```
# Program to display months and days for entered no. of days

days = int(input("Enter days: "))
months = days / 30
days = days % 30
print("Months = ",int(months),"Days = ", days)

RUN
>>>
Enter days: 365
Months =  12 Days =  5
>>>
```

Figure 3.36 Program to Display Months and Days for Entered no. of Days

Example 15 –**Program to find selling price.**

```
#Program to find selling price
costprice=int(input("Enter Cost Price: "))
profit=int(input("Enter profit: "))
sellingprice = costprice+profit
print ("Selling price: ",sellingprice)

RUN
>>>
Enter Cost Price: 100
Enter profit: 20
Selling price:  120
>>>
```

Figure 3.37 Program to Find Selling Price

Example 16 –**Program to calculate Bonus, Commission and Gross salary.**

```
# Program to calculate Bonus, Commission and Gross salary
basic_salary = 1500
bonus_rate = 200
commision_rate = 0.02
```

(Conti...)

```
sold = int(input("Enter the number of inputs sold: "))
price = float(input("Enter the total prices: "))
bonus = (bonus_rate * sold)
commission = (commision_rate * sold * price)
print("Bonus = %6.2f" % bonus)
print("Commision = %6.2f" % commission)
print("Gross salary = %6.2f" % (basic_salary + bonus + commission) )

RUN
>>>
Enter the number of inputs sold: 2
Enter the total prices: 5
Bonus = 400.00
Commission =   0.20
Gross salary = 1900.20
>>>
```

Figure 3.38 Program to Calculate Bonus, Commission and Gross salary

Example 17 –**Program to convert the time given into minutes in hours and minutes.**

```
# Program to convert the time given in minutes in hours and minutes
time = int(input("Enter time in minutes: "))
hours= time/60
minutes = time%60
print("Hours : ",round(hours))
print("Minutes :",minutes)

RUN
>>>
Enter time in minutes: 70
Hours :  1
Minutes : 10
>>>
```

Figure 3.39 Program to Convert the Time Given into Minutes in Hours and Minutes

☞ *Python 2 has two versions of input functions, input() and raw_input(). The input() function treats the received data as string if it is included in quotes '' or "", otherwise the data is treated as number. In Python 3, raw_input() function is deprecated. Further, the received data is always treated as string.*

REVIEW QUESTIONS WITH ANSWERS

1. Multiple Choice Questions

1. Feature of Python program:
   a. Easy-to-learn and read
   b. Interactive Mode
   c. Free and Open Source
   d. All of the above
2. Which of the following is not true about an interpreter?
   a. Interpreter generates an object program from the source program.
   b. Interpreter is a kind of translator.
   c. Interpreter analyses each source statement every time it is to be executed.
   d. None of the above
3. Comment in Python starts with:
   a. ! c. #
   b. & d. *
4. Python is being used in many diverse fields as:
   a. Scripting c. Web Application
   b. GUI Programming d. All of these
5. Limitation of Python:

a. Not the fastest language
b. Lesser libraries
c. Both (a) and (b)
d. None of these

6. The plus (+) is :
a. Concatenation operator
b. Repetition operator
c. Both (a) and (b)
d. None of these

7. An example of a literal constant is:
a. 5
b. 1.23
c. 'This is a string'
d. All of the above

8. Examples of valid identifier names are:
a. i
b. __my_name
c. Both (a) and (b)
d. 67Jim

9. Strings are defined using:
a. Single quote (')
b. Double quote (")
c. Triple quote (""")
d. All of the above

10. Which of the following is not a keyword in Python?
a. for
b. if
c. print
d. All are keywords

11. What is the maximum possible length of an identifier?
a. 31 characters
b. 63 characters
c. 79 characters
d. None of the above

2. State True or False for the following:

1. To indicate hexadecimal literals, you will use the prefix '0X' or '0x".
2. Booleans can have three permissible values.
3. Square brackets can be used to access elements of the string.
4. Python has a special function called *type* that tells us the data type of any value.
5. Python does not need to be compiled before it is run.
6. Complex numbers are always represented as two floating point numbers, the real and imaginary part.
7. Float can also be scientific numbers with an "e" to indicate the power of 10.
8. Int, or integer, is a whole number, positive or negative, without decimals, of unlimited length.
9. Strings can be displayed on screen using the print() function.
10. Every value in Python has a data type.

3. Match the following:

1. Python	a. start with a # character
2. Indentation	b. ...
3. Comments	c. a case sensitive language
4. Multi-line	d. a block of code
5. Identifiers	e. comments appear in more than one line
6. Primary prompt	f. can be of any length
7. Secondary prompt	g. >>>
8. Python strings	h. to verify the type of any object
9. A variable name	i. cannot be changed
10. type() function	j. cannot start with a number

4. Fill in the blanks:

1. Converting one data type to another data type is called __________.
2. ________ are defined using quotes (", ', or """).
3. In Python, _________ symbol is used to add comment.
4. In Python, ________ is used to request and get information from the user.
5. ________ can be defined as a data which is given in a variable or constant.
6. ________ is the basic editor and interpreter environment.
7. ________ is the default Python prompt of the interactive shell.
8. ________ is a program that the computer can directly execute.

9. A program stored in a file (usually one that will be interpreted) is called ________.

10. ________ are the entries in a computer program for the purpose of documentation or explanation.

Answers

1.	1. d	2. a	3. c	4. d	5. c	6. a
	7. d	8. c	9. d	10. d	11 d	
2.	1. T	2. F	3. T	4. T	5. T	6. T
	7. T	8. T	9. T	10. T		
3.	1. c	2. d	3. a	4. e	5. f	6. g
	7. b	8. i	9. j	10. h		

Short Answers Questions

4.	1. Typecasting	2. Strings
	3. #	4. input
	5. Literals	6. IDLE
	7. >>>	8. Object code
	9. Script	10. Comments

1. What is Python?

Ans Python is a high-level, interpreted, interactive and object oriented-scripting language. It was designed to be easily readable; uses English keywords frequently whereas other languages use punctuation. It has fewer syntactical constructions than other languages.

2. Discuss some characteristics of Python Language.

Ans Python has following features:

(a) *Easy-to-learn:* Python has relatively few keywords, simple structure, and a clearly defined syntax. So, it is easy to learn and use.

(b) *Easy-to-read:* Python code is much more clearly defined and visible to the eyes. So, programs written in Python are easily readable and understandable.

(c) *Interactive Mode:* It supports an interactive mode in which we can enter results from a terminal right to the program, allowing interactive testing and debugging of code.

(d) *Portable:* Python can run on a wide variety of hardware platforms and has the same interface on all platforms. So, it is called platform independent programming language.

3. What do you mean by the statement 'Python is Interactive'?

Ans This statement means that we can actually work at a Python prompt and interact with the interpreter directly to execute our programs and get the output.

4. Is Python case-sensitive?

Ans Yes, Python is a case-sensitive programming language. Thus *AGE, Age* and *age* are three different identifiers in Python. Some legal identifiers are x, age, marks2, Total_Marks, etc.

5. What are comments in a Python program?

Ans In programming, comment is the text that we insert into the program for documentation purpose.

A hash sign (#) that is not inside a string literal begins a comment. All characters after the sign # and up to the end of the physical line (a physical line is what we see as a line when we write a program) are part of the comment, and the Python interpreter ignores them.

6. What is multi-line statement?

Ans Statements in Python typically end with a new line, i.e., at the end of the line. Python does, however, allow the line to continue by using the line continuation character (\) at the end of the line. Such a statement is called multi-line statement.

7. Why is indentation important in Python?

Ans Python programmers almost always use *four* spaces for the first level of indentation, *eight* spaces for the next level (a code block nested inside another code block), and so on. The indentation must be the same for every line of a block. We get an Indentation Error message (syntax error) if we use, for example, four spaces on one line of a block and three spaces on another line in the same block.

8. Why is Python called interpreted language? How is it different from C++?

Ans A program written in a compiled language, like C or C++, is converted from the source language, i.e., C or C++ into a language that is understood by our computer (binary code, i.e., 0s and 1s) using a compiler with various flags and options. When we run the program, the linker/loader software copies the program from hard disk to memory and starts executing.

Python, on the other hand, does not need to be converted into binary. we just run the program directly from the source code. Internally, Python converts the source code into an intermediate form called bytecodes and then translates this into the native language of our computer and then runs it. All this, actually, makes using Python much easier since we don't have to worry about compiling the program, making sure that the proper libraries are linked and loaded, etc. This also makes our Python programs much more portable.

9. Python is free and open source. Comment.

Ans Python is an example of FLOSS (Free/Libre and Open Source Software). In simple terms, we can freely distribute copies of this software, read its source code, make changes to it, and use pieces of it in new free programs. FLOSS is based on the concept of a community which shares knowledge. This is one of the reasons why Python is so good-it has been created and is constantly improved and upgraded by a community to make it better.

10. Why is Python considered an ideal language for scripting and rapid application development?

Ans Python is an easy to learn, powerful programming language. It has efficient high-level data structures and a simple but effective approach to object-oriented programming. Python's elegant syntax and dynamic typing, together with its interpreted nature, make it an ideal language for scripting and rapid application development in many areas on most platforms.

11. 'Python is a true cross-platform language'. Comment.

Ans Python can run equally well on a variety of platforms such as Windows, Linux/UNIX, Macintosh, Supercomputer, and smart phones. So, It is a portable and true cross-platform language.

12. The only prompt used by the Python interactive system is the one consisting of three right-angle brackets (>>>). Is it True or False?

Ans False. Python interactive system also uses a secondary prompt consisting of three periods (...).

13. Write one advantage of using triple quoted strings.

Ans The use of triple quoted strings makes it possible for us to continue a string on a new line, and to preserve the line break in the string.

14. What is a script?

Ans A script is a text file containing Python program.

15. Indentation in Python is used for cosmetic purposes only. Is it True or False?

Ans False. Indentation is used in Python to determine the grouping of statements, which is critical to the success of a program.

16. Write the output for the following:

```
city = input ("Enter your City Name :
")
print("My city name is ", city)
```

Ans
```
Enter your City Name : New Delhi
My city name is  New Delhi
```

17. Write the output for the following:

```
# Program to accept a string as input
from the user
string = input("Enter a String :")
print ("Input string is", string)
print ("Type is:", type(string))
```

Ans
```
Enter a String :Welcome
Input string is Welcome
Type is: <class 'str'>
```

18. Write the following program code and check output. What is the difference between x and 'x'?

```
x = 10
print x
print 'x'
```

Ans
```
10
'x'
```

Here, 'x' is a character whereas x is a variable. This means that 'x' is simple (x) and x (without quotes) will print the value of x, i.e., 10.

19. What is a string?

Ans A string is a sequence of characters. It is basically just a bunch of words.

20. What is meant by Single Quote string and Double Quotes string?

Ans We can specify strings using single quotes such as 'Quote me on this'. All whitespace, i.e., spaces and tabs are preserved as it is.
Strings in double quotes work exactly the same way as strings in single quotes, such as "What's your name?"

21. "Strings are Immutable". What do you mean by this?

Ans This means that once we have created a string, we cannot change it.

22. What are the rules for naming Identifier?

Ans Rules for naming identifier are as follows:

(a) The first character of the identifier must be a letter or an underscore.

(b) The rest of the identifier name can consist of letters, underscores (_) or digits (0-9).

(c) Identifier names are case-sensitive. For example, myname and myName are not the same.

23. A variable is the same as a constant. Is it True or False?

Ans False. The value of a variable is intended to change during the execution of the program whereas the value of a constant is not intended to change.

24. Python programmers must declare all variables. Is it True or False?

Ans False. Variable declarations are not required in Python. All that is required to cause a variable to come into existence is to invent a new name for the variable and assign a value to it.

25. Variable names can begin with the digit characters. True or False?

Ans False. Variable names must begin with a letter or an underscore character.

26. Describe three different ways to format string literals.

Ans Surround them with matching pairs of single quotes, double quotes, or triple quotes.

27. What are keywords? Explain with example.

Ans At the time of designing a language, some words are reserved to do specific tasks. Such words are called as keywords or reserved words. Keywords cannot be used as variable. For example, *def, for, print*, etc.

28. What is the difference between keyword and identifier?

Ans Keywords are the words used by Python interpreter to recognize the structure of program. As these words have specific meaning for the interpreter, they cannot be used for any other purpose. So, keywords are reserved.
An identifier is a unique name that enables us to identify something. Identifiers are used to label variables, functions, classes, objects, and modules. They begin with either a letter or an underscore, and they can contain letters, underscores, or digits. They cannot contain punctuation marks. They are user-defined.

29. What do you mean by Assignment?

Ans Assignment is the operation of setting a value to a variable.

30. What is expression?

Ans Expression refers to a section of code that can be worked out to produce a value.

31. Differentiate between lvalue and rvalue.

Ans Lvalues are the objects to which we assign value or expressions. Lvalues expression can come on the left or right hand side of an assignment statement.
Rvalues are the literals and expressions that are assigned to lvalues. Rvalue expressions comes only on the right hand side of the assignment statement.

32. What do you mean by an Integer?

Ans An integer is a fundamental (i.e., built-in) type used to define numeric variables holding whole numbers.

33. Immutable value cannot be modified. (True/False)

Ans True

34. What is the value of variable num after the following assignment statements are executed?

```
num = 10
num = num + 2
print(num)
```

Ans 12

35. Do variables x and y refer to the same memory location after the following instructions are executed? (YES/NO)

(a)
```
x = 10
y = x
x = x + 1
print(x)
print(y)
```

Ans No, x=11 and y=10

36. Can you use keyword as variable name in Python? Why?

Ans No, we cannot use a keyword as variable name, function name or any other identifier as keywords are the reserved words in Python.

37. What is mixed-type expression?

Ans A mixed-type expression is an expression containing operands of different type.

38. Classify each of the following as valid or invalid variable names:
percent%, a_1, sum of numbers, hint_, date_of_birth

Ans percent% -> invalid
a_1 -> valid
sum of numbers -> invalid
hint_ -> valid
date_of_birth -> valid

39. Define data type.

Ans The kind of data that a variable may hold in a programming language is called the *data type*.

40. Computer programs are composed of expressions, which are made up of statements. Is it True or False?

Ans False. Just the reverse is true. Programs are made up of statements, which are composed of expressions.

41. In the following expression, 2+5, what is the common jargon for the plus sign? What is the common jargon for the 2 and the 5?

Ans The plus sign is commonly called the operator. The 2 and the 5 are commonly called operands. More specifically, the 2 is the left operand, and the 5 is the right operand.

42. What is the use of type()?

Ans To verify the type of any object in Python, use the type() function.

43. The modulus operator is used to produce the quotient in division. Is it True or False?

Ans False. The modulus operator is used to produce the remainder.

44. Describe the use of parentheses in expressions.

Ans Parentheses can be used to group terms in an expression so as to provide control over the order in which the operations are performed.

45. Explain *None* data type with example.

Ans In Python, None is a special data type with a single value. For example,

```
begin = None
```

The line assigns a special value called None to variable begin. None is Python's way of representing nothing. It makes a good placeholder for a value. It also evaluates to false when treated as a condition.

46. Explain different functions used for casting.

Ans The functions which used for casting are:

(a) int(): It is used to specify integer literal. It constructs an integer number from a string literal and float.

(b) str(): It is used to specify the string literal. It constructs a string type from integer literal or float literal.

(c) float(): It is used to specify the float data types. It constructs float literal from integer and string literal.

47. Explain the difference between tuples and lists.

Ans A tuple is an immutable linear data structure. Thus, in contrast to lists, once a tuple is defined, it cannot be altered. Tuples are denoted by parentheses whereas lists are denoted by square brackets

48. Describe how Python evaluates an expression containing parentheses.

Ans A Python expression is evaluated by first evaluating each of the sub-expressions in the parentheses, and then using those values to complete the evaluation. If the expression contains nested parentheses, the evaluation is performed by evaluating the innermost parentheses first and working outwards from there.

49. Explain the use of the assignment operator.

Ans The assignment operator causes the value of its right operand to be stored in the memory location identified by its left operand.

50. What numeric types are supported by Python?

Ans There are three numeric types in Python:
int
float
complex
Variables of numeric types are created when we assign a value to them:

x = 1 # int
y = 2.8 # float
z = 1j # complex

51. What is the use of print statement?

Ans To print the result of a Python program in the terminal window, we apply the print command, i.e., the word print followed by a string enclosed in quotes, or just a variable.

52. How Python evaluates an expression containing parentheses?

Ans Expression in python is evaluated by evaluating each of the sub-expressions in the parentheses first, and then using those values to complete the evaluation. If the expression contains nested parentheses, the evaluation is performed by evaluating the innermost parentheses first and then it evaluates outward parentheses.

53. What is a statement?

Ans A statement is a unit of code that the Python interpreter can execute.

54. What is the use of comment?

Ans Comments are the entries in a computer program for the purpose of documentation or explanation. They should be written so that the logic of a program becomes understandable easily. However, the compiler ignores comments.

55. Differentiate between comment and indentation.

Ans Comment is used to provide internal documentation to a program whereas indentation makes a program or a function clear and readable.

56. Discuss any two rules to create a variable name.

Ans A variable can have a short name (like x and y) or a more descriptive name (like age, carname, total_volume). Rules for Python variables:

(a) A variable name must start with a letter or the underscore character. It cannot start with a number.

(b) Variable names are case-sensitive (age, Age and AGE are three different variables).

57. Write a short note on identifiers.

Ans Identifier is the user-defined name given to a part of a program viz. variable, object, function etc. It is not reserved. It can have letters, digits and a symbol underscore. It must begin with either a letter or underscore. For instance, _chk, chess, trial etc. are valid identifiers.

58. Write a short note on input() function.

Ans In Python, input is used to request and get information from the user. For example:
print("Enter your name:")
x = input()
print("Hello, " + x)

59. What is the result of each of the following when evaluated?

```
n=10
m=2
print(n/m)
print(n//m)
print(n%m)
```

Ans 5.0
5
0

60. Write a program to obtain three numbers and print their sum.

```
# Program to obtain three numbers and print their sum
num1=int(input("Enter number 1:"))
num2=int(input("Enter number 2:"))
num3=int(input("Enter number 3:"))
sum = num1 + num2 + num3
print("Three numbers are :" , num1, num2, num3)
print("Sum is :" , sum)
```

(Conti...)

```
RUN
>>>
Enter number 1:19
Enter number 2:16
Enter number 3:14
Three numbers are : 19 16 14
Sum is : 49
>>>
```

Figure 1 Program to obtain three numbers and print their sum

61. Write a program to obtain length and breadth of a rectangle and calculate its area.

```
# Program to obtain length and breadth of a rectangle and calculate its
area

length= float(input("Enter length of the rectangle:"))
breadth = float(input("Enter breadth of the rectangle:"))
area = length * breadth
print("Rectangle specifications")
print("Length : ", length)
print("breadth : ",breadth)
print("Area : ",area)

RUN
>>>
Enter length of the rectangle:4.8
Enter breadth of the rectangle:2.4
Rectangle specifications
Length :  4.8
breadth :  2.4
Area :  11.52
>>>
```

Figure 2 Program to obtain length and breadth of a rectangle and calculate its area

62. Write program to read height in cm and convert the height to feet and inches.

```
# Program to Read Height in cm and Convert the Height to Feet and Inches
cm=int(input("Enter the height in centimeters:"))
inches=0.394*cm
feet=0.0328*cm
print("The length in inches",round(inches,2))
print("The length in feet",round(feet,2))

RUN
>>>
Enter the height in centimeters:55
The length in inches 21.67
The length in feet 1.8
>>>
```

Figure 3 Program to Convert the Height to Feet and Inches

EXERCISE

1. Discuss few features of Python language.
2. Is Python case-sensitive? Comment.
3. What is indentation? Is it necessary to indent statements in Python?
4. In Python programming, comments are ignored by the computer. Is it True or False?
5. How is interactive mode different from script mode?
6. Write short notes on the following:
   (a) Interactive mode
   (b) Physical line
   (c) Script
   (d) IDLE
7. How would you create multi-line comment in Python?
8. "Python is an interpreted language". Justify.
9. "Python is Interactive". Comment.
10. Explain syntax error with an example.
11. Write the following program code and check the output. What is the difference between x and 'x'?
```
x = "Hello Friends!"
print(x)
print ('x')
```
12. What is Python?
13. Write any two features of Python.
14. What are the characteristics of Python language?
15. Write the process of downloading and installing Python.
16. How would you exit interactive mode?
17. Write Python shortcut to quit interactive mode.
18. Explain print() with an example.
19. What is the difference between int() and float()?
20. Which function will you use to convert number into string?
21. Define type() function.
22. What is the significance of a variable?
23. Mention the sign which is used to assign values to variables.
24. Write the difference between mutable and immutable variables.
25. Name any five Python keywords.
26. What do you mean by constants?
27. Write an example of a literal constant.
28. What is the use of escape sequence?
29. What do you mean by L-value?
30. What do you mean by escape character \" ?
31. What do you mean by data type?
32. Which type of data is stored by Number data type?
33. What is type() function?
34. Differentiate between the following:
    (a) Mutable variable and Immutable variable
    (b) Constant and Variable
    (c) Integer and Character constant
35. Write short notes on:
    (a) Literals
    (b) Keyword
36. Python supports four different numerical types. Explain each with example.
37. What are Literal Constants? Explain with an example.
38. What is the difference between keyword and identifier?
39. What is an integer?
40. Differentiate between int and float numerical types.
41. What is the significance of a variable?
42. State True or False:
    (a) None is a special data type with single value.
    (b) A value when stored as floating point will have 53 bits of precision.
    (c) A sequence of digits starting with 0 (zero) is taken to be an octal integer.
    (d) Python does not have any keywords.
    (e) \\ is an escape sequence to represent backslash.
43. Differentiate between float and complex numbers.
44. Explain the difference between static and dynamic typing.
45. How is a meaningful identifier useful?
46. State the basic rules to declare variables in Python.
47. Explain multiple assignment with an example.
48. Explain dynamic typing with an example.
49. How are strings in Python identified?
50. Write the function of slice operator.
51. How will you define tuple?
52. How will you make an empty dictionary?
53. Can set accept duplicate values?
54. What is the difference between type casting and automatic type conversion? Explain with suitable example.
55. What is the purpose of comment and indentation in a program?

56. Explain any two escape sequences with example.

LAB EXERCISE

1. Type the following expression one by one at Python Prompt >>> and press Enter key.
(a) `2 + 4 + 7`
(b) `2 * 6`
(c) `5 + 3 * 7`
(d) `2 ** 3`
(e) `8 - (6 * 4)`

2. Give the output of the following statements:
(a) `print(2 + 4 + 7)`
(b) `print(2 * 6)`
(c) `print("Hello! how are you")`
(d) `print("Sum of 2 + 5 = ",2+5)`
(e) `print(5 * 7, (10 - 2) * 4)`
(f) `print(2 ** 4)`
(g)
```
message = "Welcome"
print(type(message))
```
(h)
```
num = 1972
print(type(num))
```
(i)
```
pi = 3.14
print(type(pi))
```

3. Write the output of the following statements:

(a)
```
>>> x=8
>>> y=4
>>> print(x + y)
>>> print(x - y)
>>> print(x * y)
```
(b)
```
name = input ("Enter your Name : ")
print("My name is ", name)
```

4. Write the following code in a new window opened by IDLE and get the output.
```
maths = 97
english = 88
hindi = 75
total = maths + english + hindi
average = total /3
print("Total :",total)
print("Average :", average)
```

5. Write the following program and get the output.
```
# Calculation
num1 = 70
num2 = 10
sum = num1 + num2
sub = num1 - num2
product = num1 * num2
div = num1/num2
print("Sum : ", sum)
print("Subtraction: ", sub)
print("Product : ", product)
print("Division : ", div)
```

6. Given the following assignment: x = 2. What would each of the following Python statements print?
(a) `print("x")`
(b) `print('x')`
(c) `print(x)`
(d) `print("x + 1")`
(e) `print('x' + 1)`
(f) `print(x + 1)`

7. What will be the output of the following?

(a)
```
print(3+4)
print(3, 4, 3 + 4)
print()
print(3, 4,)
print(3+4)
print("The answer is", 3 + 4)
```
(b)
```
x=20
x= x+10
x= x-5
print(x)
```

8. Type the following at the Python prompt and write the output:
```
>>> int(4.5)
>>> int(3.9)
>>> long(3.9)
>>> float(int(3.3))
>>> int(float(3.3))
>>> int(float(3))
```

9. What will be the output of the following?

a.
```
>>> a = 5.0; b = -5.0; c = 1.9856; d = 33
>>> print('a is', a, 'b is', b, 'c and d are', c, d)
```
b.
```
>>> print ("Hello\nWorld\n\nGoodbye 32\n")
```

10. Write the output of the following Python code:

a.
```
>>> print(6.3)
>>> print(755)
>>> print('Hello! World')
>>> name = "Shiv"
>>> print(name)
```
b.
```
num = 3
num = num + 2
print(num)
```
c.
```
x = 2
y = x
x = x + 1
print(x)
print(y)
```

d.
```
x=10
print (x)
x = "**"
print (x)
```
e.
```
x, y, z = 2.5, 4, "Hello"
print (x)
print (y)
print (z)
```
f.
```
print (2+5)
print ('2+5')
```
g.
```
eval("8*2+7")
eval("8/2+5")
```
11. What is the value of variables num1 and num2 after the following instructions are executed?

num1= 0
k = 5
num1 = num1 + k * 2
num2 = num1 + k * 2

12. Write a code in Python to print your name, class, and DOB as separate strings.
13. Write a program to find the simple interest for given principal (P), rate of interest (R) and number of years (T). The formula is:

$$I = \frac{PRT}{100}$$

14. Write a program to assign two numeric variables as N1 and N2 and perform arithmetic operations, such as addition, subtraction, multiplication and division on these variables. Finally, display the result.
15. Repeat the above program by accepting N1 and N2 from the user through the keyboard and display the result on the screen.
16. Write a program that takes height in centimeters and then converts your height into feet and inches. [Note 1 foot = 12 inches and 1 inch = 2.54 cm]
17. Write a program to enter length and breadth of rectangle and then print area of rectangle.
18. Write a program to compute profit earned. Cost price and selling price are to be inputted from keyboard.
19. Write a program to compute discount amount and net amount on the sale inputted from the keyboard.
20. Write a program to find the area of a square.

CHAPTER 4

Operators, Expressions and Python Statements

4.1 OPERATORS

An *operator* is a particular symbol which is used on some values and produces an output as a result. In other words, the *operator* in Python specifies an operation to be performed on the variables that yields a resultant value. The operator works on operands. An *operand* is an entity on which the operator acts. For example, in the expression:

```
a + b
```

the sign + is an operator which specifies the operation of addition on the two operands **a** and **b**.

Operators can be unary, binary or ternary. The operator which requires a single operand is known as a unary operator; the operator which requires two operands is known as a binary operator; and which requires three operands is called ternary operator. For example,

```
-x # here - is unary operator


7 + 2 = 9 # here + is binary operator


# Assign minimum value using ternary
operator
x, y = 5, 7
minimum = x if x < y else y
print(minimum)
```

Two operators, + and -, can be used as unary operators. The unary operator has only one operand. It expects a single numeric expression (literal number, variable, or more complicated numeric expression within parentheses) immediately to its right; it computes the additive inverse of its operand.

☞ *A binary operator is an operator that takes two arguments (for example, + or /). A unary operator operates on a single value. (For example, -).*

Python language operators are classified into the following types. These are:

(a) Arithmetic Operators
(b) Relational (Conditional) Operators
(c) Logical/Boolean Operators
(d) Assignment Operators
(e) Bitwise Operators
(f) Membership Operators
(g) Identity Operators

4.2 ARITHMETIC OPERATORS

Arithmetic operators perform basic arithmetic operations. Arithmetic operators, such as +, -, *, / , % (modulus), ** (exponent), etc., are used for mathematical calculations. An arithmetic expression is made up of constants, variables, a combination of both or a function call, connected by arithmetic operators. Some of these operators also work on data types other than numbers, but they may work differently. For example, + adds two numbers (2 + 2 gives the result 4). But concatenating numbers gives a string ('2' + '2' gives the result '22').

You cannot use an operator with two incompatible data types. For example, if you try to use + with an integer and a string, Python returns an error. An arithmetic expression is made up of constants, variables, a combination of both or a function call, connected by arithmetic operators. (See Figure 4.1).

Normally, operators are said to be either unary or binary. A unary operator has only one operand while a binary operator has two operands. In its unary mode with a single operand, a minus sign is usually a sign changing operator, while in its binary mode with two operands, a minus sign is usually a subtraction operator.

4.2.1 Working with Arithmetic Operators

The binary arithmetic operator requires two operands to operate upon them. Assuming variable *a* holds 10 and variable *b* holds 20 then:

(a) + (addition or plus) say a + b, will give 30.
(b) – (subtraction or minus) say a – b, will give -10.
(c) * (multiplication) say a * b, will give 200.
(d) / (slash for division) say b / a will give 2.0.
(e) % (modulus operator for remainder), say b % a will give 0.
(f) ** [exponent - Performs exponential (power) calculation on operators]
a = 2
b = 3
c = a**b will give 8.
(g) // (Floor division) - It refers to division of operands where the result is the quotient in which the digits after the decimal point are removed. In other words, the operation that divides two numbers and chops off the fraction part is called floor division.
a=9
b=2
9//2 will give 4
and
a=9.0
b=2.0
9.0//2.0 will give 4.0

Example 1 –**Demo of arithmetic operators.**

```
# Demo of arithmetic operators
a = 20
b = 10
c = 0
c = a + b
print("Sum of a + b is ", c)
c = a - b
print("Difference a - b is ", c)
c = a * b
print("Multiplication a * b is ", c)
c = a / b
print("Division a/b is ", c)
c = a % b
print("Remainder a%b is ", c)
a = 2
b = 3
c = a**b
print("Exponent a**b is ", c)
a = 10
b = 5
c = a//b
print("Floor division a//b is ", c )

RUN
Sum of a + b is   30
Difference a - b is  10
Multiplication a * b is  200
Division a/b is  2.0
Remainder a%b is  0
Exponentiation a**b is  8
Floor division a//b is  2
```

Figure 4.1 Demo of arithmetic operators

Let's Try

Exponentiation refers to finding powers. Python uses ** before a power. Exponents do not need to be integers. For example, 0.5 power will produce a square root. Try the following in the Shell:

>>> 3**4 >>> 5*2**3	>>> 9**.5 >>> 2**.5	>>> (1+1)**(5-2) >>> 3*1**3

Write the output of following binary arithmetic operations:

```
# Working with binary arithmetic operators
a = 4
b = 2
sum = a+b
sub = a-b
mult = a*b
divi = a/b
modu = a%b
expo = a**2
print("Sum of a + b is ", sum)
print("Subtraction of a - b is ", sub)
print("Multiplication of a * b is ", mult)
print("Division of a / b is ", divi)
print("Modulus of a % b is ", modu)
print("Exponent of a ** b is ", expo)
```

Example 2 –**Program to calculate area of a triangle using formula 1/2*base*height.**

```
# Program to calculate area of a triangle using formula 1/2*base*height
base = float(input("Enter base of a triangle : "))
height = float(input("Enter height of a triangle : "))
area_of_triangle = (1/2* base * height)
print("Area of a triangle: ",area_of_triangle)

RUN
>>>
Enter base of a triangle : 3.5
Enter height of a triangle : 5.5
Area of a triangle:  9.625
>>>
```

Figure 4.2 Program to calculate area of a triangle

Example 3 –**Program to print quotient.**

```
# Program to print Quotient
a = int(input ("Enter first number: "))
b = int(input ("Enter second number: "))
print("Quotient : ", a/b)

RUN
>>>
Enter first number: 5
Enter second number: 2
Quotient :  2.5
>>>
```

Figure 4.3 Program to print Quotient

Example 4 –**Program to calculate simple interest.**

```
# Program to calculate simple interest
principal = int(input ("Enter any principal amount: "))
rate = int(input ("Enter rate of interest: "))
time = int(input ("Enter time: "))
si = (principal*rate*time)/100
print("Simple Interest = ",si)

RUN
>>>
Enter any principal amount: 3000
Enter rate of interest: 10
Enter time: 12
Simple Interest =  3600.0
>>>
```

Figure 4.4 Program to calculate simple interest

Example 5 –**Program to calculate area of a triangle using Heron's formula.**

```
# Program to calculate area of a triangle using Heron's formula
side1 = float(input("Enter first side of a triangle : "))
side2 = float(input("Enter second side of a triangle : "))
side3 = float(input("Enter third side of a triangle : "))

s=(side1+side2+side3)/2
area =(s*(s-side1)*(s-side2)*(s-side3))**0.5
print("Area of a triangle is :", area)

RUN
>>>
Enter first side of a triangle : 6
Enter second side of a triangle : 4
Enter third side of a triangle : 4
Area of a triangle is : 7.937253933193772
>>>
```

Figure 4.5 Program to calculate area of a triangle

Example 6 – **Program to calculate area and perimeter of a parallelogram.**

```
# Program to calculate area and perimeter of parallelogram
l = float(input("Enter length: "))
w = float(input("Enter width: "))
h = float(input("Enter height: "))
```

(Conti...)

```
area_parallelogram = l*h
peri_parallelogram = 2*l + 2*w
print( "The area of the parallelogram is  ", area_parallelogram)
print( "The perimeter of the parallelogram is  ", peri_parallelogram)

RUN
>>>
Enter length: 5.2
Enter width: 2.0
Enter height: 1.5
The area of the parallelogram is   7.800000000000001
The perimeter of the parallelogram is   14.4
>>>
```

Figure 4.6 Program to calculate area and perimeter of parallelogram

Example 7 –**Program demonstrating working with power operator.**

```
# Program demonstrating working with power operator
x = int(input("Please enter an integer: "))
print('value of x = ', x)
print('x**2 = ', x**2)
print('x**3 = ', x**3)
print('x**4 = ', x**4)

RUN
>>>
Please enter an integer: 2
value of x =  2
x**2 =  4
x**3 =  8
x**4 =  16
>>>
```

Figure 4.7 Program demonstrating working with power operator

Example 8 –**Demo of division operator (/).**

```
# Demo of division operator (/)
dividend, divisor = eval(input('Please enter two numbers to divide: '))
print(dividend, '/', divisor, "=", dividend/divisor)


RUN
>>>
Please enter two numbers to divide: 8,2
8 / 2 = 4.0
>>>
Please enter two numbers to divide: 2,8
2 / 8 = 0.25
>>>
```

Figure 4.8 Demo of division operator (/)

Example 9 –**Demo of modulus operator (%).**

```
# Demo of modulus operator (%).
num1 = int(input("Enter first number : "))
num2 = int(input("Enter second number : "))
remainder = num1%num2
print("Remainder: ",remainder)

RUN
>>>
Enter first number : 7
Enter second number : 2
Remainder: 1
>>>
Enter first number : 10
Enter second number : 2
Remainder: 0
>>>
```

Figure 4.9 Demo of modulus (%) operator

4.2.2 Hierarchy of Arithmetic Operators

Calculations in Python are done in a specific order, which is called *operator precedence*. In arithmetic, operations in parentheses are performed first. Operators in higher rows are evaluated before operators in lower rows. If multiple operators appear in a single cell in the table which are equal in precedence they are evaluated from left to right.

When two or more operators appear in an expression, the order of evaluation depends on the rules of precedence. For mathematical operators, Python follows the mathematical convention. The acronym PEMDAS (Parentheses Exponentiation Multiplication Division Addition and Subtraction) is a useful way to remember the rules.

Precedence of Arithmetic Operators

() (Parentheses) — **Highest**

**** (Exponentiation)**

- (Negation)

/(Division) //(Integer division) *(Multiplication) %(Modulus)

+ (Addition) - (Subtraction) — **Lowest**

The hierarchy or *order* of operation of arithmetic operators is as follows:

(a) Parentheses have the highest precedence. Since expressions in parentheses are evaluated first, 2 * (4-1) is 6, and (1+1)**(4-2) is 4.

(b) Exponentiation has the next highest precedence and is evaluated from right to left, so 2**1+1 is 3, not 4, and 3*1**3 is 3, not 27.

(c) Multiplication and Division have the same precedence, which is higher than Addition and Subtraction, which also have the same precedence. So, when you have a multiple expressions like 2*3-1 multiplication and division are performed before addition and subtraction. Hence, the result is 5, not 4. The result of 6+4/2 is 8.0, not 5.0.

(d) Operators with the same precedence are evaluated from left to right (except exponentiation). So in the expression degrees / 2 * pi, the division happens first and then the result is multiplied by pi. To divide by 2π, you can use parentheses or write degrees / 2 / pi.

Precedence of operators decides the order in which different operators are applied. Associativity of operators decides the order in which multiple occurrences of the same level operator are applied.

Example 10

```
1 + ((3 + 1)/(8 – 4) – 5)
```

Evaluation of the expression is shown in Figure 4.10

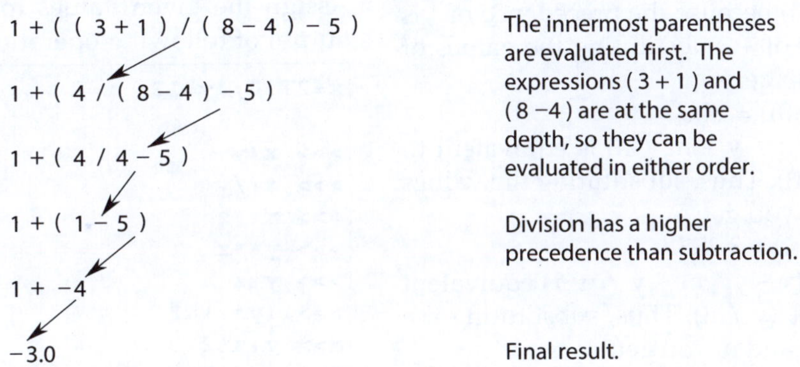

Figure 4.10 Evaluation of the expression enclosed by parentheses

4.2.3 Division and Remainder

The division operator (/) is used for division. It divides left hand operand by right hand operand. For example:

`5/2`	evaluates to	2.5
`7/2`	evaluates to	3.5
`1/3`	evaluates to	0.3333333333333333
`5.0/2`	evaluates to	2.5
`99/100`	evaluates to	0.99
`99/100.0`	evaluates to	0.99
`99.0/100`	evaluates to	0.99
`–5/2`	evaluates to	–2.5
`7/–2`	evaluates to	–3.5
`1/3`	evaluates to	0.3333333333333333

Python also provides int() functions that can be used to convert numbers into ints. Conversion to an *int* simply discards the fractional part of a float; the value is truncated, not rounded. For example,

```
>>> int(4.5)
4
>>> int(3.9)
3
>>> float(int(3.3))
3.0
>>> int(float(3.3))
3
>>> int(float(3))
3
```

☞ *In Python 2, the result of division of two integers is rounded to the nearest integer. As a result, 3/2 will show 1. In order to obtain a floating-point division, numerator or denominator must be explicitly used as float. Hence, use of either 3.0/2 or 3/2.0 or 3.0/2.0 will result in 1.5.*
Python 3 evaluates 3/2 as 1.5 by default.

Example 11

Given the following declarations:

```
m = 3
n = 4
x = 2.5
y = 1.0
```

Evaluate the values for the following expressions:

(a) m + n + x + y
(b) m + x * n + y
(c) x / y + m / n
(d) x – y * m + y / n
(e) x / 0

Solution

(a) The expression (m + n + x + y) is equal to 3 + 4 + 2.5 + 1.0 = 10.5.
(b) The expression (m + x * n + y) is equivalent to ((m + (x * n) + y)) because the precedence of * is higher than that of +. Substituting the values of the variables, you get:
((3 + (2.5 * 4) + 1.0)) = 14.0
(c) The expression (x / y + m / n) is equivalent to ((x / y) + (m / n)). Thus, substituting the values of x, y, m and n, you get:
(2.5 / 1.0) + (3 / 4) = 3.25
(d) The expression (x – y * m + y / n) is equivalent to (x – (y * m)) + (y / n). Thus, substituting the values of x, y, m and n, you get:
(2.5 – (1.0 * 3) + (1.0 / 4)), i.e., 2.5 – 3.0 + .25, i.e., –0.25.
(e) x / 0 is undefined. Any number divided by zero is infinite and hence the value is not defined, so, you will get error message.

☞ *Note: Python 2 displays long integers with an uppercase L, but in Python 3 it is not used.*

Let's Try

Given the following declarations:

```
m = 5
n = 4
x = 2.5
y = 2.0
```

Evaluate the values for the following expressions:

(a) m + n + x + y
(b) m + x * n + y
(c) x / y + m / n
(d) x – y * m + y / n
(e) x / 0

4.2.4 Remainder Operator (%)

Unlike the other arithmetic operators which accept both integer and floating point operands, the *remainder operator* (also called the *modulus operator*) accepts only integer value of operands. The resulting value is the remainder of the first operand divided by the second operand. In Python, the modulus operator is a percent sign(%). For example, the expression:

```
9 % 5
```

has a value of 4 because 5 goes into 9 once, with a remainder of 4. The expression:

```
10 % 5
```

has a value of zero because 5 goes into 10 two times, with no remainder.

Let's Try

Assign the given values to variable and write the output of following operations:

```
x=27.0; y=12; z=2

>>> x/y
>>> x//y
>>> x**z
>>> y**z
>>> y%z
>>> (y*z)%2
>>> y+z%2
>>> y/z*2
```

4.3 RELATIONAL / CONDITIONAL OPERATORS

Relational Operators are used to compare values. They are used to test the relation between two values and then return a boolean value either True or False. All Python relational operators are binary operators and hence, require *two* operands. A relational expression is made up of two arithmetic expressions connected by a relational operator. Comparison operators produce a Boolean result (type bool, either True or False). When a Boolean expression is evaluated, it produces a value of either true (the condition holds) or false (it does not hold). Conditions may compare either numbers or strings. If you compare strings, you get result based on alphabetical order. For example, "apple" < "orange"

Table 4.1 Relational Operators

Operator	Symbol	Form	Result
greater than	>	a > b	True if a is greater than b; else False
less than	<	a < b	True if a is less than b; else False
greater than or equal to	>=	a >=b	True if a is greater than or equal to b; else False
less than or equal to	<=	a <= b	True if a is less than or equal to b; else False
equal to	==	a == b	True if a is equal to b; else False
not equal to	!=	a != b	True if a is not equal to b; else False

is true, because "apple" is alphabetically less than "orange".

While comparing strings, the ordering is lexicographic (as in dictionary). Basically, this means that strings are put in alphabetic order according to the underlying ASCII (American Standard Code for Information Interchange) codes. Lexicographical ordering is implemented using corresponding ordinal value. So, all upper-case letters are considered lesser than lower case letters (For example, 'A' is less than 'a' because ASCII value of 'A' (65) is lesser than 'a'(97)).

The list of relational operators is given in Table 4.1

☞ *You can check the ordinal value using ord(<character>), for example ord("A") is 65.*

For example,

```
>>> 5 < 8
True
>>> 5 < 3
False
>>> 5 < 7 < 10
True
>>> "Apple" < "Mango"
True
>>> "Orange" < "Mango"
False
>>> 7 > 3
True
>>> 5 <= 8
True
>>> 7 <= 5
False

>>> 5 != 6
True
>>> 4 != 4
False
>>> 5==5
True
>>> 4==5
False
>>> 'Good' == 'Good'
True
>>> 'Good' == 'Very Good'
False
>>> 'a' == 'A'
False
>>> 'a' > 'A'
True
# because ordinal value of 'a' is 97 and 'A' is 65
>>> 'a' < 'A'
False
>>> 'python' == 'Python'
False
>>> 'Python' == 'Python'
True
>>> 'Cat' == ' Cat'
False
# because space is in the beginning, and ordinal value of space is 32.
>>> 'Cat' == 'Cat'
True
# remove space before Cat, now the strings are equal
>>> ord('P')
80
>>> ord('p')
112
>>> 'P'<'p'
True
# 'P' is less than 'p' because ASCII value of 'P' (80) is lesser than 'p'(112))
```

All the relational operators have lower precedence than the arithmetic operators. For example, the expression:

```
a + b * c < d / f
```

is evaluated as if it had been written as follows:

```
( a + (b * c )) < (d / f)
```

Example 12

Consider the following declarations:
j = 0
m = 1
n = –1;
x = 2.5
y = 0.0
Evaluate the following expressions:
(a) j > m
(b) m / n < x
(c) j <= m >= n
(d) -x + j == y > n >= m

Solution

(a) j > m is not true because the value of j = 0 and value of m = 1. Hence, the result is False.
(b) The expression m / n < x is equivalent to (m / n) < x because the precedence of / is higher than that of <. Substituting the values of the variables, you get the result as True.
(c) The expression j <= m >= n is equivalent to ((j <= m) >= n). Substituting the values of the variables, you get the result as True.
(d) The expression -x +j == y > n >= m is equivalent to ((-x) +j) == ((y > n) >= m). Substituting the values of the variables you get the result as False.

Let's Try

Assign the given values to variable and write the output of following relational operations:

a=""
b="good"
c="Good"
d="good"
e="GOOD"
 	
>>> a==b
>>> a=b
>>> a==b
>>> c==d
>>> e>d
>>> e<d
>>> a
	x=2
	y=2.0
	
	>>> x<y
	>>> x<=y
	>>> x==y
	>>> x>y
	>>> x>=y
	>>> x!=y

4.4 LOGICAL/BOOLEAN OPERATORS

Logical operators are also called Boolean operators. It combines the results of one or more expressions, and these are called logical expressions. After testing the conditions, they return logical status True or False. Python tests an expression with *and* and *or* operators from left to right and returns, the last value tested.
There are three logical operators: *and*, *or*, and *not*.

4.4.1 and

The *and* operator evaluates to True, if both the expressions are true; False if either or both operands evaluate to False. For example, x > 0 *and* x < 10 is true only if x is greater than 0 and less than 10.

4.4.2 or

The *or* operator evaluates to True, if either of operands evaluates to true; False if both operands evaluate to False. For example, n%2 == 0 *or* n%3 == 0 is true if either of the expression is true, that is, if the number is divisible by 2 or 3.

4.4.3 not

The *not* operator is used to reverse the logical state of its expression. Logical not returns *True* if the expression is false and *False* if the expression is true. For example, the not operator negates a Boolean expression, so not (x > y) is true if x > y is false, that is, if x is less than or equal to y.
Comparisons may be combined using the Boolean operators **and** and **or**, and the outcome of the comparison may be negated with **not**. These have lower priorities than comparison operators.

```
# Logical operator examples
a = True
b = False
print(a and b) # False
print(a or b) # True
print(not b) # True
```

☞ *A Boolean expression is an expression that is either True or False.*

Let's Try

Assign the given values to variable and write the output of following logical operations:

`>>> (2==2) or (3==5)`
`>>> 2>5 or 2<1`
`>>> 5>2 or 1<2`
	`>>> (2==2) and (3==5)`
	`>>> 2>5 and 2<1`
	`>>> 5>2 and 1<2`
	
	`>>> not(5>2)`
	`>>> not(2>5)`

4.4.4 Hierarchy of Logical Operators

The logical *not* operator has a higher precedence than the others. The *and* operator has higher precedence than the *or* operator. Both the logical *and* & *or* operators have lower precedence than the relational and arithmetic operators.

Precedence of Logical Operators

Operator	Precedence
not	**Highest** ↑
and	
or	**Lowest**

Example 13

Consider the following declarations:

j = 0

m = 1

n = -1

Evaluate the following expressions:

(a) j and m

(b) j < m and n <m

(c) m + n or not j

Solution

(a) The expression j and m is not true because the value of j = 0 and the value of m = 1. Hence, the result is 0 (zero),i.e, false.

(b) The expression j < m and n < m is equivalent to (j < m) and (n < m) because the precedence of relational operators is higher than that of logical operators. Substituting the values of the variables, you get the result as true.

(c) The expression m + n or not j is equivalent to (m + n) or (not j). Substituting the values of the variables, you get the result as true.

4.5 OPERATORS AND THEIR PRECEDENCE AND ASSOCIATIVITY

All operators have two important properties called precedence and associativity. Both properties affect how operands are attached to operators. *Precedence* means the order in which two different kinds of operators should be applied in an expression. *Associativity* means the order in which the two operators with the same precedence should be applied in an expression.

☞ *Note: When more than one operator appears in an expression, the order of evaluation depends on the rules of precedence.*

To understand how precedence works, consider the expression :

`2+3 *4`

Should it be interpreted as

`(2+3) *4`

(that is, 20), or rather is

`2+(3 *4)`

(that is, 14) the correct interpretation?

```
num3=int(input("Enter number 3:"))
sum = num1 + num2 + num3
print("Three numbers are :" , num1, num2,
num3)
print("Sum is :" , sum)
```

As in normal arithmetic, multiplication and division in Python have equal importance and are performed before addition and subtraction. You can say multiplication and division have precedence over addition and subtraction. In the following expression:

`2+3 *4`

the multiplication is performed before addition, since multiplication has precedence over addition. The result is 14. The multiplicative operators(*, /, //, and %) have equal precedence with each other, and the additive operators (binary + and -) have equal precedence with each other. The multiplicative operators have precedence over the additive operators.

As in standard arithmetic, in Python if the addition is to be performed first, parentheses can override the precedence rules. The expression:

```
(2+3) *4
```

evaluates to 20. Multiple sets of parentheses can be arranged and nested in any ways that are acceptable in standard arithmetic.

All binary operators, except assignment, are left associative. The assignment operator supports a technique known as chained assignment. The code:

```
w = x = y = z
```

can also be read right-to-left. First y gets the value of z. Both w and x also get the value of z.

In the case of precedence, parentheses can be used to override the natural associativity within an expression.

The unary operators have higher precedence than the binary operators, and the unary operators are right associative. This means the statements:

```
print(-3 + 2)
print(-(3 + 2))
```

will display

```
-1
-5
```

☞ *Note: In the case where operators have the same precedence, associativity (sometimes called binding) is used to determine the order in which operands are grouped with operators. Grouping occurs in either (right-to-left) or (left-to-right) order, depending on the operator.*

A mixed-type expression is an expression containing operands of different types. When mathematical operations are performed with mixed operators in Python expression, Python uses rules and regulations to determine which operations to perform first, based on a pre-determined precedence. The rule of operator precedence follows a similar precedence as applied in most computer programming languages. Table 4.2 summarizes the operator precedence applied in Python programming.

Table 4.2 Operator Precedence

Operator	**Description**
lambda	Lambda expression
or	Boolean OR
and	Boolean AND
not	Boolean NOT
in, notin	Membership tests
is, is not	Identity tests
<, <=, >, >=, !=, ==	Comparisons
|	Bitwise OR
^	Bitwise XOR
&	Bitwise AND
<<, >>	Shifts
+, -	Addition and subtraction
*, /,%	Multiplication, division, remainder
+x, -x	Positive, negative
~x	Bitwise not
**	Exponentiation

Let's Try

Consider the following code containing mixed arithmetic expression. What will be the final result and the final data type?

```
x = 7
y = 2
z = 5.0
k = 36.0
A = (x + y) / z
B = k /z * x / 2
print(A)
print(B)
```

```
x = 4
y = 2
z = 4.0
k = 49.0
A = (x + y) / z
B = k /z * x / 2
print(A)
print(B)
```

Let's Try

What will be the output produced by the following code?

```
A, B, C, D = 9.2,
2.0, 6, 24
print(A/4)
print(A//4)
print(B ** C)
print(D//B)
print(A%C)
```

```
a, b = 10, 20
print(a==b)
print(a<b)
print(a<=b)
print(a!=b)
```

4.6 ASSIGNMENT (AUGMENTED) OPERATORS

Assignment operators are used to assign values to the variables. They combine the effect of arithmetic and assignment operator. Augmented assignments can make your code more compact, concise, and more readable. Instead of writing x = x + 1, you can just put the expression operator + before the assignment operator (=) and write x += 1. This is called an augmented assignment, and it works with all the standard operators, such as *, /, %, and so on. For example,

```
>>> x = 2
>>> x += 1
>>> x *= 2
>>> x
6
```

If you try to update a variable that doesn't exist, you get an error "**NameError: name 'x' is not defined**", because Python evaluates the right side before it assigns a value to x. Also note before you can update a variable, you have to initialize it.

☞ *Note: Updating a variable by adding 1 is called an increment; subtracting 1 is called a decrement.*

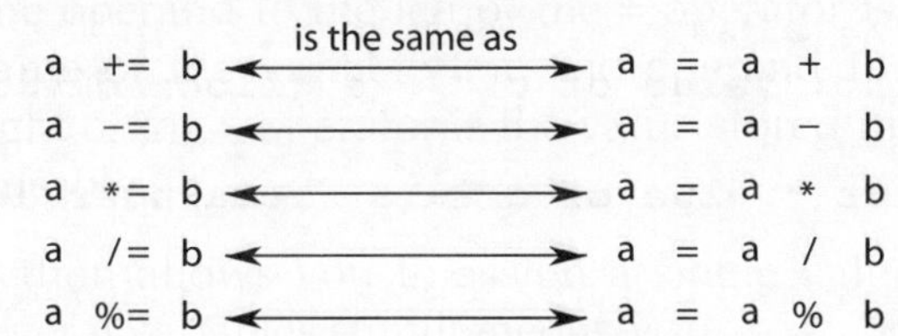

Figure 4.11 Arithmetic Assignment Operator Equivalence

Python language offers special shorthand operators that combine assignment with each of the arithmetic operations to simplify the coding. The operators are given in Table 4.3. The equivalences are shown in Figure 4.12.

Table 4.3 Assignment Operators

Operator	Symbol	Form	Operation
assign	=	a = b	put the value of b into a
add-assign	+=	a += b	put the value of a+b into a
subtract-assign	-=	a -= b	put the value of a-b into a
multiply-assign	*=	a * = b	put the value of a*b into a
divide-assign	/=	a /= b	put the value of a/b into a
remainder-assign	%=	a %= b	put the value of a%b into a

Example 14 –**Demo of assignment operator.**

```
# Demo of assignment operator
a = 2
b = 10
c = 0
c = a + b
print("Value of c is ", c)
c += a
print("Value of c += a (add-assign) is ", c)
c *= a
print("Value of c *= a (multiply-assign) is ", c)
c /= a

print("Value of c /= a (divide-assign) is ", c)
c **= a
print("Value of c **= a (exponential assign) is ", c)
c //= a
print("Value of c //= a (floor division assign) is ", c)
c %= a
print("Value of c %= a (remainder-assign) is ", c )


RUN
Value of c is  12
Value of c += a (add-assign) is  14
Value of c *= a (multiply-assign) is  28
Value of c /= a (divide-assign) is  14.0
Value of c **= a (exponential assign) is  196.0
Value of c //= a (floor division assign) is  98.0
Value of c %= a (remainder-assign) is  0.0
```

Figure 4.12 Demo of Assignment Operator

For example, the expression:

`j = j * 5`

can be written as

`j *= 5`

One of the main reasons for using the arithmetic assignment operators is to avoid spelling mistakes and make code more readable. For example, the expression:

`op_big_x_dimension = op_big_x_dimension * 2`

can be written as

`op_big_x_dimension *= 2`

The second version is easier to read and write, and contains fewer chances of spelling errors.

Let's Try

Execute the following codes and write their output:

a=2 a+1 print(a)	a=2 a += 1 print(a)	a=2 a= a+1 print(a)

Assuming the value of variable x as 10, execute the following codes and write their output:

>>> a+=2
>>> x-=2
>>> x*=2
	>>> x/=2
	>>> x%=2
	>>> x**=2
		>>> x//=2

4.7 BITWISE OPERATORS

A bit is the smallest possible unit of data storage, and it can have only one of the two values : 0 and 1.

Bitwise operator works on bits and performs bit-by-bit operation, instead of whole.

Table 4.4 shows the bitwise operators and their meaning.

Table 4.4 Bitwise Operators and their Meaning

<table>
<tr><th>Bitwise Operator</th><th>Meaning</th></tr>
<tr><td>>></td><td>Right shift</td></tr>
<tr><td><<</td><td>Left shift</td></tr>
<tr><td>&</td><td>AND</td></tr>
<tr><td>|</td><td>OR</td></tr>
<tr><td>^</td><td>XOR</td></tr>
<tr><td>~</td><td>One's complement</td></tr>
</table>

☞ *In some other languages, ^ is used for exponentiation, but in Python it is bitwise operator called xor.*

In order to understand the bitwise operators, let us first consider the SHIFT operators. There are two types of shift operators that shift the bits in any integer variable by a specified number of positions. The '>>' operator shifts bits to the right, and the '<<' operator shifts bits to the left.

4.7.1 Right Shift Operator '>>'

The right shift operator (>>) shifts the bits of the number to the right by the number of bits specified. This means that those many bits are lost.

In general, the right shift operator is used in the form:

```
variable >> number-of-bits
```

11 >> 1 gives 5. 11 is represented in bits by 1011 which when right shifted by 1-bit gives 101, which is the decimal 5. Take another example; you know that the decimal number 8 is represented in binary form as:

```
1000
```

Similarly, the decimal number 4 is represented as:

```
100
```

If data is represented in a computer using 8 bits form, then decimal digits 8 and 4 will be represented by 00001000 and 00000100, respectively. The only difference between these two numbers is that the "1" in the second number is shifted one bit to your right. If the variable "a" holds the value "8", then you can shift it right by one position, with the following statement:

```
a >> 1
```

This expression when converted to decimal value would be evaluated as "4". You can shift a number by several bits. For example, you can change "8" into "2" by shifting the digit '1' by two bits to the right by using the expression:

```
a >> 2
```

4.7.2 Left Shift Operator '<<'

The left shift (<<) operator shifts bits of the number to the left for a specified number of bit positions. This means it adds 0s to the empty least-significant places. Each number is represented in memory by bits or binary digits, i.e., 0 and 1. The expression takes the form:

```
variable << number-of-bits
2 << 2 gives 8.
```

2 is represented by 10 in bits. Left shifting by 2 bits gives 1000 which represents the decimal 8.

Example 15

Assume a = 60, and b = 11; Now in binary format they will be as follows:
a = 0011 1100, b = 0000 1011
Solve the following bitwise operators a>>2, a<<2, b>>2 and b<<2.

Solution

The left operand value is moved right by the number of bits specified by the right operand.
a >> 2 = 15
(means 0000 1111)
The left operands value is moved left by the number of bits specified by the right operand.
a << 2 = 240
(means 1111 0000)
Same as above; the left operand value is moved right by the number of bits specified by the right operand.
b >> 2 = 2
(means 0000 0010)
The left operands value is moved left by the number of bits specified by the right operand.
b << 2 = 44
(means 0010 1100) See Figure 4.13

Let's Try

```
Assume a = 60, and b = 13; Now in binary
format they will be as follows:
a = 0011 1100
b = 0000 1101
Write the output of the following bit-
wise operations:
Find a>>2, a<<2, b>>2, b<<2.
```

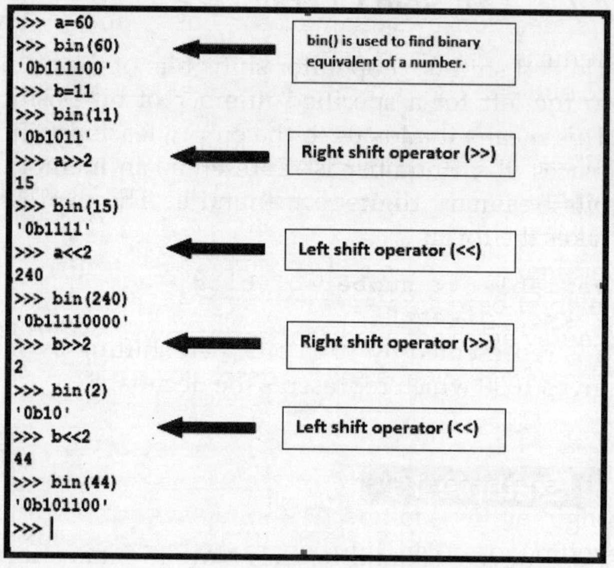

Figure 4.13 Working of shift operators

☞ *The bin() method converts and returns the binary equivalent string of a given integer.*

4.7.3 & (Bitwise AND)

Bitwise AND returns 1 if both the bits are 1, otherwise 0. For example, numbers 5 & 9 gives 1.

4.7.4 | (Bitwise OR)

Bitwise OR returns 1 if any of the bits is 1. If both the bits are 0, then it returns 0. For example, numbers 5 | 9 gives 13.

4.7.5 ^ (Bitwise XOR)

Bitwise XOR returns 1 if one of the bits is 0 and the other bit is 1. If both the bits are 0 or 1, then it returns 0. For example, the numbers 5 ^ 9 gives 12.

4.7.6 ~ (Bitwise invert)

The bitwise inversion of number ~5 gives -6 and ~9 gives -10. (See Figure 4.14).

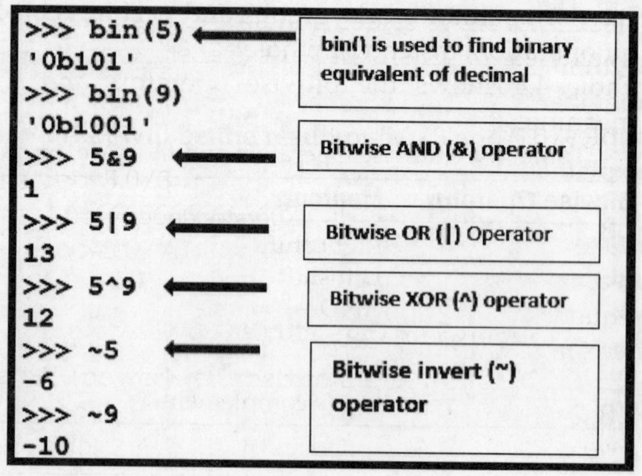

Figure 4.14 Working of bitwise &, |, ^ and ~ operators

Example 16

Assume a = 60, and b = 11; now in binary format they will be as follows:
a = 0011 1100
b = 0000 1011
Solve the following bitwise operations:
a&b, a|b, a^b, ~a and ~b.

Solution

a&b = 0000 1000 →8 # Operator copies a bit to the result if it exists in both

a|b = 0011 1111 →63 # It copies a bit if it exists in either operand.

a^b = 0011 0111 →55 # It copies the bit if it is set in one operand but not both.

~a = -0011 1101 →-61 # It returns complement of a number.

~b = -0000 1100 →-12 # It returns complement of a number.

Let's Try

Write the output of following bitwise operations:

```
Assume if a = 60, and b = 13; Now in
binary format they will be as follows:
a = 0011 1100
b = 0000 1101
Find a&b, a|b, a^b, ~a, ~b.
```

4.8 MEMBERSHIP OPERATORS

Python has membership operators, which test for membership in a sequence, such as strings, lists, or tuples. There are two membership operators explained below:

4.8.1 in Operator

Evaluates to true if it finds a variable in the specified sequence and false otherwise. For example, x *in* y; here, *in* results in a 1 if x is a member of sequence y.

4.8.2 not in Operator

Evaluates to true if it does not find a variable in the specified sequence and false otherwise. For example,
x *not in* y. Here *not in* results in a 1 if x is not a member of sequence y.

Example 17

Boolean test to find whether a value is inside a container or not:

```
>>> t = [1, 2, 4, 5]
>>> 3 in t
False
>>> 4 in t
True
>>> 4 not in t
False
```

For strings, tests for substrings:

```
>>> a = 'abcde'
>>> 'c' in a
True
>>> 'cd' in a
True
```

Example 18 **–Demo of working of Membership Operators.**

```
From the Python Shell, enter the following and observe the results:

>>> 10 in (40, 20, 10)
True
>>> 10 not in (40, 20, 10)
False
>>> grade = 'B+'
>>> grade in ('A','A+','B','B+','C','C+','D')
True
>>> >>> grade = 'E'
>>> grade in ('A','A+','B','B+','C','C+','D')
False
>>>
```

Figure 4.15 Demo of working of Membership Operators

Let's Try

Write the output of following membership operators operations:

```
# Working with membership operators
>>> t = [2, 4, 6, 8]
>>> 3 in t
>>> 4 in t
>>> 4 not in t
```

```
# Working with membership operators
>>> a='abcde'
>>> b in a
>>> 'b' in a
>>> 'ab' in a
>>> 'ac' in a
>>> 'de' in a
```

4.9 IDENTITY OPERATORS

Identity operators compare the memory locations of two objects. There are two Identity operators explained below:

4.9.1 is Operator

Evaluates to true if the variables on either side of the operator point to the same object and false otherwise. For example, x is y; here result is 1 if is(x) equals is(y).

```
>>> x = y = [1, 2, 3]
>>> z = [1, 2, 3]
>>> x == y
True
>>> x == z
True
>>> x is y
True
>>> x is z
False
>>> x = [1, 2, 3]
>>> y = [2, 4]
>>> x is not y
True
```

4.9.2 is not Operator

Evaluates to false if the variables on either side of the operator point to the same object and true otherwise. For example, x *is not* y; here, is not results in 1, if is(x) is not equal to is(y).

Example 19 –**Demo of Identity operators.**

```
# Demo of Identity operators
>>> s1='xyz'
>>> s2=input("Enter a string: ");
Enter a string: abc
>>> s1==s2
False
>>> s1 is s2
False
>>> s3 = 'xyz'
>>> s1 is s3
True
```

Figure 4.16 Demo of *Identity* operator

Let's Try

Write the output of following code :

```
# Working with Identity operators
>>> s1='xyz'
>>> s2=input("Enter a string: ");
Enter a string: xyz
>>> s1==s2
>>> s1 is s2
>>> s3 = 'xyz'
>>> s1 is s3
```

Write the output of following code :

```
>>> x = [2, 4, 6]
>>> y = [1, 2]
>>> x is not y
```

4.10 EXPRESSIONS

Expressions consist of combinations of values, which can be constant values, such as a string ("Shiva") or a number (12), and operators, which are symbols that act on the values in some way. The following are the examples of expressions:

```
10 - 4
11 * (4 + 5)
x - 5
a / b
```

In other words, the expression consists of one or more operands and one or more operators linked together to compute a value. For example:

```
a=5 # assume a=5
a + 2
```

is a legal expression that results in the sum of the value in the variable **a** and **2**. The variable **a** is also an expression as is the constant 2, since they both represent the value. Expression values, in turn, can act as Operands for Operators. For example, 9+6 and 8+5+2 are two expressions which will result in value 15.

Taking another example, 6.0/5+(8-5.0) is an expression in which values of different data types are used. These types of expressions are also known as *mixed type* expressions. When mixed type expressions are evaluated, Python promotes the result of lower data type to higher data type, i.e., to float. So, the result of the above-mentioned expression will be 4.2. This is known as *implicit typecasting*. Implicit typecasting is done without any intimation to the user. Sometimes, you may want to perform a type conversion ourselves. The programmer may instruct the Python interpreter to convert one type of data to another type, which is known as *explicit conversion*. The float() function converts an *int* into *float*. Python also provides int() and long() functions that can be used to convert numbers into ints and longs, respectively. For example,

```
>>> float(22)
22.0
>>> int(4.8)
4
```

Expression can also contain another expression. When you have an expression consisting of sub expression(s), Python decides the order of operations based on precedence of operator. When an expression contains two different kinds of operators, the order in which the operators should be applied is known as *Operator Precedence*. Higher precedence operator is applied before lower precedence operator.

When an expression contains two operators with the same precedence, the order in which the operators should be applied first is known as *Associativity*. Operator associativity determines the order of evaluation when the operators are of same precedence, and are not grouped by parentheses.

An operator may be left associative or right associative. In left associative, the operator appearing on the left side will be evaluated first, while in right associative, operator appearing on the right will be evaluated first. In Python '=' and '**' are right associative. The following list describes the basic rules of operator precedence in Python:

(a) Expressions are evaluated from left to right.

(b) Exponentiation, multiplication, and division are performed before addition and subtraction.

(c) Expressions in parentheses are evaluated first. Parentheses can be used to group terms in an expression to provide control over the order in which the operations are performed.

(d) Mathematical expressions are performed before Boolean expressions (and , or , not). Table 4.5 summarizes the precedence of operators from higher precedence to lower precedence.

When at least one of the operands is itself an expression (as in 2 * 7 + 5), the expression is a compound expression. Python follows the standard mathematical order of operations, so 2 * 7 + 5 is equivalent to (2 * 7) + 5.

Table 4.5 Precedence of Operators from Higher Precedence to Lower Precedence

Operator Name	Operators Symbols
Exponentiation	**
Unary plus and minus	+, -
Multiply, divide, modulus, floor division	*, /, %, //
Addition and subtraction	+, -
Relational (comparison) operators	<, <=, >, >=
Equality operators	==, !=
Assignment operators	%=, /=, //=, -=, +=, *=
Logical operators	not, and, or

Let's Try

Evaluate the following expression with precedence of operator:

```
x = 2* 3/ 5 + 10 //3 -1
print(x)
```

```
x = 3* 3/ 2 + 9 //3 - 2
print(x)
```

4.11 STATEMENTS

A Python statement is an instruction or a unit of code that the Python interpreter can execute. In computer language, complete command is called statement. Examples of statement are:

```
>>> print(12 + 15)
27
```

This is because you told the system to print the result of the expression 12 + 15, which is a complete statement. However, if you type :

```
>>> print(12 +)
```

you will get a syntax error.

Other statements could be the following:

```
>>> print("Welcome to the world of Python")
Welcome to the world of Python
>>> print("Sum of 2 + 5 = ", 2+5)
Sum of 2 + 5 = 7
```

The first statement asks Python to display string literal *Welcome to the world of Python*. In the second print statement, Python prints the part within quotes "Sum of 2 + 5 = " followed by the result of adding 2 + 5, which is 7. To print multiple items on the same line, separate them with comma.

It is possible to have a single statement span multiple lines when the line is too long to read on a screen. To do this, simply put a space and a backslash at the end of the line as explained earlier. Note that Python allows you to put multiple statements on a line by separating each statement with a semicolon:

```
>>> x = 1; y = 2
```

REVIEW QUESTIONS WITH ANSWERS

1. Multiple Choice Questions

1. Operator precedence determines which operator:
   a. Operates on the largest numbers
   b. Is used first
   c. Is most important
   d. None of these

2. Indicate which of the following is true about 'Python' operators:
   a. Operators must have one or more operands
   b. Operators are either unary or binary
   c. Operators have some precedence
   d. All of the above

3. Escape sequence:
   a. \n
   b. \"
   c. \a
   d. All of the above

4. The expression, i=30*10+27; evaluates to:
   a. 327
   b. -327
   c. 810
   d. 0

5. Identity operators:
   a. is
   b. is not
   c. Both (a) and (b)
   d. None of the above

6. The operator & is used for:
   a. Bitwise AND b. Bitwise OR
   c. Logical AND d Logical OR

7. A "Python" expression contains relational, assignment and arithmetic operators. There are no parentheses used. They will be evaluated in:
   a. Assignment Relational Arithmetic order
   b. Arithmetic Relational Assignment order
   c. Relational Arithmetic Assignment order
   d. Assignment Arithmetic Relational order

8. The && and || operators:
   a. Compare two numeric values b. Combine two numeric values
   c. Compare two boolean values d None of the above.

9. Operators can be:
   a. Unary b. Binary
   c. Ternary d All of these.

10. Signed right shift enables to:
    a. Shift right by pushing copies of the leftmost bit in from the left, and lets the rightmost bits fall off
    b. Shift left by pushing zeros in from the right and lets the leftmost bits fall off
    c. Both (a) and (b)
    d. None of these

11. Identify the data type for the value 2+0j:
    a. Integer
    b. Float-point number
    c. Complex number
    d. String

12. The value of the expressions 4/(3*(2-1)) and 4/3*(2-1) is the same. State whether true or false.
    a. True
    b. False
    c. Error
    d. None of these

13. The value of the expression 4 + 3 % 2 is:
    a. 7
    b. 5
    c. 2
    d. 0

14. Which of the following operators has its associativity from right to left?
    a. + b. //
    c. % d **.

15. What is the value of x in the following expression?
```
x = int(42.25+2/2)
print(x)
```
a. 44
b. 43
c. 22
d. 23

16. What is the value of the following expression?
2+4.00, 2**4.0
a. (6.0, 16.0)
b. (6.00, 16.00)
c. (6, 16)
d. (6.00, 16.0)

17. Which of the following is the truncation division operator?
a. /
b. %
c. //
d. #

18. What is the order of precedence in Python?
i) Parentheses
ii) Exponential
iii) Multiplication
iv) Division
v) Addition
vi) Subtraction
a. i,ii,iii,iv,v,vi
b. ii,i,iii,iv,v,vi
c. ii,i,iv,iii,v,vi
d. i,ii,iii,iv,vi,v

19. Which of the following has the same precedence level?
a. Addition and Subtraction
b. Multiplication, Division and Addition
c. Multiplication, Division, Addition and Subtraction
d. Addition and Multiplication

20. Which of the following has the highest precedence in the expression?
a. Exponential b. Addition
c. Multiplication d Parentheses

21. Which of the following has the same precedence level?
a. Multiplication and Division
b. Addition and Multiplication
c. Division and Addition
d. All of the above

2. State True or False for the following:

1. The Ternary operator is the operator that is used to show the conditional statements.
2. Operators are used to perform operations on variables and values.
3. Logical operators are used to combine conditional statements.
4. Identity operators are used to compare the objects, not if they are equal, but if they are actually the same object, with the same memory location.
5. is operator returns false if both variables are the same object.
6. The operand to the left of the = operator is the name of the variable and the operand to the right of the = operator is the value stored in the variable.
7. Python allows you to assign a single value to several variables simultaneously.
8. Bitwise operator works on bits and performs bit by bit operation.
9. In computer language complete command is called statement.
10. Associativity operators are usually evaluated from right to left.

3. Match the following:

1. Single operand	a. in and not in
2. Two operands	b. And, Or, and Not
3. Logical operators	c. Binary operator
4. Membership operators	d. %
5. Identity Operators	e. Unary operator
6. Modulus	f. is and is not
7. Exponentiation	g. Sets each bit to 1 if one of two bits is 1
8. Floor division	h. **
9. AND	i. //

10. OR	j. Sets each bit to 1 if both bits are 1

4. Fill in the blanks

1. An operator which requires three operands is called ________.
2. ________ operators are used for comparing the values.
3. ________ operators are used to assigning values for the variables.
4. Bitwise operators are used for performing operations over the ______.
5. ________ operators are used with numeric values to perform common mathematical operations.
6. ________ operators are used to assign values to variables.
7. In the expression 4 + 5 = 9, 4 and 5 are called ________ and + is called operator.
8. ________ performs exponential (power) calculation on operators.
9. Calculations in Python are done in a specific order, which is called ________.
10. ________ operator combines the effect of arithmetic and assignment operator.
11. The expression int(x) implies that the variable x is converted to ______.
12. The output of the expression 3*1**3 is ________.

Answers

1. 1. b 2. d 3. d 4. a 5. c 6. a
7. b 8. c 9. d 10. a 11 c 12 a
13. b 14. d 15. b 16. a 17. c 18. a
19. a 20. d 21. a

2. 1. T 2. T 3. T 4. T 5. F 6. T
7. T 8. T 9. T 10. F

3. 1. e 2. c 3. b 4. a 5. f 6. d
7. h 8. i 9. j 10. g

4. 1. Ternary operator 2. Relational
3. Assignment 4. Bits
5. Arithmetic 6. Assignment
7. Operands 8. **
9. Operator precedence 10. Augmented
11. Integer 12. 3

Short Answer Questions

1. Define Operator and Operand.

Ans An *operator* is a particular symbol which is used on some values and produces an output as a result. An *operand* is an entity on which an operator acts. For example, in the following expression:

c=a+b

the sign + is an operator which specifies the operation of addition on the two operands **a** and **b**.

2. What is the use of type()?

Ans To verify the type of any object in Python, use the type() function.

3. The modulus operator is used to produce the quotient in division. Is it True or False?

Ans False, the modulus operator is used to produce the remainder.

4. Describe the use of parentheses in expressions.

Ans Parentheses can be used to group terms in an expression so as to provide control over the order in which the operations are performed.

5. Describe how Python evaluates an expression containing parentheses.

Ans A Python expression is evaluated by first evaluating each of the sub-expressions in the parentheses, and then using those values to complete the evaluation. If the expression contains nested parentheses, the evaluation is performed by evaluating the innermost parentheses first and working outwards from there.

6. Explain the use of the assignment operator.

Ans The assignment operator causes the value of its right operand to be stored in the memory location identified by its left operand.

7. What is the difference between Expressions and Operators?

Ans Most statements (logical lines) that you write will contain expressions. A simple example of an expression is 2 + 3. An expression is a combination of operators and operands.

Operators are functionality that do something and can be represented by symbols, such as + or by special keywords. They require some data to operate on and such data is called operands.

8. What is the difference between * and **? Explain with an example.

Ans * (multiply) gives the multiplication of the two numbers or returns the string repeated that many times. For example,

2 * 3 gives 6.
'la' * 3 gives 'lalala'.

** (power) returns x to the power of y. For example,

3 ** 4 gives 81 (i.e., 3 * 3 * 3 * 3)

9. What is the difference between / , // and % operators?

Ans / (divide) Divides x by y. For example:
4 / 3 gives 0.75

// (floor division) Returns the floor of the quotient by truncating the fractional part. For example:
4 // 3 gives 1

% (modulus) Returns the remainder of the division. For example:
8 % 3 gives 2.
-25.5 % 2.25 gives 1.5.

10. What is the difference between << (left shift) and >> (right shift) operators?

Ans << (left shift) Shifts the bits of the number to the left by the number of bits specified. (Each number is represented in memory by bits or binary digits, i.e., 0 and 1)
For example, 2 << 2 gives 8. 2 is represented by 10 in bits.
Left shifting by 2 bits gives 1000 which represents the decimal 8.

>> (right shift) Shifts the bits of the number to the right by the number of bits specified.
For example, 11 >> 1 gives 5.
11 is represented in bits by 1011, which when right shifted by 1 bit gives 101 which is the decimal 5.

11. What is the difference between & (bit-wise AND), and | (bit-wise OR) operators?

Ans Bit-wise AND (&) returns 1 if both the bits are 1, otherwise 0. For example, the numbers 5 & 3 gives 1.
Bit-wise OR (|) returns 1 if any of the bits is 1. If both the bits are 0, then it returns 0. For example, the numbers 5 | 3 gives 7.

12. Explain *not* (boolean NOT) with an example.

Ans The *not* operator is used to reverse the logical state of its expression. Logical not returns *True* if the expression is false and *False* if the expression is true. For example,
If x is True, it returns False.
If x is False, it returns True.
x = True;
not x returns False.

13. Explain *and* (boolean AND) with example.

Ans The *and* operator evaluates to True, if both the expressions are true; False if either or both operands evaluate to False. For example,
x and y returns False if x is False, else it returns evaluation of y
x = False;
y = True;
x **and** y returns False since x is False.
In this case, Python will not evaluate y since it knows that the left hand side of the 'and' expression is False which implies that the whole expression will be False irrespective of the other values.

14. Explain **or** (boolean OR) with example.

Ans The *or* operator evaluates to True, if either of operands evaluates to true; False if both operands evaluate to False. For example,
If x is True, it returns True, else it returns evaluation of y
x = True;
y = False;
x **or** y returns True.

15. Explain Associativity of operators with example.

Ans *Associativity* means the order in which the two operators with the same precedence should be applied in an expression. It is usually associated from left to right. This means that operators with the same precedence are evaluated from left to right manner. For example, 2 + 3 - 4 is evaluated as (2 + 3) - 4.
Some operators like assignment operators have right to left associativity. i.e., a = b = c is treated as a = (b = c).

16. What is an expression?

Ans An expression is a combination of values, variables, and operators. A value all by itself is considered an expression, and so is a variable. Hence the following are all legal expressions (assuming that the variable x has been

assigned a value):
17
x
x + 17

17. What is a statement?

Ans A statement is a unit of code that the Python interpreter can execute.

18. What do you mean by floor division?

Ans The operation that divides two numbers and chops off the fractional part. For example, assuming a=15.9, b= 3, c=a//b gives value 5.0, not 5.3.

19. What is the difference between "=" and "=="?

Ans "=" is the assignment operator whereas "==" is the equality operator. The assignment operator is used to assign a value to an identifier, whereas the equality operator is used to determine if two expressions have the same value.

20. What do you mean by precedence and associativity of operators?

Ans The operators in Python are grouped hierarchically according to their precedence (i.e, order of evaluation). Operations with a higher precedence are carried out before operations having a lower precedence. Assignment operators have a lower precedence than any of the other operators.

The order in which consecutive operations within the same precedence group are carried out is known as associativity.

21. What are Identity and Membership operators?

Ans Identity operators are used to compare the objects, not if they are equal, but if they are actually the same object, with the same memory location.
Membership operators are used to test if an object is present in a sequence.

22. Explain different bitwise operators.

Ans **& (AND)** : Sets each bit to 1 if both bits are 1
| (OR) : Sets each bit to 1 if one of two bits is 1
^(XOR): Sets each bit to 1 if only one of two bits is 1
~ (NOT): Inverts all the bits
<< (Left Shift): Zero fill left shift enables to shift left by pushing zeros in from the right and lets the leftmost bits fall off.
>> (Right Shift): Signed right shift enables to shift right by pushing copies of the leftmost bit in from the left, and lets the rightmost bits fall off.

23. What will be the result of 5.0/3 and 5.0//3?

Ans >>> 5.0/3
1.6666666666666667
>>> 5.0//3
1.0

24. How will you calculate 2.5^2 in Python?

Ans ** (power) returns x to the power of y.
>>> 2.5**2
6.25

25. What is the difference between + and * operators of List?

Ans The plus (+) sign is the list concatenation operator, while the asterisk (*) is the repetition operator.

26. What is boolean data type? Explain with an example.

Ans Comparisons in Python can only generate one of the two possible responses: True or False. These data types are called booleans.
To illustrate, you can create several variables to store Boolean values and print the result:

```
bool_1=4==2*3
bool_2=10<2*2**3
bool_3=8>2*4+1
print(bool_1)
print(bool_2)
print(bool_3)

RUN
False
True
False
```

27. Evaluate the following expressions in Python.

(a) 10 - (5 * 4)

Ans -10

(b) 20%5

Ans 0

(c) -4 *(6/2)

Ans -12.0

28. What is the result of each of the following when evaluated?

(a)
```
n=10
m=2
print(n/m)
print(n//m)
print(n%m)
```

Ans 5.0
5
0

(b)
```
a, b = 2,4
a,b = b,a+2
print(a,b)
```

Ans 4 4

29. What is the difference between pow() and **?

Ans Both pow() and the double star (**) operator perform exponentiation. ** is an operator whereas pow() is a built-in function.

30. What is the difference between expression and statement?

Ans An expression is a combination of symbols, operators and operand. For example, 8*3+4 is an expression. The outcome of an expression is always a value.
Statement is an instruction or a unit of code that the Python interpreter can execute. For example, print ("Welcome") is a statement. Statement may or may not return a value as outcome.

31. What is the difference between num = 20 and num == 20?

Ans In num = 20, variable *num* is assigned the value 20
In num == 20, variable *num* is compared with the value 20

32. x, y, z = 10, 4, 8
\# evaluate the following Boolean expressions:
```
print(x == 8)
print(x < y)
print(x > y)
print( x >= 0 and x < 4)
print(x >= 0 and x < 10)
print(x < 10)
print(y < z)
print(x <= 10)
```

Ans
```
False
False
True
False
False
False
True
True
```

33. Which of the following is an invalid statement?

(a) abc = 1,00,000

(b) a b c = 100 200 300

(c) a,b,c = 100, 200, 300

(d) a_b_c = 1,00,000

Ans a b c = 100 200 300 # invalid because spaces are not allowed in variable names.

34. What are the values of the following expressions?

(a) `2**(3**2)`

Ans 512

(b) `(2**3)**2`

Ans 64

(c) `2**3**2`

Ans 512

35. Write a program to convert dollars in Rupee.

```
# Program to convert dollars in Rupee
dollars = float(input("Please enter dollars:"))
rupees = dollars * 69.45
print(rupees, " Rupees")

RUN
>>>
Please enter dollars:10
694.5  Rupees
>>>
```

Figure 1 Program to convert dollars in Rupee

36. Write a program to convert Kilometers into Miles.

```
# Program to convert Kilometers to Miles
# miles = kilometers * conv_fac
km = float(input("Enter the value in kilometers: "))
# 1 Kilometer = 0.621371 Mile
conv_fac  = 0.621371
# Converting km to mi.
miles = km * conv_fac
print("The entered value in Miles: ", miles)

RUN
>>>
Enter the value in kilometers: 2.500
The entered value in Miles:  1.5534275
>>>
```

Figure 2 Program to convert Kilometers to Miles

37. Write a program to convert the distance (in feet) into inches, yards, and miles.

```
# Program to convert the distance (in feet) to inches, yards, and miles.
dis_ft = int(input("Input distance in feet: "))
dis_inches = dis_ft * 12
dis_yards = dis_ft / 3.0
dis_miles = dis_ft / 5280.0
print("The distance in inches is %i inches." % dis_inches)
print("The distance in yards is %.2f yards." % dis_yards)
print("The distance in miles is %.2f miles." % dis_miles)

RUN
>>>
Input distance in feet: 200
The distance in inches is 2400 inches.
The distance in yards is 66.67 yards.
The distance in miles is 0.04 miles.
>>>
```

Figure 3 Program to convert the distance (in feet) to inches, yards, and miles

38. Write a program to calculate GST (Goods and Services Tax).

```
# Program to calculate GST
item=input("Enter item name: ")
sp_cost = float(input("How much is selling price of item? "))
gst_rate = float (input("What is GST rate %: "))
cgst=sp_cost * ((gst_rate/2)/100)
```

(Conti...)

```
sgst=cgst
amt = sp_cost+cgst+sgst
print("CGST (@",(gst_rate/2),"%): ",(cgst))
print("SGST (@",(gst_rate/2),"%): ",(sgst))
print("Amount payable: ",(amt))

RUN
>>>
Enter item name: mobile
How much is selling price of item? 12600
What is GST rate %: 18
CGST (@ 9.0 %):  1134.0
SGST (@ 9.0 %):  1134.0
Amount payable:  14868.0
>>>
```

Figure 4 Program to calculate GST

39. Choose the output of the following codes:

```
print(not(7>2))
print(not(6&6))
```

a. False
   False
b. True
   True
c. False
   True
d. None of the above

Ans. False
False

EXERCISE

1. **Fill in the blanks:**
   a. An entity on which an operator acts is called ________.
   b. An ________ operates on variables and constant values, and then performs an action in a program.
   c. The ________ expressions give the value "1" for TRUE result and the value "0" for FALSE result.
   d. ________ means that in the same expression if you have two operators of the same precedence, they are evaluated from left to right.
   e. In Python ________ and ________ are right associative.
2. How is * different from **? Explain with an example.
3. What do you mean by identity operators?
4. Write the logical statements for the following:
   (a) Basic_pay is more than 2200 for all employees whose category is T.
   (b) Stock below 100 for all items whose item_no is 100 and in the shop A.
5. Explain the following type of operators, each with one example List the hierarchy of operations.
   (a) Arithmetic operators
   (b) Logical operators
6. Write a short note on membership operators.
7. Differentiate between the terms operand and the operator. State different types of operators used in Python and give one example of each.
8. What do you mean by associativity? What is the associativity of different arithmetic operators?
9. Write a short note on bitwise operators.
10. What would the following code do?
    x=y=50
11. Give examples of unary and binary operators.
12. What will be the result of 7.0/3 and 7.0//3?
13. Write short note on *None* data type of Python.
14. Describe operators and expressions.
15. What is the use of operator precedence and operator associativity?

LAB EXERCISE

1. Write the output of the following program:

```
n=20
m=2
print(n/m)
print(n//m)
print(n%m)
```

2. Show the result of evaluating each expression. Ensure that the value is in the proper form to indicate its type (int, long int, or float). If the expression is illegal, give reason.
   (a) 5*6 + 7
   (b) 6*3/4
   (c) 3/4*6
   (d) 6.0*3/4
   (e) 15%4
   (f) 4.0 / 10.0 + 3.5 * 2
   (g) 10 % 4 + 6 / 2
   (h) 3 * 10 / 3 + 10 % 3
3. What will be the output of the following code:
   (a)
   ```
   a = 3 - 4 + 10
   b = 5 * 6
   c = 7.0/8.0
   print("These are the values:", a,
   b, c)
   ```
   (b)
   ```
   a=4
   print(a)
   b=12+5
   print(b)
   c=b%a
   print(c)
   ```
   (c)
   ```
   a=4
   a=a+2
   print(a)
   a=4
   a+=2
   print(a)
   ```
4. Given the following assignments: i1 = 2, i2 = 5, i3 = -3, d1 = 2.0, d2 = 5.0, d3 = -0.5; evaluate each of the following Python expressions.
   (a) i1 / i2
   (b) i1 // i2
   (c) i2 / i1
   (d) i2 // i1
5. What will be the output of the following code if input value is 8, -8, 0?
   ```
   x=int(input("Input any number "))
   if x < 0:
       print("Number is negative")
   elif x==0:
           print("Number is zero")
   else:
       print("Number is positive")
   ```
6. What will be the output of the following code?
   ```
   org_cost = 100
   n_price = 120
   Calculate_GST = ((n_price - org_cost
   ) * 100 / org_cost )
   print( "GST = " ,Calculate_GST)
   ```
7. What will be the output of the following code?
   (a)
   ```
   a, b, c = 6.3,  3,  20
   print(a/b)
   print(a//b)
   print(c% b)
   print(b**2)
   ```
   (b)
   ```
   a, b = 3,9
   a,b = b,a+2
   print(a,b)
   ```
   (c)
   ```
   a, b = 2,4
   a,b = b,a+2
   print(a,b)
   ```
8. If a=7 and b=2, evaluate the following and write the output:
   i a+b
   ii a-b
   iii a*b
   iv a/b
   v a%b
9. Write a program that accepts 5 subjects marks from the user and prints total and percentage.
10. Write a program to read a set of three real numbers from the keyboard and find out their sum and average.
11. Write a program that accepts 7 days temperature and then prints average temperature of the week.
12. The cost of fencing a circular field at the rate of Rs. 24 per meter is Rs 5280. Write a program to find the length of the fence.
    Length of fence = Total cost/Rate.
13. A car travels a distance of 300 km at the speed of 25 km/h. Write a program to find the time taken to cover the given distance.
    Time = Total distance/Speed
14. An amount of Rs. 100000 is deposited in a bank paying an annual interest rate of 7%, compounded quarterly. Find the balance after 5 years using the formula amt=p*((1+r/n)**(n*t)) where p = principal amt, r = interest rate, n= no. of times the interest is compounded per year, t= no. of years.

CHAPTER 5

Conditional and Iterative Statements

5.1 INTRODUCTION

Control statements define the direction or flow according to which execution of a program should take place. Statements that are executed one after the other or the statements that are executed sequentially are the normal flow-of-control statements in a program. Normally, Python program begins with the first statement and is executed till the end (Sequence construct). [See Figure 5.1.] Control statements also implement decisions and repetitions in programs.

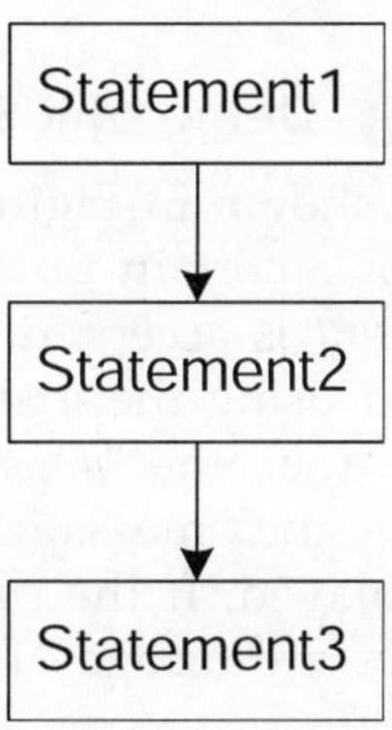

Figure 5.1 The Sequence Construct

Control statements are of the following two types:

(a) Conditional branching or statement

(b) Looping or iteration

In *Conditional branching*, a program decides whether or not to execute the next statement(s), based on the resultant value of the current expression. For example, go to IInd year if you pass Ist year exams, else repeat Ist year (See Figure 5.2).

In *Looping*, a program executes a set of instructions repeatedly till the given condition is true. Looping, for example, adds 1 to number x till current value of x becomes 100. It is also called *iteration*. Iteration is a process of executing a statement or a set of statements repeatedly, until the specified condition is true (See Figure 5.3).

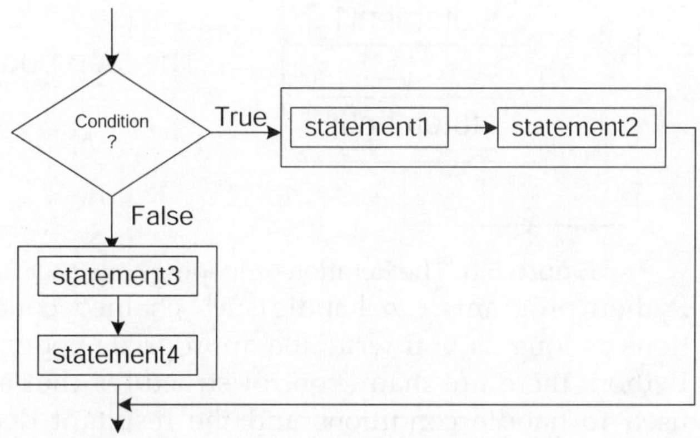

Figure 5.2 Conditional Branching or Decision Construct

All the control structures are explained further in the following sections.

5.2 CONDITIONAL STATEMENTS

When the program uses a condition to decide which set of statements is to be executed between two alternative set of statements, is called conditional statements. For example,

"If it is cold then put your coat on."

In the above statement, the resultant action is taken if the condition is evaluated to *true* (i.e., the weather is cold).

The conditions could be multiple, as in the following conversation:

"Ok then, if I come back early from work, I will see you tonight; else if it is too late I will make it tomorrow; else if my brother arrives tomorrow we can get together on Tuesday; else if Tuesday is a holiday, then let it be Wednesday; else I will call you to arrange for the next meeting!".

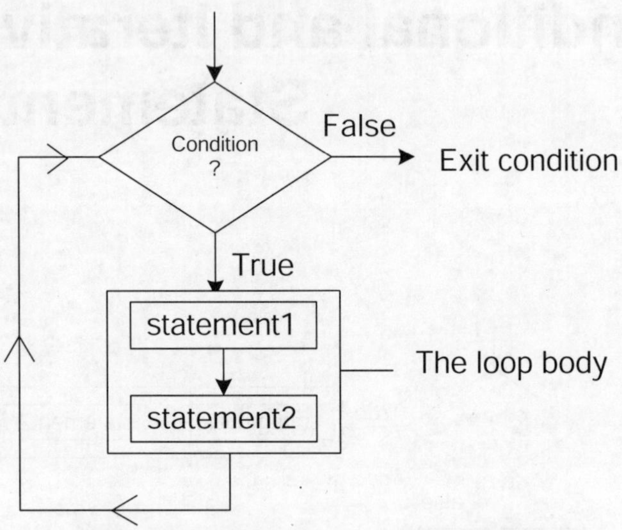

Figure 5.3 The Iteration or looping construct

Python programs can handle such chained conditions as long as you write the appropriate code. In Python, there are many control structures that are used to handle conditions and the resultant decisions. In this chapter, you will be introduced to more powerful tools, namely the *if..else*, *while*, and *for* constructs. But before developing the solution of a problem, you need to decide different tools, used to solve the problem. If efficient programming tools are used, tasks are effectively performed. We code some instructions to instruct computer for problem-solving purposes. The choice of tools depends on the nature of problems.

☞ *A program is a set of instructions, written in a computer language, to perform a specific task.*

5.3 *if* STATEMENT

The statement *if* tests a particular condition. Whenever that condition evaluates to *true*, an action or a set of actions is executed. Otherwise, the actions are ignored. The syntactic form of *if* statement is as follows:

```
if (expression):
    statement
```

The *expression* must be enclosed within parentheses. If it evaluates to a non-zero value, the condition is considered as *true*, and the *statement* following it is executed.

For example,

```
if(marks>=40):
   print("Pass")
if (num < 0):
    print("Number is negative.")
if ch=='':
   print("You entered space.")
```

5.3.1 Simple Program

Example 1 -**Demo of if Statement.**

In the program, shown in Figure 5.4, a credit card limit is tested for a certain purchase. The value of the variable *amount* is accepted from the keyboard; then it is verified using the *if* statement. When the condition is *true* (i.e., the "*amount*" is less than or equal to 1000), the message "Your charge is accepted" is displayed. If the condition is *false*, the program displays a message "The amount exceeds your credit limit".

```
# Credit Card Program
amount = int(input("Enter the amount :"))
if (amount <= 1000):
    print("Your charge is accepted.")
if (amount > 1000):
    print ("The amount exceeds your credit limit.")

RUN
>>>
Enter the amount : 1000
Your charge is accepted.
>>>
>>>
Enter the amount :1289
The amount exceeds your credit limit.
>>>
```

Figure 5.4 Credit Limit Testing Using if Statement

Let's Try

```
price=int(input("Enter Price: "))
qty=int(input("Enter Quantity: "))
amt=price*qty
if amt>1000:
  print ("10% discount is applicable")
  discount=amt*10/100
  amt=amt-discount
print ("Amount payable: ",amt)
```

5.4 *if-else* STATEMENT

The statement *if* also allows to answer for the false value by using an *else* clause. The *else* statement contains the block of code that executes if the conditional expression in the if statement evaluates to 0 or a false value. The else statement is an optional statement; if it is provided, in any situation one of the two blocks gets executed, not both.
The syntactic form of if–else statement is as follows:

```
if (expression):
    statements BLOCK 1
else:
    statements BLOCK 2
```

When the expression evaluates to a non-zero value, the condition is considered to be *true* and statements BLOCK 1 is executed; otherwise, statements BLOCK 2 is executed. Blocks can have multiple lines. As long as they are all indented with the same amount of space, they constitute one block. Figure 5.5 shows the flow diagram of if-else statement.
For example,

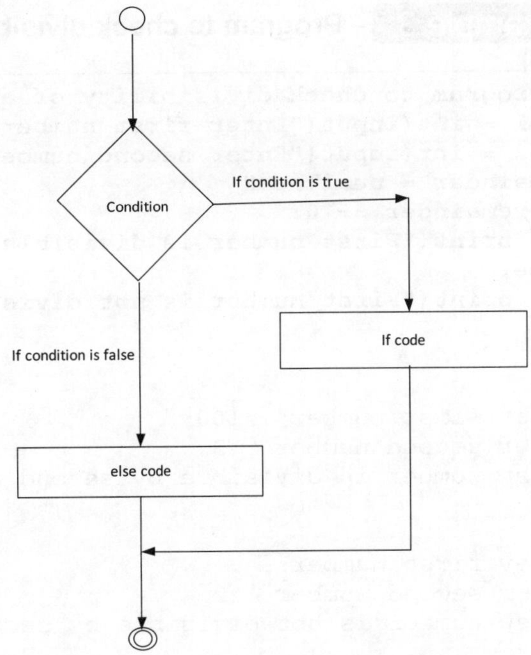

Figure 5.5 Flow Diagram of *if-else* Statement

```
if 10>100:
  print("10 is greater than 100")
else:
  print("10 is less than 100")
```

5.4.1 Simple Programs

Example 2 –**Program to print absolute value of a number provided by the user.**

```
# Take a number from the user and print its absolute value.
num = eval(input("Enter a number: "))
print('|', num, '| = ', (-num if num < 0 else num), sep='')


RUN
>>>
Enter a number: -9
|-9| = 9
>>>
>>>
Enter a number: 9
|9| = 9
>>>
```

Figure 5.6 Program to Print Absolute Value of a Number

Example 3 – **Program to check divisibility of a number.**

```
# Program to check divisibility of a number
num1 = int(input("Enter first number : "))
num2 = int(input("Enter second number : "))
remainder = num1%num2
if remainder == 0:
    print("First number is divisible by second number")
else:
    print("First number is not divisible by second number")

RUN
>>>
Enter first number : 100
Enter second number : 2
First number is divisible by second number
>>>
>>>
Enter first number : 9
Enter second number : 2
First number is not divisible by second number
>>>
```

Figure 5.7 Program to Check Divisibility of a Number

Example 4 – **Program for tax calculation.**

```
# Program for tax calculation
name=input("Enter the name of Employee :")
salary=float(input("Enter the salary :"))
if(salary>50000):
 tax=0.10*salary
 netsalary=salary-tax
 print("The net salary of "+name+" is",netsalary)
else:
 netsalary=salary
 print("No taxable Amount")
 print("The net salary of "+name+ "is",salary)

RUN
>>>
Enter the name of Employee :Swati
Enter the salary :60000
The net salary of Swati is 54000.0
>>>
>>>
Enter the name of Employee :Geeta
Enter the salary :45000
No taxable Amount
The net salary of Geeta is 45000.0
>>>
```

Figure 5.8 Program for tax calculation

Example 5 –**Program to print the largest number.**

```
# Program to print the largest no.
num1 = int(input("Enter first number: "))
num2 = int(input("Enter second number: "))
num3 = int(input("Enter third number: "))
max = num1
if num2 > max:
    max= num2
if num3> max:
    max=num3
print("Largest number is: ", max)

RUN
>>>
Enter first number: 27
Enter second number: 37
Enter third number: 17
Largest number is:  37
>>>
```

Figure 5.9 Program to Print the Largest number

Let's Try

Write a program to print the smallest number.

Example 6 –**Program to print negative or positive number.**

Suppose, you want to write a program that accepts a value of a variable from the user and prints whether the number is positive or negative using the *if-else* statement. The program is shown in Figure 5.10.

```
# Demo of if-else statement
num = int(input("Enter a number :"))
if (num < 0):
    print("Number is negative.")
else:
    print("Number is positive.")

RUN
>>>
Enter a number : 5
Number is positive.
>>>
Enter a number :-7
Number is negative.
>>>
```

Figure 5.10 Program to Print Negative or Positive Number

Example 7 –**Program to read two numbers and print quotient.**

```
# Program to print quotient
dividend, divisor = eval(input('Please enter two numbers to divide: '))
if divisor != 0:
```

(Conti...)

```
    print(dividend, '/', divisor, "=", dividend/divisor)
else:
    print('Division by zero is not allowed')

RUN
>>>
Please enter two numbers to divide: 8,2
8 / 2 = 4.0
>>>
Please enter two numbers to divide: 2,8
2 / 8 = 0.25
>>>
Please enter two numbers to divide: 8,0
Division by zero is not allowed
>>>
```

Figure 5.11 Program to Print Quotient

Example 8 –Program to display menu to calculate area of square or rectangle.

```
# Program to display menu to calculate area of square or rectangle
print("1. Calculate area of a square ")
print("2. Calculate area of rectangle ")
choice = int(input("Enter your choice (1 or 2): "))
if (choice == 1):
    side = float(input("Enter side of a square : "))
    area_square = side * side
    print("Area of a square is :", area_square)
else:
    length = float(input("Enter length of a rectangle : "))
    breadth = float(input("Enter breadth of a rectangle : "))
    area_rectangle = length * breadth
    print("Area of a rectangle is :", area_rectangle)

RUN
>>>
1. Calculate area of a square
2. Calculate area of rectangle
Enter your choice (1 or 2): 2
Enter length of a rectangle : 8
Enter breadth of a rectangle : 4
Area of a rectangle is : 32.0
>>>
>>>
1. Calculate area of a square
2. Calculate area of rectangle
Enter your choice (1 or 2): 1
Enter side of a square : 2.5
Area of a square is : 6.25
>>>
```

Figure 5.12 Program to Calculate Area of Square or Rectangle

Example 9 –Program to print larger number using swap.

In the program shown in Figure 5.13, the *if* statement rearranges any two values stored in *x* and *y* in such a way that the smaller number will always be in *x* and the larger number always in *y*. If the two numbers are already in the proper order, the compound statement will not be executed.

You will always get the larger value first and then the smaller value.

```
# Print larger number using swap
x=y=0
x=int(input("Enter the first number: "))
y=int(input("Enter the second number: "))
if(x>y):
    x,y=y,x # swap (interchange) values
    print("The larger number is : ",y)
    print("The smaller number is : ",x)
else:
    print("The larger number is : ",y)
    print ("The smaller number is : ",x)
RUN
>>>
Enter the first number: 5
Enter the second number: 7
The larger number is :  7
The smaller number is :  5
>>>
Enter the first number: 7
Enter the second number: 5
The larger number is :  7
The smaller number is :  5
>>>
```

Figure 5.13 Program to print larger number using swap

Example 10 –Program to print if the number is even or odd.

```
# Program to print no. is even or odd
num=int(input("Enter a number: "))
if (num % 2 == 0):
    print(num, "is an even number.")
else:
    print(num, "is an odd number.")

RUN
>>>
Enter a number: 2
2 is an even number.
>>>
>>>
Enter a number: 5
5 is an odd number.
>>>
```

Figure 5.14 Program to Print number is Even or Odd

Example 11 –**Program to display the menu to calculate sum or product of entered numbers.**

```
# Program to display menu to calculate sum or product of entered numbers
num1 = int(input("Enter first number : "))
num2 = int(input("Enter second number : "))
num3 = int(input("Enter third number : "))
print("1. Calculate sum")
print("2. Calculate product")
choice = int(input("Enter your choice (1 or 2): "))
if (choice == 1):
    sum = num1+num2+num3
    print("Sum of three numbers are :", sum)
else:
    product = num1*num2*num3
    print("Product of three numbers are : ",product  )
RUN
>>>
Enter first number : 2
Enter second number : 3
Enter third number : 4
1. Calculate sum
2. Calculate product
Enter your choice (1 or 2): 1
Sum of three numbers are : 9
>>>
>>>
Enter first number : 2
Enter second number : 3
Enter third number : 4
1. Calculate sum
2. Calculate product
Enter your choice (1 or 2): 2
Product of three numbers are :  24
>>>
```

Figure 5.15 Program to Display Menu to Calculate Sum or Product of Entered Numbers

5.5 *if-elif-else* STATEMENTS

In the *if* statement, the statement following the condition or the keyword *else* is a single executable statement, such as an assignment statement. If multiple tasks are to be performed depending on a condition, then they can be grouped together within *block* to form a single compound statement. Thus, you can use more than one statement by embedding the statements in a block. In the compound statement, there is no limit to number of statements that can appear inside the body, but there has to be at least one. Indentation level is used to tell Python which statement(s) belongs to which block.

If you want to check for several conditions, you can use *elif*, which is short for "else if". It is a combination of an *if* clause and an *else* clause. Like the else, the elif statement is optional. However, unlike else for which there can be at the most one statement, there can be unlimited number of elif statements following an if. The syntax of the if...elif...else statement is as follows:

```
if(expression1):
    statement(s)
elif(expression2):
    statement(s)
elif(expression3):
    statement(s)
```

```
else:
    statement(s)
```

For example,

```
grade = eval(input('Enter your score: '))
if grade>=90:
 print('A')
elif (grade>=70):
 print('B')
elif (grade>=60):
 print('C')
elif (grade>=40):
 print('D')
else:
 print('F')
```

☞ *In Python, like the else, the elif statement is optional.*

5.5.1 Simple Programs

Example 12 –Program to print the entered number is positive, negative or zero using if...elif...else statement.

```
# Program to print number is positive, negative or zero
num = int(input('Enter a number: '))
if (num > 0):
  print('The number is positive')
elif (num < 0):
  print('The number is negative')
else:
  print('The number is zero')

RUN
>>>
Enter a number: 7
The number is positive
>>>
Enter a number: -5
The number is negative
>>>
Enter a number: 0
The number is zero
>>>
```

Figure 5.16 Program to print number is positive, negative or zero

Example 13 –Program to Calculate Electricity Bill.

```
# Program to Calculate Electricity Bill
units = int(input("Enter Number of Units Consumed : "))
if(units > 500):
    amount = units * 9.25
    surcharge = 80
elif(units >= 300):
    amount = units * 7.75
    surcharge = 70
elif(units >= 200):
    amount = units * 5.25
    surcharge = 50
elif(units >= 100):
    amount = units * 3.75
    surcharge = 30
```

(Conti...)

```
else:
    amount = units * 2.25
    surcharge = 20
billtotal = amount + surcharge
print("Electricity Bill = %.2f"  %billtotal)

RUN
Enter Number of Units Consumed : 450
Electricity Bill = 3557.50
```

Figure 5.17 Program to Calculate Electricity Bill

Example 14 **–Program to calculate tax.**

```
# Program to calculate tax
name=input("Enter the name of Employee :")
salary = eval(input('Enter salary: '))
if salary <=500000:
    taxamt=0.05*salary
elif salary <=600000:
    taxamt=0.07* salary
elif salary <=700000:
    taxamt =0.08*salary
else:
    taxamt=0.10*salary
print("Name: ", name, "Salary :", salary, "Tax :", taxamt)

RUN
Enter the name of Employee :Aman
Enter salary: 770000
Name:  Aman Salary : 770000 Tax : 77000.0
```

Figure 5.18 Program to calculate tax

Example 15 **–Program to print numbers in ascending order.**

```
# Program to print numbers in ascending order
num1 = int(input("Enter first number: "))
num2 = int(input("Enter second number: "))
num3 = int(input("Enter third number: "))
if num1 < num2 and num1 < num3:
    if num2 < num3:
        x, y, z = num1, num2, num3
    else:
        x, y, z = num1, num3, num2
elif num2 < num1 and num2 < num3:
    if num1 < num3:
        x, y, z = num2, num1, num3
    else:
        x, y, z = num2, num3, num1
else:
```

(Conti...)

```
    if num1<num2:
        x, y, z = num3, num1, num2
    else:
        x, y, z = num3, num2, num1

print("Numbers in ascending order are: ", x,y,z)

RUN
>>>
Enter first number: 27
Enter second number: 25
Enter third number: 45
Numbers in ascending order are:  25 27 45
>>>
```

Figure 5.19 Program to Print Numbers in Ascending Order

Let's Try

Write a program to enter three numbers and print numbers in descending order.

5.6 NESTED *if* STATEMENT

There may be a situation when you want to check for another condition after one condition evaluates to true. In such a situation, you can use the nested if construct. In a nested if construct, you can have an *if...elif...else* construct inside another *if...elif...else* construct.

Example 16 –Program to test whether the entered character is alphabetic character or not.

Suppose you want to test the ASCII code of an entered character to check if it is an alphabetic character. After checking this, you would like to further check if it is in lowercase or uppercase. Knowing that the ASCII codes for the uppercase letters are in the range of 65-90, and those for lowercase letters are in the range of 97-122, program shown in Figure 5.20 establishes this logic.

```
# Program to test - character is alphabetic character or not
ch = input("Enter an alphabetic character: ")
if (ch>='A' and ch<='Z'):
    print("The character is an upper-case letter")
elif (ch>='a' and ch<='z'):
    print("The character is a lower-case letter")
else:
    print("This is not an alphabetic character!")

RUN
>>>
Enter an alphabetic character: A
The character is an upper-case letter
>>>
Enter an alphabetic character: b
The character is a lower-case letter
>>>
Enter an alphabetic character: 9
This is not an alphabetic character!
>>>
```

Figure 5.20 Program to test whether the entered character is alphabetic character or not

5.7 NOTION OF ITERATING COMPUTATION (LOOPS)

Many jobs that are required to be done with the help of a computer are *repetitive* in nature. For example, calculation of wages of different workers in a factory is done using the formula (No. of hours worked) × (wage rate). This calculation will be performed by an accountant for each worker every month. Such types of repetitive calculations can easily be done with the help of a program that has a built-in loop. Figure 5.21 shows the flow diagram of loop statement.

5.7.1 What is a Loop?

A loop is defined as a block of instructions repeated for a certain number of times. Figure 5.22 illustrates a flowchart showing the concept of looping. It shows the flowchart for printing values 1, 2, 3..., 20. In Step 5 of Figure 5.22, the current value of A is compared with 21. If the current value of A is less than 21, steps 3 and 4 are repeated. As soon as the current value of A becomes more than 21, the path corresponding to "NO" is followed, and the repetition process stops.

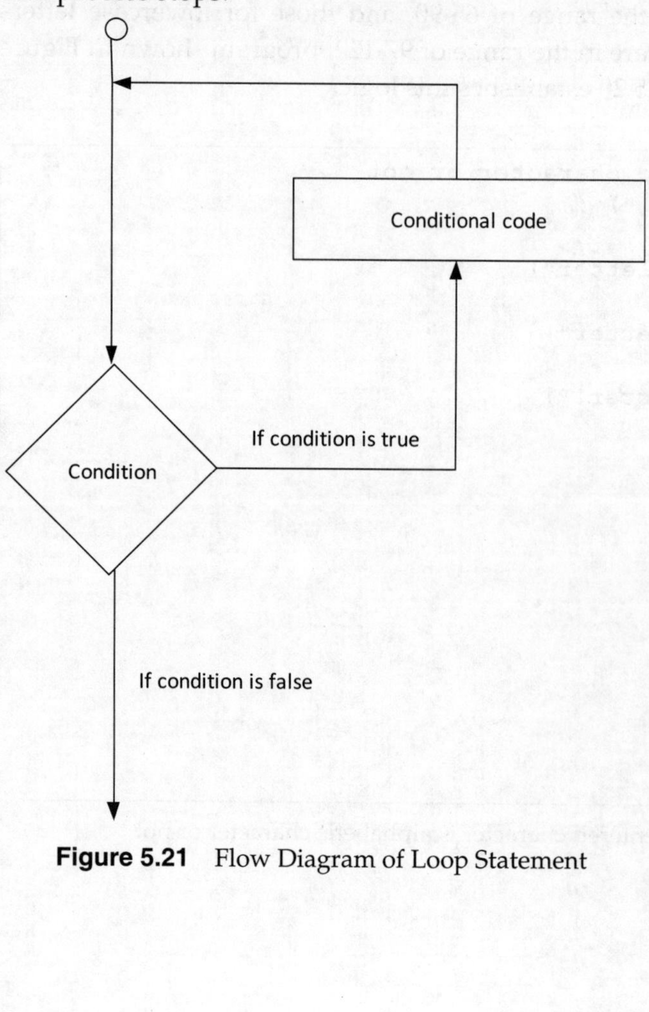

Figure 5.21 Flow Diagram of Loop Statement

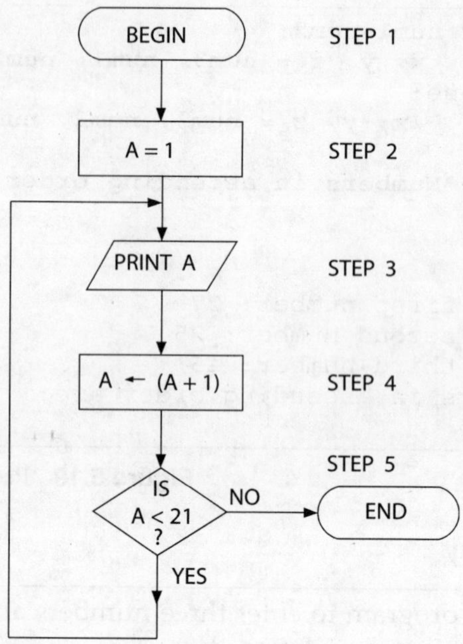

Figure 5.22 Concept of Looping using Flowchart

5.7.2 Control Flow

By default, statements in the script are executed sequentially from the first to the last. But the sequential flow can be altered either by conditional execution where a block of one or more statements will be executed if a certain expression is true or by repetitive execution where a block of one or more statements will be repetitively executed as long as a certain expression is true.
Python uses the while and for keywords to constitute a conditional loop, by which repeated execution of a block of statements is done until a Boolean expression is true.

5.8 THE *while* STATEMENT

The while loop is used to repeat a set of statements as long as the condition is true. In Python, an indefinite loop is implemented using the while statement. The indefinite loop keeps iterating until certain conditions are met. The syntax of while statement is as follows:

```
while (<condition>):
    <body>
```

Here, condition is a Boolean expression. The body of the loop executes repeatedly as long as the condition is true. When the condition becomes false, the loop terminates.

while (x < y):
 x = x + 1

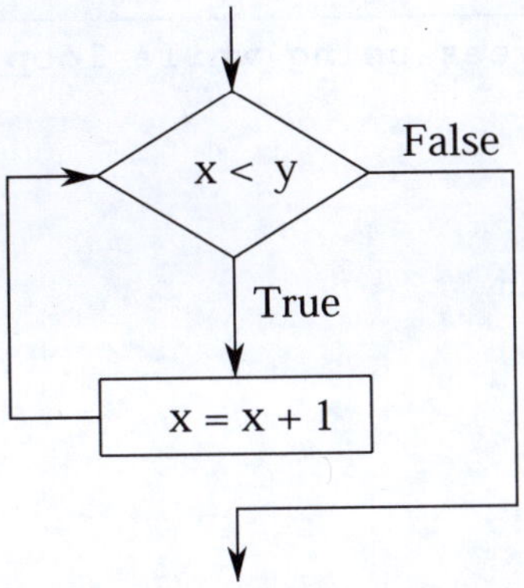

Figure 5.23 Flow control of a *while* statement

Note that the condition is always tested first, before the loop body is executed. This kind of structure is called a pre-test loop. If the loop condition is initially false, the loop body will not execute at all. Here is an example of a simple while loop that counts from 0 to 10:

```
i = 0
while (i <= 10):
      print(i)
      i = i + 1
```

The above-mentioned program will produce numbers from 1 to 10 as an output. Here the repetitive block after the while statement involves incrementing the value of an integer variable and printing it. Before the block begins, the variable *i* is initialized to 0. Till it is less than equal to 10, i is incremented by 1 and printed to display the sequence of numbers.

Figure 5.23 shows the flow of control for the *while* statement. As long as *x* is less than *y*, the program continues to execute the *while* loop. With each pass through the loop, *x* is incremented by one. When it is no longer less than *y*, control comes out of the loop and flows to the next statement.

Let's Try

```
num = 0
while (num< 10):
      num = num + 1
      print("num =", num)
```

5.8.1 Simple Programs

Example 17 –Program to display the string "Hello World" five times.

Figure 5.24 shows the program displaying the string "Hello World" five times using the *while* loop.

```
# Demonstration of while loop
count = 0
while(count <=4):
    print("Hello World")
    count= count + 1
print ("Done")

RUN
>>>
Hello World
Hello World
Hello World
Hello World
Hello World
Done
>>>
```

Figure 5.24 Program to Display 'Hello World' Five Times

Example 18 –Program to display gross pay for three employees using while loop.

The program segment shown in Figure 5.25 computes and displays gross pay of three employees. The loop body gets an employee's payroll data and computes and displays pay. After gross pay of each employee is displayed, "*All employees processed*" message will be displayed at last.

```
# Program to display gross pay of three employees using while loop
count_emp = 0
while(count_emp <3):
    hours = int(input("Hours :"))
    rate = float(input("Rate :"))
    pay = hours * rate
    print("Pay is Rs. ", pay)
    count_emp = count_emp +1
print( "All employees processed" )

RUN
>>>
Hours :2
Rate :200
Pay is Rs.  400.0
Hours :4
Rate :500.25
Pay is Rs.  2001.0
Hours :8
Rate :750.75
Pay is Rs.  6006.0
All employees processed
>>>
```

Figure 5.25 Computing Gross Pay of 3 Employees

Let's Try

What is the output of following code fragments?

<table>
<tr>
<td><pre>count = 0
while(count < 5):
    print("Hello")
    count= count + 1</pre></td>
<td><pre>i=100
while(i<=200):
    print(i)
    i+=40</pre></td>
<td><pre>n=30
i=5
s=0
while (i<n):
    s+=i
    i+=5
print("i=",i)
print("sum=",s)</pre></td>
</tr>
</table>

Example 19 –Calculation of factorial.

In Figure 5.26, the *while* loop is used to calculate the factorial of a number in this program. The number is entered from the keyboard using the *input* function and is assigned to the variable "number".

```
# Calculation of factorial
factorial = 1
number = int(input("Enter the number : "))
while(number > 1):
    factorial = factorial * number
```

(Contd...)

```
    number = number -1
print ("The factorial is ", factorial)

RUN
>>>
Enter the number : 5
The factorial is  120
>>>
```

Figure 5.26 Program to Calculate Factorial of a Number using *while* Loop

Example 20 –Program to print numbers 1 to 10 on different lines.

```
# Print numbers 1 to 10 using while loop
count = 0
while(count <=10):
    print(count)
    count= count + 1
print("Done")

RUN
>>>
0
1
2
3
4
5
6
7
8
9
10
Done
>>>
```

Figure 5.27 Printing numbers 1 to 10 using *while* Loop

The Python print() function by default ends with a newline. Python has a predefined format for using print() function; if you use print(a_variable) then it will go to next line automatically. In Python 2, for printing code on the same line, comma is used; but Python 3 provides one extra argument, i.e., end =" " to print code on the same line.

Example 21 –Program to print numbers 1 to 10 on the same line.

```
# Print numbers 1 to 10 on the same line using while loop
count = 0
while(count <=10):
    print(count, end =" " )
    count= count + 1
print("\nDone")
```

(Contd...)

```
RUN
>>>
0 1 2 3 4 5 6 7 8 9 10
Done
>>>
```

Figure 5.28 Printing Numbers 1 to 10 on the same line using *while* Loop

Example 22 –Program to print even numbers series.

```
# Print even numbers using while loop
count = 0
while(count <=20):
    print(count, end =" " )
    count= count + 2
print("\nDone")

RUN
>>>
0 2 4 6 8 10 12 14 16 18 20
Done
>>>
```

Figure 5.29 Printing Even Number Series using while Loop

Example 23 –Program to print odd numbers series.

```
# Print odd numbers using while loop
count = 1
while(count < 20):
    print(count, end =" " )
    count= count + 2
print ("\nDone")

RUN
>>>
1 3 5 7 9 11 13 15 17 19
Done
>>>
```

Figure 5.30 Printing Odd Number Series using while Loop

Example 24 –Program to print average of entered numbers.

```
# Program to print average of entered numbers
counter = 0
total = 0
number = 0
```

(Contd...)

```
while number >= 0:
    number = int(input("Enter a positive number or a negative to exit: "))
    total += number
    counter += 1
avg = total / counter
print("Average = : ",avg )

RUN
>>>
Enter a positive number or a negative to exit: 4
Enter a positive number or a negative to exit: 2
Enter a positive number or a negative to exit: 4
Enter a positive number or a negative to exit: -4
Average = :  1.5
>>>
```

Figure 5.31 Program to Print Average of Entered Numbers

Example 25 –**Program to find sum of all even and odd numbers up to specified number.**

```
# Program to find sum of all even and odd numbers up to specified number
num = int(input("Enter any number : "))
count= 1
sum_even=sum_odd=0
while (count<=num):
    if (count% 2) ==0:
        sum_even += count
    else:
        sum_odd += count
    count += 1
print("Sum of all even numbers up to ",num ," is ",sum_even)
print("Sum of all odd numbers up to ",num ," is ",sum_odd)

RUN
>>>
Enter any number : 15
Sum of all even numbers up to  15  is  56
Sum of all odd numbers up to  15  is  64
>>>
```

Figure 5.32 Program to find sum of even and odd numbers

Let's Try

What is printed by the following code fragments?

```
a = 0
while a > 100:
    print(a)
    a += 1
print()
```

```
i = 1
while True:
    if i%2 == 0:
        break
    print(i)
    i += 2
```

Let's Try

What is the output of following code fragments?

<table>
<tr>
<td>

```
result = 1
while result < 100:
    result *= 2
    print (result)
```

</td>
<td>

```
i = 1
while True:
    if i%3 == 0:
        break
    print(i)
    i += 1
```

</td>
</tr>
</table>

5.9 THE *for* STATEMENT

Python provides *for* statement as another form for accomplishing control using loops. The *for* loop statement is used to repeat a statement or a block of statements a specified number of times.
A Python *for* loop has this general form.

```
for <var> in <sequence>:
   <body>
```

The body of the loop can be sequence of Python statements. The start and end of the body can be indicated by its indentation under the loop heading. The variable after the keyword for is called the loop index. It takes on each successive value in the sequence, and the statements in the body are executed once for each value.
Usually, the sequence portion is a list of values. You can build a simple list by placing a sequence of expressions in square brackets. Some interactive examples help to illustrate the point:

```
>>> for i in [0,1,2,3]:
    print(i)

0
1
2
3

>>> for odd in [1, 3, 5, 7, 9]:
    print(odd * odd)

1
9
25
49
81
```

The for loop specification ends with a colon, and after the colon (:) comes a block of statements which works on the current element. Each statement in the block must be indented.

```
>>> little_list = ['the', 'quick',
'brown', 'fox']
>>> for the_item in little_list:
  print(the_item, "*", end =" " )

the * quick * brown * fox *
```

This example takes each item in little_list one at a time and prints it.

5.9.1 Operation of the *for* Loop

First the initialization expression is executed, and then the test condition is examined. If the test expression is false to begin with, the statements in the body of the loop will not be executed at all. If the condition is true, the statements in the body of the loop are executed and, following that, the increment expression is executed. That is why the first number printed by the program is 0, not 1. Printing takes place before the number is incremented by increment (++) operator. Finally, the loop recycles, and the test expression is queried again. This continues until the test expression becomes false, and the loop will end.

5.10 THE range() FUNCTION

Python range() function generates a list of numbers, which is generally used to iterate over with for loops. Python range() function examples:

```
>>> # One parameter
>>> for i in range(5):
...     print(i)
...
0
1
2
3
4
```

```
>>> # Two parameters
>>> for i in range(3, 6):
...     print(i)
...
3
4
5
>>> # Three parameters
>>> for i in range(4, 10, 2):
...     print(i)
...
4
6
8
>>> # Going backwards
>>> for i in range(0, -10, -2):
...     print(i)
...
0
-2
-4
-6
-8
```

Let's Try

What is the output of following code fragments?

`>>> for i in range(10):` `...     print(i)`	`>>> for i in range(0, -12, -2):` `...     print(i)`

`sum = 0`
`for i in range(16,2,-2):`
`    sum+=i`
`print (sum)`
	`for x in range(-300, 300, 100):`
	`    print(x)`

Python range() vs xrange() Functions

You may have heard of a function known as xrange(). This is a function which is present in Python 2.x; however, it was renamed to range() in Python 3.x, and the original range() function was deprecated in Python 3.x. In Python 2.x, range() produced a list, while xrange() returned an iterator – a sequence object.

5.10.1 The for Loop and the range() Built-in Function

The for statement acts more like a traditional loop; that is, a numerical counting loop.

```
>>> for eachNum in [0, 1, 2, 3, 4, 5]:
        print(eachNum)
0
1
2
3
4
5
```

Within our loop, *eachNum* contains the integer value that you are displaying, and you can use it in any numerical calculation you wish. Since your range of numbers may differ, Python provides the range() built-in function to generate such a list for you. It does exactly what you want, taking a range of numbers and generating a list.

```
>>> for eachNum in range(6):
        print(eachNum)

0
1
2
3
4
5
```

Note that range(n) generates integers 0, 1, 2, ..., n-1. For example,

range(start, stop, step) generates a sequence of integers as start, start+step, start+2*step, and so on, but not including stop. For example, range(2, 8, 3) returns 2 and 5 (and not 8), while range(1, 11, 2) returns 1, 3, 5, 7, 9.

range(start, stop) is the same as range(start, stop, 1).

A *for* loop over integers is written as:

```
for i in range(start, stop, step):
```

The following program writes the numbers from 1 to 100:

```
for number in range(1,101,1):
    print(number)
```

An integer to be added to the current number to generate the next number is called a step. If left out, it defaults to 1. So, the previous program can be written as:

```
for number in range(1,101):
    print(number)
```

5.10.2 Simple Programs

Example 26 –**Program to print numbers 1 to 10 using for loop.**

```
# A loop to print values 1 to 10
for i in range(1,11,1):
    print(i, end =" ")

RUN
>>>
1 2 3 4 5 6 7 8 9 10
>>>
```

Figure 5.33 Program to Print Numbers 1 to 10

Example 27 –**Program to print even number series up to 20.**

```
# A loop to print even number series up to 20
for i in range(0,21,2):
    print(i,end =" ")

RUN
>>>
0 2 4 6 8 10 12 14 16 18 20
>>>
```

Figure 5.34 Program to Print Even Numbers

Example 28 –**Program to print sum of even number series up to 10.**

```
# Print sum of even number series up to 10
sum=0
for i in range(0,11,2):
    sum +=i
    print("Sum of even numbers <= ", i, "is", sum)
RUN
>>>
Sum of even numbers <=  0 is 0
Sum of even numbers <=  2 is 2
Sum of even numbers <=  4 is 6
Sum of even numbers <=  6 is 12
Sum of even numbers <=  8 is 20
Sum of even numbers <=  10 is 30
>>>
```

Figure 5.35 Program to Print Sum of Even Numbers

Let's Try

Write a program to print sum of odd number series up to 11.

Example 29 –**Program to generate multiplication table of the entered number.**

```
# Generation of Multiplication Table
num =int(input("Enter number for which you want table : "))
for i in range(1,11):
    print(num, 'X', i,'=', num * i    )

RUN
>>>
Enter number for which you want table : 5
5 X 1 = 5
5 X 2 = 10
5 X 3 = 15
5 X 4 = 20
5 X 5 = 25
5 X 6 = 30
5 X 7 = 35
5 X 8 = 40
5 X 9 = 45
5 X 10 = 50
>>>
```

Figure 5.36 Program to Print Table of Desired Number

Example 30 –**Program to print letters of a word.**

```
# Printing letters of word
letter = input("Enter word : ")
for word in letter:
    print(word)

RUN
>>>
Enter word : Python
P
y
t
h
o
n
>>>
```

Figure 5.37 Program to Print Letters of Entered Word

Example 31 –**Program to print ASCII code for entered message.**

```
# Printing ASCII code
message = input("Enter message to encode : ")
print("ASCII code for message :")
for ch in message:
    print(ord(ch),end =" ") # ord function returns the numeric code
```

(Contd...)

```
RUN
>>>
Enter message to encode : Apple
ASCII code for message :
65 112 112 108 101
>>>
```

Figure 5.38 Program to Print ASCII Code for Entered Message

Example 32 –Program to find sum of natural numbers up to specified number.

```
# Program to input number and find sum of all natural numbers up to given number
num = int(input("Enter any number : "))
sum= 0
for i in range(1,num+1):
    sum = sum+i
print("Sum of all natural numbers up to ",num ," is ",sum)

RUN
>>>
Enter any number : 5
Sum of all natural numbers up to  5  is  15
>>>
```

Figure 5.39 Program to Find Sum of All Natural Numbers up to the given number

Example 33 –Program to check whether the entered number is prime or not.

```
# Program to check number is prime or not
num = int(input("Enter any number: "))
# prime number is always greater than 1
if num > 1:
    for i in range(2, num):
        if (num % i) == 0:
            print(num, "is not a prime number")
            break
    else:
        print(num, "is a prime number")# if number is less than or equal to 1,then
it is not prime number
else:
    print(num, "is not a prime number")

RUN
>>>
Enter any number: 5
5 is a prime number
>>>
Enter any number: 8
8 is not a prime number
>>>
```

Figure 5.40 Program to Check Entered Number is Prime or Not

Example 34 –**Program to print all the Prime Numbers within a given range.**

```
# Program to print all the Prime Numbers within a given range
num=int(input("Enter upper limit: "))
for a in range(2,num+1):
    k=0
    for i in range(2,a//2+1):
        if(a%i==0):
            k=k+1
    if(k<=0):
        print(a)

RUN
>>>
Enter upper limit: 17
2
3
5
7
11
13
17
>>>
```

Figure 5.41 Program to Print all the Prime Numbers within a Given Range

Example 35 –**Program to display first ten Mersenne numbers. Numbers in the form 2n-1 are called Mersenne numbers. For example, the first Mersenne number is 21-1 = 1, the second Mersenne number is 22-1 = 3, etc.**

```
# Program to display first ten Mersenne numbers
print("First ten Mersenne numbers are :")
for n in range (1,11):
    mersenne = 2**n-1
    print(mersenne, end=' ')


RUN
>>>
First ten Mersenne numbers are :
1 3 7 15 31 63 127 255 511 1023
>>>
```

Figure 5.42 Program to display first ten Mersenne numbers

5.11 NESTED LOOPS

A loop may also contain another loop within its body. This form of a loop inside another loop is called *nested loop*. In a nested loop construction, the inner loop must terminate before the ending of outer loop.

Example 36 –**Program to print pyramid of stars using for loop.**

```
*
* *
* * *
* * * *
* * * * *
```

```
# Nested for loop
n = int(input("Enter a number to form pyramid :"))
for i in range(1,n):
    for j in range(1,i):
        print("*",end =" ")
    print()
```

Figure 5.43 Program to print pyramid of stars using for loop

Example 37 –**Program to print inverted triangle of stars using for loop.**

```
* * * * *
* * * *
* * *
* *
*
```

```
# Print the pattern
for a in range(5, 0, -1):
    for b in range(1,a+1):
        print("*", end=' ')
    print(" ")
```

Figure 5.44 Program to print inverted triangle of stars using for loop

Example 38 –**Program to print pattern of stars.**

```
* * * * *
* * * * *
* * * * *
```

```
# Print the pattern
for a in range(1, 4):
    for b in range(1,6):
        print("*", end=' ')
    print(" ")
```

Figure 5.45 Program to print pattern of stars

Let's Try

Write a program to print the following pattern:

`* * *`
`* * *`
`* * *`
	`    *`
	`  * * *`
	`* * * * *`
		`*`
		`* *`
		`* * *`

Example 39 –Program to print pattern of numbers.

1 2 3 4 5
1 2 3 4 5
1 2 3 4 5

```
# Print the pattern
for a in range(1, 4):
    for b in range(1,6):
        print(b, end=' ')
    print(" ")
```

Figure 5.46 Program to print pattern of numbers

Example 40 –Program to print pattern of numbers.

1 1 1 1 1
2 2 2 2 2
3 3 3 3 3

```
# Print the pattern
for a in range(1, 4):
    for b in range(1,6):
        print(a, end=' ')
    print(" ")
```

Figure 5.47 Program to print pattern of numbers

Example 41 –Program to print pattern of numbers.

1
1 2
1 2 3
1 2 3 4

```
# Print the pattern
for a in range(1, 5):
    for b in range(1,a+1):
        print(b, end=' ')
    print(" ")
```

Figure 5.48 Program to print pattern of numbers

Example 42 –Program to print pattern of numbers.

1
2 2
3 3 3
4 4 4 4

```
# Print the pattern
for a in range(1, 5):
    for b in range(1,a+1):
        print(a, end=' ')
    print(" ")
```

Figure 5.49 Program to print pattern of numbers

Example 43 –**Program to print pattern of numbers.**

5 5 5 5 5
4 4 4 4
3 3 3
2 2
1

```
# Print the pattern
for a in range(5, 0, -1):
    for b in range(1,a+1):
        print(a, end=' ')
    print(" ")
```

Figure 5.50 Program to print pattern of numbers

Let's Try

What is the output of following code fragments?

```
# Print the pattern
for a in range(5, 0, -1):
    for b in range(1,a+1):
        print(b, end=' ')
    print(" ")
```

```
# Print the pattern
for a in range(0, 5):
    for b in range(1,a+1):
        print("*", end=' ')
    print(" ")
```

5.12 JUMP STATEMENTS

Those statements which transfer the program control, unconditionally within the program, from one place to another are called *jump* statements. These statements include the following:

(a) *break* Statement
(b) *continue* Statement
(c) *pass* Statement

5.13 *break* STATEMENT

The *break* statement causes an immediate *exit* from the innermost loop structure. It transfers control out of *while* or *for* statement. It is mostly required when, due to some external condition, you need to exit from a loop.

If you need to come out of a running program immediately without letting it perform any further operation in a loop, then you can use *break* statement. The *break* statement exits the current loop (for or while) and transfers control to the statement immediately following the control structure.

Figure 5.51 shows the use of *break* statement.

Example 44 –**Demo of break statement.**

```
# Demo of using break statement
count = 1
while(count > 0):
```

(Contd...)

```
    print("Count :",count)
    count += 1
    #Breaks out of the while loop when count >5
    if(count>5):
        break
print("End of Program")

RUN
>>>
Count : 1
Count : 2
Count : 3
Count : 4
Count : 5
End of Program
>>>
```

Figure 5.51 Demo of using *break* Statement

Note that in the following example, *break* statement causes the program to immediately exit the loop; so it will print COMP.

Example 45 –**Demo of break statement.**

```
# Demo of using break statement
for ch in 'COMPUTER':
    if ch == 'U':
        break
    print(ch)
RUN
>>>
C
O
M
P
>>>
```

Figure 5.52 Demo of using *break* Statement

5.14 *continue* STATEMENT

The *continue* statement forces the next iteration of the loop to take place, skipping any statement(s) that follows the *continue* statement in the current iteration, i.e., *continue* statement jumps back to the top of the loop for the next iteration.

The syntax of the *continue* statement is :

continue

The *continue* statement can be considered as the opposite of *break* statement. It is used to skip the rest of the body of the loop and the next iteration after the loop begins immediately.

Example 46 –**Demo of continue statement.**

```
# Demo of continue statement
count=0
```

(Contd...)

```
while True:
    count= count +1
    # End loop if count is greater than 10
  if (count > 10):
        break
    # Skip 5
    if (count == 5):
        continue
    print(count)


RUN
>>>
1
2
3
4
6
7
8
9
10
>>>
```

Figure 5.53 Demonstration of Using *continue* Statement

Figure 5.53 shows the use of continue statement. At the top of the loop, the *while* condition is tested, and the loop is entered, if it's true. Here, when count is equal to 5, the program does not get to the print (count) statement. So, the number 5 is skipped with the *continue* statement, and loop ends with the *break* statement. Note in Figure 5.54, *U* is skipped due to the use of *continue* statement.

Example 47 –Demo of continue statement.

```
# Demo of using continue statement
for ch in 'COMPUTER':
    if (ch == 'U'):
        continue
    print(ch)
RUN
>>>
C
O
M
P
T
E
R
>>>
```

Figure 5.54 Demonstration of Using *continue* Statement

Example 48 –**Program to print square of positive numbers.**

```
# Program to print square of positive numbers
while True:
    n = int(input("Please enter an Integer: "))
    if n< 0:
        continue #this will take the execution back to the starting of the loop
    elif n == 0:
        break
    print("Square is ", n ** 2)
print("Goodbye")
RUN
>>>
Please enter an Integer: -4
Please enter an Integer: 2
Square is  4
Please enter an Integer: 3
Square is  9
Please enter an Integer: 0
Goodbye
>>>
```

Figure 5.55 Printing square of positive numbers

Difference between break and continue statements

The *continue* statement skips the remainder of the statements in the body of a current iteration and starts execution immediately from the beginning of the next iteration.

The *break* statement in the body of a loop terminates the loop. It exits from the current loop and starts execution from the statement following the loop.

☞ *break and continue can be used in both for and while statements.*

5.15 *pass* STATEMENT

The *pass* statement in Python is used when a statement is required syntactically, but you do not want any command or code to execute. This statement is a null operation; nothing happens when it executes. The pass is also useful in places where your code will eventually go, but it has not been written yet. For example,

```
if (condition):
    pass
```

It can be used as a placeholder while you are writing code. For example, you may have written an if statement and you want to try it, but you do not have the code for one of your blocks. Consider the following:

```
name=input('Enter your name: ')
if(name=='Ram'):
    print('Welcome!')
elif(name=='Ramesh'):
# Not finished yet...
elif(name=='Rohan'):
    print('Access Denied')
```

This code will not run because an empty block is illegal in Python. To fix this, simply add the pass statement to the middle block:

```
name=input('Enter your name: ')
if(name=='Ram'):
    print('Welcome!')
elif(name=='Ramesh'):
# Not finished yet...
    pass
elif(name=='Rohan'):
    print('Access Denied')
```

5.16 *assert* STATEMENT

The assert statement checks if a given logical expression is true; or false. Program executes only if the expression is true and otherwise it raises the AssertionError. The syntax of assert is:

```
assert Expression[, Arguments]
```

Example 49 –**Demo of assert statement.**

```
# Demo of assert statement
num=int(input('Enter a number: '))
assert num>=0
print('You entered: ', num)
RUN
>>>
Enter a number: 8
You entered:  8
>>>
>>>
Enter a number: -4
Traceback (most recent call last):
  File "C:\Users\shash\AppData\Local\Programs\Python\Python37-32\assert.py", line
2, in <module>
    assert num>=0
AssertionError
>>>
```

Figure 5.56 Demo of *assert* statement

The print statement will display if the entered number is greater than or equal to 0. Negative numbers result in aborting the program after showing the AssertionError as shown in Figure 5.56. So, Assertions are simply boolean expressions that check if the condition returns true or not. If it is true, the program does nothing and moves to the next line of code. However, if it's false, the program stops and throws an error.

☞ *Python assert statement is a debugging aid that tests a condition, it brings the program on halt as soon as any error is occurred and shows the point of the program where error has occurred.*

The AssertionError is also a built-in exception and can be handled using the try...except construct. An expression is tested, and if the result comes up false, an exception is raised. For example,

```
try:
    num=int(input('Enter a number: '))
#if condition returns False, AssertionError is raised:
    assert(num >=0), "Only positive numbers accepted."
    print(num)
except AssertionError as msg:
    print(msg)
```

REVIEW QUESTIONS WITH ANSWERS

1. Multiple Choice Questions

1. We can go back to the start of the loop by using:
   a. break
   b. pass
   c. continue
   d. None of these
2. The condition on which the execution or exit of the loop depends is called :
   a. exit condition
   b. test condition
   c. Both (a) and (b)
   d. None of these
3. What is true about break statement?
   a. It is used to terminate the execution of the current loop.

b. It always breaks the current execution and transfers control to outside the current block.
c. If the break is in a loop, it exits from the loop; and if the break is in a nested loop, it exits from the innermost loop.
d. All the statements are true.

4. Which is not true about Python quotes?
a. Python recognizes both single quotes(') and double quotes(") as valid ways to delimit a string value.
b. If a single quote marks the beginning of a string value, the single quote must delimit the end of the string.
c. The double quotes if used must appear in pairs.
d. You may mix the quotes while representing a string.

5. If x has the value 10, the statement print('x') will print:
a. 10
b. x
c. It will print both
d. None of these

6. Which is true about the variables?
a. A variable can be reassigned at anytime.
b. A variable must be assigned before it can be used within a program.
c. A variable represents a location in memory capable of storing a value.
d. All of the above.

7. An ________ loop is a loop that executes its block of statements repeatedly until the user forces the program to quit.
a. Infinite
b. Finite
c. Both a and b
d. None of these

8. How many asterisks does the following code fragment print?
```
for a in range(-10, 10):
    print('*', end='')
print()
```
a. 20   b. 0
c. 10   d None of the above

9. How many asterisks does the following code fragment print?
```
for a in range(-10, 10, 5):
    print('*', end='')
print()
```
a. 10   b. 4
c. 20   d None of these

10. What is printed by the following code fragment?
```
a = 0
while a < 4:
    print(a, end='')
    a += 1
print()
```
a. 0123   b. It will display an error
c. 01234   d None of these

11. What is the output of the following?
```
i = 3
while True:
    if i%2 == 0:
        break
    print(i, end=" ")
    i + = 1
```
a. 3   b. 1 2 3
c. error   d None of the above

12. What is the output of the following?
```
i = 1
while True:
    if i%007 == 0:
        break
    print(i, end=" ")
    i += 1
```
a. 1 2 3 4 5 6   b. 1 2 3 4 5 6 7
c. error   d None of the above

13. What is the output of the following?
```
i = 5
while True:
    if i%0011 == 0:
        break
    print(i, end=" ")
    i += 1
```
a. 5 6 7 8 9 10   b. 5 6 7 8
c. 5 6   d error

14. What is the output of the following?

```
i = 1
while True:
    if i%2 == 0:
        break
    print(i, end=" ")
    i += 2
```

a. 1 b. 1 2
c. 1 2 3 4 5 6 d infinite loop

15. What is the output of the following?

```
i = 4
while True:
    if i%3 == 0:
        break
    print(i)
    i += 2
```

a. 2 4 b. 4
c. 2 3 d error

16. What is the output of the following?

```
i = 1
while False:
    if i%2 == 0:
        break
    print(i)
    i += 2
```

a. 1 b. 1 3 5 7
c. 1 2 3 4 d Nothing will be printed

2. State True or False for the following:

1. The break statement is allowed only inside a loop body.
2. There can be zero or more elif parts, and the else part is optional.
3. The keyword elif is short for else if, and is useful to avoid excessive indentation.
4. The elif keyword is Python's way of saying "if the previous conditions were not true, then check this condition".
5. With the while loop, we can execute a set of statements as long as a condition is true.
6. With the break statement, we can stop the loop even if the while condition is true.
7. In general, Python statements are not executed sequentially.
8. A loop statement allows us to execute a statement or group of statements multiple times.
9. Loop control statements change execution from its normal sequence.
10. In Python, like the else, the elif statement is optional.

3. Match the following:

1. The pass statement	a. continues with the next iteration of the loop
2. The break statement	b. nested loop
3. The continue statement	c. used as a placeholder
4. while loop	d. breaks out of for or while loop
5. for loop	e. break and continue
6. An assignment statement	f. tests the condition before executing the loop body
7. Infinite loops	g. executes a sequence of statements multiple times
8. A loop contained with in another loop	h. binds a variable name to an object
9. Jump statements	i. converts string to number
10. int()	j. usually are accidental

4. Fill in the blanks:

1. _______ allows loop termination when some condition is met and the control is transferred to the next statement.
2. _______ enables to skip rest of the current iteration when some specific condition is met and the control is transferred to the beginning of the next iteration.
3. _______ is used when you need some block of code syntactically, but you want to skip its execution.
4. The _______ loop executes as long as the condition remains true.

5. The ______ function returns a sequence of numbers, starting from 0 by default and increments by 1 (by default), and ends at a specified number.
6. If the while condition is initially ______, the body is not executed at all.
7. In an infinite loop, the while condition ______ becomes false.
8. Infinite loops are created by accident and represent _______ errors in their programs.
9. The ______ loop is used for fixed iterations.
10. A while loop is ______ loop.
11. The ______ statement can optionally include an error message string, which gets displayed along with the AssertionError.
12. Python uses the _______ keyword to implement decision control.
13. The _______ statement is simply ignored by the Python interpreter and can be seen as a null statement.
14. In Python, the _______ method returns an immutable sequence of numbers.

Answers

1. 1. c 2. c 3. d 4. d 5. b 6. d
7. a 8. a 9. b 10. a 11 c 12 a
13. b 14. d 15. b 16. d

2. 1. T 2. T 3. T 4. T 5. T 6. T
7. F 8. T 9. T 10. T

3. 1. c 2. d 3. a 4. f 5. g 6. h
7. j 8. b 9. e 10. i

4. 1. break 2. continue
3. pass 4. while
5. range() 6. False
7. Never 8. Logical
9. for 10. Pre-test
11. assert 12. if
13. pass 14. range()

Short Answer Questions

1. What is conditional branching?

Ans In Conditional branching, a program decides whether or not to execute the next statement(s), based on the resultant value of the current expression. For example, go to IInd year if you pass Ist year exams, else repeat Ist year.

2. What is looping?

Ans In looping, a program performs a set of actions or operations repeatedly till the given condition is true. Looping, for example, adds 1 to number x till current value of x becomes 100. It is also called *iteration*. Iteration is a process of executing a statement or a set of statements repeatedly, until the specified condition is true.

3. Explain if statement.

Ans The statement *if* tests a particular condition. Whenever that condition evaluates to *true*, an action or a set of actions is executed. Otherwise, the actions are ignored.

4. Explain range() function.

Ans Python range() function generates a list of numbers, which is generally used to iterate over with for loops.

5. Mention the similarity and difference between *break* and *continue* statements.

Ans **Similarity**: Both *break* and *continue* are jump statements.

Difference: The *break* statement terminates the entire loop body whereas *continue* statement forces the next iteration of the loop to take place, skipping any code following continue statement in the current iteration of the loop.

6. What is the function of *break* statement in a while or for loop?

Ans If the *break* statement is included in the while, or for, loop then control will immediately be transferred out of the loop when the *break* statement is encountered. This provides a convenient way to terminate the loop if an error or other irregular condition is detected.

7. What is the use of Control structures?

Ans Control structures allow us to change the sequence of instructions for execution. They also implement decisions and repetitions in programs.

8. How many types of control structures are there? Explain.

Ans There are mainly two types of control structures. These are:

(a) Conditional Controls: They allow the computer to take decision as to which statement is to be executed next.
(b) Looping: It allows the computer to execute a group of statements repeatedly till the condition is satisfied.

9. Explain Selection logic.

Ans Selection logic, also known as decision logic, is used for making decisions. It is used for selecting the proper path out of the two or more alternative paths in the program logic. It is depicted as either an IF...THEN...ELSE or IF.....THEN structure.

10. Write a program to print the first few numbers in a Fibonacci series.

Ans

```
# Generation of Fibonacci series
number=int(input("Enter no. up to which you want fibonacci series: "))
num1=0;num2=1
print(num1)
print(num2)
for i in range(1,number):
        num3 = num1+num2
        print(num3)
        num1,num2 = num2, num3

RUN
>>>
Enter number up to which you want fibonacci series : 6
0
1
1
2
3
5
8
>>>
```

Figure 1 Program for Q10

11. Write a program to calculate sum of the series.

Ans

```
num= int(input('Enter number : '))
n= int(input('Enter limit: '))
sum= 0
for i in range(1, n+1):
    r= num*i
    sum =sum + r
    print(r,'+' ,end=' ')
    print('Sum of series is', sum)

RUN
>>>
Enter number : 2
Enter limit: 3
2 + Sum of series is 2
4 + Sum of series is 6
6 + Sum of series is 12
>>>
```

Figure 2 Program for Q11

12. Give the output of the following programs:

(a)
```
x=2
if x == 3:
    print("X equals 3.")
elif x == 2:
    print("X equals 2.")
else:
    print ("X equals something else.")
print("This is outside the 'if'.")
```

(b)
```
x = 3
while (x < 10):
    if (x > 7):
        x += 2
        continue
    x = x + 1
    print("Still in the loop.")
    if (x == 8):
        break
print("Outside of the loop.")
```

(c)
```
for x in range(10):
    if x > 7:
        x += 2
        continue
    x = x + 1
    print "Still in the loop."
    if x == 8:
        break
print "Outside of the loop."
```

The outputs of (a), (b) and (c) are as follows:

Ans a

```
>>>
X equals 2.
This is outside the 'if'.
>>>
```

Figure 3 Output for Q12(a)

Ans b

```
>>>
Still in the loop.
Still in the loop.
Still in the loop.
Still in the loop.
Still in the loop.
Outside of the loop.
```

Figure 4 Output for Q12(b)

Ans c

```
>>>
Still in the loop.
Still in the loop.
Still in the loop.
Still in the loop.
Still in the loop.
Still in the loop.
Still in the loop.
Still in the loop.
Outside of the loop.
```

Figure 5 Output for Q12(c)

13. Write a program using while loop that asks the user for a number and prints a countdown from that number to zero. Note: Decide what your program will do, if user enters a negative number.

Ans

```
# Program to print countdown from the entered number to 0
count = 0
number = int(input("Enter the number : "))
if(number < 0):
    print("Number entered below 0. Aborting!")
while(number >= 0):
    count = count +1
    print("The number is ", number)
    number = number - 1

RUN
>>>
Enter the number : 5
The number is  5
The number is  4
The number is  3
The number is  2
The number is  1
The number is  0
>>>
Enter the number : -5
Number entered below 0. Aborting!
>>>
```

Figure 6 Program for Q13

14. Give the output of the following programs:

(a)

```
# Pattern
row = int(input("Enter the number of rows: "))
n = row
while n >= 0:
    x= "*"*n
    print(x)
    n -= 1
```

(b)

```
# Pattern
n = int(input("Enter the number of rows: "))
i=1
while i <= n:
    print("*" * i)
    i += 1
```

(c)

```
# Power Series
x = float(input("Enter the value of x: "))
n = term= num= 1
sum = 1.0
while n <= 100:
    term*= x / n
    sum += term
    n += 1
    if term < 0.0001:
        break
print("No of Times= %d and Sum= %f" % (n, sum))
```

(d)

```
# Fibonacci Series
a,b = 0, 1
while b < 100:
    print(b, end='')
    a, b = b, a + b
```

Ans(a)

```
>>>
Enter the number of rows: 3
***
**
*
>>>
```

Figure 7 Output for Q14(a)

Ans(b)

```
>>>
Enter the number of rows: 3
*
**
***
>>>
```

Figure 8 Output for Q14(b)

Ans(c)

```
>>>
Enter the value of x: 0
No of Times= 2 and Sum= 1.000000
>>>
>>>
Enter the value of x: 0.1
No of Times= 5 and Sum= 1.105171
>>>
```

Figure 9 Output for Q14(c)

Ans(d)

```
>>>
1 1 2 3 5 8 13 21 34 55 89
>>>
```

Figure 10 Output for Q14(d)

15. Give the output of the following programs:

(a)

```
print('A')
print('B')
for i in range(5):
    print('C')
    print('D')
print('E')
```

(b)

```
print('A')
print('B')
for i in range(5):
    print('C')
for i in range(5):
    print('D')
print('E')
```

Ans

```
>>>
A
B
C
D
C
D
C
D
C
D
C
D
E
>>>
```

Figure 11 Output for Q15(a)

Ans

```
>>>
A
B
C
C
C
C
C
D
D
D
D
D
E
>>>
```

Figure 12 Output for Q15(b)

16. Write a program to print all multiples of 13 that are smaller than 100. Use the range function in the following manner: range (start, end, step) where "start" is the starting value of the counter, "end" is the end value and "step" is the integer value by which the counter is increased each time.

Ans

```
# Program to print multiples of 13 smaller than 100
print ("Multiples of 13 are :")
for i in range(13,100,13):
    print(i,end =" ")

RUN
>>>
Multiples of 13 are :
13 26 39 52 65 78 91
>>>
```

Figure 13 Program for Q16

17. Write a program that accepts two numbers from the user to divide if the divisor is 0, it should print message "Division by zero is not allowed".

Ans

```
# Program to print message "Division by zero is not allowed" if divisor is
0

dividend, divisor = eval(input('Please enter two numbers to divide: '))
if divisor != 0:
    print(dividend, '/', divisor, "=", dividend/divisor)
else:
    print('Division by zero is not allowed')

RUN
>>>
Please enter two numbers to divide: 8,2
8 / 2 = 4.0
>>>
Please enter two numbers to divide: 2,8
2 / 8 = 0.25
>>>
Please enter two numbers to divide: 8,0
Division by zero is not allowed
>>>
```

Figure 14 Program for Q17

18. Write a program to enter a number from the keyboard and then print the sum of the digits of the number. It also reverses the number.

Ans

```
#Program to print reverse and sum of digits
sum = 0
rev = 0
number=int(input("Enter a number: "))
n = number
while (number):
    digit = number % 10
    sum += digit
    rev = rev * 10 + digit
    number //= 10
print("Reverse of number is : ",rev)
print ("Sum of digits of the number is : ",sum)

RUN
>>>
Enter a number: 759
Reverse of number is :  957
Sum of digits of the number is :  21
>>>
```

Figure 15 Program for Q18

19. Write a program to input an integer and print whether it is negative, zero, single or more, using if-elif-else statement.
x< 0 Negative, x == 0 'Zero', x == 1 'Single', else display 'More'.

Ans

```
x = int(input("Please enter an integer: "))
if x< 0:
    print('Negative')
elif x == 0:
    print('Zero')
elif x == 1:
    print('Single')
else:
    print('More')

RUN
>>>
Please enter an integer: -5
Negative
>>>
```

Figure 16 Program for Q19

20. Write a program to print multiplication Table up to 10.

Ans

```
# Multiplication Table up to 10
i=1
print("-" * 50)
while i < 11:
    n = 1
    while n <= 10:
        print("%4d" % (i * n), end=' ')
        n += 1
        print()
    i +=1
    print("-" * 50)
```

Figure 17 Program for Q20

21. How many asterisks do the following code fragments print?

Ans

```
x = 0
while x < 5:
    print('*', end='')
    x += 1
print()

RUN
>>>
*****
>>>
```

```
x = 0
while x < 5:
    print('*', end='')
print()
RUN
>>>
infinite * will be
printed
>>>
```

```
x = 0
while x > 5:
    print('*', end='')
    x += 1
print()

RUN
>>>
No * will be printed
>>>
```

Figure 18 Program for Q21

22. Write the output of the following code fragments:

Ans

```
i = 1
while True:
    if i%3 == 0:
        break
    print(i)
    i += 1

RUN
>>>
1
2
>>>
```

```
for i in [1, 2, 3, 4][::-1]:
    print (i)

RUN
>>>
4
3
2
1
>>>
```

```
i = 5
while True:
    if i% 10 == 0:
        break
    print(i)
    i += 1

RUN
>>>
5
6
7
8
9
>>>
```

Figure 19 Program for Q22

23. How many times are the following loops executed?

Ans

```
i = 1
while True:
    if i%2 == 0:
        break
    print(i)
    i += 2

RUN
>>>
Infinite loop
>>>
```

```
i=100
while(i<=200):
    print(i)
    i+=40

RUN
>>>
3 times
>>>
```

```
i = 20
while i < 50:
    print(i)
    i += 5

RUN
>>>
6 times
>>>
```

Figure 20 Program for Q23

24. Write a program to display menu to calculate area or perimeter of a circle.

Ans

```
# Program to calculate area or perimeter of a circle
radius = float(input("Enter radius of a circle : "))
print("1. Calculate area of a circle ")
print("2. Calculate perimeter of a circle")
choice = int(input("Enter your choice (1 or 2): "))
if (choice == 1):
    area = 3.14 * radius * radius
    print("Area of a circle is :", area)
else:
    peri = 2 *3.14* radius
    print("Perimeter of a circle is : ",peri)

RUN
>>>
Enter radius of a circle : 3.5
1. Calculate area of a circle
2. Calculate perimeter of a circle
Enter your choice (1 or 2): 1
Area of a circle is : 38.465
>>>
```

(Conti...)

```
>>>
Enter radius of a circle : 3.5
1. Calculate area of a circle
2. Calculate perimeter of a circle
Enter your choice (1 or 2): 2
Perimeter of a circle is :  21.98
>>>
```

Figure 21 Program for Q24

25. Write a program to display menu to calculate Volume or Surface area of a sphere.

Ans

```
# Program to calculate Volume or Surface area of a sphere
radius = float(input("Enter radius of a circle : "))
print("1.Calculate Surface area of a sphere ")
print("2 Calculate Volume of a sphere ")
choice = int(input("Enter your choice (1 or 2): "))
if (choice == 1):
    surface_area = 4 * 3.14 * radius * radius
    print("Surface Area of a sphere is :", surface_area)
else:
    volume = (4/3 *(3.14 * radius * radius * radius))
    print("Volume of a sphere: ",volume)
>>>
Enter radius of a circle : 2.5
1.Calculate Surface area of a sphere
2 Calculate Volume of a sphere
Enter your choice (1 or 2): 1
Surface Area of a sphere is : 78.5
>>>
Enter radius of a circle : 2.5
1.Calculate Surface area of a sphere
2 Calculate Volume of a sphere
Enter your choice (1 or 2): 2
Volume of a sphere:  65.41666666666666
>>>
```

Figure 22 Program for Q25

26. Write a program to print numbers in descending order.

Ans

```
# Program to print numbers in descending order
num1 = int(input("Enter first number: "))
num2 = int(input("Enter second number: "))
num3 = int(input("Enter third number: "))
if num1 > num2 and num1 > num3:
    if num2 > num3:
        x, y, z = num1, num2, num3
    else:
        x, y, z = num1, num3, num2
elif num2 > num1 and num2 > num3:
    if num1 > num3:
        x, y, z = num2, num1, num3
    else:
```

(Contd...)

```
        x, y, z = num2, num3, num1
else:
    if num1>num2:
        x, y, z = num3, num1, num2
    else:
         x, y, z = num3, num2, num1
print("Numbers in descending order are: ", x,y,z)

RUN
>>>
Enter first number: 27
Enter second number: 25
Enter third number: 45
Numbers in descending order are:  45 27 25
>>>
```

Figure 23 Program for Q26

27. Write a program to print if the year is a leap year or not.

Ans

```
# Program to print if the year is leap or not
year=int(input("Enter 4-digit year : "))
if(year%4==0 and year%100!=0 or year%400==0):
    print(year, "is a leap year!")
else:
    print(year, "is not a leap year!")
RUN
>>>
Enter 4-digit year : 2016
2016 is a leap year!
>>>
Enter 4-digit year : 1900
1900 is not a leap year!
>>>
```

Figure 24 Program for Q27

28. Write a program to count the number of Digits in entered Number.

Ans

```
# Program to count the number of digits in entered Number
num=int(input("Enter number:"))
count=0
while(num>0):
    count=count+1
    num=num//10
print("The number of digits in the number are:",count)

RUN
>>>
Enter number:573
The number of digits in the number are: 3
>>>
Enter number:8854
The number of digits in the number are: 4
>>>
```

Figure 25 Program for Q28

29. Write a program to check whether the entered number is palindrome or not.

Ans

```
# Program to check number is palindrome or not
num = int(input("Enter a number: "))
rev_num = 0
temp = num
while temp > 0:
    rev_num = rev_num*10 + (temp%10)
    temp = temp//10
if num == rev_num:
    print(num,"is a palindrome.")
else:
    print(num,"is not a palindrome.")

RUN
>>>
Enter a number: 1331
1331 is a palindrome.
>>>
```

Figure 26 Program for Q29

30. Write a program to check whether the entered number is buzz number or not. A number is said to be Buzz number if it ends with 7 or is divisible by 7.

Ans

```
#Program to check whether a number is buzz or not
num =int(input("Enter number to be checked for Buzz: "))
if(num % 10 == 7 or num % 7 == 0):
    print(num, "is a Buzz Number")
else:
   print(num, "is not a Buzz Number")
RUN
>>>
Enter number to be checked for Buzz: 63
63 is a Buzz Number
>>>
>>>
Enter number to be checked for Buzz: 65
65 is not a Buzz Number
>>>
```

Figure 27 Program for Q30

31. Write a program to input principal amount, rate and time, and calculate the compound interest and amount after each year.

Ans

```
# Program to calculate the compound interest and amt after each year
p= int(input( "Enter Principal Amount : "))
r= int(input( "Enter Rate of interest : "))
t= int(input( "Enter Time period : "))
for i in range (1,t+1):
    interest= (p*r*1)/100
    p= p+ interest
    print  ("After ",i, " Year ", " Interest = ",interest, "Amount = ",p)
```

(Conti...)

```
RUN
>>>
Enter Principal Amount  : 5000
Enter Rate of interest  : 7
Enter Time period : 3
After  1  Year   Interest =  350.0 Amount =  5350.0
After  2  Year   Interest =  374.5 Amount =  5724.5
After  3  Year   Interest =  400.715 Amount =  6125.215
>>>
```

Figure 28 Program for Q31

32. Write a program to input a number and check whether it is an armstrong number or not. An Armstrong number is a number such that the sum of its digits raised to the power three is equal to the number itself. For example, 371 is an Armstrong number since 3**3 + 7**3 + 1**3 = 371.

Ans

```
# Program to input a no and check armstrong no or not.
num = int(input("Enter a number :"))
sum=0
temp= num
while temp>0:
    digit = temp % 10
    sum += digit**3
    temp //=10
if  num == sum:
    print (num, "is Armstrong no.")
else:
    print (num, "is not Armstrong no.")

RUN
>>>
Enter a number :371
371 is Armstrong no.
>>>
```

Figure 29 Program for Q32

33. Write a Python program to find the factors of entered number x.

Ans

```
# Program to find the factors of a number x
x= int(input("Enter  a number:"))
print("The factors of",x,"are:")
for i in range(1, x + 1):
       if x % i == 0:
           print(i)
RUN
>>>
Enter  a number:25
The factors of 25 are:
1
5
25
>>>
```

Figure 30 Program for Q33

34. Write the output for the following:

Ans

```
n = 5
while n > 0:
    print(n)
    n = n - 1
print('Done!')

RUN
>>>
5
4
3
2
1
Done!
>>>
```

Figure 31 Program and output for Q34

35. What is the output of the following?

Ans

```
i = 0
while i < 7:
     print(i, end= " ")
    i += 1
    if i == 4:
        break
else:
    print(0)

RUN
>>>
0 1 2 3
>>>
```

```
i = 1
while False:
    if i%2 == 0:
        break
    print(i)
    i += 2

RUN
>>>
Nothing will be printed
>>>
```

```
i = 0
while i < 5:
    print(i, end= " ")
    i += 2
else:
    print(0)

RUN
>>>
0 2 4 0
>>>
```

Figure 32 Program for Q35

36. Write the output of the following codes:

(a)

```
if (5 > 0) and (0 > -5):
    print("I")
elif (5 < 0) or True:
    print("love")
else:
    print("INDIA")
```

Ans I

(b)

```
if (5 < 0) and (0 < -5):
    print("I")
elif (5 > 0) or False:
    print("love")
else:
    print("INDIA")
```

Ans love

```
(c) if (8 < 2) and (2 > 5):
        print("I")
    elif (5 > 7) or False:
        print("love")
    else:
        print("INDIA")
```

Ans INDIA

37. What do you mean by flow-of-control?

Ans The flow-of-control of a program is the order in which the statements are executed one after the other sequentially.

38. What do you mean by selection statements?

Ans In some programs, you may need to change the sequence of execution of instructions according to specified conditions. This is done by selection statements.

39. What is the minimum number of iteration that *while* loop could make?

Ans *while* loop could make 0 iteration.

40. What is the difference between entry-controlled loop and exit-controlled loop?

Ans In an entry-controlled loop, the loop control condition is evaluated at the entry point of the loop. However, in an exit-controlled loop, the loop control condition is evaluated at the exit point of the loop.

If the loop control condition is false in the beginning, the entry-controlled loop is never executed. However, the exit-controlled loop would be executed at least once.

41. What are jump statements?

Ans Jump statements are the statements that allow us to transfer control to another part of our program.

42. What is Iteration?

Ans It is a process of executing a statement or a set of statements repeatedly, until the specified condition is true.

EXERCISE

1. What is selection statement? Explain with an example.
2. Explain the difference between selection and repetition.
3. What do you mean by finite and infinite loops?
4. What is the purpose of pass statement?
5. Explain if-else statement with an example.
6. Write a single *if* statement that examines two integer variables and changes the larger to the smaller, using only one *else* clause.
7. State various loop control structures supported by Python and compare them with one another.
8. State the use of the following statements, giving an example of each.
   (a) break (b) continue (c) pass
9. Name the types of jump statements.
10. What is the significance of range() function?
11. Write python code for the following:
    (a) Find the roots of the quadratic equation given below:
    $ax^2 + bx + c = 0$
    (b) Determine the simple interest using the formula:
    $$SI = \frac{PRT}{100}$$
    where SI = Simple Interest, T = Period in years, R = Rate of interest per year, P = Principal amount taken on loan.
    (c) Determine the compound interest using the formula:
    CI = P*((1+R/N)**(N*T)) where CI = Compound Interest, T = Period in year, R = Rate of interest per year,
    N = Number of times the interest is compounded per year
    P = Principal amount taken on loan.
12. Define the following terms:
    (a) Selection
    (b) Iteration
13. What do you mean by looping control in a program? Explain the different terms which are used in looping.
14. Write the syntax of *while* loop.
15. Why is an if statement used in Python programming?
16. What is the difference between *for* loop and *while* loop?
17. What is nested loop?
18. Explain looping with the help of an example.

LAB EXERCISE

1. Write a program in Python to compute a sales person's commission based on the following table:

Amount of Sales	Commission Rate (% of sales)
Less than Rs. 500	2%
Rs. 500 or more, but less than Rs. 5000	5%
Rs. 5000 and above	10%

2. Write a program to print first 100 prime numbers using *while* loop.
3. Salesman's commission is calculated using the following Pseudocode. Use this for writing a program in Python.

   Input sales
   IF sales < 1500
   THEN
      Commission = 2% of sales
   ELSE
      Commission = 5% of sales
   END IF
   Print Commission

4. Write a program to find the sum of odd and even numbers between 1 and 100.
5. Write a program in Python to calculate volume and surface area of a sphere. Make the program as general as possible.
6. Write an appropriate control structure that will examine value of a floating point variable called temp and print one of the following messages, depending on the value assigned to temp:
   (a) ICE, if the value of temp is less than or equal to zero.
   (b) WATER, if the value of temp is > 0 and < 100.
   (c) STEAM, if the value of temp is equal to or exceeds 100.
7. Write a program to input a digit and print it in words.
8. Write a program to input three angles and check if it forms a triangle or not.
9. Write a program to input number N, and then check whether the number is Automorphic number or not. A number is called Automorphic number if its square ends with the same digits as the number itself. For example:
   Input : N = 25
   Output : Automorphic as 25*25 = 625
10. Write a program to input numbers and print Highest Common factor.
11. Write the output of the following programs:

a)

```
sub1=int(input("Enter marks of the first subject: "))
sub2=int(input("Enter marks of the second subject: "))
sub3=int(input("Enter marks of the third subject: "))
sub4=int(input("Enter marks of the fourth subject: "))
sub5=int(input("Enter marks of the fifth subject: "))
avg=(sub1+sub2+sub3+sub4+sub4)/5
if(avg>=90):
    print("Grade: A")
elif(avg>=80&avg<90):
    print("Grade: B")
elif(avg>=70&avg<80):
    print("Grade: C")
elif(avg>=60&avg<70):
    print("Grade: D")
else:
    print("Grade: F")
```

Figure 33 Program for Q11(a)

b)

```
# Program to print all numbers in a range divisible by a given number
lower=int(input("Enter lower range limit:"))
upper=int(input("Enter upper range limit:"))
num=int(input("Enter the number to be divided by:"))
for i in range(lower,upper+1):
    if(i%num==0):
        print(i)
```

Figure 34 Program for Q11(b)

c)

```
#  Program to check if a number is a Perfect number.
num = int(input("Enter any number: "))
sum1 = 0
for i in range(1, num):
    if(num % i == 0):
        sum1 = sum1 + i
if (sum1 == num):
    print("The number is a Perfect number!")
else:
    print("The number is not a Perfect number!")
```

Figure 35 Program for Q11(c)

d)

```
#Program to find whether a number is prime or composite number
num = int(input("Enter any number : "))
if num > 1:
    for i in range(2, num):
        if (num % i) == 0:
            print(num, "is NOT a prime number")
            break
    else:
        print(num, "is a PRIME number")
elif num == 0 or 1:
    print(num, "is a neither prime NOR composite number")
else:
    print(num, "is NOT a prime number it is a COMPOSITE number")
```

Figure 36 Program for Q11(d)

e)

```
num=int(input("Enter a number: "))
temp=str(num)
t1=temp+temp
t2=temp+temp+temp
compute=num+int(t1)+int(t2)
print("The value is:",compute)
```

Figure 37 Program for Q11(e)

f)

```
#Program to find the sum of series: 1 + 1/2 + 1/3 + ... + 1/N.
n=int(input("Enter the number of terms:"))
x=int(input("Enter the value of x:"))
sum1=1
for i in range(2,n+1):
    sum1=sum1+((x**i)/i)
print("The sum of series is",round(sum1,2))
```

Figure 38 Program for Q11(f)

g)

```
#Nested loop to print the pattern
i = 1
while(i<=5):
    j=1
    while(j<=i):
        print(j,end =" ")
        j = j+1
    print()
    i = i +1
```

Figure 39 Program for Q11(g)

h)

```
# Nested loop
i = 1
while(i<=5):
    j=1
    while(j<=i):
        print("*",end =" " )
        j = j+1
    print()
    i = i +1
```

Figure 40 Program for Q11(h)

i)

```
i = 11
while i> 1 :
  if (i % 2 == 0):
    x = i%2
    i = i-1
  else:
    i = i-2
    x = i
    print(x**2)
```

```
i = 20
while i < 50:
    print(i)
    i += 5
```

```
i = 1
while True:
    if i%3 == 0:
        break
    print(i)
    i += 1
```

Figure 41 Program for Q11(i)

12. Write the output of the following Python codes fragments:

```
n=30
i=5
s=0
while i<n:
    s+=i
    i+=5
print("i=",i)
print("sum=",s)
```

```
sum = 0
for i in range(16,2,-2):
    sum+=i
print (sum)
```

```
while(i<=200):
    print(i)
    i+=40
```

Figure 42 Program for Q12

13. Write the output of the following Python codes fragments:

```
for i in range(1, 6):
    for j in range(i):
     print(i, end=' ')
    print()
```

```
for x in range(100, 200):
    if (x%7==0) and (x%5==0):
        print (x)
```

Figure 43 Program for Q13

14. Write the output of the following Python codes fragments:

```
#Program to print Fibonacci series of
first 8 elements.
a,b=0,1
print(a,b,end=' ')
for x in range(3,9):
    c=a+b
    print(c,end=' ')
    a,b=b,c
```

```
for i in range(0,12,2):
    print(i,"#", end=' ')
```

Figure 44 Program for Q14

15. Rewrite the following Python program after removing all the syntactical errors (if any), underlining each correction:

```
x = int(input("Enter a number "))
if (x%2 =0):
    print(x,"is  even")
elif x<0 :
    print(x,"should be positive")
else ;
    print(x,"is odd")
```

Figure 45 Program for Q15

CHAPTER 6

Strings in Python

6.1 SEQUENCE DATA TYPES

A sequence is an ordered collection of items, indexed by positive integers. It is a combination of mutable (a mutable variable is one, whose value may change) and immutable (an immutable variable is one, whose value may not change) data types. There are three types of sequences available in Python; they are Strings, Lists and Tuples. They share much of the same syntax and functionality.
String is an ordered sequence of letters/characters. For example, your name can be considered a string. Strings are defined using quotes - single quotes (' '), double quotes (" ") or triple quotes (""""). List is also a sequence of values of any type. Lists are defined using square brackets and commas. Tuples are a sequence of values of any type and are indexed by integers. They are defined using parentheses (and commas). You can access individual members of a string, list or tuple using square bracket "array" notation. We will cover Sequence Data Types – List and Tuple in Chapters 7 and 8, respectively.

6.2 STRING

A string is a sequence of one or more characters (letters, numbers, symbols) that can be either a constant or a variable. Strings are the form of data used in programming for storing and manipulating text, such as words, names and sentences. They are immutable data types, i.e., they are unchanging. You can write them in Python using single quotes, double quotes, or triple quotes. The quotes are not part of string. They only tell the computer where the string constant begins and ends. String literals are written by enclosing a sequence of characters in single quotes ('hello'), double quotes ("hello") or triple quotes ('''hello''' or """hello"""). Strings are objects of Python's built-in class 'str'.

☞ *A string value is a collection of one or more characters put in single, double or triple quotes.*

6.2.1 Creating String

To create a string, put the sequence of characters inside single quotes, double quotes, or triple quotes and then assign it to a variable. The single quotes and double quotes work in the same manner for the string creation. Triple quotes can be used in Python to represent multiline strings and docstrings.
To store a string inside a variable, you simply need to assign a string to a variable (See Figure 6.1 and Figure 6.2). Following examples show different ways to initialize strings:

Example 1 –Different ways of string initialization.

```
# Python string examples - all assignments are identical

my_str1 = 'This is a string in single quotes'
my_str2 = "This is a string in double quotes"
my_str3 = """This is a string in triple quotes"""

# With triple quotes strings can extend to multiple lines
String_var = """ This section will help you to
explore all the concepts
of Python Strings """
```

Figure 6.1 Different ways of string Initialization

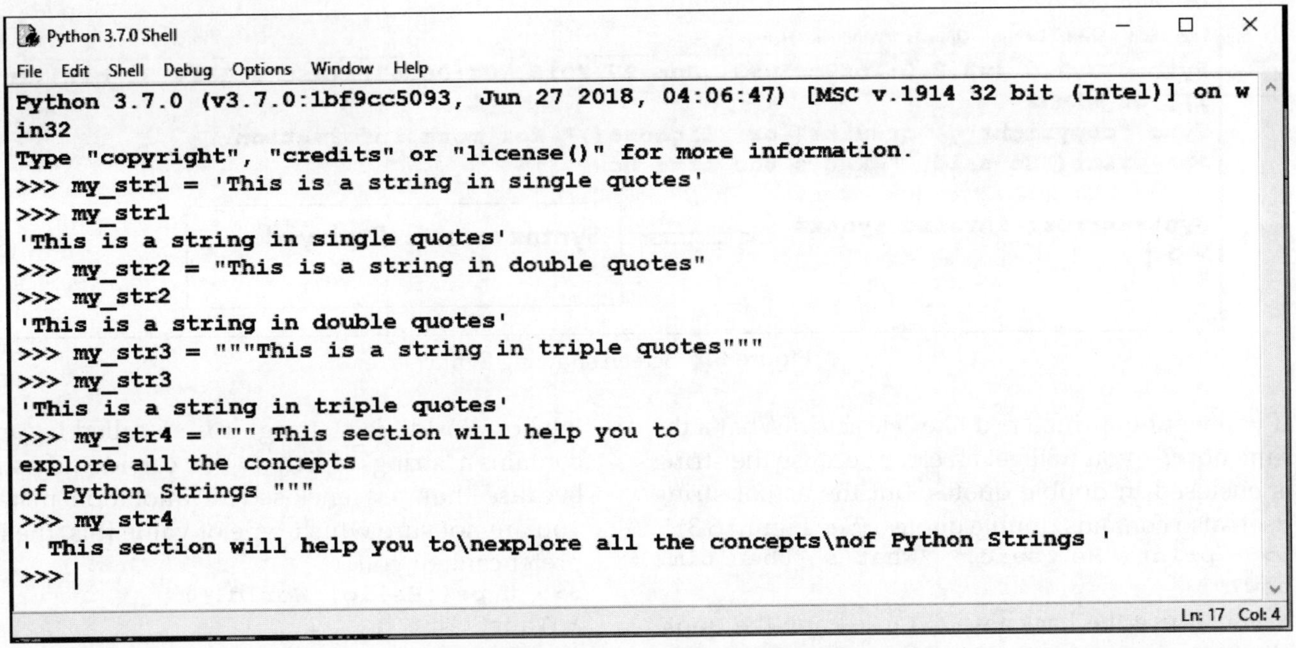

Figure 6.2 String creation with output

Single Quotes

You can write strings using single quotes, such as 'This is a string in single quotes.'. They can have any character or sign, including space in them.

Double Quotes

Strings in double quotes work in the same manner as strings in single quotes. For example, "This is a string in double quotes.", "What's the time now?" etc.

Triple Quotes

You can write multi-line strings using triple quotes (""""). You can also use single quotes and double quotes within the triple quotes. For example,

```
'''This is a multi-line string. This is
the first line.
This is the second line. "What's the
time now?", I asked.
He said, "It's quarter to three."
'''
```

Docstrings

Python has a feature called documentation strings, usually referred to by its short name, docstrings. Docstring is an important tool that helps document the program better and makes it easier to understand.

6.3 LOGICAL AND PHYSICAL LINE

A physical line is what you see when you write the program. A logical line is what Python sees as a single statement. Python implicitly assumes that each physical line corresponds to the logical line. An example of the logical line is a statement like print("Hello World") – if this is on a line by itself (as you see it in an editor), then this also comply with to a physical line.

Implicitly, Python encourages the use of a single statement per line which makes code more readable.

If you have a long line of code, you can break it into multiple physical lines by using the backslash (\). The backslash in the string makes the string continue on the next line without a newline. This is referred to as explicit line joining. For example,

```
s = 'This is a string. \
This continues the string.'
print(s)
```

This gives the output:

```
This is a string. This continues the
string.
```

Note that even though text is written in two lines the text is considered continuous.

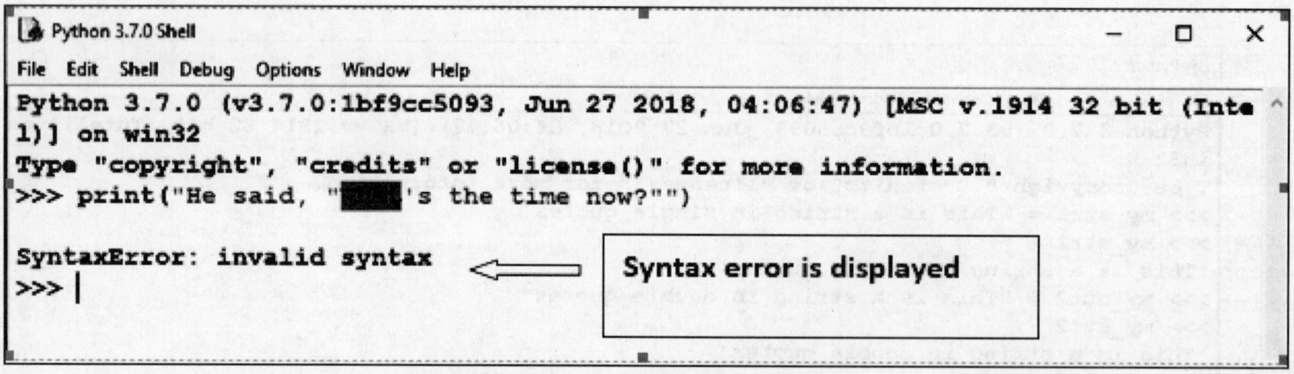

Figure 6.3 Screen showing Syntax error

If you want to print a text like "He said, "What's the time now?"" you will get an error because the string is enclosed in double quotes, but the actual string itself also contains double quotes. (See Figure 6.3).

```
>>> print("He said, "What's the time now?"")
```

You can use the backslash (\) to escape the quote characters within the string. You can insert double quotes and single quotes inside a string by using escape sequence backslash(\) character. An escape sequence starts with a backslash and is interpreted differently. If you use single quote to represent a string, all the single quotes inside the string must be escaped. Similar is the case with double quotes. So you can change the above code as this:

```
>>> print("He said, \"What's the time now?\"")
He said, "What's the time now?"
>>> print('He said, "What\'s the time now?"')
He said,"What's the time now?"
```

Just as you used the backslash to escape the double quotes, you can use an escape sequence '\n' to force a string to span multiple lines.

```
>>> print("This is printed\nin two lines")
This is printed
in two lines
```

6.4 WORKING WITH STRINGS

String is an ordered sequence of letters/characters. It is enclosed in single (′′) or double (" ") or triple quotation(′′′) marks. The quotes are not a part of string. They only tell the computer where the string constant begins and ends. They can have any character or sign, including space in between them.

'Hello, World!' is a string; it is so-called because it contains a 'string' of letters. You can identify strings because they are enclosed in quotation marks. If you are not sure which type of value it is, the interpreter can tell you.

```
>>> type('Hello, World!')
<class 'str'>
```

It is possible to change one type of value/variable to another type. It is known as *type conversion* or *typecasting*. The conversion can be done explicitly (programmer specifies the conversion) or implicitly (interpreter automatically converts the data type).

An empty string contains no characters and has length 0, represented by two quotation marks. The string with length 1 represents a character in Python. For example 'a', 'b', 'c' are strings of length one.

In general, you cannot perform mathematical operations on strings, even if the strings look like numbers. So, the following are invalid:

```
'8'-'2'
'apples'/'easy'
'third'*'first'
```

If you need to store numbers that may have calculations performed on them, do not make them a string. There's a difference between the following two declarations:

```
a = 1
a = "1"
```

In the first line, the value 1 is a number. In the second line, it's a string.

The + operator works with strings, but it might not do what you expect; it performs concatenation, which means joining the strings by linking them end-to-end. For example:

str	P	Y	T	H	O	N
Positive index	0	1	2	3	4	5
Negative index	-6	-5	-4	-3	-2	-1

Figure 6.4 Structure of PYTHON str

```
first = 'Lakhan'
second = 'lal'
print(first + second)
```

The output of this program is Lakhanlal.

The * operator also works on strings; it performs repetition. For example, 'Save'*3 is 'SaveSaveSave'. If one of the operands is a string, the other has to be an integer.

This use of + and * makes sense by analogy with addition and multiplication. Just as 4*3 is equivalent to 4+4+4, you expect 'Save'*3 to be the same as 'Save'+'Save'+'Save'. The plus (+) sign is the string concatenation operator, and the asterisk (*) is the repetition operator.

The string is a sequence of characters. You can access the characters one at a time with the bracket operator. An individual character in a string is accessed using a subscript (index). The subscript should always be an integer (positive or negative). It starts with 0. To access the first character of the string, consider the following:

```
>>> str = 'PYTHON'
>>> print(str[0])
P
```

☞ *String indices are zero-based, i.e., the first character in a string has index 0.*

The second statement selects character at number 0 from str and prints the character P. The expression in square brackets is called an *index*. The index indicates which character in the sequence you want.

Index is an offset from the beginning of the string, and the offset of the first letter is zero. To access the second character of the string, consider the following:

```
>>> print(str[1])
Y
```

You can use any expression, including variables and operators, as an index, but the value of the index has to be an integer. If you try to access index out of the range or use decimal number, you will get errors.

```
>>> print(str[8])
IndexError: string index out of range
>>> print(str[1.5])
TypeError: string indices must be integers
```

Alternatively, you can use negative indices, which count backward, i.e., from the end of the string to the beginning. The expression str[-1] yields the last letter, str[-2] yields the second last letter, and so on.

To access the last character of the string, consider the following:

```
>>> print(str[-1])
N
```

To access the third last character of the string, consider the following:

```
>>> print(str[-3])
H
```

Strings in Python are stored by placing each character separately in contiguous locations as shown in Figure 6.4.

The index, also called *subscript*, is the numbered position of letter in the string. In Python, indices begin from 0 onwards in the forward direction also called positive index, and from -1, -2, and so on in the backward direction, also called negative index. Positive subscript helps in accessing the string from the beginning. Negative subscript helps in accessing the string from the end.

☞ *The index is the numbered position of an alphabet in the given string.*

You can access any character using <stringname>[<index>]. Index 0 or -ve n (where, n is length of the string) displays the first element.

For example : str[0] or str[-6] will display the first element 'P'.

Subscript 1 or -ve (n-1) displays the second element.

For example : str[1] or str[-5] will display the second element 'Y'.

The built-in function len() returns the length of a string:

```
>>> str = "PYTHON"
>>> len(str)
6
```

Since length of string variable can be determined using len(<string>), you can say that:

(a) The first character of the string is at index 0 or -length. So in example given in Figure 6.4, at index 0 or -6, character stored is **P**.

(b) The second character of the string is at index 1 or -(length-1). So in example given in Figure 6.4, at index 1 or -(6-1)= -5, character stored is **Y**.

(c) The second last character of the string is at index (length-2) or -2. So in example given in Figure 6.4, at index (6-2)= 4 or -2, character stored is **O**.

(d) The last character of the string is at index (length-1) or -1. So in example given in Figure 6.4, at index (6-1)= 5 or -1, character stored is **N**.

Let's Try

Write the output of the following code segments:

>>> name = 'Abhishek' **>>> letter = name[1]**	**>>> name = 'Abhishek'** **>>> letter = name[1.5]** **>>> print(letter)**

Example 2 – **Accessing Python String items.**

```
# Access Python String items
x = 'BPB PUBLICATIONS'
# Positive Indexing
print(x[0])
print(x[1])
print(x[2])

# Negative Indexing
print(x[-1])
print(x[-2])
print(x[-3])

RUN
>>>
B
P
B

S
N
O
>>>
```

Figure 6.5 Program for accessing string

6.4.1 Strings are Immutable

Strings are immutable means that the contents of the string variable cannot be changed after it is created. Let us understand the concept of immutability with the help of an example.

```
>>> greeting = 'Hello, world!'
>>> greeting[0] = 'J'
TypeError:'str' object does not support
item assignment
```

The *object* in this case is the string, and the *item* is the character you tried to assign. Python does not allow the programmer to change a character in a string. As shown in the above example, greeting has the value 'Hello, world!'. An attempt to replace 'H' in the string by 'J' displays a TypeError.

The reason for the error is that strings are immutable, which means you cannot change an existing string. The best you can do is create a new string that is a variation on the original:

```
>>> greeting = 'Hello, world!'
>>> new_greeting = 'J' + greeting[1:]
>>> print (new_greeting)
Jello, world!
```

This example concatenates a new first letter to a slice (a part of a string specified by a range of indices) of greeting. It has no effect on the original string. You will study string slice later in this chapter. Python strings cannot be changed. Assigning a character to an indexed position in the string results in an error.

☞ *A segment of a string is called a slice. Selecting a slice is similar to selecting a character.*

You cannot delete or remove characters from a string. This will cause an error because item assignment or item deletion from a string is not supported. Although deletion of entire string is possible with the use of a built-in del keyword.

```
>>> my_string = 'Hello'
>>> my_string
'Hello'
>>> del my_string
```

Further, if you try to print the string, this will produce an error-`"NameError: name 'my_string' is not defined"` because String is deleted and is unavailable to be printed.

```
>>> my_string
```

You can assign string to another string or an expression that returns a string using assignment. For example,

```
>>> str1 = 'Teena'
```

6.4.2 Traversing a String

Traversing a string means accessing all the elements of the string one after the other by using the subscript or index. The string can be traversed character-by-character using for loop or while loop. Example 3 demonstrates string traversal using for loop. In this program, each character of string "PYTHON" will be accessed one-by-one. In the each iteration of for loop, the next character in the string str is assigned to the variable, i. The loop continues until no character is left.

Example 3 –**String traversal using for loop.**

```
# String traversal using for loop
str = "PYTHON"
for i in str:
    print(i)

RUN
>>>
P
Y
T
H
O
N
>>>
```

Figure 6.6 Program for String Traversal Using for Loop

Example 4 –**String traversal using while loop.**

```
# String traversal using while loop
str = "PYTHON"
i=0
while i < len(str):
    print(str[i])
    i = i+1
```

(Conti...)

```
RUN
>>>
P
Y
T
H
O
N
>>>
```

Figure 6.7 Program for String Traversal Using while Loop

The while loop traverses the string and displays each letter on a line by itself. The loop condition is i < len(str); so when i is equal to the length of the string, the condition becomes false, and the body of the loop is not executed. (See Figure 6.7).

Example 5 –**Finding the length of entered string.**

```
# Program to find the length of entered string
while True:
    s = input('Enter something : ')
    if s == 'quit':
        break
    print('Length of the string is', len(s))
print('Done')

RUN
>>>
Enter something : Hello PYTHON
Length of the string is 12
Enter something : WELCOME
Length of the string is 7
Enter something : quit
Done
>>>
```

Figure 6.8 Program for Finding Length of String

In this program, you repeatedly take the user's input and print the length of each input. You are providing a special condition to stop the program by checking if the user input is 'quit'. If it is so, stop the program by breaking out of the loop and reach the end of the program. The length of the input string can be found out using the built-in len() function. (See Figure 6.8).

Example 6 –**Program to check length of a string with suitable message.**

```
# Program to check length of a string with suitable message
while True:
    s = input('Enter something : ')
    if s == 'quit':
        break
```

(Conti...)

```
    if len(s) < 3:
        print('Too small')
        continue
    print('Input is of sufficient length')

RUN
>>>
Enter something : C
Too small
Enter something : Ca
Too small
Enter something : Cat
Input is of sufficient length
Enter something : Elephant
Input is of sufficient length
Enter something : quit
>>>
```

Figure 6.9 Program to Check Length of a String

In this program, you accept input from the user, but you process the input string only if it is at least 3 characters long. So, you use the built-in len() function to get the length and if the length is less than 3, you skip the rest of the statements in the loop by using the continue statement. Otherwise, the rest of the statements in the loop are executed, doing any kind of processing you want to do here. (See Figure 6.9).

Example 7 –**Program to replace character in a string with a symbol.**

```
# Python program to replace character in a string with a symbol
input_string = str(input("Enter a string : "))
st=input("Enter a character you want to change in the entered string : ")
symbol = input("Enter the symbol you want to replace with : ")
changed_str = input_string.replace(st,symbol)
print("Modified String is : ",changed_str)

RUN
>>>
Enter a string : Hello
Enter a character you want to change in the entered string : e
Enter the symbol you want to replace with : @
Modified String is :  H@llo
>>>
```

Figure 6.10 Program to Replace Character in a String with a Symbol

Example 8 –**Program which accepts a string as input and prints "Yes" if the string is "yes" or "YES" or "Yes", otherwise prints "No".**

```
# Program which accepts a string as input and print "Yes" or "No"
input_string = str(input("Enter a string : "))
```

(Conti...)

```
if input_string=="yes" or input_string=="YES" or input_string=="Yes":
    print("Yes")
else:
    print ("No")

RUN
>>>
Enter a string : yes
Yes
>>>

>>>
Enter a string : Hello
No
>>>
```

Figure 6.11 Program which Accepts a String as Input to print "Yes" or "No"

String Formatting

String formatting syntax has changed from Python 2 to Python 3.
Python 2 "%d %s" % (i, s)
Python 3 "{} {}".format(i, s)
Python 2 "%d/%d=%f" % (355, 113, 355/113)
Python 3 "{:d}/{:d}={:f}".format(355, 113, 355/113)
For example,

```
>>> "{} comes before {}".format('a','b')
'a comes before b'
```

```
num1 = int(input("Enter first number: "))
num2 = int(input("Enter second number: "))
product = num1 * num2
print('The product of', num1, 'and', num2, 'is', product)

RUN
>>>
Enter first number: 5
Enter second number: 8
The product of 5 and 8 is 40
>>>
```

But program shown above is cumbersome. To accomplish the same thing, specify any variables to be interpolated in curly braces ({}). Specify either a lowercase f or uppercase F directly before the opening quote of the string literal. This tells Python it is an f-string instead of a standard string. (See Figure 6.12).

```
num1 = int(input("Enter first number: "))
num2 = int(input("Enter second number: "))
product = num1 * num2
print(f'The product of {num1} and {num2} is {product}')
```

(Conti...)

```
RUN
>>>
Enter first number: 5
Enter second number: 8
The product of 5 and 8 is 40
>>>
```

Figure 6.12 String formatting

The format() is one of the string formatting methods in Python3, which allows multiple substitutions and value formatting. Format string contains curly braces {} as placeholders or replacement fields which get replaced. It is separated from field name using colon(:). For example, you can left-justify <, right-justify > or center ^ a string in the given space. You can also format integers as binary, hexadecimal etc, and floats can be rounded or displayed in the exponent format. You can use positional arguments or keyword arguments to specify the order. Figure 6.13 demonstrates different ways of string formatting.

Example 9 –**Program for formatting of string.**

```
# Program for formatting of strings

# Default order
str1 = "{} {} {}".format('Work', 'Is', 'Worship')
print("String in default order: ")
print(str1)

# Positional Formatting
str1 = "{1} {0} {2}".format('Work', 'Is', 'Worship')
print("\nString in Positional order: ")
print(str1)

# Keyword Formatting
str1 = "{l} {f} {g}".format(g = 'Work', f = 'Is', l = 'Worship')
print("\nString in order of Keywords: ")
print(str1)

# Formatting of Integers
str1 = "{0:b}".format(12)
print("\nBinary representation of 12 is ")
print(str1)

# Formatting of Floats
str1 = "{0:e}".format(154.6347)
print("\nExponent representation of 154.6347 is ")
print(str1)
```

(Conti...)

```
# Rounding off Integers
str1 = "{0:.2f}".format(1/4)
print("\nOne-fourth is : ")
print(str1)

# String alignment
str1 = "|{:<10}|{:^10}|{:>10}|".format('Work','Is','Worship')
print("\nLeft, center and right alignment with Formatting: ")
print(str1)

RUN
>>>
String in default order:
Work Is Worship

String in Positional order:
Is Work Worship

String in order of Keywords:
Worship Is Work

Binary representation of 12 is
1100

Exponent representation of 154.6347 is
1.546347e+02

One-fourth is :
0.25

Left, center and right alignment with Formatting:
|Work      |    Is    |   Worship|
>>>
```

Figure 6.13 Program for formatting of strings

Let's Try

Write the output of the following Python codes:

# Iterate Python String 	
str = 'SCHOOL'
for word in str:
  print("Letters are: ", word)
	# Iterate Python String
	str ="SCHOOL"
	for word in range(len(str)):
	  print("Letters at index {0} is = {1}".format(word, str[word]))

6.5 SPECIAL STRING OPERATORS

Strings can be manipulated using operators like concatenation(+), repetition(*), and membership operators like *in* and *not in*. Different special string operators are discussed in the following sections:

6.5.1 Concatenation (+) Operator

The + operator is known as concatenation operator used to join the strings given on either side of the operator. For example,

```
>>> 'Work' + 'Hard'
'WorkHard'
```

To give a white space between the two words, insert a space before the closing of first string within quotes.

```
>>> 'Work ' + 'Hard'
'Work Hard'
```

Note that the interpreter gives back the string with single quotes, regardless of whether you enter strings with single quotes or double quotes.

The + operator can work with numbers and strings separately for addition and concatenation, respectively. However, you cannot combine numbers and strings as operands with a + operator. It will produce an error.

```
>>> 7 + 7
14 # (valid) + operator is used as addition
>>>'7' + '7' # (valid) + operator is used as concatenation
'77'
>>> 7 + '7'# (invalid) it will produce an error
```

You cannot concatenate integers and strings together.

☞ *The + operator must have both operands of the same type. It cannot work with one operand as number and the other as string.*

6.5.2 Replication (*) Operator

There may be times when you need to use Python to automate tasks, and one way you may do this is through repeating a string several times. Replication * (multiply) gives the multiplication of the two numbers or returns the string repeated that many times. For example,

```
>>> 5 * 7
35
>>> "Save!" * 3
'Save!Save!Save!'
```

When the * (multiplication) operator works with number, it returns the product of two numbers. The * (replication) operator used with string produces multiple copies of the same string. For replication, if one of the operands is a string, the other has to be a number, i.e., "string" * number or number * "string". It cannot work with both operands of string types. It will display an error.

```
>>> 7 * 7
49 # (valid) * operator is used as multiplication
>>> 'Stop ' * 2
'Stop Stop' # (valid) * operator is used as replication
>>> 5 * '$'
'$$$$$' # (valid) * operator is used as replication
>>> '2' * '5'# (invalid) it will produce an error
```

☞ *Strings can include any characters, including digits. Quotes turn digits into strings.*

☞ *You can concatenate strings with the "+" operator and create multiple concatenated copies of the string with the "*" operator.*

6.5.3 Membership Operator (in)

Membership operator *in* returns true if a character exists in the given string, false otherwise. For example,

```
>>> str = "Work Hard"
>>> 'W' in str
True
>>> 'Work' in str
True
>>> 'work' in str
False # because w of work is in small case
>>> 'We' in str
False
```

Let's Try

Write the output of the following code segments:

`print ('black'+ 'white')`	`print("Hello" * 3)`
`print (('h') in 'elephant')`	`print (('i') in 'elephant')`

Comparisons	Result	Reason
"abc" == "abc"	True	Because letter case is same.
"a" == "A"	False	Because letter case is different.
"a" != "A"	True	Because letter case is different.
"abc" > "ABC"	True	Because uppercase letters are considered smaller than the lower-case letters due to their ASCII values.
'123' > '456'	False	Because ASCII value of 123 is lower than 456.

Figure 6.14 Working of Comparison Operators with Strings

6.5.4 Membership Operator (not in)

The *not in* membership operator returns true if a character does not exist in the given string. For example,

```
>>> str = "Work Hard"
>>> 'W' not in str
False
>>> 'Word' not in str
True
```

☞ *The in and not in are membership operators that test for the presence of a substring in the string.*

6.5.5 Comparison Operators

All the comparison operators (<, <=, >, >=, !=, ==) are applied to strings also. The comparisons using these operators follow the standard character-by-character comparison rules for ASCII and Unicode. ASCII values of numbers 0 to 9 are from 48 to 57, uppercase (A to Z) are from 65 to 90, and lowercase (a to z) are from 97 to 122. Python has the two boolean values, True and False. Many comparison operators return True and False as depicted in Figure 6.14.

At the most basic level, computers store all information as numbers. To represent character data, a translation scheme is used which maps each character to its representative number.

Normal strings in Python are stored internally as 8-bit ASCII, while Unicode strings are stored as 16-bit Unicode. This extension allows the strings to include characters from the different languages of the world. Python 3 supports Unicode extensively, including allowing Unicode characters within strings. Python provides a set of built-in functions that allows you to switch back and forth between characters and their corresponding ASCII and Unicode values. The *ord()* function returns the numeric ("ordinal") code of a single-character string, while *chr()* is the inverse of *ord()*. *chr()* returns a single character string referring to the given numeric code. (See Figure 6.15). Here are also some interactive examples:

```
>>> ord("a") # ord() function will return numeric values
97
>>> ord("A")
65
>>> ord('#')
35
>>> chr(97) # chr() returns an integer to a character
'a'
>>> chr(90)
'Z'
```

☞ *ord() function returns the ASCII or Unicode value of a character and requires single character only.*

☞ *chr() function takes ASCII or Unicode value in integer form and returns the character corresponding to the ASCII or Unicode value.*

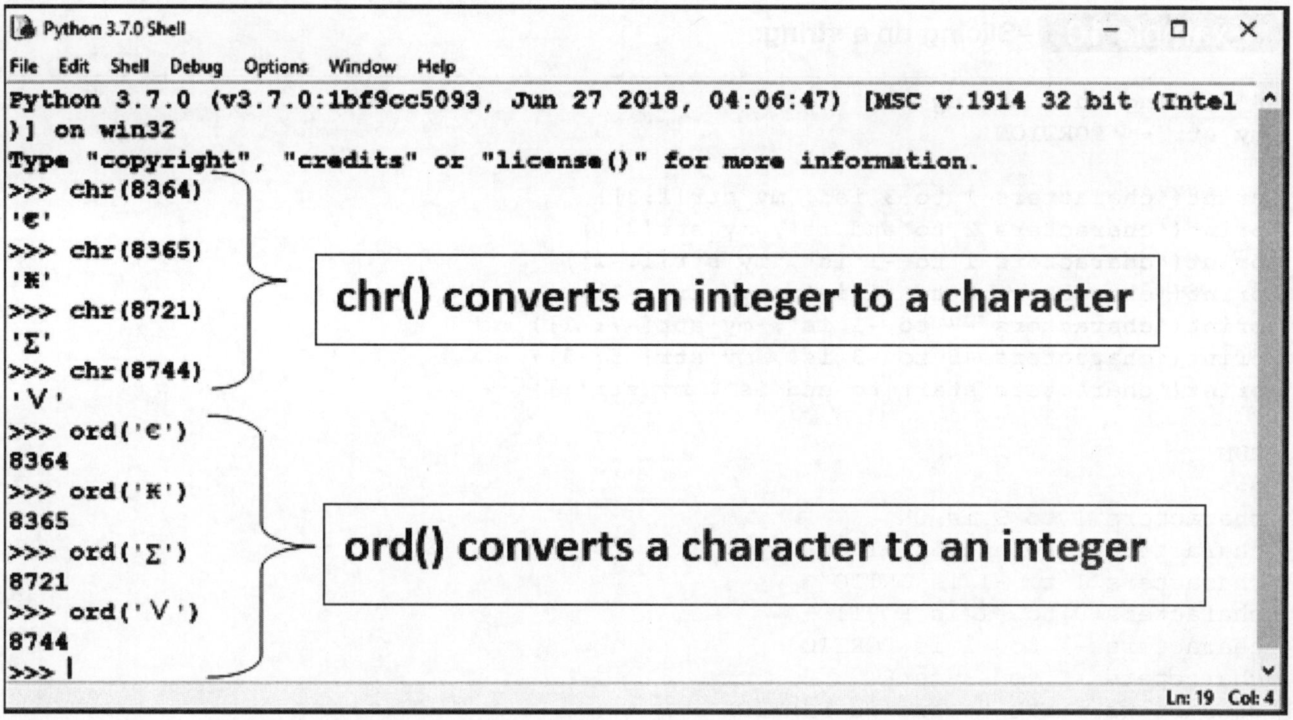

Figure 6.15 Screen showing demo of ord() and chr()

6.6 STRING SLICES

Slicing is a mechanism used to select a range of items from sequence. You can retrieve a slice (substring) of a string with a slice operation. The slicing operation is used by specifying the name of the sequence followed by an optional pair of numbers separated by a colon enclosed within [](square brackets). The slice operator [] is used to access the individual characters of the string. However, you can use the : (colon) operator in Python to access the substring. Note that this is very similar to the indexing operation you have been using till now. Characters are accessible using their position in the string which has to be enclosed in brackets following the string. The position number can be positive or negative, which means starting at the beginning or the end of the string. Substrings are extracted by providing values of the start and end positions separated by a colon. Both positions are optional, which means you can choose to start extracting at the beginning of the string or to extract the substring until the end. While accessing characters, it is prohibited to access a position that does not exist. During substring extraction, the longest possible string is extracted. Figure 6.16 summarizes the arrangement of a string 'PORTION'.

str	P	O	R	T	I	O	N
Positive index	0	1	2	3	4	5	6
Negative index	-7	-6	-5	-4	-3	-2	-1

Figure 6.16 Structure of str PORTION

Example 10 –**Slicing on a string.**

```
# Slicing on a string
my_str = 'PORTION'

print('characters 1 to 3 is', my_str[1:3])
print('characters 2 to end is', my_str[2:])
print('characters 1 to -1 is', my_str[1:-1])
print('characters 0 to -1 is', my_str[:-1])
print('characters -7 to -1 is', my_str[-7:-1])
print('characters -5 to -3 is', my_str[-5:-3])
print('characters start to end is', my_str[:])

RUN
>>>
characters 1 to 3 is OR
characters 2 to end is RTION
characters 1 to -1 is ORTIO
characters 0 to -1 is PORTIO
characters -7 to -1 is PORTIO
characters -5 to -3 is RT
characters start to end is PORTION
>>>
```

Figure 6.17 Program for Slicing on a String

☞ *[] is known as slice operator. It is used to access the sub-strings of a particular string.*
[:] is known as range slice operator. It is used to access the characters from the specified range.

Remember the following points while accessing elements in the strings using subscripts:

(a) The first number (before the colon) in the slicing operation refers to the position from where the slice starts, and the second number (after the colon) indicates where the slice will stop.
(b) If the first number is not specified, Python will start extracting characters from the beginning of the sequence.
(c) If the second number is left out, Python will stop at the end of the sequence.
(d) Note that the slicing starts at the start position and ends just before the end position, i.e., the start position is included, but the end position is excluded from the sequence slice. Thus, my_str[1:3] returns a slice of the sequence starting at position 1, includes position 2 but stops at position 3. Therefore, a slice of two items is returned.
(e) Omitting both the indices directs the Python interpreter to extract the entire string starting from 0 till the last index. Thus, my_str[:] returns a copy of the whole sequence.
(f) Positive subscript helps in accessing the string from the beginning. You can also do slicing with negative positions. Negative numbers are used for positions from the end of the sequence, i.e., count backward from the end of the string. For example, my_str[:-1] will return a slice of the sequence, which excludes the last item of the sequence but contains everything else.
(g) If the first index is greater than or equal to the second, the result is an empty string, represented by two quotation marks.
(h) Note that -0 is the same as 0, so it does not count from the right.

Let's Try

Write the output of the following code segments:

`>>> word="language"`
`>>> word[1:3]`
`>>> word[5:]`
`>>> word[-1]`
`>>> word[-1:]`
`>>> word[::-1]`
	`>>> s="ten"`
	`>>> rev_str = s[len(s)::-1]`
	`>>> print(rev_str)`

Let's Try

Write the output of the following Python code.

```
# Slicing Python String
x ="BPB PUBLICATIONS"
# Slicing the String using two indexes
a = x[0:3]
print("Both Indexes = ", a)
# Slicing the String using Second indexes
b = x[:10]
print("No First Index = ", b)
# Slicing the String using First indexes
c = x[4:]
print("No Second Index = ", c)
# Slicing the String without using two indexes
d = x[:]
print("No Indexes = ", d)
# Slicing the String using Negative indexes
e = x[-3:]
print("Negative First Index = ", e)
# Slicing the String using Negative indexes
f = x[:-2]
print("Negative Second Index = ", f)
```

Specifying a stride in a String Slice

There is one more variant of the slicing syntax. Adding an additional : and a third index designates a stride (also called a step), which indicates the number of characters to jump after retrieving each character in the slice. For example, for the string 'PORTION', the slice 0:7:2 starts with the first character and ends with the last character (the whole string), and every second character is skipped.

```
>>> my_str = 'PORTION'
>>> my_str[0:7:2]
'PRIN'
```

6.7 STRING FUNCTIONS AND METHODS

Python provides built-in functions and methods that allow us to do string manipulation. Every string object that you create in Python is actually an instance of String class. The string manipulation methods that are discussed below use the following syntax:

`<stringObject>.<method name>()`

6.7.1 len()

len() is a built-in function that returns the number of characters in a string.

```
>>> fruit = 'apple'
>>> len(fruit)
5
```

An empty string contains no characters and has length 0, but other than that, it is the same as any other string. A string with length 1 represents a character in Python.

The len() method counts the total number of characters within a string. If you want to count the number of times either one particular character or a sequence of characters shows up in a string, you can do so with the count() method. Let's count the number of times the character "S" appears in our string s1 = "Shashi Singh":

```
>>> s1="Shashi Singh"
>>> print(s1.count("S"))
2
```

Although the total number of capital and small letter *s* is 3 but it is showing 2, as each character is case-sensitive. If you want to search for all the letters in a string regardless of case, you can use the str.lower() method to convert the entire string to lower-case first.

```
>>> str.lower(s1)
'shashi singh'
>>> s2=str.lower(s1)
>>> print(s2.count("s"))
3
```

You can also find at which position a character or a character sequence occurs in a string. You can do this with the str.find() method, and it will return the position of the character based on index number. You can check to see where the first "a" occurs in the string s1:

```
>>> print(s1.find("a"))
2
```

The character "a" first occurs at the index position of 2 in the string "Shashi Singh".

Let's Try

Write the output of the following code segments:

<table>
<tr><td><pre>a = ['apple', 'banana', 'pomegranate']
for x in a:
    print(x, len(x))</pre></td><td><pre>str1 = 'Hello World'
  len(str1)</pre></td></tr>
</table>

<table>
<tr><td><pre>str1 = 'Apple is healthy. Apple is also good
for health.'
print()
print(str1.count("Apple"))
print()</pre></td><td><pre>str = "elephant"
count = 0
for i in str:
  count = count+1
print(count)</pre></td></tr>
</table>

6.7.2 capitalize()

The method capitalize() returns a copy of the string with only its first character capitalized.

```
>>> str = "this is string"
>>> str.capitalize()
'This is string'
```

6.7.3 find()

The find() method is used to locate the position of the given substring within the string; it returns -1 if it is unsuccessful in finding the substring.

```
find(str, beg=0 end=len(string))
>>> str= "This is a simple sentence"
>>> str.find('tan')
-1
```

In other words, it returns -1 because substring is not found in the given string. On omitting the start parameter, the function starts the searching process from the very beginning.

```
>>> str.find('ten')
20
>>> str.find('is',0,4)
2
>>> str.find('is',4,15)
5
```

6.7.4 isalnum()

It returns true if string contains only letters and digits, i.e., all characters are alphanumeric and false otherwise if the string contains any special character, such as _, @,#,*, including space.

```
>>>str1='Work Hard'
>>>str1.isalnum()
False
```

because it has a space which is a special character.

```
>>>str2='Work'
>>>str2.isalnum()
True
```

```
>>>str3='Work1'
>>>str3.isalnum()
True

>>>str4='1234'
>>>str4.isalnum()
True
```

6.7.5 isalpha()

It returns true if the string contains only letters, otherwise returns false.

```
>>>str2='Work'
>>>str2.isalpha()
True

>>>str3='Work1'
>>>str3.isalpha()
False

>>>str4='1234'
>>>str4.isalpha()
False
```

6.7.6 isdigit()

It returns true if the string contains only digits, and false otherwise.

```
>>>str2='Work'
>>>str2.isdigit()
False

>>>str3='Work1'
>>>str3.isdigit()
False

>>>str4='1234'
>>>str4.isdigit()
True
```

6.7.7 lower()

It converts all the uppercase letters into a string to lowercase.

```
>>> 'Save Water'.lower()
save water
```

6.7.8 islower()

It returns true if the string is in lowercase, and false otherwise.

```
>>>str1='Work Hard'
>>>str1.islower()
False

>>>str2='hello'
>>>str2.islower()
True

>>>str3='ROHAN'
>>>str3.islower()
False
```

6.7.9 isupper()

It returns true if the string is in uppercase and false otherwise.

```
>>>str1='Work Hard'
>>>str1.isupper()
False

>>>str2='hello'
>>>str2.isupper()
False

>>>str3='ROHAN'
>>>str3.isupper()
True
```

6.7.10 upper()

It returns the exact copy of the string with all letters in uppercase.

```
>>> 'Save Water'.upper()
'SAVE WATER'
```

6.7.11 lstrip()

It removes all the leading (left side) whitespace in a string.

```
>>> str = "   Save Water"
>>> str.lstrip()
'Save Water'
```

It removes characters from the left based on the string argument passed (including default white-space characters) and then returns a copy of the string.

```
>>> str='ABC International'
>>> print(str)
'ABC International'

>>> str.lstrip('A')
'BC International'

>>> str.lstrip('ABC ')
'International'
```

6.7.12 rstrip()

It returns a copy of the string with trailing characters removed based on the string argument passed. It also removes default whitespace characters from the right.

```
>>> str2 = "Hello World    "
>>> str2.rstrip()
'Hello World'
>>> str = "Television"
>>> str.rstrip('vision')
'Tele'
```

6.7.13 isspace()

It returns true if the string contains only whitespace characters, and false otherwise.

```
>>> '    '.isspace()
True
>>> ''.isspace()
False
>>> str='w'
>>> print(str.isspace())
False
```

It will return false if the string contains even one character.

6.7.14 istitle()

It checks whether the string is title-cased, i.e., the first letter of each word is capitalized. It returns true if string is properly title-cased, and false otherwise.

```
>>> 'This Is A Title'.istitle()
True
>>> 'This is A title'.istitle()
False
```

6.7.15 replace(old,new)

It replaces all occurrences of old substring in a string with the new substring.

```
>>> str = 'This is just a simple string.'
>>> str.replace ('simple', 'short')
'This is just a short string.'

>>> 'This is a test'.replace('is', 'eez')
'Theez eez a test'
```

The replace() works like a search and replace feature of a word processing software.

6.7.16 split()

It splits the string according to delimiter *str* (space, if not provided) and returns a list of substrings, i.e., it splits the string into a list of "words".

```
>>> s1 = "Work is Worship"
>>> words = s1.split()
>>> words
['Work', 'is', 'Worship']
```

Example 11 -**Program to read a line and count number of words.**

```
#Program to read line and count number of words
my_line=input("Enter a line: ")
x=my_line.split()
count=0
for i in x:
    count = count+1
print(count)

RUN
>>>
Enter a line: Clean and Green Delhi
4
>>>
```

Figure 6.18 Program to read a line and count number of words

Let's Try

Write the output of following program to check if the word 'work' is present in the string "work is worship" or not.

```
str = "work is worship"
print ('work' in str.split())
```

6.7.17 join()

The join() method concatenates words from a list of words to form a single string. Elements can be joined using any separator.

```
>>> str1 = ('Raja', 'Ram', 'Mohan',
'Rai')
>>> str1
('Raja', 'Ram', 'Mohan', 'Rai')
>>> str = ' '
>>> str.join(str1)
'Raja Ram Mohan Rai'
```

6.7.18 swapcase()

It returns a copy of the string with lowercase letters turned into uppercase and vice versa.

```
>>> str='COMPUTER'
>>> print(str.swapcase())
computer

>>> str='computer'
>>> print(str.swapcase())
COMPUTER
```

6.7.19 partition()

This function splits the strings at the first occurrence of separator and returns the string in three parts, i.e., before the separator (head), the separator itself, and the part after the separator (tail). If the separator is not found, it returns the string itself, followed by two empty strings.

```
>>> str = "The Golden Star"
>>> str.partition('Gold')
('The ', 'Gold', 'en Star')

>>> str.partition('ne')
('The Golden Star', '', '')

>>> str.partition('e')
('Th', 'e', ' Golden Star')
```

6.7.20 str()

A string is a sequence of one or more characters (letters, numbers, symbols). It is a common form of data in computer programs, and you may need to convert strings into numbers or numbers into strings. You can convert numbers into strings using the str() method. You pass either a number or a variable into the parentheses of the method, and then that numeric value will be converted into a string value. Let us first convert integer into string. To convert the integer 17 into a string value, you can pass 17 into the str() method:

```
>>> str(17)
'17'
```

The quotes around the number '17' signify that the number is no longer an integer but is now a string value.

Similarly, when you pass a float into the str() method, the string value of the float will be returned.

Strings can be converted to numbers by using the int() and float() methods. int() method converts the strings into integer and allows you to do calculations. You can also convert the numbers to float by using the float() method.

REVIEW QUESTIONS WITH ANSWERS

1. Multiple Choice Questions

1. Converts all uppercase letters in a string to lowercase.
   a. islower()
   b. swapcase()
   c. lower()
   d. None of the above
2. The method _____ returns a copy of the string with only its first character capitalized.
   a. upper()
   b. capitalize()

c. swapcase()
d. None of the above

3. Returns true if string contains only letters and digit.
a. isalnum()
b. isdigit()
c. isalpha()
d. None of the above

4. Replication (*) means:
a. It gives the multiplication of the two numbers
b. The string is repeated that many times.
c. Both (a) and (b)
d. None of the above

5. The find() method returns -1 if it is:
a. Unsuccessful in finding the substring
b. Successful in finding the substring
c. Both (a) and (b)
d. None of the above

6. Which of the following are string literals?
a. "Mohan" b. 'class'
c. '12345' d. All of the above

7. Types of numeric literal(s) supported by Python:
a. integer b. complex
c. float d. All of the above

8. Python uses ______ quotes at the beginning and end of the docstring.
a. Single b. Double
c. Triple d. All of these

9. Slicing requires a ______ which separates the start and end index of the field.
a. # b. @
c. : d. *

10. ______ function converts an integer expression to a string.
a. int() b. str()
c. Both a and b d. None of these

11. The chr() method:
a. Converts an integer to a character:
b. Converts a character to an integer
c. Returns the length of a string
d. Returns a string representation of an object

12. What will be the result of the len() function given below?
```
>>> s = 'I am a string.'
>>> len(s)
```
a. 11 b. 14
c. 16 d. 10

13. What is output of following codes?
```
>>> 'the total number of characters'.title()
```
a. The total number of characters
b. The Total Number Of Characters
c. THE TOTAL NUMBER OF CHARACTERS
d. None of the above

14. Write the output of following code:
```
>>> my_str='PORTION'
>>> my_str[2:5]
```
a. ORT b. ORTIO
c. RTI d. RTION

15. Write the output of following code:
```
str1 = "Once again he asked \"How long is a piece of string?\""
print(str1)
```
a. "Once again he asked \"How long is a piece of string?\""
b. Once again he asked "How long is a piece of string?"
c. 'Once again he asked "How long is a piece of string?"'
d. Error

16. Write the output of following code:
```
str = "HELLO"
str[0] = "h"
print(str)
```
a. HELLO b. hELLO
c. hello d. TypeError

17. Write the output of following code:
```
str = "HELLO"
print(str)
str = "hello"
print(str)
```
a. HELLO
hello b. hello
HELLO
c. Both (a) and (b) d. Error

18. What is the output when following statement is executed ?
```
>>>"x"+"yz"
```
a. 'x' b. 'yz'
c. 'yzx' d. 'xyz'

19. What is the output when following statement is executed ?
```
>>>"ABCD"[2:]
```
a. A b. AB
c. CD d. DC

20. What is the output when following code is executed ?

```
>>> str1 = 'hello'
>>> str2 = ','
>>> str3 = 'python'
>>> str3[-1:]
```

a. 'n' b. 'hello'
c. 'o' d. 'python'

21. Which arithmetic operator cannot be used with strings ?

a. + b. *
c. / d. None of the above

22. What is the output when following statement is executed ?

```
>>>print('hello' 'world')
```

a. helloworld b. hello world
c. hello
world d. Error

23. Which of the following is the correct way to declare string variable in Python?

a. fruit = 'mango' b. fruit = "mango"
c. fruit = mango d. Both (a) and (b)

24. Which pre-defined Python function is used to find length of string?

a. len() b. strlen()
c. length() d. stringlength()

2. State True or False for the following:

1. Python does not have a character data type.
2. strip([str]) removes the whitespaces and trailing spaces from the string.
3. Docstring phrase ends with a period (.) and can be multiple lines.
4. Python 3 stores strings as Unicode, by default.
5. Docstrings can be one line or multiline.
6. A single character is simply a string with a length of 2.
7. Strings most often contain non-numeric characters.
8. Traversing a string means accessing all the elements of the string one after the other.
9. isupper() and upper() are same.
10. A logical line is what you see when you write the program.
11. [:] is known as range slice operator.
12.
```
string_var = 'Python'
string_var = "Python"
string_var = """Python"""
```
All assignments are identical.
13. String literal separated by whitespace are concatenated.
14. The index must be an integer.
15. The index of -1 refers to the last item.
16. We can access individual characters using indexing and a range of characters using slicing.
17. If we try to access index out of the range, we will get error.
18. Strings are un-modifiable.

3. Match the following:

1. Integer literal	a. y = 12.3
2. Float Literal	b. x = 10
3. lstrip()	c. docstring
4. join()	d. remove leading white-spaces
5. Python documentation string	e. returns the string in upper case
6. lower()	f. concatenate a string
7. upper()	g. Inverts case for all letters in string
8. split()	h. returns the string in lowercase
9. len(string)	i. splits the string into substrings
10. swapcase()	j. returns the length of the string

4. Fill in the blanks:

1. ________ function converts all uppercase characters into lowercase and vice versa.
2. _______ is a mechanism used to select a range of items from sequence type.
3. Python has extended documentation capability, called _________.
4. ______ constructs a string from a wide variety of data types.
5. ________ creates new strings, concatenating multiple copies of the same string.

6. ________ returns true if string has only letters and digits and false otherwise.
7. _______ returns true if string has all alphabetic characters, and false otherwise.
8. _______ returns "titlecased" version of string, that is, all words begin with uppercase and the rest are lowercase.
9. Non-zero numbers and non-empty strings represent _______ Boolean values.
10. _________ are immutable.
11. ________ returns an integer value for the given character.
12. _______ returns a string representation of an object.
13. The first character in a string has index _______.
14. Omitting both indices returns the original _______.
15. A string cannot be _______ once it has been assigned.
16. We _______ delete or remove characters from a string.

Answers

1. 1. c 2. b 3. a 4. c 5. a 6. d
7. d 8. c 9. c 10. b 11 a 12 b
13. b 14. c 15. b 16 d 17 a 18 d
19. c 20. a 21 c 22 a 23 d 24 a

2. 1. T 2. T 3. T 4. T 5. T 6. F
7. T 8. T 9. F 10. F 11 T 12 T
13. T 14. T 15. T 16 T 17 T 18 T

3. 1. b 2. a 3. d 4. f 5. c 6. h
7. e 8. i 9. j 10. g

4. 1. swapcase() 2. Slicing
3. docstrings 4. str()
5. Repetition 6. isalnum()
7. isalpha() 8. title()
9. true 10. Strings
11. ord() 12. str()
13. 0 14. string
15. Changed 16. Cannot

Short Answers Questions

1. What are strings?

Ans A string is a sequence of characters. It is basically just a bunch of words. It is the form of data used in programming for storing and manipulating text, such as words, names and sentences. We can write it in Python using single quotes, double quotes, or triple quotes.

2. A palindrome is a word that is spelled the same backward and forward. Write a program that checks whether the word is palindrome or not.

Ans

```
# program to check the word is palindrome or not
string=input("Enter string:")
if(string==string[::-1]):
        print("The string is a palindrome")
else:
        print("The string is not a palindrome")

RUN
>>>
Enter string:DAD
The string is a palindrome
>>>
>>>
Enter string:Mohan
The string is not a palindrome
>>>
```

Figure 1 Program for Q2

3. Write a program that takes your full name as input and displays the abbreviations of the first and middle names leaving the last name as it is.

Ans

```
# program to take full name as input and displays the abbreviations of the
first and middle names
a = input("Enter string :")
a = a.split()
b = a[0][0]+". "+a[1][0]+". "+a[2]
print(b)

RUN
>>>
Enter string :Vivek Kumar Singh
V. K. Singh
>>>
```

Figure 2 Program for Q3

4. Write a program to find the largest word in the string entered by user.

Ans

```
# program to find the largest word in the string entered by user
a =input("Enter string :")
a = a.split()
lar = a[0]
max_len = len(a[0])
for i in a:
  if len(i)>max_len:
    max_len = len(i)
    lar = i
print(lar)

RUN
>>>
Enter string :Programming is fun.
Programming
>>>
```

Figure 3 Program for Q4

5. Write a program that counts total characters in a string.

Ans

```
# Count total characters in string
input_string = input("Enter a string : ")
count = 0
for c in input_string :
    if c.isspace() != True:
        count = count + 1
print("Total number of characters : ",count)

RUN
>>>
Enter a string : Green and Clean India
Total number of characters :  18
>>>
```

Figure 4 Program for Q5

6. Write a program to count alphabets, digits and special characters in a string.

Ans

```
# Program to Count alphabets, digits and special characters in a String
input_string = input("Enter a string : ")
alphabets = digits = special = 0
for i in range(len(input_string)):
    if(input_string[i].isalpha()):
        alphabets = alphabets + 1
    elif(input_string[i].isdigit()):
        digits = digits + 1
    else:
        special = special + 1

print("\nTotal Number of Alphabets in this String :  ", alphabets)
print("\nTotal Number of Digits in this String :  ", digits)
print("\nTotal Number of Special Characters in this String :  ", special)

RUN
>>>
Enter a string : India won match by 5 runs!

Total Number of Alphabets in this String :   19
Total Number of Digits in this String :   1
Total Number of Special Characters in this String :   6

>>>
```

Figure 5 Program for Q6

7. Write a program to make a new string with all the consonants deleted from the string.

Ans

```
# Program to make a new string with all the consonants deleted from the
string
a = ['a','e','i','o','u','A','E','I','O','U',' ']
b =input("Enter string :")
for i in b:
  if i not in a:
    b = b[:b.index(i)]+b[b.index(i)+1:]
print(b)


RUN
>>>
Enter string :Eat Apples every day.
Ea Ae ee a
>>>
```

Figure 6 Program for Q7

8. Write a program to find the length of the string without using len() function.

Ans

```
# Program to find the length of the string without using len function.
string = input("Enter string :")
count= 0
for i in string:
    count = count+1
print (count)

RUN
>>>
Enter string :Python
6
>>>
```

Figure 7 Program for Q8

9. Write a program to print every character of a string entered by user in a new line.

Ans

```
# Program to print every character of a string entered by user in a new line
string = input("Enter string :")
for i in string:
    print(i)

RUN
>>>
Enter string :Program
P
r
o
g
r
a
m
>>>
```

Figure 8 Program for Q9

10. Write a program to print reverse order of the entered string.

Ans

```
# Program to print reverse order of a string
s = input("Enter a string: ")
rev_str = s[len(s)::-1]
print(rev_str)

RUN
>>>
Enter a string: BAT
TAB
>>>
```

Figure 9 Program for Q10

11. Find the output of the following program segments:

(a)
```
>>> str1 = 'Computer World'
>>> len(str1)
```

Ans 14

(b)
```
word = 'banana'
count = 0
for letter in word:
 if letter == 'a':
   count = count + 1
print(count)
```

Ans 3

(c)
```
>>> word = 'banana'
>>> new_word = word.upper()
>>> print(new_word)
```

Ans BANANA

(d)
```
str1 = str(input("Enter a string : "))
sub_str = input("Enter the substring : ")
print(str1.count(sub_str))
```

Ans Enter a string : Apple is good. Apple is also healthy.
Enter the substring : Apple
2

12. What is the significance of triple quotes?

Ans We can specify multi-line strings using triple quotes - ("""). We can use single quotes and double quotes freely within the triple quotes. An example is:
'''This is a multi-line string. This is the first line.
This is the second line. "What's your name?," I asked.
He said "Ram, Raja Ram."
'''

13. Differentiate between physical line and logical line.

Ans A physical line is what we see when we write the program. A logical line is what Python sees as a single statement. Python implicitly assumes that each physical line corresponds to a logical line.

14. What is the difference between lstrip() and rstrip()?

Ans lstrip() removes characters (including whitespace characters) from the left, based on the argument passed whereas rstrip() removes characters (including whitespace characters) from the right, based on the argument passed.

15. Explain membership operator *in* with example.

Ans Membership operator *in* returns true if a character exists in the given string, and false otherwise. For example,

```
>>> str = "Work Hard"
>>> 'W' in str
True
>>> 'Work' in str
True
>>> 'work' in str
False # because w of work is in small case
>>> 'We' in str
False
```

16. What do you mean by 'strings are immutable'?

Ans Strings are immutable means that the contents of the string variable cannot be changed after it is created.

17. What is the function of slicing operation?

Ans We can retrieve a slice (substring) of a string with a slice operation. The slicing operation is used by specifying the name of the sequence, followed by an optional pair of numbers separated by a colon, enclosed within square brackets.

18. What is the use of Docstrings?

Ans Python has a feature called documentation strings, usually referred to by its short name, docstrings. Docstring is an important tool that we should make use of since it helps document the program better and makes it easier to understand.

19. "The quotes are not a part of string". Comment.

Ans The quotes are not a part of string. They only tell the computer where the string constant begins and ends. They can have any character or sign, including space in between them.

20. How are empty strings represented in Python?

Ans An empty string contains no characters and has length 0, represented by two quotation marks in Python.

21. What is the difference between (+) and (*) operators?

Ans The plus (+) sign is the string concatenation operator, while the asterisk (*) is the repetition operator. We can concatenate strings with the "+" operator and create multiple concatenated copies of the string with the "*" operator. The use of + and * makes sense by analogy with addition and multiplication. Just as 4*3 is equivalent to 4+4+4, we expect 'Save'*3 to be the same as 'Save'+'Save'+'Save'.

22. Differentiate between ord() and chr() functions.

Ans ord() function returns the ASCII value of a character and requires single character only whereas chr() function takes ASCII value in integer form and returns the character corresponding to the ASCII value.

23. Write short note on subscript.

Ans A string is a sequence of characters. We can access the characters one at a time with the bracket operator. An individual character in a string is accessed using a subscript (index). The subscript should always be an integer (positive or negative).

24. What do you mean by positive and negative indices?

Ans In Python, indices that begin from 0 onwards in the forward direction are called positive indices, and the indices which begin from -1, -2, -3 in the backward direction are called negative indices. Positive subscript helps in accessing the string from the beginning. Negative subscript helps in accessing the string from the end.

25. 'String indices must be an integer'.Comment.

Ans We can use any expression, including variables and operators, as an index, but the value of the index has to be an integer. Otherwise, we might get an error. We can also use negative indices, which count backward, i.e., from the end of the string to the beginning.

26. What do you mean by traversing a string?

Ans Traversing a string means accessing all the elements of the string one after the other by using the subscript or index.

27. Write short note on membership operators.

Ans in and not in are membership operators. in operator returns true if a particular sub-string is present in the specified string.
not in operator does the exact reverse of in. It returns true if a particular substring is not present in the specified string.

28. Consider the string my_str= "Green and Clean INDIA". Write statements in Python to do the following:

(a) To display the last five character.

(b) To display the starting index for the substring 'an'.

(c) To check whether the string contains substring 'NDI' or not.

(d) To repeat string two times.

Ans Figure 10 shows the statements in Python and their output.

```
>>> my_str="Green and Clean INDIA"
>>> my_str[-5:]
'INDIA'                         ⇨ To display last five characters
>>> my_str.find('an')
6                               ⇨ To display starting index of substring 'an'
>>> 'NDI' in my_str
True                            ⇨ To check strine contains 'NDI' or not
>>> my_str*2
'Green and Clean INDIAGreen and Clean INDIA'
>>> |                             To repeat string two times
```

Figure 10 Python statements and output for Q28

EXERCISE

1. Suggest the appropriate functions for the following tasks:
   (a) Capitalize all letters of a string.
   (b) Remove whitespace from the beginning of a string.
   (c) Split a string into a list of "words".
   (d) Remove all trailing (right side) whitespace of string.
   (e) Find length of a string.
2. What do you mean by string and substring?
3. What are indices?
4. How are strings internally stored?
5. What do you mean by subscripts? How are they written?
6. What do you mean by string slices? Explain with an example.
7. Write the role of isaplha(), isalnum(), isdigit(), and isspace() functions.
8. Differentiate between islower() and lower() functions.
9. Write a program to compute the length of string.
10. Differentiate between lstrip() and rstrip() functions.
11. Differentiate between *in* and *not in* membership operators.
12. How can you use single quotes and double quotes freely within the triple quotes?
13. What is a logical line in Python?
14. Write one feature of negative subscript.
15. Write the slicing structure of 'PYTHON' string.
16. What is an index?
17. What do you mean by traversing a string?

LAB EXERCISE

1. Write the output of the following program segments:

(a)
```
>>> word = 'banana'
>>> index = word.find('a')
>>> print(index)
```
(b)
```
>>> word = 'banana'
>>> word.find('na')
```
(c)
```
str = 'Hello World!'
print(str[0])
print(str[2:5])
print(str * 2)
```
(d)
```
var1 = 'Hello World!'
var2 = "Python Programming"
print("var1[0]: ", var1[0])
print("var2[1:5]: ", var2[1:5])
```
(e)
```
>>> str1 = 'World of Computers'
>>> len(str1)
```
(f)
```
>>> 'Save Plants'.lower()
```
(g)
```
>>> 5 * 7
>>> "Work!" * 3
```
(h)
```
>>> str='pooja'
>>> print(str.swapcase())
```
(i)
```
sample_str = 'Python String'
print (sample_str[0])
print (sample_str[-1])
print (sample_str[-2])
```
(j)
```
sample_str = 'Python String'
print (sample_str[3:5])
print (sample_str[:6])
print (sample_str[7:])
```
(k)
```
sample_str = 'Python String'
sample_str[2] = 'a'
```

2. Write a program that reads a string and prints whether it is palindrome or not.
3. Write a program to check if the given substring is present in the string.
4. Write a program to enter a string and print the reversed string.
5. Write a program to count no. of 'a' in the string 'banana'.
6. Write a program to count no. of vowels in the string 'apple'.
7. Write a program to read a string of characters of the maximum size of 255 characters and then perform the following operations on the string:
   (a) Print the string in the reverse.
   For example, if the input string is : Computer Science
   Then, the output should be as shown below:
   ecneicS retupmoC
   (b) Find the total number of words in the string.
8. Write a program to count the number of words in a string as well as the number of characters other than the space.
9. Write a program to reverse a string.
10. Write a program that converts first letter of a string to uppercase.

11. Write a program to read a line and print:
(a) No. of uppercase letters
(b) No. of lowercase letters
(c) No. of digits

12. Write a program to find the largest word in the string entered by user.

13. Write the following programs given in Q13(a), Q13(b), Q13(c), Q13(d) and Q13(e) and find the output:

(a)

```
# Program that accepts a string and count number of digits and letters.
s = input("Enter a string :")
d=l=0
for c in s:
    if c.isdigit():
        d=d+1
    elif c.isalpha():
          l=l+1
    else:
        pass
print("No. Of Letters :", l)
print("No. Of Digits", d)
```

Figure 11 Program for Q13(a)

(b)

```
# Programs that reads a line & Prints no. of lowercase, uppercase letters
and digits
line = input("Enter a line: ")
lowercount = uppercount = digitcount = 0
for a in line:
    if a.islower() :
        lowercount += 1
    elif a.isupper() :
        uppercount += 1
    elif a.isdigit() :
        digitcount += 1
print ("No. Of uppercase letters:", uppercount)
print ("No. Of lowercase letters:", lowercount)
print ("No. Of digits: ", digitcount)
```

Figure 12 Program for Q13(b)

(c)

```
# Program that accepts a word from the user and reverse it.
Word = input("Input a word to reverse: ")
for char in range(len(word) - 1, -1, -1):
    print(word[char], end="")
```

Figure 13 Program for Q13(c)

(d)

```
# Program to input name and print each character with a single space
str=input("Enter any string: ")
ctr=0
while ctr < len(str):
    ch=str[ctr]
    print (ch, end= "")
    ctr=ctr+1
```

Figure 14 Program for Q13(d)

(e)

```
#Program to reads a string and capitalizes every alternate letter in it
my_str1=input("Enter a string: ")
length=len(my_str1)
my_str2=""
for i in range(0,length):
    if i%2==0:
        my_str2 += my_str1[i]
    else:
        my_str2 += my_str1[i].upper()
print(my_str2)
```

Figure 15 Program for Q13(e)

CHAPTER 7

List Manipulation

7.1 LIST

The most basic data structure in Python is the sequence. Each element of a sequence is assigned a number - its position or index. The first index is zero, the second index is one, and so forth.

A list is a sequence of multiple values in an ordered sequence. It is the most versatile datatype available in Python, which can be written as a list of comma-separated values (items) between square brackets. Each element or value that is inside of a list is called an item. Like a string, a list is a sequence of values. In the string, the values are characters; in a list, they can be of any type. Lists are more general than strings.

a. Strings are always sequences of characters between quotes, whereas lists can contain values of any type between square brackets [ ]. Lists can contain values of mixed data types. A single list can contain numbers, strings, or other lists.

b. Unlike strings, which are immutable, it is possible to change individual elements of a list. Lists are mutable, which means that items in a list can be modified by assigning new values.

c. Like string indices, list indices start at 0, and lists can be sliced, concatenated and so on.

d. List is a sequence that can be indexed into, and that can grow and shrink by adding elements or deleting elements from the list.

☞ *A list is an ordered collection of values.*

7.2 CREATING LISTS

There are several ways to create a new list; the simplest way is to enclose the elements in square brackets [ ], separated by commas. It can have any number of items and they may be of different types (integer, float, string etc.).

The syntax for creating a list is:

<list_name> = [<value>, <value>, <value>]

For example, you can create a list of cities having three items such as Delhi, Mumbai, and Chennai, separated by comma and enclosed inside square brackets.

City=['Delhi', 'Mumbai', 'Chennai']

Other examples of Python lists are:

```
>>> L1 = [10, 20, 30, 40] # list of 4 integer elements
>>> L2 = ["Raj", "Govind", "Abdul"] # list of 3 strings
>>> L3 = [1, 1.5, 2.5, 7] # list of integer and float numbers
>>> L4 = ['a', 'b', 'c'] # list of characters
>>> L6 = [] # list with no values i.e., empty list
>>> L7 = ['Orange', 2.0, 5, [10,20]] # nested list
>>> L8 = [7, "Hello", 3.14] # list with mixed datatypes
```

Note that for string values you can use either single or double quotes with comma separator and numeric values are separated simply by comma separator.

A list within another list is called nested list. Although a list can contain another list, the nested list still counts as a single element. So, the length of list L7 is four. A list that contains no elements is called an *empty list*; you can create one with empty brackets [], as shown above. You can also create long list containing many elements by splitting the list across several lines. Note that opening and closing square brackets appear just in the beginning and at the end of the list.

```
evennum = [0, 2, 4, 6, 8, 10, 12, 14, 16,
18, 20, 22, 24, 26, 28, 30, 32, 34, 36,
38]
```

You can also create lists of single characters or digits using keyboard input. For example,

```
list1 = list(input('Enter elements of
list: '))
Enter elements of list: 2468
>>> list1
['2', '4', '6', '8']
```

Notice you have entered integers, but the data type of all entered characters entered is string. To enter a list of integers, you use eval() method as given below:

```
list2= eval(input("Enter list: " )
print(list2)
```

The string is a sequence of characters and a list is a sequence of values, but the list of characters is not the same as a string. To convert from the string to the list of characters, you can use list():

```
>>> s = 'hello'
>>> t = list(s)
>>> print(t)
['h', 'e', 'l', 'l', 'o']
```

To create an empty list (the list with no items, its length is 0), you can also use the built-in list type object :

```
>>> L = list() # empty list
>>> L
[]
>>> len(L)
0
```

Since list is the name of a built-in function, you should avoid using it as a variable name.

The list function breaks a string into individual letters. If you want to break a string into words, you can use the split method:

```
>>> s = 'work is worship'
>>> t = s.split()
>>> print(t)
['work', 'is', 'worship']
```

Lists can be multidimensional, i.e., nested inside other lists. Lists containing other lists can be used as a way of storing a matrix or table of information. A 3X3 matrix could be created by assigning a list of lists to a variable.

```
>>> matrix = [[1,2,3],[4,5,6],[7,8,9]]
```

Example 1 –**Creating list of five integers.**

```
# Creating list
list_of_elements = [] #empty list
print("Enter list of five integers")
for i in range(5):
    print("Enter integer", i)
    userinput=int(input())
    list_of_elements.append(userinput)
print("The list is: ",list_of_elements)

RUN
>>>
Enter list of five integers
Enter integer 0
4
Enter integer 1
7
Enter integer 2
9
Enter integer 3
3
Enter integer 4
2
The list is:  [4, 7, 9, 3, 2]
>>>
```

Figure 7.1 Creating List of Five Integers

7.2.1 Concept of Mutable Lists

Lists are mutable. This means that the value of an item in a list can be modified with an assignment statement. In other words, you can change the contents of a list without creating a new list. Strings, on the other hand, cannot be changed or modified.

```
>>> num = [17, 12, 18]
>>> num[1] = 5
>>> print(num)
[17, 5, 18]
```

The second element of num, which used to be 12, is now changed to 5. You can consider a list as a relationship between indices and elements. This relationship is called a mapping; each index "maps to" one of the elements.

Let's Try

Consider the following examples to update the values inside the list:

```
>>> List = [1, 2, 3, 4, 5, 6]
>>> print(List)
[1, 2, 3, 4, 5, 6]
>>> List[2] = 10;
>>> print(List)
[1, 2, 10, 4, 5, 6]
```

```
>>> a = [1,2,"anything",4.0]
>>> print(a)
[1, 2, 'anything', 4.0]
>>> a[2]='something'
>>> print(a)
[1, 2, 'something', 4.0]
```

7.3 ACCESSING LISTS

Lists are a container data type that acts as a dynamic array. In other words, the list is a sequence that can be indexed into and can grow and shrink. List elements have index numbers. Indexing and slicing operations on lists mostly work in the same way as they do with strings. List indexing is zero-based as it is with strings. Working from left to right, the first element has the index 0, the next has the index 1, and so on.

```
Num =[45,67,56,34]
print(Num(0))
45
```

it prints 45, because the location of a list starts at position 0.

7.3.1 Indexing

List data type is a container that holds a number of elements in a given order. For accessing an element of the list, indexing is used. Each item in a list corresponds to an index number, which is an integer value, starting with the index number 0 goes to length - 1.. You can use indexing to change items within the list, by setting an index number equal to a different value. This example shows the items at index 0 and 1 of the list x.

```
>>> x = ['apple', 'banana', 'pear']
>>> x[0]
'apple'
>>> x[1]
'banana'
```

Python allows negative indexing for its sequences. The negative indices are counted from the right. The index of -1 refers to the last item, -2 to the second last item and so on until the left most element is encountered. The following example shows the items at index -1 and -2.

```
>>> x[-1]
'pear'
>>> x[-2]
'banana'
```

The literal representation of a list is square brackets containing zero or more items, separated by commas.

An individual element of a list can also be accessed through their indexes. For example,

```
>>> ch = ['l','o','w','e','r']
>>> ch[0]
'l'
>>> ch[4]
'r'
>>> ch[-1]
'r'
>>> ch[-5]
'l'
```

Note that while accessing individual elements, if you give index outside the legal indices, Python will raise IndexError as shown below:

```
>>> ch[5]
Traceback (most recent call last):
  File "<pyshell#5>", line 1, in <module>
    ch[5]
IndexError: list index out of range
```

☞ *Accessing elements in a list is called indexing.*

Let's Try

Consider the following examples to understand indexing in a better way:

```
# Positive indexing
>>> List = [10, 20, 30, 40, 50]
>>> print(List)
[10, 20, 30, 40, 50]
>>> List[0]
10
>>> List[1]
20
>>> List[2]
30
>>> List[3]
40
>>> List[4]
50
```

```
# Negative indexing
>>> List = [10, 20, 30, 40, 50]
>>> print(List)
[10, 20, 30, 40, 50]
>>> List[-1]
50
>>> List[-2]
40
>>> List[-3]
30
>>> List[-4]
20
>>> List[-5]
10
```

Consider the following examples and write outputs:

```
>>> List=["first", "second", "third"]
>>> List[0]
>>> List[1]
>>> List[-1]
>>> List[-3]
```

```
>>> my_list = ['n','o','t','e']
>>> print(my_list[0])
>>> print(my_list[-4])
>>> print(my_list[3])
>>> print(my_list[-1])
```

7.3.2 Slicing

You know that a slice of a list is its sub-list. Just as you use indexing to access individual elements, you can use slicing to access range of elements. You do this by using two indices, separated by a colon (:). Slicing is very useful for extracting parts of a sequence. The numbering here is very important. The first index is the number of the first element you want to include.

List slicing is an operation that extracts certain elements from a list and forms them into another list, possibly with different number of indices and different index ranges. Slices are treated as boundaries, and the result will include all the elements between boundaries. The syntax for list slicing is as follows:

```
seq = L [start: stop: step]
```

The start, stop, step parts of the syntax are integers. Each of them is optional. They can be both positive and negative. If you omit first index, slice starts from 0, and omitting of stop will take it to end. Default value of step is 1.

You supply two indices as limits for your slice, where the first is included and the second is excluded.

Consider the following:

```
>>> numbers = [1, 2, 3, 4, 5, 6, 7, 8, 9, 10]
>>> numbers[3:6]
[4, 5, 6]
>>> numbers[0:1]
[1]
```

Let's say you want to access the last three elements of the list.

```
>>> numbers[7:10]
[8, 9, 10]
```

Now, the index 10 refers to element 11 which does not exist, but is one step after the last element you want.

In a regular slice, the step size is one, which means that the slice moves from one element to the next, returning all the elements between the start and end:

```
>>> numbers[0:10:1]
[1, 2, 3, 4, 5, 6, 7, 8, 9, 10]
```

In the above example, you can see that the slice includes another number, the step size, made explicit.

If the step size is set to a number greater than one, elements will be skipped accordingly. For example, a step size of two will include only alternate elements of the list between the start and the end:

```
>>> numbers[0:10:2]
[1, 3, 5, 7, 9]
numbers[3:6:3]
[4]
```

You can use the shortcuts, for example, if you want every fourth element of a sequence, you need to supply only a step size of four:

```
>>> numbers[::4]
[1, 5, 9]
```

The step size cannot be zero as that would not get you anywhere. However it can be negative, which means extracting the elements from right to left:

```
>>> numbers[8:3:-1]
[9, 8, 7, 6, 5]
>>> numbers[10:0:-2]
[10, 8, 6, 4, 2]
>>> numbers[0:10:-2]
[]
>>> numbers[::-2]
[10, 8, 6, 4, 2]
>>> numbers[5::-2]
[6, 4, 2]
>>> numbers[:5:-2]
[10, 8]
```

☞ *A negative index means traversal from the end of the list.*

As you can see, the first limit (the leftmost) is still included, while the second (the rightmost) is excluded. While using a negative step size, you need to have the first limit (start index) higher than the second one.

☞ *Accessing parts of segments is called slicing.*

Let's Try

Consider the following examples to understand slicing in a better way:

```
>>> list_x = [1, 2, 3, 4, 5]
>>> list_y = list_x[2:5]
>>> print(list_y)
[3, 4, 5]
>>> print(list_x)
[1, 2, 3, 4, 5]
```

```
>>> x = [1, 2, 3, 4]
>>> x[0:2]
[1, 2]
>>> x[1:4]
[2, 3, 4]
>>> x[0:-1]
[1, 2, 3]
```

Consider the following examples and write outputs:

```
n = [1, 2, 3, 4, 5, 6, 7, 8]
print(n[1:5])
print(n[:5])
print(n[1:])
print(n[:])
```

```
ind=['zero','one','two','three','four',
'five']
print(ind[2:4])
print(ind[:4])
print(ind[4:])
print(ind[:])
```

7.3.3 Traversing

The sequential accessing of each element in a list is called traversing. This can be done by using either *for* or *while* loop statements. This can be done in two as shown in the following examples:

Using 'in' operator inside for loop

'in' operator using for loop Iterates each element of a list in sequence. For example:

```
for x in [1,2,3]:
    print (x)

>>>
1
2
3
>>>
```

You can also use for/in to work on a string. The string acts like a list of its chars, prints all the chars in a string. For example,

```
str="Hello"
for ch in str:
    print(ch)
>>>
H
e
l
l
o
>>>
for ch in ['p', 'y', 't', 'h', 'o', 'n']:
   print (ch)
>>>
p
y
t
h
o
n
>>>
```

Note that each letter is accessed and displayed on a new line till all the elements are traversed and displayed.

The *in* construct on its own is an easy way to test if an element appears in a list or not.

```
Rainbow = ['Red', 'Orange', 'Yellow',
'Green', 'Blue', 'Indigo', 'Violet']
if 'Orange' in Rainbow:
       print("Yes")
>>>
Yes
>>>
```

Let's Try

Consider the following examples to understand traversing in a better way:

```
for Rainbow in ['Red', 'Orange', 'Yel-
low', 'Green', 'Blue', 'Indigo', 'Vio-
let']:
    print("I like",Rainbow)
>>>
I like Red
I like Orange
I like Yellow
I like Green
I like Blue
I like Indigo
I like Violet
>>>
```

```
namelist = ['Aman', 'Beena', 'Deepak']
for x in namelist:
  print("Hello", x)

>>>
Hello Aman
Hello Beena
Hello Deepak
>>>
```

Consider the following examples and write outputs:

```
for fruit in
['apple','banana','mango']:
    print("I like",fruit)
```

```
squares = [1, 4, 9, 16, 25]
sum = 0
for num in squares:
    sum += num
print (sum)
```

Using range() function

The range() gives a sequence of numbers in between the two integers given to it. The combination of the for-loop and the range() function allow you to build a traditional numeric for loop:

```
# print the numbers from 0 through 10
for i in range(11):
    print(i)
>>>
0
1
2
3
4
5
6
7
8
9
10
>>>
```

You can convert it to a list by using list(). Let's make it clear by following examples:

```
print(list(range(1,5)))
print(list(range(10)))
print(list(range(1,11)))
print(list(range(0)))
print(list(range(1,10,2)))
print(list(range(2,12,2)))
>>>
[1, 2, 3, 4]
[0, 1, 2, 3, 4, 5, 6, 7, 8, 9]
[1, 2, 3, 4, 5, 6, 7, 8, 9, 10]
[]
[1, 3, 5, 7, 9]
[2, 4, 6, 8, 10]
>>>
```

Note that range(1,5) includes 1 but not 5 and range(1,10,2) will create a sequence of numbers but with a step of 2.

len() is an useful function which you use on a list. It gives us the length (number of elements) of a list. For example:

```
# Use of len() on a list
a = list(range(1,5))
print(a)
print(len(a))
b = [12,23,27,33]
print(b)
print(len(b))

>>>
[1, 2, 3, 4]
4
[12, 23, 27, 33]
4
>>>
```

More examples of list traversal are discussed below:

Example 2 –**List traverse using while loop.**

```
# List traversing
numbers = [1 ,2, 3, 4, 5, 6, 7, 8, 9, 10]
i = 0
while i < 10:
    print(numbers[i],end=" ")
    i = i + 1


RUN
>>>
1 2 3 4 5 6 7 8 9 10
>>>
```

Figure 7.2 List Traversing Using while Loop

Example 3 –**Traversing list using for loop.**

```
# Traversing list using for loop
numbers = [1, 2, 3, 4, 5, 6, 7, 8, 9, 10]
for i in numbers:
    print(i, end =" ")

RUN
>>>
1 2 3 4 5 6 7 8 9 10
>>>
```

Figure 7.3 Traversing list Using for Loop

Example 4 –**Traversing list using while loop and len() function.**

```
# Traversing list using while loop and len() function
numbers = [1, 2, 3, 4, 5, 6, 7, 8, 9, 10]
i=0
while i < len(numbers):
    print(numbers[i],end =" ")
    i += 1

RUN
>>>
1 2 3 4 5 6 7 8 9 10
>>>
```

Figure 7.4 Traversing List Using while Loop and len() Function

Example 5 –**Traversing list and Printing even numbers.**

```
# Traversing list and printing even numbers
numbers = [1, 2, 3, 4, 5, 6, 7, 8, 9, 10]
i=1
while i < len(numbers):
    print(numbers[i],end =" ")
    i += 2

RUN
>>>
2 4 6 8 10
>>>
```

Figure 7.5 Traversing List and Printing even numbers

☞ *Note that len() is a built-in function, so you do not need to import it.*

Example 6 –**Program to print elements of list along with their indices.**

Program to print elements of a list with their positive and negative indices.

```
# Program to print elements of list along with their indices
ch = ['l', 'o', 'w', 'e', 'r']
length = len(ch)
for i in range(length):
    print("At positive index", i, "and negative index", (i-length), "element is :
", ch[i])

RUN
>>>
At positive index 0 and negative index -5 element is :  l
At positive index 1 and negative index -4 element is :  o
At positive index 2 and negative index -3 element is :  w
At positive index 3 and negative index -2 element is :  e
At positive index 4 and negative index -1 element is :  r
>>>
```

Figure 7.6 Program to Print Elements of List Along with Their Indices

Example 7 –**Program to find sum of the elements in a list.**

```
# To find sum of the elements in a list
a = [10,20,30,40]
s = 0
i = 0
while (i<len(a)):
  s = s+a[i]
  i=i+1
print("sum: ",s)

RUN
>>>
sum:  100
>>>
```

Figure 7.7 Program to find sum of the elements in a list.

Example 8 –**Program to display total and the average value of the elements in the list.**

```
# To display total and the average value of the elements in the list.
list = [93,79,73,56,59]
total = 0
i = 0
while i < len(list):
    total = total + list[i]
    i = i + 1
average = total / len(list)
print("Total: ", total)
print("Average: ",average)

RUN
>>>
Total:  360
Average:  72.0
>>>
```

Figure 7.8 Program to Print Elements of List Along with Their Indices

7.4 LIST OPERATIONS

There are several operations that are applicable to lists. These are discussed in the following sections:

7.4.1 Joining Lists

Joining list means to concatenate (add) two lists together. The plus (+) operator, applied to two lists, produces a new list that is a combination of them:

```
>>> a = [1, 2, 3]
>>> b = [4, 5, 6]
>>> c = a + b
>>> print(c)
[1, 2, 3, 4, 5, 6]
```

The + operator when used with lists requires both the operands to be of list type, other wise it will produce error. For example,

```
>>> li = [10, 20 ,30]
>>> li + 2
TypeError: can only concatenate list (not "int") to list
>>> li + "xyz"
TypeError: can only concatenate list (not "str") to list
```

7.4.2 Repeating Lists

Multiplying a list by an integer *n* creates a new list that repeats the original list *n* times. The * operator repeats a list the given number of times.

```
>>> [0] * 4
[0, 0, 0, 0]
>>> [1, 2, 3] * 3
[1, 2, 3, 1, 2, 3, 1, 2, 3]
```

The first example repeats [0] four times. The second example repeats the list [1, 2, 3] three times.

7.4.3 Slicing Lists

The slice operator also works on lists. If you omit the first index, the slice starts at the beginning. If you omit the second, the slice goes to the end. So if you omit both, the slice is a copy of the whole list.

```
>>> t = ['a', 'b', 'c', 'd', 'e', 'f']
>>> t[1:3]
['b', 'c']
>>> t[:4]
['a', 'b', 'c', 'd']
>>> t[3:]
['d', 'e', 'f']
>>> t[:]
['a', 'b', 'c', 'd', 'e', 'f']
```

The slice operator on the left side of an assignment operator can modify multiple elements:

```
>>> t = ['a', 'b', 'c', 'd', 'e', 'f']
>>> t[1:3] = ['x', 'y']
>>> print(t)
['a', 'x', 'y', 'd', 'e', 'f']
```

☞ *List slicing leads to an extracted part of a list because list slice is a list in itself.*

7.4.4 Comparing Lists

You can test whether the contents of two or more lists are the same or not. The comparison operators can be used to compare lists.

```
>>> [11, 22] == [11, 22]
True
>>> [11, 22] < [11, 33]
True
```

Let's Try

Find and write the output of the following Python codes:

```
for i in [1, 2, 3, 4][::-1]:
    print (i)
```

```
>>> [21, 22] == [21, 22]
>>> [21, 42] > [21, 33]
```

7.5 OBJECTS AND VALUES

If you execute these assignment statements:

```
a = 'apple'
b = 'apple'
```

You know that a and b both refer to a string, but you do not know if they refer to the same string. There are two possible states:

(a) In the first case, a and b refer to two different objects that have the same value.

(b) In the second case, they refer to the same object.

To check whether two variables refer to the same object or not, you can use the *is* operator.

```
>>> a = 'apple'
>>> b = 'apple'
>>> a is b
True
```

In this example, Python only created one string object, and both a and b refer to it.

But when you create two lists, you get two objects:

```
>>> a = [1, 3, 5]
>>> b = [1, 3, 5]
>>> a is b
False
```

In this case, you can say that two lists are equivalent because they have the same elements, but not identical, as they do not refer to the same object. If two objects are identical, they are also equivalent, but if they are equivalent, they are not necessarily identical.

7.5.1 Aliasing

A circumstance where two or more variables refer to the same object is called aliasing. If *a* refers to an object and you assign a to b, then both variables refer to the same object:

```
>>> a = [1, 3, 5]
>>> b = a
>>> b is a
True
```

The association of a variable with an object is called a reference. In this example, there are two references to the same object.

An object with more than one reference has more than one name, so you say that the object is aliased.

If the aliased object is mutable, changes made with one alias affect the other:

```
>>> b[1] = 7
>>> print(a)
[1, 7, 5]
```

7.6 LIST FUNCTIONS AND METHODS

Python provides various methods that operate on lists. For example, *append()* adds a new element to the end of a list, *extend()* takes a list as an argument and appends all of the elements, *sort()* arranges the elements of the list from low to high, and *pop()* modifies the list and returns the element that was removed.

Every list object that you create in Python is actually an instance of List class. The syntax of using it is discussed below:

```
<listObject>.<method name>()
```

7.6.1 len()

The built-in len() function is used to get the length of list.

```
>>> lst = ['a', 'b', 'c', 'd']
>>> len(a)
4
```

It is possible to nest lists (create list containing other lists), for example:

```
>>> q = [2, 3]
>>> p = [1, q, 4]
>>> len(p)
3
```

☞ *len() returns the number of items in the list.*

Let's Try

Find and write the output of the following Python codes:

```
a = ["Red", "Blue", "Green"]
print(len(a))
```

```
List = [1, 2, 3, 3, 2, 1]
print(len(List))
```

7.6.2 count()

To find out the number of times a value occurs in a list, use the count(value) method.

```
>>> basket = ['apple', 'banana', 'orange', 'apple']
>>> basket.count('apple')
2
>>> a_list = [47, "47", 47, 4747]
>>> a_list.count(47)
2
```

☞ *count() returns the number of occurrences of the specified object in the list.*

Let's Try

Find and write the output of the following Python codes:

```
>>> a_list = ['she', 'sells', 'seashells']
>>> a_list.count('she')
```

```
n = [1, 1, 2, 3, 4, 4, 4, 5]
print(n.count(4))
print(n.count(1))
print(n.count(2))
print(n.count(6))
```

Example 9 – **Demo of List count using count() Method.**

```
# Python List count using count() Method
colours = ['Red', 'Orange', 'Green', 'Blue', 'Red', 'Blue']
numbers = [7, 2, -5, 0, 7, -1, 2, 7]

print("Original List : ", colours)
print('Number of Times Colour Red is repeated = ', colours.count('Red'))
print('Number of Times Colour Blue is repeated = ', colours.count('Blue'))
print('Number of Times Colour Green is repeated ', colours.count('Green'))

print("\nOriginal number List : ", numbers)
print('Number of Times no.7 is repeated = ', numbers.count(7))
print('Number of Times no. 2 is repeated = ', numbers.count(2))
print('Number of Times no. 0 is repeated = ', numbers.count(0))

RUN
>>>
Original List :  ['Red', 'Orange', 'Green', 'Blue', 'Red', 'Blue']
Number of Times Colour Red is repeated =  2
Number of Times Colour Blue is repeated =  2
Number of Times Colour Green is repeated  1

Original number List :   [7, 2, -5, 0, 7, -1, 2, 7]
Number of Times no.7 is repeated =  3
Number of Times no. 2 is repeated =  2
Number of Times no. 0 is repeated =  1
>>>
```

Figure 7.9 Python List count using count() Method

7.6.3 append()

To add an item to the end of a list, use the append() method. This method changes the list in place. The syntax of append() method is:

```
list.append(item)
```

The item can be numbers, strings, another list, dictionary etc.

This example adds the string 'apple' to a list:

```
>>> basket = ['apple', 'banana', 'orange']
>>> basket.append('apple')
>>> basket
['apple', 'banana', 'orange', 'apple']
```

This example adds the integer 444 to a list:

```
>>> items = [111, 222, 333]
>>> items.append(444)
>>> items
[111, 222, 333, 444]
```

Remember, list methods modify the target list in place. They do not return a new list:

```
>>> a = ['a', 'b']
>>> x = a.append(17)
>>> print(x)
None
>>> a
['a', 'b', 17]
```

Also, append() allows you to append a string as a single entity:

```
>>> a = ['a', 'b']
>>> a.append('cat')
>>> a
['a', 'b', 'cat']
```

Let's Try

Find and write the output of the following Python codes:

```
a = ["Red", "Blue"]
print(a)
a.append("Green")
print(a)
```

```
odd = [1, 3, 5]
odd.append(7)
print(odd)
```

☞ *append() adds an item to the end of the list.*

7.6.4 extend()

To add the items of one list i.e., iterable object to an existing list, use the extend() method. In other words, all the items of a list are added at the end of already created list. The syntax is:

list.extend(list2)

Here *list* is primary list, which will be extended and list2 will be added to list.

This example adds elements of list y to x.

```
>>> x = ['apple', 'banana', 'orange']
>>> y= ['pear', 'mango']
>>> x.extend(y)
>>> x
['apple',  'banana',  'orange',  'pear',
'mango']
```

This example adds elements of list b to a.

```
>>> a = [11, 22, 33,]
>>> b = [44, 55]
>>> a.extend(b)
>>> a
[11, 22, 33, 44, 55]
```

If the iterable object is a string, each character is added individually. This example adds each character of the string 'pear'.

```
>>> x = ['apple', 'banana', 'orange']
>>> x.extend('pear')
>>> x
['apple',  'apple',  'banana',  'orange',
'p', 'e', 'a', 'r']
```

This example adds all elements of a list to the another list:

```
>>> odd = [1, 3, 5, 7]
>>> odd.extend([9, 11, 13])
>>> print(odd)
[1, 3, 5, 7, 9, 11, 13]
```

☞ *One common pattern is to start a list a the empty list [], then use append() or extend() to add elements to it.*

Let's Try

Find and write the output of the following Python codes:

```
>>> x = [1, 2, 3]
>>> y = [4, 5, 6]
>>> x.extend(y)
>>> print(x)
```

```
>>> t1 = ['a', 'b', 'c']
>>> t2 = ['d', 'e']
>>> t1.extend(t2)
>>> print (t1)
```

7.6.5 insert()

You have learned that you can put an element to the end of a list by using the method "append". To work efficiently with a list, you need also a way to add elements to arbitrary positions inside of a list. This can be done with insert() method. It Inserts an item at a specified position and move the remaining items to the right. The syntax is as follows:

list.insert(<position, element)

Note: Position mentioned should be within the range of List

This example inserts an item at the beginning of a list:

```
>>> items
[111, 222, 333, 444]
>>> items.insert(0, 1)
>>> items
[1, 111, 222, 333, 444]
```

This example inserts a string in the middle of the list:

```
>>> numbers = [1, 2, 3, 5, 6, 7]
>>> numbers.insert(3, 'four')
>>> numbers
[1, 2, 3, 'four', 5, 6, 7]
```

☞ *insert() method inserts the element/item at the given index, shifting elements to the right.*

Let's Try

Find and write the output of the following Python codes:

```
a = ["green", "blue"]
print(a)
a.insert(0, "red")
print(a)
a.insert(2, "yellow")
print(a)
```

```
>>> a = [2, 1, 3, 4]

#inserts element 5 at index 3
>>> a.insert(3,5)
>>> a
```

```
>>> a = [1, 5, 3, 4]
>>> a.insert(2,7)
>>> a
```

Example 10 –**Demo of append(), insert() and extend() methods.**

```
# Demo of append(), insert() and extend() methods
colours = ['Red', 'Orange', 'Green']
print(colours) # print original list

# Adding items using Python append() method
colours.append('Black')
print(colours)

# inserting items using Python insert() method
colours.insert(2, 'Yellow')
print(colours)

# Extending List using Python extend() method
colours_new = ['Blue','Pink']
colours.extend(colours_new)
print(colours)

RUN
>>>
['Red', 'Orange', 'Green']
['Red', 'Orange', 'Green', 'Black']
['Red', 'Orange', 'Yellow', 'Green', 'Black']
['Red', 'Orange', 'Yellow', 'Green', 'Black', 'Blue', 'Pink']
>>>
```

Figure 7.10 Demo of append(), insert() and extend() methods

7.6.6 pop()

To delete one or more elements, i.e., remove an element, many built in functions can be used, such as pop(), remove() and keywords such as del. The pop() removes the item at the given position in the list, and returns it. If no index is specified, pop() removes and returns "rightmost", i.e., the last item in the list. So, you can push items onto the right end of a list and pop items off the right end of a list with append() and pop() respectively. This enables us to use the list as a stack like data structure. It syntax is:
`list.pop([index])`
Note Index is not a necessary parameter, if not mentioned takes the last index. If the optional <index> parameter is specified, the item at that index is removed and returned. <index> may be negative. <Index> defaults to -1, so list.pop(-1) is equivalent to list.pop(). The method 'pop' raises an IndexError exception if the list is empty or the index is out of range.

```
# Example 1: No index specified
a = ["red", "blue", "green"]
print(a)
a.pop()
print(a)
>>>
['red', 'blue', 'green']
['red', 'blue']
>>>
# Example 2: Index specified
a = ["red", "blue", "green"]
print(a)
a.pop(1)
print(a)
a.pop(-2)
```

```
print(a)
>>>
['red', 'blue', 'green']
['red', 'green']
['green']
>>>
# Example 3: No index specified
>>> items = [111, 222, 333, 444, ]
>>> items
[111, 222, 333, 444]
>>> items.append(555)
>>> items
[111, 222, 333, 444, 555]
>>> items.pop()
555
>>> items
[111, 222, 333, 444]

>>> a = [11, 22, 33, 44, ]
>>> b = a.pop()
>>> a
[11, 22, 33]
>>> b
44
>>> b = a.pop()
>>> a
[11, 22]
>>> b
33

>>> x = [1, 2, 3]
>>> x.pop()
3
>>> x
[1, 2]
>>> x.pop(0)
1
>>> x
[2]
```

Note that when calling pop() without any arguments, the last member of the list is removed from the list and returned.

☞ *The pop() method is the only list method that both modifies the list and returns a value (other than None).*

Using pop(), you can implement a common data structure called a stack. A stack like this works just like a stack of plates. You can put plates on top, and you can remove plates from the top. The last one you put into the stack is the first one to be removed. (This principle is called Last-In, First-Out or LIFO).

☞ *The pop() method removes and returns an element at the given index.*

Let's Try

Find and write the output of the following Python codes:

```
>>> fruits = ["Apple", "Banana", "Mango", "Pears"]
>>> fruits.pop(0) # first item
'Apple'
>>> fruits
["Banana", "Mango", "Pears"]
>>> fruits.pop(1)
'Mango'
>>> fruits
['Banana', 'Pears']
```

7.6.7 remove()

The remove() method is used to remove the first occurrence of a value. If you know the List item or the value inside the List then, you can use remove() method to remove the list item. The syntax is:

```
list.remove(element)
```

Element to be deleted is mentioned using list name and element.

```
>>> x = ['to', 'be', 'or', 'not', 'to', 'be']
>>> x.remove('be')
>>> x
['to', 'or', 'not', 'to', 'be']
```

Note that you have two 'be' items in this list but remove() method removed only one item. This is because, remove() method will only remove the first instance of the item and ignores the remaining.

```
>>> x.remove('bee') # Removing Non Existing Item from List
Traceback (most recent call last):
  File "<pyshell#3>", line 1, in <module>
    x.remove('bee')
NameError: name 'bee'is not defined
```

As you can see, you cannot remove something (in this case, the string 'bee') if it is not there in the list. That's why it is throwing an error.

☞ *The pop() method removes and returns an element with a specified index or the last element if the index number is not given. The remove() method removes a particular item from a list.*

Let's Try

Find and write the output of the following Python codes:

```
>>> a=[2,1,3,5,2,4]
>>> a.remove(2)
>>> a
```

```
# Removing Blue Item from Colours List
Colours   =   ['Red',   'Blue',   'Green',
'Pink']
Colours.remove('Blue')
print(Colours)
```

7.6.8 del statement

The del statement allows you to remove specific items from the list or to remove all items identified by a slice. To delete a single element from a Python list, use its index and use the slicing operator to delete a slice. The syntax is:

```
del list[i]
del ist[i:j]
>>> num = ['one', 'two', 'three', 'four',
'five', 'six']
>>> del num[3] # Deleting a single ele-
ment
>>> num
['one', 'two', 'three', 'five', 'six']
```

You can delete multiple elements out of the middle of a list by assigning the appropriate slice to an empty list. You can also use the del statement with the same slice:

```
>>> colours = ['red', 'blue', 'green',
'orange', 'pink', 'black']
>>> colours[1:5] = []
>>> colours
['red', 'black']
>>> colours = ['red', 'blue', 'green',
'orange', 'pink', 'black']
>>> del colours[1:5] # Deleting a few
elements
>>> colours
['red', 'black']
```

Use the del statement/keyword to delete the entire Python list.

```
>>> del colours # Deleting the entire
Python list
```

☞ *The del statement and the pop() method does somewhat the same thing, except that pop returns the removed item.*

Let's Try

Find and write the output of the following Python codes:

```
List = [0,1,2,3,4]
print(List)
del List[0]
print(List)
del List[3]
print(List)
```

```
fruits   =   ['Apple',   'Mango',   'Grape',
'Banana']
del fruits[3]
print(fruits)
```

7.6.9 reverse()

The reverse() method reverses the order of items/elements in the list. It's syntax is:

```
list.reverse()
>>> x = [1, 2, 3]
>>> x.reverse()
>>> x
[3, 2, 1]
a1 = ["bear", "lion", "tiger", "ele-
phant"]
a1.reverse()
print(a1)
['elephant', 'tiger', 'lion', 'bear']
```

Let's Try

Find and write the output of the following Python codes:

```
a = [3,7,5,2,6,1]
a.reverse()
print(a)
```

```
a1 = ["bee", "wasp", "butterfly"]
a1.reverse()
print(a1)
```

7.6.10 sort()

The sort() method is used to sort list in place. Sorting 'in place' means changing the original list so its elements are in sorted order, rather than simply returning a sorted copy of the list. It does not create a new list. It's syntax is:

```
list.sort()
```

For example,

```
>>> x = [4, 6, 2, 1, 7, 9]
>>> x.sort()
>>> x
[1, 2, 4, 6, 7, 9]
```

The confusion usually occurs when users want a sorted copy of a list while leaving the original alone.

```
>>> x = [4, 6, 2, 1, 7, 9]
>>> y = x.sort() # Don't do this!
>>> print(y)
None
```

Since sort() modifies x but returns nothing, you end up with the sorted x and the y containing None. One correct way of doing this would be to first bind y to a copy of x, and then sort y, as shown below:

```
>>> x = [4, 6, 2, 1, 7, 9]
>>> y = x[:]
>>> y.sort()
>>> x
[4, 6, 2, 1, 7, 9]
>>> y
[1, 2, 4, 6, 7, 9]
```

x[:] is a slice containing all the elements of x, effectively a copy of the entire list.

If the Python list members are strings, it sorts them according to their ASCII values.

```
>>> L1 = ['red', 'Blue', 'Green', 'Red', 'pink']
>>> L1.sort()
>>> print(L1)
['Blue', 'Green', 'Red', 'pink', 'red']
>>> sorted(['hello','HELLO','Hello'])
['HELLO', 'Hello', 'hello']
>>>
```

The sort() method sorts the elements in ascending order. With the reverse parameter set to True, the list is sorted in a descending order.

```
list.sort(reverse=True)
>>> names=['Vivek', 'Mohan', 'Swati', 'Krishna']
>>> names.sort(reverse=True)
>>> print(names)
['Vivek', 'Swati', 'Mohan', 'Krishna']
```

The built-in function sorted returns a new sorted list without modifying the source list. In other words, it returns a sorted version of the list, but does not change the original one. It's syntax is :

```
list.sorted()
>>> a = [4, 3, 5, 9, 2]
>>> sorted(a)
[2, 3, 4, 5, 9]
>>> a
[4, 3, 5, 9, 2]
```

The behavior of sort method and sorted function is exactly same except that sorted returns a new list instead of modifying the given list.

Example 11 –Program to sort list in ascending and descending order using sort() method.

```
# Program to sort list in ascending and descending order using sort() method.
n = [6, 7, 2, 1, 2, 9, 5, 6]

print("Original List")
print(n)

print("Sorted List in ascending order")
n.sort()
print(n)

print("Sorted List in descending order")
n.sort(reverse=True)
print(n)
```

(Contd...)

```
RUN
>>>
Original List
[6, 7, 2, 1, 2, 9, 5, 6]
Sorted List in ascending order
[1, 2, 2, 5, 6, 6, 7, 9]
Sorted List in descending order
[9, 7, 6, 6, 5, 2, 2, 1]
>>>
```

Figure 7.11 Program to sort list in ascending and descending order

Let's Try

Find and write the output of the following Python codes:

```
>>> a = [3,6,5,2,4,1]
>>> a.sort(reverse=True)
>>> print(a)
```

```
>>> t = ['d', 'c', 'e', 'b', 'a']
>>> t.sort()
>>> print(t)
```

☞ *sort() sorts items in a list in ascending order.*

7.6.11 clear()

When you are done with a list, you can remove all values contained in it by using the list.clear() method. clear() removes all items/elements from the list. It is equivalent to del a[:].

```
>>> x = [4, 6, 2, 1, 7, 9]
>>> x.clear()
[]
```

Note that after executing this method, it returns empty list.

☞ *You can also use the clear() method to empty a list.*

Let's Try

Find and write the output of the following Python codes:

```
>>> a = [3,6,5,2,4,1]
>>> a.clear()
>>> print(a)
```

```
>>> t = ['d', 'c', 'e', 'b', 'a']
>>> t.clear()
>>> print(t)
```

7.6.12 max() and min()

max() returns the largest item in an iterable (Eg, list) or the largest of two or more arguments. If more than one item shares the maximum value, only the first one encountered is returned.

min() returns the smallest item in an iterable (Eg, list) or the smallest of two or more arguments.

```
>>> x = [4, 6, 2, 1, 7, 9]
>>> max(x)
9
>>> min(x)
1
a = [11, 12, 13, 14, 15]
b = [11, 12, 13, 14]
print(max(a, b))
print(min(a,b))
>>>
[11, 12, 13, 14, 15]
[11, 12, 13, 14]
>>>
```

Example 12 –**Use of max() & min().**

```
# Use of max() & min()
names = ["Meera","Aman", "Sangeeta", "Preeti", "Upma","Nitika"]
print("Original List")
print(names)
print("Maximum ", max(names))
print("Minimum ", min(names))

RUN
>>>
Original List
['Meera', 'Aman', 'Sangeeta', 'Preeti', 'Upma', 'Nitika']
Maximum  Upma
Minimum  Aman
>>>
```

Figure 7.12 Use of max() & min()

Example 6 –**Program to find maximum and minimum in list**

```
# Program to find maximum and minimum in list
n = [6, 7, 2, 1, 2, 9, 5, 6]
print("Original List")
print(n)
print("\nMaximum ", max(n))

print("\nMinimum ", min(n))

RUN
>>>
Original List
[6, 7, 2, 1, 2, 9, 5, 6]
Maximum  9
Minimum  1
>>>
```

Figure 7.13 Program to find maximum and minimum in list

☞ *max() returns the largest item in the list where as min() returns the smallest item in the list.*

Let's Try

Find the outputs for the following:

```
y = [10, 42, 72, 16, 27]
m = max(y)
p = y.index(m)
print(m, p)
```

```
lst = [0, 1, 2, 3, 'four', 0x101]
print( len(lst))
```

```
Num_List = [4,13,22,29,30,44,52]
Num_List.sort()
print("Sorted list is ",Num_List)
print("Mid        value        is        ",
Num_List[int(len(Num_List)/2)])
```

```
TXT   = ["20","50","30","40"]
CNT   = 3
TOTAL = 0
for C in [7,5,4,6]:
    T = TXT[CNT]
    TOTAL = float (T) + C
    print(TOTAL)
    CNT-=1
```

```
Name=["Amar","Shveta","Parag"]
for i in Name:
    if i[0]=='S':
      print(i)
```

7.7 LINEAR SEARCH ON LIST

Locating a particular data item in a list is known as *Searching*. The application of search occurs in computer when a particular data item is required from a set of stored data. The search is said to be *successful* if the desired data is located otherwise the search is considered to be *unsuccessful*.

Linear or Sequential searching is finding or searching an element in a linear i.e. one after the other or traversing each and every element and checking if it is the one required.

In sequential search, each element of a list is compared one by one with the given ITEM to be searched, until either the desired element is found or the end of the list is reached.

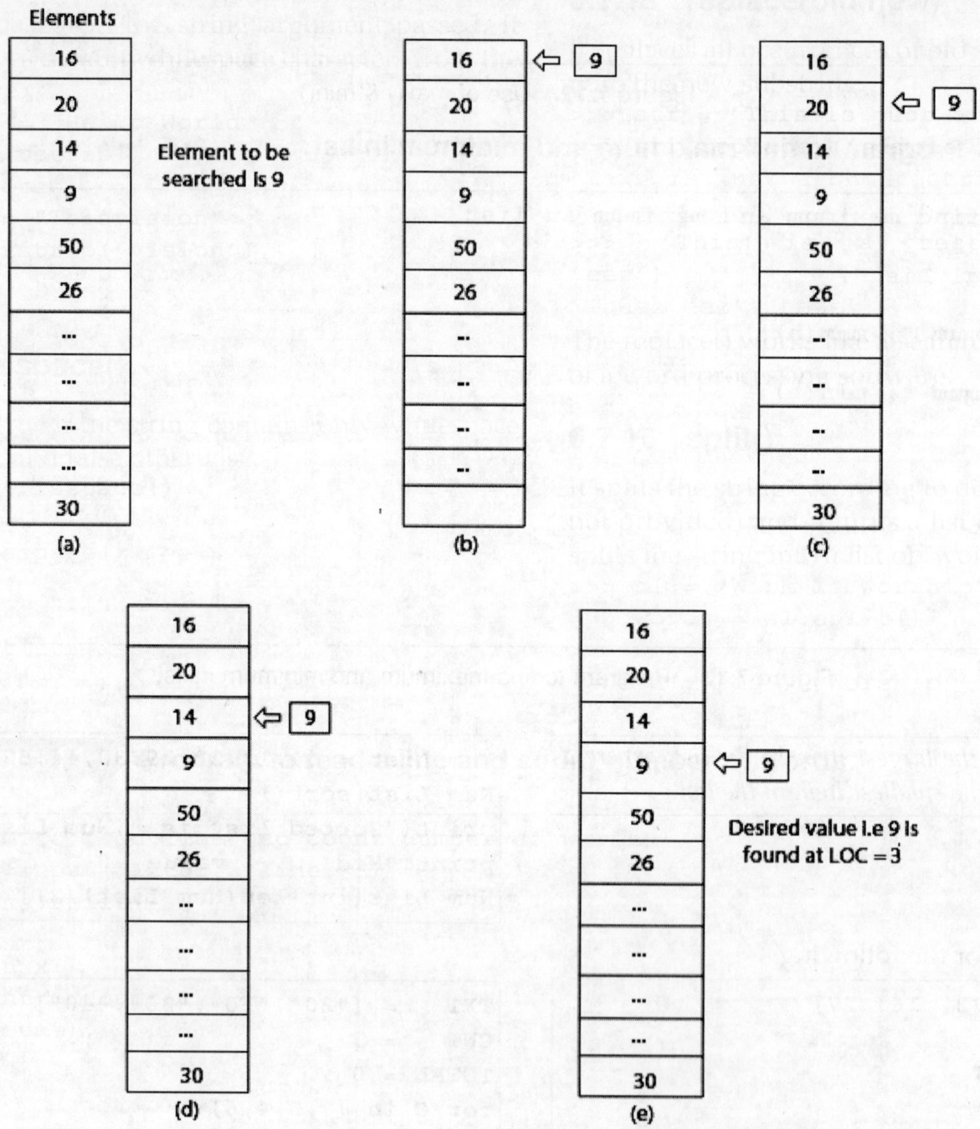

Figure 7.14 Illustration of linear search

Let us take an example to understand linear search in a better way. Consider the unsorted list shown in Figure 7.14 which contains *n* elements. Suppose the element that is to be searched is 9. The concept of sequential search states that the element 9 is matched with each element of list. If it matches, then the search is completed. Otherwise, next element from the list is fetched and compared. This process is continued until either the desired element is found or list is exhausted. (See Figure 7.14).

To access individual elements of a list, you should use the index position. The first location or index of a list is 0. So element 9 is located at index position or location 3.

Sequential search is a simple and easy method, but is efficient only for small size of list and highly inefficient for large sized list because if the list is big, then the number of comparisons are more. In the worst case, you will have to make N comparisons, to search for the record in the end of the list, where N is the maximum number of elements in the list.

Example 13 –**Searching Element in a List Using for Loop.**

```
# Searching element in a list
list_of_elements = [14, 12, 18, 19, 13, 17]
print("list of items is", list_of_elements)
x = int(input("Enter number to search: "))
found = False
for i in range(len(list_of_elements)):
 if(list_of_elements[i] == x):
  found = True
  print("%d found at %dth position"%(x,i))
  break
if(found == False):
 print("%d is not in list"%x)

RUN
>>>
list of items is [14, 12, 18, 19, 13, 17]
Enter number to search: 13
13 found at 4th position
>>>
```

Figure 7.15 Program for Linear Search Using for Loop

Example 14 –**Searching Element in a List Using while Loop.**

```
# Searching element in a list
items = [2, 8, 9, 12, 17]
print("list of items is", items)
x = int(input("enter item to search:"))
i = flag = 0
while i < len(items):
 if items[i] == x:
     flag = 1
     break
 i = i + 1

if flag == 1:
     print(x,"found at position:", i)
else:
     print(x,"not found in a list")
```

(Contd...)

```
RUN
>>>
list of items is [2, 8, 9, 12, 17]
enter item to search:12
12 found at position: 3

list of items is [2, 8, 9, 12, 17]
enter item to search:7
7 not found in a list
>>>
```

Figure 7.16 Program for Linear Search Using while Loop

7.8 COUNTING FREQUENCY OF ELEMENTS IN A LIST

Example 15 –Program to Find the Frequency of Numbers in a List.

```
# To find the frequency of numbers in a list
my_list = [] #empty list
print("Enter list of five integers")
for i in range(5):
    print("Enter integer", i)
    userinput=int(input())
    my_list.append(userinput)
print("The list is: ",my_list)
length=len(my_list)
element=int(input("Enter element :"))
c=0
for i in range(0,length-1):
   if element==my_list[i]:
         c+=1
if c == 0:
   print(element, "not found in a given list")
else:
   print(element, "has frequency as", c, "in given list")
RUN
>>>
Enter list of five integers
Enter integer 0
2
Enter integer 1
3
Enter integer 2
2
Enter integer 3
2
Enter integer 4
5
The list is:  [2, 3, 2, 2, 5]
Enter element :2
2 has frequency as 3 in given list
>>>
```

Figure 7.17 Program to Find Frequency of Numbers in a List

Let's Try

Write the output of following program given in Figure 7.18.

```
#To find the frequency of elements in a list
my_list=eval(input("Enter list: "))
#print('Original List : ',my_list)
length=len(my_list)
element=int(input("Enter element :"))
c=0
for i in range(0,length-1):
  if element==my_list[i]:
        c+=1
if c == 0:
   print(element, "not found in a given list")
else:
   print(element, "has frequency as", c, "in given list")
```

Figure 7.18 Program to Find Frequency of elements in a List

REVIEW QUESTIONS WITH ANSWERS

1. Multiple Choice Questions

1. List are similar to string in a way(s) like:
   a. Indexing
   b. Slicing
   c. Accessing individual elements
   d. All of the above
2. An empty list is indicated by:
   a. {}   b. []
   c. ()   d. None of the above
3. Which of the following statement is true?
   a. Lists is immutable
   b. Strings and tuples are mutable
   c. Lists are mutable
   d. None of these
4. We can have list of following type:
   a. List of strings
   b. List of mixed value types
   c. List of numbers
   d. All of the above
5. List containing another list is known as:
   a. Nested list   b. Empty list
   c. Joint list   d. None of these
6. If you omit the first index, the slice starts at the ______.
   a. Beginning
   b. End
   c. Middle
   d. None of these
7. What will be the output of the following Python code:
```
>>> numbers = [17, 123]
>>> numbers[1] = 5
>>> print numbers
```
   a. [17, 5, 123]
   b. [5, 17, 123]
   c. [17, 5]
   d. None of the above
8. An empty list is represented by:
   a. []   b. ()
   c. {}   d. !
9. What will be the output of following code:
```
a=[1,2,3,4,5]
print(a[::2])
```
   a. [4, 5]
   b. [1, 3, 5]
   c. [1, 2]
   d. [1, 2, 3, 4]
10. **What will be the output of following code:**
```
a=[1,2,3,4,5]
print(a[::])
```
   a. [1, 2, 3, 4, 5]   b. [1, 5]
   c. [1, 2, 3, 4]   d. None of these

2. State True or False for the following:

1. Individual elements of a list can accessed through their indexes.
2. A string is a sequence of characters and a list is a sequence of values.
3. clear() method after executing returns empty list.
4. Slicing list using negative indexes is not allowed.
5. If we specify list[1:4] then slicing will start at index position 1 and ends at index position 3.
6. In list an omitted first index defaults to zero, an omitted second index defaults to the size of the list being sliced.
7. **>>> x = [1, 2, 3, 4]**
   >>> x[0:2]
   displays
   [1, 2, 3]
8. Negative indices can be used to index the list from left.
9. When a wrong index is used, Python gives an error.
10. The built-in function len() can be used to find the length of a list.

3. Match the following:

1. Element	a. A sequence of values
2. Index	b. Sequential accessing of each element
3. List	c. Adds a new element to the end of a list
4. Traversal	d. One of the values in sequence
5. >>> nums = [3, 12, 74] >>> print len(nums)	e. An integer value
6. >>> nums = [3, 12, 74] >>> print max(nums)	f. Concatenates lists
7. sort()	g. 3
8. append()	h. 74
9. * operator	i. Low to high
10. + operator	j. Repeats a list

4. Fill in the blanks:

1. _______ is very useful for extracting parts of a sequence.
2. One of the values in a list (or other sequence), also called _______.
3. A list that is an element of another list is called _______.
4. A circumstance where two or more variables refer to the same object is called _______.
5. The association of a variable with an object is called a _______.
6. The list function breaks a string into _______ letters.
7. To convert from a string to a list of characters, you can use _______.
8. If an index has a _______ value, it counts backward from the end of the list.
9. A list that contains no elements is called an _______.
10. _______ a Python list by an integer makes copies of its items that a number of times while preserving the order.

Answers

1. 1. d 2. b 3. c 4. d 5. a 6. a 7. c 8. a 9. b 10. a

2. 1. T 2. T 3. T 4. F 5. T 6. T 7. F 8. F 9. T 10. T

3. 1. d 2. e 3. a 4. b 5. g 6. h 7. i 8. c 9. j 10. f

4. 1. Slicing 2. Item/element 3. Nested list 4. Aliasing 5. Reference 6. Individual 7. list() 8. Negative 9. Empty list 10. Multiplying

Short Answer Questions

1. What is the significance of list?

Ans A list is a collection of a number of values or variables in an ordered sequence. These values are called elements. The element can be any Python object, including numbers, strings, functions, and other lists.

2. What is the difference between string and list?

Ans The difference between string and list are as follows:

(a) Strings are always sequences of characters whereas lists can contain values of any type, i.e., mixed data types. A single list can contain numbers, strings, other lists.
(b) Strings are immutable whereas lists are mutable i.e., it is possible to change individual elements of a list or can be modified by assigning new values.

3. Lists are mutable. Comment.

Ans Lists are mutable. This means that the value of an item in a list can be modified with an assignment statement.

4. Why are Python Lists called dynamic arrays?

Ans Lists are dynamic arrays. They are arrays in the sense that we can index items in a list (for example, mylist[3]), and we can select sub-ranges (for example, mylist[2:4]).
They are dynamic in the sense that we can add and remove items after the list is created.

5. How will we extract different parts of a list? Explain with an example.

Ans Python uses slicing for extracting parts of a list structure. Such parts are known as sublists or slices. For example,

A[i:] is the sublist starting with index i in A and continuing to the end of A:

```
>>> A = [2, 3.5, 8, 10]
>>> A[2:]
[8, 10]
```

A[i:j] is the sublist starting with index i in A and continuing up to index j-1. Make sure we remember that the element corresponding to index j is not included in the sublist:

```
>>> A[1:3]
[3.5, 8]
```

A[:i] is the sublist starting with index 0 in A and continuing up to the element with index i-1:

```
>>> A[:3]
[2, 3.5, 8]
```

A[1:-1] extracts all elements except the first and the last (recall that index -1 refers to the last element), and A[:] is the whole list:

```
>>> A[1:-1]
[3.5, 8]
>>> A[:]
[2, 3.5, 8, 10]
```

6. What is an empty list in Python?

Ans A list that contains no elements is called an empty list; we can create one with empty brackets, [].

7. How do list indices work in Python?

Ans List indices work in the same way as string indices:

(a) Any integer expression can be used as an index.
(b) If we try to read or write an element that does not exist, we get an IndexError.
(c) If an index has a negative value, it counts backward i.e., from the end of the list.

8. Explain the working of + and * operators in a list.

Ans The + operator concatenates lists. For example,

```
>>> a = [1, 2, 3]
>>> b = [4, 5, 6]
>>> c = a + b
>>> print(c)
[1, 2, 3, 4, 5, 6]
```

The * operator repeats a list a given number of times. For example,:

```
>>> [0] * 4
[0, 0, 0, 0]
>>> [1, 2, 3] * 3
[1, 2, 3, 1, 2, 3, 1, 2, 3]
```

The first example repeats [0] four times. The second example repeats the list [1, 2, 3] three times.

9. What happens when you do following with the list?

(a) If you omit the first index.
(b) If you omit the second.
(c) if you omit both.

Ans

(a) If we omit the first index, the slice starts at the beginning.
(b) If we omit the second, the slice goes to the end.
(c) If we omit both, the slice is a copy of the whole list.

10. How does append() method differ from extend() method?

Ans append() method adds a new element to the end of a list. For example,

```
>>> t = ['a', 'b', 'c']
```

>>> t.append('d')
>>> print(t)
['a', 'b', 'c', 'd']

extend() method takes a list as an argument and appends all of the elements. For example,:
>>> t1 = ['a', 'b', 'c']
>>> t2 = ['d', 'e']
>>> t1.extend(t2)
>>> print(t1)
['a', 'b', 'c', 'd', 'e']
This example leaves t2 unmodified.

11. Explain count() method with example.

Ans The count method counts the occurrences of an element in a list. For example,
>>> ['to', 'be', 'or', 'not', 'to', 'be'].count('to')
2

12. What is index() method used for?

Ans The index() method is used for searching lists to find the index of the first occurrence of a value. For example,
>>> knights = ['We', 'are', 'the', 'knights', 'who', 'say', 'ni']
>>> knights.index('who')
4

13. What is aliasing? Explain with an example.

Ans A circumstance where two or more variables refer to the same object is called aliasing. If variable a refers to an object and we assign b to a, then both variables refer to the same object. For example,
>>> a = [1, 3, 5]
>>> b = a
>>> b is a
True

14. What do you mean by sequence?

Ans A sequence is an ordered collection of items, indexed by positive integers. It is combination of mutable and non-mutable data types. Three types of sequence data types available in Python are strings, lists, and tuples.

15. What is indexing?

Ans All elements in a sequence are numbered as from 0,1,2, and so on. We can access them individually with their respective number. This is called indexing. We use an index to fetch an element. All sequences can be indexed in this way. When we use a negative index, Python counts from the right, that is, from the last element. The last element is at position -1.

16. Write a program that asks you to enter a year, a month (as a number from 1 to 12), and a day (1 to 31), and then prints out the date with the proper month name.

Ans

```
# Print out a date, given year, month, and day as numbers
months = [
'January',
'February',
'March',
'April',
'May',
'June',
'July',
'August',
'September',
'October',
'November',
'December'
]
# A list with one ending for each number from 1 to 31
endings = ['st', 'nd', 'rd'] + 17 * ['th'] \
+ ['st', 'nd', 'rd'] + 7 * ['th'] \
+ ['st']
year = input('Year: ')
```

(Contd...)

```
month = input('Month (1-12): ')
day = input('Day (1-31): ')
month_number = int(month)
day_number = int(day)
# Remember to subtract 1 from month and day to get a correct index
month_name = months[month_number-1]
ordinal = day + endings[day_number-1]
print(month_name + ' ' + ordinal + ', ' + year)


RUN
>>>
Year: 2018
Month (1-12): 07
Day (1-31): 25
July 25th, 2018
>>>
```

Figure 1 Program for Q16

17. Write a program to print domain name using slice operation.

Ans

```
# Split up a URL of the form http://www.myschool.org
url = input('Please enter the URL: ')
domain = url[11:-4]
print("Domain name: " + domain)

RUN
>>>
Please enter the URL: http://www.myschool.org
Domain name: myschool
>>>
```

Figure 2 Program for Q17

18. Write a program that reads in a user name and checks the entered password against a database (a list) that contains pairs of names and password. If the name and password pair is found in the database, the string 'Access granted' is printed, otherwise "Access denied" is printed.

Ans

```
# Check a user name and password
database = [
['Ajay', '1111'],
['Suman', '2222'],
['Abhishek', '3333'],
['Vivek', '4444']
]
username = input('User name: ')
password = input('Password: ')
```

(Contd...)

```
if [username, password] in database:
    print('Access granted')
else:
    print('Access denied'   )

RUN
>>>
User name: Vivek
Password: 4444
Access granted.
>>>
>>>
User name: Mona
Password: 5555
Access denied.
>>>
```

Figure 3 Program for Q18

19. Write a program to print average of entered numbers using two different methods.

Ans a

```
total = 0
count = 0
while True :
    inp = input('Enter a number: ')
    if inp == 'done' : break
    value = float(inp)
    total = total + value
    count = count + 1
average = total / count
print('Average:', average)
RUN
>>>
Enter a number: 5
Enter a number: 7
Enter a number: 8
Enter a number: done
Average: 6.66666666667
>>>
>>>
Enter a number: 8.8
Enter a number: 9.7
Enter a number: 9.5
Enter a number: done
Average: 9.333333333333334
>>>
```

Figure 4 Program for Q19

Ans b

```
# Averaging with a list
numlist = list()
while True :
    inp = input('Enter a number: ')
    if inp == 'done' : break
    value = float(inp)
    numlist.append(value)
average = sum(numlist) / len(numlist)
print('Average:', average)

RUN
>>>
Enter a number: 5
Enter a number: 8
Enter a number: 9
Enter a number: 8
Enter a number: 9
Enter a number: done
Average: 7.8
>>>
```

Figure 5 Program for Q19

20. What is the default value for the first index if you omit the first index value in a slice?

Ans The default value is zero (0).

21. What is the default value for the second index if you omit the second index value in a slice?

Ans The default value for the second index is the length of the string (the actual number of characters in the string).

22. What is the purpose of negative slice indices?

Ans Negative indices can be used to count from the right end of the string.

23. Explain the functions of del statement, pop() and remove().

Ans The del statement can be used to remove an individual item, or to remove all items identified by a slice. The pop() method removes an individual item and returns it, while remove() searches for an item, and removes the first matching item from the list.

24. If two list are equivalent, is it necessary that they are identical also. Explain with an example.

Ans

```
>>> a = [2, 4, 6]
>>> b = [2, 4, 6]
>>> a is b
False
```

Above two lists are equivalent, because they have the same elements, but not identical, because they are not the same object. If two objects are identical, they are also equivalent, but if they are equivalent, they are not necessarily identical.

25. Name three types of sequence objects.

Ans The types of sequence objects are string, tuple, and list.

26. Which item in the sequence is selected for an index value of -1?

Ans The last item in the sequence is selected for an index value of -1.

27. Just like C, C++, and Java, Python supports character type; True or False?

Ans False. There is no character type in Python. Rather, a string items are characters.

28. How are lists formed?

Ans Lists are formed by placing a comma-separated sequence of expressions in square brackets.

29. What are the characteristics of list?

Ans A list is a sequence of items stored as a single object. Characteristics of list are as follows:

(a) Items in a list can be accessed by indexing, and sublists can be extracted by slicing.

(b) Lists are mutable; individual items or entire slices can be replaced through assignment statements.

(c) Lists can grow and shrink as needed.

30. Write a program to find sum of all elements in a list.

Ans

```
# Program to find sum of all elements in a list
Num_List = []
Number = int(input("Enter total number of elements in a List: "))
for i in range(1, Number + 1):

    value = int(input("Enter element : "))
    Num_List.append(value)
    print(Num_List)
sum = 0
for item in Num_List:
    sum = sum + item
print("Sum of all elements in a List: ",sum)

RUN
>>>
Enter total number of elements in a List: 3
Enter element : 4
[4]
Enter element : 6
[4, 6]
Enter element : 5
[4, 6, 5]
Sum of all elements in a List:  15
>>>
```

Figure 6 Program for Q30

31. Write a program to find product of all elements in a list.

Ans

```
# Program to find product of all elements in a list
Num_List = []
Number = int(input("Enter total number of elements in a List: "))
for i in range(1, Number + 1):
    value = int(input("Enter element : "))
    Num_List.append(value)
    print(Num_List)
product = 1
for item in Num_List:
    product = product * item
print("Product of all elements in a List: ",product)

RUN
>>>
Enter total number of elements in a List: 3
Enter element : 2
[2]
```

(Contd...)

```
Enter element : 6
[2, 6]
Enter element : 4
[2, 6, 4]
Product of all elements in a List:  48
>>>
```

Figure 7 Program for Q31

32. Write a program to find the middle element in a random number list.

Ans

```
#Program to find the middle element in a random number list
Num_List = []
Number = int(input("Enter total number of elements in a List: "))
for i in range(1, Number + 1):
    value = int(input("Enter element : "))
    Num_List.append(value)
    Num_List.sort()
print("Sorted list is ",Num_List)
print("Mid value is ",Num_List[int(len(Num_List)/2)])

RUN
>>>
Enter total number of elements in a List: 5
Enter element : 22
Enter element : 66
Enter element : 33
Enter element : 11
Enter element : 55
Sorted list is  [11, 22, 33, 55, 66]
Mid value is  33
>>>
```

Figure 8 Program for Q32

33. Write a program to find sum of even and odd numbers in a List.

Ans

```
# Program to find Sum of Even and Odd Numbers in a List
Num_List = []
Even_Sum = 0
Odd_Sum = 0
Number = int(input("Enter total number of elements in a List: "))
for i in range(1, Number + 1):
    value = int(input("Enter element : "))
    Num_List.append(value)
for j in range(Number):
    if(Num_List[j] % 2 == 0):
        Even_Sum = Even_Sum + Num_List[j]
    else:
        Odd_Sum = Odd_Sum + Num_List[j]
print("\nThe Sum of Even Numbers in the List =  ", Even_Sum)
print("The Sum of Odd Numbers in the List =  ", Odd_Sum)
```

(Contd...)

```
RUN
>>>
Enter total number of elements in a List: 6
Enter element : 2
Enter element : 5
Enter element : 4
Enter element : 6
Enter element : 3
Enter element : 5

The Sum of Even Numbers in the List =   12
The Sum of Odd Numbers in the List =   13
>>>
```

Figure 9 Program for Q33

34. Write a program to find maximum and minimum number in a list.

Ans

```
# To find Maximum and Minimum number in a list.
lst = []
num = int(input('How many numbers: '))
for n in range(num):
    numbers = int(input('Enter number '))
    lst.append(numbers)
print("Maximum element in the list is :", max(lst))
print("Minimum element in the list is :", min(lst))

RUN
>>>
How many numbers: 5
Enter number 45
Enter number 67
Enter number 23
Enter number 12
Enter number 53
Maximum element in the list is : 67
Minimum element in the list is : 12
>>>
```

Figure 10 Program for Q34

35. Write a program to add two matrices.

Ans

```
# Program to add two matrices using nested loop
X = [[2,4,3],
     [4 ,5,6],
     [7 ,8,9]]
Y = [[3,4,1],
     [2,7,8],
     [4,3,5]]
add = [[0,0,0],
          [0,0,0],
          [0,0,0]]
```

(Contd...)

```
for i in range(len(X)):
   for j in range(len(X[0])):
       add[i][j] = X[i][j] + Y[i][j]
for k in add:
   print(k)

RUN
>>>
[5, 8, 4]
[6, 12, 14]
[11, 11, 14]
>>>
```

Figure 11 Program for Q35

36. Write a program to transpose a matrix.

Ans

```
X = [[17,72],
     [14 ,65],
     [43 ,23]]
trans = [[0,0,0],
         [0,0,0]]
for i in range(len(X)):
for j in range(len(X[0])):
       trans[j][i] = X[i][j]
for k in trans:
  print(k)

RUN
>>>
[17, 14, 43]
[72, 65, 23]
>>>
```

Figure 12 Program for Q36

37. Write outputs for the following:

a.

```
li=["A1","A2","B1","B2","C1","C2"]
length=0
for i in li :
  length +=1
print ('Length of the list is :',length)
```

Figure 13 Program for Q37(a)

Ans a 6
2

b.

```
li=[11,22,55,77]
length=0
for i in li :
  length +=1
print ('Length of the list is :',length)
```

Figure 14 Program for Q37(b)

Ans b Length of the list is : 4

c.

```
stringLen='Python'
print(len(stringLen))
listLen=['one','two']
print(len(listLen)
```

Figure 15 Program for Q37(c)

Ans c Length of the list is : 6

38. Write the output for the following list:

```
Num_List = [4,13,22,29,30,44,52]
Num_List.sort()
print("Sorted list is ",Num_List)
print("Mid value is ",Num_List[int(len(Num_List)/2)])
```

Figure 16 Program for Q38

Ans Sorted list is [4, 13, 22, 29, 30, 44, 52]
Mid value is 29

39. Write the output for the following list:

```
STATES = ["MP","UP","WB","TN","MH","MZ","DL","BH","RJ","HR"]
for i in STATES:
    if i[0]=='M':
      print(i)
```

Figure 17 Program for Q39

Ans MP
MH
MZ

40. Find and write the output of the following Python code:

```
Numbers = [9,18,27,36]
for Num in Numbers:
        for N in range(1, Num%8):
                print(N,"#", end="")
        print()
```

Figure 18 Program for Q40

Ans 1 #
1 #2 #
1 #2 #3 #

41. Find and write the output of the following Python code:

```
STR   = ["90","10","30","40"]
COUNT = 3
SUM   = 0
for I in [1,2,5,4]:
      S = STR[COUNT]
      SUM = float (S)+I
      print(SUM)
      COUNT-=1
```

Figure 19 Program for Q41

Ans 41.0
32.0
15.0
94.0

42. Find and write the output of the following Python code:

```
STR   = ["10","30","50","70"]
COUNT = 3
SUM   = 0
for I in [1,2,5,4]:
      S = STR[COUNT]
      SUM = float (S)+I
      print(SUM)
      COUNT-=1
```

Figure 20 Program for Q42

Ans 71.0
52.0
35.0
14.0

43. Find and write the output of the following Python code:

```
n = [1, 2, 3, 4, 5]
print("There are {0} items".format(len(n)))
print("Maximum is {0}".format(max(n)))
print("Minimum is {0}".format(min(n)))
print("The sum of values is {0}".format(sum(n)))
```

Figure 21 Program for Q43

Ans There are 5 items
Maximum is 5
Minimum is 1
The sum of values is 15

44. Find and write the output of the following Python code:

```
# Find Maximum and Minimum in list
list = [107, 101, 250, 501, 205, 175]
print("List Items : ", list)

# Minimum list element
minimum = min(list)
print("\nThe Minimum item in this list = ", minimum)

# Maximum list element
maximum = max(list)
print("\nThe Maximum item in this list = ", maximum)
```

Figure 22 Program for Q44

Ans List Items : [107, 101, 250, 501, 205, 175]
The Minimum item in this list = 101
The Maximum item in this list = 501

45. Rewrite the following code in Python after removing all syntax error(s). Underline each correction done in the code and also write output.

```
STRING=""WELCOME
NOTE""
for S in range[0,8]:
        print STRING(S)
print(S+STRING)
```

Ans

```
STRING="WELCOME"
NOTE=""
for S in range(0,8):
    print(STRING[S])
print(S,STRING)

RUN
>>>
W
E
L
C
O
M
E
>>>
Also range(0,8) will give a runtime error as the index is out of range. It
should be range(0,7)
```

Figure 23 Program for Q45

46. Find and write the output of the following Python code:

```
for Name in ['John', 'Garima','Seema','Karan']:
     print(Name)
     if Name[0]=='S':
          break
     else:
      print('Completed!')
print('Well done!')
```

Figure 24 Program for Q46

Ans John
Completed!
Garima
Completed!
Seema
Well done!

47. Find and write the output of the following Python code:

```
# Use of sort()
names = ["Meera","Aman", "Sangeeta", "Preeti", "Upma","Nitika"]
print("Original List")
print(names)
print("Sorted List in ascending order")
names.sort()
print(names)
print("Sorted List in decending order")
names.sort(reverse=True)
print(names)
```

Figure 25 Program for Q47

Ans Original List
['Meera', 'Aman', 'Sangeeta', 'Preeti', 'Upma', 'Nitika']
Sorted List in ascending order
['Aman', 'Meera', 'Nitika', 'Preeti', 'Sangeeta', 'Upma']
Sorted List in decending order
['Upma', 'Sangeeta', 'Preeti', 'Nitika', 'Meera', 'Aman']

48. What are the capabilities of lists?

Ans Capabilities of lists are as follows:

(a) Appending an item.
(b) Inserting an item (at the beginning or into the middle of the list).
(c) Adding a list of items to an existing list.

49. Find the outputs of the following Python codes:

(a)
```
>>> numbers = [1, 2, 3, 4, 5, 6, 7,
8, 9, 10]
>>> numbers[0:1]
```

Ans [1]

(b)
```
>>> x = [11, 22, 33]
>>> x.reverse()
>>> x
```

Ans [33, 22, 11]

(c)
```
>>> x = [4, 6, 2, 1, 7, 9]
>>> x.sort()
>>> x
```

Ans [1, 2, 4, 6, 7, 9]

(d)
```
>>> x = [[1, 2], 1, 1, [2, 1, [1,
2]]]
>>> x.count(1)
```

Ans 2

(e)
```
# Add the squares given in the list
squares = [1, 4, 9, 16]
sum = 0
for num in squares:
    sum += num
print(sum)
```

Ans 30

(f)
```
# Access every 3rd element in a list
a = [1, 2, 3, 4, 5, 6, 7, 8, 9, 10]
i = 0
while i < len(a):
    print(a[i])
    i = i + 3
```

Ans 1
4
7
10

(g)
```
>>> li = ['x', 'ab', 'd', 'cde']

# no switch: alphabetical order
>>> sorted(li)
```

Ans ['ab', 'cde', 'd', 'x']

(h)
```
>>> li = ['x', 'ab', 'd', 'cde']

# reverse alphabetical order
>>> sorted(li, reverse=True)
```

Ans ['x', 'd', 'cde', 'ab']

(i)
```
>>> li = ['x', 'ab', 'd', 'cde']

# order by string length
>>> sorted(li, key=len)
```

Ans ['x', 'd', 'ab', 'cde']

(j)
```
>>> li = ['x', 'ab', 'd', 'cde']

# string length, reverse
>>> sorted(li, key=len, reverse=True)
```

Ans ['cde', 'ab', 'x', 'd']

EXERCISE

1. What are elements?
2. What is a list? Why list is used in Python programming?
3. How can you create a new list?
4. What is known as an empty list?
5. How is the step size useful in slicing process?
6. What is known as traversing?
7. Write the function used for of joining lists.
8. Write the result of [0] * 8.
9. What is known as aliasing?
10. What does an append() function return?
11. Why is the remove() method used in a list?
12. Why are lists called mutable type?
13. What are different ways of creating a list?
14. What is the difference between append() and insert() methods of a list?
15. What is the difference between pop() and remove() methods of a list?
16. What are nested lists? Explain with an example.
17. What do you mean by comparing lists?
18. Differentiate between Concatenate operator (+) and extend() method.
19. What is the difference between slicing with insert and insert() method.
20. Write the most appropriate method for the following:
    (a) To delete given element from the list.
    (b) To add element at the end of the list.
    (c) To add element at the beginning of the list.

LAB EXERCISE

1. Create a list of integers up to 20 using for loop.
2. Write a program to traverse a list and print all odd numbers from the list.
3. Write a function that receives two lists and creates third list, containing all elements from the first and the second list.
4. How will you create the following lists:
   (a) [-11,13,14]
   (b) [1, 1, 2, 3, 5, 8, 13]
   (c) [7, 8, 9]
5. If l = [19, 18, 17, 16, 15, 14] then evaluate the following expressions by using Python lists:
   (a) l[0]
   (b) l[1]
6. If variable v is assigned as
   >>> v = ['a', 'e', 'i', 'o', 'u']
   then write the result of >>> v[1:3].
7. If variable toy is assigned as
   >>> toy = ['doll', 'car', 'bat', 'car', 'ball', 'car', 'car']
   then write the result of
   >>>toy.count('car').
8. What would be the output of the following programs?

(a)
```
degrees = [0, 10, 20, 40, 100]
for C in degrees:
        print("list element: ", C)
print("The degrees list has", len(degrees), 'elements')
```

(b)
```
>>> A = [2, 3.5, 8, 10]
>>> A[2:]
>>> A[:3]
```

(c)
```
list = [400, 500, 100, 2000]
# Reversed
list.reverse()
print(list)

# Sorted
list.sort()
print(list)
```

(d)
```
names = ["Tina", "Binay", "Jayant",
"Binay", "Seema"]
# Remove this value
names.remove("Binay")
print(names)

# Delete all except first two ele-
ments
del names[2:]
print(names)

# Delete all except last element
del names[:1]
print(names)
```

(e)
```
# Two lists.
a = [10, 20, 30]
b = [40, 50, 60]

# Add all elements in list b to list
a.
a.extend(b)

# List a now contains six elements.
print(a)
```

(f)
```
list = []
list.append(1)
list.append(2)
list.append(6)
list.append(3)
print(list)
```

(g)
```
names = ['a', 'a', 'b', 'c', 'a']
# Count the letter a.
value = names.count('a')
print(value)
```

(h)
```
number_list = [x ** 2 for x in ran-
ge(10) if x % 2 == 0]
print(number_list)
```

(i)
```
my_list = []
for x in [20, 40, 60]:
    for y in [2, 4, 6]:
            my_list.append(x * y)
print(my_list)
```

(j)
```
Data    = ["P",20,"R",10,"S",30]
Times   = 0
Alpha   = ""
Add     = 0
for C in range(1,6,2):
    Times= Times + C
    Alpha= Alpha + Data[C-1]+"$"
    Add  = Add + Data[C]
    print(Times,Add,Alpha)
```

(k)
```
colors = ['yellow', 'red', 'blue',
'green', 'black']
print colors[0]
print colors [1:]
```

9. Create the lists to perform the following tasks:

(a) Add integers and display their sum.

(b) Calculate and display sum of all even integers.

10. Write a program to add two matrices.

## CHAPTER 8

Tuples

8.1 TUPLE

Tuple is a compound data type in Python. It is a sequence of multiple values in an ordered sequence. Tuples are very similar to lists, but tuples cannot be changed. In other words, the tuple can be viewed as a "constant list". While lists use square brackets[], tuples are written with standard parentheses() or no parentheses, and elements are separated with comma as given below:

```
# elements written without parentheses
>>> t1 = 'a', 'b', 'c', 'd', 'e'

# elements written within parentheses
>>> t2 = ('a', 'b', 'c', 'd', 'e')

# tuple of numbers
>>> tuple1 = (0, 1, 2, 3)

# tuple of mixed numbers
>>> tuple2 = (33, 3.3, 3+3j)

# tuple of mixed data types
>>> T1 = (101, "Aman", 77])

# tuple of srtings
>>> T2 = ("Apple", "Banana", "Orange")

# a tuple containing a single
  element or item
>>> t3 = 'a',
>>> type(t3)
<type 'class'>

# An empty tuple
>>> empty_tup = ()
()
```

a. Syntactically, the tuple is a comma-separated list of values. For example,
   `>>> t1 = 'a', 'b', 'c', 'd', 'e'`

b. Although parentheses is not necessary, it is common to enclose tuples in parentheses. For example,
   `>>> t2 = ('a', 'b', 'c', 'd', 'e')`

c. To create a tuple with a single element/item, you have to include the final comma after the item:

   `>>> t3 = 'a', <-- note trailing comma`

☞ *Unlike Python Strings, Tuple allow you to store different types of data such as integer, float, string etc.*

8.2 DIFFERENCE BETWEEN LIST AND TUPLE

Differences between lists and tuples are as follows:

(a) Lists are enclosed in square brackets [ ], and their elements and size can be changed, while tuples are enclosed in parentheses ( ) and cannot be updated.
(b) Tuples can be thought as read-only lists. They protect against accidental changes of their contents whereas lists can grow and shrink as needed. In other words the list has the variable length and tuple has the fixed length.
(c) Tuples are immutable like strings, i.e., you cannot modify them. However, lists are mutable; individual items or entire slices can be replaced through assignment statements.
(d) Tuples can hold both homogeneous as well as heterogeneous values. You generally use tuple for heterogeneous (different) datatypes and list for homogeneous (similar) datatypes.
(e) Tuples are faster than lists. Iterating over the elements of a tuple is faster compared to iterating over a list.

8.3 TUPLES ARE IMMUTABLE

Tuples are immutable which means you cannot update them or change values of their elements. A new object has to be created if a different value has to be stored. You can take portions of an existing tuple to create a new tuple as given below:

```
>>> tup1 = (1, 2, 3)
>>> tup2 = (5, 6, 7)
>>> tup1
(1, 2, 3)
>>> tup2
(5, 6, 7)
>>> tup2[0]  = 4 # action is not valid for tuples, error will be displayed
Traceback (most recent call last):
  File "<pyshell#15>", line 1, in <module>
    tup2[0] = 4
TypeError: 'tuple' object does not support item assignment
```

So, let's create the new tuple as given below:

```
>>> tup3 = tup1 + tup2
>>> tup3
(1, 2, 3, 5, 6, 7)
>>>
```

Using the addition operator(+), with two or more tuples, adds up all the elements into a new tuple.

☞ *Tuples respond to the + and * operators much like strings since they mean concatenation and repetition operators, respectively, except that the return value is a new tuple, not a string.*

Let's Try

```
# Zero-element tuple.
a = ()
# One-element tuple.
b = ("one",)
# Two-element tuple.
c = ("one", "two")
print(a)
print(b)
print(c)
```

```
tup1 = (10,20,30)
tup2 = (40,50,60)
tup3 = tup1 + tup2
print  ("The  third  tuple  elements:"
,tup3)
```

```
tup1 = ('abc', 'xyz')
tup2 = (72, 3.14)
tup3 = tup1 + tup2
print (tup3)
```

8.4 CREATION, INITIALIZATION AND ACCESSING THE ELEMENTS IN A TUPLE

To create a tuple with zero elements, use only a pair of parentheses "()". For a tuple with one element, use a trailing comma. For a tuple with two or more elements, use a comma between elements. No ending comma is needed here.

8.4.1 Tuple Creation

Creating a tuple means placing different comma-separated values within parentheses. However, the parentheses are optional. Also, the elements of a tuple can be of any valid Python data types ranging from numbers, strings, lists, etc. For example:

```
>>> tup1 = ('C++', 'Python', 1997, 2013)
>>> tup2 = (1, 2, 3, 4, 5 )
>>> tup3 = "a", "b", "c", "d"
```

Once a tuple is created, you cannot change its values. Tuples are unchangeable.

☞ *You cannot delete or add elements in a tuple, once it is created.*

The empty tuple is formed with a pair of parentheses containing nothing. For example:

```
# Demo of zero-element/empty tuple
tup4 = ()
>>> len(tup4)
0
```

☞ *You may get the length of a tuple by using the len function. Simply, provide a tuple name in the parenthesis after len keyword.*

To write a tuple containing a single value you have to include a trailing comma, even though there is only one value. For example:

```
# Demo of one-element tuple
tup5 = (20,)
>>> len(tup5)
1
```

Take another example to understand it in better way:

```
>>> t3 = (1,)
>>> t3
(1,)
>>> type(t3)
<type 'tuple'>
```

It is important to note that declaring a tuple consisting a single element requires a comma after the first element. If you miss out the comma, t3 would become an integer because 1 itself is an integer.

```
>>> t3 = (1)
>>> type(t3)
<type 'int'>
```

```
# Two-element tuple
tup6 = ("one", "two")
>>> len(tup6)
2
```

```
# Tuple of numbers
>>> tuple1 = (0, 1, 2, 3)
>>>   print("A   tuple   of   numbers:",
tuple1)
A tuple of numbers: (0, 1, 2, 3)
>>>
```

The tuple in Python is immutable. An immutable object cannot be changed. Once created, it always has the same values. Trying to make an item assignment in a tuple will display the following error:

```
>>> tup = ('a', 'b', 'd', 'd')
>>> tup[2] = 'c' # This causes an error
Traceback (most recent call last):
  File "<pyshell#14>", line 1, in <mod-
ule>
    tup[2] = 'c' # This causes an error
TypeError: 'tuple' object does not sup-
port item assignment
```

☞ *To declare a tuple, you must type a list of items separated by commas, inside parentheses. Then assign it to a variable. For example, marks=(97,88,92)*

```
# Creating nested tuples
tuple1 = (0, 1, 2, 3)
tuple2 = ('Hello', 'Python')
tuple3 = (tuple1, tuple2)
print(tuple3)

>>>
((0, 1, 2, 3), ('Hello', 'Python'))
>>>
```

Let's Try

```
tup_eg = (11,12,13,14,15)
print  ("Total  number  of  elements  in
tuple = ", len(tup_eg))
```

```
# Create tuples (one with brackets, one
without) and print them
weekdays   =   ("Mon",   "Tues",   "Wed",
"Thur", "Fri")
weekends = "Sat", "Sun"

# Print the tuples
print(weekdays)
print(weekends)
```

8.4.2 Tuple Assignment

You can assign all the elements in a tuple using a single assignment statement. Tuple assignment occurs in parallel rather than in sequence, which makes it useful for swapping values.

To swap the values of two variables with conventional assignment statements, you have to use a temporary variable. For example, to swap x and y:

```
>>> temp = x
>>> x = y
>>> y = temp
```

In Python, you can assign all the elements in a tuple using a single assignment statement:

```
>>> x, y = y, x
```

The left side is tuple variables; and the right side is tuple values. Each value is assigned to its respective variable. All the expressions on the right side are evaluated before allocating any assignment.

The number of variables on the left and the number of values on the right have to be the same:

```
>>> x, y = 1, 2, 3
ValueError: too many values to unpack
```

8.4.3 Accessing Elements in Tuples

Tuple items can be accessed by referring to the index number, inside square brackets. Like string indices, tuple indices begin at 0. Accessed items can be either single elements or in groups, known as *slices*. Subsets can be accessed with the slice operator ([] and [:]) as in strings. The slice notation in Python uses a colon. On the left side of the colon, you have the starting index. If no starting index is present, the program uses 0. And on the right side of the colon, you have the ending index. If no ending index is present, the last possible index is used. For example,

```
tup1 = ('Mona', 'Monty', 1997, 2003)
>>> tup1[0]
'Mona'
>>> tup1[1]
'Monty'
```

Note: Indexes starts with 0 that is why you use 0 to access the first element of tuple, 1 to access second element and so on.

☞ *When using positive indices, you traverse the list from the left.*

Python allows negative indexing for its sequences. Similar to list and strings you can use negative indexes to access the tuple elements from the end. If you want to access value 2003, you can write either tup1[-1] or tup1[3]. The index of -1 refers to the last item, -2 to the second last item and so on.

```
>>> tup1[-1] # Negative index
2003
>>> tup1[3] # Positive index
2003
```

☞ *Unlike positive indexing, negative indexing begins traversing from the right.*

To access values in tuple, use the square brackets along with the index:

```
>>> t1 = (1, "abc", 7.0)
>>> t1[0] # accessing first element
1
>>> t1[1]
'abc'
>>> t1[2]
7.0
>>> t1[3]
Traceback (most recent call last):
  File "<pyshell#9>", line 1, in <module>
    t1[3]
IndexError: tuple index out of range
```

This error occurs when you mention the index which is not in the range. For example, if a tuple has 3 elements and you try to access the 4th element then this error would occur.

You can use negative indexes to access the tuple elements from the end; -1 to access last element, -2 to access second last and so on as shown in the example below:

```
>>> t1[-1]
7.0
>>> t1[-2]
'abc'
>>> t1[-3]
1
```

Likewise, nested tuples are accessed using nested indexing, as shown in the example below:

```
# Accessing Nested Tuple Items
Tuple = ((1, 2, 3), [4, 5, 6], 'Hello')
print(Tuple[0][0])
print(Tuple[1][0])
print(Tuple[2][0])
print(Tuple[2][4])
>>>
1
4
H
o
>>>
```

Example 1 – **Demo of accessing nested tuple.**

```
# Accessing nested tuples
Tuple = ([7,4,3], "Raj", (10, 11, 12))
print(Tuple[0][0])
print(Tuple[0][1])
print(Tuple[0][2])
```

(Contd...)

```
print(Tuple[1][0])
print(Tuple[1][1])
print(Tuple[1][2])

print(Tuple[2][0])
print(Tuple[2][1])
print(Tuple[2][2])
RUN
>>>
7
4
3
R
a
j
10
11
12
>>>
```

Figure 8.1 Demo of accessing nested tuple

Slices are treated as boundaries, and the result will contain all the elements between these boundaries. So, a tuple having 5 elements will have indices from 0 to 4. Trying to access an element outside of tuple will raise an IndexError.

```
>>> tup2 = (1, 2, 3, 4, 5)
>>> tup2[1:5]
(2, 3, 4, 5)
>>> tup2[3:7]
(4, 5)
>>> tup2[8]
Traceback (most recent call last):
  File "<pyshell#4>", line 1, in <module>
    tup2[8]
IndexError: tuple index out of range
```

The index must be an integer; so you cannot use float or other types. This will result in TypeError.

☞ *A slice is created using the subscript notation, [] with colons between starting and ending index.*

Let's Try

Write the output for the following Python code:

```
tuple1 = (1, 2, 3, 4, 5)
print(tuple1[-1])
print(tuple1[-4])
```

```
>>> fruits = "apple", "orange", "ba-
nana", "berry", "mango"
>>> fruits[0]
```

```
>>> t1 = (1, "abc", 3.0)
>>> t1
>>> type(t1)
```

Example 2 –**Write a program that uses tuple slices.**

```
values = (1, 3, 5, 7, 9, 11, 13)
# Copy the tuple
print(values[:])
# Copy all values at index 1 or more
print(values[1:])
```

(Contd...)

```
# Copy one value, starting at first
print(values[:1])

# Copy values from index 2 to 4
print(values[2:4])

RUN
>>>
(1, 3, 5, 7, 9, 11, 13)
(3, 5, 7, 9, 11, 13)
(1,)
(5, 7)
>>>
```

Figure 8.2 Program that Uses Tuple Slices

8.4.4 Membership Test in Tuples

Membership operators "*in*" and "*not in*" checks whether the given element is contained in the tuple or not. For example:

```
>>> 4 in (2, 4, 6, 8)
True
>>> 5 in (2, 4, 6, 8)
False
>>> 4 not in (2, 4, 6, 8)
False
>>> 5 not in (2, 4, 6, 8)
True
>>> 'a' in tuple("python")
False
>>> 'a' not in tuple("python")
True
```

Identity operator "*is*" returns *true,* if the variables on either side of the operator point to the same memory location, and *false* otherwise. For example,

Example 3 –**Demo of identity operator.**

```
a = 'Janak Puri'
b = 'Dwarka'
c = 'Dwarka'
if a is b:
   print ('a is b')
else:
   print ('a is not b')
if b is c:
   print('b is c')
else:
   print ('b is not c')

RUN
>>>
a is not b
b is c
>>>
```

Figure 8.3 Demo of identity operator

Identity operator "*is not*" returns true if both the operand point to different memory location. It is opposite of "*is*" operator.

Let's Try

Write the output for the following Python code:

```
>>> tuple = ('p', 'y', 't', 'h', 'o',
'n')
>>> for item in tuple:
  print("Item:", item)
```

8.5 TUPLE FUNCTIONS

Unlike Python lists, tuples do not have methods/functions such as append(), remove(), extend(), insert() and pop() due to their immutable nature. However, there are many other built-in methods to work with tuples:
count() ,len(), max(), min(), etc.

8.5.1 cmp()

cmp() does not exist in Python 3. If you really want it, you can define it yourself, and it gives the same result. For example,

```
def cmp(a, b):
    return (a > b) - (a < b)
```

In Python 2, cmp() function compares elements of both tuples. It checks whether the given tuples are same or not. If both the tuples are same, it will return 0, otherwise 1 or -1. If the first tuple is bigger than the second one then it returns 1, otherwise -1.

Syntax:

```
cmp(tup1,tup2) #tup1 and tup2 are tuples
```

Example

```
>>> tup1=(11,22,33)
>>> tup2=(50,60,70)
>>> tup3=(11,22,33)
>>> cmp(tup1,tup2) # first tuple is small
-1
>>> cmp(tup1,tup3) //same
0
>>> cmp(tup2,tup1) //first tuple is big
1
```

8.5.2 count()

count() returns the number of occurrences of an item in the tuple. For example,

```
a = (1,2,2,3,4,5,5,5)
a.count(2)
2
a.count(5)
3
```

☞ *Use count() method to calculate the number of times a specified value appears in the tuple.*

8.5.3 len()

The method len() returns the number of elements in the tuple.

Syntax:

```
len(tup)
```

Example:

```
>>> tup1=(11,22,33)
>>> len(tup1)
3
```

8.5.4 max() and min()

The max() and min() built-in functions used to find the largest and the smallest elements in a sequence, respectively. For strings, the comparison performed is alphabetical, e.g., "Anu" comes before "Zyan". So, "Anu" would be less than "zero". For numbers, the comparison is numeric, e.g., 10 comes before 20. These comparisons are logical.

Syntax:

```
max(args)  #Returns the maximum of a
sequence or set of arguments
min(args)  #Returns the minimum of a
sequence or set of arguments
```

Example:

```
>>> max(10,20,30)
30
>>> min(10,20,30)
10
>>> students = ("shiv", "vivek",
"neelam", "shashi")
>>> max(students)
vivek
>>> min(students)
neelam
```

Example 4 –**Program that uses max() and min() functions.**

```
# Use of max() and min() for strings
friends = ("sanjay", "morris", "ajay", "suman")
print(max(friends))
print(min(friends))
# Max and min for numbers
earnings = (1000, 2020, 500, 400)
print(max(earnings))
print(min(earnings))

RUN
>>>
suman
ajay

2020
400
>>>
```

Figure 8.4 Program for Example 4

Example 5 –**Program that uses max() function to get maximum value in tuples.**

```
tup_num = (23,-4,55,550,250,505)
tup_str = ('Mona', 'Monu', 'Mohan', 'Meena')
print ("The maximum value in numbered tuple = ", max(tup_num))
print ("The maximum value in string tuple = ", max(tup_str))

RUN
>>>
The maximum value in numbered tuple =  550
The maximum value in string tuple =  Monu
>>>
```

Figure 8.5 Program for Example 5

Example 6 –**Program that uses min() function to get minimum value in tuples.**

```
tup_num = (23,-4,55,550,250,505)
tup_str = ('Mona', 'Monu', 'Mohan', 'Meena')
print ("The minimum value in numbered tuple = ", min(tup_num))
print ("The minimum value in string tuple = ", min(tup_str))

RUN
>>>
The minimum value in numbered tuple =  -4
The minimum value in string tuple =  Meena
>>>
```

Figure 8.6 Program for Example 6

Let's Try

Type the following Python codes and write the output:

```
a=(10,20,30,40,50)
print(len(a))
print(min(a))
print(max(a))
```

```
tup_num = (23,-4,-5,55,25,50)
print (max(tup_num))
print (min(tup_num))
```

8.5.5 sorted()

This function returns a sorted version of the tuple. The sorting is in ascending order, just like in the following example:

```
a = (6,7,4,2,1,5,3)
sorted(a)
[1, 2, 3, 4, 5, 6, 7]
```

☞ *sorted() function doesn't modify the original tuple.*

8.5.6 tuple( )

It is used to create tuples from different types of values.

```
# Creating empty tuple
>>> t=tuple()
>>> t
()
```

```
# Creating tuple from string
>>> t=tuple("xyz")
>>> t
('x','y','z')
```

```
# Creating tuple from list
>>> t=tuple([2,4,6])
>>> t
(2,4,6)
```

```
# Creating tuple from dictionary
>>> t=tuple({1:"1", 2:"2"})
>>> t
(1,2)
```

☞ *The empty tuple is formed with a pair of parentheses containing nothing.*

8.5.7 index()

The index() method works with tuple the same way it works with lists. It takes one argument and returns the index of the first appearance of an item in a tuple. If you use index() on a value that is not found, an error results.

Syntax:

```
<tuplename>.index(<item>)
```

Example:

```
>>> tup=(2,5,7,7,2,1)
>>> tup.index(7)
2
>>> tup.index(2)
0
```

☞ *Use index() method to get first occurrence of the specified value in the tuple.*

Let's Try

Write the output for the following Python code:

```
# Get index of element with value
"ball".
items = ("bat", "ball", "chess")
index = items.index("ball")
print(index, items[index])
```

8.5.8 sum()

The sum() returns the arithmetic sum of all the items in the tuple.

```
>>> tup=(2,5,7,7,2,1)
>>> sum(tup)
24
```

You can not apply sum() function on a tuple with strings, it will generate a TypeError error:

```
>>> tup2=('2','5','7','7','2','1')
>>> sum(tup2)
Traceback (most recent call last):
  File "<pyshell#8>", line 1, in <module>
    sum(tup2)
TypeError: unsupported operand type(s)
for +: 'int' and 'str'
>>>
```

8.6 COMMON TUPLE OPERATIONS

Python provides you with a number of ways to manipulate tuples.

8.6.1 Tuple Slicing

If you want a part(slice) of a tuple, use the slicing operator []. The first value in a tuple is at index 0. Similar to Python lists, you can use the index values in combination with square brackets [] to access items in a tuple. When using positive indices, you traverse the list from the left. For example,

```
numbers = (0,1,2,3,4,5,6)
numbers[0]
0
numbers[3]
3
```

You can also use negative indexing with tuples:

```
numbers[-1]
6
```

Indexing is used to obtain individual items, whereas slicing allows you to obtain a subset of items. When you enter a range that you want to extract, it is called *range slicing*. The general format of range slicing is:

[Start index (included):Stop index (excluded):Increment]

Here, Increment is an optional parameter, and by default, the increment is 1. For example,

```
# Item at index 5 is excluded
numbers[1:5]
(1, 2, 3, 4)
# This provides all the items in the tuple
numbers[:]
(0, 1, 2, 3, 4, 5, 6)
# Increment = 2
numbers[::2]
(0, 2, 4, 6)
```

You can also use the negative increment value to reverse the tuple.

```
numbers[::-1]
(6, 5, 4, 3, 2, 1, 0)
```

Let's Try

Type the following Python codes and write the output:

```
>>> grade_point=(10,9,8,7,6,5,4,0)
>>> grade_point[2:4]
```

```
>>> grade_point=(10,9,8,7,6,5,4,0)
>>> grade_point[:4]
>>> grade_point[4:]
>>> grade_point[2:2]
```

```
>>> grade_point=(10,9,8,7,6,5,4,0)
>>> grade_point[:-4]
>>> grade_point[-4:]
```

```
>>> grade_point=(10,9,8,7,6,5,4,0)
>>> grade_point[4:-4]
>>> grade_point[-4:4]
```

8.6.2 Tuple Addition

You can combine tuples to form a new tuple. The addition operation simply performs a concatenation with tuples. For example,

```
x = (1,2,3,4)
y = (5,6,7,8)
# Combining two tuples to form a new tuple
z = x + y
print(z)

>>>
(1, 2, 3, 4, 5, 6, 7, 8)
>>>
```

Let's Try

Type the following Python code and write the output:

```
>>> t = (1, 2, 3, 4, 5)
>>> t = t + (6,)
>>> print (t)
```

Hence, you can add any kind of element to a tuple, using the + operator.

8.6.3 Tuple Multiplication

The multiplication operation simply leads to repetition of the tuple by the given number of times. For example,

```
x = (1,2,3,4)
z = x*2
print(z)
```

```
>>>
(1, 2, 3, 4, 1, 2, 3, 4)
>>>
```

Let's Try

Type the following Python codes and write the output:

```
a=(10,20,30,40,50)
b = (60,70)
c = a + b
print(c)
```

```
a=(10,20,30)
b = (60,70)
print(a * 2)
print(b * 3)
```

8.6.4 Deleting a Tuple

Since tuples are immutable, it is not possible to delete individual elements of a tuple, however, you can delete the whole tuple itself. In order to explicitly remove an entire tuple, the del keyword is used with the tuple name.

For example,

```
tuple1 = (1, 2, 3, 4, 5, 6)
print(tuple1)
(1, 2, 3, 4, 5, 6)

del tuple1[0]   # not possible it will
raise error
print(tuple1)
Traceback (most recent call last):
  File "C:/Users/shash/AppData/Local/Pro
grams/Python/Python37-32/tup4.py", line
5, in <module>
    del tuple1[0]
TypeError: 'tuple' object doesn't sup-
port item deletion

>>> del tuple1 # tuple1 will be deleted
from the memory
>>>  print(tuple1)  # NameError because
tuple1 is deleted

Traceback (most recent call last):
  File "<pyshell#2>", line 1, in <module>
    print(tuple1)
NameError: name 'tuple1' is not defined
>>>
```

Note an exception raised, this is because after using `del tuple1` tuple does not exist any more.

8.7 PACKING AND UNPACKING TUPLES

You can also create a Python tuple without parentheses. This is called *tuple packing*.

Multiple assignments can be performed using tuples. Let us take an example:

```
>>> lyrics, songs, music, videos, obj = o
# o is already defined
>>> songs
'tuple'
```

Note that either or both sides of an assignment operator (=) consist of tuples. For example,

```
>>> i, j = 11, 12
>>> j
12
```

In the above example, lyrics, songs, music, videos, obj = o is called "tuple unpacking" because the tuple o was unpacked, and its values were assigned to each of the variables on the left. The concept of "Tuple packing" is considered as the reverse process, i.e., o = lyrics, songs, music, videos, obj. Python tuples unpacking is when you assign values from a tuple to a sequence of variables in python. While unpacking the tuple, or performing multiple assignments, you must have the same number of variables being assigned to values being assigned.

Let us discuss more examples of packing and unpacking of tuples. In packing, you place values into a new tuple. And in unpacking you extract those values back into variables i.e., tuples items value assigned to variables.

```
# Python Tuples Packing
>>> b= 1, 2.0, 'three'
# Python Tuples Unpacking
>>> percentages=(99,95,90,89)
>>> a,b,c,d=percentages
>>> b
95
```

☞ *Python tuple unpacking is when you assign values from a tuple to a sequence of variables in python.*

Let's Try

Type the following Python codes and write the output:

```
fruitlist = ("Apple", "Mango", "Ba-
nana", "Grapes")
app, man, ban, gra =fruitlist

print(app)
print(man)
print(ban)
print(gra)
```

Note that Tuple's items have been assigned to app, man, ban, and gra variables correspondingly.

REVIEW QUESTIONS WITH ANSWERS

1. Multiple Choice Questions

1. To declare a Tuple with one item:
   a. Tuple_Name = (456,)
   b. Tuple_Name = (456;)
   c. Tuple_Name = (456:)
   d. All of the above
2. >>> max(('Hi','hi','Hello')) will produce:
   a. Hi b. Hello
   c. hi d. None of the above
3. min( ) returns:
   a. Largest item in the tuple.
   b. Number of items in the tuple.
   c. Its smallest item in the tuple.
   d. None of these
4. Tuples cannot be:
   a. Added b. Multiplied
   c. Changed d. None of the above
5. If we need to create a tuple with a single element, we need to include a final:
   a. Comma b. Semicolon
   c. Full stop d. None of these
6. Create empty tuple:
   a. T=tuple[] b. T=tuple()
   c. T=tuple{} d. None of these
7. The items in a tuple can be accessed using an index enclosed in:
   a. [] b. {}
   c. () d. None of these
8. The len() function can be used on any sequence such as:
   a. string b. tuple
   c. list d. All of the above
9. What will be the output of the following:
   ```
   tuple_a = '1', '2'
   tuple_b = ('3', '4')
   print (tuple_a + tuple_b)
   ```
   a. (1, 2, 3, 4) b. ('1', '2', '3', '4')
   c. ['1', '2', '3', '4'] d. All of the above
10. Which of the following statements is/are True?
    a. Tuples have structure, lists have an order.
    b. Tuples are homogeneous, lists are heterogeneous.
    c. Tuples are immutable, lists are mutable.
    d. All of these

2. State True or False for the following:

1. tup1[0] = 100; is not valid for tuples.
2. The items in the tuple can be accessed by using their specific index value.
3. Python tuple supports reverse indexing, i.e., accessing elements using the (-ve) index values.
4. The tuple elements can be accessed from one direction only.
5. To determine if a specified item is present in a tuple use the *is* keyword.
6. You cannot remove items in a tuple.
7. The 'tuple' object does not support item assignment.
8. A tuple can have any number of items and they may be of different types.
9. Nested tuples are accessed using nested indexing.
10. We cannot change the elements in a tuple.

3. Match the following:

1. The index -1 represents	a. repetition of the tuple.
2. Empty tuple	b. unchangeable
3. count()	c. last item
4. Multiplication	d. parentheses containing nothing
5. Immutable	e. returns the number of occurrences
6. Membership	f. must be an integer
7. tuple()	g. not in
8. sorted()	h. converts another construct into a tuple
9. index	i. access a range of items

10. Colon ":" j. doesn't modify the original tuple

4. Fill in the blanks:

1. If you want to declare a Tuple with one item then, we have to specify ________ after the item.
2. The elements from left to right are traversed using the ________ indexing.
3. The right most element (last) of the tuple can be accessed by using the index ______.
4. Index value starts at 0 and end at n-1 where n is the Tuple ________.
5. The tuple(seq) converts a list into ________.
6. To determine how many items a tuple has, use the ______ method
7. ________ searches the tuple for a specified value and returns the position of where it was found.
8. A tuple created without using parentheses is known as ________.
9. The tuple has the ______ length.
10. We can store list inside tuple or tuple inside the list up to ______ number of level.

Answers

1. 1. a 2. c 3. c 4. c 5. a 6. b 7. a 8. d 9. b 10. d

2. 1. T 2. T 3. T 4. F 5. F 6. T 7. T 8. T 9. T 10. T

3. 1. c 2. d 3. e 4. a 5. b 6. g 7. h 8. j 9. f 10. i

4. 1. comma 2. negative 3. -1 4. size 5. tuple 6. len() 7. index() 8. tuple packing 9. fixed 10. any

Short Answer Questions

1. What is tuple?

Ans Tuples are a sequence of values of any type, indexed by integers. They are immutable. They are enclosed in ().

2. A tuple in Python is immutable. Comment.

Ans A tuple in Python is immutable. This means, it cannot be modified as immutable object cannot be changed. Once created, it always has the same values.

3. What is the difference between objects and methods?

Ans Strings, lists, and tuples are objects, which means that they not only hold values, but they also have built-in behaviors called methods, that act on the values in the object.

4. Is an item assignment in a tuple possible?

Ans No, an item assignment statement in tuple is not possible.

5. What is len() function used for in list and tuple?

Ans With lists and tuples, len() function returns the number of elements in the sequence, For example,

```
>>> len(['a', 'b', 'c', 'd'])
4
>>> len((2, 4, 6, 8, 10, 12))
6
```

6. What is the use of *in* operator?

Ans The *in* operator checks whether the given element is contained in the tuple or not. For example,

```
>>> 4 in (2, 4, 6, 8)
True
>>> 5 in (2, 4, 6, 8)
False
```

7. Write short note on tuple assignment.

Ans An assignment to all the elements in a tuple is done using a single assignment statement. Tuple assignment occurs in parallel rather than in sequence, making it useful for swapping values.

8. How will you create tuple with zero element and 1 element?

Ans Zero element: To create a tuple with zero elements, use only a pair of parentheses "()". For example,

```
# Zero element tuple
x = ()
```

One element: For a tuple with one element, use a trailing comma.

```
# One-element tuple
y = ("Sunday",)
```

9. Compare and contrast tuples and list.

Ans Tuples are very similar to lists, but tuples cannot be changed, i.e., no change in the contents of the tuple is allowed. A tuple can be viewed as a 'constant list'. While lists employ square brackets, tuples are written with standard parentheses or no parentheses.

10. Can we update tuples?

Ans Like numbers and strings, tuples are immutable which means we cannot update them or change values of their elements.

11. Differentiate between following two Python statements:

```
>>> t1 = 'a',
>>> t2 = ('a')
```

Ans To create a tuple with a single element, we have to include the comma:

```
>>> t1 = 'a',
>>> type(t1)
<class 'tuple'>
```

A value in parentheses is not a tuple:

```
>>> t2 = ('a')
>>> type(t2)
<class 'str'>
```

12. What is the difference between list and tuple?

Ans Lists are enclosed in brackets [ ], and their elements and size can be changed, whereas tuples are enclosed in parentheses ( ) and cannot be updated. Tuples can be thought of as "read-only" lists.

13. Identify the following as mutable or immutable:
lists, numbers, strings, tuples, and dictionaries.

Ans Mutable : lists, dictionaries
Immutable : numbers, strings, tuples

14. How will you swap values in Python?

Ans Python "multiple assignment" will swap values in Python. For example,

```
# swapping variables in Python
>>> (x, y) = (1, 2)
>>> x
1

>>> y
2

>>> (x, y) = (y, x)
>>> x
2
>>> y
1
```

15. Can you create a tuple from other tuples? Explain.

Ans Yes, we can create a tuple from other tuples as well. The third tuple is created based on first two tuples as shown in the example below:

```
tup1 = (1,2,3)
tup2 = (4,5,6)
tup3 = tup1 + tup2
print ("The third tuple elements:"
,tup3)

>>>
The third tuple elements: (1, 2, 3,
4, 5, 6)
>>>
```

16. How will you access tuple elements by index numbers? Explain with an example.

Ans

```
# Demo of accessing tuple elements by index numbers
vowels = ('a','e','i','o','u')
print(vowels[0],vowels[1], vowels[2], vowels[3], vowels[4])
print(vowels[0],vowels[-4], vowels[-3], vowels[-2], vowels[-1])
RUN
>>>
a e i o u
a e i o u
>>>
```

Figure 1 Program for Q16

17. Write a python code to demonstrate working with string tuple. Assign following string to tup:
tup=('python','tuples','are','immutable')
and find total length, maximum element, minimum element and number of occurrences of word "are" in a string.

Ans

```
# Working with string tuple
tup=('python','tuples','are','immutable')
#len(tuple) gives total length of a tuple
print("Total length of a tuple : ",len(tup))
#max(tuple) gives maximum element of a tuple
print("Maximum element of a tuple : ",max(tup))
#min(tuple) gives minimum element of a tuple
print("Minimum element of a tuple : ",min(tup))
#count(x) gives number of occurrences of x in the tuple
print("Number of occurrences of are :",tup.count('are'))

RUN
>>>
Total length of a tuple :  4
Maximum element of a tuple :  tuples
Minimum element of a tuple :  are
Number of occurrences of are : 1
>>>
```

Figure 2 Program for Q17

18. Can you append in tuple? Explain.

Ans No, we can not append in a tuple. If we try to add something to a tuple, we will get an *AttributeError* error. For example,

```
colours = ('red', 'blue', 'green')
colours.append('pink')
```

It will display following error message:

```
Traceback (most recent call last):
  File "C:/Python34/dic6.py", line 2, in <module>
    colours.append('pink')
AttributeError: 'tuple' object has no attribute 'append'
```

19. How will you create an empty tuple?

Ans We can create an empty tuple using built-in function tuple() as follows:

```
>>> t = tuple()
>>> print t
()
```

20. Find the output of the following programs:

(a)

```
>>> numbers = [1, 2, 3, 4]
>>> [(x, x**2, x**3) for x in numbers]
```

Ans [(1, 1, 1), (2, 4, 8), (3, 9, 27), (4, 16, 64)]

(b)

```
checks = (10, 20, 30)
# Add two tuples
more = checks + checks
print(more)
```

Ans (10, 20, 30, 10, 20, 30)

(c)

```
checks = (10, 20, 30)
# Multiply tuple
total = checks * 3
print(total)
```

Ans (10, 20, 30, 10, 20, 30, 10, 20, 30)

(d)

```
tup_eg = (11,12,13,14,15)
print ("Total number of elements in tuple = ", len(tup_eg))
```

Ans Total number of elements in tuple = 5

(e)

```
>>> cmp(1,2)
>>> cmp("a","b")
>>> cmp(3,1)
>>> cmp(3.1,3.1)
```

Ans -1
-1
1
0

(f)
```
>>> 3*(40+2)
>>> 3*(40+2,)
```

Ans 126
(42, 42, 42)

(g)
```
list = ['X','Y','Z']
tup_eg = tuple(list)
print ("New tuple elements after conversion = ", tup_eg)
```

Ans New tuple elements after conversion = ('X', 'Y', 'Z')

(h)
```
colours = ('red', 'green', 'blue')
print("The available colours are:")
for colour in colours:
    print("- " + colour)
print("\nThe first colour is: " + colours[0])
print("The second colour is: " + colours[1])
print("The third colour is: " + colours[2])
```

Ans The available colours are:
- red
- green
- blue
The first colour is: red
The second colour is: green
The third colour is: blue

EXERCISE

1. What is the difference between lists and tuples?
2. How tuple in Python is immutable?
3. A tuple is constructed by enclosing a series of comma-separated items in square brackets. Is it True or False?
4. What is the use of tuple() method?
5. The items in a tuple are accessed using a key, as in looking for things in a dictionary. Is it True or False?
6. How can you create a tuple with zero element?
7. How can you access the elements in tuples?
8. What does the statement >>> max (111, 222, 999, 333) return?
9. What does statement >>> min (9999, 8888, 1111, 2222, 5555) return?
10. What do you mean by packing and unpacking tuples?
11. When unpacking, the number of variables on the left must match the number of values in the tuple. Is it True or False?

LAB EXERCISE

1. What would be the output of the following programs?

(a)
```
t=tuple()
print(t)
```

(b)
```
t=(1,2,3,4,5)
print len(t)
```

(c)
```
t=(1,2,3,4,5)
max(t)
min(t)
```

(d)
```
t1=(1,2,3,4,5)
t2=(10,20,30)
t3=t1+t2
print(t3)
```

(e)
```
tuple = (1, 2, 3)
print("tuple:", tuple)
```

(f)
```
#Data Type
tuple = (1, 2, 3)
print("tuple:", type(tuple))
```

(g)
```
# tuples maintain order
tuple = ("one", "two", "three")
print("tuple:", tuple)
```

(h)
```
# tuples allow duplication
tuple = (11, 11, 11)
print("tuple:", tuple)
```

(i)
```
>>> vowels = ('a','e','i','o','u')
>>> vowels
>>> vowels[-1]
>>> vowels[-2]
>>> vowels[-5]
```

(j)
```
# create a tuple of mixed data types
tuple1 = (33, "33", [3, 3])
print("A tuple of mixed data types:", tuple1)
```

(k)
```
>>> t = ('x', 'y', 'z')
>>> t[0]
>>> t[-1]
```

2. Write a program to input marks of 'n' students and find out the minimum and maximum marks among them.
3. Write a program to store name and class of 5 students in tuples and display them.
4. How will you swap two values using tuples?
5. Write a program to input names of 'n' employees in tuple and display them.

CHAPTER 9

Dictionaries

9.1 DICTIONARIES

Dictionaries (or dict in Python) are a way of storing elements just like you would in a Python list. But, rather than accessing elements using its index, you assign a fixed key to it and access the element using the key.

Dictionaries are like address books. It is used to hold data that are related. For example, if you know person's name, you can easily get person's details. The person's name is technically referred to as a key, and any corresponding detail is referred to as the value. Note that the key must be unique as you cannot find the correct information if you have two persons with the same name.

The dictionary is Python's built-in mapping type. This means that dictionaries map keys to values and these key-value pairs are a useful way to store data in Python. Keys will be a single element. Values can be a list or list within a list, numbers, etc. To declare a dictionary, you use curly braces on either side { }. Inside these curly brackets, keys and values are declared. Each key is separated from its value by a colon (:) while each element is separated by commas. In other words, a dictionary is:

a. An associative array.
b. A mapping from keys to values.
c. A container (collection) that holds key:value pairs.

9.2 CONCEPT OF KEY : VALUE PAIR

Python dictionary (its keyword is *dict*) is a data type that stores multiple data items (elements) of different types.

Let's Try

Write the output of the following:

```
>>> myDict = {"A":"Ant", "B":"Bat",
"C":"Cow"}
>>> myDict
```

The dictionary is like a list, but more general. In the list, the indices have to be integers; in the dictionary they can be (almost) of any type.

You can think of a dictionary as a mapping between a set of indices (which are called keys) and a set of values. Each key maps to a value. The association of a key and a value is called a key:value pair or sometimes an item. Pairs of keys and values are specified in the dictionary by using the notation:

```
d = {key1 : value1, key2 : value2 }
```

Notice that the key:value pairs are separated by a colon, and the pairs themselves are separated by commas, and all this is enclosed in a pair of curly braces. For example, here is an empty dictionary and several dictionaries containing key:value pairs:

```
d1 = {}
d2 = {'width': 8.5, 'height': 11}
d3 = {1: 'RED', 2: 'GREEN', 3: 'BLUE', }
```

Note that a comma after the last pair is optional.

Python does not store dictionary elements in any particular order. If you enter elements in one order, they may be stored in another (essentially random) order inside Python. The order of the key:value pairs is not the same. In fact, if you type the same example on your computer, you might get a different result. In general, the order of items in the dictionary is unpredictable. But that's not a problem, as the elements of the dictionary are never indexed with integer indices. Instead, you use the keys to look up the corresponding values. For example,

```
>>> info = {'Name': 'Mona', 'Age': 7,
'Class': 'First'};
>>> print(info)
{'Name': 'Mona', 'Class': 'First','Age':
7 };
```

☞ *Note that the order of elements while the dictionary was being created is different from the order in which they are actually stored and displayed.*

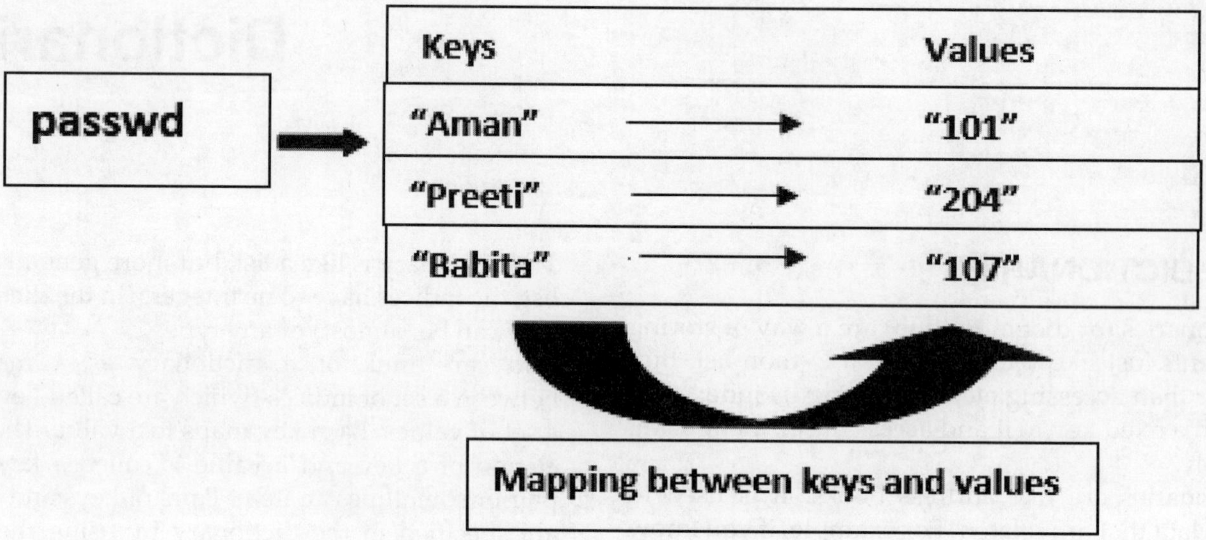

Figure 9.1 Mapping between keys and values

9.2.1 Characteristics of a Dictionary

(a) The dictionary is an unordered collection of objects.
(b) Values are accessed using a key.
(c) The dictionary can shrink or grow as required.
(d) The contents of dictionaries can be modified.
(e) Dictionaries can be nested.
(f) Sequence operations, such as slice, cannot be used with dictionaries.
(g) More than one entry per key is not allowed (no duplicate key is allowed).
(h) The values in the dictionary can be of any type while the keys must be immutable like numbers, tuples or strings.
(i) Dictionary keys are case sensitive - Same key name with the different case are treated as different keys in Python dictionaries.

☞ *A dictionary is used as container type that can store any number of Python objects, including other container types.*

9.3 CREATION, INITIALIZATION AND ACCESSING THE ELEMENTS IN A DICTIONARY

A collection that allows us to look up information associated with arbitrary keys is called a *mapping*. Python dictionaries are mappings. Some other programming languages provide similar structures called hashes or associative arrays. The dictionary can be created in Python by listing key:value pairs inside curly braces. A simple dictionary shown in Figure 9.1 stores some usernames and passwords.

```
# Creating a Dictionary
>>>   passwd   =   {"Aman":"101",   "Preeti":"204", "Babita":"107"}
```

Notice that keys and values are joined together with a ":" and commas are used to separate the pairs. The main use of the dictionary is to look up the value associated with a particular key. This is done through indexing notation. More than one entry per key is not allowed, which means no duplicate key is allowed.

☞ *Dictionaries are collections of data that associate a unique key with each value.*

An empty dictionary (without any items) is written with just two curly braces, like this: {}.

```
>>> dict1 = {} # it is an empty dictionary with no elements
>>> dict1
{}
```

type() returns the type of the passed variable. If passed variable is dictionary, then it would return the object representing the 'dict' class.

```
>>> type(dic1)
<class 'dict'>
```

To create an empty dictionary, you can either use the dict() function with no inputs, or assign a pair of curly brackets with nothing in between to a variable. You can confirm that both methods will produce the same result. For example,

```
empty = {}
my_empty = dict()
empty == my_empty
True
```

To create dictionary using built-in function dict(), the argument to dict() should be a sequence of key-value pairs.

```
# using built-in function dict()
my_dict = dict({1:'apple', 2:'banana'})
```

The following examples store employee information as a dictionary:

```
>>> dict2 = {'name': 'Raj', 'deptcode': 7} # Creating a Dictionary
>>> dict1, dict2
({}, {'deptcode': 7, 'name': 'Raj'})
```

To access dictionary elements, you use the familiar square brackets along with the key to obtain its value:

```
>>> dict2['name'] # accessing a element using key
'Raj'
```

Dictionary dict1 is empty while dict2 has two data items. The keys in dict2 are 'name' and 'deptcode', and their associated value items are 'Raj' and 7, respectively. Access to the value is through the key, as you can see from the explicit access to the 'name' key.

If you attempt to access a data item with the key which is not a part of the dictionary, you get an error:

```
>>> dict2['salary']
Traceback (most recent call last):
  File "<pyshell#1>", line 1, in <module>
    dict2['salary']
KeyError: 'salary'
```

☞ *You can also access a value for a key using get() method. The difference while using get() is that it returns None instead of KeyError, if the key is not found.*

In this example, you tried to access a value with the key 'salary' which, as you know, does not exist in the code given above. The best way to check if the dictionary has the specific key or not is by using the following syntax:

```
'keyname' in dictionary
```

It will return *True* if the dictionary has that key and *False* otherwise.

```
>>> 'salary' in dict2
False
>>> 'name' in dict2
True
>>> dict2['name']
'Raj'
```

Once the *in* has returned True, meaning that the key exists, then you can access it without having to worry about getting the KeyError.

☞ *In Python 2, has_key() method checks whether a dictionary has a given key or not. The expression d.has_key(k) is equivalent to k in d. The has_key() method has been removed from Python 3.*
Instead of:
dictionary.has_key('keyname')
you should use:
'keyname' in dictionary

Let us take a look at another dictionary example, using keys other than strings:

```
>>> dict3 = {}
>>> dict3[1] = 'abc'
>>> dict3['1'] = 3.14159
>>> dict3[3.2] = 'xyz'
>>> dict3
{3.2: 'xyz', 1: 'abc', '1': 3.14159}
```

Rather than adding each key:value pair individually, you could also enter all the data for dict3 at the same time. For example,

```
dict3 = { 3.2: 'xyz', 1: 'abc', '1': 3.14159 }
```

9.3.1 Traversing a Dictionary

Traversing a dictionary means visiting each element of the dictionary to display its values on the screen. Similar to the lists, you can use a "for in" loop to traverse through a dictionary. In general, it is the keys which enable iteration.

Example 1 –Demo of traversing a dictionary.

```
# Traversing a Dictionary
mydict = {1: 'Apple', 2: 'Banana' , 3: 'Orange', 4: 'Grapes'}
for i in mydict:
    print(i, ":",mydict[i])
```

(Contd...)

```
RUN
>>>
1 : Apple
2 : Banana
3 : Orange
4 : Grapes
>>>
```

Figure 9.2 Demo of traversing a dictionary

In Figure 9.2 'in' operator is used with for loop to iterates each key of a dictionary.

9.3.2 Appending Values in a Dictionary

Python allowed the dictionary object to be mutable. Hence, the add or update operations are permissible. In Python dictionary, addition of elements can be done in multiple ways. One value at a time can be added to a dictionary by defining value along with the key e.g. Dict[Key] = "Value". For example,

```
>>> dict2['name'] = 'Raju' # update existing entry
>>> dict2['deptcode'] = 5 # update existing entry
>>> dict2['deptname'] = 'Sales' # add new entry
```

If the key does exist, then its previous value will be overridden by its new value. You may also add the contents of an entire dictionary to another dictionary by using the update() built-in method.

Whenever you add an element whose key already exists, it's value will get changed to the new value. On adding a fresh "key: value" pair, a new element will get added to the dictionary. For example,

```
>>> d1 = {'a': 10, 'b': 200, 'c': 30}
>>> d1.update([('b', 20), ('d', 40)])
>>> d1
{'a': 10, 'b': 20, 'c': 30, 'd': 40}
```

In the example, key 'b' already exists in d1, so its value is updated from 200 to 20, and however, there is no key 'd' in d1, so that key-value pair is added.

Example 2 –Demo of append and update the dictionary.

```
#Demo of append and update the dictionary
# Original dictionary created with name, class and year
mydict={"name": "Aman", "class":"XII", "year":2019}
print(mydict)

# Dictionary appended with "stream = Science"
mydict["stream"] = "Science"
print(mydict)

# Dictionary updated with "stream = Commerce" instead of Science
mydict.update({"stream":"Commerce"})
print(mydict)

RUN
>>>
{'name': 'Aman', 'class': 'XII', 'year': 2019}
{'name': 'Aman', 'class': 'XII', 'year': 2019, 'stream': 'Science'}
{'name': 'Aman', 'class': 'XII', 'year': 2019, 'stream': 'Commerce'}
>>>
```

Figure 9.3 Demo of append and update the dictionary

9.3.3 Removing Dictionary Elements and Dictionaries

You can remove item from the existing dictionary by using *del* statement. You can either remove individual dictionary elements or clear the entire contents of the dictionary. If you really want to "remove" the entire dictionary, use the del statement. Here are some deletion examples for dictionaries and dictionary elements:

```
del dict2['name'] # remove entry with key 'name'
dict2.clear() # remove all entries in dict2
del dict2 # delete entire dictionary, i.e., dict2
```

Note- del dict2 will delete the entire dictionary and hence printing it after deletion will raise an Error.

☞ *The del keyword removes the item with the specified key name or can also delete the dictionary completely.*

Let's Try

Write the output of the following:

```
>>> month = {'Jan': 1, 'Feb': 2, 'Mar': 3, 'Apr': 4,  'May': 5, 'June': 6}
>>> month['Feb']
```

```
>>> di = {'a': 10, 'b': 20, 'c': 30}
>>> print(di.get('b'))
>>> print(di.get('x'))
```

```
d1   =   {'Rohan':   18,'Raj':24,'Dev':-22,'Robert':27}
del d1 ['Dev']
print(d1)
```

```
numbers = range(10)
dict1 = {}
# Add values to 'dict1' using for loop
for i in numbers:
    if i%2==0:
        dict1[i] = i**2
    else:
        dict1[i] = i**3
print(dict1)
```

```
dict1 = {'a': 5, 'b': 10, 'c': 15, 'd': 20, 'e': 25}
# Check for items greater than 2
dict2 = {x:y for (x,y) in dict1.items() if y>10}
print(dict2)
```

9.4 COUNTING THE FREQUENCY OF ELEMENTS IN A LIST USING A DICTIONARY

Dictionaries can be used wherever you want to store attributes and values that describe some concept or entity. For example, you can use the dictionary to count instances of particular objects or states. Since each key must have a unique identifier, there cannot be duplicate values for the same key. Therefore, you can use the key to store the items of input data, leaving the value part to store the results of our calculations. For example, suppose you want to find out the frequency of each letter in a sentence, such as "Computer is a machine." You could iterate through the characters of the sentence and assign each one to a key in the dictionary.

Example 4 –**Program using dictionary to iterate through the characters.**

```
# Program using dictionary to iterate through the characters
sentence = "Computer is a machine."
characters = {}
for character in sentence:
   characters[character] = characters.get(character,0) + 1
print(characters)
```

(Contd...)

```
RUN
>>>
{'C': 1, 'm': 2, 'o': 1, 'u': 1, 's': 1, 'r': 1, 'h': 1, 'i': 2, 'p': 1, 'c': 1,
'.': 1, 'a': 2, 't': 1, 'n': 1, ' ': 3, 'e': 2}
>>>
```

Figure 9.4 Program for Example 4

Example 5 –**Program to Count the frequency of elements in a list using a dictionary.**

```
# Program to Count the frequency of elements
list=[2,3,3,5,4,4,2,2]
print('Original List : ',list)
my_set=set(list)
d=dict.fromkeys(my_set,0)
#print('Dictionary with 0 values :')
#print(d)
for n in list:
    d[n]=d[n]+1
print('Element : Frequency')
print(d)
RUN
>>>
Original List :   [2, 3, 3, 5, 4, 4, 2, 2]
Element : Frequency
{2: 3, 3: 2, 4: 2, 5: 1}
>>>
```

Figure 9.5 Program for Example 5

Let's Try

Type the following program to count frequency of letters and see the output:

```
# Program to count frequency of letters
letter_counts = {}
for letter in "Programming":
    letter_counts[letter] = letter_counts.get(letter, 0) + 1
print(letter_counts)
```

9.5 SORTING KEY AND VALUE

Creating the dictionary with a set of key:value pairs can be accomplished if all the data items are known in advance.

Dictionaries do not have an inherent order. To impose an order while processing a dictionary, you have to sort it using the sorted() function. Looping over the sorted list of keys using sorted(ls), the dictionary content is printed out with the keys in alphabetical order as given below:

```
ls = {'Uma':76, 'Mohan':85, 'Beena':92, 'Lisa':28}
for s in sorted(ls):        # s iterates over sorted list of keys
        print(s, 'is', ls[s], 'years old.')
```

(Contd...)

```
>>>
Beena is 92 years old.
Lisa is 28 years old.
Mohan is 85 years old.
Uma is 76 years old.
>>>
```

But what if you want to sort by member's age here, the dictionary value can be achieved by specifying the key= option, i.e., key=ls.get to be exact. For example,

```
for s in sorted(ls, key=ls.get):     # value-based sorting
      print(s, 'is', ls[s], 'years old.')
>>>
Lisa is 28 years old.
Uma is 76 years old.
Mohan is 85 years old.
Beena is 92 years old.
>>>
```

Example 6 –Program to enter and display information in a dictionary.

```
# Program using dictionary to enter and display information on the screen
rec=dict()
num=int(input("Enter number of students :"))

i=1
while i<=num:
    name=input("Enter name of student :")
    per=input ("Enter marks% of student :")
    rec[name]=per
    i=i+1
print("Name of Student","\t","marks%")
for i in rec:
    print("\t",i,"\t\t",rec[i])

RUN
>>>
Enter number of students :3
Enter name of student :Gagan
Enter marks% of student :87%
Enter name of student :Geeta
Enter marks% of student :69%
Enter name of student :Anita
Enter marks% of student :95%
Name of Student   %marks
  Gagan              87%
  Geeta              69%
  Anita              95%
>>>
```

Figure 9.6 Program for Example 6

Example 7 –**Program to enter name and percentage of marks in a dictionary, and then display information according to marks percentage, i.e., value based.**

```
# Program using dictionary to enter and display information in sorted order
according to marks%
rec=dict()
num=int(input("Enter number of students :"))
i=1
while i<=num:
    name=input("Enter name of student :")
    per=int(input ("Enter marks% of student :"))
    rec[name]=per
    i=i+1
    ls = rec.keys()
print ("Name of Student","\t","marks%")
for i in sorted(ls,key=rec.get) :
    print ("\t",i,"\t\t",rec[i])

RUN
>>>
Enter number of students :4
Enter name of student :Uma
Enter marks% of student :56
Enter name of student :Tina
Enter marks% of student :84
Enter name of student :Sonu
Enter marks% of student :98
Enter name of student :Yash
Enter marks% of student :45
Name of Student  marks%
   Yash  45
   Uma   56
   Tina   84
   Sonu   98
>>>
```

Figure 9.7 Program for Example 7

☞ *Dictionary Keys are case sensitive i.e., same key name but with different case are treated as different keys in python dictionaries.*

9.6 DICTIONARY FUNCTIONS AND METHODS

Just like the other built-in types, dictionaries also have methods and functions.

9.6.1 dict()

The dict() constructor builds dictionaries directly from lists of key:value pairs stored as tuples. When the pairs form a pattern, list comprehensions can compactly specify the key:value list.

```
>>> dict([('Amit', 4139), ('Ramesh', 4127), ('John', 4098)])
{'Amit': 4139, 'John': 4098, 'Ramesh': 4127}
```

Since dict() is the name of a built-in function, you should avoid using it as a variable name. You can create a dictionary during run time using dict(), also called dynamic allocation.

9.6.2 cmp()

cmp() is not supported by Python 3; however, if you

are using Python 2 then, cmp() is used to check whether the given dictionaries are same or not. If both are same, it will return 0, otherwise it will return 1 or -1. If the first dictionary has more number of items, than the second one it will return 1, otherwise return -1. For example,

```
>>> D1 = {'Sun': 1, 'Mon': 2, 'Tue': 3,
'Wed': 4, 'Thurs': 5,
        'Fri': 6, 'Sat': 7 }
>>> D2 = {'Sun': 1, 'Mon': 2, 'Tue': 3,
'Wed': 4, 'Thurs': 5,
         'Fri': 6, 'Sat': 7 }
>>> D3 = {'Sun': 1, 'Mon': 2, 'Tue': 3,
'Wed': 4, 'Thurs': 5 }
>>> cmp(D1,D3) #both are not equal
1
>>> cmp(D1,D2) #both are equal
0
>>> cmp(D3,D1)
-1
```

☞ *In Python 2, cmp() is used to check whether the given dictionaries are same or not. cmp() is not supported by Python 3.*

9.6.3 len()

The len() built-in function gives us the number of items in a dictionary, i.e., it returns the number of key:value pairs. For example,

```
>>> temps = {'Delhi': 20.2, 'Allahabad':
15.4, 'Goa': 10.5}
>>> len(temps)
3
```

Let's Try

```
>>> week = {'Mon' : 1, 'Tues':2, 'Wed' :
3, 'Thurs' :4, 'Fri' :5, 'Sat' :6, 'Sun'
:7}
>>> len(week)
```

9.6.4 clear()

The clear() method removes all items from the dictionary. For example,

```
>>> d = {}
>>> d['name'] = 'Vivek'
>>> d['age'] = 18
>>> d
{'age': 18, 'name': 'Vivek'}
>>> returned_value = d.clear()
>>> d
{}
>>> print(returned_value)
None
```

☞ *The dict.clear() method is used to remove all elements of dictionary dict, and the dict.copy() method is used to return a shallow copy of dictionary dict.*

9.6.5 get()

The get() method is an easy way to get a value from a dictionary. Ordinarily, when you try to access an item that is not present in the dictionary, things go very wrong. For example,

```
>>> d = {}
>>> print(d['name'])
Traceback (most recent call last):
  File "<pyshell#2>", line 1, in <module>
    print(d['name'])
KeyError: 'name'
```

But, when you use get() function, it displays None:

```
>>> print(d.get('name'))
None
```

As you can see, when you use get() to access a non-existent key, there is no exception. Instead, you get the value None. You may supply your own "default" value, which is then used instead of None. For example,

```
>>> d.get('name', 'N/A')
'N/A'
```

9.6.6 pop()

The pop() method first gives the value corresponding to the given key, and then removes the key:value pair from the dictionary. For example,:

```
>>> d = {'x': 1, 'y': 2}
>>> d.pop('x')
1
>>> d
{'y': 2}
```

9.6.7 popitem()

The popitem() method is similar to list.pop() method, which pops off the last element of a list. Unlike list.pop(), popitem() pops off an arbitrary item because dictionaries do not have the "last element" or any order whatsoever. This may be very useful if you want to remove and process the items one-by-one in an efficient way (without retrieving a list of the keys first). For example,

```
d1={'publisher':   'BPB',   'price':   99,
'title': 'Computer Science'}
>>> d1.popitem()
('publisher', 'BPB')
>>> d1
{'title': 'Computer Science', 'price':
99}
>>>
```

Although popitem() is similar to the list method pop(), there is no dictionary equivalent of append (which adds an element to the end of a list). Since dictionaries have no order, such a method would not make any sense.

9.6.8 keys()

The keys and values can be extracted as lists from a dictionary. The keys() method of a dictionary object returns a list of all the keys used in the dictionary, in arbitrary order. For example,

```
>>> temps = {'Delhi': 20.2, 'Allahabad':
15.4, 'Goa': 10.5}
>>> temps.keys()
dict_keys(['Goa', 'Allahabad', 'Delhi'])
```

Let's Try

```
>>> month = {'Jan': 1, 'Feb': 2, 'Mar':
3, 'Apr': 4,   'May': 5, 'June': 6}
>>> month.keys()
```

9.6.9 values()

The values() method returns list of values.

```
>>> temps = {'Delhi': 20.2, 'Allahabad':
15.4, 'Goa': 10.5}
>>> temps.values()
dict_values([10.5, 15.4, 20.2])
```

Let's Try

```
>>> month = {'Jan': 1, 'Feb': 2, 'Mar':
3, 'Apr': 4,   'May': 5, 'June': 6}
>>> month.values()
```

9.6.10 items()

It returns a list of tuples (key,value) representing the key:value pairs. It is useful when you wish to iterate through the keys or values of a dictionary, even though in no particular order.

```
>>> temps = {'Delhi': 20.2, 'Allahabad':
15.4, 'Goa': 10.5}
>>> temps.items()
dict_items([('Allahabad',          15.4),
('Delhi', 20.2), ('Goa', 10.5)])
```

Example 8 -Program that converts dictionary into list of tuples.

```
# Convert dictionary to list of tuples
vegetables = {"carrot" : 1, "peas" : 2, "onion" : 4}
items = list(vegetables.items())
for item in items:
    print(len(item), item)


RUN
>>>
2 ('carrot', 1)
2 ('peas', 2)
2 ('onion', 4)
>>>
```

Figure 9.8 Program for Example 8

9.7 CHECKING FOR EXISTENCE OF A KEY

Membership operators *in* and *not in* work with dictionaries, but they can check for existence of *keys* only. The *in* operator returns *True* if the given key is present in the dictionary, otherwise *False*. The *not in* operator will return *True* if the given key is not present in the dictionary otherwise *False*.

```
>>> d = {}
>>> 'name' in d
False
>>> d['name'] = 'Mohan'
>>> 'name' in d
True
>>>    stu1={'name'   :   'Raj',   'age':17,
'Marks':97}
>>> 'Raj' in stu1 # 'Raj' is not a key,
hence it returned False
False
>>> 'Raj' not in stu1
True
```

☞ *The operators in and not in do not apply on values of a dictionary.*

REVIEW QUESTIONS WITH ANSWERS

1. Multiple Choice Questions

1. `dict1 = {'a': 1, 'b': 2, 'c': 3, 'd': 4}`
   `dict1.keys()`
   a. Put all keys of 'dict1' in a list and returns the list
   b. Put all values saved in 'dict1' in a list and returns the list
   c. Displays both keys and values
   d. None of these
2. In Python, a Dictionary can be created by placing sequence of elements within _______ braces.
   a. {} b. []
   c. () d. None of these
3. This is an example of:
   `Dic = {'Name': 'Aman', 1: [1, 2, 3, 4]}`
   a. Dictionary with Integer Keys b. Empty Dictionary
   c. Dictionary with Mixed keys d. None of the above
4. ______ function(s) can also be used for deleting specific values and arbitrary values from a Dictionary.
   a. pop() b. popitem()
   c. Both (a) and (b) d. None of the above
5. Python Dictionary are defined into ______ element(s).
   a. Keys b. Values
   c. Both keys and values d. None of these
6. In dictionary, index value can be of:
   a. integer b. Any data type
   c. float d. None of the above
7. Sequence operations:
   a. Slicing can be applied on dictionary
   b. Concatenation can be applied on dictionary
   c. Cannot be applied to dictionaries
   d. None of the above
8. In general, the order of items in a dictionary is:
   a. Unpredictable
   b. Predictable
   c. known
   d. None of these
9. `>>> a = {'x': 1, 'y': 2, 'z': 3}`
   `>>> a['z']`
   returns:
   a. 1 b. 2
   c. 3 d. None of these
10. What will be the output of the following code:
   `x = {(2,4):1,(4,6):2}`
   `print(x[2,4])`
   a. Key Error b. 1
   c. 2 d. 0
11. What will be the output of the following
   `a = {'a':1,'b':2,'c':3}`
   `print (a['a','b'])`
   a. [1,2] b. {'a':1,'b':2}
   c. (1,2) d. Key Error

2. State True or False for the following:

1. for loops are used to repeat a certain operation or a block of instructions in a program for a given number of times.

2. It is possible to create a new dictionary from a given dictionary but with items.
3. Dictionaries can not be nested.
4. Each key-value pair in a Dictionary is separated by comma.
5. Keys of a Dictionary must be unique.
6. Dictionary keys are case sensitive.
7. Items in a nested dictionary can also be deleted by using del keyword.
8. No duplicate key is allowed in a dictionary.
9. Same key name but with the different case are treated as different keys in Python dictionaries.
10. You cannot copy the entire dictionary to new dictionary.

3. Match the following:

1.	Key-value pair is separated by	a.	comma (,)
2.	Each key is separated by	b.	colon (:)
3.	An empty dictionary	c.	clear()
4.	Removes all the elements from the dictionary	d.	curly braces{}
5.	It function gives the number of pairs in the dictionary.	e.	"=" equal sign
6.	Assign values to variable	f.	len()
7.	It returns None instead of KeyError	g.	hashes
8.	A dictionary is an associative array	h.	get()
9.	Check if a key exists	i.	any data type
10.	Index value of dictionary	j.	in

4. Fill in the blanks:

1. Dictionary in Python is an _______ collection of data values, used to store data values like a map.
2. _______ holds key:value pair.
3. Dictionary can also be created by the built-in function ______.
4. Updating an existing value in a Dictionary can be done by using the built-in ______ method.
5. The ______ method will also help in accessing the element from a dictionary.
6. Using ______, specific values from a dictionary as well as whole dictionary can be deleted.
7. All the items from a dictionary can be deleted at once by using ______ method.
8. ______ removes the element with the specified key.
9. ______ removes the last inserted key-value pair.
10. ______ returns a list containing the dictionary's keys.

Answers

1. 1. a 2. a 3. c 4. c 5. c 6. b 7. c 8. a 9. c 10. b 11. d

2. 1. T 2. T 3. F 4. F 5. T 6. T 7. T 8. T 9. T 10. F

3. 1. b 2. a 3. d 4. c 5. f 6. e 7. h 8. g 9. j 10. i

4. 1. Unordered 2. Dictionary 3. dict() 4. update() 5. get() 6. del keyword 7. clear() 8. pop() 9. popitem() 10. keys()

Short Answer Questions

1. What is dictionary?

Ans A dictionary is another container type that can store any number of Python objects, including other container types. It is mutable. It consists of pairs (called items) of keys and their corresponding values. It is also known as associative array or hash table.

2. Compare and contrast dictionaries (dicts) with other Python data types.

Ans

(a) Dictionaries are a container type that stores data, like lists and tuples.

(b) Dictionaries are a mapping data type indexed by text(keys). The dictionary's elements (the items it contains) are key:value pairs. In contrast, lists and tuples store data by using numeric indexes (they are sequence data types) and support indexing and slicing.

(c) Dictionaries are mutable. That means, a dictionary can be modified in place; we do not have to create a copy of it to modify it (as we do with strings and tuples). However, a dict's keys must be immutable.

3. What are the advantages of hash?

Ans Hashes are used for space-efficient storage, for security and cryptography, and so on. Another benefit of hashing is that after the hash value is computed, keys can be looked directly; there's no need for the computer to search through a whole list of keys. In Python, this feature makes dictionaries very fast.

4. Does Python store dictionary elements in any particular order?

Ans No, python does not store dictionary elements in any particular order. If we enter elements in one order, they may be stored in another (essentially random) order inside Python. For example,

```
>>> D1 = {'sleep': "All night", 'work': "All day"}
>>> D1
{'work': 'All day', 'sleep': 'All night'}
```

5. What is a mapping?

Ans A mapping is a structure in which values are stored and retrieved according to a key. This data type is unordered and mutable. However keys of a dictionary must be unique and immutable. This is often called a dictionary, as it behaves similar to a common dictionary.

6. What is another name for mapping?

Ans A dictionary.

7. What are the characteristics of a Python dictionary?

Ans The characteristics of a Python dictionary are as follows:

(a) A dictionary is an unordered collection of objects.

(b) Values are accessed using a key rather than an ordinal numeric index.

(c) The dictionary can shrink or grow as needed.

(d) It can be nested.

(e) The contents of dictionaries can be modified.

8. A dictionary is an mutable object. Comment.

Ans A dictionary is mutable as its existing items can be modified, new items can be added to it, and existing items can be deleted from it.

9. A dictionary is an unordered collection of objects. Comment.

Ans The items in a dictionary are not maintained in any specific order, and the dictionary can contain references to any type of objects.

10. Can sequence operations, such as slicing and concatenation, be applied to dictionaries?

Ans No, the dictionary is not a sequence. Since it is not maintained in any specific order, operations that depend on the specific order cannot be used.

11. Write the syntax of a dictionary.

Ans A dictionary consists of one or more key:value pairs, separated by commas, and enclosed in a pair of curly braces. It can be empty also, i.e., having no items.

12. Can you remove key:value pairs from a dictionary. If so, how?

Ans We can use del statement to remove an existing key:value pair from a dictionary.

13. What do you mean by traversing a dictionary?

Ans Traversing a dictionary means visiting each element of the dictionary to display its values on the screen.

14. Can you merge two dictionaries? If so, how?

Ans Two dictionaries can be merged into one by using update( ) method. It merges the keys and values of one dictionary with that of another and overwrites values of the same key.

15. Discuss the properties of Dictionary Keys.

Ans There are few properties which should be considered while using dictionary keys:

(a) More than one entry per key is not allowed (no duplicate key is allowed).

(b) The values in the dictionary can be of any type while the keys must be immutable like numbers, tuples, or strings.

(c) Dictionary keys are case sensitive. Same key name but with the different case are treated as different keys in Python dictionaries.

16. What do the keys(), values() and items() functions do?

Ans keys(): Returns a list of the keys.
values(): Returns a list of the values.
items(): Returns a list of tuples (key,value) representing the key:value pairs.

17. Write different capabilities of dictionary.

Ans A dictionary has the following capabilities:

(a) Ability to iterate over keys or values or key-value pairs.
(b) Ability to add key-value pairs dynamically.
(c) Ability to look for a value by key.

18. Write difference between lists and dictionaries.

Ans The difference between lists and dictionaries are:

(a) In dictionary, index value can be of any data type and is called key, but in list index value is an integer.
(b) No sequence operation such as slicing and concatenation be applied to dictionaries as dictionary is not a sequence. Since it is not maintained in any specific order, operation that depends on a specific order cannot be used where as slicing and concatenation are applied on lists.
(c) List are sequential collections (ordered) and dictionaries are non-sequential collections (unordered).

19. Write a program to traverse a dictionary and display its elements on the different lines.

Ans

```
DAYS = {
'Sunday': 1,
'Monday': 2,
'Tuesday': 3,
'Wednesday': 4,
'Thursday': 5,
'Friday': 6,
'Saturday': 7,
}
for i in DAYS:
    print(i,":", DAYS[i])

RUN
>>>
Monday : 2
Tuesday : 3
Friday : 6
Wednesday : 4
Thursday : 5
Sunday : 1
Saturday : 7
>>>
```

Figure 1 Program for Q19

20. Write a program to traverse a dictionary and display its elements on the same line.

Ans

```
DAYS = {
'Sunday': 1,
'Monday': 2,
'Tuesday': 3,
'Wednesday': 4,
```

(Contd...)

```
'Thursday': 5,
'Friday': 6,
'Saturday': 7,
}
for i in DAYS:
    print(i,":", DAYS[i], end= ' ')

RUN
>>>
Monday : 2 Tuesday : 3 Friday : 6 Wednesday : 4 Thursday : 5 Sunday : 1
Saturday : 7
>>>
```

Figure 2 Program for Q20

21. Write a program to create dictionary and display information on the screen.

Ans

```
# Program to create dictionary and display information on the screen
compscience=dict()
num=int(input("Enter no. of students opted for Python Language :"))
i=1
while i<=num:
    name=input("Enter name of student :")
    grade=input ("Enter grade of student :")
    compscience[name]=grade
    i=i+1
print ("Computer Science","\t","Name of Student","\t","Grade")
for i in compscience:
    print ("Python","\t\t\t",i,"\t\t",compscience[i])

RUN
>>>
Enter no. of students opted for Python Language :2
Enter name of student :Vivek
Enter grade of student :A1
Enter name of student :Abhishek
Enter grade of student :A2
Computer Science     Name of Student     Grade
Python               Abhishek                A2
Python               Vivek                   A1
>>>
```

Figure 3 Program for Q21

22. Write a program to display information on the screen in ascending order of names.

Ans

```
# Program to information on the screen in ascending order of names
compscience=dict()
num=int(input("Enter number of students opted for Python Language :"))
i=1
while i<=num:
```

(Contd...)

```
    name=input("Enter name of student :")
    grade=input ("Enter grade of student :")
    compscience[name]=grade
    i=i+1
    ls = compscience.keys()
print ("Computer Science","\t","Name of Student","\t","Grade")
for i in sorted(ls,key=None, reverse=False):
  print ("Python","\t\t\t",i,"\t\t",compscience[i])

RUN
>>>
Enter number of students opted for Python Language :3
Enter name of student :Seema
Enter grade of student :B2
Enter name of student :Vivek
Enter grade of student :A1
Enter name of student :Abhishek
Enter grade of student :A2
Computer Science          Name of Student          Grade
Python                      Abhishek               A2
Python                      Seema                  B2
Python                      Vivek                  A1
>>>
```

Figure 4 Program for Q22

23. Write a program to input students details in a dictionary and then delete particular roll no. using name.

Ans

```
# Program to input students details and then delete particular roll no.
using name
details=dict()
num=int(input("Enter number of students whose information you want to enter
:"))
i=1
while i<=num:
    name=input("Enter name of the student :")
    rno=input ("Enter roll number of the student :")
    details[name]=rno
    i=i+1
name= input("Enter name of student you want to delete :")
del details[name]
ls=details.keys()
print (" Student information after deleting"     )
print ("Name of Student","\t","Rno")
for i in ls:
    print("\t",i,"\t\t",details[i])
```

(Contd...)

```
RUN
>>>
Enter number of students whose information you want to enter :3
Enter name of the student :Rahul
Enter roll number of the student :6
Enter name of the student :Suman
Enter roll number of the student :9
Enter name of the student :Tina
Enter roll number of the student :15
Enter name of student you want to delete :Suman
Student information after deleting
Name of Student          Rno
  Tina                    15
  Rahul                   6
>>>
```

Figure 5 Program for Q23

24. Find the output of the following programs:

(a)

```
>>> dict2 = { 'name': 'Ajay', 'rno':
8 }
>>> len(dict2)
```

Ans 2

(b)

```
>>> d = {'publisher': 'BPB',
'price': 99, 'title': 'Computer
Science'}
>>> d.keys()
```

Ans ['publisher', 'price', 'title']

(c)

```
>>> d = {'publisher': 'BPB',
'price': 99, 'title': 'Computer
Science'}
>>> d.values()
```

Ans ['BPB', '99', 'Computer Science']

(d)

```
>>> d = {'publisher': 'BPB',
'price': 99, 'title': 'Computer
Science'}
>>> d.item()
```

Ans [('publisher': 'BPB'), ('price': 99), (title': 'Computer Science')]

(e)

```
>>> dict1 = {}
>>> dict1
```

Ans {}

(f)

```
>>> cmp(1,2)
>>> cmp("a","b")
>>> cmp(3,1)
>>> cmp(3.1,3.1)
```

Ans -1
-1
1
0

(g)

```
>>> week = {'Mon' : 1, 'Tues':2,
'Wed' : 3, 'Thurs' :4, 'Fri' :5,
'Sat' :6, 'Sun' :7}
>>> week.keys()
```

Ans dict_keys(['Tues', 'Wed', 'Thurs', 'Sun', 'Fri', 'Mon', 'Sat'])

(h)

```
dict_keys(['Tues', 'Wed', 'Thurs',
'Sun', 'Fri', 'Mon', 'Sat'])
>>> week.values()
```

Ans dict_values([2, 3, 4, 7, 5, 1, 6])

(i)

```
dictionary = {
    'Aman': 'A+',
    'Veena': 'B',
    'Deepak': 'O',
}
print("Dictionary:")
for item in dictionary:
    print(item)
print()
```

Ans Dictionary:
Aman
Veena
Deepak

(j)
```
dictionary = {
    'Aman': 'A+',
    'Veena': 'B',
    'Deepak': 'O',
}
for key in dictionary:
        print("dictionary[%s]:  %s" %
(key, dictionary[key]))
print()
```

Ans dictionary[Aman]: A+
dictionary[Veena]: B
dictionary[Deepak]: O

(k)
```
dictionary = {1: "one", 2: "two", 3:
"three"}
print("dictionary:",   type(diction-
ary))
```

Ans dictionary: <class 'dict'>

(l)
```
dictionary  =  {11:  'eleven',  11:
'eleven', 11: 'eleven'}
print("dictionary:", dictionary)
```

Ans dictionary: {11: 'eleven'}
Note that Dictionary items are unique i.e., no duplication. However, in case of duplicate keys rather than giving an error, Python will take the last instance of the key to be valid and simply ignoring previous key-value pair.

EXERCISE

1. Discuss the concept of key-value pair with the help of examples.
2. How dictionaries are different from list?
3. What do you understand by mapping?
4. How will you append values to the dictionary?
5. What is the difference between keys() and values() functions?
6. What is the difference between pop() and remove() methods of a list?
7. How can you specify the pairs of keys and values in a dictionary?
8. How will you remove an item from dictionary?
9. Write the statement to create an empty dictionary.
10. Write the statement to update the dictionary.
11. Write the significance of del statement.
12. How is dict() constructor useful in creating dictionary?
13. What does clear() method return?
14. If variable weekday is assigned as:
    `>>> weekday = ['Sunday' : 1, 'Monday' : 2, 'Tuesday': 3, 'Wednesday' : 4, 'Thursday' : 5, 'Friday' : 6, 'Saturday' : 7]`
    then write the result of
    `>>> weekday.values()`
15. What is difference between string and dictionary?
16. How clear() function different from del() statement?

LAB EXERCISE

1. What would be the output of the following programs?

(a)
```
>>>  d  =  {'publisher':  'BPB',
'price': 99, 'title':
        'Computer Science'}
>>> len(d)
```

(b)
```
>>> d = {'x': 4, 'y': 5}
>>> d.pop('x')
```

(c)
```
hits  =  {"home"  :  124,  "sitemap"  :
26, "about" :  32}
# Sort the keys from the dictionary
keys = sorted(hits.keys())
print(keys)
```

(d)
```
>>>  week  =  {'Mon'  :  1,  'Tues':2,
'Wed'  :  3,  'Thurs'  :4,  'Fri'  :5,
'Sat' :6, 'Sun' :7}
>>> week.keys()
```

(e)
```
dictionary = {
    'one': 'first',
    'two': 'second',
    'three': 'third',
}
print("dictionary:", dictionary)
```

(f)
```
dictionary = {1: 'one', 2: 'two', 2:
'Two', 3: 'three'}
print("dictionary:", dictionary)
```

(g)
```
# Program to count frequency of
letter
letter_counts = {}
for letter in "madam":
   letter_counts[letter]=letter_coun
ts.get(letter,0)+1
print(letter_counts)
```

2. Write a program to read in five names and their addresses to store in a dictionary and then print them on the screen.
3. Write a program to enter all the party names, such as BJP, AAP and Congress, and the number of seats they got in assembly election in Delhi. Then display entire information on the screen.
4. Write a program to enter account details, such as name and account_no. Then delete name using account number.
5. Write a program to enter account details, such as name and account_no. Then display all account holders information in ascending order, based upon their account_no.
6. Write a program to enter account details, such as name , amount and account_no. Then update account using account number.

CHAPTER 10

Functions

10.1 TOP-DOWN APPROACH OF PROBLEM SOLVING

Top-down design is the technique of breaking down a problem into various major tasks needed to be performed. Each of these tasks is further broken down into separate *subtasks*, and so on till each subtask is sufficiently simple to be written as a self contained or procedure module. The entire solution of the problem will then consist of a series of simple modules.

In top-down design, you initially describe the problem you are working on at the highest or most general level. The description of the problem at this level will usually be concerned with what must be done – not how it must be done. The description will be in terms of complex, higher-level operations. You must take all of the operations at this level and individually break them down into simpler steps that begin to describe how to accomplish the tasks. If these simple steps can be represented as acceptable algorithmic step, you need not split them any further. If that is not the case, then you split each of these second level operations individually into still simpler steps. This stepwise refinement continues until each of the original top-level operations have been described in terms of acceptable shortest (primitive) statements.

☞ *Top-down approach is used in the system analysis and design process.*

The top-down approach, starting at the general levels to gain an understanding of the system and gradually moving down to levels of greater detail is done in the analysis stage. In the process of moving from top to bottom, each component is exploded into more and more details.

Thus, the problem at hand is analysed or broken down into major components, each of which is again broken down if necessary.

☞ *Top-down process involves working from the most general down to the most specific.*

The design of modules is reflected in hierarchy charts such as, the one shown in Figure 10.1. The purpose of procedure *Main* is to co-ordinate the three branch operations e.g. *Get*, *Process* and *Put* routines. These three routines communicate only through *Main*. Similarly, *Sub1* and *Sub2*, can communicate only through the Process routine.

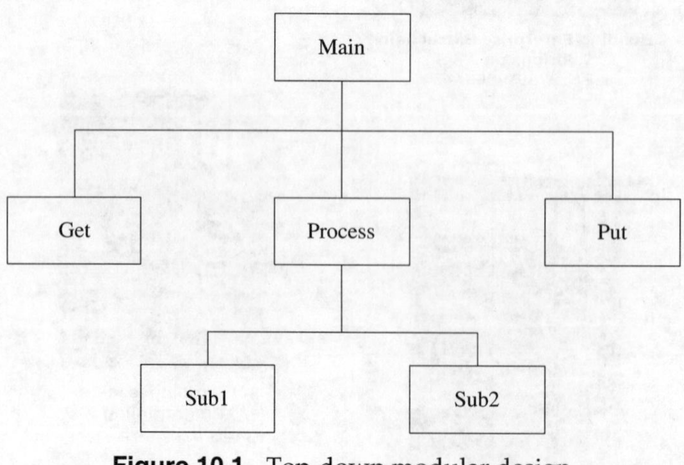

Figure 10.1 Top-down modular design

☞ *Using the top-down approach, attention is first focussed on global aspects of the overall system. As the design progress takes place, the system is decomposed into subsystems and more consideration is given to specific issues.*

Advantages of Top-down Approach

The advantages of top-down approach are as follows:

a. This approach allows a programmer to remain "on top of" a problem and view the developing solution in context. The solution always proceeds from the highest level downwards. With other techniques, you may find yourselves bogged down with very low-level decisions at a very early stage. It will be difficult to make these decisions if it is not clear as to how they may affect the overall solution of the problem.
b. This would be a very good way to delay decisions on problems whose solution may not be readily available. At each stage in the development, the individual operation will be split up into a number of more elementary steps. If you are not sure how to proceed with Step 1 you can still work on Step 2.
c. By dividing the problem into a number of subproblems, it is easier to share problem development. For example, one person may solve one part of the problem and the other person may solve another part of the problem.
d. Since debugging time grows quickly when the program is longer, it will be to our advantage to debug a long program divided into a number of smaller segments or parts rather than one big chunk. The top-down development process specifies a solution in terms of a group of smaller, individual subtasks. These subtasks thus become the ideal units of program for testing and debugging.

   If you add a new piece of code, say "p" to the overall program "P", and an error condition occurs, you can definitely state that the error must either be in "p" itself or in the interface between "p" or "P", because "P" has been previously checked and certified.

☞ *By testing the program in small pieces, you greatly simplify the debugging process. In addition, you will have the satisfaction of knowing that everything you have coded so far is correct.*

e. Another advantage of top-down development process is that it becomes an ideal structure for managing and implementing a program using a team of programmers. A senior programmer can be made responsible for the design of a high-level task and its decomposition into subtasks. Each of those subtasks can then be "given out" to a junior programmer who works under the direction of the senior staff. Since almost all software projects are done by teams of two or more programmers, this top-down characteristic helps in faster completion of the system.

In summary, top-down method is a program design technique that analyses a problem in terms of more elementary subtasks. Through the technique of stepwise splitting, you expand and define each of the separate subtasks until the problem is solved. Each subtask is tested and verified before it is expanded further. Thus, there are additional advantages:

a. Increased comprehension of the problem.
b. Unnecessary lower-level detail are removed.
c. Reduced debugging time.

10.1.1 Bottom-up Approach of Problem Solving

When faced with a large and complex problem, it may be difficult to see how the *whole* thing can be done. It may be easier to solve parts of the problem individually, taking the easier aspects first and thereby gaining the insight and experience to tackle the more difficult tasks, and finally to try and join them all together to form the complete solution. This is called a bottom-up approach.

This approach suffers from the *disadvantage* that the parts of the program may not fit together easily. There may be a lack of consistency between modules, and considerable re-programming may have to be carried out. Hence, this approach is not much favoured.

10.2 MODULAR PROGRAMMING

One way to improve the structure of a system is to break down the original problem to be solved into independent tasks called *modules*, and then execute each module in a pre-defined sequence. The resulting design would then contain a network of modules.

☞ *Breaking down a problem into smaller pieces (modules) allows you to focus more easily on a particular piece of the problem without worrying about the overall problem.*

In this way, the various tasks can be solved easily. They are more manageable since each module performs a very specific function. Typically, you can code each module independently of the others and test or debug each module separately. Once all modules are working properly, you can link them together by writing the coordinating module (generally called the root segment or the main module). The coordinating code activates the various modules in a pre-determined sequence (See Figure 10.2). Note that in this Figure, the resulting problem consists of five modules: the coordinating module and the four modules A, B, C, and D. It is, of course, conceivable that a particular module itself might be broken down into further sub-modules, down the line.

☞ *By breaking down a problem into independent modules, a system designer incharge of a very complex problem can easily assign various members of a team the responsibility for developing one or more modules.*

Such modules can be run and tested independent of one another. Making one change in one module is a very local intervention that does not require an understanding of all other modules.

In a modular environment, each module can be specified again as a sequence of smaller modules describing what is to be done at increasing levels of detail. The technique of expanding a problem solving plan into several levels of detailed subplans and presenting the system structure as a hierarchy of tasks is also called top-down design. The hierarchy chart, also called a structured diagram, is a useful tool for illustrating module relationships and the hierarchies. Figure 10.3 shows a hierarchy chart for the problem shown in Figure 10.2.

☞ *A subroutine can also reduce the code required for writing tasks that are to be performed repeatedly at different places in a program.*

In summary, modularization helps the problem solver to write better structured solutions that are more compact and thus easier to work with and more readable.

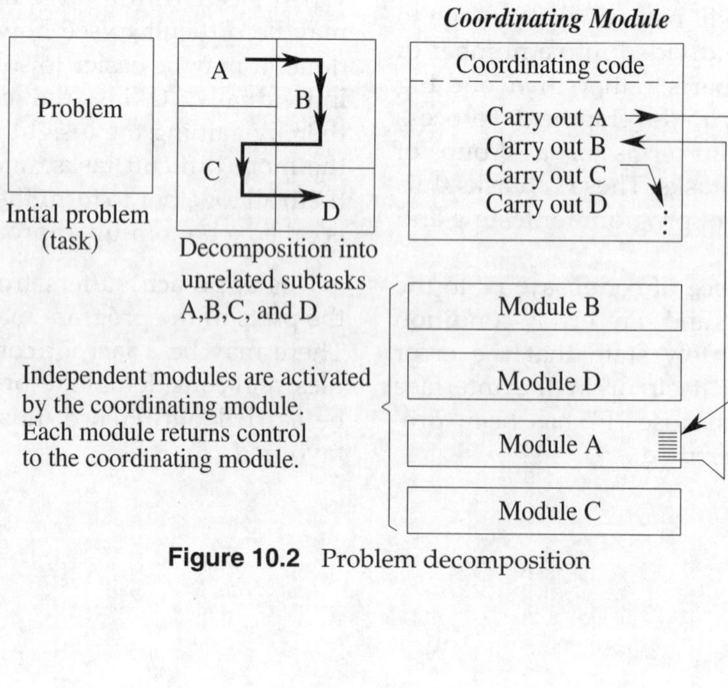

Figure 10.2 Problem decomposition

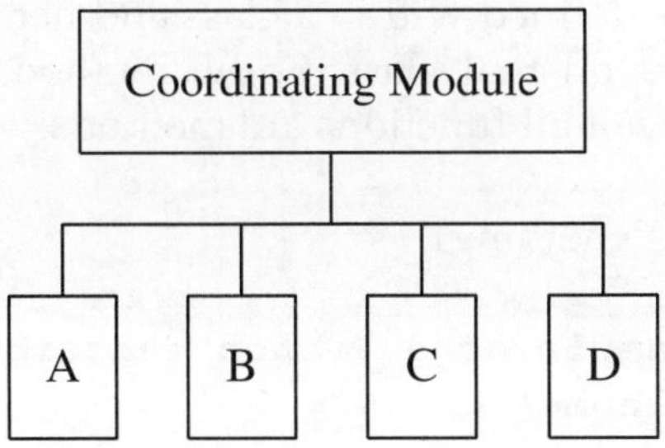

Figure 10.3 A Hierarchy chart

10.2.1 Modular Design

In industry, the problems that are to be solved with the help of computers need thousands of lines of code. The importance of splitting a problem into a series of self-contained modules then becomes important. A module should not exceed about 100 or so lines and should preferably be short enough to fit on a single page or two.

Advantages of Modular Design

a. Rather than focusing on the entire problem at hand, a module typically focuses on one relatively small portion of the problem.
b. Since module is small, it is simpler to understand it as a unit of code. It is therefore easier to test and debug, especially if its purpose is clearly defined and documented.
c. Program maintenance becomes much easier because the modules that are likely to be affected are quickly identified.
d. In a very large project, several programmers may be working on a single problem. Using a modular approach, each programmer can be given a specific set of modules to work on. This enables the whole project to be completed faster.
e. More experienced programmers can be given a more complex module to write, and the junior programmers can work on simpler modules.
f. Modules can be tested independently, thereby shortening the time taken to get the whole project working.
g. If a programmer leaves a project, it is easier for someone else to take over a set of self-contained modules.
h. A large project becomes easier to monitor as well as to control.

10.3 FUNCTIONS

A *function* is a routine, or set of instructions, that performs a specific task and can be processed independently. When the program passes control to a function, the function performs that task and *returns* control to the instruction following the *calling* instruction. Python function is a grouping of program statements put into a single unit to carry out tasks at a given level. Each Python function can be activated through the execution of a function call.

☞ *The collection of functions creates a program. The function is also known as procedure or subroutine in other programming languages.*

A *function* can be equated to a "blackbox" to which *one or more input values are passed, some processing is done,* and *output value is then returned* automatically. Figure 10.4 illustrates this sequence for the call to a function *sqrt*. The value of *x(16.0)* is the function input, and the function result or output is the square root of 16.0, i.e., 4 (See Figure 10.4).

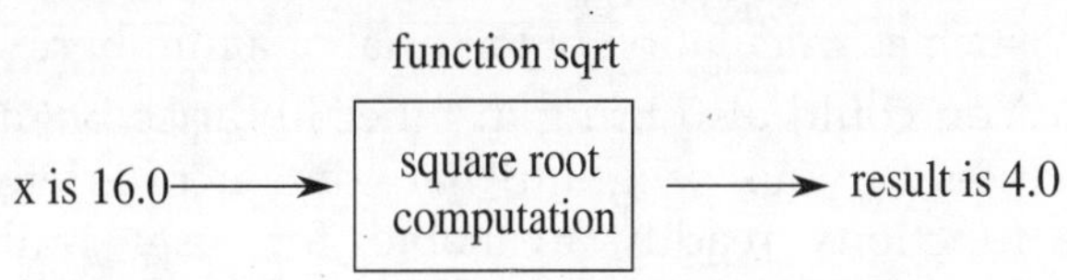

Figure 10.4 Function *sqrt* as a "Black Box"

Suppose you want to calculate Total marks of various students in a class. If you write a program without using function, you have to write same code again and again. But if you use a function say *total*, then you need not write the code again and again. Instead, you can jump to the section of code that calculates *Total* marks and come back to normal program flow when you have finished.

10.3.1 Advantages of using Function

Functions in Python are used because of the following reasons:

a. The use of functions enables you to write Python program in logically independent sections in the same way as you develop the solution algorithm. So, functions provide better modularity for your application and a high degree of code reusing.

b. Functions may be executed more than once in a program. Also if you have written and tested a function subprogram, you may use it in other programs or other functions. By using functions, you can avoid rewriting same logic/code again and again in a program. So a function can be called as a section of a program that is written once and can be executed whenever required in the program, thus making code reusability.
c. As the program grows larger and larger, functions make it more organized and manageable. You can track a large Python program easily when it is divided into multiple functions i.e., the complexity of a program can be divided into simple subtasks and function subprograms can be written for every subtasks. The subprograms are easier to write, understand and debug.
d. Multiple persons can work on same program by assigning different functions to each of them. Programmers reduce coding time and debugging time, thereby reducing overall development time, by using functions.
e. In Python, a function can call the same function again. It is called *recursiveness*. Many calculations can be done easily using recursive process, such as calculation of factorial of a number.
f. You could also bring in other libraries or modules to your program that contain pre-defined functions readily available for use. Built-in function, are the function(s) that are built into Python and can be accessed by a programmer. For example len(), type(), int(), etc. A library of functions can be designed and tested for use of every programmer.

☞ *The most important reason to use functions is to make program handling easier as only a small part of the program is dealt with at a time. It also reduces the size of the program and makes the program more readable and understandable.*

Functions vs Methods

A function just refers to a standalone function. Functions can be called only by its name, as it is defined independently. A method refers to a function which is part of a class. You can access it with an instance or object of the class. Methods can't be called by its name only, you need to invoke the class by a reference of that class in which it is defined, i.e., method is defined within a class and hence they are dependent on that class. So all methods are functions, but not all functions are methods.

Syntax

function(something)

Example

```
# An example of a Python function
a = 'Welcome'
len(a)
>>>
 7
>>>
```

Syntax

something.method()

Example

```
# An example for a Python method
a.upper()
>>>
'WELCOME'
>>>
```

Relation between Module, Package and Library

A module is a file containing Python definitions, functions, variables, classes and statements with .py extension which you intend to reuse in different codes of your program. To reuse the functions of a given module you simply need to import the module.

A Python package refers to a directory of Python module(s). This feature comes in handy for organizing modules of one type at one place. You can think of packages as the directories on a file system and modules as files within directories. For example, NumPy is a Python package for scientific computing which can deal with large data sizes.

The term library is simply a common term for a bunch of code that was designed with the aim of being usable by many applications. It provides some common functionality that can be used by specific applications.

In Python, a library is used loosely to describe a collection of the core modules. The term 'standard library' in Python language refers to the collection of exact syntax, token and semantics of the Python language which comes bundled with the core Python distribution. The Python installers for the Windows automatically adds the standard library and some additional libraries.

☞ *Script means series of commands within a single file.*

10.4 TYPES OF FUNCTIONS

Python comes preloaded with many function-definitions that you can use or create new function as per your requirement. Functions are of three types. These are:
(a) Module
(b) Built-in Functions
(c) User Defined Functions

10.4.1 Module

A module is a file that contains a collection of related functions and other definitions. Python comes loaded with some pre-defined modules that you can use or you even create your own modules. The Python modules that come preloaded with Python are called standard library modules. Three such standard library modules are math module, random module and statistics module. You can make a module available to another program by importing it. For example, if you want pre-defined function pi(), inside your module, you need to first import the module math which contains definitions of pi() in your program. Here's how you import:

```
>>> import math
```

Here's how you access the name pi that it defines:

```
>>> math.pi
3.141592653589793
```

Note that you can import modules with the import command. To use a module, you can import it. Usually import statements occur at the beginning of the Python module. Importing modules is a fairly simple operation, but it requires a little explanation. Modules are discussed in detail in Chapter 12.

The math Module

This module contains a set of commonly-used mathematical functions, including number-theoretic functions (such as factorial); logarithmic and power functions; trigonometric (and hyperbolic) functions; angular conversion functions (degree/radians); and some special functions and constants.

The random Module

The random module provides tools for making random selections. Random numbers are used for games, simulations, testing, security, and privacy applications. The random module must be imported before it can be used.

The statistics Module

The statistics module provides functions to mathematical statistics of numeric data. The popular statistical functions are defined in this module are mean(), median() and mode().

10.4.2 Built-in Functions

Built-in functions are those which come along with Python installation as libraries and always available for use, without importing any module (file). Built-in functions in Python Programming Language are called as Library function. You don't have to bother about the logic inside the Library functions. The Python interpreter has a number of built-in functions. They are loaded automatically as the interpreter starts and are always available. For example, print() and input() for I/O, number conversion functions int(), float(), complex(), data type conversions list(), tuple(), set(), etc.

10.4.3 User Defined Functions

Instead of depending on built-in functions, Python programming language allows you to create your own functions called as user defined functions. For example, if you want to perform some mathematical calculations then you can place them in separate function with proper function name and then you can call that function multiple time.

Python function is the grouping of program statements into a single unit. Each Python function can be activated through the execution of a function call. Execution always begins at the first statement of the program. Statements are executed one at a time, in order, from top to bottom. Order in which statements are executed, is called the flow of execution.

So far you have only seen the functions which come with Python either in some file (module) or in interpreter itself (built in), but it is also possible for programmer to write their own function(s). These functions can then be combined to form a module which can then be used in other programs by importing them.

10.5 DEFINING A FUNCTION

You can define functions to provide the required functionality. Here are simple rules to define a function in Python:

(a) Function blocks begin with the keyword *def* followed by an identifier, i.e., name of the function followed by parenthesized list of parameters and a colon (:) to mark the end of function header.Next follows the block of statement(s) that are the part of function.

(b) A name used inside a function to refer to the value passed as an argument is called *parameter*. Any input parameters or arguments should be placed within these parentheses. You can also define parameters inside these parentheses.

(c) Optional documentation string (docstring) is used to describe what the function does.

(d) One or more valid Python statements that make up the function body. The function body consists of indented statements and statements must have same indentation level (usually 4 spaces). The function body gets executed every time the function is called.

(e) An optional return statement to return a value from the function. It can be anywhere in the function body. This statement ends the execution of the function call and "returns" the result, i.e., the value of the expression following the return keyword, to the caller. If there is no return statement in the function code, the function ends, when the control flow reaches the end of the function body.

☞ *The statement return [expression] exits a function, optionally passing back an expression to the caller. A return statement with no arguments is the same as return None.*

The syntax for defining function is as follows:

```
def functionname( parameters ):
   """function_docstring"""
   function_suite i.e. the function body
   return [expression]
```

You create a function with a *def* statement. This provides the name, parameters and the suite of statements that creates the function's result. By default, parameters have a positional behavior, and you need to inform them in the same order that they were defined.

The function name is the name by which the function is known. The parameters is a list of variable names; these names are the local variables to which actual argument values will be assigned when the function is applied. The suite (which must be indented) is a block of statements that computes the value for the function.

There is a convention in Python to insert a documentation string right after the def line of the function definition. The documentation string, known as a docstring, should contain a short description of the purpose of the function and explain what the different arguments and return values are. Interactive sessions from a Python shell are also common to illustrate how the code is used. Docstrings are usually enclosed in triple double quotes """""", which allow the string to span several lines or summary section of exactly one line.

The return statement specifies the result value of the function. This value will become the result of applying the function to the argument values. This value is sometimes called the effect of the function.

10.5.1 Function Header

It begins with the keyword *def* and ends with colon (:), and contains the function identification details. The first line of a function definition is called function header.

10.5.2 Function Body

Consisting of sequence of indented (4 space) Python statement(s), to perform a task. The body can contain any number of statements. The body of the function gets executed only when the function is called/invoked. The first statement of the function body can optionally be a string constant, docstring, enclosed in triple quotes. It contains the essential information that someone might need about the function. The last statement of the function, i.e., return statement returns a value from the function. Return statement may contain a constant/literal, variable, expression or function, if return is used without anything, it will return None.

☞ *The sequence of statements inside a function definition is called function body.*

Here is the simplest form of a Python function. This function takes a string as input parameter and prints it on standard screen.

In the program given in Figure 10.5,

```
def printme( str ): # Line 1
```

The first line of function definition, i.e., Line 1 is called header and the rest, of the lines in our example, is known as body.

Example 1 –**Demo of Python function.**

```
def printme(str):
   """This prints a passed string into this function"""
   print(str)
   return
```

Figure 10.5 Python function

10.5.3 Calling/Invoking a Function

Defining a function only gives it a name, specifies the parameters that are to be included in the function, and structures the blocks of code.

Once the basic structure of a function is finalized, you can execute it by calling it from another function or directly from the Python prompt. Following is the example to call printme() function.

Example 2 –**Demo of function definition.**

```
# Function definition
def printme( str ): # Function definition
   """This prints a passed string into this function"""
   print(str)
   return
# Now you can call printme function
printme("Call to user defined function") # Function calling /invoking

RUN
Call to user defined function
```

Figure 10.6 Function Definition

10.6 STRUCTURE OF A PYTHON PROGRAM

In Python, all function definitions are given at the top followed by statements also called top level statement. Internally Python gives a special name to top level statements as _main_. Python begins execution of a program from top level statements, i.e., from _main_. def statements are also read but ignored until called. The top level statements are not indented at all. In the following example line 5, 6, 7 and 8 are called top level statements. Lets study the program given in Example 3 to see how statements are executed one at a time.

(a) The first statement of a function can be an optional statement - the documentation string of the function or docstring. Python starts execution from the first statement, i.e., line 1. Since it is comment line so ignored by the browser.

(b) *def* statement is also read but ignored until called. So, in line 2, Python just executes the function header line to determine that it is proper function header and entire function body, i.e., line 3 and line 4 are not executed by Python.

(c) So actual program execution begins with first statement of _main_ segment,. i.e., line 5 and it will print *testing*...on console.

(d) Next line 6 will be executed which is again a print statement so, it will print *passing the value 2* on the console.

(e) Statement 7, i.e., z = f(2) is a function call statement. Whenever a function call statement is encountered, function call will send the control flow to the function definition, i.e., line 2 and the value from _main_ i.e 2 is passed to it. Now the function f(x) receives the value 2 in variable x.

(f) Now the statements (line 3 and line 4) in the function body are executed and with the return statement or the last statement of function body, the control returns to the statement from where the function was called. Since the last statement of function body is *return* statement returning a value of y, i.e., 4, which will be given back to _main_ . Now the value returned will be stored in the variable z.

(g) Now the statement in line 8 which is the print statement will be executed and it will display the result :

the function returns 4

Example 3 –Program for exponentiation (power) calculation.

```
# Program for exponentiation (power) calculation          # line 1
def f(x):                                                 # line 2
    y = x**x                                              # line 3
    return y                                              # line 4
print("testing...")                                       # line 5
print("passing the value 2")                              # line 6
z = f(2)                                                  # line 7
print("the function returns", z)                          # line 8

RUN
>>>
testing...
passing the value 2
the function returns 4
>>>
```

Figure 10.7 Program to perform exponentiation (power) calculation

Let's consider another example. Assume you want to calculate powers, just like the built-in function pow, or the operator **. You can define the (integer) power of a number in several different ways, but let's start with a simple one: power(x,n) (x to the power of n) is the number x multiplied by itself n-1 times (so that x is used as a factor n times). So power(2,3) is 2 multiplied with itself twice, or 2 X 2 X 2 = 8.

Example 4 –Program for power calculation.

```
def power(x, n):
    result = 1
    for i in range(n):
        result *= x
    return result
a = int(input("Enter number "))
b = int(input("Raise to power "))
pw = power(a, b)
print(a, "raise to power", b, "is", pw)

RUN
>>>
Enter number 2
Raise to power 3
2 raise to power 3 is 8
>>>
>>>
Enter number 3
Raise to power 4
3 raise to power 4 is 81
>>>
```

Figure 10.8 Program for power calculation

10.7 DOCSTRINGS

Docstrings serve as documentation for your function to describe what the function does in the program so that anyone who reads the function's docstring understands what your function does, without having to go through all the code in the function definition. These are optional constructs enclosed by triple quotes. It is a comment in the programming language.

10.8 FUNCTION PARAMETERS AND ARGUMENTS

Parameters are the value(s) provided in the parenthesis when you write function header. You can add as many parameters as you want, just separate them with a comma.

☞ *In other words, parameter is a name used inside a function to refer to the value passed as an argument.*

Arguments are the value(s) provided in function call/invoke statement. This value is assigned to the corresponding parameter in the function. The variables you write after your function name in *def* statements are often called the *formal parameters* of the function. The values you supply when you call the function are called the *actual parameters*, or arguments. By default, parameters have a positional behavior and you need to inform them in the same order that they were defined.

It is common to say that the function takes arguments and return the result. The return statement can contain expression which gets evaluated and the value is returned. If there is no expression in the statement or the return statement itself is not present inside a function, then the function will return the None object.

☞ *The parameter passed by the client is known as the **actual parameter**. The parameter specified by the function is called the **formal parameter**.*

☞ *Argument is a value provided to a function when the function is called. This value is assigned to the corresponding parameter in the function.*

Parameters are placeholders for information that you give to a function so it can carry out an action. For example, if a function is defined as follows:

```
def display(message):
```

then, *message* is a parameter or formal argument. Although display has only one parameter, function can have many. To define function with multiple parameter, list them out, separated by commas.

In the following statement, *It will display message for you* is an argument or actual argument.

```
display("It will display message for you")
```

Here are a few things to know about function parameters:

(a) A function can have any number of parameters (or no parameters).
(b) When you define a function, you specify how many parameters it has.
(c) You can define default values for any or all of the parameters.

Here are a few things to know about arguments:

(a) Arguments are passed when you call the function.
(b) If the parameter has a default value, you don't have to pass an argument.
(c) You can pass an argument as a literal or as a name.

☞ *The values being passed through a function-call statements are called arguments or actual arguments. The values received in the function definition or header is called parameters or formal parameters.*

In the Example 4 shown above i.e. def power(x, n): *x* and *n* are known as parameters or formal parameters.

Whereas in pw = power(a, b)

a and *b* are known as arguments or actual arguments.

Arguments in Python can be literals, variables or expressions.

☞ *Function header cannot contain expressions.*

10.9 TYPES OF PARAMETERS OR FORMAL ARGUMENTS

You can call a function by using the following types of formal arguments:

(a) Required arguments
(b) Keyword arguments

(c) Default arguments
(d) Variable-length arguments

10.9 1 Required Arguments

Required arguments are the arguments passed to a function in correct positional order. Here the number of arguments in the function call should match exactly with the function definition.

To call the function printme(), you definitely need to pass one argument otherwise it would give a syntax error. See Example 5.

Example 5 –Demo of required arguments.

```
# Function definition is here
def printme(str):
   "This prints a passed string into this function"
   print(str)
   return
# Now you can call printme function
printme("This function will print passed function")

RUN
>>>
This function will print passed function
>>>
```

Figure 10.9 Demo of required arguments

When you do not pass argument to function call, i.e., you write printme() function without argument then, it will give syntax error:

```
Traceback (most recent call last):
  File "test.py", line 11, in <module>
    printme();
TypeError: printme() takes exactly 1
argument (0 given)
```

Using Positional Parameters and Positional Arguments

If you just list out a series of variable names in a function's header, you create positional parameter.
`def birthday1(name, age):`
If you call a function with just a series of values, you create positional parameter:
`birthday1 ("Sai",7)`
Using positional parameters and positional arguments means that parameters get their value based only on the position of the values sent. The first parameter gets the first value sent, the second parameter gets the second value sent and so on. With this particular function call it means name gets "Sai" and age gets 7.

If you switch the positions of two arguments, the parameters get different values. So with the call
`birthday1(7, "Sai")`
i.e., name gets the first value 7 and age gets the second value "Sai" which is wrong. Thus the values of arguments must match with parameters, position-wise (Positional) and order-wise. And the arguments must be provided for all parameters (Required).

10.9.2 Keyword Arguments

Keyword arguments are the named arguments with assigned values being passed in the function call statement, i.e., when you use keyword arguments in a function call, the caller identifies the arguments by the parameter name.

This allows you to skip arguments or place them out of order because the Python interpreter is able to use the keywords provided to match the values with parameters. You can also make keyword calls to the printme() function in the following ways:

Example 6 –Demo of keyword arguments.

```
# Function definition
def printme(str):
   "This prints a passed string into this function"
   print(str)
   return
# Now you can call printme function
printme(str = "My string")

RUN
My string
```

Figure 10.10 Demo of keyword arguments

Example 7 –Demo of keyword argument.

```
# Function definition
def info(name, age ):
   "This prints a passed info into this function"
   print("Name: ", name)
   print("Age: ", age)
   return
# Now you can call printinfo function
info(age=17, name="Vivek" )

RUN
>>>
Name: Vivek
Age: 17
>>>
```

Figure 10.11 Demo of keyword argument

Example 7 gives more clear picture. Note, here order of the parameter does not matter.

Using Keyword(named) Arguments

You can tell the function to assign certain values to specific parameters, regardless of order, if you use keyword arguments. With keyword argument, you use the actual parameter names from the function header to link a value to a parameter. So by calling the same function birthdat1() with

`birthday1(name="Sai", age=7)`

name gets "Sai" and age gets 7. The importance of keyword argument is that their order doesn't matter. It's the keywords that link values to parameter. So, the call

`birthday1(age=7, name="Sai")`

will produce the same result as above, i.e., name gets "Sai" and age gets 7, even though the values are listed in opposite order.

10.9.3 Default arguments

Default arguments are those that take a default value if no argument value is passed during the function call. You can assign this default value by with the assignment operator =.

If any of the formal parameters in the function definition are declared with the format "arg = value," then you will have the option of not specifying a value for those arguments when calling the function. If you do not specify a value, then that parameter will have the default value given when the function executes. In the above code, the variable age is not passed into the function however the default value of age is considered in the function.

Example 8 –**Demo of Default argument.**

```
# Function definition
def info(name, age = 19 ):
   "This prints a passed info into this function"
   print("Name: ", name)
   print("Age: ", age)
   return
# Now you can call printinfo function
info(age=17, name="Vivek" )
info(name="Vivek" )

RUN
>>>
Name:  Vivek
Age:  17
Name:  Vivek
Age:  19
>>>
```

Figure 10.12 Demo of Default argument

Using Default Parameter Values

A parameter having default value in the function header is known as a default parameter. In case the user does not want to provide values (argument) at the time of calling, you can provide default argument values. Following is an example of function header with default values:

`def birthday2(name= "Raj", age=5):`

This means that if no value is supplied to name, it gets "Raj". And if no value is supplied for age, it gets 5. So the call

`birthday2()`

will not generate an error, instead the default values are assigned to the parameters.

You can override the default values of any or all the parameter. With the call:

`birthday2(name="Dev")`

The default value of name is overridden, name gets "Dev", age still gets the value 5.

Using Multiple Argument Types Together

Python allows you to combine multiple argument types in a function call. You can combine keyword argument and positional argument in a single function. But while using keyword arguments, following should be kept in mind:

(a) An argument list must first contain positional arguments followed by any keywords arguments.

(b) Keywords in argument list should be from the list of parameters name only.

(c) You cannot specify a value for an argument more than once.

(d) Parameter names corresponding to positional arguments cannot be used as keywords in the same calls.

Some function arguments can be given a default value so that you may leave out these arguments in the call, if desired. A typical function may look as:

```
>>> def somefunc(arg1, arg2, kwarg1=4, kwarg2=8):
>>> print (arg1, arg2, kwarg1, kwarg2)
```

The first two arguments, arg1 and arg2, are ordinary or positional arguments, while the latter two are keyword arguments or named arguments. Each keyword argument has a name (in this example kwarg1 and kwarg2) and an associated default value. The keyword arguments must always be listed after the positional arguments in the function definition.

When calling somefunc(), you may leave out some or all of the keyword arguments. Keyword arguments that do not appear in the call get their values from the specified default values. You can demonstrate the effect through some calls has summarized in Table 10.1.

Table 10.1 somefunc() legal function calls

Function Call Statement	Legal/illegal	Result
somefunc(3,2)	Legal	3 2 4 8
somefunc(10,20,30,40)	Legal	10 20 30 40
somefunc(25,50,kwarg2=100)	Legal	25 50 4 100
somefunc(kwarg2=2,arg1=3,arg2=4	Legal	3 4 4 2

Notice that 1st and 2nd call to function is based on default argument value, and the 3rd and 4th call are using keyword arguments.

In the first usage, values 3 and 2 are passed on to arg1 and arg2, respectively. Thus, they all work with default values.

In second call, all the four parameters get values in function call statement.

In third usage, variable arg1 gets the first value 25, arg2 gets the value 50 due to the position of the argument. And parameter kwarg2 gets the value 100 due to naming, i.e., keyword arguments. The parameter kwarg1 uses the default value, i.e., 4.

In the fourth usage, you use keyword argument for all specified value. Keyword arguments can be used in any order and for argument skipped, there is a default value. Table 10.2 illustrates some illegal function calls.

Table 10.2 somefunc() illegal function calls

Function call statement	Legal/illegal	Result
somefunc()	illegal	Required or positional argument missing, i.e., somefunc() takes at least 2 arguments (0 given).
somefunc(kwarg1=10,kwarg2=20,30,40)	illegal	Keyword arguments are placed before positional arguments.
somefunc(4,5,arg2=6)	illegal	somefunc() got multiple values for keyword argument 'arg2'.
somefunc(4,5,kwarg1=5,kwarg3=6)	illegal	Undefined name kwarg3 used.

Let's Try

```
def info(name,age=17):
   print("My name is ",name,"and age
        is ",age)
info(name = "Dev")
```

10.9.4 Variable-Length Arguments

You may need to process a function for more arguments than you specified while defining the function. These arguments are called variable length arguments and are not named in the function definition, unlike required and default arguments.

The general syntax for a function with non-keyword variable arguments is as follows:

```
def functionname([formal_args,] *var_args_tuple ):
    "function_docstring"
    function_suite
    return [expression]
```

An asterisk (*) is placed before the variable name that will hold the values of all non-keyword variable arguments. You use *args as a parameter in the function header. It gives us the ability to pass N (variable) number of arguments. You use *args when you aren't sure how many arguments are going to be passed to a function, or if you want to pass a stored list or tuple of arguments to a function. You can also use the **kwargs syntax in a Python function declaration. It let us pass N (variable) number of arguments which can be named or keyworded. **kwargs is used when you don't know how many keyword arguments will be passed to a function.

Example 9 –**Python code to demonstrate *args.**

```
# Python code to demonstrate *args
def fn(*argList):
      for argx in argList:
            print (argx, end=' ')

fn('Learning', 'Python', 'is', 'Fun')
RUN
>>>
Learning Python is Fun
>>>
```

Figure 10.13 Python code to demonstrate *args

Example 10 –**Python code to demonstrate **kwargs.**

```
# Python code to demonstrate **kwargs
def fn(**kwargs):
      for stu, age in kwargs.items():
            print(stu,"'s Age is",age)
fn(Dev=17, Shiv=16, Karan=18)

RUN
>>>
Dev 's Age is 17
Shiv 's Age is 16
Karan 's Age is 18
>>>
```

Figure 10.14 Python code to demonstrate **kwargs

This tuple remains empty if no additional arguments are specified during the function call. Following is a simple example.

Example 11 –**Demo of variable length arguments.**

```
# Function definition
def info(arg1, *vartuple ):
```

(Contd...)

```
    "This prints a variable passed arguments"
    print("Output is: ")
    print(arg1)
    for var in vartuple:
       print(var)
    return

# Now call info function
info(10 )
info(70, 60, 50 )

RUN
>>>
Output is:
10
Output is:
70
60
50
>>>
```

Figure 10.15 Demo of variable length arguments

Let's Try

```
# Python Function with No Arguments, and No Return Value  FUNCTION 1
def Add1():
    a = 2
    b = 3
    Sum = a + b
    print("After Calling the Function:", Sum)
Add1()
# Python Function with Arguments, and No Return Value FUNCTION 2
def Add2(a,b):
    Sum = a + b
    print("Result:", Sum)
Add2(2,3)
# Python Function with Arguments, and Return Value FUNCTION 3
def Add3(a,b):
    Sum = a + b
    return Sum
Z=Add3(10,20)
print("Result ",Z)
# Python Function with No Arguments, but with  Return Value FUNCTION 4
def Add4():
    a=11
    b=20
    Sum = a + b
    return Sum
Z=Add3(10,12)
print("Result ", Z)
```

10.10 ANONYMOUS FUNCTIONS

You can use the lambda keyword to create small anonymous functions. These functions are called anonymous because they are not declared in the standard manner by using the def keyword.

(a) Lambda forms can take any number of arguments but return just one value in the form of an expression. They cannot contain commands or multiple expressions.
(b) An anonymous function cannot be a direct call to print because lambda requires an expression.
(c) Lambda functions have their own local namespace and cannot access variables other than those in their parameter list and those in the global namespace.
(d) Although it appears that lambda's are a one-line version of a function, they are not equivalent to inline statements in C or C++, whose purpose is bypassing function stack allocation during invocation for performance reasons.

Syntax:

The syntax of lambda functions contains only a single statement, which is as follows:

`lambda [arg1 [,arg2,.....argn]]:expression`

Following is the example to show how lambda form of function works:

Example 12 –Demo of Anonymous function.

```
# Function definition
sum = lambda arg1, arg2: arg1 + arg2;
# call sum as a function
print("Value of total : ", sum( 10, 20 ))
print("Value of total : ", sum( 20, 20 ))

RUN
>>>
Value of total :  30
Value of total :  40
>>>
```

Figure 10.16 Demo of Anonymous function

10.11 The return STATEMENT

A Python function could also optionally return a value. This value could be a result produced from your function's execution or even be an expression or value that you specify after the keyword 'return'. And, after a return statement is executed, the program flow goes back to the state next to your function call and gets executed from there. So, to call a Python function at any place in your code, you will only have to use its name and pass arguments in its parentheses, if any. A return statement with no arguments is the same as return *None*.

Example 13 –Demo of return statement.

```
# Function definition
def sum( arg1, arg2 ):
   # Add both the parameters and return them.
   total = arg1 + arg2
   print("Inside the function : ", total)
   return total
# Now you can call sum function
total = sum( 10, 20 )
print("Outside the function : ", total )
```

(Contd...)

```
def add_num(x,y):
    sum = x + y
    return sum
num1 = 2
num2 = 5
print("The sum is", add_num(num1, num2))

RUN
>>>
Inside the function :  30
Outside the function :  30
The sum is 7
>>>
```

Figure 10.17 Demo of return statement

Let's Try

```
def add_num(x,y):
   sum = x + y
   return sum
num1 = 2
num2 = 5
print("The    sum   is",    add_num(num1,
num2))
```

10.12 GLOBAL AND LOCAL VARIABLES

Variable names initialized and used inside one function are invisible to other functions. Such variables are called local variables. Whereas global variables defined outside of any function definition and are visible inside all of your functions.

Global variables are the one that are defined and declared outside a function and you can use them anywhere. These variables can be accessed by any function in the program. A global variable exists for the life of the program, but local variables are created during a function call and are discarded when the function's execution has completed.

Local variables are the one that are defined and declared inside a function/block and you can use them only within that function or block. This variable is present in the local space and not in the global space. During a program's execution, local variables live only when the function is executing. When a particular function call is finished, the space allocated for its local variables is freed up and can be used for a local variable in another function when that function is invoked. For example,

```
a=5 #Global Variable
def add():
  b=2  #Local Variable
  c=a+b
  print(c)
add()
```

It will display 7 as output.

10.13 LIFETIME AND SCOPE OF VARIABLES

A variable's lifetime is the period of time for which it resides in the memory. The lifetime of variables inside a function is as long as the function executes. They are destroyed once you return from the function. Hence, a function does not remember the value of a variable from its previous calls.

All variables in a program may not be accessible at all locations in that program. This depends on where you have declared a variable. The variable declared in one part of the program may not be accessible to the other parts. The scope of a variable determines the portion of the program where you can access a particular identifier. There are two basic scopes of variables in Python.

(a) Global scope
(b) Local scope

Variables that are defined inside a function body have a local scope. In other words, it is local to that function and those defined outside have a global scope.

This means that local variables can be accessed only inside the function in which they are declared, If you then try to access the variable x outside the function, it will give NameError.

Global variables can be accessed throughout the program body by all functions. When you call a function, the variables declared inside it are brought into scope.

```
def func1():
        x=9 # Local scope
        print(x)
func1()
>>>
9
>>>
y=9 # Global scope
def func2():
      print(y)
func2()
>>>
9
>>>
```

Let us discuss about global scope of a variable in brief.

(a) The global names are variables assigned at the top level of the enclosing module file. It means that it is visible everywhere within the program.
(b) The global names must be declared only if they are assigned within a function.
(c) Global variables must be referenced within a function without being declared. See Example 14.

Example 14 –**Demo of local and global variables.**

```
total = 0; # This is global variable.
# Function definition
def sum( arg1, arg2 ):
   # Add both the parameters and return them.
   total = arg1 + arg2; # Here total is local variable
   print("Inside the function local total : ", total)
   return total
# Now you can call sum function
sum( 20, 40 )
print("Outside the function global total : ", total)
```

Figure 10.18 Demo of local and global variables

When the above code is executed, it produces following result:
Inside the function local total : 60
Outside the function global total : 0

10.13.1 global Statements

The global statements are remotely like declaration statements in Python. They are not type or size declarations, though they are namespace declarations. The global statement tells Python that a function plans to change one or more global names, i.e., names that live in the enclosing module's scope (namespace).

☞ *A namespace is a practical approach to define the scope, and it helps to avoid name conflicts.*

10.14 void FUNCTION

A function that doesn't return a value is called void function or non-fruitful function whereas a function that returns a value is called fruitful function.

void functions might display something on the screen or have some other effect, but they don't have a return value. If you try to assign the result to a variable, you get a special value called *None.*

☞ *A void function internally returns an empty value None.*

10.15 LIBRARY FUNCTIONS

10.15.1 Input()

Input() is built-in functions, used to obtain information from the user.

```
>>> input("Enter a number: ")
Enter a number: 57
'57'
```

Note that this returns the input as a string. If you want to take 57 as an integer, you need to apply the int() function to it. The int() converts a value to an integer.

```
>>> int(input("Enter a number"))
Enter a number: 57
57
```

Example 15 –**Demo of Input() function.**

```
#Demo of Input() function
print('Please enter some text:')
x = input()
print('Text entered is:', x)
print('Type:', type(x))
print('Please enter an integer value:')
x = input()
print('Please enter another integer value:')
y = input()
num1 = int(x)
num2 = int(y)
print(num1, '+', num2, '=', num1 + num2)

RUN
>>>
Please enter some text:
Hello
Text entered is: Hello
Type: <class 'str'>
Please enter an integer value:
4
Please enter another integer value:
2
4 + 2 = 6
>>>
```

Figure 10.19 Demo of Input() function

10.15.2 eval()

The eval() function converts a string containing a valid expression to an object. For example,

```
x = 9
print(eval('x + 1'))
>>>
10
>>>
>>> c = eval("3, 5, 6") # c = (3,5,6)
>>> c
(3, 5, 6)
>>>
```

10.15.3 print()

The print() function enables a Python program to display textual information to the user.

```
print("Hello, World!")
print("I am learning Python")
```

10.16 STRING FUNCTIONS

Python has several built-in functions associated with the string data type. These functions let us easily modify and manipulate strings. Every string object that you create in Python is actually an instance of String class. Most of the string manipulation methods are already discussed in chapter 6.

Syntax

```
<stringObject>.<method name>()
```

10.16.1 count()

count() returns the number of times a specified value occurs in a string.

10.16.2 find()

The find() method is used to locate the position of the given substring within the string; it returns -1 if it is unsuccessful in finding the substring.

10.16.3 rfind()

Searches the string for a specified value and returns the last position of where it was found.

10.16.4 capitalize()

The method capitalize() returns a copy of the string with only its first character capitalized.

10.16.5 title()

The method title() converts the first character of each word to uppercase.

10.16.6 lower()

It converts all the uppercase letters in a string to lowercase.

10.16.7 upper()

It returns the exact copy of the string with all letters in uppercase.

10.16.8 swapcase()

It returns a copy of the string with lowercase letters turned into uppercase and vice-versa.

10.16.9 islower()

It returns true if the string is in lowercase and false otherwise.

10.16.10 isupper()

It returns true if the string is in uppercase and false otherwise.

10.16.11 istitle()

It checks whether the string is title-cased i.e., the first letter of each word is capitalized. It returns true if string is properly title-cased, and false otherwise.

10.16.12 replace(old,new)

It replaces all occurrences of old substring in a string with the new substring.

10.16.13 strip()

It removes whitespaces from start and end of string.

10.16.14 lstrip()

It removes all the leading (left side) whitespace in a string.

10.16.15 rstrip()

It returns a copy of the string with trailing characters removed based on the string argument passed. It also removes default whitespace characters from the right.

10.16.16 split()

The split method returns a list of the words of a string. The method assumes that words are separated by whitespace, which can be either spaces, tabs or newline characters.

10.16.17 partition()

This function splits the strings at the first occurrence of separator and returns the string in three parts, i.e., before the separator (head), the separator itself, and the part after the separator (tail). If the separator is not found, it returns the string itself, followed by two empty strings.

10.16.18 join()

The join() method takes a list of strings and joins them together into a single string. Elements can be joined using any separator.

10.16.19 isspace()

It returns true if the string contains only whitespace characters, and false otherwise.

10.16.20 isalpha()

It returns true if the string contains only letters, otherwise returns false.

10.16.21 isdigit()

It returns true if the string contains only digits, and false otherwise.

10.16.22 isalnum()

It checks whether string consists of only alphanumeric characters.

10.16.23 startswith()

The startswith() check whether that string starts with a particular string and returns true if the string starts with the specified string, i.e., it determines if the string is a prefix of the string.

```
>>> str1='Work Hard'
>>> str1.startswith('Work')
True
```

Note that startswith requires case to match.

```
>>> str1='Work Hard'
>>> str1.startswith('work')
False
```

10.16.24 endswith()

endswith() check whether that string ends with a particular string and returns true if the string ends with the specified string, i.e., it determines if the string is a suffix of the string.

```
>>> str1='Work Hard'
>>> str1.endswith('Hard')
True
>>> str1.endswith('hard')
False
```

10.16.25 encode() and decode()

The encode() and decode() methods are used to transform string data to and from a specified character encoding. As input, these accept an encoding name such as 'ascii', 'utf-8', or 'utf-16'. These methods are most commonly used to convert Unicode strings into a data encoding suitable for I/O operations. The encode() method is only available on strings, and the decode() method is only available on the bytes datatype.

```
>>> str1='Hello World'
>>> str1.encode()
b'Hello World'
```

Note that literal *b* is added in front of a string declaration, for creating a bytes object.

10.16.26 str()

str() takes an argument and returns the string equivalent of it.

10.16.27 split()

It splits the string according to delimiter *str* (space, if not provided) and returns a list of substrings, i.e., it splits the string into a list of "words".

String Slicing

Slicing is a string operation for extracting a part of the string. To extract a single character from a string, follow the string with the index of the desired character surrounded by square brackets ([ ]), remembering that the first character of a string has index zero. The syntax is s[i:j] meaning the substring starting at index i, running up to but not including index j.

Example 16 –**Demo of String Slicing.**

```
MyString = "ABCDEF"
print(MyString) # Prints a whole string.
print(MyString[0:3]) # Prints characters 0 to 3.
print(MyString[3::]) # Prints from character 3 to the end.
print(MyString[0:6:2]) #Prints every alternate character.
print(MyString[-1:-7:-1]) #Prints every character backwards
print(MyString[0:-2]) #Print until -2 from the end.

RUN
>>>
ABCDEF
ABC
DEF
ACE
FEDCBA
ABCD
>>>
```

Figure 10.20 Demo of String Slicing

Membership

Membership operator *in;* returns true if a character exists in the given string, false otherwise.

10.17 PATTERN MATCHING

Regular expressions, called regexes for short, are descriptions for a pattern of text. A regular expression in a programming language is a special text string used for describing a search pattern. It is extremely useful for extracting information from text such as code, files, log, spreadsheets or even documents. They are used at the server side to validate the format of email addresses or password during registration, used for parsing text data files to find, replace or delete certain string, etc. It is also used for webpage "Scraping" (extract large amount of data from websites).

In Python, a regular expression is denoted as RE (REs, regexes or regex pattern) are imported through re module. "re" module included with Python primarily used for string searching and manipulation. In order to use search() function, you need to import re first and then execute the code.

```
>>> import re
```

10.17.1 re attribute

The re attribute of a matched object returns a regular expression object.

10.17.2 string attribute

string attribute returns the passed string.

10.17.3 Using r prefix before RegEx

When r or R prefix is used before a regular expression, it means raw string. For example, '\n' is a new line whereas r'\n' means two characters: a backslash \ followed by n. Backlash \ is used to escape various characters including all metacharacters. However, using r prefix makes \ treat as a normal character.

10.17.4 Metacharacters

Each character in a Python Regex is either a metacharacter or a regular character. A metacharacters are characters with a special meaning, while a regular character matches itself. Python has the following metacharacters as listed in Table 10.3.

Table 10.3 Python Metacharacters

<table>
<tr><th>Metacharacter</th><th>Description</th></tr>
<tr><td>^</td><td>Matches a pattern at the start of the string</td></tr>
<tr><td>$</td><td>Matches end of string.</td></tr>
<tr><td>.</td><td>Matches a single character, except a newline.</td></tr>
<tr><td>[ ]</td><td>A bracket expression matches a single character from the ones inside it.</td></tr>
<tr><td>[^]</td><td>Matches a single character from those except the ones mentioned in the brackets.</td></tr>
<tr><td>( )</td><td>Parentheses define a marked subexpression, also called a block, or a capturing group.</td></tr>
<tr><td>\t, \n, \r, \f</td><td>Tab, newline, return, form feed.</td></tr>
<tr><td>*</td><td>Checks for zero or more characters to its left.</td></tr>
<tr><td>{m,n}</td><td>Matches the preceding character minimum m times, and maximum n times.</td></tr>
<tr><td>{m}</td><td>Matches the preceding character exactly m times.</td></tr>
<tr><td>?</td><td>Checks for exactly zero or one character to its left.</td></tr>
<tr><td>+</td><td>Checks for one or more characters to its left.</td></tr>
<tr><td>|</td><td>The choice operator matches either the expression before it, or the one after.</td></tr>
</table>

When using wildcards, ? matches any single character, and * matches any series of characters. So for instance:
a?a matches aaa, aba, aca but not aa or abba.
a*a matches aaa, aba, aca, aa or abba.
a.a matches aaa, aba, aca, etc.
a..a matches aaaa, aaba, abba, etc.
[abc] matches a or b or c. You can also give a range: [a-d] means a b c or d.
[^abc] matches everything but a or b or c.
[a-zA-Z0-9] - Matches any letter from (a to z) or (A to Z) or (0 to 9).

Example 17 –Demo of . metacharacter.

```
# Demo of . metacharacter
import re
str1 = "Hello World"
if re.search(r".....", str1):
  print (str1 + " has length >= 5")
else:
  print (str1 + "has length <=5")

RUN
>>>
Hello World has length >= 5
>>>
```

Figure 10.21 Demo of . metacharacter

Example 12 Demo of . metacharacter.

```
# Demo of . metacharacter
import re
str1 = "Cat"
if re.search(r".....", str1):
  print (str1 + " has length >=5")
else:
  print (str1 + " has length <=5")

RUN
>>>
Cat has length <=5
>>>
```

Figure 10.22 Demo of . metacharacter

Example 12 Demo of [.]

```
# Demo of [.]
import re
str1 = "Hello, Python."
if re.search(r"....[.]", str1):
   print (str1 + " has length >= 5 and ends with a ." )

RUN
>>>
Hello, Python. has length >= 5 and ends with a .
>>>
```

Figure 10.23 Demo of [.]

☞ *The | character is called a pipe. You can use it anywhere you want to match one of many expressions.*

10.17.5 Special Sequences

If the character following the backslash is a recognized escape character, then the special meaning of the term is taken. For example, \n is considered as newline. However, if the character following the \ is not a recognized escape character, then the \ is treated like any other character. A special sequence is a \ followed by one of the characters in the list below, and has a special meaning:

Table 10.4 Python Special Sequences

Character	Description
\A (start of string)	Returns a match if the specified characters are at the beginning of the string. It works across multiple lines as well.
\b (empty string at the beginning or end of a word)	Returns a match where the specified characters are at the beginning or at the end of a word.
\B (empty string not at the beginning or end of a word)	Returns a match where the specified characters are present, but not at the beginning (or at the end) of a word.
\d (a digit)	Returns a match where the string contains digits (numbers from 0-9).
\D (a non-digit)	Returns a match where the string does not contain digits.
\s (whitespace)	Returns a match where the string contains a single whitespace character like: space, newline, tab, return.
\S (non-whitespace)	Returns a match where the string does not contain a white space character.
\w (alphanumeric)	Returns a match where the string contains any word characters (any single letter, digit or underscore).
\W (non-alphanumeric)	Returns a match where the string does not contain any word characters.
\Z (end of string)	Returns a match if the specified characters are at the end of the string.

10.17.6 Rules for a Match

The basic rules of regular expression search for a pattern within a string are:

(a) The search proceeds through the string from start to end.
(b) All of the pattern must be matched, but not all of the string.
(c) The search stops at the first match.

10.17.7 Python Regular Expression Functions

All the regex functions in Python are in the re module. Regular expression methods include re.match(), re.search() & re.findall(). Many Python regex methods and Regex functions take an optional argument called Flags.

match()

The match() function returns a match object if the text matches the pattern. Otherwise it returns None. The match() functions looks for a pattern at the beginning of a string:

```
>>> import re
>>> re.match(r'foot', 'football') # Match
<re.Match object; span=(0, 4), match='foot'>
>>> re.match(r'ball', 'football')  # No match
```

search()

The search() function checks for a match anywhere in the string. If there is more than one match, only the first occurrence of the match will be returned.

```
>>> re.search(r'foot', 'football')
<re.Match object; span=(0, 4), match='foot'>

>>> re.search(r'ball', 'football')
<re.Match object; span=(4, 8), match='ball'>
```

The behaviour of regular expression matching can be subtly modified by using flags. For instance by specifying the re.IGNORECASE (or simply re.I), you make your regular expressions blind to the difference between lower and uppercase characters:

```
>>> re.search(r'Hello','HELLO',  flags=re.I)
<re.Match object; span=(0, 5), match='HELLO'>
```

Example 18 –**Demo of search().**

```
import re
str1 = "Hello, world."
if re.search(r"l+", str1):
    print('There are one or more consecutive letter "l"' +\
            "'s in " + str1)
RUN
>>>
There are one or more consecutive letter "l"'s in Hello, world.
>>>
```

Figure 10.24 Demo of search()

Compilation Flags

You can change the way the matching engine processes an expression using option flags. The flags can be combined using a bitwise or operation, and passed to compile(), search(), match(), and other functions that accept a pattern for searching.
Compilation flags let you modify some aspects of how regular expressions work. Flags are available in the re module under two names, a long name such as IGNORECASE, and a short, one-letter form such as I. Various flags used in Python includes
IGNORECASE [re.I] performs case-insensitive matching; character class and literal strings will match letters by ignoring case.
MULTILINE [re.M] flag controls how the pattern matching code processes anchoring instructions for text containing newline characters. Within a string made of many lines, allow ^ and $ to match the start and end of each line.
DOTALL [re.S] is the other flag related to multiline text. Normally the dot character . matches everything in the input text except a newline character. The flag allows dot to match newlines as well.

findall()

Both match() and search() return the first match. If you want all matches, you need to use findall() function.

```
>>> re.findall(r't.o', 'two cats too cute')
['two', 'too']
```

Sometimes you would like to access specific parts of the matched string-this can be achieved by groups. To create a group put the interesting part of a pattern in parentheses. For instance, you can use three groups to match the month, day and year part of a date:

```
>>> import re
>>> re.search(r'\b(\d{2})-(\d{2})-(\d{4}
```

```
)\b', '17-06-2019')
<re.Match object; span=(0, 10),
match='17-06-2019'>
```

To access the groups you can query the match object returned by the search function:

```
>>> mo = re.search(r'\b(\d{2})-(\d{2})-(
\d{4})\b', '17-06-2019')
>>> mo.group()
'17-06-2019'
>>> mo.group(0)
'17-06-2019'
>>> mo.group(1)
'17'
>>> mo.group(2)
'06'
>>> mo.group(3)
'2019'
>>> mo.groups()
('17', '06', '2019')
```

Groups can also be used with findall():

```
>>> re.findall(r'w(..)k', 'week weak')
['ee', 'ea']
```

split()

split method splits the string where there is a match and returns a list of strings where the splits have occurred.

```
>>> re.split(r'[,:]', 'red,blue:green')
['red', 'blue', 'green']
```

sub()

You can use the sub() function to substitute the part of a string with another. The method returns a string where matched occurrences are replaced with the content of replace variable. sub() takes three arguments- pattern, substring, and string. For example,

```
>>> re.sub('^a','an','a apple')
'an apple'
```

Here, you used ^ so it won't change apple to anpple.

subn()

The subn() is similar to sub() expect it returns both the modified string and the number of substitutions made. For example,

Example 19 –Demo of subn().

```
import re
# string
str = 'abc 123  xyz'
# matches all whitespace characters
pattern = '\s+'
# empty string
replace = ''
new_str = re.subn(pattern, replace, str)
print(new_str)

RUN
>>>
('abc123xyz', 2)
>>>
```

Figure 10.25 Demo of subn()

Compiling Regular Expressions

Regular expressions are compiled into RegexObject instances, which then have methods for various operations such as searching for pattern matches or performing string substitutions. You can learn about this by interactively experimenting with the re module. It allows you to enter REs and strings, and displays whether the RE matches or fails. First, run the Python interpreter, import the re module, and compile a RE.

```
>>> import re
>>> p.re.compile('[a-z]+')
>>> p
re.compile('[a-z]+')
```

Now, you can try matching various strings against the RE '[a-z]+'. An empty string should not match at all since + means 'one or more repetitions'. match() should return None in this case, which will cause the interpreter to print no output. You can explicitly print the result of match() to make this clear.

```
>>> p.match("")
>>> print(p.match(""))
None
```

Now, let's try it on a string that it should match, such as "hello". In this case, match() will return a MatchObject, so you should store the result in a variable for later use.

```
>>> m=p.match('hello')
>>> print(m)
<re.Match object; span=(0, 5), match='hello'>
```

Now you can query the MatchObject for information about the matching string. MatchObject instances also have several methods and attributes; the most important ones are:

group()

The group() method returns the part of the string where there is a match. If a match is found, if not, it returns None.

```
>>> m.group()
'hello'
```

start()

The start() function returns the index of the start of the matched substring.

end()

The end() returns the end index of the matched substring.

```
>>> m.start(), m.end()
(0, 5)
```

span()

The span() function returns a tuple containing start and end index of the matched part.

```
>>> m.span()
(0, 5)
```

10.17.8 Greedy and Non-greedy

When a special character matches as much of the search sequence (string) as possible, it is said to be a "Greedy Match". Non greedy matches the smallest number of repetitions.

By default the + and * operators are greedy, i.e. they will match as much as possible. For instance:

```
>>> re.search(r'\(.*\)', '(foot) (football)')
<re.Match object; span=(0, 17), match='(foot) (football)'>
```

will not stop on the first closing parenthesis and will match the whole string '(foot) (football)'.

Sometimes, however, you want our regular expression to be non-greedy and to match as little as possible. The non-greedy counterparts of + and * are +? and *?, respectively.

```
>>> re.search(r'\(.*?\)', '(foot) (football)')
<re.Match object; span=(0, 6), match='(foot)'>
```

will only match '(foot)'.

10.18 NUMERIC FUNCTIONS

Math functions are very helpful in calculating some of the complex mathematical expressions like power, sine/cosine, factorials etc.

10.18.1 eval()

The eval() function dynamically translates the text provided by the user into an executable form that the program can process. This allows users to provide input in a variety of flexible ways; for example, users can enter multiple entries separated by commas, and the eval function evaluates it as a Python tuple.

10.18.2 max()

Python built-in function max() returns the largest of its parameters. Here is the simplest version of the program.

Example 20 –**Demo of max() function.**

```
def main():
    x1  = int(input("Please enter first value(x1) : "))
    x2  = int(input("Please enter second value(x2) : "))
    x3  = int(input("Please enter third value(x3) : "))
```

(Contd...)

```
    print("The largest value is", max(x1,x2,x3))
main()

RUN
>>>
Please enter first value(x1) : -80
Please enter second value(x2) : -20
Please enter third value(x3) : -10
The largest value is -10
>>>
>>>
Please enter first value(x1) : 56
Please enter second value(x2) : 43
Please enter third value(x3) : 23
The largest value is 56
>>>
```

Figure 10.26 Demo of max() function

10.18.3 min()

Python built-in function min() returns the smallest of its parameters. Here is the simplest version of our program.

Example 21 –**Demo of min() function.**

```
def main():
    x1  = int(input("Please enter first values(x1) : "))
    x2  = int(input("Please enter second values(x2) : "))
    x3  = int(input("Please enter third values(x3) : "))
    print("The smallest value is", min(x1,x2,x3))
main()
RUN
>>>
Please enter first values(x1) : -80
Please enter second values(x2) : -20
Please enter third values(x3) : -10
The smallest value is -80
>>>
Please enter first values(x1) : 56
Please enter second values(x2) : 43
Please enter third values(x3) : 23
The smallest value is 23
>>>
```

Figure 10.27 Demo of min() function

10.18.4 pow()

The **pow(x,y)** function returns the value of *x* raised to the power of *y*, i.e.,x^y. Both pow() and the double star (**) operator perform exponentiation. ** is an operator and pow() is a built-in function.

Unlike the built-in ** operator, math.pow() converts both its arguments to type float. Use ** or the built-in pow() function for computing exact integer powers.

Example 22 –**Demo of pow() function.**

```
print("pow(2,0)  : ", pow(2, 0))
print("pow(2,2)  : ", pow(2, 2))
print("pow(2,3)  : ", pow(2, 3))
print("pow(2,4)  : ", pow(2, 4))
print("pow(3,4)  : ", pow(3, 4))
print("pow(2,-2)  : ", pow(2, -2))

RUN
>>>
pow(2,0)  :  1
pow(2,2)  :  4
pow(2,3)  :  8
pow(2,4)  :  16
pow(3,4)  :  81
pow(2,-2)  :  0.25
>>>
```

Figure 10.28 Demo of pow() function

10.18.5 round()

The round() built-in function has a syntax of round (flt,ndig=0). It normally rounds a floating point number to the nearest integral number and returns that result (still) as a float. When the optional third ndig option is given, round() will round the argument to the specific number of decimal places.

Example 23 –**Demo of round() function.**

```
>>> round(3)
3
>>> round(3.45)
3
b>>> round(3.4999999)
3
>>> round(3.4999999, 1)
3.5
```

Figure 10.29 Use of round() function

10.18.6 int()

It constructs an integer number from an integer literal, a float literal (by rounding down to the previous whole number) or a string literal (provided that the string represents a whole number). For example,

```
x = int(1)    # x will be 1
y = int(2.8) # y will be 2
z = int("3") # z will be 3
```

10.18.7 abs()

abs() returns the absolute value of the given argument. Here are some examples of using the abs() built-in function:

Example 24 –**Demo of abs() function.**

```
>>> abs(-1)
1
>>> abs(10.0)
10.0
```

Figure 10.30 Demo of abs() function

10.18.8 ceil()

The method **ceil()** returns the smallest whole number greater than or equal to *x*. The general form is:
math.ceil(x)

Example 25 –**Demo of ceil() function.**

```
import math # This will import math module
print("math.ceil(-35.18) : ",math.ceil(-35.18))
print("math.ceil(100.12) : ", math.ceil(100.12))
print("math.ceil(100.83) : ", math.ceil(100.83))
print("math.ceil(1.13) : ", math.ceil(1.13))
print("math.ceil(-1.13) : ", math.ceil(-1.13))
RUN
>>>
math.ceil(-35.18) :  -35
math.ceil(100.12) :  101
math.ceil(100.83) :  101
math.ceil(1.13) :  2
math.ceil(-1.13) :  -1
>>>
```

Figure 10.31 Demo of ceil() function

10.18.9 floor()

The **floor()** method returns the largest whole number less than or equal to *x*. For example,

Example 26 –**Demo of floor() function.**

```
import math # This will import math module
print("math.floor(-35.18): ",math.floor(-35.18))
print("math.floor(100.12): ", math.floor(100.12))
print("math.floor(100.83): ", math.floor(100.83))
print("math.floor(1.3): ", math.floor(1.3))
print("math.floor(2.0): ", math.floor(2.0))
RUN
>>>
math.floor(-35.18):-36
math.floor(100.12):100
math.floor(100.83):100
math.floor(1.3):1
math.floor(2.0):2
>>>
```

Figure 10.32 Demo of floor() function

10.18.10 fabs()

The fabs() function returns the absolute value of x.

The general form is:

`math.fab(x)`

Example 27 –Demo of fab() function.

```
import math # This will import math module
print("math.fabs(-35.18) : ",math.fabs(-35.18))
print("math.fabs(100.12) : ", math.fabs(100.12))
print("math.fabs(100.83) : ", math.fabs(100.83))
print("math.fabs(1.13) : ", math.fabs(1.13))
print("math.fabs(2.0) : ", math.fabs(2.0))

RUN
>>>
math.fabs(-35.18) :  35.18
math.fabs(100.12) :  100.12
math.fabs(100.83) :  100.83
math.fabs(1.13) :  1.13
math.fabs(2.0) :  2.0
>>>
```

Figure 10.33 Demo of fab() function

10.18.11 sqrt()

The **sqrt()** function returns the non-negative square root of *x*. If *x* is negative, a domain error occurs.

For example,

`math.sqrt(x)`

Example 28 –Demo of sqrt() function.

```
import math # This will import math module
print("math.sqrt(49) : ", math.sqrt(49))
print("math.sqrt(5) : ", math.sqrt(7))
print("math.sqrt(64) : ", math.sqrt(64))

RUN
>>>
math.sqrt(49) :  7.0
math.sqrt(5) :  2.6457513110645907
math.sqrt(64) :  8.0
>>>
```

Figure 10.34 Use of sqrt() function

Example 29 Program to compute the real roots of a quadratic equation.

The program shown in Figure 10.35 uses the *sqrt* (square root) to compute the roots of a quadratic equation of the form:

$ax^2 + bx + c = 0$

```
# A program that computes the real roots of a quadratic equation.
# Illustrates use of the math library.
# Note: this program crashes if the equation has no real roots.
import math # Makes the math library available.
def main():
    print("This program finds the real solutions to a quadratic")
    print()
    a = int(input("Please enter the coefficient a: "))
    b = int(input("Please enter the coefficient b: "))
    c = int(input("Please enter the coefficient c: "))
    discRoot = math.sqrt(b * b - 4 * a * c)
    root1 = (-b + discRoot) / (2 * a)
    root2 = (-b - discRoot) / (2 * a)
    print()
    print("The solutions are:", root1, root2)
main()

RUN
>>>
This program finds the real solutions to a quadratic
Please enter the coefficient a: 3
Please enter the coefficient b: -4
Please enter the coefficient c: -2
The solutions are: 1.7207592200561266 -0.38742588672279316
>>>
```

Figure 10.35 Program to compute the real roots of a quadratic equation

10.18.12 exp()

The **exp()** function returns the exponential number E raised to the power of *a*. For example,

Example 30 –Demo of exp() function.

```
import math # This will import math module
print("math.exp(-35.18) : ",math.exp(-35.18))
print("math.exp(100.12) : ", math.exp(100.12))
print("math.exp(100.83) : ", math.exp(100.83))
print("math.exp(1.13) : ", math.exp(1.13))
print("math.exp(2.0) : ", math.exp(2.0))

RUN
>>>
math.exp(-35.18) :  5.266476209220732e-16
math.exp(100.12) :  3.0308436140742566e+43
math.exp(100.83) :  6.164709417352325e+43
math.exp(1.13) :  3.0956565001247114
math.exp(2.0) :  7.38905609893065
>>>
```

Figure 10.36 Demo of exp() function

10.18.13 divmod()

divmod() built-in function combines division and modulus operations into a single function call that returns the pair (quotient, remainder) as a tuple. For example,

```
>>> divmod (14,5)
(2,4)
>>> divmod (2.7, 1.5)
(1.0, 1.2000000000000002)
```

Example 31 –**Demo of divmod() function using integer values.**

```
def main():
    x1  = int(input("Please enter first value(x1) : "))
    x2  = int(input("Please enter second value(x2) : "))
    print("The quotient and remainder are", divmod(x1,x2))
main()

RUN
>>>
Please enter first value(x1) : 10
Please enter second value(x2) : 3
The quotient and remainder are (3, 1)
>>>
>>>
Please enter first value(x1) : 3
Please enter second value(x2) : 10
The quotient and remainder are (0, 3)
>>>
```

Figure 10.37 Demo of divmod() function using integer value

Example 32 –**Demo of divmod() function using float value.**

```
def main():
    x1  = float(input("Please enter first value(x1) : "))
    x2  = float(input("Please enter second value(x2) : "))
    print("The quotient and remainder are", divmod(x1,x2))
main()

RUN
>>>
Please enter first value(x1) : 2.5
Please enter second value(x2) : 10
The quotient and remainder are (0.0, 2.5)
>>>

>>>
Please enter first value(x1) : 10
Please enter second value(x2) : 2.5
The quotient and remainder are (4.0, 0.0)
>>>
```

Figure 10.28 Demo of divmod() function using float value

10.19 THE random MODULE

Modules are files that contain code meant to be used in other programs. These modules usually group together a collection of programming related to one another. The random module contains function related to generating random numbers and producing random results. Random numbers have many applications in science and computer programming, especially when there are significant uncertainties in a phenomenon of interest. The first line of code in the program introduces the import statement. The statement allows you to import or load modules. In case of random module:

```
import random
```

10.19.1 random()

The random module contains functions that return random numbers, which can be useful for simulations or any program that generates random output. Python has a module random for generating random numbers. The numbers generated by random.random() tend to be equally distributed between 0 and 1. The random function can be used to generate pseudorandom floating point values. It requires no parameters and returns values uniformly distributed between 0 and 1 (including 0, but excluding 1). The following example shows the usage of random() function:

☞ *The random() function is part of the random package which returns a floating-point value.*

Example 33 **-Demo of random() function.**

```
import random # This will import random module
print(random.random())
print(random.random())
print(random.random())

RUN
>>>
0.03843263415457954
0.5650010796211149
0.27553471708860566
>>>
```

Figure 10.39 Demo of random() function

10.19.2 randint()

If you want a random integer, you can use the randint function. Randint accepts two parameters: a lowest and a highest number and returns an integer between lowest and highest (including both).

This function is not accessible directly so you need to import random module and then you need to call this function using random static object. Generate integers between 1,5. The first value should be less than the second. This will output either 1, 2, 3, 4 or 5.

Example 34 **-Demo of randint() function.**

```
import random # This will import random module
print(random.randint(0, 5))
print(random.randint(-4, 20))
RUN
>>>
3
13
>>>
```

(Contd...)

```
>>>
4
8
>>>
```

Figure 10.40 Demo of randint() function

10.19.3 uniform()

The function random.uniform, when supplied with two numerical parameters a and b, returns a random (uniformly distributed) real number.

Example 35 –Demo of uniform() function.

```
import random # This will import random module
print(random.uniform(0, 5))
print(random.uniform(-4, 20))

RUN
>>>
3.9638451355692887
-3.1520760763005606
>>>
```

Figure 10.41 Demo of uniform() function

10.19.4 randrange()

randrange([start], stop, [step]) returns a random number from range(start, stop, step). The function random.randrange is the standard function for generating a random integer in the range you would get by calling range with the same arguments. For example, to get a random number in the range from 1 to 10 (inclusive), you would use randrange(1,11) (or, alternatively, randrange(10)+1), and if you want a random odd positive integer lower than 20, you would use randrange(1,20,2).

Example 36 –Demo of randrange() function.

```
import random # This will import random module
print(random.randrange(6))
print(random.randrange(1,20,2))

RUN
>>>
1
1
>>>
>>>
4
19
>>>
```

Figure 10.42 Demo of randrange() function

Example 37 -Demo of randrange() function.

Let's ask the user how many dice to throw, and how many sides each one should have. The dice-throwing mechanism is implemented with randrange and a for loop.

```
from random import randrange
num = int(input('How many dice? '))
sides = int(input('How many sides per dice? '))
sum = 0
for i in range(num):
    sum += randrange(sides) + 1
print('The result is', sum)

RUN
>>>
How many dice? 3
How many sides per dice? 6
The result is 11
>>>
```

Figure 10.43 Demo of randrange() function

Let's Try

Observe the following Python code and find out, which out of the given options i) to iv) are the expected correct output(s). Also assign the maximum and minimum value that can be assigned to the variable 'Go'.

i. 100 $$ 75 $$ 10 ii. 75 $$ 10$$ 125 $$
iii. 75 $$ 10 $$ iv. 10 $$ 125 $$ 100

```
import random
X =[100,75,10,125]
Go = random.randint(0,3)
for i in range(Go):
    print (X[i],"$$",)
>>>
100 $$ 75 $$ 10 $$
>>>
```

Minimum Value that can be assigned to Go is 0.
Maximum Value that can be assigned to Go is 3.

10.20 DATE AND TIME FUNCTIONS

Python has a module named datetime to work with dates and times. In Python, date, time and datetime classes provide a number of function to deal with dates, times and time intervals. Date and datetime are an object in Python, so when you manipulate them, you are actually manipulating objects and not string or timestamps. Whenever you manipulate dates or time, you need to import datetime function. The datetime module enables you to create the custom date objects, perform various operations on dates like the comparison, etc. To work with dates as date objects, you have to import datetime module into the Python source code.

10.20.1 The concept of Ticks

In Python, the time instants are counted since 12:00 am, January 1, 1970. It is the beginning of an era. and is used to start counting time. This special moment is called epoch. In Python, the time between the present moment and the special time above is expressed in seconds. That time period is called Ticks. A tick can be seen as the smallest unit to measure the time. The time() function in the time module returns the number of seconds from 12 am on January 1, 1970 to the present.

Example 38 –**Demo to calculate number of ticks using time() function.**

```
# Import time module
import time

# prints the number of ticks spent since 12 AM, 1st January 1970
ticks = time.time()
print ("Number of ticks since 12:00am, January 1, 1970: ", ticks)

RUN
>>>
1560653863.8000364
>>>
```

Figure 10.44 Demo to calculate number of ticks using time() function

10.20.2 time()

To get how many ticks have passed since the epoch, you call the Python time() method.

```
>>> import time
>>> time.time()
1514472318.761928
```

A time object instantiated from the time class represents the local time.

Example 39 –**Demo of time() function.**

```
from datetime import time
# time(hour = 0, minute = 0, second = 0)
a = time()
print("a =", a)
# time(hour, minute and second)
b = time(9, 32, 52)
print("b =", b)
# time(hour, minute and second)
c = time(hour = 9, minute = 32, second = 52)
print("c =", c)
# time(hour, minute, second, microsecond)
d = time(9, 32, 52, 224565)
print("d =", d)
RUN
>>>
a = 00:00:00
b = 09:32:52
c = 09:32:52
d = 09:32:52.224565
>>>
```

Figure 10.45 Demo of time() function

Example 40 –**Program to print hour, minute, second and microsecond.**

```
# Print hour, minute, second and microsecond
from datetime import time
```

(Contd...)

```
a = time(9, 32, 52)

print("hour =", a.hour)
print("minute =", a.minute)
print("second =", a.second)
print("microsecond =", a.microsecond)

RUN
>>>
hour = 9
minute = 32
second = 52
microsecond = 0
>>>
```

Figure 10.46 Program to print hour, minute, second and microsecond

Once you create a time object, you can easily print its attributes such as hour, minute etc. Note that you have not passed microsecond argument, so, its default value 0 is printed.

10.20.3 localtime()

localtime() returns the current time according to your geographical location, in a more readable format. Consider the following example.

Example 41 –**Demo of localtime() function.**

```
import time

#returns a time tuple

print(time.localtime(time.time()))

RUN
>>>
time.struct_time(tm_year=2019, tm_mon=6, tm_mday=16, tm_hour=8, tm_min=28, tm_sec=59, tm_wday=6, tm_yday=167, tm_isdst=0)
>>>
```

Figure 10.47 Demo of localtime() function

10.20.4 asctime()

The time can be formatted by using the asctime() function of time module. It returns the formatted time for the time tuple being passed.

```
>>> import time
>>> time.asctime()
'Sun Jun 16 11:18:09 2019'
```

10.20.5 clock()

It returns the number of seconds elapsed since the first call made to it. It returns the value as a floating number.

```
>>> time.clock()
1392.736455535
>>> time.clock()
1409.408693707
```

10.20.6 sleep()

The sleep() method of time module is used to stop the execution of the script for a given amount of time. The output will be delayed for the number of seconds. Consider the following example.

Example 42 –**Demo of sleep() function.**

```
import time
for i in range(0,5):
    print(i)
    #Each element will be printed after 2 second
    time.sleep(2)
RUN
>>>
0
1
2
3
4
>>>
```

Figure 10.48 Demo of sleep function

10.20.7 now()

The now() method to create a datetime object containing the current local date and time. The date contains year, month, day, hour, minute, second, and microsecond.

Example 43 –**Demo of now() function.**

```
# Get Current Date and Time
import datetime;

#returns the current datetime object

print(datetime.datetime.now())

RUN
>>>
2019-06-16 08:36:33.975566
>>>
```

Figure 10.49 Demo of now() function

10.20.8 today()

today() method defined in the date class to get a date object containing the current local date.

Example 44 –**Demo of today() function.**

```
# Get Current Date

import datetime;
date_object = datetime.date.today()
print(date_object)
```

(Contd...)

```
RUN
>>>
2019-06-16
>>>
```

Figure 10.50 Demo of today() function

Example 45 –Demo of today() function.

```
# Print today's year, month and day
from datetime import date
today = date.today()
print("Current year:", today.year)
print("Current month:", today.month)
print("Current day:", today.day)

RUN
>>>
Current year: 2019
Current month: 6
Current day: 16
>>>
```

Figure 10.51 Demo of today() function

10.20.9 date()

The date() is a constructor of the date class. It takes three arguments: year, month and day.

Example 46 –Demo of date() function.

```
# Date object to represent a date
import datetime
d = datetime.date(2019, 7, 12)
print(d)

RUN
>>>
2019-07-12
>>>
```

Figure 10.52 Demo of date() function

10.20.10 dir()

The dir() function to get a list containing all attributes of a module.

Example 47 –Demo of dir() function.

```
import datetime
print(dir(datetime))
```

(Contd...)

```
RUN
>>>
['MAXYEAR', 'MINYEAR', '__builtins__', '__cached__', '__doc__', '__file__',
'__loader__', '__name__', '__package__', '__spec__', 'date', 'datetime', 'dateti-
me_CAPI', 'time', 'timedelta', 'timezone', 'tzinfo']
>>>
```

Figure 10.53 Demo of dir() function

10.20.11 timestamp()

You can also create date objects from a timestamp. You can convert a timestamp to date using from timestamp() method.

Example 48 –**Demo of timestamp() function.**

```
from datetime import date
print("Date :", timestamp)

RUN
>>>
Date : 2021-07-14
>>>
```

Figure 10.54 Demo of timestamp() function

10.20.12 strftime()

The strftime() method takes one or more format codes and returns a formatted string based on it. A reference of some format codes are used in following example:

Example 49 –**Demo of strftime() function.**

```
import datetime
x = datetime.datetime.now()
print(x.year)
print(x.strftime("%a")) #Weekday, short version i.e. Sun
print(x.strftime("%A")) #Weekday, full version i.e. Sunday
print(x.strftime("%w")) #Weekday as a number 0-6  i.e. 0
print(x.strftime("%d")) #Day of month 01-31  i.e. 16
print(x.strftime("%b")) #Month name, short version i.e. Jun
print(x.strftime("%B")) #Month name, full version  i.e. June
print(x.strftime("%m")) #Month as a number 01-12  i.e.  06
print(x.strftime("%y")) #Year, short version, without century  i.e. 19
print(x.strftime("%Y")) #Year, full version i.e., 2019
print(x.strftime("%H")) #Hour 00-23 i.e.  11
print(x.strftime("%I")) #Hour 00-12 i.e.  11
print(x.strftime("%p")) #AM/PM  i.e.   AM
print(x.strftime("%M")) #Minute 00-59 i.e.  02
print(x.strftime("%S")) #Second 00-59  i.e. 59
print(x.strftime("%c")) #Local version of date and time i.e. Sun Jun 16 11:02:59
2019
```

(Contd...)

```
print(x.strftime("%x")) #Local version of date  i.e. 06/16/19
print(x.strftime("%X")) #Local version of time i.e.  11:02:59

RUN
>>>
2019
Sun
Sunday
0
16
Jun
June
06
19
2019
11
11
AM
02
59
Sun Jun 16 11:02:59 2019
06/16/19
11:02:59
>>>
```

Figure 10.55 Demo of strftime() function

Date Arithmetic

Example 50 -Demo of Date Arithmetic.

```
import datetime
today = datetime.date.today()
print('Today     :', today)
one_day = datetime.timedelta(days=1)
print('One day   :', one_day)
yesterday = today - one_day
print ('Yesterday:', yesterday)
tomorrow = today + one_day
print ('Tomorrow :', tomorrow)

RUN
>>>
Today     : 2019-06-16
One day   : 1 day, 0:00:00
Yesterday: 2019-06-15
Tomorrow : 2019-06-17
>>>
```

Figure 10.56 Demo of Date Arithmetic

10.20.13 The calendar module

Python provides a calendar object that contains various methods to work with the calendars.

Example 51 -**Demo of month() function.**

```
#Program to print the calendar of July 2019
print(calendar.month(2019,7))

RUN
>>>
     July 2019
Mo Tu We Th Fr Sa Su
 1  2  3  4  5  6  7
 8  9 10 11 12 13 14
15 16 17 18 19 20 21
22 23 24 25 26 27 28
29 30 31
>>>
```

Figure 10.57 Demo of month() function

```
>>> print(calendar.month(2020,1))
    January 2020
Mo Tu We Th Fr Sa Su
       1  2  3  4  5
 6  7  8  9 10 11 12
13 14 15 16 17 18 19
20 21 22 23 24 25 26
27 28 29 30 31
```

You can also print the calendar of whole year. The prcal() method of calendar module is used to print the calendar of the whole year. (See Figure 10.58).

```
# Printing the calendar of whole year
import calendar

#printing the calendar of the year 2019
calendar.prcal(2019)
```

10.20.14 isleap()

The isleap() takes a 4-digit year as an argument, and returns True if it is a leap year. Otherwise, False.

```
>>> calendar.isleap(2019)
False
>>> calendar.isleap(2020)
True
```

10.20.15 leapdays(y1,y2)

The leapdays() returns the total number of leap days from year y1 to year y2.

```
>>> calendar.leapdays(1990,2020)
7
```

10.20.16 firstweekday()

The firstweekday() returns which day is currently set as the first day of the week.

```
>>> calendar.setfirstweekday(0)
>>> calendar.firstweekday()
0
```

Python 3.7.0 Shell

File Edit Shell Debug Options Window Help

```
      January                   February                   March
Mo Tu We Th Fr Sa Su      Mo Tu We Th Fr Sa Su      Mo Tu We Th Fr Sa Su
    1  2  3  4  5  6                   1  2  3                   1  2  3
 7  8  9 10 11 12 13       4  5  6  7  8  9 10       4  5  6  7  8  9 10
14 15 16 17 18 19 20      11 12 13 14 15 16 17      11 12 13 14 15 16 17
21 22 23 24 25 26 27      18 19 20 21 22 23 24      18 19 20 21 22 23 24
28 29 30 31               25 26 27 28               25 26 27 28 29 30 31

       April                      May                       June
Mo Tu We Th Fr Sa Su      Mo Tu We Th Fr Sa Su      Mo Tu We Th Fr Sa Su
 1  2  3  4  5  6  7             1  2  3  4  5                      1  2
 8  9 10 11 12 13 14       6  7  8  9 10 11 12       3  4  5  6  7  8  9
15 16 17 18 19 20 21      13 14 15 16 17 18 19      10 11 12 13 14 15 16
22 23 24 25 26 27 28      20 21 22 23 24 25 26      17 18 19 20 21 22 23
29 30                     27 28 29 30 31            24 25 26 27 28 29 30

        July                     August                  September
Mo Tu We Th Fr Sa Su      Mo Tu We Th Fr Sa Su      Mo Tu We Th Fr Sa Su
 1  2  3  4  5  6  7                1  2  3  4                         1
 8  9 10 11 12 13 14       5  6  7  8  9 10 11       2  3  4  5  6  7  8
15 16 17 18 19 20 21      12 13 14 15 16 17 18       9 10 11 12 13 14 15
22 23 24 25 26 27 28      19 20 21 22 23 24 25      16 17 18 19 20 21 22
29 30 31                  26 27 28 29 30 31         23 24 25 26 27 28 29
                                                    30

      October                   November                  December
Mo Tu We Th Fr Sa Su      Mo Tu We Th Fr Sa Su      Mo Tu We Th Fr Sa Su
    1  2  3  4  5  6                   1  2  3                         1
 7  8  9 10 11 12 13       4  5  6  7  8  9 10       2  3  4  5  6  7  8
14 15 16 17 18 19 20      11 12 13 14 15 16 17       9 10 11 12 13 14 15
21 22 23 24 25 26 27      18 19 20 21 22 23 24      16 17 18 19 20 21 22
28 29 30 31               25 26 27 28 29 30         23 24 25 26 27 28 29
                                                    30 31
```

Figure 10.58 Use of calendar.prcal to print Calendar of 2019

10.21 RECURSION

Recursion is the process of defining something in terms of itself. A physical world example would be to place two parallel mirrors facing each other. Any object in between them would be reflected recursively.

You know that in Python, a function can call other functions. It is even possible for the function to call itself. These type of construct are termed as recursive functions. For example, the factorial of 5 (denoted as 5!) is 1*2*3*4*5 = 120 is a recursive function to find the factorial of an integer. The factorial function is widely used in combinatorial analysis (counting theory in mathematics), probability theory, and statistics. The factorial of n usually is expressed as n!. Factorial is defined for non-negative integers.

Example 52 –**Program to find factorial using recursion.**

```
def calc_fact(x):
    if x == 1:
        return 1
    else:
        return (x * calc_fact(x-1))

num = 5
print("The factorial of", num, "is", calc_fact(num))

RUN
>>>
The factorial of 5 is 120
>>>
```

Figure 10.59 calc_fact() recursive function

In the above example, calc_fact() is a recursive function as it calls itself. When you call this function with a positive integer, it will recursively call itself by decreasing the number. Each function call multiples the number with the factorial of number 1 until the number is equal to one. The recursion ends when the number reduces to 1, which is called the base condition. Every recursive function must have a base condition that stops or terminates the recursion or else the function calls itself infinitely.

Example 53 –**Program to find the power of a number using recursion.**

```
# To find the power of a number using recursion
def power(base,exp):
   if (exp==1):
       return base
   if (exp!=1):
       return (base*power(base,exp-1))
base = int(input("Enter base: "))
exp = int(input("Enter exponential value: "))
print ("Result:",power(base,exp))

RUN
>>>
Enter base: 4
Enter exponential value: 3
Result: 64
>>>
```

Figure 10.60 Program to find the power of a number using recursion

In the above example, power() is a recursive function as it calls itself. When user enters the base and exponential value, the numbers are passed as arguments to a recursive function to find the power of the number. The base condition is given that if the exponential power is equal to 1, the base number is returned. If the exponential power is not equal to 1, the base number multiplied with the power function is called recursively with the arguments as the base and power minus 1 and the final result is printed.

10.21.1 Advantages of Recursion

(a) Recursive functions make the code look clean and refined.

(b) A complex task can be broken down into simpler sub-problems using recursion.
(c) Sequence generation is easier with recursion than using some nested iteration

10.21.2 Disadvantages of Recursion

(a) Sometimes the logic behind recursion is difficult to follow through.
(b) Recursive calls are expensive (inefficient) as they take up a lot of memory and time.
(c) Recursive functions are hard to debug.

REVIEW QUESTIONS WITH ANSWERS

1. Multiple Choice Questions

1. The math.sqrt(49) returns:
   a. 7.0
   b. 8.0
   c. 2.64
   d. None of these
2. Directive %a represents:
   a. Weekday, short version
   b. Weekday, full version
   c. Weekday as a number 0-6
   d. None of these
3. The ceil() returns _____ whole number greater than or equal to x.
   a. Smallest b. Largest
   c. Any d. None of the above
4. A module:
   a. Is independent grouping of code and data
   b. Can be re-used in other programs
   c. Can depend on other modules
   d. All of the above
5. Named block of statements within a program is known as:
   a. Module
   b. Function
   c. Namespace
   d. None of these
6. Built-in function:
   a. len() b. input()
   c. type() d. All of the above
7. Standard library module:
   a. math module b. random module
   c. Both (a) and (b) d. None of these
8. What is the final value of x?

```
x = 7
def func():
    global x
    print('x is', x)
    x = 2
    print('Changed global x to', x)
func()
print('Value of x is', x)
```

   a. Value of x is 7
   b. Value of x is 2
   c. Value of x is 0
   d. None of these
9. Which keyword is used for function?
   a. Fun b. Define
   c. def d. All of these
10. What is the output of the following:

```
>>>    re.split(r'[,:]',       'red,blue:-
green')
```

   a. ['red', 'blue', 'green'] b. ['red'; 'blue'; 'green']
   c. ('red', 'blue', 'green') d. All of the above

2. State True or False for the following:

1. A module in Python is a .py file.
2. It's possible to import more than one module in one import statement.
3. split('delimiter') splits your string into a list.
4. A function may or may not have parameters inside the parentheses.
5. The code block within every function starts with a colon (;).
6. A return statement with no arguments is the same as return None.
7. Parameters are specified after the function name, inside the square brackets.
8. [abc] matches 'a', 'b', and 'c'.
9. Metacharacters are characters with a special meaning.
10. In order to use search() function, you need to import re first and then execute the code.

3. Match the following:

1. Package	a. converts a value to an integer.
2. strip()	b. a directory of Python module(s)
3. int()	c. replaces a given string with another string.
4. input()	d. returns the value of x to the power of y.
5. pow()	e. reads and returns a line of string
6. lambda	f. the first line of a function definition
7. header	g. anonymous Python function
8. doctsring	h. way to define a function
9. def	i. built-in function
10. print()	j. brief about the function and its operation

4. Fill in the blanks:

1. A _______ is a file containing Python definitions and statements.
2. _______ removes whitespaces at the beginning or at the end of the string.
3. A variable that's declared inside a function has a _____ scope.
4. A variable's lifetime is the period of time for which it resides in the _______.
5. _______ statement that reads a module file and creates a module object.
6. A function that you define yourself in a program is known as ________ function.
7. The first statement of the body function is a documentation string called _______.
8. Keyword _____ marks the start of function header.
9. _____ matches the end of the string.
10. _______ matches the preceding character zero or more times.

Answers

1. 1. a 2. a 3. a 4. d 5. b 6. d
7. c 8. b 9. c 10. a

2. 1. T 2. T 3. T 4. T 5. F 6. T
7. F 8. T 9. T 10. T

3. 1. b 2. c 3. a 4. e 5. d 6. g
7. f 8. j 9. h 10. i

4. 1. module 2. strip()
3. local 4. memory
5. import 6. user defined
7. doctsring 8. def
9. $ 10. *

Short Answer Questions

1. What is the purpose of a header file in a Python program?

Ans A header file provides a centralized location for the declaration of all extern variables, function prototypes, etc. Files that must use or define a variable or a function, include header file(s). By using header files, two main safeguards are provided.

2. What is function?

Ans A named sequence of statements that performs some useful operation. Functions may or may not take arguments and may or may not produce a result.

3. What are the advantages of using functions.

Ans Functions let us write code only once.

Functions hide unnecessary complexity from the user.

Functions make our code easier to understand.

Functions help us organize our program logically.

4. What is function definition?

Ans A statement that creates a new function, specifying its name, parameters, and the statements it executes is called function definition.

5. Write a short note on built-in function.

Ans Built-in functions are the functions that are built into Python and can be accessed by programmer any time without importing any module (file) such functions are input(), int(), float(), type(), help() etc.

6. How is built-in function accessed?

Ans Built-in function is accessed simply by writing the function name, followed by an optional list of arguments that represent information being passed to the function.

7. How will you import all functions in the math module?

Ans `from math import *`

8. What is difference between ceil() and floor() functions?

Ans The function **ceil()** returns the smallest whole number greater than or equal to x. The **floor()** function returns the largest whole number less than or equal to x.

9. What is Python module?

Ans A module is a file that contains a collection of related functions and other definitions. We can make a module available to another program by importing it.

10. How will you import specific names only within a module?

Ans We can import specific names only within a module, without importing the whole module, by using the `from <module> import <name>` statement.

11. Write short note on user defined function.

Ans Apart from the library functions that are in-built in Python, users can also define functions to do a task relevant to their programs. Such functions are called user-defined functions. These functions should be codified by the user, so that any call to the function can refer to it.

12. What is difference between pow() and **?

Ans Both pow() and the double star (**) operator perform exponentiation. ** is an operator and pow() is a built-in function.

13. What do you mean by Regular expressions?

Ans Regular expressions, called regexes for short, are descriptions for a pattern of text. For example, a \d in a regex stands for a digit character. They allow us to specify a pattern of text to search for.

14. What is a metacharacter?

Ans Each character in a Python Regex is either a metacharacter or a regular character. A metacharacters are characters with a special meaning, while a regular character matches itself.

15. How match() function is different from search() function?

Ans The match() function returns a match object if the text matches the pattern. Otherwise it returns None. The match() functions looks for a pattern at the beginning of a string. The search() function checks for a match anywhere in the string. If there is more than one match, only the first occurrence of the match will be returned.

16. What do you mean by greedy match and non greedy match?

Ans When a special character matches as much of the search sequence (string) as possible, it is said to be a greedy match. Non greedy matches the smallest number of repetitions.

17. Differentiate between max() and min() functions?

Ans Python built-in function max() returns the largest of its parameters. Python built-in function min() returns the smallest of its parameters.

18. Write a short note on random module.

Ans The random module contains function related to generating random numbers and producing random results. Random numbers have many applications in science and computer programming, especially when there are significant uncertainties in a phenomenon of interest.

19. Write a short note on randint().

Ans If we wanted a random integer, we can use the randint() function. Randint accepts two parameters: a lowest and a highest number, and returns an integer between lowest and highest (including both).

20. Observe the following Python functions and write the name(s) of the module(s) to which they belong:

a. uniform() b. findall()

Ans **a.** random **b.** re

21. Rewrite the following Python program after removing all the syntactical errors (if any), underlining each correction.:

```
def checkval:
    x = int(input("Enter a number"))
    if x % 2 = 0 :
        print(x,"is  even")
    else if x<0 :
        print(x,"should be positive")
    else ;
         print(x,"is odd" )
```

Ans

```
def checkval():
    x = int(input("Enter a number: "))
    if x % 2 == 0 :
        print(x," is  even")
    elif x<0 :
        print(x," should be positive")
    else :
         print(x," is odd" )
```

Figure 1 Program for Q21

22. Find the output of the following program

```
def calcresult():
  i = 9
  while(i>1):
    if (i%2 == 0):
       x = i%2
       i = i-1
    else:
       i = i-2
       x = i
    print(x**2)
calcresult()
```

Ans 49
25
9
1

23. Observe the following Python code and find out, the expected correct output(s). Also assign the maximum and minimum value that can be assigned to the variable "N".

```
import random
SIDES=["EAST","WEST","NORTH","SOUTH"];
N=random.randint(1,3)
OUT=""
for I in range(N,1,-1):
    OUT=OUT+SIDES[I]
    print(OUT)
```

a. SOUTHNORTH b. SOUTHNORTHWEST

c. SOUTH d. EASTWESTNORTH

Ans SOUTH
SOUTHNORTH

Maximum value of N = 3
Minimum value of N = 1

24. Name the function/method required to:
(a) check if a string contains only alphabets.
(b) give the total length of the list.

Ans **a.** isalpha() **b.** len()

25. Observe the following Python functions and write the name(s) of the module(s) to which they belong:
(a) uniform()
(b) findall()
(c) ceil()
(d) randint()

Ans **a.** random **b.** .re **c.** math **d.** random

26. Write definition of a Method AFIND(CITIES) to display all the city names from a list of cities starting with alphabet A. For example:
CITIES contains ["AHMEDABAD","CHENNAI","NEW DELHI","AMRITSAR","AGRA"]

Ans

```
def AFIND(CITIES):
    for i in CITIES:
        if i[0]=='A':
            print(i)
CITIES= ["AHMEDABAD","CHENNAI","NEW DELHI","AMRITSAR","AGRA"]
AFIND(CITIES)

>>>
AHMEDABAD
AMRITSAR
AGRA
>>>
```

Figure 2 Program for Q26

27. What are the possible outcome(s) executed from the following code? Also specify the maximum and minimum values that can be assigned to variable N.

```
import random
NAV  = ["LEFT","FRONT","RIGHT","BACK"];
NUM  = random.randint(1,3)
NAVG = ""
for C in range(NUM,1,-1):
    NAVG = NAVG+NAV[C]
print(NAVG)
```

a. BACKRIGHT b. BACKRIGHTFRONT

c. BACK d. LEFTFRONTRIGHT

Ans BACKRIGHT
Max value 3 and minimum value 1 for variable NUM.

28. Write definition of a Method MSEARCH(STATES) to display all the state names from a list of STATES, which are starting with alphabet M.
STATES=["MP","UP","WB","TN","MH","MZ","DL","BH","RJ","HR"]

Ans

```
def MSEARCH(STATES):
    for i in STATES:
        if i[0]=='M':
            print(i)
STATES=["MP","UP","WB","TN","MH","MZ","DL","BH","RJ","HR"]
MSEARCH(STATES)

>>>
MP
MH
MZ
>>>
```

Figure 3 Program for Q28

29. Write definition of a method/function TenTimesEven(VALUES) to add and display the sum of ten times of the even values present in the list of 'VALUES'. For example, If the Nums contain [5,2,3,6,3,4], the method/function should display Twice of even Sum: 120 (i.e. 2x10 + 6x10 + 4x10).

Ans

```
def TenTimesEven(VALUES):
    se=0
    for i in range(6): # range(0,6):
        if VALUES[i]%2==0:
            se=se+VALUES[i]*10
    print("Even Sum:",se)
Nums=[5,2,3,6,3,4]
TenTimesEven(Nums)

>>>
Even Sum: 120
>>>
```

Figure 4 Program for Q29

30. Write definition of a method/function TenTimesOdd(VALUES) to add and display the sum of ten times of the odd values present in the list of 'VALUES'. For example, If the Nums contain [5,2,3,6,3,4], the method/function should display Twice of odd Sum: 110 (i.e. 5x10 + 3x10 + 3x10).

Ans

```
def TenTimesOdd(VALUES):
    se=0
    for i in range(6): # range(0,6):
        if VALUES[i]%2 !=0:
            se=se+VALUES[i]*10
    print("Odd Sum:",se)
Nums=[5,2,3,6,3,4]
TenTimesOdd(Nums)

>>>
Odd Sum: 110
>>>
```

Figure 5 Program for Q30

31. Write definition of a method/function EndingA(Names) to search and display those strings from the list of Names, which are ending with 'A'.
Names=["JAYA","KAREEM","TARUNA","LOVISH"]

Ans

```
def Ending(Names):
    for N in Names:
        if N[len(N)-1]=='A':
            print(N)
Names=["JAYA","KAREEM","TARUNA","LOVISH"]
Ending(Names)

>>>
JAYA
TARUNA
>>>
```

Figure 6 Program for Q31

32. Write definition of a method/function AddOddEven(VALUES) to display sum of odd and even values separately from the list of VALUES. For example, If the VALUES contain :[15,26,37,10,22,13], the function should display Even Sum: 58 Odd Sum: 65.

Ans

```
def AddOddEven(VALUES):
    so=0
    se=0
    for i in VALUES:
        if i%2==0:
            se=se+i
        else:
            so=so+i
    print("Even Sum:",se)
    print("Odd Sum:",so)
VALUES=[15,26,37,10,22,13]
AddOddEven(VALUES)
>>>
Even Sum: 58
Odd Sum: 65
>>>
```

Figure 7 Program for Q32

33. Write short note on Anonymous Function.

Ans These functions are called anonymous because they are not declared in the standard manner by using the def keyword. We can use the lambda keyword to create small anonymous functions. Lambda forms can take any number of arguments but return just one value in the form of an expression.

34. Type the following Python Recursive Function and test the output for following:
>>> facto(5)
>>> facto(4)

Ans

```
>>> def facto(n):
  if n==1:
     return 1
  return n*facto(n-1)

>>> facto(5)
120
>>> facto(4)
24
>>>
```

Figure 8 Program for Q34

35. Write a Python program to add two numbers using function.

Ans

```
#Python program to add two numbers using function
def add(a,b):
    sum=a+b;
    return sum;
num1=int(input("Enter first number: "))
num2=int(input("Enter second number: "))
print("The sum is",add(num1,num2))

RUN
>>>
Enter first number: 20
Enter second number: 25
The sum is 45
>>>
```

Figure 9 Program for Q35

36. Write a Python program to find product of two numbers using function.

Ans

```
#Python program to find product of two numbers using function
def prod(a,b):
    multi=a*b;
    return multi;
num1=int(input("Enter first number: "))
num2=int(input("Enter second number: "))
print("The product is",prod(num1,num2))
```

(Contd...)

```
RUN
>>>
Enter first number: 20
Enter second number: 5
The product is 100
>>>
```

Figure 10 Program for Q36

37. Write a program to calculate area of the parallelogram, area of the square, area of the circle and the volume of the cone. Import pi constant from math module.

Ans

```
from math import pi
h = 5.0 # height
b = 2.0 # base
r = 1.5 # radius
area_parallelogram = h*b
print("The area of the parallelogram is ", area_parallelogram)
area_square = b**2
print( "The area of the square is   ", area_square)
area_circle = pi*r**2
print ("The area of the circle is   ", area_circle)
volume_cone = 1.0/3*pi*r**2*h
print( "The volume of the cone is ", volume_cone)

RUN
>>>
The area of the parallelogram is   10.0
The area of the square is   4.0
The area of the circle is   7.0685834705770345
The volume of the cone is  11.780972450961723
>>>
```

Figure 11 Program for Q37

38. Write a program, using if-else, to print roots are imaginary or not.

Ans

```
import math
a = int(input("Enter value of a: "))
b = int(input("Enter value of b: "))
c = int(input("Enter value of c: "))
d=b*b-4*a*c
if d < 0:
    print("ROOTS are imaginary" )
else:
    root1 = (-b + math.sqrt(d)) / (2.0 * a)
    root2 = (-b -math.sqrt(d)) / (2.0 * a)
    print("Root 1 = ", root1)
    print("Root 2 = ", root2)
```

(Contd...)

```
RUN
>>>
Enter value of a: 2
Enter value of b: 8
Enter value of c: 3
Root 1 =   -0.41886116991581024
Root 2 =   -3.58113883008419
>>>
```

Figure 12 Program for Q38

39. Write a Python function to calculate sum of all the numbers in a list.

Ans

```
# A Python function to calculate sum of all the numbers in a list
def sum(num):
    total = 0
    for x in num:
        total += x
    return total
print(sum((6, 4, 2, 0, 5)))

RUN
>>>
17
>>>
```

Figure 13 Program for Q39

40. Write a Python function to calculate product of all the numbers in a list.

Ans

```
# A Python function to find product of all the numbers in a list
def prod(num):
    total = 1
    for x in num:
        total *= x
    return total
print(prod((2, 4, 2, 5)))

RUN
>>>
80
>>>
```

Figure 14 Program for Q40

41. Write a Python function that accepts a string and calculate the number of upper case letters and lower case letters.

Ans

```
# A Python function that accepts a string and calculate the number of upper
case letters and lower case letters.

def str_test(str1):
    x={"UCASE":0, "LCASE":0}
    for i in str1:
        if i.isupper():
           x["UCASE"]+=1
        elif i.islower():
           x["LCASE"]+=1
        else:
           pass
    print ("Original String : ", str1)
    print ("No. Of UPPER CASE characters : ", x["UCASE"])
    print ("No. Of lower case Characters : ", x["LCASE"])
str_test("I am Learning Functions")

RUN
>>>
Original String :  I am Learning Functions
No. Of UPPER CASE characters :  3
No. Of lower case Characters :  17
>>>
```

Figure 15 Program for Q41

42. Write a Python function to check the number is prime or not.

Ans

```
# A Python function to check the number is prime or not.
def test(Number):
    count = 0
    for i in range(2, (Number//2 + 1)):
        if(Number % i == 0):
            count = count + 1
    return count
num = int(input(" Enter a number: "))
cnt = test(num)
if (cnt == 0 and num != 1):
    print(num, "is a Prime Number")
else:
    print(num,"is not a Prime Number")

RUN
>>>
Enter a number: 5
5 is a Prime Number
>>>
 Enter a number: 8
8 is not a Prime Number
>>>
```

Figure 16 Program for Q42

43. Write a Python function to check the number is even or odd.

Ans

```
# A Python function to check the number is even or odd
num=int(input("Enter a number to check odd or even: "))
def chk_evenodd(num):

    if(num%2==0):
        print(num," is an even number")
    else:
        print(num," is an odd number")
chk_evenodd(num);

RUN
>>>
Enter a number to check odd or even: 4
4  is an even number
>>>
Enter a number to check odd or even: 7
7  is an odd number
>>>
```

Figure 17 Program for Q43

44. Write a Program to find largest number using function.

Ans

```
# Program to find largest number
num1=int(input("Enter the first number: "));
num2=int(input("Enter the second number: "));
num3=int(input("Enter the Third number: "));
def find_largest():
    if(num1>num2):
        if(num1>num3):
            largest=num1
        else:
            largest=num3
    else:
        if num2>num3:
            largest=num2

        else:
            largest=num3

        print("Largest number is: ",largest)

find_largest();

RUN
>>>
Enter the first number: 24
Enter the second number: 48
Enter the Third number: 12
Largest number is:  48
>>>
```

Figure 18 Program for Q44

45. Write a Program to find smallest number using function.

Ans

```
# Program to find smallest number
num1=int(input("Enter the first number: "));
num2=int(input("Enter the second number: "));
num3=int(input("Enter the Third number: "));
def find_smallest():
    if(num1<num2):
        if(num1<num3):
            smallest=num1
        else:
            smallest=num3
    else:
        if num2<num3:
            smallest=num2

        else:
            smalest=num3

        print("Smalest number is: ",smallest)

find_smallest();

RUN
>>>
Enter the first number: 27
Enter the second number: -27
Enter the Third number: 0
Smalest number is:  -27
>>>
```

Figure 19 Program for Q45

46. Write a Python program to find factorial using function.

Ans

```
#Python program to find factorial using function
#def factorial(num):
    fact=1;
    i=1
    while (i<=num):
        fact=fact*i
        i=i+1
    return fact
num=int(input("Enter a number: "));
result=factorial(num)
print("Factorial of the number is",result)
factorial(num)

RUN
>>>
Enter a number: 5
Factorial of the number is 120
>>>
```

Figure 20 Program for Q46

EXERCISE

1. What is a function? What are its types?
2. What is a module? What is the file extension of a Python module?
3. How are modules useful in a programming language?
4. Define module and package.
5. What is an argument? Give an example.
6. Explain any two built-in functions with the help of suitable example.
7. Write a short note on fabs() function of math module.
8. The sqrt() function returns the non-negative square root of x. What happens when x is negative?
9. Differentiate between degrees() and radians().
10. Explain any three Python built-in functions with example.
11. What are actual arguments?
12. What is a default argument?
13. Write the syntax for a function with non-keyword variable arguments.
14. Write the advantages of Recursion.
15. Name the prime types of functions.
16. Write the significance of module in Python programming.
17. Which keyword is used to begin the function blocks?
18. Write the syntax for defining the function.
19. Why it is needed to pass one argument, if an user defined function printline() is called?
20. Write the syntax for a function with non-keyword variable arguments.
21. What are docstrings? How are they useful?
22. What is the significance of return statement?
23. Differentiate between Global and Local variables.

LAB EXERCISE

1. What would be the output of the following programs?

(a)
```
#Python program to add two numbers
using function
def add(a,b):
    sum=a+b;
    return sum;
num1=20
num2=25
print("The sum is",add(num1,num2))
```

(b)
```
#Python program to find product of
two numbers using function
def prod(a,b):
    mul=a*b;
    return mul;
num1=20
num2=25
print("The sum is",prod(num1,num2))
```

(c)
```
def Hello():
    print('Hello Python')
Hello()
Hello()
```

(d)
```
def chk(x, y):
    if x > y:
        print(x, 'is maximum')
    elif x == y:
        print(x, 'is equal to', y)
    else:
        print(y, 'is maximum')
chk(7,9)
chk(7,7)
```

(e)
```
x = 10
def func(x):
    print('x is', x)
    x = 5
    print('Changed local x to', x)
func(x)
print('x is now', x)
```

(f)
```
def chk(x, y):
    if x < y:
        print(x, 'is mininmum')
    elif x == y:
        print(x, 'is equal to', y)
    else:
        print(y, 'is minimum')
chk(77,99)
```

(g)
```
x = 10
def func():
    global x
    print('x is', x)
    x = 5
    print('Changed global x to', x)
func()
print('Value of x is', x)
```

(h)
```
def HowMany(ID,Val):
    c=0
    for i in ID:
        if i==Val:
            c=c+1
    print(Val,"found",c,"Times")
ID=[115,122,137,110,122,113]
Val=122
HowMany(ID,Val)
```

(i)
```
def Count3and7(N):
    c=0
    for i in range(1,N+1):
        if i%3==0 or i%7==0:
            c=c+1
    print("Numbers which are between
1 and", N,"is", c)
N=15
Count3and7(N)
```

(j)
```
Data = ["P",20,"R",10,"S",30]
Times = 0
Alpha = ""
Add = 0
for C in range(1,6,2):
    Times= Times + C
    Alpha= Alpha + Data[C-1]+"$"
    Add  = Add + Data[C]
    print(Times,Add,Alpha)
```

(k)
```
import random
POINTS=[20,40,10,30,15];
POINTS=[30,50,20,40,45];
BEGIN=random.randint(1,3)
LAST=random.randint(2,4)
for C in range(BEGIN,LAST+1):
    print(POINTS[C],"#", )
```

(l)
```
def Convert(X=45,Y=30):
    X=X+Y
    Y=X-Y
    print(X,"&",Y)
    return X
A=250
B=150
A=Convert(A,B)
print(A,"&",B)
B=Convert(B)
print(A,"&",B)
A=Convert(A)
print(A,"&",B)
```

2. Write a Python function to calculate volume of the sphere.
3. Using random module, simulate tossing a coin N times. You can use zero for head and 1 for tail.
4. Enter two values and find quotient and remainder using divmod() function.
5. Write a Python function which converts uppercase letters to lowercase.
6. Write a Python function to calculate area of the circle.
7. Write a Python that takes a number and calculate and display the log, square, sin and cosine of it.
8. Write a Python function that takes a number and displays it log, sine and cosine. When the routine terminates, execution automatically returns to the point from where it was called.
9. Write the output for the following:
   (a) print(pow(2, 2))
   (b) print(pow(-2, 2))
   (c) print(pow(2, -2))
   (d) print(pow(-2, -2))

CHAPTER 11

File Processing

11.1 CONCEPT OF FILES

File is a named location on the system storage which records data for later access. It is used to store data permanently for future use to perform various file operations like opening, reading, writing etc. Usually a file is kept on a permanent storage media, e.g. a hard drive disk. A unique name and path is used by users to access a file for reading, writing and modification purposes. The most basic tasks involved in file manipulation are reading data from files and writing or appending data to files.

Python supports file handling and allows users to read, write and append files, along with many other file handling options that operates on files. In Python, file processing takes place in the following order:

(a) Open a file that returns a file handle.

(b) Use the handle to perform read or write action.

(c) Close the file handle.

Before you do a read or write operation to a file in Python, you need to open it first. And as the read/write transaction completes, you should close it to free the resources tied with the file.

☞ *File is a named location on disk to store related information.*

A file is a contiguous set of bytes used to store data. This data is organised in a specific format and can be simple as a text file or as complicated as a program executable.

11.1.1 Types of File

There are two types of files in Python. They are:

(a) Text file

(b) Binary file

A text file is simply a file which stores sequences of characters using an encoding like utf-8, latin1 etc., whereas in the case of binary file, data is stored in the same format as in Computer memory. Examples of text files are Python source code, HTML file, etc. Whereas executable files, images, audio etc. are examples of binary files. Inside the disk both types of files are stored as a sequence of 0s and 1s. So at the lowest level, text file will be collection of bytes. The only difference is that when a text file is opened the data is decoded back using the same encoding scheme they were encoded in. However, in the case of binary files no such thing happens.

A text file is the most common file. Each line of text file is terminated by a special character, known as End of Line (EOL). In Python, the new line character (\n) is default EOL terminator.

Binary files store data in 0s and 1s i.e., machine readable format. One character stores one byte in the memory i.e., 8-bits.

Since binary files store data after converting it into binary language (0s and 1s), there is no EOL character. This file type returns bytes. This is the file to be used when dealing with non-text files such as images files, Document files, Video files, Audio files, Executable files etc.

All binary files follow a specific format. You can open some binary files in the normal text editor but you cannot read the content present inside the file, because all the binary files are encoded in the binary format, which can be understood by us. Binary format is understood by a computer or machine only. For opening such binary files you need a specific type of software. For example, you need Microsoft word software to open .doc binary files, pdf reader software to open .pdf binary files and a photo editor software to read the image files and so on.

11.2 FILE OPENING IN VARIOUS MODES

The access mode determines the mode in which the file has to be opened, i.e., read, write, append, etc. You specify the access mode of a file through the mode argument. You use 'r', to read the file, and use 'w' or 'a', to write or append, respectively. The mode argument if not passed, then Python will assume it to be 'r' by default.

Mode is an optional string that specifies the mode in which the file is opened. The mode you choose will depend on what you wish to do with the file. The Table 11.1 shows the details about the access mode to open a file.

Table 11.1 Access Mode

Access mode	Description
r	It opens the file for reading only. Starts reading from beginning of file. This is the default mode.
rb	It opens the file for reading only in binary format. The file pointer exists at the beginning of the file.
r+	It opens the file for reading and writing both. The file pointer exists at the beginning of the file. If you want to open an existing file for read and write, you should better use "r+", because this will not delete the content of the file.
rb+	It opens the file for reading and writing both in binary format. The file pointer exists at the beginning of the file.
x	It creates a new file with the specified name. It causes an error when a file exists with the same name.
w	It opens the file to write only. It will overwrite the file if any file exists. The file pointer is at the beginning of the file.
wb	It opens the file to write only in binary format. It overwrites the file if it exists previously or creates a new one if no file exists with the same name. The file pointer exists at the beginning of the file.
w+	It opens the file to write and read both. It is different from r+ as it overwrites the previous file if one exists whereas r+ doesn't overwrite the previously written file. It creates a new file if no file exists. The file pointer exists at the beginning of the file.
wb+	It opens the file to write and read both in binary format. The file pointer exists at the beginning of the file. If the file does not exist, creates a new file for reading and writing.
a	It will append the existing file. The file pointer is at the end of the file. It creates a new file if no file exists.
ab	It opens the file in the append mode in binary format. The file pointer is at the end of the file if the file exists. If the file does not exist, it creates a new file for writing.
a+	It opens a file to append and read both. The file pointer remains at the end of the file if a file exists. If the file does not exist, it creates a new file for reading and writing.
ab+	It opens a file to append and read both in binary format. The file pointer remains at the end of the file if the file exists. If the file does not exist, it creates a new file for reading and writing.

11.3 OPENING AND READING A FILE

So far you have seen the various Python programs, which took the input from the keyboard and delivered the output on the screen. The programs which run for a short period of time, give some output and after that data disappears. And when you run the programs again, you have to provide new inputs. This is because the data is entered in primary memory which is temporary in nature. Those programs which are persistent i.e., they are always in running then their data is to be stored in permanent storage device (say, harddisk) . If the program is closed or restarted then the same data can be retrieved. In this chapter, you will learn to take input from files and write result to the files. The data stored within a file is known as persistent data because this data is permanently stored in the system.

To open a file in Python, you first need some way to associate the file on disk with a variable in Python. This process is called opening a file. You begin by telling Python where the file is. The location of your file is often referred to as the file path. When you access a file on an operating system, a file path is required. If the path is in current working directory, you can just provide the filename. If the file resides in a directory other than that, you have to provide the full path with the file name. It is broken up into three major parts:

(a) **Folder Path**: It specifies the file folder location.
(b) **File Name**: It is the actual name of the file.
(c) **Extension**: It is extension with a period (.) to indicate the file type.

Python has an in-built function called open() to open a file. You can specify the mode while opening a file. In mode, you specify whether you want to read 'r', write 'w' or append 'a' to the file. You also specify if you want to open the file in text mode or binary mode. The default is reading in text mode. In this mode, you get strings when reading from the file. The syntax is:

```
file_object = open(file_name, mode);
```

Here, file_name is the name of the file or the location of the file that you want to open, and file_name should include the file extension.

Let's suppose you created a file named "abc.txt" present at the location "C:/Documents/python/" with following contents inside it:

```
This is first sentence of code.
This is second sentence of code.
This is third sentence of code.
```

Following Python program shown in Figure 11.1 asks the user to enter the filename, read and display the content, and finally, it closes the file.

Example 1 –**Program to read and display content.**

```
# Program to read and display content
print("Enter 'x' for exit.");
filename = input("Enter filename with extension to read: ");
if filename == 'x':
    exit();
else:
    r = open(filename, "r");
    print("\nThe file,",filename,"opened successfully!");
    print("The file",filename,"contains:\n");
    print(r.read())
    r.close()

RUN
>>>
Enter 'x' for exit.
Enter filename with extension to read: c:\documents\python\abc.txt
The file, c:\documents\python\abc.txt opened successfully!
The file c:\documents\python\abc.txt contains:
This is first sentence of code.
This is second sentence of code.
This is third sentence of code.
>>>
```

Figure 11.1 Program to read and display content

11.4 CLOSING A FILE

Once all the operations are done on the file, you must close it using the close() method. Any unwritten information gets destroyed once the close() method is called on a file object. The syntax of close() is:

```
file_object.close();
```

Python automatically closes a file when the reference object of a file is re-assigned to another file.

☞ *It is always the best practice to close a file when your work gets finished. While closing a file, the system frees up all resources allocated to it.*

11.5 WRITING ONTO A FILE

The write() method writes any string to an open file. The write() method does not add a newline character ('\n') to the end of the string. If you want the newline character you have to add it manually. Its syntax is:

`file_object.write(string);`

To write some content to a file in Python, you have to ask users to enter the name of file along with their extension like filename.txt. Then open that file if it exists, or create a file with that name and again ask from the user to enter some content into line of sentences to put those sentences into that file as the content of the file.

Following Python program asks the user to enter the file name to open/create a file and asks them to enter three sentences as the content to be added in the file.

Here is the Python program, used to create a new file and writes some content entered by the user. (See Figure 11.2).

Example 2 –Program to write to file.

```
#Program to write to file
print("Enter 'x' for exit.");
filename = input("Enter filename to create & write content: ");
if filename == 'x':
    exit();
else:
    w = open(filename, "w");
    print("The file,",filename,"created successfully!");
    print("Enter 3 sentences to write on the file: ");
    s1 = input();
    s2 = input();
    s3 = input();
    w.write(s1);
    w.write("\n");
    w.write(s2);
    w.write("\n");
    w.write(s3);
    w.close();
    print("Content written successfully ");

RUN
>>>
Enter 'x' for exit.
Enter filename to create & write content: c:\documents\python\xyz.txt
The file, c:\documents\python\xyz.txt created successfully!
Enter 3 sentences to write on the file:
I am writing my first sentence.
This is my second sentence.
And, finally my last sentence.
Content written successfully
>>>
```

Figure 11.2 Program to write to file

11.6 FILE FUNCTIONS

Different file functions are discussed in the following sections.

11.6.1 open()

In Python, a physical file must be mapped to a built-in file object with the help of built-in function open().

```
file_object = open(filename[, access_mode] [, buffersize])
```

Python has in-built functions to create and manipulate files. The io module is the default module for accessing files and you do not need to import it. The module consists of open(filename, access_mode, buffersize) that returns a file object, which is called "handle". You can use this handle to read from or write to a file. Python treats the file as an object, which has its own attributes and methods.

In the open() method, the first parameter is the name of a file including its path. The file path is a string that represents the location of a file. The access mode parameter is an optional parameter which decides the purpose of opening a file, i.e., read, write, append, etc. The optional buffersize argument specifies the file's desired buffer size: 0 means unbuffered, 1 means line buffered.

If the path is in current working directory, you can just provide the filename, as shown below:

```
file_object = open("textfile.txt")
```

If the file resides in some other directory, you have to provide the full path with the file name. Make sure file name and path given is correct, otherwise you will get a FileNotFoundError.

11.6.2 close()

It closes the opened file. The file once closed, cannot be read or written to. For example,

```
my_file = open("C:/Documents/python/abc.txt", 'r')
  print(my_file.read())
  my_file.close()
my_file = open("C:/Documents/Python/xyz.txt", 'w')
  my_file.write("Hello")
  my_file.close()
```

11.6.3 read()

To read a file Python provides the read() method. The read() method reads a string from the file. It can read the data in the text as well as binary format. When you read the file with read(), you read strings from file. When you read numbers, you need to convert them to integers with data type conversion functions like int().

☞ *read() reads at a specified number of bytes from the file.*

Example 3 –Demo of read() function.

```
# Demo of read() function
my_file = open("c:/Documents/Python/abc.txt","r")
print(my_file.read())

RUN
>>>
This is first sentence of code.
This is second sentence of code.
This is third sentence of code.
>>>
```

Figure 11.3 Demo of read() function

Let's Try

```
# Reading the entire file at once
my_file = "c:/Documents/Python/abc.txt"
file_handle = open(my_file, 'r')
file_data = file_handle.read()
print(file_data)
```

In order to read character from the file, you can pass the argument to the read() function, for example, read(22) would read the first twenty two characters of the file. Let's understand the sample code given in figure 11.4.

Example 4 –Program to read first 22 characters from file.

```
#Program to read first 22 characters from file
my_file = open("c:/Documents/Python/abc.txt","r")
print(my_file.read(22))

RUN
>>>
This is first sentence
>>>
```

Figure 11.4 Program to read few characters

Let's Try

```
#Program to read first few characters from file
my_file = open("c:/Documents/Python/abc.txt","r")
print(my_file.read(4))
```

11.6.4 readline()

Python enable us to read the file line by line by using a function readline(). It reads one line from the file and places the file pointer to the beginning of the new line. If you use the readline() method twice, then you get the first two lines of the file.

Example 5 –Demo of readline() function.

```
# Demo of readline() function
my_file = open("c:/Documents/Python/abc.txt","r")
print(my_file.readline())
print(my_file.readline())
print(my_file.readline())

RUN
>>>
This is first sentence of code.
This is second sentence of code.
This is third sentence of code.
>>>
```

Figure 11.5 Demo of readline() function

11.6.5 readlines()

Another way you could iterate over each line in the file is to use the Python readlines() method of the file object. The readlines() reads all lines until the end of file and returns a list object. readlines() reads until EOF and returns a list containing the lines. (See Figure 11.6).

Example 6 –**Demo of readlines() function.**

```
# Demo of readlines() function
my_file = open("c:/Documents/Python/abc.txt","r")
print(my_file.readlines())

RUN
>>>
['This is first sentence of code.\n', 'This is second sentence of code.\n', 'This
is third sentence of code.\n']
>>>
```

Figure 11.6 Demo of readlines() function

readlines() function reads all the lines of text file including the newline characters. In Figure 11.7, you are trying to read only the 3rd line from the "abc.txt" file using a "for loop".

☞ *Python provides a string method called strip() which removes whitespace, or non-printable characters, from both ends of a string.*

Example 7 –**Program to read a specific line from a File.**

```
# Program to read a specific line from a File
line_number = 3
my_file = open("c:/Documents/Python/abc.txt","r")
current_line = 1
for line in my_file:
        if(current_line == line_number):
                print(line)
                break
        current_line = current_line +1

RUN
>>>
This is third sentence of code.
>>>
```

Figure 11.7 Program to read a specific line

Let's try

```
# First open the file to read(r)
inp = open("c:/documents/python/abc.txt","r")
# read the file into a list then print  each item
for line in inp.readlines():
   print (line)
# Now close it
inp.close()
```

11.6.6 write()

The write() function writes a fixed sequence of characters to a file. The write() does not actually write data to a file but to a buffer. When the close() function is called, it is written in file.

☞ *In order to write data into a file, you must open the file in write mode.*

You need to be very careful while writing data into the file as it overwrites the content present inside the file that you are writing, and all the previous data is erased.
Before writing data to a sample.txt file, file appears as shown in Figure 11.8.

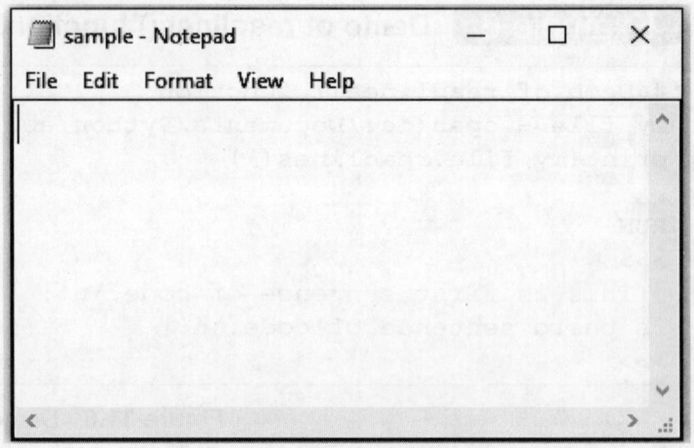

Figure 11.8 Blank sample.txt file

Now write one sentence using write() function as given in Example 8.

Example 8 –**Demo of write() function.**

```
# Demo of write() function
my_file = open("c:/Documents/python/sample.txt","w")
my_file.write("I am writing my first sentence")
my_file.close()
```

Figure 11.9 Demo of write() function

The above code writes the string "I am writing my first sentence" into the "sample.txt" file. Now sample.txt file will be displayed as shown in Figure 11.10.
Note that the first line in Figure 11.11 is "I am writing my first sentence\n" ending with \n character, the cursor will move to the next line of the file and then write "I am writing my second sentence".
Remember if you do not mention \n character, then the data will be written continuously without any space in the text file.

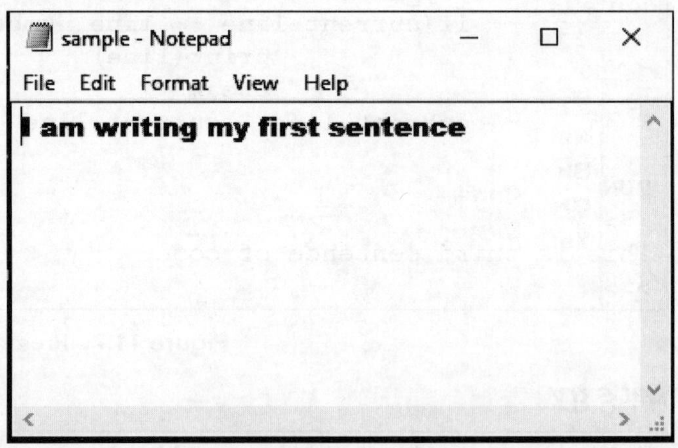

Figure 11.10 A sample.txt file with one line of text

Example 9 –**Demo of write() function.**

```
# Demo of write() function in the file sample.txt
my_file = open("c:/Documents/python/sample.txt","w")
my_file.write("I am writing my first sentence\n")
my_file.write("I am writing my second sentence")
```

Figure 11.11 Demo of write() function

The output of Figure 11.11 is shown in Figure 11.12.

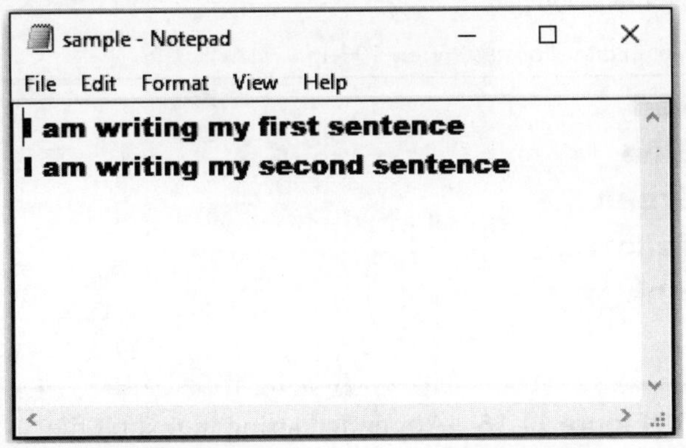

Figure 11.12 Output of sample.txt file

11.6.7 writelines()

The writelines writes a sequence of the strings to a file. It's syntax is:

`file_object.writelines(seq)`

So, whenever you have to write a sequence of string, you will use writelines(), instead of write(). (See Figure 11.13).

Example 10 –Demo of writelines() function.

```
# Demo of writelines() function to write list of data
colours = ["Red\n", "Blue\n", "Green\n", "Yellow"]
my_file = open("C:/Documents/python/test.txt", "w")
my_file.writelines(colours)
my_file.close()
```

Figure 11.13 Program to write sequence of strings in a file

The output of program shown 11.13 is shown in Figure 11.14.

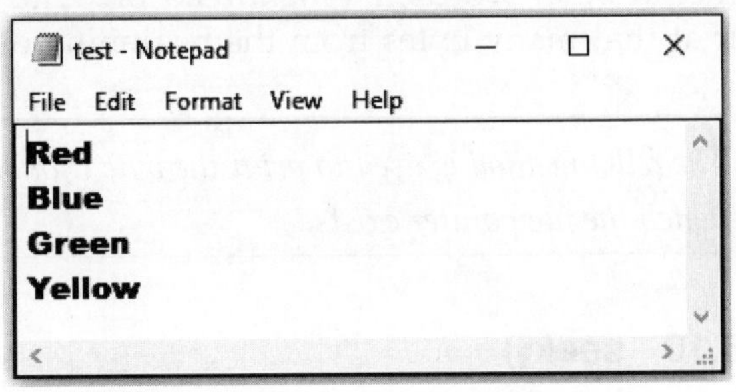

Figure 11.14 Output of text.txt file

11.6.8 append()

Appending is writing data at the end of the file. In this mode, file pointer is placed at the end in an existing file. It can also be used for creating a file, by opening a non existing file using this mode. In order to write into a file in Python, you need to open it in write 'w', append 'a' or exclusive creation 'x' mode. You need to be careful with the 'w' mode as it will overwrite into the file if it already exists. All previous data are erased. Writing a string or sequence of bytes (for binary files) is done using write() method. This method returns the number of characters written to the file.

Let's see how the append mode works:

To append data into a file you must open the file in "a+" mode so that you have access to both append as well as write modes.

Example 11 –Demo of append() function.

```
# Demo of appending string
my_file = open("C:/Documents/python/test.txt", "a+")
my_file.write("\nPink")
my_file.close()
```

Figure 11.15 Appending in the file text.txt

The output of program shown in Figure 11.15 is shown in Figure 11.16. Note that code in Figure 11.15 appends a string "pink" into a "test.txt" file.

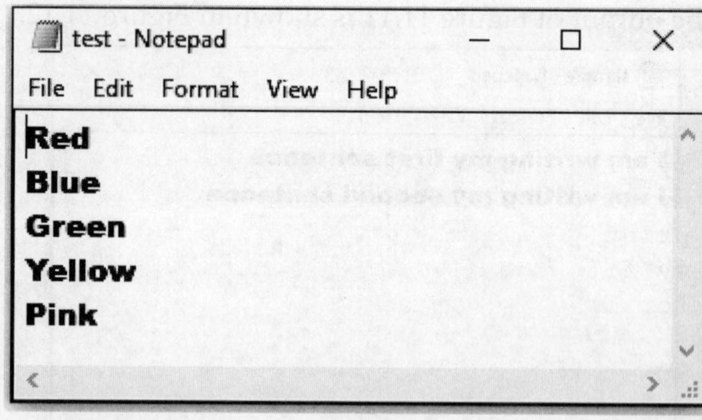

Figure 11.16 Appended string in text.txt file

Example 12 – **Demo of appending list of data.**

```
# Appending list of data in the file test.txt
colours = ["\nWhite", "\nBlack", "\nIndigo", "\nPurple"]
my_file = open("C:/Documents/python/test.txt", "a+")
my_file.writelines(colours)
my_file.close()
```

Figure 11.17 Appending list of data in the file

The output of program shown in Figure 11.17 is shown in Figure 11.18.

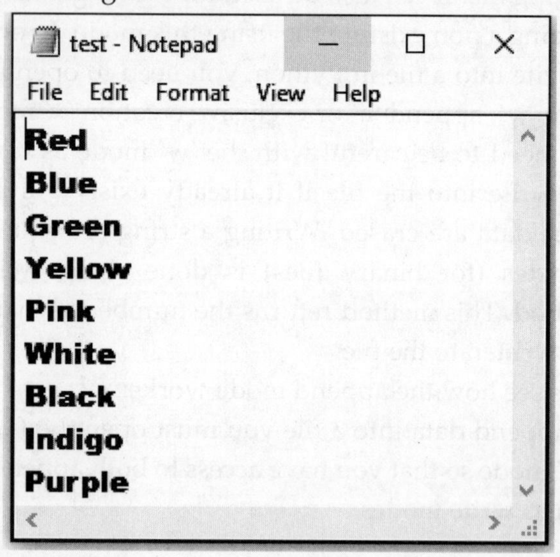

Figure 11.18 Appended list of data in text.txt file

11.6.9 tell()

The tell() method tells the current position within the file; in other words, the next read or write will occur at that many bytes from the beginning of the file.

☞ *The tell() method is used to print the byte number at which the file pointer exists.*

11.6.10 seek()

The seek() method enables you to modify the file pointer position externally.

The syntax to use the seek() method is:

`<file-ptr>.seek(offset[, from_what)`

offset refers to the new position of the file pointer. *from_what* shows the reference position from where the bytes are to be moved. The reference point 0 indicates the beginning of the file and is default, 1 (the current position of file) and 2 (the end of the file).

☞ *seek() sets the file's current position.*

Example 13 –**Demo of tell() and seek() methods.**

```
# Demo of tell() and seek() methods
text=["\nDifferent","Colours","Name"]
my_file = open("C:/Documents/python/test.txt", mode="a+")
my_file.writelines(text)
print("Position of  the file cursor :",my_file.tell())
my_file.seek(0)
for line in my_file:
        print(line)
RUN
>>>
Position of  the file cursor : 88
Red
Blue
Green
Yellow
Pink
White
Black
Indigo
Purple

DifferentColoursName
>>>
```

Figure 11.19 Demo of tell() and seek() methods

11.6.11 rename()

Python provides us with an "os" (Operating System) module which has some in-built methods that would help us in performing the file operations such as renaming and deleting the file.
In order to use this module, first of all, you need to import the "os" module in your program and then call the related methods.

This rename() method accepts two arguments i.e. the current file name and the new file name. Its syntax is:

`os.rename(current_file_name, new_file_name)`

You can specify the location as well as shown in example 14.

Example 14 –**Demo of rename() function.**

```
# Demo of rename()
import os
os.rename("C:/Documents/python/test.txt", "C:/Documents/python/test1.txt")
```

Figure 11.20 Demo of rename()

11.6.12 remove()

The remove() method is used to delete the file by supplying the file name or the file location that you want to delete. Its syntax is:

`os.remove(file_name)`

For example:

```
import os
os.remove("test.txt")
```

Here "test.txt" is the file that you want to remove. Similarly, you can pass the file location as well to the arguments as shown in the example:

```
import os
os.remove("C:/Documents/Python/
test.txt")
```

11.7 WORKING WITH BINARY FILES

You know that text files are composed of octets, or bytes, of binary data whereby each byte represents a character and the end of the file is marked by a special byte pattern, known generically as end of file, or eof. A binary file contains arbitrary binary data and thus no specific value can be used to identify end of file, thus a different mode of operation is required to read these files. Python adds 'b' to the mode parameter, like this:

```
bin_file = file("BinaryFile.bin","rb")
```

You can use any of the other modes too, simply adding 'b', i.e.,"wb" to write, "ab" to append. rb+ will open a binary file, for both reading and writing purpose. The file pointer is placed at the beginning of the file when it is opened using rb+ mode. wb+ will open in binary format, for both writing and reading. File pointer will be placed at the beginning for writing into it, so an existing file will be overwritten. A new file can also be created using this mode. The ab+ opens a binary file, for both appending and reading. File pointer is placed at the end of the file, in an already existing file. Using this mode a non existing file may be created.

If you want to write structure such as list, dictionary etc. and also want to read it then you have to use a module in Python known as pickle . Pickling means converting structure into byte stream before writing the data into file. When you want to work on binary file, conversion of data at the time of reading, as well as writing is required. Pickle module can be used to store any kind of object in file as it allows you to store Python objects with their structure. So for storing data in binary format, you will use pickle module. First you need to import the module. It provides two main methods for the purpose, dump and load. For creation of binary file you will use pickle.dump() to write the object in file, which is opened in binary access mode. Once data is stored using dump(), it can then be used for reading. When you read a file then a opposite operation is to be done known as unpickling. For reading data from file you will use pickle.load() to read the object from pickle file.

☞ *Importing pickle module, required to work on binary file.*

Example 15 –**Demo of writing binary file.**

```
# Program to write list sequence in binary file
def bin_oper():
    import pickle
    list=[27,46,72,98,23]
    f=open("c:/documents/python/listdata.dat",'wb')
    pickle.dump(list,f)
    print("Data added to Binary file successfully.")
    f.close()
bin_oper()

RUN
>>>
Data added to Binary file successfully.
>>>
```

Figure 11.21 Program to write list sequence in binary file

When you try to open listdata.dat in notepad, it will opened as shown in Figure 11.22.

To read Binary file use load ( ) function as shown in Figure 11.22.

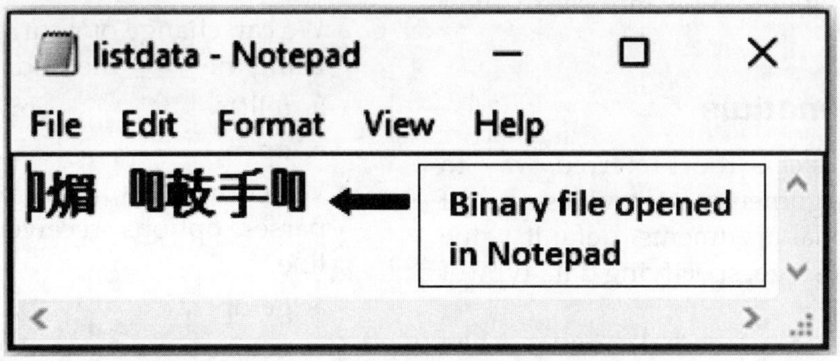

Figure 11.22 Binary file opened in notepad

Example 16 – **Demo to read binary file.**

```
# Program to read binary file using load() function
def bin_oper():
    import pickle
    f=open("c:/documents/python/listdata.dat",'rb')
    dict=pickle.load(f)
    f.close()
    print(dict)
bin_oper()

RUN
>>>
[27, 46, 72, 98, 23]
>>>
```

Figure 11.23 Program to read binary file using load() function

☞ *Pickle module has two methods - dump( ) to write and load( ) to read.*

11.8 COMMAND LINE ARGUMENTS

Python Command line arguments are input parameters passed to the script when executing them. In other words, it is an argument sent to a program being called. A program can take any number of command line arguments. Python supports the creation of programs that can be run on the command line, completely with command-line arguments. Almost every modern programming language has the ability to take in arguments from the command line. It is very important feature because it allows for dynamic inputs from users, whether they wrote the program or not.

Python comes with several different libraries that allow your Python code to take user input from the command line. The three most common ones are sys.argv, getopt, and argparse.

11.8.1 sys.argv

Python sys module stores the command line arguments in the form of a list, you can access it using sys.argv. The first element in the list is the name of the file. The arguments always come in the form of a string. This is very useful and simple way to read command line arguments as String. The program will accept an arbitrary number of arguments passed from the command-line (or terminal) while getting executed. The program will print all the arguments that were passed and the total number of arguments.

11.8.2 getopt module

Python getopt module is useful in parsing command line arguments where you want user to enter some options too.

11.8.3 argparse module

Python argparse module is the preferred way to parse command line arguments. It provides a lot of option such as positional arguments, default value for arguments, help message, specifying data type of argument etc.
Python argparse is the recommended command-line argument parsing module in Python. It is very common to the getopt module but that is a little complicated and usually need more code for the same task.

REVIEW QUESTIONS WITH ANSWERS

1. Multiple Choice Questions

1. What is the value stored in sys.argv[0]?
   (a) null
   (b) You cannot access it
   (c) The program's name
   (d) The first argument
2. The ______ method returns our current position (in number of bytes).
   a. tell() b. seek()
   c. close() d. None of the above
3. The most basic task(s) involved in file manipulation are:
   (a) Reading data from file
   (b) Writing data into file
   (c) Appending data to file
   (d) All of these
4. f.seek(0) is used to:
   (a) Bring file cursor to initial position
   (b) Get the current file position
   (c) Read the entire file
   (d) None of these
5. If <from> argument is 0, then:
   (a) The end of the file would serve as the reference position
   (b) The shift will start from the root level
   (c) The reference position will become the current position
   (d) None of these
6. We can change our current file cursor (position) using the _____method.
   a. tell() b. seek()
   c. open() d. close()
7. Which module in the python standard library parses options received from the command line?
   a. getopt b. os
   c. getarg d. main
8. What is the type of sys.argv?
   a. set b. list
   c. tuple d. string
9. Access mode(s) supported by Python
   a. read b. write
   c. append d. All of the above
10. The unpickling denotes
    (a) The byte stream is converted back into an object hierarchy.
    (b) The process which converts a Python object hierarchy into a byte stream.
    (c) Both (a) and (b)
    (d) None of these

2. State True or False for the following:

1. Read-Write mode is also called updating mode.
2. The pickle.load() recognizes automatically, which format had been used for writing the data.
3. Use the read() function to read the entire contents of a file.
4. The binary mode returns bytes.
5. 'a' mode data will be appended in the beginning of the file pointer.
6. 'rb' opens a file for the read-only mode in the binary format.
7. 'ab+' opens a file for appending and read-only mode in the binary format.
8. seek(offset) takes only two types of arguments namely 1 and 2.
9. seek(offset) 2 reference will be pointed at the end of the file.

10. When you open a file in the binary mode it does not accept the encoding parameter.

3. Match the following:

1.	tell()	a.	Refer documentation
2.	<offset>	b.	Returns the current file location
3.	<from>	c.	Represents the size of the displacement
4.	The program's name	d.	Indicates the start point
5.	sys.argv	e.	Default mode
6.	Read-only mode	f.	It is a list of elements
7.	Pickling	g.	Access to both the append as well as write modes
8.	'a+' mode	h.	dump() function
9.	rename() method	i.	Both reading and writing
10.	'r+' mode	j.	Accepts two arguments

4. Fill in the blanks:

1. _______ is the argument list to be parsed.
2. _________ parses options received from the command line.
3. ________ method returns an integer giving the current position of object in the file.
4. Each line of a file is terminated with a special character, called the _______.
5. The ______ function in Python to open a file in read or write mode.
6. The ______ method reads a string from an open file.
7. Closing a file will free up the resources that were tied with the file and is done using Python _______ method.
8. ______ method to read individual lines of a file.
9. _______ denotes the process which converts a Python object hierarchy into a byte stream.
10. Use the _________ function to read the content of the file one by one.

Answers

1. 1. c 2. a 3. d 4. a 5. b 6. b 7. a 8. b 9. d 10. a

2. 1. T 2. T 3. T 4. T 5. F 6. T 7. T 8. F 9. T 10. T

3. 1. b 2. c 3. d 4. a 5. f 6. e 7. h 8. g 9. j 10. i

4. 1. args 2. getopt 3. tell() 4. EOL 5. open() 6. read() 7. close() 8. readline() 9. Pickling 10. readlines

Short Answer Questions

1. What is file pointer?

Ans When a file is opened using method, the operating system associates a pointer that points to a character in the file. The file pointer determines from where the read and write operation will take place. Initially, the file pointer points at the start of the file.

2. Discuss various modes to open a file.

Ans 'r' : This mode indicates that file will be open for reading only.

'w' : This mode indicates that file will be open for writing only. If file, does not exists, it will create a new one.

'a' : This mode indicates that the output of that program will be append to the previous output of that file.

'r+' : This mode indicates that file will be open for both reading and writing.

3. Write short note on binary mode of opening a file.

Ans Binary mode returns bytes and this is the mode to be used when dealing with non-text files like image or exe files.

4. Differentiate between read() and readline().

Ans read() function reads the entire file and returns a string.

readline() function reads lines from that file and returns as a string. It fetches the line n, if it is being called n^{th} time.

5. Write function of a+ mode.

Ans The a+ mode opens a file for both appending and reading. The file pointer is at the end of the file if the file exists. The file opens in the append mode. If the file does not exist, it creates a new file for reading and writing.

6. What are different ways to read from a file?

Ans To read a file Python provides different reading methods. There are three ways to read from a file.
read([n])
readline([n])
readlines()
where *n* is the number of bytes to be read.
The read() method just outputs the entire file if number of bytes are not given in the argument. The readline(n) outputs at most n bytes of a single line of a file. It does not read more than one line. The readlines() returns a list where each element is single line of that file.

7. What are command line arguments?

Ans Command line arguments are flags given to a program/script at runtime. They contain additional information for our program so that it can execute.

8. Why do we use command line arguments?

Ans Command line arguments give additional information to a program at runtime. This allows us to give our program different input without changing the code.

9. What is the use of getopt method?

Ans This method parses command line options and parameter list.

10. What are the different file processing modes supported by Python?

Ans Python provides different modes to open files. The read-only, write-only, read-write and append mode. 'r' is used to open a file in read-only mode, 'w' is used to open a file in write-only mode, 'rw' is used to open in reading and write mode, 'a' is used to open a file in append mode. If the mode is not specified, by default file opens in read-only mode.

11. What is pickling and unpickling in Python?

Ans Pickling is a process in which a pickle module accepts any Python object, converts it into a string representation and dumps it into a file by using dump() function.
Unpickling is a process of retrieving original Python object from the stored string representation for use.

12. What is the use of offset?

Ans The offset refers to the byte count which determines the position relative to which the offset will move the file pointer. In other words offset is used to calculate the position of fileobject in the file in bytes. Offset is added to from_what (reference point) to get the position.

13. Write a statement in Python to open a text file DATA.TXT so that new contents can be written in it.

Ans file= open("DATA.TXT","w") OR file= open("DATA.TXT","w+")

14. Differentiate between readlines() and readline() functions.

Ans Python's readlines() function reads all the lines in a file, while readline() only reads one line at a time, which may help save memory.

15. Name two functions which allow us to access a file in a non-sequential or random mode.

Ans seek() and tell()

16. Name the file which is stored in human readable form and can also be created using any text editor.

Ans Text files are stored in human readable form and also be created using any text editor.

17. What is the use of seek() and tell() methods?

Ans To access the contents of file randomly - seek and tell methods are used. tell() method returns an integer giving the current position of object in the file. The integer returned specifies the number of bytes from the beginning of the file till the current position of file object.

18. What is the use of close() method?

Ans The close() will be used to close the file object, once we have finished working on it. The method will free up all the system resources used by the file, this means that once file is closed, we will not be able to use the file object any more.

19. Write a program to write users data such as name and age in a file.

Ans

```
# Program to write user data into a file
ch=’y’
f=open("c:/documents/python/abc.txt","a")
while ch==’y’ or ch ==’Y’:
    name=input("Enter your name: ")
    age=int(input("Enter your age: "))
    f.write(name)
    f.write("\n")
    f.write(str(age))
    f.write("\n")
    print("Data saved successfully")
    ch=input("Do you want to enter more records Y/N :")
f.close()

RUN
Enter your name: Abhishek
Enter your age: 17
Data saved successfully
Do you want to enter more records Y/N :y
Enter your name: Rahul
Enter your age: 21
Data saved successfully
Do you want to enter more records Y/N :n
>>>
```

Figure 1 Program for Q19

20. Write a program to make duplicate of file abc.txt as abc.bak as shown in following Figure.

Name	Date modified	Type	Size
abc.bak	1/4/2020 9:31 AM	BAK File	1 KB
abc	1/2/2020 10:05 PM	Text Document	1 KB

Ans

```
# Create the equivalent of: COPY abc.txt and abc.bak
# First open the files to read(r) and write(w)
inp = open("c:/documents/python/abc.txt","r")
outp = open("c:/documents/python/abc.bak","w")
# read file, copying each line to new file
for line in inp:
    outp.write(line)
print ("1 file copied...")
# Now close the files
inp.close()
outp.close()

RUN
>>>
1 file copied...
>>>
```

Figure 2 Program for Q20

EXERCISE

1. What is a file?
2. Differentiate between Text and binary files?
3. Why the files are used?
4. What are command line arguments?
5. Consider the following code and Explain statement 1 and give output of 2:

```
f = open ("mytry", "w+")
f.write ("0123456789abcdef")
f.seek (-3,2)        //1
print(f.read(2))   //2
```

6. Differentiate between the following: f = open('diary.txt', 'a') and f = open('diary.txt', 'w')
7. Write a statement in Python to open a text file WRITEUP.TXT so that new content can be written in it.
8. Compare & contrast read(), readline() and readlines().
9. How is write() different from writelines().
10. How many file modes can be used with the open() function to open a file?

LAB EXERCISE

1. What would be the output of the following programs?

(a)

```
# First open the file to read(r)
inp = open("c:/documents/python/abc.txt","r")
# iterate over the file printing each item
for line in inp:
    print (line)
# Now close it
inp.close()
```

(b)

```
# First open the file to read(r)
inp = open("c:/documents/python/abc.txt","r")
# iterate over the file printing each item
for line in inp:
    print ((line).rstrip())
# Now close it
inp.close()
```

2. Write a method in Python to read the content from a text file story.txt line by line and display the same on screen.
3. Write a program to prompt for a file name, and then read through the file line-by-line.
4. Write a statement in Python to open a text file MARKER.TXT so that existing content can be read from it.
5. Write a statement in Python to open a text file Score.txt so that new contents can be written in it.
6. Write a method/function ISTOUPCOUNT() in Python to read contents from a text file WRITER.TXT, to count and display the occurrence of the word "IS" or "TO" or "UP".
   For example, if the content of the file is:
   IT IS UP TO US TO TAKE CARE OF OUR SURROUNDING.
   IT IS NOT POSSIBLE ONLY FOR THE GOVERNMENT TO TAKE RESPONSIBILITY.
   The method/function should display Count of IS TO and UP is 6.

CHAPTER 12

Scope and Module

12.1 INTRODUCTION

Variables are reserved memory locations to store values. When you assign a variable with = to an instance, you are binding or mapping the variable to that instance. Python keeps track of all these mappings with namespaces. Roughly speaking, namespaces are just containers for mapping names to objects, i.e., these are containers for mapping names of variables to objects. You can think of them as dictionaries, containing name:object mappings, where the dictionary keys represent the names and the dictionary values the object itself. Such a "name-to-object" mapping allows you to access an object by a name that you have assigned to it. For example, if we make a simple string assignment via a_string = "Hello", you created a reference to the "Hello" object, and hereafter you can access via its variable name a_string.

Also you have multiple independent namespaces in Python, and names can be reused for different namespaces with unique objects. Namespaces also have different levels of hierarchy called "scope".

The "scope" in Python defines the "hierarchy level" in which you search namespaces for certain "name-to-object" mappings. A scope represents the textual area of a Python program where a namespace is directly accessible.

12.2 SCOPE OF OBJECTS AND NAMES

The scope of a variable determines the portion of the program where you can access a particular identifier. There are two basic scopes of variables in Python:

(a) Local scope
(b) Global scope

Variables that are defined inside a function body have a local scope. In other words, it is local to that function and those defined outside have a global scope. This means that local variables can be accessed only inside the function in which they are declared, If you then try to access the variable x outside the function, it will give NameError.

☞ *A local scope refers to the local objects available in the current function.*

Example 1 –**Demo of local scope.**

```
def func1():
        x=9 # Local scope
        print(x)
func1()

RUN
>>>
 9
>>>
```

Figure 12.1 Demo of local scope

Global variables can be accessed throughout the program body by all functions. When you call a function, the variables declared inside it are brought into scope.

Let us discuss global scope of a variable in brief:

(a) The global names are variables assigned at the top level of the enclosing module file. It means that it is visible everywhere within the program.

(b) The global names must be declared only if they are assigned within a function.

(c) Global variables must be referenced within a function without being declared.

☞ *A global scope refers to the objects available through the code execution since their inception.*

Example 2 –**Demo of global scope.**

```
y=9 # Global scope
def func2():
      print(y)
func2()

RUN
>>>
 9
>>>
```

Figure 12.2 Demo of global scope

Example 3 –**Demo of local and global variables.**

```
total = 0; # This is global variable.
# Function definition
 def sum(arg1, arg2):
      # Add both the parameters and return them
      total = arg1 + arg2; # Here total is local variable
     print("Inside the function local total : ", total)
     return total
     # Now you can call
sum function sum(20, 40)
print("Outside the function global total : ", total)

RUN
>>>
Inside the function local total : 60
Outside the function global total : 0
>>>
```

Figure 12.3 Demo of local and global variables

Here, you just defined the variable name total twice. So, how does Python know which namespace it has to search if you want to print the value of the variable total? This is where Python's LEGB-rule comes into play. The order for name resolution (for names inside a function) is: local, enclosing function for nested def, global, and then the built-in namespaces (i.e., LEGB).

However, if you assign a new value to a name, a local name is created, which hides the global name. The global statement is necessary if you are changing the reference to an object (e.g. with an assignment).

In Example 4, to modify the contents of the array, the global statement is not needed because you are only modifying the object. Whereas in Example 5, you are modifying the reference to the variable, global is needed, otherwise, a local variable will be created inside the function.

☞ *If you want to print out the dictionary mapping of the global and local variables, you can use the functions global() and local().*

Example 4 –**Demo of local variable.**

```
>>> x = []
>>> def myfun():
        x.append('Hello')    # Don't need global, no change of reference for x
>>> myfun()
>>> x

RUN
>>>
['Hello']
>>>
```

Figure 12.4 Demo of local variable

Example 5 –**Demo of global variable.**

```
>>> x = 1
>>> def myfun():
        global x
        x = 5
>>> myfun()
>>> x

RUN
>>>
5
>>>
```

Figure 12.5 Demo of global variable

12.2.1 The global keyword

In Python global keyword is used to globally defined variable instead of locally defining it. This is useful when you want to change the value of a variable through a function. To use it, simply type global followed by the variable name, as shown in Figures 12.6 and 12.7.

Example 6 –**Demo of global keyword.**

```
x=10
def change(y):
    global x #global keyword
    x = y
change(11)
print (x)
```

(Contd...)

```
RUN
>>>
11
>>>
```

Figure 12.6 Demo of global keyword

Example 7 –Demo of global keyword.

```
x = "i"
def outside():
    x = "j"
    def inside():
        global x
        x = "k"
        print("inside:", x)
    inside()
    print("outside:", x)
outside()
print("global:", x)

RUN
>>>
inside: k
outside: j
global: k
>>>
```

Figure 12.7 Demo of global keyword

In Finger 12.7, using global keyword, the x in inside() will refer to the global variable. That one will be changed, but not the one in outside(), because you are only referring to the global x.

12.2.2 The nonlocal keyword

The nonlocal keyword is useful in nested functions. It causes the variable to refer to the previously bound variable in the closest enclosing scope. In other words, it will prevent the variable from trying to bind locally first, and force it to go a level 'higher up'. (See Figure 12.8).

Example 8 –Demo of nonlocal keyword.

```
def outside():
    x=10
    def inside():
        nonlocal x
        x = 11
        print (x)
    inside()
    print (x)
outside()
```

(Contd...)

```
RUN
>>>
11
11
>>>
```

Figure 12.8 Demo of nonlocal keyword

Example 9 –**Demo of nonlocal keyword.**

```
x = "i"
def outside():
    x = "j"
    def inside():
        nonlocal x
        x = "k"
        print("Inside:", x)
    inside()
    print("Outside:", x)
outside()
print("global:", x)

RUN
>>>
Inside: k
Outside: k
global: i
>>>
```

Figure 12.9 Demo of nonlocal keyword

In Figure 12.9, using the nonlocal keyword, x in the inside() function should actually refer to the x defined in the outside() function, which is one level higher. So, x in both inside() and outside() is defined as "k", because it could be accessed by inside().

12.3 LEGB RULE

We know that variables need to be defined before they can be used in a program. Depending on how and where it was defined, a variable will have to be accessed in different ways. Some variables are defined globally, and others locally. This means that a variable referring to an entity in a certain part of a program, may refer to something different in another part of the program. Depending on where you are in a program, a different namespace will be used.

The "scope" defines on which hierarchy level Python searches for a particular "variable name" for its associated object. It uses the LEGB-rule to search the different levels of namespaces before it finds the name-to-object' mapping. LEGB stands for Local Enclosed Global Built-in. LEGB tells us the order in which Python accesses the variable in a program. First, Python will check if the variable is present in the local scope, if not then checks in enclosing scope. If the search in the enclosed scope is unsuccessful, too, Python moves on to the global namespace, and finally, it will search the built-in namespace: **`Local -> Enclosed -> Global -> Built-in,`** where the arrows denote the direction of the namespace-hierarchy search order. (See Figure 12.10).

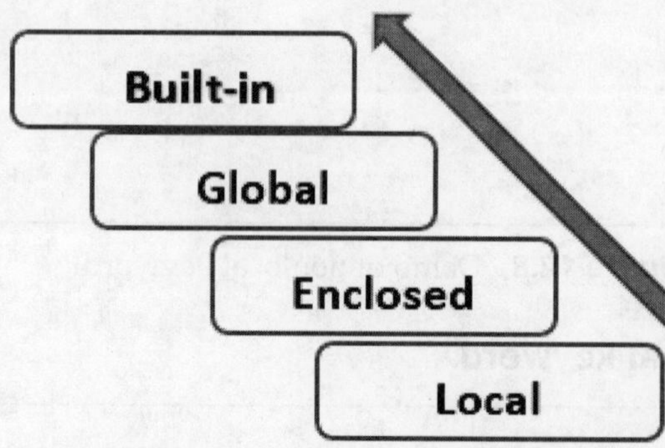

Figure 12.10 Python's LEGB hierarchy

Python namespaces can be divided into four types. Let's understand the LEGB terms one by one:

12.3.1 Local

Local can be inside a function or class method. A function, for-loop, try-except block are some examples of a local namespace. The name references create or change Local names by default. Python first tries to search for an identifier(variable) in Local scope. The local variable exists only within the block/function that it is declared in. The local namespace is deleted when the function or the code block finishes its execution. You cannot use it outside the function where it is declared. For example in the code given in Figure 12.11, x=5 is local to the num() function means you cannot access that variable outside this function. So, the output of the last print(x) will be an error saying name 'x' is not defined.

Example 10 –Demo of Local namespace.

```
# Demo of Local namespace
def num():
    x=5
    print(x)
num()
print (x)

RUN
>>>
5
Traceback (most recent call last):
  File "C:/Users/shash/AppData/Local/Programs/Python/Python37-32/local.py", line
5, in <module>
    print (x)
NameError: name 'x' is not defined
>>>
```

Figure 12.11 Demo of Local namespace

12.3.2 Enclosed

Enclosed can be its enclosing function, i.e., if a function is wrapped inside another function. Python checks the enclosing feature, such as if there is a variable with the same name. If Python does not find an identifier(variable) within the local scope, it will examine the Enclosing scope to see if it can find the variable there. Its lifecycle is the same as the local namespace. Let's understand this by an example discussed in Figure 12.12.

Example 11 –**Demo of Enclosed namespace.**

```
# Demo of Enclosed namespace
def outside():
    x=5
    def inside():
      print( x)
    inside()
    print (x)
outside()

RUN
>>>
5
5
>>>
```

Figure 12.12 Demo of Enclosed namespace

12.3.3 Global

Global refers to the uppermost level. If you define a variable at the top of your script, it will be a global variable. This means that it is accessible from anywhere in your script, including from within a function. The global namespace for a module is created when the module definition is read. Generally, module namespaces also last until the interpreter quits. If Python fails to find the variable in both above scopes, then it will check the global scope. Let's understand this by an example discussed in Figure 12.13. As you have no x in the local and enclosing scope, so Python checks the global scope and outputs 5 for both print x statements.

Example 12 –**Demo of Global namespace.**

```
#Demo of Global namespace
x=5
def outside():
    def inside():
        print (x)
    inside()
    print( x)
outside()

RUN
>>>
5
5
>>>
```

Figure 12.13 Demo of Global namespace

Let's Try

Write the output of the following code where global variable name can be changed by change_name():

```
name = 'Mohan'
def change_name(new_name):
    global name
    name = new_name
print(name)
change_name('Sohan')
print(name)
```

12.3.4 Built-in

Built-in are special names that Python reserves for itself. Built-in means the function and variables that are already defined in Python. If an identifier is not found in any of the above scopes within a module, then Python will examine the built-in identifiers to see if it is defined there. (See Figure 12.14).

Example 13 –Demo of Built-in namespace.

```
#Demo of Built-in namespace
x = len ( 'VIVEK' )
print(x)

RUN
>>>
5
>>>
```

Figure 12.14 Demo of Built-in namespace

If len is not found in any of the scopes, then Python would consult the Built-in scope, where it will find the len function and outputs 5. But if you create your own len function then it will have precedence over Built-in len function. Let's see example 14.

Example 14 –Demo of Built-in namespace.

```
#Demo of Built-in namespace
def len(x):
    return (1)
x = len ( 'VIVEK' )
print(x)

RUN
>>>
1
>>>
```

Figure 12.15 Demo of Built-in namespace

Note that your len function precedes over built-in len and thus the output of print x statement equals 1.

12.4 MODULE BASICS

A Python module is a file containing Python codes - including statements, variables, functions and classes. It shall be saved with file extension of ".py". The module name is the filename, i.e., a module shall be saved as "<module_name>.py".

☞ *A module in Python is just a file containing Python definitions and statements.*

Advantages of Python modules are:

(a) Module allows to logically organize your Python codes.
(b) Groping related code into a module makes the code easier to understand and use.
(c) Similar types of attributes can be categorized and placed in a single module.
(d) Module provides facility of reusability of codes.

12.5 MODULE FILES AS NAMESPACES

Namespaces are just containers for mapping names to objects. You know that everything in Python literals, lists, dictionaries, functions, classes, etc., is an object. Also namespaces can exist independently from each other and that they are structured in a certain hierarchy. The name references create or change local names by default. The global declarations are used to design assigned names to an enclosing module's scope. In Python programming, all function names assigned inside a def statement are locals by default whereas the functions written in Python can use global but they must be declared as global.

☞ *A namespace is a naming system used to make sure that names are unique to avoid naming conflicts.*

12.6 IMPORT MODEL

A package is just a directory tree with some Python files in it. To use any package in your code, you must first make it accessible. You have to import it. In Python, modules are accessed by using the *import* statement. When you do this, you execute the code of the module, keeping the scopes of the definitions so that your current file(s) can make use of these. Some modules are available through the Python Standard Library which contains many modules that provide access to system functionality or provide standardized solutions and are therefore installed with your Python installation. Others can be installed with Python's package manager pip. Additionally, you can create your own Python modules since modules are comprised of Python .py files.

There are a number of modules that are built into the Python Standard Library. Some of the commonly used built-in modules are os, sys, math, random, data time etc. Import statement is used to get a module as a whole. When you use the from statement, you copy names from the module to the importer.

☞ *Python packages are namespaces containing multiple modules.*

12.6.1 Writing and Importing Modules

A module is a file that contains a collection of related functions and other definitions. Writing a module is just like writing any other Python file. Modules can contain definitions of functions, classes, and variables that can then be utilized in other Python programs. You can make a module available to another program by importing it. For example, Python has a math module that includes a number of specialized mathematical tools, and it also defines some names, including pi. Here's how you import:

```
>>> import math
```

Here's how you access the name pi that it defines:

```
>>> math.pi
3.1415926535897931
```

Note that you can import modules with the *import* command. To use a module, you can import it. Usually import statements occur at the beginning of the Python module. Importing modules is a fairly simple operation, but it requires a little explanation. Consider the following examples:

(a) import math
(b) import os, sys
(c) from math import sqrt
(d) import os as operatingSystem

These examples highlight some variations in how you can import modules:

(a) This first example is the simplest and easiest to understand. It is merely the keyword *import* followed by the module name (in this case, math). The standard way to import a module, say math, is to write:

```
import math
```

and then access individual functions in the module with the module name and prefix as given below:

```
x = math.sqrt(y)
```

(b) Multiple modules can be imported with the same import command, with the modules separated by a comma.

(c) You can import specific names only within a module, without importing the whole module, by using the `from <module> import <name>` statement. This can be useful for performance reasons if you only need one function from a large module. Now you can work with sqrt directly, without the math prefix. More than one function can be imported:

```
from math import sqrt, exp, log, sin
```

Sometimes one just writes:

```
from math import *
```

to import all functions in the math module. This includes sin, cos, tan, asin, acos, atan, sinh, cosh, tanh, exp, log (base e), log10 (base 10), sqrt, as well as the famous numbers e and pi. Importing all functions from a module, using the asterisk (*) syntax, is convenient, but this may result in a lot of extra names in the program that are not used.

It is in general recommended not to import more functions than those that are really used in the program

(d) If a module has a name that is difficult to work with or remember, and you want to use a name to represent it that is meaningful to you, simply use the *as* keyword and *import <module-name> as <specific-name>*.

Let's look at few examples to use import:

Create a Python module area.py as shown in Figure 12.16. This module import the "math" module. It contains multiple mathematical functions. Among them is the pi() function, which provides the value of pi which is used to calculate area of circle.

Example 15 –Demo of import.

```
# To create area module area.py
import math
def area_circle(radius):
    return math.pi*radius*radius
def area_square(side):
     return side*side
def area_rectangle(length,breadth):
     return length * breadth
```

Figure 12.16 Demo of import

Example 16 –Demo of Importing module area.py in math1.py module.

Now let us use area.py module in another module math1.py to calculate area_circle, area_square, and area_rectangle.

```
# Importing module area.py in math1.py module
import area
print(area.area_circle(2))
print(area.area_square(5))
print(area.area_rectangle(8,4))

RUN
>>>
12.566370614359172
25
32
>>>
```

Figure 12.17 Importing module area.py in math1.py module

Example 17 –Demo of dir().

You can use dir() function which list all objects such as sub-modules, variables, constants defined in the module. To list all the objects present in area.py, type :

```
>>> import area
>>> dir(area)
```

It will display all objects as shown in Figure 12.18.

```
>>> import area
>>> dir(area)
['__builtins__', '__cached__', '__doc__', '__file__', '__loader__', '__name__', '__package__',
'__spec__', 'area_circle', 'area_rectangle', 'area_square', 'math']
>>>
                                                                    Ln: 9  Col: 56
```

Figure 12.18 Demo of dir()

Example 18 –Demo of from-import statement.

With the from-import statement, you can select specific functions from the module. For example, to calculate area of circle only, that call specific sub-module from-import statement is used as shown in Figure 12.19.

```
# To call specific function module in math2.py module
from area import area_circle
print(area_circle(3))
RUN
>>>
28.274333882308138
>>>
```

Figure 12.19 Demo of from-import statement

Example 19 –Demo of import * statement.

We can also import all the attributes from a module by using *. For example you can import all the sub-module from module "area.py" as shown in Figure 12.20.

```
# To import all the sub-modules from module "area.py" in "math3.py"
from area import *
print(area_circle(5))
print(area_square(4))
print(area_rectangle(5,3))
```

(Contd...)

```
RUN
>>>
78.53981633974483
16
15
>>>
```

Figure 12.20 Demo of import * statement

12.6.2 Python Module Search Path

Whenever you import Python modules, say hello, the interpreter searches a built-in version. If not found, it searches for a file named hello.py under a list of directories given by variable sys.path. The sys.path is initialized from the environment variable PYTHONPATH. PYTHONPATH is also looked up to check for the presence of the imported modules in various directories. The interpreter uses it to determine which module to load. The environment variable PYTHONPATH is empty by default.

☞ *PYTHONPATH is an environment variable which is used when a module is imported.*

12.7 RELOADING MODULES

As you know that, a module is loaded once despite of the number of times it is imported into the Python source file. If you want to reload the already imported module to re-execute the top-level code, Python provides you the reload() function. This is useful if you have edited the module source file using an external editor and want to try out the new version without leaving the Python interpreter. The syntax to use the reload() function is as below:
reload(<module-name>)

REVIEW QUESTIONS WITH ANSWERS

1. Multiple Choice Questions

1. To determine in which order Python should access namespaces, you can use the:
   a. LEGB rule
   b. LGBE rule
   c. LBGE rule
   d. LGEB rule
2. LEGB stands for:
   a. Local Enclosed Global Built-in
   b. Logical Enclosed Global Built-in
   c. Linear Enclosed Global Built-in
   d. None of the above
3. A Python variable name must:
   a. Begin with an alphabetic character or an underscore
   b. May contain alphanumeric characters and an underscore
   c. The name of the variable should not coincide with the keyword
   d. All of the above
4. Which of the following is false about import modulename form of import?
   a. The namespace of imported module becomes part of importing module
   b. This form of import prevents name clash
   c. The namespace of imported module becomes available to importing module
   d. The identifiers in module are accessed as: modulename.identifier
5. Which of the following is not an advantage of using modules?
   a. Provides a means of reuse of program code
   b. Provides a means of dividing up tasks
   c. Provides a means of reducing the size of the program
   d. Provides a means of testing individual parts of the program
6. Which of the following is not a valid namespace?
   a. Global namespace
   b. Private namespace
   c. Built-in namespace
   d. Local namespace

2. State whether True or False

1. A name declared at Global scope, is not enclosed in a function.

2. A global variable can be declared in a function using the keyword global.
3. When searching for a variable, first search Global, and then search Enclosing scopes.
4. If a name is not found using Local, Enclosing, or Global, then the built-in names are searched.
5. Built-in scope searched last.
6. It is usually a bad idea to modify global variables inside the function scope.
7. Python modules can get access to code from another module by importing the file/function using import.
8. A module is a piece of software that has a specific functionality.
9. The namespace of imported module becomes part of importing module.
10. The namespace of imported module becomes available to importing module.

3. Match the following:

1. Local	a. Defined inside enclosing functions
2. Enclosed	b. Defined inside function/class
3. Global	c. Reserved names in Python builtin modules
4. Built-in	d. Defined at the uppermost level
5. namespace	e. Hierarchy level
6. Scope	f. Python dictionary structure

4. Fill in the blanks:

1. A __________ is a container where names are mapped to objects.
2. In Python, the _______ rule is used to decide the order in which the namespaces are to be searched for scope resolution.
3. The ___________defines on which hierarchy level Python searches for a particular "variable name" for its associated object.
4. If a name is not found in the namespace hierarchy, ________ error is raised.
5. A _________ is a reference to a memory address that contains the value.
6. _______ means the function and variables that are already defined in Python.

Answers

1. 1. a 2. a 3. d 4. a 5. c 6. b

2. 1. T 2. T 3. F 4. T 5. T 6. T 7. T 8. T 9. F 10. T

3. 1. B 2. A 3. D 4. C 5. F 6. E

4. 1. Namespace 2. LEGB 3. Scope 4. NameError 5. Variable 6. Built-in

Short Answer Questions

1. What do you understand by module and package?

Ans A module is a file containing Python codes - including statements, variables, functions and classes. It shall be saved with file extension of ".py". On the other hand a Package is simply a directory of Python modules.

2. What do you mean by LEGB?

Ans The order for name resolution (for names inside a function) is: local, enclosing function for nested def, global, and then the built-in namespaces (i.e., LEGB).
L: Local namespace which is specific to the current function.
E: for nested function, the Enclosing function's namespace.
G: Global namespace for the current module.
B: Built-in namespace for all the modules.

3. What is namespace in Python?

Ans A namespace is a naming system used to make sure that names are unique to avoid naming conflicts.

4. Name any two commonly used built-in modules.

Ans math and random

5. What do you mean by Global variable?

Ans Global variable means that it is accessible from anywhere in our script, including from within a function. It is usually defined at the top of the script or outside of the function.

6. What do you mean by Built-in?

Ans Built-in means the function and variables that are already defined in Python.

7. What do you understand by following import statement:
`from X import a, b, c`

Ans It imports the module X, and creates references in the current namespace to the given objects. Or in other words, we can now use a, b and c in our program.

8. What do you mean by reloading module?

Ans In reloading module, instead of creating a new module object, the existing module is re-used. By re-using the same object, existing references to the module are preserved even if class or function definitions are modified by the reload.

9. How will you import all the attributes from a module?

Ans We can also import all the attributes from a module by using *. The syntax is given below:
`from <module> import *`
For example, from math import *

10. Write short note on from-import statement.

Ans Instead of importing the whole module into the namespace, Python provides the flexibility to import only the specific attributes of a module. This can be done by using from import statement. The syntax to use the from-import statement is given below:
from < module-name> import <name 1>, <name 2>..,<name n>

11. Write the output for the following:

(a)
```
x = 10
y = 27
def fun(x):
        y = 20
        print( x, y)
fun(33)
print( x, y)
```

Figure 1 Program for Q11(a)

Ans 33 20
10 27

(b)
```
def fun():
    global x
    x = 10
fun()
print( x)
```

Figure 2 Program for Q11(b)

Ans 10

(c)
```
print( pow(2,3))
print (len("hello"))
```

Figure 3 Program for Q11(c)

Ans 8
5

EXERCISE

1. What are local variables and global variables in Python?
2. What are Python modules? Name some commonly used built-in modules in Python? Also what is the file extension of Python module?
3. What is the difference between locals() and globals()?
4. What is a from import statement and write the syntax for it?
5. What is namespace in Python? Explain with an example.

6. What is PYTHONPATH?
7. How does Python resolve the scope of a name or identifier?
8. What is the significance of assigning namespace to Python modules?
9. What is the difference between import statement and from import statement?
10. Write any two advantages of Python modules.
11. Why is the use of import all statements not recommended?

LAB EXERCISE

1. What would be the output of the following programs?

(a)
```
a = 'global'        # Global file-scope
def myfun():
    b = 'local'     # Function local-scope
    print(b)
    print(a)        #  global variable can be read
myfun()
print(a)
```

(b)
```
a = 'global'      # Global file-scope
def myfun():
   a = 'change'    # Local a is created & hides the global a
   print(a)        # Show local

myfun()
print(a)             # Global unchanged
```

(c)
```
temp = 10  # global-scope variable
def func():
     temp = 20    # local-scope variable
     print(temp)
print(temp)
func()
print(temp)
```

(d)
```
temp = 10
def func():
     global temp
     temp = 20    # local-scope variable
     print(temp)
print(temp)
func()
print(temp)
```

CHAPTER 13

NumPy Basics

13.1 INTRODUCTION TO NUMPY

NumPy stands for 'Numerical Python' or 'Numeric Python'. It is an open source module of Python which provides fast mathematical computation on arrays and matrices. Since, arrays and matrices are an essential part of the Machine Learning ecosystem, NumPy along with Machine Learning modules like Scikit-learn, Pandas, Matplotlib, TensorFlow, etc., complete the Python Machine Learning Ecosystem. NumPy is also useful in linear algebra, random number capability etc.

In order to use Numpy, you must import in your module by using a statement like:

import numpy as np

The above statement has given *np* as alias name for numpy module. Once imported you can use both names i.e., numpy or np for functions, e.g. numpy.array( ) is same as np.array( ).

Arrays, in general refers to a named group of homogeneous (of same type) elements. For example, students array containing 5 entries as [84, 87, 63, 74, 52] then students is an array. Each item stored in an array is called an *element*. Each location of an element in an array has a numerical index, which is used to identify the element. Numpy refers to the dimensions of its arrays as *axes*. Axes are always numbered 0 onwards. The shape of an array depends upon the list of integers giving the size of the array along each dimension.

A NumPy array is simply a grid that contains values of the same/homogeneous type. NumPy Arrays come in two forms:

(a) 1-D(one dimensional) arrays known as Vectors(having single row/column only). To create a one-dimensional NumPy array, you can simply pass a Python list to the array method. For example,

```
# Creating a 1-D Numpy array
import numpy as np
x = [2,4,6,8]
nums=np.array(x)
print(nums)
```

```
>>>
[2 , 4 , 6 , 8]
>>>
```

In the script above you first imported the NumPy library as np, and created a list x. We then passed this list to the array function of the NumPy library. Finally, you printed the nums array on screen.

(b) Multidimensional arrays known as Matrices(can have multiple rows and columns). For example,

```
# Creating a 2-D Numpy array
import numpy as np
nums    =    np.array([   [1,2,3,4]    ,
[11,12,13,14] ])
print(nums[1,3])
print(nums[1][3])
print(nums)
```

```
>>>
14
14
[[1,2,3,4]
[11,12,13,14]]
>>>
```

The above script results in a matrix where every inner list in the outer list becomes a row. The number of columns is equal to the number of elements in each inner list.

Individual elements of array can be accessed using arrayname[index] and multi-dimension arrays can be accessed as arrayname[row][col] or arrayname[row,col].

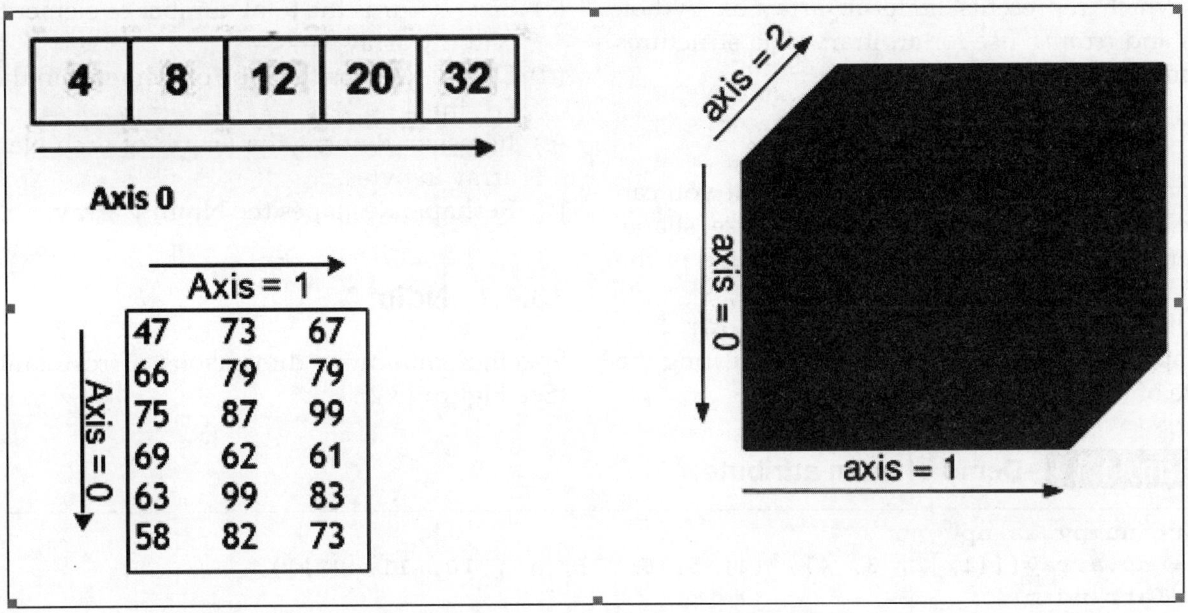

Figure 13.1 Types of NumPy Array

13.2 ndarray

NumPy works with Python objects called multi-dimensional!arrays. Arrays are basically collections of values, and they have one or more dimensions. NumPy array data structure is also called *ndarray*, short for n-dimensional array. It is also known by the alias array. An array with one dimension is called a *vector* and an array with two dimensions is called a!*matrix*.

NumPy's main object is the homogeneous multidimensional array. It is a table of elements (usually numbers), all of the same type, indexed by positive integers. In NumPy dimensions are called *axes*. The number of axes is *rank*.

For example, the coordinates of a point in 3D space [1, 2, 1] has one axis. That axis has 3 elements in it, so you can say it has a length of 3. In the example given below, the array has 2 axes. The first axis has a length of 2, the second axis has a length of 3.

```
[[ 1., 0., 0.],
 [ 0., 1., 2.]]
```

Difference between NumPy Array and List

(a) Once a Numpy array is created, you cannot change its size, However, size can be changed in list.
(b) NumPy array contains elements of homogeneous(same) types. Python list contains elements of heterogeneous(different) types.
(c) Numpy array occupies much less space and memory consumption than a Python list.

13.3 DATA TYPES

A data type describes what type data is to be stored in a variable, or in any Python object. A data type object is an instance of numpy.dtype class which describes how the bytes in the fixed-size block of memory corresponding to an array item should be interpreted. dtypes can be referenced by their class, long name or short name. It describes the following aspects of the data:

(a) Type of the data such as integer, float, Python object, etc.
(b) Size of the data which lists the size (in bytes) of each array element.
(c) Byte order of the data.

NumPy supports a much greater variety of numerical types. There are 5 basic numerical types representing booleans (bool), integers (int), unsigned integers (uint), floating point (float) and complex. Those with numbers in their name indicate the bitsize of the type (Number of bits needed to represent a single value in memory). One bit can hold the value 0 or 1, and computers organize memory in units of bytes, which are 8 bits, allowing for $2^8 = 256$ different values per byte. Along with above numerical types it also supports *strings* (str, unicode), *object*, which represents items in array as Python objects and *records*, use for arbitrary data structures in record arrays.

13.4 ARRAY ATTRIBUTES

NumPy arrays have a set of attributes that you can access. These attributes includes array's size, shape, number of dimensions, and data type. Some of the important attributes of a NumPy object are:

(a) Ndim: Displays the dimension of the array.
(b) Shape: Returns a tuple of integers indicating the size of the array.
(c) Size: Returns the total number of elements in the NumPy array.
(d) Dtype: Returns the type of elements in the array, i.e., int64.
(e) Itemsize: Returns the length of each element of array in bytes.
(f) Reshape: Reshapes the NumPy array.

13.4.1 Ndim

Specifies minimum dimensions of resultant array. (See Figure 13.2).

Example 1 –Demo of ndim attribute.

```
import numpy as np
arr = np.array([[1, 2, 3, 4], [4, 5, 6, 7], [9, 10, 11, 23]])
print(arr.ndim)

RUN
>>>
2
>>>
```

Figure 13.2 Demo of ndim attribute

13.4.2 Shape

The shape of an ndarray tells about the number of elements along each axis of it.

The 'Shape' function returns the shape of array. It is a tuple of integers. These numbers denote the lengths of the corresponding array dimension. You can say that the "shape" of an array is a tuple with the number of elements per axis (dimension). In our example, the shape is equal to (6, 3), i.e., you have 6 lines and 3 columns.

np.shape = returns a tuples of integers indicating the size of array.

Example 2 –Demo of shape attribute.

```
import numpy as np
x = np.array([[47,73,67],
             [66,79,79],
             [75,87,99],
             [69,62,61],
             [63,99,83],
            [58,82,73]])
print(np.shape(x))
x.shape = (2,9)
print(x)
```

(Contd...)

```
RUN
>>>
(6, 3)
[[47 73 67 66 79 79 75 87 99]
 [69 62 61 63 99 83 58 82 73]]
>>>
```

Figure 13.3 Demo of shape attribute

The shape of an array also tells us something about the order in which the indices are processed, i.e., first rows, then columns and after that the further dimensions.

Output

```
[[47 73 67 66 79 79 75 87 99]
 [69 62 61 63 99 83 58 82 73]]
```

"shape" can also be used to change the shape of an array for example,

```
>>> x.shape = (2,9)
>>> print(x)
```

13.4.3 Size

To get the size of the array, the size function associated with the numpy array is used. (See Figure 13.4).

Example 3 –**Demo of size attribute.**

```
import numpy as np
a = np.array([[1,2,3,4,5,6,7]])
print("Array Size:",a.size)

RUN
>>>
Array Size: 7
>>>
```

Figure 13.4 Demo of size attribute

Let's Try

```
import numpy as np
a  =  np.array([[11,12,13,14,15,16,17]])
print("Array Size:",a.size)
print("Shape:",a.shape)
```

13.4.4 Dtype

It tells about the type of data stored in the ndarray. By default, ndarrays have the datatype as float. Every array has one and only one dtype. All items in it should be of that dtype. An integer is a value without decimal. If you create an array with decimal, then the type will change to float.

Example 4 –**Demo of dtype attribute.**

```
import numpy as np
a  = np.array([1,2,3])
print(a.dtype)
RUN
>>>
int32
>>>
```

Figure 13.5 Demo of dtype attribute

Let's Try

```
import numpy as np
x = np.array([1.1,2.0,3.2])
print(x.dtype)
```

13.4.5 Itemsize

The itemsize attribute returns the length of each element of array in byte. (See Figure 13.6).

Example 5 –Demo of itemsize attribute.

```
import numpy as np
a = np.array([[11,12,13]])
print("Each item contains",a.itemsize,"bytes")

RUN
>>>
Each item contains 4 bytes
>>>
```

Figure 13.6 Demo of itemsize attribute

13.4.6 Reshape

You can use reshape method to reshape an array. The reshape() function associated with the ndarray object is used to reshape the array. It accepts the two parameters indicating the row and columns of the new shape of the array. The only required condition is original size of array remains unchanged. (See Figure 13.7).

Example 6 –Demo of reshape attribute.

```
import numpy as np
a = np.array([[1,2],[3,4],[5,6]])
print("original array")
print(a)
a=a.reshape(2,3)
print("reshaped array")
print(a)
RUN
>>>
original array
[[1 2]
 [3 4]
 [5 6]]
reshaped array
[[1 2 3]
 [4 5 6]]
>>>
```

Figure 13.7 Demo of reshape attribute

13.5 ARRAY CREATION

There are several ways to create an array in NumPy like np.array, np.zeros, np.ones, etc. Each of them provides some flexibility. Syntax to create an array with important attributes of a Numpy object is:

Syntax: numpy.array(object, dtype=None, copy=True, order='K', subok=False, ndmin=0)

Parameters:

Object: An array, any object exposing the array interface.

Dtype: Desired data type of array.

Copy: If true(default), then the object is copied.

Order 'K', 'A','C','F': Specify the memory layout of the array. If object is not an array, the newly created array will be in C order (row major) unless 'F' is specified, in which case it will be in Fortran order.

Subok: If True, then sub-classes will be passed-through, otherwise the returned array will be forced to be a base-class array.

ndmin: Specifies minimum dimensions of resultant array.

Take a look at the following examples to understand better.

For example, to convert a list of numeric value into one-dimensional Numpy array as shown in Figure 13.8.

```
import numpy as np
List = [1,2,3,4]
a1 = np.array(List)
print(a1)
```

The above code written in Python is shown in Figure 13.9:

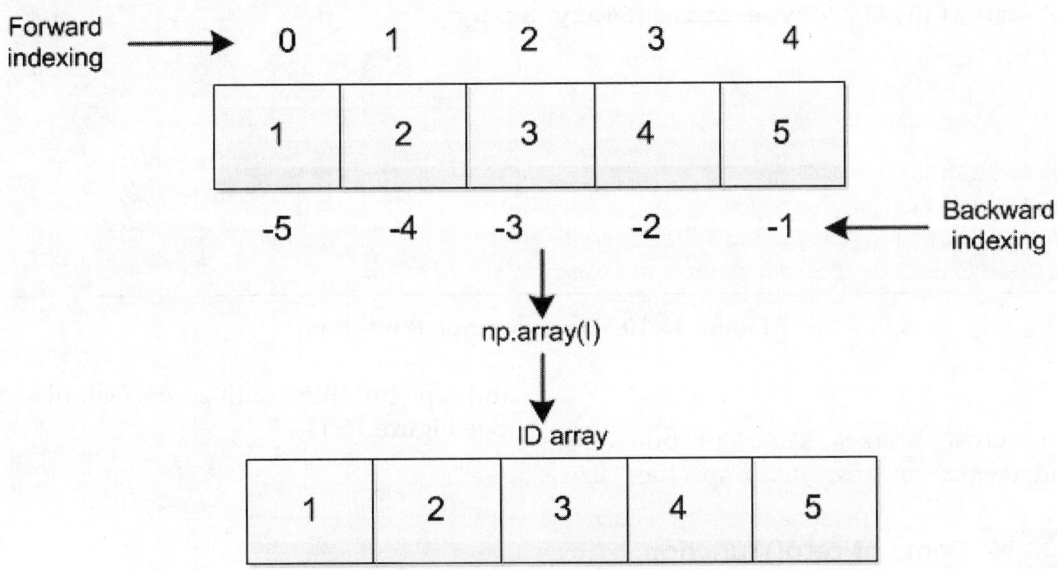

Figure 13.8 Creation of NumPy array

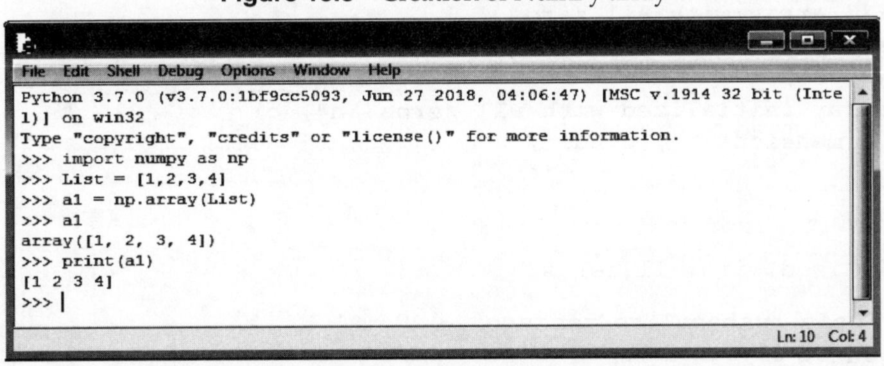

Figure 13.9 Python code to create NumPy array

Simplest way to create an array in Numpy is to use Python List:

myPythonList = [1,9,8,3]

To convert Python list to a numpy array by using the object np.array:

numpy_array_from_list = np.array(myPythonList)

To display the contents of the list:

numpy_array_from_list

```
>>>
array([1, 9, 8, 3])
>>>
```

13.5.1 Methods used to create Numpy Array

Different methods used to create Numpy array are discussed in the following sections.

empty( )

empty( ) function is used to create empty arrays or an uninitialized array of specified shape and dtype, in which you can store actual data as and when required. (See Figure 13.10). Note that empty( ) created array with random garbage values.

Example 7 –Demo of empty() function.

```
import numpy as np
arr1 = np.empty([3,2], dtype=int) #Empty array
print(arr1)

RUN
>>>
[[6357069 6815843]
 [7209065 4653157]
 [6881397     100]]
>>>
```

Figure 13.10 Demo of empty() function

zeros( )

The function zeros( ) takes same attributes as empty( ), and creates an array with specifies size and type but filled with zeros. Default dtype is float. (See Figure 13.11).

Example 8 –Demo of zero() function.

```
# Creating a 2X3 array with all zeros
import numpy as np
c = np.zeros((2, 3))
print ("\nAn array initialized with all zeros:\n", c)
print("No. of dimensions: ", c.ndim)

RUN
>>>
An array initialized with all zeros:
 [[0. 0. 0.]
 [0. 0. 0.]]
No. of dimensions:  2
>>>
```

Figure 13.11 Demo of zero() function

Let's Try

```
import numpy as np
x = np.zeros((5,), dtype = int)
print(x)
```

Example 9 –Demo of one() function.

```
import numpy as np
arr1 = np.ones([3,2],dtype=np.int64)
print(arr1)

RUN
>>>
[[1 1]
 [1 1]
 [1 1]]
>>>
```

Figure 13.12 Demo of one() function

Let's Try

```
import numpy as np
x = np.ones(5)
print(x)
```

copy()

If you just assign a portion of an array to another array, the new array you just created actually refers to the parent array in memory. That means, if you make any changes to the new array, it will reflect in the parent array as well. So to avoid disturbing the parent array, you need to make a copy of it using copy(). All numpy arrays come with the copy() method. (See Figure 13.13).

ones( )

The function ones( ) takes same attributes as empty( ), and creates an array with specified size and type but filled with ones. (See Figure 13.12).

Example 10 –Demo of copy() function.

```
import numpy as np
x=np.array([11,12,13])
y=x
z=np.copy(x)
x[0]=22
print(x)
print(y)
print(z)

RUN
>>>
[22 12 13]
[22 12 13]
[11 12 13]
>>>
```

Figure 13.13 Demo of copy() function

13.6 ARRAY CREATION ROUTINES

NumPy offers a lot of array creation routines for different circumstances. arange() is one such function based on numerical ranges. It's often referred to as np.arange() because *np* is a widely used abbreviation for NumPy.

This function takes the start index of the array, the end index, and the step size (which is optional) and returns an ndarray object containing evenly spaced values within a given range. The format of the function is as follows:

```
numpy.arange(start, stop, step, dtype)
```

The first three parameters determine the range of the values, while the fourth specifies the type of the elements:

(a) start is the number (integer or decimal) that defines the first value in the array.
(b) stop is the number that defines the end of the array and is not included in the array.
(c) step is the number that defines the spacing (difference) between each two consecutive values in the array and defaults to 1.
(d) The dtype specifies the datatype for the Numpy array.

For example,

```
>>> np.arange(start=1, stop=10, step=3)
array([1, 4, 7])
```

In the above example, start is 1; so, the first element of array is 1. step is 3, i.e., your second value is 1+3, that is 4, while the third value in the array is 4+3, which equals 7.

You can pass start, stop, and step as positional arguments as well:

```
>>> np.arange(1, 10, 3)
array([1, 4, 7])
```

You can omit step. In this case, arange() uses its default value of 1. The following two statements are equivalent:

```
>>> np.arange(start=1, stop=10, step=1)
array([1, 2, 3, 4, 5, 6, 7, 8, 9])
>>> np.arange(start=1, stop=10)
array([1, 2, 3, 4, 5, 6, 7, 8, 9])
```

The start, stop and step attribute provide the values for a numerical range. start and step values are optional. When only stop value is given, the numerical range is generated from zero to stop value with step 1. dtype is the type of the elements of the output array. (See Figure 13.14).

```
>>> np.arange(7, dtype=float)
array([0., 1., 2., 3., 4., 5., 6.])
>>> arr1 = np.arange(10,20,2, np.float32)
>>> arr1
array([10., 12., 14., 16., 18.], dtype=float32)
>>> |
```

Figure 13.14 Use of arange function

☞ *Remember that the arange method returns an array that starts with the starting index and ends at one index less than the end index.*

Let's Try

```
>>> np.arange(1, 10)
>>> np.arange(start=0, stop=10, step=1)
>>> np.arange(0, 10, 1)
>>> np.arange(10)
```

13.6.1 Providing Negative Arguments

If you provide negative values for start or both start and stop, and have a positive step, then arange() will work the same way as with all positive arguments:

```
>>> np.arange(-5, -1)
array([-5, -4, -3, -2])
>>> np.arange(-8, -2, 2)
array([-8, -6, -4])
>>> np.arange(-5, 6, 4)
array([-5, -1,  3])
```

13.6.2 Counting Backwards

Sometimes you want an array with the values decrementing from left to right. In such cases, you can use arange() with a negative value for step, and with a start greater than stop:

```
>>> np.arange(5, 1, -1)
array([5, 4, 3, 2])
>>> np.arange(7, 0, -3)
array([7, 4, 1])
```

13.7 ARRAY FROM EXISTING DATA

An array is created from existing data by the following functions:

numpy.asarray

This array is used for converting the Python sequence into ndarray. This routine is used to create an array by using the existing data in the form of lists, or tuples.

numpy.asarray(sequence, dtype = None, order = None)

It accepts the following parameters.

(a) sequence: It is the Python sequence which is to be converted into the Python array. Input data can be in any form such as list, list of tuples, tuples, tuple of tuples or tuple of lists.

(b) dtype: It is the data type of each item of the array.

(c) order: It can be set to C (row major) or F (column major). The default is C.

Example 11 –**Program to convert list to ndarray.**

```
# Convert list to ndarray
import numpy as np
x = [1,2,3]
a = np.asarray(x)
print(type(a))
print(a)

RUN
>>>
<class 'numpy.ndarray'>
[1 2 3]
>>>
```

Figure 13.15 Convert list to ndarray

Example 12 –**Program to Create a numpy array using Tuple.**

```
#Creating a numpy array using Tuple
import numpy as np
l=(1,2,3,4,5,6,7)
a = np.asarray(l);
print(type(a))
print(a)

RUN
>>>
<class 'numpy.ndarray'>
[1 2 3 4 5 6 7]
>>>
```

Figure 13.16 Creating a numpy array using Tuple

Let's Try

```
# Creating numpy array using the list
import numpy as np
l=[1,2,3,4,5,6,7]
a = np.asarray(l);
print(type(a))
print(a)
```

The dtype specifies the datatype for the Numpy array.

13.8 ARRAY FROM NUMERICAL RANGES

Numerical ranges: np.arange, np.linspace, np.logspace

13.8.1 np.arange

arange( ) returns an ndarray object containing evenly spaced values within a given range. The format of the function is as follows:
numpy.arange(start, stop, step, dtype)
The start, stop and step attribute provide the values for a numerical range. start and step values are optional. When only stop value is given, the numerical range is generated from zero to stop value with step 1.

13.8.2 np.linspace

linspace( ) is used to generate evenly spaced elements between two given limits. The format of function is as follows:
numpy.linspace(start, stop, num, endpoint, retstep, dtype)
The *start* and *stop* attributes provides start and end values of the sequence. *num*, provides the number of evenly spaced samples to be generated. By default it is 50. The *endpoint* is True by default, hence the stop value is included in the sequence. If false, it is not included. *retstep*, if true, returns samples and step between the consecutive numbers. *dtype* is a data type of output ndarray. (See Figure 13.17 and 13.18).

Example 13 –Demo of linespace() function.

```
import numpy as np
x = np.linspace(10,20,5)
print(x)

RUN
>>>
[10.  12.5 15.  17.5 20. ]
>>>
```

Figure 13.17 Demo of linespace() function

Example 14 –Demo of linspace() function.

```
# endpoint set to false
import numpy as np
x = np.linspace(10,20,5, endpoint = False)
print(x)
RUN
>>>
[10. 12. 14. 16. 18.]
>>>
```

Figure 13.18 Demo of linspace() function

Let's Try

```
import numpy as np
arr1 = np.linspace(2,10,3)
print(arr1)
```

```
import numpy as np
arr2 = np.linspace(1,2,4)
print(arr2)
```

13.8.3 numpy.logspace

logspace() function creates an array by using the numbers that are evenly separated on a log scale. Start and stop endpoints of the scale are indices of the base, usually 10. The format of function is as follows:

numpy.logspace(start, stop, num, endpoint, base, dtype)

The *start* and *stop* define the starting and final value of sequence in the base. *num* defines the number of values between the range. *endpoint,* is a boolean type value. If true, stop is the last value in the range. *base* represents the base of log space. Its default is 10. *dtype* is data type of the array items.

Example 15 –**Demo of logspace() function.**

```
import numpy as np
arr = np.logspace(10, 20, num = 5, endpoint = True)
print("The array over the given range is ",arr)

RUN
>>>
The array over the given range is  [1.00000000e+10 3.16227766e+12 1.00000000e+15
3.16227766e+17
 1.00000000e+20]
>>>
```

Figure 13.19 Demo of logspace() function

13.9 INDEXING AND SLICING

NumPy creates an appropriate scale index at the time of array creation. In order to access a single or multiple items of an array, you need to pass array of indexes in square brackets.

Indexing in two-dimensional array is represented by a pair of values, where the first value is the index of the row and the second is the index of the column.

Integer array indexing: In this method, lists are passed for indexing for each dimension. One to one mapping of corresponding elements is done to construct a new arbitrary array.

Boolean array indexing: This method is used when you want to pick elements from array which satisfy some condition.

Example 16 –**Demo of indexing.**

```
import numpy as np

array1d = np.array([1, 2, 3, 4, 5, 6])
print(array1d[0])    # Get first value
print(array1d[-1])   # Get last value
print(array1d[3])    # Get 4th value from first
print(array1d[-5])   # Get 5th value from last
```

(Contd...)

```
# Get multiple values
print(array1d[[0, -1]])
print("-" * 10)
array2d = np.array([[1, 2, 3], [4, 5, 6], [7, 8, 9]])
print(array2d)
print("-" * 10)
print(array2d[0, 0])   # Get first row first col
print(array2d[0, 1])   # Get first row second col
print(array2d[0, 2])   # Get first row third col
print(array2d[0, 1])   # Get first row second col
print(array2d[1, 1])   # Get second row second col
print(array2d[2, 1])   # Get third row second col

RUN
>>>
1
6
4
2
[1 6]
----------
[[1 2 3]
 [4 5 6]
 [7 8 9]]
----------
1
2
3
2
5
8
>>>
```

Figure 13.20 Demo of indexing

Just like lists in Python, NumPy arrays can be sliced. Slicing allows to extract portions of an array or select a subset of an existing array to generate new arrays. For slicing a sequence of numbers separated by colons (:) within square brackets. Syntax for performing slicing :

<Arrayname>[<start>: <stop> : <step>]

When <start>, <stop> or <step> values are not specified then Python will assume their default values as : start = 0, stop = dimension size, and step = 1. A single item respective to that index is returned for only one parameter. If a : is inserted in front of it, all items from that index onwards will be extracted. If two parameters (with : between them) is used, items between the two indexes (not including the stop index) with default step one are sliced.

Example 17 –Demo of slicing.

```
import numpy as np
array1d = np.array([0, 1, 2, 3, 4, 5, 6, 7, 8, 9])
print(array1d[4:])  # From index 4 to last index
```

(Contd...)

```
print(array1d[:4])   # From index 0 to 4 index
print(array1d[4:7])  # From index 4(included) up to index 7(excluded)
print(array1d[:-1])  # Excluded last element
print(array1d[:-2])  # Up to second last index(negative index)
print(array1d[::-1])  # From last to first in reverse order(negative step)
print(array1d[::-2])  # All odd numbers in reversed order
print(array1d[-2::-2]) # All even numbers in reversed order
print(array1d[::])  # All elements

RUN
>>>
[4 5 6 7 8 9]
[0 1 2 3]
[4 5 6]
[0 1 2 3 4 5 6 7 8]
[0 1 2 3 4 5 6 7]
[9 8 7 6 5 4 3 2 1 0]
[9 7 5 3 1]
[8 6 4 2 0]
[0 1 2 3 4 5 6 7 8 9]
>>>
```

Figure 13.21 Demo of slicing

Example 18 –**Demo of slicing and Indexing.**

```
arr = np.array([[1, 2, 0, -4],
                [4, 6, 7, 0],
                [3, -7, 8, 5]])
# Slicing array
temp = arr[:2, ::2]
print ("Array with first 2 rows and alternate columns(0 and 2):\n", temp)
# Indexing array
temp = arr[[0, 1, 2, 1], [3, 2, 1, 0]]
print ("\nElements at indices (0, 2), (1, 2), (2, 1),(2, 0):\n", temp)

RUN
>>>
Array with first 2 rows and alternate columns(0 and 2):
 [[1 0]
 [4 7]]
Elements at indices (0, 2), (1, 2), (2, 1),(2, 0):
 [-4  7 -7  4]
>>>
```

Figure 13.22 Demo of slicing and Indexing

As arrays can be multidimensional, you need to specify a slice for each dimension of the array.

13.10 JOINING AND SPLITTING

Joining(concatenation) of arrays means combining multiple arrays into one and splitting of arrays means splitting one array into many. Concatenation, or joining of two arrays in NumPy, is primarily accomplished using the routines np.concatenate, np.vstack, and np.hstack. np.concatenate takes a tuple or list of arrays as its first argument.

Example 19 –**Demo of concatenation.**

```
# Concatenation
import numpy as np
x = np.array([1, 2, 3])
y = np.array([5, 6, 7])
z=np.concatenate([x, y])
print(z)

RUN
>>>
[1 2 3 5 6 7]
>>>
```

Figure 13.23 Demo of concatenation

You can also concatenate more than two arrays at once.

In addition to concatenation function, Numpy also offers two convenient functions hstack(horizontal stack) and vstack(vertical stack) which allows you to concatenate two multi-dimensional arrays vertically or horizontally. (See Figure 13.24).

Example 20 –**Demo of vstack and hstack functions.**

```
import numpy as np
a = np.array([[1,2,30],[10,15,4]])
b = np.array([[1,2,3],[12, 19, 29]])
print("Arrays vertically concatenated\n",np.vstack((a,b)))
print("Arrays horizontally concatenated\n",np.hstack((a,b)))

RUN
>>>
Arrays vertically concatenated
 [[ 1  2 30]
 [10 15  4]
 [ 1  2  3]
 [12 19 29]]
Arrays horizontally concatenated
 [[ 1  2 30  1  2  3]
 [10 15  4 12 19 29]]
>>>
```

Figure 13.24 Demo of vstack and hstack functions

Let's Try

```
import numpy as np
a = np.array([[1,2,3],[11,12,13]])
b = np.array([[4,5,6],[14, 15, 16]])
print("Arrays vertically concatenated\n",np.vstack((a,b)))
print("Arrays horizontally concatenated\n",np.hstack((a,b)))
```

The opposite of concatenation is splitting, i.e., to split a single array into multiple arrays which is implemented by the functions np.split, np.hsplit, and np.vsplit. For each of these, you can pass a list of indices giving the split points. (See Figure 13.25).

Example 21 –**Demo of splitting.**

```
# Splitting
import numpy as np
x = [1, 2, 3, 99, 99, 3, 2, 1]
x1, x2, x3 = np.split(x, [3, 5])
print(x1, x2, x3)

RUN
>>>
[1 2 3] [99 99] [3 2 1]
>>>
```

Figure 13.25 Demo of splitting

Let's Try

```
# Splitting
import numpy as np
x = [1, 2, 3, 4, 5, 6, 7, 8]
x1, x2, x3 = np.split(x, [2, 4])
print(x1, x2, x3)
```

13.11 ARITHMETIC OPERATIONS ON ARRAY

NumPy is not only about efficient storing of data but also makes it extremely easy to perform the arithmetic operations on multi-dimensional arrays directly. In the following example, the arithmetic operations are performed on the two multi-dimensional arrays.

Example 22 –**Demo of arithmetic operations.**

```
import numpy as np
a = np.array([[10,20,30],[10,15,4]])
b = np.array([[2,4,8],[5, 19, 29]])
print("Sum of array a and b\n",a+b)
print("Product of array a and b\n",a*b)
print("Division of array a and b\n",a/b)

RUN
>>>
Sum of array a and b
 [[12 24 38]
 [15 34 33]]
Product of array a and b
 [[ 20  80 240]
 [ 50 285 116]]
```

(Contd...)

```
Division of array a and b
 [[5.         5.         3.75      ]
 [2.         0.78947368 0.13793103]]
>>>
```

Figure 13.26 Demo of arithmetic operations

Let's Try

```
import numpy as np
x = np.array([[12,16,15],[10,15,4]])
y = np.array([[2,4,5],[5, 3, 2]])
print("Sum of array\n",x+y)
print("Product of array \n",x*y)
print("Division of array\n",x/y)
```

REVIEW QUESTIONS WITH ANSWERS

1. Multiple Choice Questions

1. Attributes of array determines
   a. size, shape
   b. memory consumption
   c. data types of arrays
   d. All of these
2. Getting and setting the value of individual array elements:
   a. Indexing   b. Slicing
   c. Reshaping   d. None of the above
3. Getting and setting smaller subarrays within a larger array:
   a. Indexing   b. Slicing
   c. Reshaping   d. None of the above
4. The number of axes in an ndarray is called its ________.
   a. rank   b. dtype
   c. shape   d. None of these
5. Numpy arrays used over lists because:
   a. Numpy arrays have contiguous memory location
   b. They are more speedy to work with
   c. They are more convenient to deal with
   d. All of the above

2. State whether True or False

1. Multi-dimensional slices work in the same way, with multiple slices separated by commas.
2. The opposite of concatenation is splitting.
3. We can initialize NumPy arrays from nested Python list and access its elements.
4. NumPy array elements can be accessed using indexing.
5. A numpy array is a collection of heterogeneous values.
6. The last value is not included in slicing.
7. Axes are always numbered 0 onwards for ndarrays.

3. Match the following:

1. Joining of arrays	a. Displays the dimension of the array
2. Splitting of arrays	b. Returns the total number of elements in the NumPy array
3. Ndim	c. Combining multiple arrays into one
4. Shape	d. Splitting one array into many
5. Size	e. Returns a tuple of integers indicating the size of the array
6. [:-1]	f. Reverses the order
7. [::-1]	g. Mean drop the last element

4. Fill in the blanks

1. In a one-dimensional array, the ith value (counting from zero) can be accessed by specifying the desired ______ in square brackets.

2. To index from the end of the array, you can use ______ indices.
3. In a multi-dimensional array, items can be accessed using a comma-separated tuple of ________.
4. _______ returns the number of axes (dimensions) of the array.
5. NumPy array holds elements of the _______ kind.
6. Numpy refers to the dimensions of its arrays as _______.
7. _________ function in NumPy is used to check the type of objects in Python.

Answers

1. 1. d 2. a 3. b 4. a 5. d

2. 1. T 2. T 3. T 4. T 5. F 6. T 7. T

3. 1. c 2. d 3. a 4. e 5. b 6. g 7. f

4. 1. index 2. negative 3. indices 4. ndim 5. same 6. axes 7. type()

1. What is numpy?

Ans NumPy("Numerical Python" or "Numeric Python") is an open source module of Python that offers functions and routines for fast mathematical computation on array and matrices.

2. Name the module you will import to use numpy?

Ans In order to use Numpy, we must import in your module by using a statement like: import numpy as np

3. What is slicing?

Ans Slicing in the NumPy array is the way to extract a range of elements from an array. Slicing in the array is performed in the same way as it is performed in the Python list.

4. Write the output for the following:

```
import numpy as np
a = np.array([[1,2],[3,4],[5,6]])
print(a[0,1])
print(a[2,0])
```

Ans 2
5

The above program prints the 2nd element from the 0th index and 0th element from the 2nd index of the array.

5. What do you mean by Axes in numpy?

Ans Numpy refers to the dimensions of its arrays as axes. Axes are always numbered 0 onwards for ndarrays.

6. What do you mean by Rank in numpy?

Ans The number of axes in an ndarray is called its rank.

7. Write the output for the following:

```
import numpy as np
arr = np.array([[1, 2, 3, 4], [4, 5, 6, 7], [9, 10, 11, 23]])
print(arr.ndim)
```

Ans 2

8. Write short note on slicing.

Ans Just like lists in Python, NumPy arrays can be sliced. As arrays can be multidimensional, you need to specify a slice for each dimension of the array. Slicing can be done over multiple dimensions. It cannot be used to expand the size of an array (unlike lists).

9. What is the purpose of negative index values in NumPy?

Ans NumPy also supports negative index values. Using a negative index allows us to retrieve or reference locations starting from the end of the array.

10. Explain different types of array with a diagram.

Ans

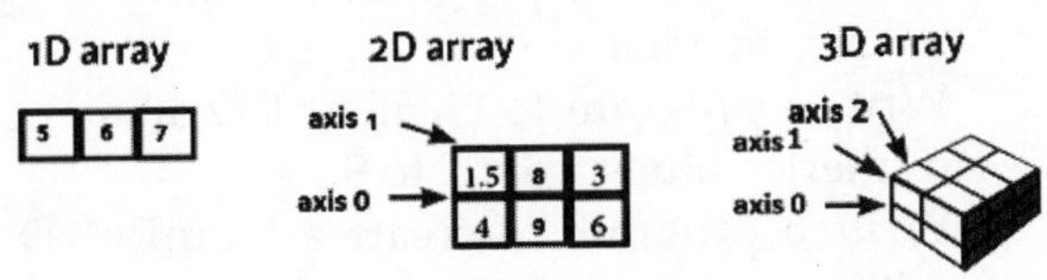

11. Define Array and NumPy array.

Ans Array: Group or collection of similar type of elements. For example, scores of players in a cricket match, marks of students in a class etc. NumPy array: A grid contains value of same type (homogeneous elements).

12. Write the output for the following:

```
import numpy as np
a = np.array([[1,2,3],[11,12,13]])
b = np.array([[4,5,6],[14, 15, 16]])
print("Arrays vertically concatenated\n",np.vstack((a,b)));
print("Arrays horizontally concatenated\n",np.hstack((a,b)))
```

Ans Arrays vertically concatenated
[[1 2 3]
[11 12 13]
[4 5 6]
[14 15 16]]
Arrays horizontally concatenated
[[1 2 3 4 5 6]
[11 12 13 14 15 16]]

EXERCISE

1. NumPy is a tool for data visualization. (True/False)
2. Discuss various features of NumPy array.
3. What is a NumPy array. How they are different from lists?
4. Discuss different attributes of NumPy arrays.
5. How an array is created from the numerical ranges in NumPy?
6. What is the purpose of using arange()?
7. What is the use of reshape() function?

LAB EXERCISE

1. Write a NumPy program to find the most frequent value in an array.
2. Take two NumPy arrays having two dimensions. Concatenate the arrays on axis 1.
3. Write a NumPy program to create an array of 10 zeros, 10 ones, 10 sevens.
4. Write a NumPy program to convert a given array into a list.
5. Write a program to create a 1 D array holding numeric values from 0 to 9.
6. Write a program to create a NumPy 1D array with all elements as Boolean false
7. Write a NumPy program to extract all even numbers from an array.
   Input:[1,2,3,4,5,6,7,8]
   Output:[2,4,6,8]
8. Write output of the following code:

(a)
```
>>> import numpy as np
>>> L=[10, 20, 30, 40]
>>> A=np.array(L)
>>> A
>>> A.ndim
>>> A.shape
>>> A.size
```

(b)
```
>>> A=np.arange(10)
>>> A
>>> B=np.arange(1,20,3)
>>> B
```

(c)
```
>>> L=[10, 20, 30, 40, 50, 60]
>>> Arr=np.array(L)
>>> Arr
>>> Arr[:]
>>> Arr[:5]
>>> Arr[2:4]
>>> Arr[2:]
>>> Arr[2:-1]
>>> Arr[1:5:2]
```

(d)
```
>>> Z=np.linespace(2.5,5,6)
>>> Z
```

(e)
```
>>> A=np.arange(2,50,2).reshape(4,6)
>>> print(A)
```

GLOSSARY

Important Definitions and Terminologies

... The default Python prompt of the interactive shell while entering code for an indented code block or within a pair of matching left and right delimiters

>>> The default Python prompt of the interactive shell.

Algorithm A set of instructions which describes the steps to be followed to carry out an activity.

Aliases Multiple variables that contain references to the same object.

Axes The dimensions of NumPy arrays.

Binary operators Operators that act upon two operands are referred to as binary operators.

Boolean Variables of this type can take only one of the two values, True or False.

Boolean Data Type Comparisons in Python can generate only one of two possible responses: True or False. These data types are called booleans.

Bug An error in a computer program that causes it to produce an incorrect or unexpected result.

clear() Delete all entries.

Coercion Implicit type conversion.

Comment Any text to the right of # symbol in Python.

Compiler A system software package that converts a high-level language program to machine language codes.

Compound statement Group of statements.

Concatenation Adds values on either side of the operator.

Conditional Branching It is the ability of a program to decide whether or not to execute code based on the value of an expression.

Conditional Transfer An instruction that may change the sequence of instructions being followed, depending upon the result of an operation.

Connector A symbol used to transfer flow between different pages of a lengthy flowchart.

Constants Fixed values in a program.

Counter A variable used to count something, usually initialized to zero and then incremented.

Data type The kind of data that a variable may hold in a programming language is called the *data type*.

Debugging A process of finding and removing the bugs from a computer program.

Definite Loops The simplest kind of loop is called a definite loop. This is a loop that will execute a definite number of times.

Delimiter A character or string used to indicate where a string should be split.

Dict A keyword used in Python programming.

Dictionary An unordered collection of key:value pairs.

Element One of the values in a list (or other sequence), also called items.

Empty string A string with no characters and length 0, represented by two quotation marks.

Error A procedure that leads to an incorrect result.

Exceptions An exception is an error that occurs when a program is executed.

Expression Any valid combination of operators, literals and variables.

File A named location on the system storage which records data for later access.

Flag A flag is a Boolean variable used to record whether or not something has happened.

float Numbers with fractions or decimal points.

Flowchart A diagram representing an algorithm to show the steps of the given problem.

Folder Path Specifies the file folder location.

Function A named sequence of statements.

Global scope A global scope refers to the objects available through the code execution since their inception.

Identifiers Names given to program elements, such as variables, functions, and arrays.

IDLE An Integrated Development Environment for Python. IDLE is a basic editor and interpreter environment.

Immutable A compound data type whose elements cannot be changed by assigning new values to them.

Immutable variable An object with a fixed value. Immutable objects include numbers, strings and tuples. Such an object cannot be altered.

Import A way to use modules in Python code.

in A keyword through which a tuple is searched.

In Membership Operator Returns true if a character exists in the given string.

Incrementation A process wherein numerical value added to the variable each time one goes round the loop.

Index An integer value used to select an item in a sequence.

Infinite loop A loop that never ends.

int Basic integer data type.

Interpreter An interpreter is a program that translates one statement of a high-level language program in to machine codes and executes it and then translates and executes the next statement of the program and so forth.

items() Returns a list of tuples (key,value) representing the key-value pairs.

Iteration A process of executing a statement or a set of statements repeatedly.

key-value pair Representation of mapping from a key to a value.

keys() Returns a list of the keys.

List A compound data type.

List Traversing The sequential accessing of each element in a list.

Local scope A local scope refers to the local objects available in the current function.

Logical operators Symbols used to show a logical relationship between two data items.

Loop A sequence of instructions that is executed repeatedly until a terminal condition occurs.

Looping A process of repeating a series of steps a certain number of times.

Mapping A collection that allows us to look up information associated with arbitrary keys.

MFC Microsoft Foundation Class(es).

Module A file containing Python definitions, i.e., functions and statements.

Modulus operator(%) The % operator finds the modulus of its first operand relative to the second.

Mutable Type A data type in which the elements can be modified. All mutable types are compound types. Lists are mutable data types; strings are not.

Mutable variable A *mutable variable* is one whose value may change in place.

Namespace A namespace is a naming system used to make sure that names are unique to avoid naming conflicts.

Nested List A list that is an element of another list.

Nested Loop A loop that contains another loop inside its body.

NumPy An open source module of Python which provides fast mathematical computation on arrays and matrices.

Object A thing to which a variable can refer.

Operand An entity on which an operator acts.

Output Result produced by the computer.

Pseudocode A program analysis tool that is used for planning program logic. It is an imitation of actual computer instructions written in ordinary English language.

Python A high-level, interpreted, interactive and object oriented-scripting language.

Python packages Python packages are namespaces containing multiple modules.

raise Raise statement allows the programmer to force a specified exception to occur.

Regular expression This refers to a pattern that can match a piece of text.

Relational operators It compares the values of its operands.

Repetition Creates new string by concatenating multiple copies of the same string.

Scope The scope of a variable determines the portion of the program where you can access a particular identifier.

seek() Sets the file's current position.

Sequences A sequence is a data structure in which the elements are numbered (starting with zero). Examples of sequence types are lists, strings, and tuples.

Slice A part of a string specified by a range of indices.

Statement A unit of code.

String A string is an ordered sequence of characters.

Substring A part or a subset of another string.

tell() A method used to print the byte number at which the file pointer exists.

Traceback A list of the functions that are executing, printed when an exception occurs.

Traversal A process of iterating through a sequence of the given string.

try and catch Preventing an exception from terminating a program using the try and except statements.

Tuple A sequence of immutable Python objects.

Tuple Assignment An assignment with a sequence on the right side and a tuple of variables on the left. The right side is evaluated, and then its elements are assigned to the variables on the left.

Unicode Strings Unicode strings give us a consistent way to process character data from a variety of character encodings.

values() Returns a list of the values.

Variable A variable is a programming construct that uses a certain part of memory to represent a specific item of data that we wish to keep track of in a program.

while Loop It evaluates a test expression before allowing entry into the loop.

write() A method writes any string to an open file.

writelines() A method that writes a sequence of the strings to a file.

Solved Sample Paper–1

Total Time : 3 Hours

Total Marks 100
(Part One - 40 Part Two - 60)

PART – ONE

1. Multiple Choice Questions

1.1 The ________ provides pictorial representation of given problem.
a. Algorithm b. Flowchart
c. Pseudocode d. All of these

1.2 A sequence of instructions, in a computer language, to get the desired result is known as:
a. An algorithm b. A decision table
c. A program d. None of the above

1.3 Which type of errors are flagged by compilers?
a. Logical errors b. Syntax errors
c. Both a and c d. None of these

1.4 An algorithm is best described as:
a. A computer language
b. A step by step procedure for solving a problem
c. A branch of mathematics
d. None of the above

1.5 Bug means:
a. A logical error in a program.
b. A difficult syntax error in a program.
c. Both a and b
d. None of the above

1.6 No value can be skipped from the function call or you cannot change the order is called:
a. Positional arguments b. Required arguments
c. Mandatory argument d. All of the above

1.7 Write the output for the following Python code:
>>> str = "PYTHON"
>>> print(str[1.5])
a. TypeError: string indices must be integers
b. IndexError: string index out of range
c. TypeError:'str' object does not support item assignment
d. None of the above

1.8 Types of numeric literal(s) supported by Python:
a. integer
b. complex
c. float
d. All of the above

1.9 To declare a Tuple with one item:
a. Tuple_Name = (556,)
b. Tuple_Name = (556;)
c. Tuple_Name = (556:)
d. All of the above

1.10 What will be the output of the following:
```
tuple_a = '1', '2'
tuple_b = ('3', '4')
print (tuple_a + tuple_b)
```
a. (1, 2, 3, 4) b. ('1', '2', '3', '4')
c. ['1', '2', '3', '4'] d. None of the above.

2. State True or False:

2.1 Tuples are immutable like strings.

2.2 Iterating over the elements of a tuple is faster compared to iterating over a list.

2.3 This is an example of:
Dic = {'Name': 'Aman', 1: [1, 2, 3, 4]}
Dictionary with Integer Keys

2.4 In general, the order of items in a dictionary is Predictable.

2.5 NumPy is a Python package for scientific computing which can deal with large data sizes.

2.6 Default arguments are those that take a default value if no argument value is passed during the function call.

2.7 Slicing is a string operation for extracting a part of the string.

2.8 In Python, a regular expression is denoted as RE.

2.9 Parameters are specified after the function name, inside the square brackets.

2.10 Metacharacters are characters with a special meaning.

3. Match the following:

3.1	print (9//2)	a. +
3.2	The operator used for concatenating two strings	b. writelines()
3.3	Function takes a list of lines to be written to file	c. 4
3.4	Key value pair	d. pow()
3.5	The function used to find power of a number	e. Dictionary
3.6	The function that yields current position in the file	f. Stack
3.7	Data structure used in recursion	g. tell()
3.8	Statement used for error checking	h. Numpy
3.9	Array processing package	i. Assert
3.10	Immutable object	j. String

4. Fill in the blanks:

a. int	b. eval	c. Get
d. Input	e. Continue	f. *
g. { }	h. Module	i. Dictionary
j. [ ]	k. Convert	l. random
m. pass	n. Range	o. ( )

4.1 The __________ command is used to take input from the keyboard.

4.2 The __________function is used to convert a string value to int.

4.3 The function used to evaluate the value of a string is ________.

4.4 The ____________ function takes the parameter filename and the mode during file processing.

4.5 List structure in Python where elements are stored in __________ parenthesis.

4.6 The __________ statement lets the program go through the piece of code without performing any action.

4.7 _________ operator repeats a list for the given number of items.

4.8 ________ is a set of functions you want to include in your application.

4.9 The structure having keys and values is called ___________.

4.10 The ________ function generates a sequence of numbers from 1 to n.

PART – TWO

(Answer any four questions)

5. a. Write a program to print all Armstrong numbers in a given range. Note: An Armstrong number is a number whose sum of cubes of digits is equal to the number itself.
   b. Accept the name of the labourer and no. of hours worked. Calculate and display the wages.

6. Explain the following with example:
   a. tell()
   b. String in Python
   c. Slicing

7. a. Write a program to find product of two numbers using repetitive addition For example:
   Multiplying first number (10), second number (4) times
   Multiplication is = 10 + 10 + 10 + 10 = 40
   b. Write a program to print if the year is a leap year or not.

8. a. Write a program to count the number of Digits in entered Number.
   b. Write a program that accepts a string and count number of digits and letters.

9. a. Write a NumPy program to find the number of rows and columns of the following matrix.
   b. Take two NumPy arrays having two dimensions. Concatenate the arrays on axis 1.

Answers to Objective Type Questions

1.	1.1	b	1.2	c	1.3	b	1.4	b	1.5	c
	1.6	d	1.7	a	1.8	d	1.9	a	1.10	b
2.	2.1	T	2.2	T	2.3	F	2.4	F	2.5	T
	2.6	T	2.7	T	2.8	T	2.9	F	2.10	T
3.	3.1	c	3.2	a	3.3	b	3.4	e	3.5	d
	3.6	g	3.7	f	3.8	i	3.9	h	3.10	j
4.	4.1	d	4.2	a	4.3	b	4.4	c	4.5	j
	4.6	e	4.7	f	4.8	h	4.9	i	4.10	l

Answers to Descriptive Type Questions

5.a

```
# Program to check Armstrong numbers in certain interval
low_range = int(input("Enter lower range: "))
upper_range = int(input("Enter upper range: "))

for num in range(low_range, upper_range + 1):
    sum = 0

    temp = num
    while temp > 0:
         digit = temp % 10
         sum += digit ** 3
         temp //= 10
    if num == sum:
         print(num)

RUN
>>>
Enter lower range: 100
Enter upper range: 1000
153
370
371
407
>>>
```

5.b

```
#Accept name and no. of hours worked and calculate the wages
name = input("Enter name: ")
hours = int(input("How many hours did you work?:"))
payrate = int(input("How much is the payrate?:"))
wage = hours*payrate
print("Name: ", name, "\nWages are Rs.: ",wage)

RUN
>>>
Enter name: Aman
How many hours did you work?:6
How much is the payrate?:70
Name:  Aman
Wages are Rs.:  420
>>>
```

6.a tell() method returns an integer giving the current position of object in the file. The integer returned specifies the number of bytes from the beginning of the file till the current position of file object.

6.b A string in Python is a sequence of alpha-numeric characters. They are immutable objects. It means that they do not allow modification once they get assigned a value.

6.c. Slicing is a string operation for extracting a part of the string, or some part of a list.

7.a

```
# Program to find product of two numbers using repetitive addition
def prod(x,y):
    if(x<y):
        return prod(x,y)
    elif(y!=0):
        return(x+prod(x,y-1))
    else:
        return 0
x=int(input("Enter the first number: "))
y=int(input("Enter second number: "))
print("Product of two numbers is: ",prod(x,y))

RUN
>>>
Enter the first number: 10
Enter second number: 4
Product of two numbers is:  40
>>>
```

7.b

```
# Program to print if the year is leap or not
year=int(input("Enter 4-digit year : "))
if(year%4==0 and year%100!=0 or year%400==0):
    print(year, "is a leap year!")
else:
    print(year, "is not a leap year!")

RUN
>>>
Enter 4-digit year : 2016
2016 is a leap year!
>>>
Enter 4-digit year : 1900
1900 is not a leap year!
>>>
```

8.a

```
# Program to count the number of digits in entered Number
num=int(input("Enter number:"))
count=0
while(num>0):
    count=count+1
    num=num//10
print("The number of digits in the number are:",count)
```

(Contd...)

```
RUN
>>>
Enter number:573
The number of digits in the number are: 3
>>>
Enter number:8854
The number of digits in the number are: 4
>>>
```

b

```
# Program that accepts a string and count number of digits and letters.
s = input("Enter a string :")
d=l=0
for c in s:
    if c.isdigit():
        d=d+1
    elif c.isalpha():
            l=l+1
    else:
        pass
print("No. Of Letters :", l)
print("No. Of Digits", d)
```

9.a

```
import numpy as np
x= np.arange(10,22).reshape((3, 4))
print("Matrix:")
print(x)
print("Number of rows and columns in the matrix:")
print(x.shape)

RUN
>>>
Matrix:
[[10 11 12 13]
 [14 15 16 17]
 [18 19 20 21]]
Number of rows and columns in the matrix:
(3, 4)
>>>
```

b

```
import numpy as np
x = np.array([[2, 4, 3], [5, 9, 8]])
y = np.array([[7, 4, 4], [3, 8, 12]])
z = np.concatenate((x, y), 1)
print(z)

RUN
>>>
[[ 2  4  3  7  4  4]
 [ 5  9  8  3  8 12]]
>>>
```

Solved Sample Paper–2

Total Time : 3 Hours

Total Marks 100
(Part One - 40 Part Two - 60)

PART – ONE

1. Multiple Choice Questions

1.1 The errors that can be pointed out by the compiler are:

a. Syntax errors b. Semantic errors
c. Logical errors d. None of the above

1.2 A compiler is:

a. A machine-independent and OS-independent
b. Machine-dependent and OS-dependent
c. Machine-dependent and OS-independent
d. Machine-independent and OS-dependent

1.3 Strings are defined using quotes (", ', or """):

a. Single quote (')
b. Double quote (")
c. Triple quote (""")
d. All of the above

1.4 Examples of valid identifier names are:

a. i b. __my_name
c. Both (a) and (b) d. 67Kim

1.5 The expression, i=30*10+27; evaluates to:

a. 327 b. -327
c. 810 d. 0

1.6 The && and || operators:

a. Compare two numeric values b. Combine two numeric values
c. Compare two boolean values d. None of these

1.7 We can go back to the start of the loop by using:

a. break b. continue
c. pass d. None of the above

1.8 Indicate which of the following is true about Python operators:

a. Operators must have one or more operands
b. Operators are either unary or binary
c. Operators have some precedence
d. All of the above

1.9 Standard library module:

a. math module
b. random module
c. Both (a) and (b)
d. None of the above

1.10 The alternative name for argument is:

a. Actual parameter b. Formal parameter
c. Formal argument d. None of the above.

2. State True or False for the following:

2.1 The scope rule in Python are summarized as ELGB (enclosed, local, global, built-in).

2.2 Strings in Python are mutable.

2.3 Python allows you to assign a single value to multiple variables simultaneously.

2.4 Python is the interpreted language.

2.5 Python is a dynamic-typed language.

2.6 Tuples are mutable built-in datatypes of Python.

2.7 Python provides a break statement to exit from a loop.

2.8 The continue statement makes the loop to resume from the next iteration.

2.9 The pass statement convey to do nothing, and the remainder of the code executes as usual.

2.10 The len() determines the length of an input string.

3. Match the following:

3.1	Algorithm	a. Flowchart
3.2	Pictorial representation of an	b. A sequence of instructions

	algorithm	which when followed properly, solves a problem.
3.3	Mutable datatypes	c. Numbers
3.4	Immutable datatypes	d List
3.5	Regular expression module	e. Stop
3.6	The upper limit of the sequence	f. The first statement
3.7	The docstring	g. Jump statement
3.8	Function	h. re
3.9	Built-in function	i. Reusable entity
3.10	continue	j. dir()

4. Fill in the blanks:

a. Algorithm b. Program c. Flowchart
d. Terminal e. Connector f. Bugs
g. Debugging h. Slicing i. zeroth
j. dictionary k. tuple m. list

4.1 A set of instructions which describes the steps to be followed to carry out an activity is called ________ .

4.2 Algorithm if written in computers language, then such set of instructions is called a ________ .

4.3 ________ is a graphical representation of a program.

4.4 The ________ symbol is used to indicate the starting and stopping in the flowchart.

4.5 A ________ symbol is represented by a circle and a letter or digit placed within the circle.

4.6 Program errors are called ________ .

4.7 The process of removing bugs is known as ________ .

4.8 The range() function in Python starts from the _____ index.

4.9 _____ is a string operation for extracting a part of the string.

4.10 A ______ is a data structure known as an associative array.

PART – TWO
(Answer any four questions)

5. a. Write a program to print Fibonacci series upto n terms.
b. Write a program to input two numbers as input and compute the greatest common divisor.

6. Explain the following with example:
a. LEGB rule
b. Seek() function
c. Namespaces

7. a. Write a NumPy program to find the most frequent value in an array.
b. Write definition of a method/function AddOddEven(VALUES) to display sum of odd and even values separately from the list of VALUES. For example, If the VALUES contain :[15,26,37,10,22,13], the function should display Even Sum: 58 Odd Sum: 65.

8. a. Write a program to print numbers in descending order.
b. Write a Python function to calculate sum of all the numbers in a list.

9. a. Write a program to enter a number from the keyboard and then print the sum of the digits of the number. It also reverses the number.
b. Draw a flow chart to print the factorials of numbers from 1 to n where n is entered by user.

Answers to Objective Type Questions

1.	1.1	a	1.2	b	1.3	d	1.4	c	1.5	a
	1.6	c	1.7	b	1.8	d	1.9	c	1.10	a
2.	2.1	F	2.2	F	2.3	T	2.4	T	2.5	T
	2.6	F	2.7	T	2.8	T	2.9	T	2.10	T
3.	3.1	b	3.2	a	3.3	d	3.4	c	3.5	h
	3.6	e	3.7	f	3.8	i	3.9	j	3.10	g
4.	4.1	a	4.2	b	4.3	c	4.4	d	4.5	e
	4.6	f	4.7	g	4.8	i	4.9	h	4.10	j

Answers to Descriptive Type Questions

5.a

```
# Program to print  Fibonacci series upto n terms
number = int(input("Enter the range number: "))
First_value = 0
Second_value = 1
for i in range(0, number):
    if(i <= 1):
        Next = i
    else:
        Next = First_value + Second_value
        First_value = Second_value
        Second_value = Next
    print(Next)

RUN
>>>
Enter the range number: 5
0
1
1
2
3
>>>
```

5.b

```
#Program to input two numbers and compute the greatest common divisor
def gcd(x,y):
    if(y==0):
        return x
    else:
        return gcd(y,x%y)
x=int(input("Enter the first number:"))
y=int(input("Enter second number:"))
GCD_NO=gcd(x,y)
print("GCD Number is: ", GCD_NO)

RUN
>>>
Enter the first number:7
Enter second number:21
GCD Number is:  7
>>>
```

6.a LEGB stands for Local Enclosed Global Built-in. LEGB tells us the order in which Python accesses the variable in a program. First, Python will check if the variable is present in the local scope, if not then checks in enclosing scope. If the search in the enclosed scope is unsuccessful, too, Python moves on to the global namespace, and finally, it will search the built-in namespace

6.b The seek() method enables us to modify the file pointer position externally.

6.c A namespace is a naming system used to make sure that names are unique to avoid naming conflicts.

7.a

```
#  NumPy program to find the most frequent value in an array
import numpy as np
x = np.random.randint(0, 10, 20)
print("Original array:")
print(x)
print("Most frequent value in the array is:", np.bincount(x).argmax())

RUN
>>>
Original array:
[7 2 3 7 4 9 6 8 4 1 6 5 2 1 9 8 7 6 0 5]
Most frequent value in the array is: 6
>>>
```

7.b

```
def AddOddEven(VALUES):
    so=0
    se=0
    for i in VALUES:
        if i%2==0:
            se=se+i
        else:
            so=so+i
    print("Even Sum:",se)
    print("Odd Sum:",so)
VALUES=[15,26,37,10,22,13]
AddOddEven(VALUES)

RUN
>>>
Even Sum: 58
Odd Sum: 65
>>>
```

8. a

```
# Program to print numbers in descending order
num1 = int(input("Enter first number: "))
num2 = int(input("Enter second number: "))
num3 = int(input("Enter third number: "))
if num1 > num2 and num1 > num3:
    if num2 > num3:
        x, y, z = num1, num2, num3
    else:
        x, y, z = num1, num3, num2
elif num2 > num1 and num2 > num3:
    if num1 > num3:
        x, y, z = num2, num1, num3
    else:
        x, y, z = num2, num3, num1
```

(Contd...)

```
else:
    if num1>num2:
        x, y, z = num3, num1, num2
    else:
        x, y, z = num3, num2, num1
print("Numbers in descending order are: ", x,y,z)

RUN
>>>
Enter first number: 27
Enter second number: 25
Enter third number: 45
Numbers in descending order are:  45 27 25
>>>
```

b

```
# A Python function to calculate sum of all the numbers in a list
def sum(num):
    total = 0
    for x in num:
        total += x
    return total
print(sum((6, 4, 2, 0, 5)))

RUN
>>>
17
>>>
```

9. a

```
#Program to print reverse and sum of digits
sum = 0
rev = 0
number=int(input("Enter a number: "))
n = number
while (number):
    digit = number % 10
    sum += digit
    rev = rev * 10 + digit
    number //= 10
print("Reverse of number is : ",rev)
print ("Sum of digits of the number is : ",sum)

RUN
>>>
Enter a number: 759
Reverse of number is :  957
Sum of digits of the number is :  21
>>>
```

Ans b

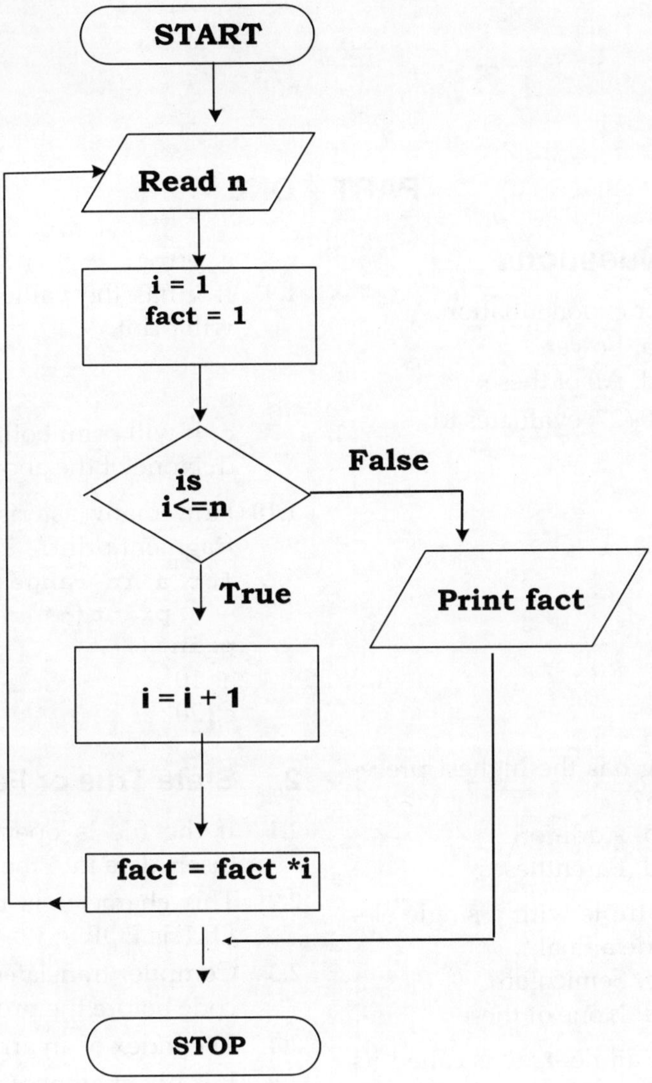

Figure 1 Flowchart to print factorial of a number

Sample Paper–1

Total Time : 3 Hours

Total Marks 100
(Part One - 40 Part Two - 60)

PART – ONE

1. Multiple Choice Questions

1.1 Python uses _______ for exponentiation.
a. **   b. Power
c. ^   d. All of these

1.2 The expression, i=30*10+27; evaluates to:
a. 327
b. -327
c. 810
d. 0

1.3 Operators can be:
a. Unary
b. Binary
c. Ternary
d. All of these

1.4 Which of the following has the highest precedence in the expression?
a. Exponential   b. Addition
c. Multiplication   d. Parentheses

1.5 If we need to create a tuple with a single element, we need to include a final:
a. Comma   b. Semicolon
c. Full stop   d. None of these

1.6 The number of axes in an ndarray is called its ______.
a. rank   b. dtype
c. shape   d. None of these

1.7 Which of the following is not a valid namespace?
a. Global namespace   b. Private namespace
c. Built-in namespace   d. Local namespace

1.8 What is the output of the following?

```
i = 1
while True:
    if i%007 == 0:
        break
    print(i, end=" ")
    i += 1
```

a. 1 2 3 4 5 6   b. 1 2 3 4 5 6 7
c. error   d. None of the above

1.9 If x has the value 10, the statement print('x') will print:
a. 10
b. x
c. It will print both
d. None of the above

1.10 How many asterisks does the following code fragment print?

```
for a in range(-10, 10, 5):
    print('*', end='')
print()
```

a. 10   b. 4
c. 20   d. None of the above.

2. State True or False for the following:

2.1 If the file is open in read mode, we cannot insert data into the file.

2.2 This character is used to indicate end of the FILE is EOF.

2.3 Compiler translates the source code into object code before the program can be executed.

2.4 The index of an array starts from 1.

2.5 It is not at all necessary for a function to return any value.

2.6 The continue statement is applicable for both the "while" and "for" loops.

2.7 NumPy arrays are more compact than lists.

2.8 An octal value can contain digits 0 to 8.

2.9 To indicate hexadecimal literals, you will use the prefix '0X' or '0x'.

2.10 Both the logical *and* & *or* operators have lower precedence than the relational and arithmetic operators.

3. Match the following:

3.1	raw string	a. Denotes value
3.2	Escape sequence	b. \"
3.3	L-value	c. r

3.4	R-value	d Storage area
3.5	None	e. membership operator
3.6	in	f. A special data type
3.7	/	g. Modulus
3.8	//	h. Division
3.9	%	I. Integer division
3.10	Logical operators	j. Boolean operators

4. Fill in the blanks:

a. logical operators	b. faster	c. process
d. not	e. slower	f. for
g. and	h. bin()	i. assert
j. pre-test	k. pass	l. never
m. while	n. slower	o. continue

4.1 Diamond shape is used to show ____ in a flowchart.

4.2 ________ are used when we want to test more than one condition and make a decision.

4.3 Reading and writing items is ______ with NumPy.

4.4 The logical _____ operator has a higher precedence than the others.

4.5 The ______ method converts and returns the binary equivalent string of a given integer.

4.6 The ______ loop is used for fixed iterations.

4.7 A while loop is ______ loop.

4.8 The _______ statement is simply ignored by the Python interpreter and can be seen as a null statement.

4.9 The ______ statement can optionally include an error message string, which gets displayed along with the AssertionError.

4.10 In an infinite loop, the while condition ______ becomes false.

PART – TWO
(Answer any four questions)

5. a. Write down one similarity and on dissimilarity between break and continue statements.

b. What is the difference between opening a file in w+ mode and a+ mode?

6. Explain the difference between

a. Text file and Binary file

b. local variable vs global variable

7. a. Write a program that asks filename from the user and create it. Using program insert text data into the file and display the contents of the file on screen.

b. Write a program to print only first 12 characters including blank space from file test.txt.

8. a. What is Command Line Argument? Give example.

b. Write a program which asks the user to enter the name and age of persons in his group. The number of persons is not known to the user in the beginning of the program. The user keeps on entering the data till the user enters the age as zero. The program finally prints the average age.

9. a. Write a program to calculate nCr. Define and use fact() function to calculate factorial of a number. nCr= n!/((r!) X (n-r)!)

b. Write a program which asks the user a number between 1 and 7 and prints the corresponding day of the week. (1: Sunday, 2: Monday,..).

Sample Paper–2

Total Time : 3 Hours

Total Marks 100
(Part One - 40 Part Two - 60)

PART – ONE

1. Multiple Choice Questions

1.1 The operator & is used for
a. Bitwise AND b. Logical AND
c. Bitwise OR d.

1.2 The result of a Relational operation is always
a. Either True or False
b. Is less than or is more than
c. Is equal or less or more
d. All of the above

1.3 What is the output of the following program?

```
i = 0
 while i< 3:
 print(i)
 i++
 print(i+1)
```

a. 0 2 1 3 2 4
b. 0 1 2 3 4 5
c. Infinite loop
d. 0 1 2 3

1.4 What will be the output of the following code?
Print type(type(int))
a. type 'int' b. error
c. type 'type' d. 0

1.5 np.eye() is used for creating:
a. Identity Matrix b. Upper triangle Matrix
c. Lower Triangle Matrix d. None of the above

1.6 Which of the following functions need a filename?
a. open() b. read()
c. close() d. None of these

1.7 What is the output of the code print (9//2)?
a. 4.5 b. 4
c. 4.0 d. Error

1.8 An expression contains relational, assignment and arithmetic operators. There are no parentheses used. They will be evaluated in which of the following order:
a. Assignment Relational Arithmetic
b. Arithmetic Relational Assignment
c. Relational Arithmetic Assignment
d. Assignment Arithmetic Relational

1.9 Debugging is used to:
a. Find errors from the program
b. Check the functionality of the program
c. Black box testing
d. All of the above

1.10 The function which reads one line from standards input and returns it as a string (removing the trailing newline):
a. raw_input b. eval
c. input d. accept

2. State True or False for the following:

2.1 The associativity of operator ! is from left to right.

2.2 A for loop can never be infinite.

2.3 Recursion cannot call a function itself.

2.4 An array is a group of related data item that share a common memory location in RAM.

2.5 Numpy is a tool for data visualization.

2.6 The break statement is used for exiting from the loop to the statement following the close of the loop.

2.7 if list1=[10,20,30], then operation list1*2 returns [20,40,60].

2.8 You cannot obtain a value in a dictionary using a key for a single element.

2.9 It is mandatory to have __main__ function in python.

2.10 Python allows you to assign a single value to multiple variables simultaneously.

3. Match the following:

3.1	The purpose of library function fflush() is	a. Case sensitive

3.2	A function call itself is called	b. To clear the specified buffer
3.3	Symbol used as new line character	c. Recursion
3.4	The bitwise AND operator is used for	d \n
3.5	Removing errors	e. Shifting bits
3.6	input()	f. Indentation
3.7	Blocks	g. Debugging
3.8	Python	h. Returns a string type of value
3.9	Keyword	I. #
3.10	Comment	j. Reserved word

4. Fill in the blanks:

a. call-by -value	b. Assembly language	c. Typecasting
d. Pickle	e. Reference	f. Literals
g. dictionaries	h. mapping	i. **
j. Object code	k. ^	l. List

4.1 ________ module is used in serialization of data.

4.2 In ________ the argument whether an expression or a value gets bound to the respective variable in the function.

4.3 When we pass an argument by ______ then it is available as an implicit reference to the function, rather than a simple copy.

4.4 The contents of ________ can be modified.

4.5 A collection that allows us to look up information associated with arbitrary keys is called a ________.

4.6 A program written in mnemonics is called ________ program.

4.7 ________ can be defined as a data which is given in a variable or constant.

4.8 Converting one data type to another data type is called __________.

4.9 ________ is a program that the computer can directly execute.

4.10 ________ performs exponential (power) calculation on operators.

PART – TWO
(Answer any four questions)

5. a. Write an algorithm to test whether a given number is prime or not.

b. What is the difference between opening a file in w+ mode and a+ mode?

c. Give the main advantage of storing data as a file. Describe various ways in which data files can be categorized in 'Python'.

6. a. Write a program to sort the numbers 1, 6, -1, 2, 8, 5, 7, 6, 5, 4 in ascending order. Include appropriate documentation.

b. What do understand by loading and linking of a program?

c. What is top-down approach to problem solving? What are its advantages?

7. a. A lucas sequence is given below:
1,3,4,7,11,18,29
The third number is sum of previous two numbers. Write a program to print first 10 numbers of lucas sequence.

b. Write program to print the value of numbers in words when number entered is in the range of 0 to 999.

8. a. Write a program to copy a file into another file.

b. Write a program to write a line of string a text file.

9. a. Write a program which asks for a integer from the user. It reverses the integer and prints "same" if after reversal the number is same as old number otherwise it prints "not same".

b. Write a program to print the following structure.

```
*
**
***
****
*****
******
```

The number of rows should be input from the user.

Specimen Answersheet for Writing Answers to Objective Questions

PAPER CODE ☐ DATE ☐

1. Multiple choice

(shade the box corresponding to your answer)

	a	b	c	d
1.1.	☐	☐	☐	☐
1.2.	☐	☐	☐	☐
1.3.	☐	☐	☐	☐
1.4.	☐	☐	☐	☐
1.5.	☐	☐	☐	☐
1.6.	☐	☐	☐	☐
1.7.	☐	☐	☐	☐
1.8.	☐	☐	☐	☐
1.9.	☐	☐	☐	☐
1.10.	☐	☐	☐	☐

2. Selecting TRUE or FALSE statements

(shade the box corresponding to your answer)

	True	False
2.1.	☐	☐
2.2.	☐	☐
2.3.	☐	☐
2.4.	☐	☐
2.5.	☐	☐
2.6.	☐	☐
2.7.	☐	☐
2.8.	☐	☐
2.9.	☐	☐
2.10.	☐	☐

3. Matching words/phrases in two columns

(write the alphabet corresponding to your answer in the box)

3.1.	☐
3.2.	☐
3.3.	☐
3.4.	☐
3.5.	☐
3.6.	☐
3.7.	☐
3.8.	☐
3.9.	☐
3.10.	☐

4. Fill in the blanks

(write the alphabet corresponding to your answer)

4.1.	☐
4.2.	☐
4.3.	☐
4.4.	☐
4.5.	☐
4.6.	☐
4.7.	☐
4.8.	☐
4.9.	☐
4.10.	☐

MCQ & Practical Assignment – 1

Multiple Choice Questions

1. Which function returns the strings?
   a. readline()   b. read()
   c. Both of the above   d. None of the above
2. What will be the output of the following pseudocode, where ^ represent XOR operation?
   Integer a,b,c
   Set b=4, a=3
   c=a^b
   Print c
   a. 4   b. 3   c. 5   d. 7
3. Which of the following is not a correct mode to open a file?
   a. ab   b. rw   c. a+   d. r+
4. def fun(a,b):
   for x in range(a,b+1):
   if x%3==0:
   print(x,end=" ")
   fun(100,120)
   a. 7   b. 8   c. 6   d. 9
5. What is the output of the following code?
   a={1:"A", 2:"B", 3:"C"}
   b= {4:"D", 5:"e"}
   a.update(b)
   print(b)
   a. {1:'A', 2:'B', 3:'C}
   b. {1:'A', 2:'B', 3:'C, 4: 'D', 5: 'E'}
   c. Error
   d. {4: 'D', 5:'E'}
6. Which of the following language is understood by computer?
   a. Machine language   b. Assembly Language
   c. High-level Language d. None of the above
7. What will be the output after the following statements?
   a=0
   b=3
   while a+b < 8:
   a += 1
   print(a, end="");
   a. 0 1 2 3 4   b. 1 2 3 4 5 6
   c. 1 2 3 4 5   d. None of these
8. What is the output of the following code?
   def disp(*arg):
   for i in arg:
   print(i)
   disp(name="Rajat", age="20")
   a. TypeError   b. Rajat 20
   c. Name age   d. None of these
9. A computer program that manages and controls a computer's activity:
   a. Interpreter
   b. Modem
   c. Compiler
   d. Operating System
10. How can we create an empty list in Pythom?
    a. list=()   b. list.null
    c. null.list   d. list=[]
11. What will be the output after the following statements?
    x=2
    if x<5:
    print(x)
    else:
    pass
    a. 2 3 4   b. 1 2 3 4
    c. 2   d. None of the above
12. A function used for writing data in the binary format:
    a. write   b. output
    c. send   d. dump
13. Which part of the memory does the system store the parameter and local variables of function call?
    a. heap
    b. stack
    c. Uninitialized data segment
    d. None of the above
14. What will be the output of the following?
    def iq(a,b):
    if(a==0):
    return b;

```
else:
    return iq(a-1, a+b);
print(iq(3,6))
```

a. 9 b. 10 c. 11 d. 12

15. What is the output of below program?

```
def maximum(x,y):
    if x>y:
        return x
    elif x==y:
        return 'The numbers are equal'
    else:
        return y
print(maximum(2,3))
```

a. 2
b. 3
c. The numbers are equal
d. None of the options

16. Which statement is correct to import all modules from the package?
a. from package import all
b. from package import *
c. from package include all
d. from package include *

17. What will be the output of the following?

```
import numpy as np
a = np.array([2,3,4,5])
b = np.arange(4)
print(a+b)
```

a. [2 3 4 5] b. [3 4 5 6]
c. [1 2 3 4] d. [2 4 6 8]

18. What will be the output of the following?

```
import numpy as np
print(np.maximum([2,3,4], [1,5,2]))
```

a. [1 5 2] b. [1 5 4]
c. [2 3 4] d. [2 5 4]

19. What is the output of the following?

```
print (int())
```

a. Any random number
b. 1
c. 0
d. Error

20. In which of the following data type, duplicate items are not allowed?
a. list b. dictionary
c. set d. None of the above

21. What will be the output of the following code?
a. type`int' b. type `type'
c. Error d. 0

22. What will be the output of the following code?

```
L =[`a', `b', `c', `d']
print "".join(L)
```

a. Error b. None
c. abcd d. [`a', `b', `c', `d']

23. The following symbol represents

a. Decision b. Initialization
c. Input/Output d. Start/End

24. Suppose list 1 is [3,4,5,20,5,25,1,3] what is list 1 after list 1.pop(1)?
a. [3, 4, 5, 20,5,25,1,3]
b. [1,3,3,4,5,5,20,25]
c. [3,5,20,5,25,1,3]
d. [1,3,4,5,20,5,25]

25. Which of the following is the use of id() function in python?
a. Id returns the identity of the object
b. Every object doesn't have unique id
c. All of the mentioned
d. None of the mentioned

26. What is called when a function is defined inside a class?
a. Module b. class
c. Another Function d. Method

27. What is the output of the following code?

```
print 9//2
```

a. 4.5 b. 4.0 c. 4 d. Error

28. Which of the following data types is not supported in python?
a. Numbers b. String
c. list d. Slice

29. Who developed Python Programming Language?
a. Wick van Rossum b. Rasmus Lerdorf
c. Guido van Rossum d. Niene Stom

30. Which type of Programming does Python support?
a. object-oriented programming
b. structured programming
c. functional programming
d. all of the mentioned

31. Which of the following is the correct extension of the Python file?
    a. .python b. .pl c. .py d. .p
32. All keywords in Python are in ________
    a. Capitalized b. lower case
    c. UPPER CASE
    d. None of the mentioned
33. What will be the value of the following Python expression?
    4 + 3 % 5
    a. 7 b. 2 c. 4 d. 1
34. Which of the following is used to define a block of code in Python language?
    a. Indentation b. Key
    c. Brackets d. All of the mentioned
35. Which keyword is used for function in Python language?
    a. Function b. Def
    c. Fun d. Define
36. Which of the following character is used to give single-line comments in Python?
    a. // b. # c. ! d. /*
37. What will be the output of the following Python code?

```
i = 1
while True:
    if i%3 == 0:
        break
    print(i)

    i + = 1
```

    a. 1 2 3 b. error
    c. 1 2 d. none of the mentioned
38. What is the order of precedence in python?
    a. Exponential, Parentheses, Multiplication, Division, Addition, Subtraction
    b. Exponential, Parentheses, Division, Multiplication, Addition, Subtraction
    c. Parentheses, Exponential, Multiplication, Division, Subtraction, Addition
    d. Parentheses, Exponential, Multiplication, Division, Addition, Subtraction
39. What will be the output of the following Python code snippet if x=1?
    x<<2
    a. 4 b. 2 c. 1 d. 8
40. What are the values of the following Python expressions?
    2**(3**2)
    (2**3)**2
    2**3**2
    a. 512, 64, 512 b. 512, 512, 512
    c. 64, 512, 64 d. 64, 64, 64
41. Which of the following is the truncation division operator in Python?
    a. | b. // c. / d. %
42. To determine in which order Python should access namespaces, you can use the:
    a. LEGB rule b. LGBE rule
    c. LBGE rule d. LGEB rule
43. A variable created or defined within a function body is classified as:
    a. local b. global
    c. built-in d. instance
44. Which of the following arguments works with implicit values that are used if no value is provided?
    a. keyword b. required
    c. variable-length d. default
45. Which values are used by the functions to communicate information back to the caller?
    a. local b. global
    c. return d. random
46. Which is the most appropriate definition for recursion?
    a. A function that calls itself
    b. A function execution instance that calls another execution instance of the same function
    c. A class method that calls another class method
    d. An in-built method that is automatically called
47. What happens if the base condition isn't defined in recursive programs?
    a. Program gets into an infinite loop
    b. Program runs once
    c. Program runs n number of times, where n is the argument given to the function
    d. An exception is thrown
48. What is the name given to that area of memory, where the system stores the parameters and local variables of a function call?
    a. a heap b. storage area
    c. a stack d. an array

49. Which of the following function headers is correct?
    a. def f(a = 1, b): b. def f(a = 1, b, c = 2):
    c. def f(a = 1, b = 1, c = 2):
    d. def f(a = 1, b = 1, c = 2, d):
50. Which of the following statements is not true for parameter passing to functions?
    a. You can pass positional arguments in any order.
    b. You can pass keyword arguments in any order.
    c. You can call a function with positional and keyword arguments.
    d. Positional arguments must be before keyword arguments in a function call.
51. What is a variable defined outside all the functions referred to as?
    a. A static variable b. A global variable
    c. A local variable d. An automatic variable
52. Which one of the following is the correct statement for creating a dictionary for assigning a day number to weekdays using short names?
    a. d ={1:Mon,2:Tue,3:Wed,4:Thur}
    b. d ={1:'Mon',2:'Tue',3:'Wed',4:'Thur'}
    c. d ={1;'Mon',2;'Tue',3;'Wed',4;'Thur'}
    d. d ={1-'Mon',2-'Tue',3-'Wed',4-'Thur'}
53. What is returned by math.ceil(3.4)?
    a. 3 b. 4 c. 4.0 d. 3.0
54. What is the value returned by math.floor(3.4)?
    a. 3 b. 4 c. 4.0 d. 3.0
55. Which one of the following has the same precedence level?
    a. Addition and Subtraction
    b. Multiplication, Division and Addition
    c. Multiplication, Division, Addition and Subtraction
    d. Addition and Multiplication
56. Which of these is the keyword?
    a. in b. is
    c. assert d. All of the above
57. Which python function is used to return length?
    a. len() b. length()
    c. obj.len d. none of the mention
58. The Slice operation is performed on a list using
    a. slice b. : (colon) c. .(dot) d. - (hyphen)
59. The python tuple is _____ in nature.
    a. Unchangeable b. Immutable
    c. Both A & B d. Mutable
60. Which of the following items are present in the function header?
    a. function name b. parameter list
    c. return value d. Both A and B
61. What is called when a function is defined inside a class?
    a. class b. function
    c. method d. module
62. What is a recursive function?
    a. A function that calls another function.
    b. A function which calls itself.
    c. Both A and B
    d. None of the above
63. In which part of memory does the system store the parameter and local variables of a function call?
    a. heap b. stack
    c. Uninitialized data segment
    d. None of the above
64. Which one of the following is the correct way of calling a function?
    a. function_name()
    b. call function_name()
    c. ret function_name()
    d. function function_name()
65. Which of the following functions is a built-in function in python?
    a. array() b. sqrt()
    c. factorial() d. print()
66. To use a module in another module, you must import it using an ________ statement
    a. import b. include
    c. both A and B d. none of the above
67. Which function is called an anonymous function?
    a. Lambda b. map c. filter d. reduce
68. Which of these is the definition for packages in Python?
    a. A set of main modules
    b. A folder of python modules
    c. A number of files containing Python definitions and statements
    d. A set of programs making use of Python modules
69. What will be the output of the following Python code?

```
x = 'abcd'
for i in x:
```

print(i.upper())

a. a B C D b. a b c d

c. error d. A B C D

70. To add a new element to a list we use which Python command?

a. list1.addEnd(5) b. list1.addLast(5)

c. list1.append(5) d. list1.add(5)

71. Which one of the following is the use of function in python?

a. Functions don't provide better modularity for your application

b. you can't also create your own functions

c. Functions are reusable pieces of programs

d. All of the mentioned

72. To declare a Tuple with one item:

a. Tuple_Name = (556,)

b. Tuple_Name = (556;)

c. Tuple_Name = (556:)

d. All of the above

73. Write the output for the following Python code:

>>> str = "PYTHON"

>>> print(str[1.5])

a. TypeError: string indices must be integers

b. IndexError: string index out of range

c. TypeError:'str' object does not support item assignment

d. None of the above

74. The _______ provides pictorial representation of given problem.

a. Algorithm b. Flowchart

c. Pseudocode d. All of these

75. A sequence of instructions, in a computer language, to get the desired result is known as:

a. An algorithm b. A decision table

c. A program d. None of the above

76. Which type of errors are flagged by compilers?

a. Logical errors b. Syntax errors

c. Both a and c d. None of these

77. An algorithm is best described as:

a. A computer language

b. A step by step procedure for solving a problem

c. A branch of mathematics

d. None of the above

78. Bug means:

a. A logical error in a program.

b. A difficult syntax error in a program.

c. Both a and b

d. None of the above

79. No value can be skipped from the function call or you cannot change the order is called:

a. Positional argument

b. Required arguments

c. Mandatory argument

d. All of the above

80. Types of numeric literal(s) supported by Python:

a. integer b. complex

c. float d. All of the above

81. What is the maximum possible length of an identifier in Python?

a. 79 characters b. 31 characters

c. 63 characters d. none of the mentioned

82. What will be the output of the following Python program?

```
i = 0
while i < 5:
    print(i)
    i += 1
    if i == 3:
        break
else:
    print(0)
```

a. error b. 0 1 2 0

c. 0 1 2 d. none of the mentioned

83. What are the two main types of functions in Python?

a. System function

b. Custom function

c. Built-in function & User defined function]

d. User function

84. What will be the output of the following Python program?

```
def addItem(listParam):
    listParam += [1]
mylist = [1, 2, 3, 4, 5]
addItem(mylist)
print(len(mylist))
```

a. 5 b. 6 c. 2 d. 1

85. What will be the output of the following Python code snippet?

```
z=set('abc$de')
```

'A' in z

a. Error b. True

c. False d. No output

86. What will be the output of the following Python expression?

round(4.276)

a. 4 b. 4.6 c. 5 d. 4.5

87. Which of the following is a feature of Python DocString?

a. In Python all functions should have a docstring

b. Docstrings can be accessed by the __doc__ attribute on objects

c. It provides a convenient way of associating documentation with Python modules, functions, classes, and methods

d. All of the mentioned

88. What will be the output of the following code snippet?

```
print(2**3 + (5 + 6)**(1 + 1))
```

a. 129

b. 8

c. 121

d. None of the above.

89. What will be the datatype of the var in the below code snippet?

```
var = 10
print(type(var))
var = "Hello"
print(type(var))
```

a. str and int b. int and int

c. str and str d. int and str

90. What will be the output of the following code snippet?

```
a = [1, 2, 3]
a = tuple(a)
a[0] = 2
print(a)
```

a. [2, 2, 3] b. (2, 2, 3)

c. (1, 2, 3) d. Error.

91. What will be the output of the following code snippet?

```
print(type(5 / 2))
print(type(5 // 2))
```

a. float and int b. int and float

c. float and float d. int and int

92. What will be the output of the following code snippet?

```
a = [1, 2, 3, 4, 5]
sum = 0
for ele in a:
    sum += ele
print(sum)
```

a. 15 b. 0

c. 20 d. None of these

93. What will be the output of the following code snippet?

```
count = 0
while(True):
    if count % 3 == 0:
        print(count, end = " ")
    if(count > 15):
        break;
    count += 1
```

a. 0 1 2 ..... 15 b. Infinite Loop

c. 0 3 6 9 12 15 d. 0 3 6 9 12

94. Which of the following types of loops are not supported in Python?

a. for b. while

c. do-while d. None of the above

95. Which of the following is the proper syntax to check if a particular element is present in a list?

a. if ele in list b. if not ele not in list

c. Both A and B d. None of the above

96. What will be the output of the following code snippet?

```
def check(a):
    print("Even" if a % 2 == 0 else "Odd")
check(12)
```

a. Even b. Odd c. Error d. None

97. What will be the output of the following code snippet?

```
example = ["Sunday", "Monday", "Tuesday", "Wednesday"];
print(example[-3:-1])
```

a. ['Monday', 'Tuesday']

b. ['Sunday', 'Monday']

c. ['Tuesday', 'Wednesday']

d. ['Wednesday', 'Monday']

98. What will be the output of the following code snippet?

```
a = [1, 2]
```

print(a * 3)

a. Error b. [1, 2]

c. [1, 2, 1, 2] d. [1, 2, 1, 2, 1, 2]

99. What will be the output of the following code snippet?

```
dict1 = {'first' : 'sunday', 'second' : 'monday'}
dict2 = {1: 3, 2: 4}
dict1.update(dict2)
print(dict1)
```

a. {'first': 'sunday', 'second': 'monday', 1: 3, 2: 4}

b. {'first': 'sunday', 'second': 'monday'}

c. {1: 3, 2: 4}

d. None of the above.

100. What will be the output of the following code snippet?

```
s = {1, 2, 3, 3, 2, 4, 5, 5}
print(s)
```

a. {1, 2, 3, 3, 2, 4, 5, 5} b. {1, 2, 3, 4, 5}

c. None d. {1, 5}

Answers to Multiple Choice Questions

1.	c	2.	d	3.	a	4.	a	5.	b
6.	a	7.	c	8.	a	9.	d	10.	d
11.	c	12.	d	13.	b	14.	d	15.	b
16.	b	17.	d	18.	d	19.	c	20.	d
21.	c	22.	a	23.	c	24.	c	25.	a
26.	d	27.	d	28.	d	29.	c	30.	d
31.	c	32.	d	33.	a	34.	a	35.	b
36.	b	37.	b	38.	d	39.	a	40.	a
41.	b	42.	a	43.	a	44.	d	45.	c
46.	b	47.	a	48.	c	49.	c	50.	a
51.	b	52.	b	53.	b	54.	a	55.	a
56.	d	57.	a	58.	b	59.	c	60.	d
61.	c	62.	b	63.	b	64.	a	65.	d
66.	a	67.	a	68.	b	69.	d	70.	c
71.	c	72.	a	73.	a	74.	b	75.	c
76.	b	77.	b	78.	c	79.	d	80.	d
81.	d	82.	c	83.	c	84.	b	85.	c
86.	a	87.	d	88.	a	89.	d	90.	d
91.	a	92.	a	93.	c	94.	c	95.	c
96.	a	97.	a	98.	d	99.	a	100.	b

Sample Practical Questions with Answers

Q1. Write a program to print all Armstrong numbers in a given range. Note: An Armstrong number is a number whose sum of cubes of digits is equal to the number itself. E.g. $370=3^3+7^3+0^3$

Solution:

```
# Program to check Armstrong numbers in certain interval
low_range = int(input("Enter lower range: "))
upper_range = int(input("Enter upper range: "))
for num in range(low_range, upper_range + 1):
  sum = 0
  temp = num
  while temp > 0:
    digit = temp % 10
    sum += digit ** 3
    temp //= 10
  if num == sum:
    print(num)


RUN
>>>
Enter lower range: 100
Enter upper range: 1000
153
370
371
407
>>>
```

Q2. Write a function to obtain sum n terms of the following series for any positive integer value of X

$X + X^3/3! + X^5/5! + X^7/7! + ...$

Solution:

```
# A function to obtain sum n terms


def power(a,b):
  p=1
  for i in range(1, b+1):
    p=p*a
```

```
  return p
def factorial(n):
  f=1
  for i in range(1, n+1):
    f=f*i
  return f
sum = 0
n= int(input("Enter the number of terms: "))
x= int(input("Enter value of x: "))
for i in range(1,2*n+1,2):
  sum = sum+power(x,i)/factorial(i)
print(sum)
```

```
RUN
>>>
Enter the number of terms: 2
Enter value of x: 2
3.3333333333333333
>>>
```

Q3. Write a function to obtain sum n terms of the following series for any positive integer value of X 1+x/1!+x2/2!+x3/3!+…

Solution:

```
# A function to obtain sum n terms of following series for any positive interger

def power(a,b):
  p=1
  for i in range(1, b+1):
    p=p*a
  return p
def factorial(n):
  f=1
  for i in range(1, n+1):
    f=f*i
  return f
def printSeries(x,n):
  sum = 0
  for i in range(n):
    sum = sum+power(x,i)/factorial(i)
  print(sum)
n= int(input("Enter the number of terms: "))
x=int(input("Enter the value of x: "))
printSeries(x,n)
```

```
RUN
>>>
Enter the number of terms: 5
Enter the value of x: 2
7.0
>>>
```

Q4. Write a program to multiply two numbers by repeated addition e.g. 6*7 = 6+6+6+6+6+6+6

Solution:

```
# Program to find product of two numbers using repetitive addition
def prod(a,b):
  sum=0
  for i in range(b):
    sum = sum +a
  print("The product is: ",sum)
num1=int(input("Enter the first number: "))
num2=int(input("Enter second number: "))
prod(num1,num2)
```

```
RUN
>>>
Enter the first number: 6
Enter second number: 7
The product is:  42
>>>
```

Q5. Write a program to compute the wages of a daily laborer as per the following rules:

Hours Worked Rate Applicable upto first 8 hrs Rs100/- per hr

a. For next 4 hrs Rs30/- per hr extra
b. For next 4 hrs Rs40/- per hr extra
c. For next 4 hrs Rs50/- per hr extra
d. For rest Rs60/- per hr extra

Solution:

```
# Program to compute the wages of a daily laborer
```

```
wage=0
def dailyPaid(hours_worked):
  if hours_worked <= 8:
    return hours_worked *wage
  if 8 < hours_worked <=12:
    return 8 * 100 + (hours_worked - 8) *30

  if 12 < hours_worked <=16:
   return 8 * 100 + (hours_worked - 12) *40 + (4*30)
  if 16 < hours_worked <=20:
    return 8 * 100 + (hours_worked - 16) *50 +
    (4*40) + (4*30)
  else:
    return 8 * 100 + (hours_worked - 20) *60 +
    (4*50) + (4*40) + (4*30)


employee_name = input("Enter Name of Labourer:
")
hours_worked = int (input("Enter total hours
worked: "))

pay= dailyPaid(hours_worked)

print("Total Wages: ",pay)
```

RUN
```
>>>
Enter Name of Labourer: Ravi
Enter total hours worked: 15
Total Wages: 1040
>>>
```

Q6. Accept the name of the labourer and no. of hours worked. Calculate and display the wages. The program should run for N number of labourers as specified by the user.

Solution:

```
# Program to compute the wages of a daily laborer
wage=0
def dailyPaid(hours_worked):
  if hours_worked <= 8:
    return hours_worked *wage
  if 8 < hours_worked <=12:
    return 8 * 100 + (hours_worked - 8) *30

  if 12 < hours_worked <=16:
   return 8 * 100 + (hours_worked - 12) *40 + (4*30)
  if 16 < hours_worked <=20:
    return 8 * 100 + (hours_worked - 16) *50 +
    (4*40) + (4*30)
  else:
    return 8 * 100 + (hours_worked - 20) *60 +
    (4*50) + (4*40) + (4*30)


n = int(input("Enter number of Labourer: "))
for i in range(1,n+1):
  name = input("Enter name of Labourer: ")
  hours_worked = int (input("Enter total hours
  worked: "))
  pay= dailyPaid(hours_worked)
  print("Total Wages: ",pay)
```

RUN
```
>>>
Enter number of Labourer: 2
Enter name of Labourer: Mohan
Enter total hours worked: 15
Total Wages: 1040
Enter name of Labourer: Rajiv
Enter total hours worked: 12
Total Wages: 920
>>>
```

Q7. Write a function that takes a string as parameter and returns a string with every successive repetitive character replaced by ?e.g. school may become scho?l.

Solution:

```
# Program to replace successive repetitive character
by ?
def fun1(st):
  ch=[]
  for i in st:
```

```
        ch.append(i)
    for i in range(len(ch)-1):
        if ch[i] == ch[i+1]:
            ch[i+1] = '?'
    return ''.join(ch)
st = input("Enter string: ")
print(fun1(st))

RUN
>>>
Enter string: school
scho?l
>>>
```

Q8. Write a program to display all the prime numbers within an interval.

Solution:

```
lower = int(input("Enter lower range: "))
upper = int(input("Enter upper range: "))

print("Prime numbers between",lower,"and", upper,"are:")

for num in range(lower,upper + 1):
    # prime numbers are greater than 1
    if num > 1:
        for i in range(2,num):
            if (num % i) == 0:
                break
        else:
            print(num)
RUN
>>>
Enter lower range: 1
Enter upper range: 20
Prime numbers between 1 and 20 are:
2
3
5
7
11
13
17
19
>>>
```

Q9. Program to find the factorial of a number provided by the user.

Solution:

```
# Python program to find factorial of a number provided by user
print("Enter the Number: ")
num = int(input())

fact = 1
i = 1
while i<=num:
    fact = fact*i
    i = i+1

print("\nFactorial =", fact)
RUN
>>>
Enter the Number:
5

Factorial = 120
>>>
```

Q10. Write a NumPy program to generate five random numbers from the normal distribution.

Solution:

```
# A NumPy program to generate five random numbers from the normal distribution.
import numpy as np
x = np.random.normal(size=5)
print(x)

RUN
>>>
[ 0.24437821 -0.56332225 -1.63439295 -0.649815 2.07372694]
>>>
```

MCQ & Practical Assignment – 2

Multiple Choice Questions

1. When an algorithm is written in the form of programming language, it becomes a :
   a. Flowchart
   b. Program
   c. Pseudo code
   d. Syntax
2. Which of the following is correct about Python?
   a. It supports automatic garbage collection
   b. It can be easily integrated with C, C++, COM, ActiveX, CORBA and Java
   c. Both of the above
   d. None of the above
3. Which of the following data types is not supported in python?
   a. Number b. String
   c. List d. Slice
4. In which language is Python written?
   a. English b. PHP
   c. C d. All of the above
5. ________ return the current file position after reading the first line.
   a. tell() b. seek()
   c. help() d. None of these
6. What do we use to define a block of code in Python language?
   a. Key b. Brackets
   c. Indentation d. None of these
7. Which character is used in Python to make a single line comment?
   a. / b. //
   c. # d. !
8. Which of the following statements is correct regarding the object-oriented programming concept in Python?
   a. Classes are real-world entities while objects are not real
   b. Objects are real-world entities while classes are not real
   c. Both objects and classes are real-world entities
   d. All of the above
9. What is the method inside the class in python language?
   a. Object b. Function
   c. Attribute d. Argument
10. Which of the following declarations is incorrect?
    a. _x = 2 b. __x = 3
    c. __xyz__ = 5 d. None of these
11. Which of the following is not a keyword in Python language?
    a. val b. raise
    c. try d. with
12. Which of the following statements is correct for variable names in Python language?
    a. All variable names must begin with an underscore.
    b. Unlimited length
    c. The variable name length is a maximum of 2.
    d. All of the above
13. Q. Which of the following declarations is incorrect in python language?
    a. xyzp = 5,000,000
    b. x y z p = 5000 6000 7000 8000
    c. x,y,z,p = 5000, 6000, 7000, 8000
    d. x_y_z_p = 5,000,000
14. Which of the following words cannot be a variable in python language?
    a. _val b. val
    c. try d. _try_
15. Which of the following operators is the correct option for power(ab)?
    a. a ^ b b. a**b
    c. a ^ ^ b d. a ^ * b
16. Which of the following precedence order is correct in Python?
    a. Parentheses, Exponential, Multiplication, Division, Addition, Subtraction
    b. Multiplication, Division, Addition, Subtraction, Parentheses, Exponential
    c. Division, Multiplication, Addition, Subtraction, Parentheses, Exponential
    d. Exponential, Parentheses, Multiplication, Division, Addition, Subtraction

17. Which one of the following has the same precedence level?
    a. Division, Power, Multiplication, Addition and Subtraction
    b. Division and Multiplication
    c. Subtraction and Division
    d. Power and Division
18. Which one of the following has the highest precedence in the expression?
    a. Division b. Subtraction
    c. Power d. Parentheses
19. Which of the following functions is a built-in function in python language?
    a. val() b. print()
    c. Print() d. None of these
20. Study the following function:
    round(4.576)
    What will be the output of this function?
    a. 4 b. 5 c. 576 d. 4.5
21. What is the output of the following statement?
    print((2,4) + (1,5))
    a. (2,4), (4,5) b. (3,9)
    c. (2,4,1,5) d. Invalid Syntax
22. What will be the output of following code?
    ```
    import numpy as np
    a = np.array([[1,2,3],[0,1,4],[11,22,33]])
    print(a.size)
    ```
    a. 1 b. 3
    c. 9 d. 4
23. Which of the following variable declaration is incorrect?
    a. a_=3 b. _a=3
    c. a?=3 d. All of these
24. ________ immediately terminates the current loop iteration.
    a. break b. pass
    c. continue d. None of the above
25. Which of the function takes two arguments?
    a. dump() b. load()
    c. Both of the above d. None of the above
26. What is the maximum possible length of an identifier?
    a. 16 b. 32
    c. 64 d. None of these
27. Which of the following executes the code line by line?
    a. Compiler b. Interpreter
    c. Executer d. Translator
28. What is the output?
    ```
    def calc(x):
        r= 2*x**2
    return r
    print(calc(5))
    ```
    a. Eror b. 50 c. 100 d. 20
29. What does the following code will print?
    ```
    x= 'mohan'
    for I in range(len(x)):
        x[i].upper()
    print(x)
    ```
    a. Mohan b. MOHAN
    c. Error d. None of these
30. What is the symbol used to represent start and stop of a flowchart?
    a. Oval b. Rectangle
    c. Arrow d. Diamond
31. What is the output of the following code?
    ```
    ms=('A','D','H','U','N','I','C')
        print(ms[1:4])
    ```
    a. ('D','H','U')
    b. ('A','D','H','U','N','I','C')
    c. ('D','H','U','N','I','C')
    d. None of these
32. Raw data assigned to variable is called as ________.
    a. Variable b. Literal
    c. Identifier d. Comment
33. What does the following code print?
    ```
    If 2+5 ==8:
        print('TRUE')
    else:
        print("FALSE")
    print("TRUE")
    ```
    a. TRUE b. TRUE FALSE
    c. TRUE TRUE d. FALSE TRUE
34. Algorithm cannot be represented by ________.
    a. pseudo codes b. syntax
    c. flowchart d. programs

35. Which one is not the attribute of a file?
    a. softspace b. mode
    c. closed d. rename
36. Which function is used to read all the characters?
    a. readall() b. read()
    c. readcharacters() d. read char()
37. Find the output of the following Python Programs.
```
a= "Meetmeafterparty"
b= 13
print a+b
```
    a. 29 b. 14
    c. error in code d. 15
38. Find the output of the following Python Programs
```
class Acc:
def_init_(self, id):
self.id = id
id = 555
acc = Acc(111)
print acc.id
```
    a. 111 b. 555
    c. 666 d. error in code
39. Which of the following is an invalid variable?
    a. my_string_1 b. foo
    c. _ d. 1st_string
40. Find the output of the following Python programs.
```
x=['ab','cd']
for i in x:
    i.upper()
print(x)
```
    a. ab b. cd
    c. ['ab','cd'] d. ['cd', 'ab']
41. What is the output of the following Python Program?
```
a=2
b='3.77'
c= -8
str1 ='{0:4f} {0.3d} {2} {1}'.format(a,b,c)
print(str1)
```
    a. 2.0000 2 -8 3.77 b. 2 3.77 -8 3.77
    c. 2.000 3 -8 3.77 d. 2.000 2 8 3.77
42. Find the output of the following Python Programs
```
def gfg(x,l= []):
for i in range(x):
    l.append(i*i)
print(l)
gfg(2)
```
    a. [3, 2, 1, 0, 1, 4] b. [0,1]
    c. [0, 1, 0, 1, 4] d. error in code
43. Suppose t =(1, 2, 4, 3), which of the following is incorrect?
    a. print (t[3])
    b. t[3]= 45
    c. print (max(t))
    d. print (len(t))
44. What will be the output of the following Python Program code?
```
>>> t1=(1,2,4,3)
>>> t2=(1,2,3,4)
>>> t1
```
    a. True b. False
    c. Error d. (1, 2, 4, 3)
45. Which of the following statements is false about recursion?
    a. Every recursive function must have a base case
    b. Infinite recursion can occur if the base case isn't properly mentioned
    c. A recursive function makes the code easier to understand
    d. Every recursive function must have a return value
46. What will be the output of the following Python code?
```
import functools
l=[1, 2, 3, 4, 5]
m = functools.reduce(lambda x, y: x
if x > y else y,l)
print(m)
```
    a. Error b. Address of m
    c. 1 d. 5
47. Which of the following is correctly evaluated for this function?
    pow(x,y,z)
    a. (x**y) / z b. (x / y) * z
    c. (x**y) % z d. (x / y) / z
48. Study the following statement:
    >>>"a"+"bc"
    What will be the output of this statement?
    a. a+bc b. abc
    c. a bc d. a

49. Study the following statements:
>>> print(ord('h') - ord('z'))
What will be the output of this statement?
a. 18 b. -18
c. 17 d. -17

50. Study the following program:
```
a = 1
while True:
    if a % 7 == 0:
        break
    print(a)
        a += 1
```
Which of the following is correct output of this program?
a. 1 2 3 4 5 b. 1 2 3 4 5 6
c. 1 2 3 4 5 6 7 d. Invalid syntax

51. Study the following program:
```
x = 'pqrs'
for i in range(len(x)):
    x[i].upper()
print (x)
```
Which of the following is the correct output of this program?
a. PQRS b. pqrs
c. qrs d. None of these

52. Study the following program:
```
d = {0: 'a', 1: 'b', 2: 'c'}
for i in d:
    print(i)
```
What will be the output of this statement?
a. a b c b. 0 1 2
c. 0 a 1 b 2 c d. None of these above

53. Which of the following option is not a core data type in the python language?
a. Dictionary b. Lists
c. Class d. All of the above

54. What error will occur when you execute the following code?
PEAR = BANANA
a. NameError b. SyntaxError
c. TypeError d. ValueError

55. What happens when '2' == 2 is executed?
a. False b. Ture
c. ValueError occurs d. TypeError occurs

56. Which of the following argument we need to pass in reshape() function?
a. Array b. Shape
c. only array d. Both array and shape

57. Which of the following is not a keyword?
a. eval b. assert
c. nonlocal d. pass

58. All keywords in Python are in ________
a. lower case
b. UPPER CASE
c. Capitalized
d. None of the mentioned

59. Which of the following cannot be a variable?
a. __init__ b. in
c. it d. on

60. Which is the correct operator for power(xy)?
a. X^y b. X**y
c. X^^y d. None of the mentioned

61. What is the answer to this expression, 22 % 3 is?
a. 7 b. 1 c. 0 d. 5

62. What is the output of this expression, 3*1**3?
a. 27 b. 9 c. 3 d. 1

63. What data type is the object below?
L = [1, 23, 'hello', 1]
a. list b. dictionary
c. array d. tuple

64. In order to store values in terms of key and value we use what core data type.
a. list b. tuple
c. class d. dictionary

65. Which of the following is the truncation division operator?
a. / b. % c. // d. |

66. Which of the following is a Python tuple?
a. [1, 2, 3] b. (1, 2, 3)
c. {1, 2, 3} d. {}

67. To find the length of string, python uses _____ method.
a. size() b. length()
c. len() d. sizeof()

68. We can use ____ statement to remove a list element.
a. delta b. del
c. insert d. index

69. ____ operator use to select single character from string.
a. slice b. index c. indent d. identity

70. What is the output when we execute list("hello")?
a. ['h', 'e', 'l', 'l', 'o'] b. ['hello']
c. ['llo'] d. ['olleh']

71. Name the statement that sends back a value from a function.
a. print b. input c. return d. None

72. Functions that do not return any value are known as:
a. fruitful functions b. void functions
c. library functions d. user-defined functions

73. Which of the given argument types can be skipped from a function call?
a. positional arguments b. keyword arguments
c. named arguments d. default arguments

74. What is returned by int(math.pow(3, 2))?
a. 6 b. 9
c. error, third argument required
d. error, too many arguments

75. What is the value of x if x = math.sqrt(4)?
a. 2 b. 2.0
c. (2, -2) d. (2.0, -2.0)

76. Which one of these is floor division?
a. / b. //
c. % d. None of the mentioned

77. Which of these is not a fundamental feature of OOP?
a. Encapsulation b. Inheritance
c. Instantiation d. Polymorphism

78. _____ represents an entity in the real world with its identity and behavior
a. A method b. An object
c. A class d. An operator

79. _____ is used to create an object.
a. class
b. constructor
c. User-defined functions
d. In-built functions

80. Which keyword is used to access members of the base class?
a. self b. pass
c. super d. assert

81. When will the else part of the try-except-else be executed?
a. always
b. when an exception occurs
c. when no exception occurs
d. when an exception occurs in to except block

82. When is the finally block executed?
a. when there is no exception
b. when there is an exception
c. only if some condition that has been specified is satisfied
d. Always

83. What happens when '1' == 1 is executed?
a. we get a True b. we get a False
c. an TypeError occurs
d. a ValueError occurs

84. What will be the output of the following Python expression if x=56.236?
print("%.2f"%x)
a. 56.236 b. 56.23 c. 56.0000 d. 56.24

85. What will be the output of the following Python function?
len(["hello",2, 4, 6])
a. Error b. 6 c. 4 d. 3

86. What will be the output of the following Python code snippet?
```
for i in [1, 2, 3, 4][::-1]:
    print (i)
```
a. 4 3 2 1 b. error
c. 1 2 3 4 d. none of the mentioned

87. What arithmetic operators cannot be used with strings in Python?
a. * b. -
c. + d. All of the mentioned

88. Which of the following statements is used to create an empty set in Python?
a. ( ) b. [ ] c. { } d. set()

89. What will be the output of the following Python code?
```
>>>list1 = [1, 3]
>>>list2 = list1
>>>list1[0] = 4
>>>print(list2)
```
a. [1, 4] b. [1, 3, 4]
c. [4, 3] d. [1, 3]

90. Which of the following concepts is not a part of Python?
    a. Pointers. b. Loops.
    c. Dynamic Typing. d. All of the above.

91. What will be the output of the following code snippet?

```
def solve(a, b):
    return b if a == 0 else solve(b % a, a)
print(solve(20, 50))
```

    a. 10 b. 20 c. 50 d. 1

92. What will be the output of the following code snippet?

```
def solve(a):
    a = [1, 3, 5]
a = [2, 4, 6]
print(a)
solve(a)
print(a)
```

    a. [2, 4, 6]. [2, 4, 6] b. [2, 4, 6], [1, 3, 5]
    c. [1. 3. 5], [1, 3, 5] d. None of these.

93. What will be the output of the following code snippet?

```
def func():
    global value
    value = "Local"

value = "Global"
func()
print(value)
```

    a. Local b. Global
    c. None d. Cannot be predicted

94. Which of the following statements are used in Exception Handling in Python?
    a. try b. except
    c. finally d. All of the above

95. What will be the output of the following code snippet?

```
a = 3
b = 1
print(a, b)
a, b = b, a
print(a, b)
```

    a. 3 1 1 3 b. 3 1 3 1
    c. 1 3 1 3 d. 1 3 3 1

96. What will be the output of the following code snippet?

```
example = ["Sunday", "Monday", "Tuesday", "Wednesday"];
del example[2]
print(example)
```

    a. ['Sunday', 'Monday', 'Tuesday', 'Wednesday']
    b. ['Sunday', 'Monday', 'Wednesday']
    c. ['Monday', 'Tuesday', 'Wednesday']
    d. ['Sunday', 'Monday', 'Tuesday']

97. Which of the following functions converts date to corresponding time in Python?
    a. strptime() b. strftime()
    c. Both A and B d. None of the above

98. As what datatype are the *args stored, when passed into a function?
    a. List. b. Tuple.
    c. Dictionary. d. None of the above.

99. As what datatype are the *kwargs stored, when passed into a function?
    a. Lists. b. Tuples.
    c. Dictionary. d. None of the above.

100. Which of the following blocks will always be executed whether an exception is encountered or not in a program?
    a. try b. except
    c. finally d. None of These

Answers to Multiple Choice Questions

1.	b	2.	c	3.	d	4.	c	5.	a
6.	c	7.	c	8.	b	9.	b	10.	d
11.	a	12.	b	13.	b	14.	c	15.	b
16.	a	17.	b	18.	d	19.	b	20.	b
21.	c	22.	c	23.	c	24.	b	25.	a
26.	d	27.	b	28.	b	29.	a	30.	a
31.	a	32.	b	33.	b	34.	d	35.	d
36.	b	37.	c	38.	d	39.	d	40.	c
41.	a	42.	b	43.	b	44.	b	45.	b
46.	d	47.	c	48.	b	49.	b	50.	b
51.	b	52.	b	53.	c	54.	a	55.	a
56.	d	57.	a	58.	d	59.	b	60.	b
61.	b	62.	c	63.	a	64.	d	65.	c
66.	b	67.	c	68.	b	69.	b	70.	a

Contd...

71.	c	72.	b	73.	d	74.	b	75.	b
76.	b	77.	c	78.	b	79.	b	80.	c
81.	c	82.	d	83.	b	84.	d	85.	c
86.	a	87.	b	88.	d	89.	c	90.	a
91.	a	92.	a	93.	a	94.	d	95.	a
96.	b	97.	a	98.	b	99.	c	100.	c

Sample Practical Questions with Answers

Q1. Write a program that takes in a sentence as input and displays the number of words, number of capital letters, no. of small letters and number of special symbols.

Solution:

```
str1=input("Enter a string: ")
if len(str1) == 0:
    print("String is Empty")
else:
    word=1
    capital=small=alnum=spe_ch=0
    for i in str1:
        if i.isspace():
            word+=1
        elif i.isupper():
            capital+=1
        elif i.islower():
            small+=1
        elif i.isalnum():
            alnum+=1
        else:
            spe_ch+=1
    else:
        print(str1)
        print(f"Number of Words: {word}")
        print(f"Number of Upper: {capital}")
        print(f"Number of Lower: {small}")
        print(f"Number of Digit: {alnum}")
        print(f"Number of Special Symbols: {spe_ch}")
RUN
>>>
Enter a string: I have $250 with me.
I have $250 with me.
Number of Words: 5
Number of Upper: 1
Number of Lower: 10
Number of Digit: 3
Number of Special Symbols: 2
>>>
```

Q2. Write a Python program that takes list of numbers as input from the user and produces a cumulative list where each element in the list at any position n is sum of all elements at positions upto n-1.

Solution:

```
length = int(input("Enter list length: "))
my_list= []
for i in range(length):
    element = int(input("Enter list Items: "))
    my_list += [element,]

cum_list=[]
for i, item in enumerate(my_list):
    cum_list+=[sum(my_list[:i])]

print("My list: ",my_list)
print("Cumulative list: ",cum_list)
RUN
>>>
Enter list length: 5
Enter list Items: 10
Enter list Items: 20
Enter list Items: 30
Enter list Items: 40
Enter list Items: 50
My list:  [10, 20, 30, 40, 50]
Cumulative list:  [0, 10, 30, 60, 100]
>>>
```

Q3. Write a program which takes list of numbers as input and finds:

a. The largest number in the list
b. The smallest number in the list
c. Product of all the items in the list

Solution:

```
list=[ int(l) for l in input("Enter elements of List: ").split(",")]
print("The list is: ",list)
max=min=list[0]
product=1
for x in list:
  if x>max:
    max=x
  if x<min:
    min=x
  product*=x
print(f"Largest Number in list : {max}")
print(f"Smallest Number in list: {min}")
print(f"Product of All Items in list: {product}")
```

```
RUN
>>>
Enter elements of List: 10,20,2,5
The list is:  [10, 20, 2, 5]
Largest Number in list : 20
Smallest Number in list: 2
Product of All Items in list: 2000
>>>
```

Q4. Write a Python function that takes two lists and returns True if they have at least one common item.

Solution:

```
def common_data(list1, list2):
  result = False
  for x in list1:
    for y in list2:
      if x == y:
        result = True
        return result
  return result
L1 = [10, 20, 30, 40, 50]
L2 = [50, 60, 70, 80, 90]
print(common_data(L1, L2))
L1 = [10, 20, 30, 40, 50]
L2 = [60, 70, 80, 90, 100]
print(common_data(L1, L2))
```

```
RUN
>>>
True
False
>>>
```

Q5. Write a Python program to combine two dictionary adding values for common keys.

d1 = {'a': 100, 'b': 200, 'c':300}

d2 = {'a': 300, 'b': 200, 'd':400}

Sample output: Counter({'a': 400, 'b': 400, 'd': 400, 'c': 300})

Solution:

```
d1 = {'a': 100, 'b': 200, 'c':300}
d2 = {'a': 300, 'b': 200, 'd':400}
d3 = dict(d1)
d3.update(d2)
for i, j in d1.items():
  for x, y in d2.items():
    if i == x:
      d3[i]=(j+y)
print(d3)
```

```
RUN
>>>
{'a': 400, 'b': 400, 'c': 300, 'd': 400}
>>>
```

Q6. Write a program that takes sentence as input from the user and computes the frequency of each letter. Use a variable of dictionary type to maintain and show the frequency of each letter.

Solution:

```
test_str = input("Enter a string: ")
freq_letter = {}
for i in test_str:
  if i in freq_letter:
    freq_letter[i] += 1
  else:
    freq_letter[i] = 1
```

```
print ("Count frequency of all characters in string is
:\n " + str(freq_letter))

RUN
>>>
Enter a string: banana
Count frequency of all characters in string is :
{'b': 1, 'a': 3, 'n': 2}
>>>
```

Q7. Apply recursive call to do the following:

a. Product of two numbers using repetitive addition

b. Print Fibonacci series upto term n

Solution: (a)

```
def product(num1,num2):
    if(num1<num2):
        return product(num2,num1)
    elif(num2!=0):
        return(num1+product(num1,num2-1))
    else:
        return 0

num1=int(input("Enter first number: "))
num2=int(input("Enter second number: "))
print("product is: ",product(num1,num2))

RUN
>>>
Enter first number: 8
Enter second number: 5
product is:  40
>>>
```

Solution: (b)

```
#Fibonacci series using recursive methods
first,second=0,1
n = int(input("please give a number for fibonacci
series : "))
def fibonacci(num):
    if num == 0:
        return 0
    elif num == 1:
        return 1
    else:
        return fibonacci(num-1)+fibonacci(num-2)
print("fibonacci series are : ")
for i in range(0,n):
    print(fibonacci(i))

RUN
>>>
=============
please give a number for fibonacci series : 5
fibonacci series are :
0
1
1
2
3
```

Q8. Write a program to check whether the entered character is vowel or consonant.

Solution:

```
# Python program to check character is vowel or
consonant

# input from user
ch = input('Enter any character: ')

# check vowel or constant and display result
if(ch=='A' or ch=='a' or ch=='E' or ch =='e' or
ch=='I'
    or ch=='i' or ch=='O' or ch=='o' or ch=='U' or
    ch=='u'):
    print(ch, "is a Vowel")
else:
    print(ch, "is a Consonant")
RUN
>>>
Enter any character: u
u is a Vowel

Enter any character: f
f is a Consonant
>>>
```

Q9. Write a Python program to count the number of strings where the string length is 2 or more and the first and last character are same from a given list of strings.

Solution:

```
# Sample List ['abc', 'xyz', 'aba', '1221', 'aaa', 'asdasdsada']

def compare(a):
  ctr = 0
  for i in a:
    if len(i) > 2 and i[0] == i[-1]:
      ctr+= 1
  return ctr

a = ['abc', 'xyz', 'aba', '1221', 'aaa', 'asdasdsada']
for i in a:
  z = compare(a)
print(z)
RUN
>>>
4
>>>
```

Q10. (a) Write a python program for linear search.

Solution:

```
# Linear Search
def linear_Search(list1, n, key):
# Searching list1 sequentially
  for i in range(0, n):
    if (list1[i] == key):
      return i
  return -1
# Test array
list1 = [1, 5, 3, 8, 12, 16]
key = 8
n = len(list1)
res = linear_Search(list1, n, key)
if(res == -1):
  print("Element not found")
else:
  print("Element found at index: ", res)
RUN
>>>
Element found at index: 3
>>>
```

Q10. (b) Write a python program for Binary search.

Solution:

```
# Binary Search
def binary_search(arr, x):
  low = 0
  high = len(arr) - 1
  mid = 0
  while low <= high:
    mid = (high + low) // 2
# Check if x is present at mid
    if arr[mid] < x:
      low = mid + 1
# If x is greater, ignore left half
    elif arr[mid] > x:
      high = mid - 1
# If x is smaller, ignore right half
    else:
      return mid
# If element not found
  return -1
# Test array
arr = [ 2, 3, 4, 10, 16, 25, 60 ]
x = 16
# Function call
result = binary_search(arr, x)
if result != -1:
  print("Element is found at index", str(result))
else:
  print("Element not found in array")

RUN
>>>
Element is found at index 4
>>>
```

MCQ & Practical Assignment – 3

Multiple Choice Questions

1. What will be the output of the following code?
   f=open("demo.txt","w+")
   f.write("Welcome to Python")
   f.seek(5)
   a=f.read(5)
   print(a)
   a. Welco b. me to
   c. Welcome to Python d. e to
2. Operations to be repeated a certain number of times are done by __________.
   a. Selection b. Sequential
   c. Simple d. Loop
3. lstrip() method is used for:
   a. delete all the trailing characters
   b. delete all the leading characters
   c. delete all leading and trailing characters
   d. delete upper case characters
4. What will be the output of the following expression?
   x=4
   print(x<<2)
   a. 4 b. 16 c. 6 d. 2
5. What will be the output of the following code?
   f=open("demo.txt","r")
   print(f.tell())
   a. 1 b. 2 c. -1 d. 0
6. Which of the following is not a valid identifier?
   a. student b. s12
   c. 123 d. _123
7. Which of the following symbol is used for input and output operations in a flowchart?
   a. Rectangle b. Parallelogram
   c. Circle d. Diamond
8. What is the output of following code?
   def add(a,b):
   return a+5,b+5
   result = add(3,2)
   print(result)
   a. 15 b. 8 c. (8,7) d. Error
9. Assume q=[3, 4, 5, 20, 5, 25, 1,3], then what will be the items of q list after q.pop(1)
   a. [3,4,5,20,5,25,1,3] b. [1,3,3,4,5,5,20,25]
   c. [3,5,20,5,25,1,3] d. [1,3,4,5,20,5,25]
10. What is the output of >>>float('12.6')
    a. 12.6 b. '12.6'
    c. 12 d. Syntax error
11. Testing is known as:
    a. A stage of all projects
    b. Finding broken code
    c. Evaluating deliverable to find errors
    d. None of the above
12. Flowchart and algorithms are used for __________.
    a. Better programming
    b. Easy testing and debugging
    c. Efficient coding
    d. All
13. Which module is to be imported for using randint() function?
    a. random b. randrange
    c. randomrange d. rand
14. What will be the output of the following Python program?
    def additem(listParam):
    listParam +=[1]
    mylist= [1,2,3,4]
    additem(mylist)
    print(len(mylist))
    a. 4 b. 5 c. 6 d. 7
15. What will be the output of the following?
    import numpy as np
    a = np.array([1,5,4,7,8])
    a=a+1
    print(a[1])
    a. 4 b. 5 c. 6 d. 7
16. A detailed flowchart is known as:
    a. Micro b. Union c. Macro d. Stack
17. Which is the function to read the remaining lines of the file from a file from a file object infile?
    a. infile.read(2) b. infile.read()
    c. infile.readlines() d. infile.readline()

18. Suppose a list with name arr, contains 5 elements, you can get the 2nd element from the list using:
    a. arr[-2] b. arr[2]
    c. arr[-1] d. arr[1]
19. Which symbol is used to write single line comment?
    a. * b. # c. / d. ?
20. Which one of the following is a mutable dat type?
    a. set b. tuple
    c. string d. None of these
21. What will be the output of the following expression?
```
a=2
b=8
print(a | b)
print(a>>1)
```
    a. 10 0 b. 10 2 c. 2 2 d. 10 1
22. Which of the following is not a keyword?
    a. eval b. nonlocal
    c. assert d. finally
23. What is the return type of the following function?
```
def fun1():
    return 'mnp',22
```
    a. List b. Dictionary
    c. String d. Tuple
24. What will be the output of the following code snippet?
```
from math import *
a = 2.19
b = 3.999999
c = -3.30
print(int(a), floor(b), ceil(c), fabs(c))
```
    a. 2 3 -3 3.3 b. 3 4 -3 3
    c. 2 3 -3 3 d. 2 3 -3 -3.3
25. What will be the output of the following code snippet?
```
set1 = {1, 3, 5}
set2 = {2, 4, 6}
print(len(set1 + set2))
```
    a. 3 b. 6 c. 0 d. Error
26. What keyword is used in Python to raise exceptions?
    a. raise b. try c. goto d. except
27. What will be the output of the following code snippet?
```
s1 = {1, 2, 3, 4, 5}
s2 = {2, 4, 6}
print(s1 ^ s2)
```
    a. {1, 2, 3, 4, 5} b. {1, 3, 5, 6}
    c. {2, 4} d. None of the above
28. Which of the following is not a valid set operation in python?
    a. Union b. Intersection
    c. Difference d. None of the above
29. What will be the output of the following code snippet?
```
a = [1, 2, 3, 4]
b = [3, 4, 5, 6]
c = [x for x in a if x not in b]
print(c)
```
    a. [1, 2] b. [5, 6]
    c. [1, 2, 5, 6] d. [3, 4]
30. Which of the following are valid escape sequences in Python?
    a. \n b. \t
    c. \\ d. All of the above
31. Which of the following are valid string manipulation functions in Python?
    a. count() b. upper()
    c. strip() d. All of the above
32. Which of the following modules need to be imported to handle date time computations in Python?
    a. datetime b. date
    c. time d. timedate
33. What will be the result of the following expression in Python "2 ** 3 + 5 ** 2"?
    a. 65536 b. 33
    c. 169 d. None of these
34. What will be the output of this program?
```
int1 = 10
int2 = 6
if int != int2:
    int2 = ++int2
    print(int1 - int2)
```
    a. 2 b. 4 c. 6 d. None
35. What will be the output of this program?
```
int1 = 10
int2 = 6
if int != int2:
    int2 = ++int1
    print(int1 - int2)
```
    a. 2 b. 4 c. 0 d. No Output

36. What will be the output of this program?
    print(6 + 5 - 4 * 3 / 2 % 1)
    a. 7 b. 7.0 c. 15 d. 11.0
37. What will be the output of this program?
    print(int(6 == 6.0) * 3 + 4 % 5)
    a. 22 b. 18 c. 20 d. 7
38. What will be the output of this program?
    i = 2
    j = 3.5
    add = i + j
    print(add)
    a. 5.5 b. 5
    c. (2 , 3 , 5) d. TypeError
39. How many control statements python supports?
    a. Four b. Five
    c. Three d. None of the these
40. How many keywords present in the python programming language?
    a. 32 b. 61 c. 33 d. 27
41. In the Python Programming Language, syntax error is detected by ______ at ________.
    a. Interpreter / Compile time
    b. Run time / Interpreter
    c. Interpreter / Run time
    d. Compile time / Run time
42. The value of the Python expression given below would be:
    4+2**5//10
    a. 77 b. 0 c. 3 d. 7
43. The return value for trunc() would be:
    a. bool b. float c. int d. None
44. The output of this Python code would be:
    >>> x={1:"X",2:"Y",3:"Z"}
    >>> del x
    a. the del method does not exist for dictionary
    b. the del would delete the values present in dictionary
    c. the del would delete the entire dictionary
    d. the del would delete all the keys in dictionary
45. Which one of these is NOT true about recursion?
    a. We can replace a recursive function by a non-recursive function
    b. The memory space taken by the recursive functions is more than that of non-recursive function
    c. Running a recursive function is faster as compared to a non-recursive function
    d. The process of recursion makes it easier for users to understand a program
46. In Python, the primary use of the tell() method is that:
    a. within the file, it tells the end position
    b. within the file, it tells the current position
    c. it tells us if the file is opened
    d. none of the above
47. In Python, find which one isn't an exception handling keyword.
    a. accept b. finally
    c. try d. except
48. Which statement is correct?
    a. List is mutable & Tuple is immutable
    b. List is immutable & Tuple is mutable
    c. Both are Mutable.
    d. Both are Immutable
49. Which symbol is used to test condition in a flow chart?
    a. Terminal b. Process
    c. Decision d. Input/Output
50. Python is a ___object-oriented programming language.
    a. Special purpose
    b. General purpose
    c. Medium level programming language
    d. All of the mentioned above
51. Amongst which of the following is / are the application areas of Python programming?
    a. Web Development
    b. Game Development
    c. Artificial Intelligence and Machine Learning
    d. All of the mentioned above
52. Amongst which of the following is / are the Numeric Types of Data Types?
    a. int b. float
    c. complex
    d. All of the mentioned above
53. list, tuple, and range are the ___ of Data Types.
    a. Sequence Types
    b. Binary Types
    c. Boolean Types
    d. None of the mentioned above

54. Amongst which of the following is / are the logical operators in Python?
a. and
b. or
c. not
d. All of the mentioned above

55. What is the name of the operator ** in Python?
a. Exponentiation
b. Modulus
c. Floor division
d. None of the mentioned above

56. The % operator returns the ___.
a. Quotient
b. Divisor
c. Remainder
d. None of the mentioned above

57. Which of the following is the basic I/O connections in file?
a. Standard Input b. Standard Output
c. Standard Errors d. All of the mentioned

58. What value does the following expression evaluate to?
```
x=5
while x <10:
    print(x,end='')
```
a. Closed loop b. One time loop
c. Infinite loop d. Evergreen loop

59. Which of the following function of dictionary gets all the keys from the dictionary?
a. getkeys() b. key()
c. keys() d. None of the mentioned

60. Which of the following is an invalid mode?
a. a b. ar+ c. r+ d. w

61. Which of the following environment variable for Python tells the Python interpreter where to locate the module files imported into a program?
a. PYTHONPATH b. PYTHONSTARTUP
c. PYTHONCASEOK d. PYTHONHOME

62. What are the three different types of algorithm constructions?
a. input/output, decision, repeat
b. input, output, process
c. loop, input/output, process
d. sequence, selection, repeat

63. Function defined to achieve some task as per the programmer's requirement is called a ______.
a. User defined function
b. Library function
c. Built in function
d. All of the above

64. A process is expressed in a flowchart by ______.
a. rectangle b. circle
c. parallelogram d. diamond

65. What will be the output of the following expression?
```
print(7//2)
print(-7//2)
```
a. 3 -3 b. 4 -4 c. 3 -4 d. 3 3

66. What is the purpose of zeros() function used in Numpy array?
a. To make a Matrix with all diagonal element 0
b. To make a Matrix with first element 0
c. To make a Matrix with all element 0
d. None of the above

67. What will be the output of the following Python code?
```
from math import *
floor(3,7)
```
a. 3 b. 4
c. 3.0 d. None of the above

68. What is the output of the following code?
```
def fun(a,b=6):
    a=a+b
    print(a)
fun(5,4)
```
a. 11 b. 9 c. 5 d. 4

69. What is the output of the following code?
```
import numpy as np
a=np.array([1,2,3,5,8])
b=np.array([0,1,5,4,2])
c= a+b
c= c*a
print(c[2])
```
a. 6 b. 24
c. 0 d. None of these

70. The process of finding errors in code is called as ______.
a. compiling b. running
c. testing d. debugging

71. What is the output of the following code?
```
import numpy as np
a=np.array([[1,2,3]])
print(a.shape)
```
a. (2, 3) b. (3, 1)
c. (1, 3) d. None of these

72. The process of drawing a flowchart for an algorithm is called __________.
a. Performance
b. Algorithmic representation
c. Evaluation
d. Flowcharting

73. What will be the output of the following?
```
print((range(4)))
```
a. 0,1,2,3 b. [0,1,2,3]
c. range(0,4) d. (0,1,2,3)

74. What is the output of >>> '2' + '3'
a. 2 3 b. '2+3'
c. '23' d. None of these

75. If we open a file in write mode and file does not exists, which of the error will generate?
a. File Found Error
b. File Not Exist Error
c. File Not Found Error
d. None of these

76. What is the output of the following code?
```
import numpy as np
y=np.array([[11,12,13,14], [32,33,34,35]])
print(y.ndim)
```
a. 1 b. 2 c. 3 d. 0

77. An algorithm that calls itself directly or indirectly is called as __________.
a. Sub Function
b. Recursion
c. Reverse Polish Notation
d. Traversal Algorithm

78. What will be output of the following?
```
import numpy as np
a=np.array([[1,2,3,4], [5,6,7,8],[9,10,11,12]])
print(a[2,2])
```
a. 7 b. 11 c. 10 d. 8

79. How many arguments a Python program can accept from the command line?
a. one b. two c. three d. any

80. The list.index(x[, start[, end]]) is used to ___.
a. Return zero-based index in the list
b. Raises a ValueError if there is no such item
c. Both A and B
d. None of the mentioned above

81. Python Dictionary is used to store the data in a ________ format.
a. Key value pair
b. Group value pair
c. Select value pair
d. None of the mentioned above

82. Conditional statements are also known as __________ statements.
a. Decision-making
b. Array
c. List
d. None of the mentioned above

83. Which of the following is not used as conditional statement in Python?
a. switch
b. if...else
c. elif
d. None of the mentioned above

84. In a Python program, Nested if Statements denotes?
a. if statement inside another if statement
b. if statement outside the another if statement
c. Both A and B
d. None of the mentioned above

85. What will be the output of the following Python code?
```
x=13
if x>12 or x<15 and x==16:
    print("Given condition matched")
else:
    print("Given condition did not match")
```
a. Given condition matched
b. Given condition did not match
c. Both A and B
d. None of the mentioned above

86. Consider the following code segment and identify what will be the output of given Python code?
```
a = int(input("Enter an integer: "))
b = int(input("Enter an integer: "))
if a <= 0:
    b = b +1
```

```
else:
    a = a + 1
```

a. if inputted number is a negative integer then b = b +1
b. if inputted number is a positive integer then a = a +1
c. Both A and B
d. None of the mentioned above

87. What will be the output of the following Python code?

```
num = 10
if num > 0:
    print("Positive number")
elif num == 0:
    print("Zero")
else:
    print("Negative number")
```

a. Positive number
b. Negative number
c. Real number
d. None of the mentioned above

88. Loops are known as _________ in programming.
a. Control flow statements
b. Conditional statements
c. Data structure statements
d. None of the mentioned above

89. The continue keyword is used to ___ the current iteration in a loop.
a. Initiate
b. Start
c. End
d. None of the mentioned above

90. Amongst which of the following is / are true about the while loop?
a. It continually executes the statements as long as the given condition is true
b. It first checks the condition and then jumps into the instructions
c. The loop stops running when the condition becomes fail, and control will move to the next line of code.
d. All of the mentioned above

91. The _______________ is a built-in function that returns a range object that consists series of integer numbers, which we can iterate using a for loop.
a. range()
b. set()
c. dictionary{}
d. None of the mentioned above

92. Amongst which of the following is / are true with reference to loops in Python?
a. It allows for code reusability to be achieved.
b. By utilizing loops, we avoid having to write the same code over and over again.
c. We can traverse through the elements of data structures by utilizing looping.
d. All of the mentioned above

93. Amongst which of the following is a function which does not have any name?
a. Del function
b. Show function
c. Lambda function
d. None of the mentioned above

94. The function file_object.close() is used to ___.
a. To open the existing file
b. To append in an opened file
c. To close an opened file
d. None of the mentioned above

95. The seek() method is used to ___.
a. Saves the file in secondary storage
b. Position the file object at a particular position in a file
c. Deletes the file form secondary storage
d. None of the mentioned above

96. Amongst which of the following function is / are used to create a file and writing data?
a. append()
b. open()
c. close()
d. None of the mentioned above

97. Amongst which of the following is / are the method of convert Python objects for writing data in a binary file?
a. set() method
b. dump() method
c. load() method
d. None of the mentioned above

98. Which of the following counts the number of elements in Numpy array ?
a. count()
b. return()
c. shape()
d. size()

99. Which of the following is not valid to import the numpy module ?
   a. import numpy as np
   b. import numpy as n
   c. import numpy as p
   d. None of the above

100. What is the order of namespaces in which Python looks for an identifier?
   a. Python first searches the built-in namespace, then the global namespace and finally the local namespace
   b. Python first searches the built-in namespace, then the local namespace and finally the global namespace
   c. Python first searches the local namespace, then the global namespace and finally the built-in namespace
   d. Python first searches the global namespace, then the local namespace and finally the built-in namespace

Answers to Multiple Choice Questions

1.	b	2.	d	3.	b	4.	b	5.	d
6.	c	7.	b	8.	c	9.	c	10.	a
11.	c	12.	d	13.	a	14.	b	15.	c
16.	a	17.	c	18.	d	19.	b	20.	b
21.	d	22.	b	23.	d	24.	a	25.	d
26.	a	27.	b	28.	d	29.	a	30.	d
31.	d	32.	a	33.	b	34.	b	35.	c
36.	d	37.	d	38.	a	39.	c	40.	c
41.	c	42.	d	43.	c	44.	d	45.	c
46.	b	47.	a	48.	a	49.	c	50.	b
51.	d	52.	d	53.	a	54.	d	55.	a
56.	c	57.	d	58.	c	59.	c	60.	b
61.	a	62.	d	63.	d	64.	a	65.	c
66.	c	67.	a	68.	b	69.	b	70.	d
71.	c	72.	d	73.	b	74.	c	75.	b
76.	b	77.	b	78.	b	79.	d	80.	c
81.	a	82.	a	83.	a	84.	a	85.	a
86.	c	87.	a	88.	a	89.	c	90.	d
91.	a	92.	d	93.	c	94.	c	95.	b
96.	b	97.	b	98.	d	99.	d	100.	c

Sample Practical Questions with Answers

Q1. Write a program to input two numbers as input and compute the greatest common divisor

Solution:

```
# A program to understand the GCD of two number
in python using the recursion.
def gcd_fun (x, y):
    if (y == 0):
        return x
    else:
        return gcd_fun (y, x % y)
x =int (input ("Enter the first number: "))
y =int (input ("Enter the second number: "))
num = gcd_fun(x, y)
print("GCD of two number is: ")
print(num)

RUN
>>>
Enter the first number: 52
Enter the second number: 24
GCD of two number is:
4
>>>
```

Q2. Write a function that takes two filenames f1 and f2 as input. The function should read the contents of f1 line by line and write them onto f2.

Solution:

```
def filefunc(f1,f2):
    openf1=open(f1,'r')
    openf2=open(f2,'w+')
    print("File 1 Content:\n",openf1.read())
    openf1.seek(0)
    openf2.write(openf1.read())
    openf2.seek(0)
    print("File 2 Content:\n",openf2.read())
    openf1.close()
    openf1.close()
f1=input("Enter a Frist File Name: ")
```

```
f2=input("Enter a Second File Name: ")
filefunc(f1,f2)

RUN
>>>
Enter a Frist File Name: f1.txt
Enter a Second File Name: f2.txt
File 1 Content:
 Best of Luck!
File 2 Content:
 Best of Luck!
>>>
```

Q3. Write a function that reads the contents of the file f3.txt and counts the number of alphabets, blank spaces, lowercase letters, number of words starting with a vowel.

Solution:

```
def filefunc(f3):
   file3=open(f3,'r')
   snt=file3.read()
   file3.close()
   if len(snt) == 0:
      print("String is Empty")
   else:
      alpha=space=lower=vowel=0
      for i in snt:
         if i.isalpha():
            alpha+=1
         elif i.isspace():
            space+=1
         if i.islower():
            lower+=1
      vow='aeiou'
      li=snt.split(' ')
      for word in li:
         for x in vow:
            if word.startswith(x):
               vowel+=1
      print(f"File Content:\n{snt}\n")
      print(f"Number of Alphabets: {alpha}")
      print(f"Number of Blank Space: {space}")
      print(f"Number of Lowercase: {lower}")
      print(f"Starting with a vowel: {vowel}")
filefunc("f3.txt")

RUN
>>>
File Content:
Best of luck for your exam

Number of Alphabets: 21
Number of Blank Space: 6
Number of Lowercase: 20
Starting with a vowel: 2
>>>
```

Q4. Write a program to replace 'a' with 'b', 'b' with 'c',….,'z' with 'a' and similarly for 'A' with 'B','B' with 'C', …, 'Z' with 'A' in a file. The other characters should remain unchanged.

Solution:

```
str1=input("Enter text:" )
str2=[]
for i in str1:
   if i.isalpha():
      str2.append(chr(ord(i)+1))
   else:
      str2.append(i)
str2=''.join(str2)
print(str2)

RUN
>>>
Enter text:God is One
Hpe jt Pof
>>>
```

Q5. Write a NumPy program to find the most frequent value in an array.

Solution:

```
import numpy as np
x = np.array([7,8,2,7,7,2,7])
print("Original array:")
```

```
print(x)
print("Most frequent value in the above array:")
print(np.bincount(x).argmax())

RUN
>>>
Original array:
[7 8 2 7 7 2 7]
Most frequent value in the above array:
7
>>>
```

Q6. Take two NumPy arrays having two dimensions. Concatenate the arrays on axis 1.

Solution:

```
import numpy as np
arr1 = np.arange(1,10).reshape(3,3)
arr2 = np.arange(10,19).reshape(3,3)
print(arr1)
print()
print(arr2)
print()
print(np.concatenate((arr1,arr2),axis=1))

RUN
>>>
[[1 2 3]
 [4 5 6]
 [7 8 9]]

[[10 11 12]
 [13 14 15]
 [16 17 18]]

[[ 1  2  3 10 11 12]
 [ 4  5  6 13 14 15]
 [ 7  8  9 16 17 18]]
>>>
```


Q7(a) Write a Python function to find the sum of all numbers between 100 and 500 which are divisible by 2.

Solution:

```
# Program to find the sum of numbers divisible by
M in the given range
def sumDivisibles(A, B, M):
    sum = 0
    for i in range(A, B + 1):
        if (i % M == 0):
            sum += i

    return sum

A = 100
B = 500
M = 2
print(sumDivisibles(A, B, M))

RUN
>>>
60300
>>>
```

Q7(b) Write definition of a method/function AddOddEven(VALUES) to display sum of odd and even values separately from the list of VALUES. For example, If the VALUES contain :[15,26,37,10,22,13], the function should display Even Sum: 58 Odd Sum: 65

Solution:

```
def AddOddEven(VALUES):
    so=0
    se=0
    for i in VALUES:
        if i%2==0:
            se=se+i
        else:
            so=so+i
    print("Even Sum:",se)
    print("Odd Sum:",so)
```

```
VALUES=[15,26,37,10,22,13]
AddOddEven(VALUES)

RUN
>>>
Even Sum: 58
Odd Sum: 65
>>>
```

Q8. Write a program to print numbers in descending order.

Solution:

```
# Program to print numbers in descending order
num1 = int(input("Enter first number: "))
num2 = int(input("Enter second number: "))
num3 = int(input("Enter third number: "))
if num1 > num2 and num1 > num3:
    if num2 > num3:
        x, y, z = num1, num2, num3
    else:
        x, y, z = num1, num3, num2
elif num2 > num1 and num2 > num3:
    if num1 > num3:
        x, y, z = num2, num1, num3
    else:
        x, y, z = num2, num3, num1
else:
    if num1>num2:
        x, y, z = num3, num1, num2
    else:
        x, y, z = num3, num2, num1
print("Numbers in descending order are: ", x,y,z)

RUN
>>>
Enter first number: 27
Enter second number: 25
Enter third number: 45
Numbers in descending order are:  45 27 25
>>>
```

Q9. Write a Python function to calculate sum of all the numbers in a list

Solution:

```
# A Python function to calculate sum of all the numbers in a list
def sum(num):
    total = 0
    for x in num:
        total += x
    return total
print(sum((6, 4, 2, 0, 5)))

RUN
>>>
17
>>>
```

Q10. Write a program to enter a number from the keyboard and then print the sum of the digits of the number. It also reverses the number.

Solution:

```
#Program to print reverse and sum of digits
sum = 0
rev = 0
number=int(input("Enter a number: "))
n = number
while (number):
    digit = number % 10
    sum += digit
    rev = rev * 10 + digit
    number //= 10
print("Reverse of number is : ",rev)
print ("Sum of digits of the number is : ",sum)

RUN
>>>
Enter a number: 759
Reverse of number is :  957
Sum of digits of the number is :  21
>>>
```